In the Middle

New Understandings About
Writing, Reading, and Learning

SECOND EDITION

Nancie Atwell

Boynton/Cook Publishers
HEINEMANN
Portsmouth, NH

Boynton/Cook Publishers, Inc.
A subsidiary of Reed Elsevier Inc.
361 Hanover Street
Portsmouth, NH 03801-3912

Offices and agents throughout the world

The author and publisher thank those who generously gave permission to reprint borrowed material:

"What's in My Journal" from *Passwords* by William Stafford. Copyright © 1991 by William Stafford. Published by HarperCollins. Reprinted by permission of The Estate of William Stafford.

"You Can't Write a Poem About McDonald's" from *Tunes for Bears to Dance To* by Ronald Wallace. Copyright © 1983 by Ronald Wallace. Published by the University of Pittsburgh Press. Reprinted by permission of the publisher.

"Maybe Dats Youwr Pwoblem Too" from *The Mating Reflex* by Jim Hall. Copyright © 1980 by Jim Hall. Published by the Carnegie Mellon University Press. Reprinted by permission of the publisher.

"While I Slept" from *Robert Francis Collected Poems: 1936–1976* by Robert Francis. Copyright © 1976 by Robert Francis. Published by The University of Massachusetts Press. Reprinted by permission of the publisher.

"English as a Second Language" in "Your Tired, Your Poor" from *Second Language: Poems* by Lisel Mueller. Copyright © 1986 by Lisel Mueller. Published by the Louisiana State University Press. Reprinted by permission of the publisher.

"To Be of Use" from *Circles on the Water: Selected Poems of Marge Piercy* by Marge Piercy. Copyright © 1973, 1982 by Marge Piercy and Middlemarsh, Inc. Published by Alfred A. Knopf, Inc. 1982. Reprinted by permission of Alfred A. Knopf, Inc. and the Wallace Literary Agency, Inc.

Library of Congress Cataloging-in-Publication Data
Atwell, Nancie.
    In the middle : new understandings about writing, reading, and
learning / Nancie Atwell.—2nd ed.
      p. cm.
    Includes bibliographical references and index.
    ISBN 0-86709-374-9
    1. Language arts (Secondary)—United States. 2. English language—
Study and teaching (Secondary)—United States. 3. English
language—United States—Composition and exercises. I. Title.
LB1631.A72 1998
427'.0071'2—dc21   97-51627
                                           CIP

Editor: Lois Bridges
Production: Melissa L. Inglis
Cover design: Jenny Greenleaf
Cover and interior photos: Andrew Edgar
Manufacturing: Louise Richardson

Printed in the United States of America on acid-free paper
02 01 00   RRD   6 7 8 9

for Toby,
and for Anne

CONTENTS

APPENDIXES

FOREWORD

I've eagerly waited for Nancie Atwell's second edition showing her latest thinking about the teaching of writing and reading. I set out to read with two basic questions in mind, "How has Nancie changed? What am I going to learn?" Of course, I've changed in the eleven years since reading the first edition. For that reason, I read the latest manuscript as if I'd never read the first.

The bottom line for the quality of any classroom is the student work. Start with student texts in Nancie's room and you'll soon ask, "What does she do to get such range and quality?" Instead of personal narrative writing you'll find memoir with a real understanding of the genre, based on students' reading of professional memoir. A partial list of genres includes short stories, poetry, book reviews (not book reports), letters to the editor, parodies, profiles, and essays. The writing is specific and engaging. It features multiple perspectives. The student authors read a wide range of books, magazines, and newspapers, and are able to entertain alternative opinions as they explore the complex subtleties of life. Best of all, there are many references to the work of both their classmates and the teacher. This is a literate community.

Beyond such incredible student writing works a pragmatic, literate professional. The key word is *works*. Nancie works her tail off. The fainthearted need not apply for this kind of teaching. *In the Middle* is for the professional with a strong desire to help students make sense of their world through reading, writing, and sound thinking. I'd add a second desire: the teacher's commitment to grow in her own ability to write and read with students. The two commitments can't be separated. One leads to the other.

I found much more in this edition about the conditions and discipline that make a classroom work. I don't think any of us have fully realized how much preparation is required for the responsive classroom. The quality of literacy Nancie achieves with her students begins with the establishment of a whole series of routines: notetaking, record keeping, sound entry points into reading and writing, minilessons, nightly reading at home, etc. From the outset of the school year the expectations and entry points are repeated again and again, until students can take off on their own. Effective student choice is based on extensive demonstrations, book sharing, read-alouds, teaching in minilessons, conferences with individuals, and continuous observation by the teacher. Readers will be delighted to learn more about how Nancie introduces the essential elements of the writing-reading workshop.

I was struck by how hard Nancie works to make sure students have effective entry points into both reading and writing. This requires conferences and observations to ensure that a student has chosen the right book to begin the year's reading. The same is true of the writing. How can a topic or genre connect with something the student wishes to express in writing? Miss the right curriculum for each student and management quickly breaks down.

School administrators and faculty take note: Nancie Atwell clearly shows how to foster superior thinkers. Too often in our schools reading and writing are separated and taught by different faculty. Worse yet, instructional time for writing is lost. Anxiety about reading scores drives too many decisions about curriculum.

Nancie writes with her students in this edition far more than in the first. I've long advocated that teachers write with their students, and I've seen good results when they do, but none like that effected in this latest edition of *In the Middle*. Nancie writes in all the genres and uses her texts to teach; she freely admits that she's learned much about writing and her students from this process. Teachers often say, "But I don't have time to write with my students." Nancie shows conclusively that it is time well spent. Showing through your own writing, during minilessons, is teaching that lasts. As she says, all a teacher has to do is write just a little better than our students for them to learn lessons about genre, convention, craft, and, especially, purpose.

This is a book that teaches. Not an hour goes by that Nancie is not engaged in systematic teaching. Good teaching requires good showing. The section on minilessons is a treasury of teaching to promote skillful, masterful readers and writers. The emphasis in the minilesson is on meaning, not rules. Where possible she gives good background about why certain conventions began and how they help the transaction between writer and reader. This section alone is worth the price of the book.

Once again, Nancie Atwell is riding ahead, breaking new trail on what we need to know about how to help students become lifelong readers/writers/learners. Her pragmatism implicitly asks, "What works? What makes sense? But, above all, what lasts?" She once told me, "I try to find out what each student wants, in life or tomorrow. Then my task is to show how what we're doing in the workshop, through our reading and writing, will help them get there." Read the second edition of *In the Middle* and you, too, will discover how to help your students realize their dreams—again and again.

Donald H. Graves

ACKNOWLEDGMENTS

In the Middle is a book about teaching and learning. I am eternally grateful to my best teachers, the seventh and eighth grade writers and readers at the Center for Teaching and Learning. This book wouldn't be without you.

I'm grateful, too, to the teachers who help shape the way I think about writing and reading. Engagement with their ideas makes my ideas possible. I thank Linda Rief, Donald Murray, Ken Macrorie, Dixie Goswami, Shelley Harwayne, Tom Newkirk, and, especially, Donald Graves. His foreword to this book is only the tip of a twenty-year iceberg of good ideas, hard questions, and encouraging words.

Mary Ellen Giacobbe is my unfailing source of inspiration, moral support, and long-distance laughter. What I learn from her, on those Sunday mornings when we straighten out the world together, is incalculable. I thank her with all my heart.

I don't know how to acknowledge Ron Miller; there's not enough Godiva. I may be the only writer in America who still composes by hand, and chapter by chapter he deciphered every crossed-out, cut-up, taped-together, margin-filled page and turned them into a manuscript. A writer couldn't ask for more scrupulous assistance or a more sympathetic first reader.

I feel honored, as I have from the first, to be associated with Heinemann and Boynton/Cook. I'm grateful to Bob Boynton and Peter Stillman for gambling on the first edition; to Toby Gordon for believing that a second edition was a worthwhile project; and to Michael Gibbons for his enthusiasm and thoughtfulness, in all the senses of the word: in the world of publishing, teachers couldn't ask for a better friend.

I thank Lois Bridges, my editor, for her guidance and her confidence in me. Knowing that she was waiting patiently was all the invitation I needed to write. I am especially indebted to Melissa Inglis, my production editor at

Heinemann, for her editorial expertise and the hours I know she devoted to making things right, and to Roberta Lew for dealing with the permissions. Andrew Edgar's beautiful photographs are a gift. They capture the essence of my kids as engaged writers and readers.

I'm grateful to two foundations for their support. The research reported in this second edition was assisted in part by a grant from The Spencer Foundation; and the CTL middle school program itself exists only because of a vote of confidence from the Geraldine C. Dodge Foundation. The data presented and views expressed in *In the Middle* are solely my responsibility.

Finally, I thank my family. James Whitmore, my uncle, helped me grow a miracle on a hillside in Maine. My mother, Mary Atwell, has never, ever doubted. She cheerleads my life every step of the way, and I count on her love and spirit. My daughter, Anne, gave up her mom for a summer with such grace and maturity that I have even more reason to be proud of her and love her to pieces. And I am luckiest to have Toby McLeod. He is the most literate person I know. From him I learned how to read literature, how to love it, and how to share that passion with others. He teaches me always, and he makes sure our home is a place where I can write and get the job done.

I
Always Beginning

If the angel deigns to come, it will be because you have
convinced him, not by your tears, but by your humble resolve
to be always beginning.
Rainer Maria Rilke

1

Learning How to Teach Writing

The logic by which we teach is not always the logic
by which children learn.
Glenda Bissex

I confess. I started out as a creationist. The first days of every school year I created, and for the next thirty-six weeks I maintained the creation: my curriculum. From behind my big desk I set it in motion; then I managed and maintained it until June. I wanted to be a great teacher—systematic, purposeful, in control. I wanted great results from my great practices. And I wanted to convince other teachers that this creation was superior stuff. So I studied my curriculum, conducting research designed to show its wonders. I didn't learn in my classroom. I tended my creation.

Today I learn in my classroom. What happens there has changed, and it continues to change. I've become an evolutionist. The curriculum unfolds as my kids and I learn together and as I teach them what I see they need to learn next. My aims stay constant—I want us to go deep inside language together and use it to know, shape, and play with our worlds—but my practice evolves as my students and I go deeper. This going deeper is research. Today my research shows me the wonders of my kids, not my methods. But it has also brought me full circle. Learning with students, collaborating with them as a writer and reader who both wonders and knows about writing and reading, has made me a better teacher to them than I dreamed possible.

The second edition of *In the Middle* describes what I've learned so far about teaching writing and reading over twenty-five years as a teacher of English. It shows what we do in my classroom today and why we do it. And it tells stories about teaching and learning.

The word *story* can be traced to the Greek *eidenai*, which means "to know." As a reader I look to stories to help me understand and give meaning to my life. As a writer I tell stories so I may understand, teaching myself and trying to teach others through the actions and reactions of those "people on the page," Donald Murray's "little scenes in which people reveal both themselves and the subject" (1982, 40). This book tells stories because it's the best way I know to reveal myself, my students, and my subject: helping kids put written language at the crux of their emotional, social, and intellectual worlds. Framing these is my own story, the evolution that brought me out from behind my big desk, invited my students to find their ways inside writing and reading, and challenged me to discover who I am in that classroom—as a teacher, learner, writer, reader, and grown-up.

In the Middle begins with my story because it's the best invitation I can extend to other teachers to come out from behind their own big desks. I didn't intuit or luck into this place, and I didn't arrive overnight. I paved the way—I continue to pave it—through writing and reading about writing, through uncovering and questioning my assumptions, through observing my kids and myself in action and trying to make sense of my observations, through dumb mistakes, uncertain experiments, and, underneath it all, a desire to do my best by students and a willingness to acknowledge that my definition of *best* will be *–should* be—ever changing.

Which means that a lot of the time, doing my best hurts. It means looking hard at the sense behind what I'm doing and asking kids to do. It means learning—and admitting—when I'm wrong. And, most painful of all, it means letting go of my creations when I see that they get in the way of students acting—and growing—as readers and writers.

The story begins in my seventh year of teaching, when I received a generous invitation to stop focusing on myself and my curriculum and start observing my students. When I did, I recognized the gap yawning between us—between the behaviors I expected as a language teacher and the behaviors kids engage in as language learners. I saw that my creation manipulated kids so that they bore sole responsibility for narrowing the gap. Students either found ways to make sense of, or peace with, the language arts curriculum, or they failed the course. But it was I who needed to move, to strike out for some common ground. I can learn in my classroom today because I moved, because the classroom became a reading and writing *workshop*, a territory my students and I can inhabit together.

I'm beginning with the story of how the workshop came to be, and how it has changed along the way, because its genesis sets the stage for the chapters of pedagogy that follow. All the particular methods of writing and reading workshop grow from my particular experience as a teacher, student, reader, writer, researcher, adult, and, most recently, parent. I hope that other teachers, through sharing my experience, will grow along with me. I'll begin the story twenty years ago, when the gap was at its widest, with an eighth grader who taught me that I didn't know enough.

Jeff

In 1975 I became the junior high English department at Boothbay Harbor Grammar School. My husband, Toby, and I moved to Maine from upstate New York, where I'd taught at a middle school in Tonawanda, outside Buffalo, where I had grown up and gone to college. We moved because of Maine.

That summer we wended our way up the coast, then down the twelve-mile peninsula to Boothbay Harbor. We were looking for a small, beautiful place to vacation; instead, we found a small, beautiful place we wanted to live. The combined population of the communities nestled along the peninsula is just over four thousand, and the sea is everywhere—coves and harbors, salt pond marshes and mud flats, tidal rivers and freshwater lakes—and it is everywhere surrounded by masses of pines, firs, and birches.

On the last day of our vacation, utterly depressed about heading back to Buffalo, we took a final drive around Southport Island. Toby parked at Hendricks Head, and we sat staring at our Triple-A maps—and the lighthouse and the islands and each other. I asked, "What do you suppose you could do if you wanted to live here? You know, as a job?" Toby said, "Well, you're a teacher."

I was a teacher. There was an opening. I got the job. We put a new tailpipe on our old Valiant, rented a truck, loaded our furniture, tranquilized our dog, and returned to Boothbay Harbor on Labor Day weekend. I was twenty-four years old, and I'd been teaching English for a year and a half.

The first time I saw my new classroom was the day before I was to teach in it. The junior high building was a two-story brick bunker separated from the grammar school proper—a classic, clapboard schoolhouse—by ledge, playground, and tradition. I walked up a dark stairwell and found my room—its linoleum floor half gone, bare lightbulbs hanging from a falling tile ceiling, and all the walls green and peeling. One wall, sheets of heavy plywood jerry-built to be "portable," divided what had once been a normal-sized classroom. (Later that year it collapsed into my side of the room and sent one of my students to the hospital.) Terry, the science and social studies departments, taught next door. The next morning, when our students arrived, I discovered that every word said in either room was perfectly audible in the other.

The principal handed me the junior high language arts curriculum, which turned out to be a copy of my schedule: so many periods each day of my two subjects, reading and English. Then he scurried back across the blacktop to the safety of K–6 and white clapboard. I took a good look around.

No books sat on the dusty shelves. No papers filled the rattletrap file cabinet. But there were twenty-seven desks to somehow squeeze into position in half a room. The next morning, when the first class of twenty-seven eighth graders chose their seats, one of them was Jeff. He was hard to miss.

Jeff was big, almost sixteen. His parents traveled because of their work, and they had withdrawn him from school over the years to take him with them. Because he hadn't grown up with his classmates and had missed so much school, Jeff talked to almost no one and was almost always alone. He stood out academically too. His reading and writing abilities were the lowest I have ever encountered.

Jeff could barely read the primary-level texts the reading coordinator provided. He couldn't distinguish some letters from others, *m* from *n* or *d* from *b*. He could spell his name, the names of his brothers and sisters, and maybe two dozen simple words. I talked with his previous years' teachers and heard six versions of the same report: they'd done what they could for Jeff in the limited time they had with him, tried to provide appropriate remedial work, and either kept him back or, because of his size, promoted him to the next grade. In a conference, his mother told me that Jeff was learning disabled and nothing could be done for him.

By the end of September I had banished memories of my pretty Tonawanda classroom and its suburban kids. I started to learn about life in rural Maine from my new students, whose families mostly made a hard living from the sea—small boat building, fishing and lobstering, the seasonal tourist industry. And I faced up to life in the bunker. I covered the peeling paint with Argus sensitivity posters. I demanded money for books and spent my own. I cadged paper and folders for writing. And I took up the challenge of trying to do something for Jeff.

At recess time Jeff stayed in most days to talk to me or Terry, whichever of us didn't have playground duty. I liked him. He knew about things I didn't—boats and sailing and the Southwest. But I did know something about books on those subjects. *Dove, Kon-Tiki, Ram, Survive the Savage Sea,* and *The Teachings of Don Juan* became the texts for Jeff's remedial reading course, while the other kids suffered the brand-new Scott, Foresman literature anthology. I wanted to inundate Jeff with reading experience, and I figured the best way was to endow his reading with huge measures of personal meaning. All that fall and winter I gave him time and books and conversation, and he struggled to read. All that fall and winter he took my breath away as I watched him break through to meaning and teach himself to read—as he moved his finger and lips, tracing each word, then finally abandoned pointing when it got in the way of his sheer pleasure in the stories. And, all that fall and winter, as I denied kids a similar kind of personal meaning in my English course, Jeff baffled me when it came time to write.

I brought with me, as the seventh- and eighth-grade English course, a writing program I developed with Tonawanda colleagues. In theory and practice it drew on James Moffett's hierarchy of discourse (Moffett and Wagner 1976); its basic tenet was that students learn to write by working systematically through a sequence of modes—drama to narrative to idea writing—with extensive prewriting and postwriting activities. Some of us had just co-authored an article for *English Journal* describing the methodology—my first professional publication. I was wedded to this program.

I had a dittoed writing assignment for each week of the school year, my own composition treasure trove. Students were asked to role-play assigned situations; then they wrote monologues. They talked about assigned topics in pairs and small groups, then wrote dialogues. They read selections from the literature anthology and wrote short fiction in response. Then I wrote comments all over their drafts, and they were to "revise" them accordingly. On Friday I collected the compositions. On Saturday I avoided the room where the papers lay awaiting me. On Sunday I wrote comments all over them yet again, recorrected too many of the same mistakes, then started cranking out the next set of dittoes and pumping myself up for Monday morning's prewriting activity. Whatever the ditto or activity, the results broke neatly into three groups. Six "gifted" writers made my task their own and did something wonderful with it, fifteen kids more or less fulfilled the assignment, and I threw up my hands over the poor effort and low ability of the rest.

The program fit my assumptions about middle school students and instruction in writing. I assigned topics because I believed that most kids were so intimidated by expressing themselves on paper they wouldn't write without a prompt, and because I believed that direction and structure from the teacher were necessary for kids to write well. When it came right down to it, I assigned topics because I believed that my ideas were more credible and important than any my students might possibly entertain. And from my perspective—the big desk at the front of the classroom—it looked as if real writing were going on out there. Then I came up against Jeff.

One of the weekly assignments involved discovering memories of personal experiences by brainstorming a list, talking about the list with a partner, choosing one memory, and writing about it. All the eighth graders worked through the prescribed prewriting procedures. Except Jeff. He spent the period whispering and humming as he drew a picture of a boy kneeling on a beach in front of a pitched tent. At the end of class he folded up his drawing and took it home. The next day Jeff came to school with a rough draft—an account of his baby brother's death on a Mexican beach. In fact, it was a finished piece. Although I wrote questions all over his narrative that pushed him to reflect and elaborate, Jeff just copied it over, one excruciating letter at a time.

This became his pattern. At school Jeff drew a becalmed sailboat; at home he wrote a *Dove*-like short story. He sketched a desert scene during the day, and that night wrote about peyote, witch doctors, and Don Juan. I developed a pattern, too. My voice regularly sounded on the other side of the plywood wall: "Jeff, stop drawing and *get to work*."

I coped by resorting to the only teaching strategy I knew. I made assumptions. Then I tested them. When they didn't hold water, I made new assumptions.

Since Jeff's drafts weren't badly misspelled, I asked him about their accuracy. He said, "My sister helps me when I get stuck." I decided he wasn't writing in class because asking me for help in front of the other kids embarrassed him. I told him not to worry about spelling on first drafts, that he and I could work on correctness later on. Jeff agreed not to worry. Then he drew through the next writing class.

I thought Jeff was distracted by the noisy classroom. I assumed he didn't want other kids to see how slowly he wrote. I blamed his lack of self-confidence. I guessed he was frustrated by the absence of an art program. My theories and remedies accumulated, and Jeff continued to draw in class and write at home. I never asked him why.

After suffering my remonstrations for half a school year, Jeff ran out of patience. One morning when he stayed in during recess, he let me have it: "Listen, Ms. Atwell. This is the way I do it, the way I write. As long as I get it done, what do you care?" He was so vehement I backed off, finally conceding his right to use whatever method worked for him, just so long as I got the requisite number of finished products to file away in his folder.

By the end of the year Jeff's writing folder was as fat as many of the others. And although he still drew in his spare time, he seldom drew during the last months' writing classes. Suddenly, he wrote. Maybe something in Jeff had changed. Maybe persevering in the face of his teacher's stony disapproval finally became too much for him. Whatever the reason, I didn't ask. I just held my breath each Monday that spring and hoped he'd get down to the new writing task.

Jeff moved on to high school. New kids moved in. I retrieved the folder of dittoed writing assignments for September and began to teach my curriculum all over again.

Two years after Jeff, I had reason to be grateful for his perseverance. A friend sent me a volume of papers presented at a conference at S.U.N.Y. Buffalo; among them was Donald Graves' "The Child, the Writing Process, and the Role of the Professional" (1975), in which Graves described his early observations of seven-year-old writers. One, John, wrote extremely slowly, spoke aloud as he wrote, proofread at the single-word level, and seemed to rehearse his writing through drawing. Graves concluded by suggesting that teachers look for and accommodate the behaviors of beginning writers.

His words rang in my head for days. Seven-year-old John called up too many images of sixteen-year-old Jeff, images I wanted to forget. Instead, I remembered—how I had done my level best to overlook and overcome all evidence that the structures of my writing program had served Jeff as constraints. And in Jeff's case, the evidence was blatant—all that talking to himself and all those drawings. I thought about the other students who sat in front of my big desk, writers of whom I knew little beyond the degree to which they satisfied the requirements of the Monday-morning assignments.

I was lucky Jeff had insisted I let him go his own way. But I had missed the chance to understand what I was seeing and support what he was doing, to talk with him and learn from him how to help him. And even if I'd had the background of Graves' early research, what would I have looked for and asked about? I didn't know.

What I did know was this: Students can't be the only learners in a classroom. Teachers have to learn, too. Common sense, good intentions, and the world's best writing program are not enough. As Graves observed in the conclusion of his 1975 report:

> It is entirely possible to read about children, review research and textbooks about writing, "teach" them, yet still be completely unaware of their processes of learning and writing. Unless we actually structure our environments to free ourselves for effective observation and participation in all phases of the writing process, we are doomed to repeat the same teaching mistakes again and again. (29)

I didn't want to be doomed to blunder forever at the expense of my students. Two years after Jeff I was teaching in the brand-new, consolidated regional elementary school. My room had carpeting, books and bookshelves, fluorescent lights, wall-to-wall Argus posters, and plenty of room for desks to be arranged however I chose. I had a new, supportive principal. I even had colleagues; in the new school I was one of three junior high English teachers. Yet I felt doomed. How could I learn—really learn—about writing? How could I learn to look, then make sense of what I observed? How could I learn anything at all in Boothbay Harbor, Maine?

On the Verge of Learning: Bread Loaf

The next summer I left Maine for seven weeks. Middlebury College's Bread Loaf School of English Program in Writing was in its second year. Bread Loaf had secured full-tuition grants for English teachers from rural schools, and I qualified. My qualifying essay was the story of Jeff and me.

I chose Bread Loaf because its catalog seemed to promise resources that Boothbay Harbor couldn't offer. But when I got there, my teacher persisted in inviting me to become *my own resource*, to learn about writing firsthand by becoming a writer and researcher. All that summer Dixie Goswami asked me to write, look at and describe how I write, and think about what my discoveries might mean for kids as writers. It was a summer of contradictions.

I saw that the choices I make as a writer—deciding how, when, what, and for whom I will write—were not options available to the writers in my classes. But I also saw an unbridgeable gap between my students and me. As an adult writer I knew my intentions and had a pretty good idea of how to act on them. As an English teacher I knew my assumptions about kids: they needed an English teacher's prewriting structures and postwriting strictures.

When Bread Loaf ended and school started again, I went back to my writing program. But this time around I tried to open things up. I gave kids more options and made the assignments more flexible—now they had a choice of four role-play situations and could write the required monologue as any one of six fictional characters. And this time around I started writing with my students, taking on the tasks I gave them. It was a daunting experience.

My assigned poetry was formulaic and cute: five-senses poems, feelings poems, who-what-when-where-why poems. My assigned narratives never went beyond the first draft; I wrote them at the breakfast table the day they were due. My assigned essays consisted of well-organized and earnest clichés. But the worst was the assigned daily journal entry. Every English class started with an enforced ten-minute "free" write, and I either had nothing to say or so much to say that ten minutes just left me frustrated—tantalizingly close to discovering what I wanted to say.

All the while I was writing this awful stuff, I was trying to conduct classroom research. My plan was to show the beneficial effects on their writing when students viewed the teacher as a writer. But I wasn't writing; I was performing. I did my real writing at home, mostly poetry and letters, for me and for people I cared about. I wasn't even conducting research; I was method testing, trying to prove the integrity of my creation. In January I called off the research project and buried my embarrassing writing portfolio in the back of a file drawer.

I am an expert rationalizer, and I rationalized hard that winter. What I needed were even more creative, more open topics. I needed thrilling prewriting activities. I needed better students—kids who could consistently make my assignments their own, who didn't "revise" by recopying their drafts and changing three words, who came to me prepared by their teachers to write well. *Aha.* I needed better colleagues.

The last was my favorite rationalization. I assumed the classic stance of secondary English teachers everywhere: if you K–6 teachers had taught properly, I wouldn't have to work so hard. Over the years, as a member of a series of language arts curriculum committees, I made an officious case for more creative writing in the elementary grades. The chief beneficiary of all this writing would, of course, be me. If someone else moved kids to show some imagination and take some initiative before junior high, all I would have to do when they came to me was frost the cake. So I distributed dittoes of my best creative writing recipes among my colleagues and held forth about THE writing process, that lockstep sequence I orchestrated every Monday through Friday. And I was generally, justifiably, ignored.

In 1980 not one of my colleagues—and some had master's degrees plus forty hours—had ever attended a course or workshop concerned with the teaching of writing. They needed information about writing, but the materials I shared (not to mention the way I shared them) did not help. Boothbay's K–6 students continued not to write. Their teachers continued to follow—or not—a language arts curriculum consisting of grade-level skills lists patched together from textbooks and other schools' curriculum guides. And I continued to lay blame.

In the late winter of 1980, Boothbay Region Elementary School began a new round of curriculum development. Eight of us from grades K–8 volunteered to serve on a language arts committee; our task was to produce a curriculum guide. Gloria Walter, the chair, suggested we take a new tack and pose questions the committee could investigate together. So we brainstormed questions, settling finally on the modest query: How do human beings acquire language?

The question was so ambitious it was ridiculous, but it at least set us on a different course. I couldn't lecture or condescend (although I did feel pretty confident that the answer would point toward a writing program rather like my own). We couldn't exchange gimmicks, borrow other schools' philosophies, or invent sequences of so-called skills. Instead, the committee began to search for resources that might help us find answers. Remembering Jeff, I wrote to Donald Graves. He responded by sending Susan Sowers to Boothbay Harbor.

Graves, Sowers, and Lucy Calkins were then nearing the end of their second year as researchers-in-residence at Atkinson Academy, a public elementary school in rural New Hampshire. Under a grant from the National Institute of Education, they spent two years following sixteen first- and third-grade writers and their teachers (Graves 1983). They observed students in their classrooms in the process of writing, in order to discover how children develop as writers and how schools can help.

Susan came to our curriculum committee with draft copies of reports from the NIE project. She also brought her authority as a teacher and researcher, a wealth of knowledge—and patience. What she had to say was not what I wanted to hear.

According to Susan, children in the NIE study learned to write by exercising the options available to real-world authors, including daily time for writing, conferences with teachers and peers during drafting, pacing set by the writer, and opportunities to publish what they had written. Most significantly, students decided what they would write. They wrote on a range of topics and in a variety of modes wider than their teachers had dreamed of assigning. They cared about content and correctness. And their teachers had come out from behind their big desks to write with, listen to, and learn from young writers.

Atkinson Academy sounded a lot like Camelot. As Susan extolled its merits, I rolled my eyes and ground my teeth. At the end of the meeting I stayed behind to argue.

"But, Susan, what if I individualize my assignments by asking a class to come up with a chain of memories, talk about them, choose one, and write it?"

"Well, that sounds very nice," she answered politely. "But that's really an exercise."

"Okay . . . but what if I give them a choice of four really funny dramatic monologues, and they get to role-play these, then choose one to write up?"

"Ummm, I guess I'd call that an exercise too."

"Wait, wait. I haven't told you my best . . ."

It was an exercise. They were all exercises.

For the next week I explained to anyone who would listen how Susan's recommendations couldn't possibly apply to me and my students, how all my classroom experience and secondary-English-teacher expertise argued against the anarchy she advocated. I railed at the art teacher: "Sarah, can you imagine what would happen if someone said kids should just stroll into your art room and invent their own projects?" I raged in the local service station: "Mr. Andrews, what if someone said customers should come into your garage, borrow your tools, and repair their own cars?" Sarah and Mr. Andrews and the others just shook their heads.

But all that week, on my free periods and in the evening, I waged a silent, losing battle with Susan Sowers as I read and reread the manuscripts she had left behind. Eventually I saw through my defenses to the truth. I didn't know how to share responsibility with my students, and I wasn't too sure I wanted to. I liked the vantage of my big desk. I liked being creative, setting topic and pace and mode, orchestrating THE process, taking charge. Wasn't that my job? If responsibility for their writing shifted to my students, what would I do?

And what might Jeff have done as a student in this other kind of classroom?

Learning in Earnest: Writing Workshop

What I did, finally, was talk to my kids. One day in March I gathered my courage and closed the classroom door. I told my students about this elementary school in New Hampshire where children developed their own ideas for writing and wrote for all kinds of real audiences, where writers received responses from their friends and the teacher *while* they were writing. I asked, "Could you do this? Would you like to?"

Yes. Some said it tentatively, some resoundingly, but they all said yes. Together we made an amazing discovery: they did have ideas for writing.

Even more amazing, given the nonsense I'd had them writing for the past six months, they had interesting ideas. We found out that in-school writing could actually be good for something—that it could serve kids as a way to solve problems and see the world. This was not Camelot. It was genuine, and it was happening in my classroom.

Brooke wrote a short story about the slaughter of baby seals. Doug wrote about duck hunting, and Greg told about deep-sea fishing. Shani described the night she heard the news that her brother had died in an automobile accident. Evie wrote letters of inquiry to private high schools, and Ernie wrote a parody of Stephen King. One of my Sarahs told about her experiences learning to drive a junked Oldsmobile in her parents' driveway; the other Sarah took us on a bus trip through Harlem that had shaken her rural Maine complacency. Eben's short story about the aftermath of a nuclear holocaust went through three drafts to become a letter to the editor of the *Portland Press Herald* objecting to the threat of reinstitution of selective service registration. Melissa's letter to the Society for Animal Protective Legislation was forwarded as evidence to a Congressional subcommittee. Lauren's letter to the local YMCA resulted in expanded gym hours for middle school students. Erin's letter to Louis L'Amour questioning the credibility of the plot of one of his novels brought a letter from L'Amour explaining his historic source.

Ted wrote an angry essay about the effects of time on his life, Kim wrote a loving essay about the effects of her mother on her life, and Joey wrote an essay about himself as a writer. When a Maine dairy announced a Down East story-writing contest, a group of eighth graders decided to enter. They listened to Marshall Dodge's *Bert and I* albums and made notes about dialect and story structure, then wrote draft after draft. Roy won the contest and a $250 scholarship; five of his classmates were runners-up.

There were no longer six top writers in each class. Every student could seek help in conferences, spend sustained time on individual pieces of writing, and discover that writing well is not a gift. Their commitment to their ideas and purposes made them work hard; their hard work made significant writing happen.

After the novelty of self-selected topics faded, the writing didn't always come easily. In April some students begged, "Just tell me what to write. Anything. I'll write it." But I held firm. Those days had ended. Instead I questioned, modeled, and insisted. "What do you care about? What do you know? What do you know about that others don't?"

The teaching didn't always come easily. But in spite of blocked writers, my uncertainty about what to say in conferences, and big administrative questions about grading, record keeping, and classroom management, I couldn't wait to get to school in the morning to see what my kids would do next.

I saw them take chances, trying new subjects, styles, and formats. I saw them take responsibility, sometimes judging a single draft sufficient and other times deciding the sixth draft represented their best meaning. I saw them take care, editing and proofreading so that real readers would attend to their meanings, not their mistakes. I saw them take time, writing and planning their writing outside of school as well as in. I watched as my English classes became a writing workshop. Suddenly, the pieces fit.

Goswami's teacher-as-researcher posture worked here because the context created real writing and real questions about real learning. Here, I could relate to my students as a writer because we were all acting on our intentions as writers; insights from my writing experiences helped me to help them. Here, isolated in a rural school at the end of a long peninsula, I could start to discover and support young writers' ways of learning. Maybe this was the kind of context Graves had in mind when he advised teachers to "free ourselves for effective observation and participation in all phases" of writing (1975, 29).

When Susan Sowers had described her team's findings to our committee that day in March, I had traced and retraced two words on the cover of my notebook: *naive* and *permissive*. I thought, "Here's a sure road to undisciplined writing and general chaos." But I learned this isn't true. Freedom of choice does not undercut structure. Instead, students become accountable for learning about and using the structures available to writers to serve their purposes. Everyone sits at a big desk, and everyone plans what will happen there.

This was the start of my evolution as an English teacher—after seven years of teaching to begin again, at the very beginning, with individual students and their intentions as writers. My first true inquiry as a teacher-researcher was a broad one: I wanted to learn what was possible.

I moved through a classroom filled with big desks, conferring with students about their emerging ideas and options and teaching them how to confer with each other. I expected that everyone would write, and that none of it would be an exercise performed for my benefit. I conducted minilessons—brief lectures at the start of class about procedures, conventions, craft, genre, and topic development. I organized the classroom so that students had supplies, resources, publication opportunities, and a physical layout to support their efforts. And I acknowledged that composition was difficult, time-consuming work by giving over English class time to writing.

The first edition of *In the Middle*, published in 1987, was a portrait of this classroom and my best knowledge then about my role in the workshop and my responsibilities to students. My sense of my roles and responsibilities continued to evolve over almost two decades of writing workshops—years in which I became an author of books, teacher of teachers, mother, and principal. In 1987 I left Boothbay Region Elementary School in order to spend time with my baby girl, and in 1990 I used the royalties from the first edition of *In the Middle* to begin building a school of my own, the Center for Teaching and Learning in Edgecomb, Maine.

Teaching writing as a process gave me permission to view teaching as a process, too. From writing I gained the courage to change my mind and my life and the humility to revise my practice whenever experience teaches me there's something else I can do to help kids become stronger, smarter, more purposeful. And so, ten years later, I turn to the next clean page and begin again.

Becoming a Teacher with a Capital T

The second edition of *In the Middle* differs in some significant ways from the first. I hope it is just as concrete in describing solutions to problems of managing writing instruction. I hope it invites teachers to imagine themselves and their students in new roles and relationships. I hope it shows the kind of student writing that is possible. But I also hope it is more explicit about the role of the teacher in the writing workshop—about how I present myself in the classroom so that students can learn how to put writing to work for them. And I hope, fervently, that it avoids the formulas and jargon that made it possible to read the first edition of *In the Middle* as a cookbook: one teacher's collection of recipes for whipping up a writing workshop.

For me, one of Donald Graves' best essays remains "The Enemy Is Orthodoxy" (1984). He argues that rules about the right methods for teaching writing "are substitutes for thinking. They clog our ears. We . . . cloud the issues with jargon in place of simple, direct prose about actual children" (185).

In addition to creating veritable smog banks of jargon in my earlier descriptions of writing workshop (I pledge never, ever again to *empower* students with *ownership*), I know I continued to view my students and their writing through the clouds of my own needs as a teacher and human being, however sincerely I was convinced I had cast off all assumptions and was seeing my student writers with clear eyes. In short, like any teacher, I bring who I am to my methods. It's in recognizing that, and seeking and acknowledging my professional identity by writing about my teaching, that I have come to understand teaching as a life's work, as the screen on which my life will play itself out.

I see myself two decades ago, still in my twenties, when Graves, Sowers, and Calkins began to publish their research, ecstatic to learn what my students could do without me in this new, egalitarian community, the writing workshop. Other English teachers felt the same excitement. We laid down the old, stodgy burdens of the profession—the *Warriner's Handbooks*, the forty-five minute lectures and canned assignments—and embraced new roles. We called ourselves sponsors, partners, coaches, facilitators of the process.

I needed the broad strokes of a revolution in order to break free of the old paradigm. I liberated myself as an English teacher by liberating my students as writers. In the early 1980s, when they chose their topics, genres, and audiences and wrote and wrote and wrote, I listened and listened and listened. I needed to learn how to pay attention; to stop performing and become quiet, to let myself fall in love with every one of my students. These were heady times, as many English teachers abandoned the old orthodoxies and cleared the way for our kids' voices.

But something happened to me that happens often in revolutions. As part of my transformation I embraced a whole new set of orthodoxies. As enlightened and child-centered as the new rules were, they had an effect similar to the old ones: they limited what I did as an English teacher, but from a different angle. Many of the orthodoxies I came to teach by are apparent in the 1987 edition:

- Minilessons should be between five and seven minutes long.
- Conferences with individuals are more important than minilessons to the group. Teachers should invest their energies in conferring.
- Attend to conventions—spelling, punctuation, paragraphing—only at the end of the process, when the content is set. Tell kids editorial issues don't matter until the final draft.
- Keep conferences short. Get to every writer every day.
- Don't look at or read students' writing during conferences.
- Don't tell writers what they should do or what should be in their writing.

- Don't write on students' writing.
- Don't praise.
- Students must have ownership of their writing.

The problem with orthodoxies is that even the best of them take away initiative from someone. *Rules* stand at the center of classroom interactions. Rules limit someone's role—in this case, the teacher's. Instead of working from a base of knowledge of writing and each child's need and intentions, I grounded my interactions with writers on the new rules. I measured myself and my teaching against a fresh orthodoxy, and a dangerous question framed my thinking about teaching writing:

- *Am I doing it right?*
- Did I have enough conferences today?
- Am I a bad teacher if I write on kids' writing?
- I wish I could take home these drafts that go on for pages and skim them, then talk with the writers tomorrow in class. Is that cheating?
- I hope no one finds out about my thirty-minute minilesson.
- I'd like to tell this kid to abandon his piece of writing—I think he'd be relieved if I did—but I don't want to usurp his ownership.
- Is it okay that I took dictation from a writer who was stuck?
- I'm sick and tired of unpunctuated, unparagraphed, misspelled drafts, but I'm afraid of interfering with the ideas.
- I wish I could assign the whole class to write a poem about the film we just saw.
- I wish I could tell the whole class to be quiet and write for the next half hour.
- *Am I doing it right?*

After six years of raising a child and a school, I returned to middle school teaching in 1994. The Center for Teaching and Learning had started out in 1990 as a K–3 school. As its director I added a grade each year. By the time the first group of kids made it to the seventh grade, I had had the benefit of plenty of experiences that led me to plenty of second thoughts about writing workshop and its orthodoxies.

For example, over years of writing workshops I observed the younger children at the Center, the students Linda Rief has called "Don Graves' kids." They had learned early on about writing-as-process, mastered the ubiquitous personal-experience narrative, and were looking for new inspirations and challenges as writers.

I also encountered teachers from across the country with problems I had never come up against, from a teacher in a budget-strapped urban setting trying to teach writing to thirty-five students at a time, six periods a day, to a teacher so upset that *In the Middle* "didn't work" in her classroom that she sent me four pages of questions she wanted answers to by Monday.

I read the work of other writing teachers and attended their presentations at conferences. Janet Allen, Maureen Barbieri, Ralph Fletcher, Mary Ellen Giacobbe, Donald Graves, Shelley Harwayne, Georgia Heard, Joanne Hindley, Donald Murray, Ken Macrorie, Tom Newkirk, Linda Rief, Tom Romano, Regie Routman, Jack Wilde, and William Zinsser are writing teachers who challenge my assumptions and methods. I argue with them—in my mind and out loud—as I argued with Susan Sowers. Then I reconsider and revise what I mean by writing workshop.

Perhaps most importantly, in the interim I had plenty of time to consider my relationship with my daughter, the nature of my role in her life as a grown-up, and the implications for how I might respond to other kids when I returned to the classroom.

For example, I remember teaching Anne how to tie her shoes. I asked her to watch me while I tied the laces slowly and talked her through it. Then I held her hands and molded her fingers into the positions they needed to take, over and over again, until she could make them hold the shapes on their own. I became her mentor of shoe tying before she became a shoe tier.

I recall the thousands of picture books we read together: how Toby and I read aloud to Anne and led her through the pages with our questions, answers to her questions, reminiscences about other books or times from her life, and spaces we made for her to chime in—how we became her mediators of reading before she became a reader.

And I think back to showing her how to set a table. I did it with her for a few nights and pointed out what she missed; then she took over, set the table on her own, put the cutlery where I said it belonged—and invented a beautiful way to fold the napkins. I established the model for table setting, then Anne went beyond the model.

Jerome Bruner (1986) refers to this phenomenon—when an adult intervenes and gradually provides less assistance to a learner—as the "handover phase." In handover, understandings and strategies that emerge during an interaction between a more competent person and a less competent person gradually become internalized in the learner's mind.

I like this phrase because it connotes the fluidity and subtlety of the interaction. It's not hands-off: the adult is active, directive, and involved in the task. It's not a handout: the child is active, intentional, and involved in the task. And neither one is distanced from the task. The adult and child aren't conversing philosophically about principles of shoe tying, reading, table setting—or corn-on-the-cob eating, hair washing, or long division. We're both engaged. Anne watches me, I watch her, I do it for her, she tries it, we talk, I lend a hand when I see she needs help. We get our hands dirty together until she gets it and doesn't need me to intervene anymore.

The grown-up is acting like a grown-up, like someone who is competent, has good advice, and wants to make a task as easy and meaningful as possible for a child. The adult gives over control when the child seems ready, because the goal is for the child to be able to act independently. There isn't an orthodoxy in sight; there is plenty of child intention and adult intervention. And it feels like a human interaction, not facilitation by formula.

The key to this kind of teaching is that it's based on *knowledge*, not *rules*. The assistance I give Anne is selective. I think three kinds of knowledge inform the help that I provide her. First, there's my personal experience of the thing being learned. (I've been tying my shoes for forty years.) There's my general knowledge of children at a particular age. (Babies can't tie shoes; five-year-olds can.) Finally, I have specific knowledge of this particular child and her needs and intentions. (Anne wanted to abandon Velcro and tie her shoes, but processing physical sequences was hard for her. So I invented a story to go along with the steps, since story was how she viewed the world just then.)

The experience of parenthood changes my teaching in ways I never predicted. I do not believe someone has to have children to be a good teacher; I have come to see how a good teacher takes parentlike responsibility for his or her students in terms of what they know about, what they can do, what they accomplish, and how the teacher provides explicit demonstrations and help. I have more specific expectations, and I just plain teach more, since becoming Anne's mother.

When I returned to the classroom in 1994, I began at the beginning. As before, I knew I wanted to try to create an environment conducive to writing: a writing workshop, with plenty of time to write and plenty of opportunities for choice, response, and publication. But this time I had glimmers of my new potential as a teacher of writing. In my classroom I could serve my students as a *mentor* of writing, a *mediator* of writing strategies, and a *model* of a writer at work.

In creating a classroom context for handover, for knowledge-based teaching in the writing workshop, I can bring personal knowledge of writing, which comes from my own writing experiences and from reading about writing. I can bring knowledge of young adolescents—who they are and how they see the world—which comes from my teaching experiences with this age group and from reading about adolescents. And I can work hard, from day one, to develop specific knowledge of the individual adolescents I teach so that I can understand their dreams, needs, problems, strengths, purposes, and goals as writers.

My goal in writing workshop is to act as a good parent, with all the complexities that role entails. I want to be a grown-up writer who listens to kids *and* shows kids how it's done, gives sound advice, and convinces them she knows what she's talking about.

I have become a teacher with a capital *T*. This does not mean I've reverted to playing God and making all the writing decisions from behind my big desk. But it does mean I'm no longer willing to withhold suggestions and directions from my kids when I can help them solve a problem, do something they've never done before, produce stunning writing, and, ultimately, become more independent of me.

Just as there are times when kids need a mirror, someone to reflect back their writing to them, there are times when they need an adult who will tell them what to do next or how to do it. Bottom line, what they need is a Teacher. Today I'm striving for the fluid, subtle, *exhilarating* balance that allows me to function in my classroom as a listener *and* a teller, an observer *and* an actor, a collaborator *and* a critic *and* a cheerleader.

Writing Workshop Today

A few years ago I gave a speech at a college known for its English education program. My subject was principles for organizing a classroom as a writing workshop. Afterward the graduate students, who were mostly classroom teachers, crowded around and congratulated me: "Your speech was so practical!" (which I took to mean helpful, and maybe even inspirational). Later that evening at a dinner party, members of the graduate school faculty also commented, but in a very different tone of voice, "Your speech was so *practical*" (in other words, not theoretical, not philosophical, and probably not even sufficiently intellectual). I didn't apologize.

For me, practice is the interesting part of education. I love to find and solve problems of instruction—to figure out how I want to be with students and discover what they need from me, each other, and the physical space we'll share for a school year. Of course, I also like to think about *why* I teach as I do—to articulate my theories of language learning and consider how my beliefs about kids, learning, and written language shape my practice. But the real challenge and satisfaction come when I develop a method that moves my kids forward.

The second edition of *In the Middle* still describes the nitty-gritty of writing workshop methods—the questions I ask myself every August about my practice when I start to get ready for the new school year:

- How do I help students develop ideas for writing that have meaning and purpose in their lives?
- How do we use the time available to us for maximum effect?
- What, how, and when do I teach about process, genre, craft, and convention?
- How do I talk with kids about their writing in ways that move them forward?
- How do I teach kids to confer with each other?
- How do I help individuals get control over formatting, spelling, punctuation, capitalization, and other conventions?
- How do I help kids send their writing out into the world, to audiences beyond the teacher and the classroom?
- What resources and materials will we need for them to grow as writers?
- How do we organize the physical space so it accommodates all the activities in which writers in a workshop engage?
- How do I organize myself? How do I arrange to keep track of each writer's activity, accomplishments, problems, pace, and growth, without killing myself?
- How do I provide models of the kinds of writing I want kids to consider and produce?
- How do I assess student writing so it reflects what I ask of them as writers, doesn't put them in competition with each other, and makes sense to them and to their parents?

Practices I've described in the second edition also reflect the recent developments in my thinking about my role as a teacher in the workshop and new questions for the sleepless nights of August:

- When do assignments from a teacher who writes help young writers engage and grow?
- What else can happen in minilessons besides me minilecturing?
- How do I talk to—and collaborate with—kids in conferences so that I'm showing them how to act on their intentions, not hoping they can find their way on their own?
- How important are specific expectations for productivity and experimentation? What should I ask young writers to produce over the course of a year, in terms of quantity and range of genres?
- How do I teach about genre without trotting out tired old English-teacher clichés that don't get to the heart of what makes good fiction or poetry or exposition?
- What behaviors do I want to see in the workshop? How do I encourage them? Which should be mandated?
- How and when do I demonstrate my own knowledge of writing? To what ends?

If I'm trying to act as a grown-up in a handover situation, sitting shoulder-to-shoulder with my student writers in the workshop as I do at home with Anne, wrestling with them over solutions to their writing problems, and showing them explicitly what I know and can do, what will that look like? What, exactly, will it mean?

So far it means that sometimes I do assign writing—poems of their own in response to a poet we've read, a collaborative script based on a favorite Greek myth, an ode to Mom on Mother's Day, a diary entry of a person from a time in history we're studying, profiles of local women whom my students admire. My students know I have reasons for any task I assign to them and that I'll explain how I believe the assignment serves their purposes—as young adults, as their parents' children, as citizens, writers, readers, historians, and thinking human beings. And they know that because I'll write in response to the assignment, too; I'll make it as genuine, practical, and engaging as can be for all of us.

The new stance I'm taking in the workshop has also meant a change in minilessons. On some days the lesson I present to the group at the start of the class is still a ten-minute minilecture, on, for example, the materials I expect students to have with them at the beginning of the workshop; the difference between *lie* and *lay*; why they need a comma to separate a vocative from the rest of the sentence when writing dialogue; how and why to keep a consistent point of view or verb tense in a narrative; news about a

writing contest or publication that features student writing. But on other days the minilesson runs as long as half an hour (Harwayne 1992). It might involve a demonstration by me as a writer at work, or it might become an occasion for students and me to work together on something—on an equitable schedule for access to the computers, on a series of questions that will help fiction writers flesh out main characters, on a collaborative poem that describes our reactions to a freak snowstorm on the last day of April, or on an enthusiastic critique of a *baaad* student essay that Macrorie (1988) offers as a prime example of "Engfish."

Minilessons in writing workshop have become a tool for teaching at least as powerful as my conferences with individual writers. Minilessons are my opportunity to present myself as a grown-up who knows about writing and the needs of middle school kids. Minilessons establish the group dynamic, the way I expect my kids to talk and think together about writing; they provide the context for theory building. Minilessons reach more than one writer at a time, provide frames of reference when writers and I confer, and grow from what I see my students doing, not doing, and needing next. Minilessons give me a forum for *telling*, just as engagingly as I can, about the behaviors and traditions and conventions of writers. Today I'm concentrating a big chunk of my energy as a writing teacher here, in these opening lessons, because I find the payoff to be so great in terms of the impact on the quality and range of my students' writing.

But the biggest change in writing workshop is in the directness of my approach to my kids. Handover manifests itself most explicitly in my conferences with writers and in the specificity of my expectations for the school year. When student writers aren't sure what to do next, can't figure out how to achieve an effect, or are just plain stuck, I draw on my knowledge of writing and help them. In addition to listening hard, asking open-ended questions, and reflecting back what I hear, I give advice, make suggestions, tell them what I think is working or needs more work, show them how something might work, and collaborate with them on pieces of their writing. As their teacher with a capital *T*, I also expect students to experiment with specific genres, attempt professional publication, produce minimum pages of draft each week and finished pieces of writing each trimester (Rief 1992), attend to conventions as they draft, take notes on minilessons (Rief 1992), be quiet, and work as hard in writing workshop as I do.

And they are undeterred. They know the goal: in the brief time we have together, to learn everything they can about writing—about purposes, genres, techniques, ideas, feelings, themselves, their worlds, and the accepted, grown-up way of doing things out in the world. They know I'll get my hands dirty showing them what I know about how to do the work and that next time around it's likely they'll be able to structure the writing for themselves. They come to trust my interventions because they see that I struggle, too, to figure out what I want to say and that I find my own purposes—and satisfactions—as a writer.

They know I write because I bring in drafts of my writing for students to respond to in conferences. I participate with them in collaborative writing ventures. I submit poems and stories to *Acorns*, our school literary magazine. Most importantly, I take off the top of my head and write out loud in front of them on overhead-projector transparencies. I show them how I plan, change my mind, confront problems, weigh options, make decisions, use conventions to make my writing sound and look the way I want it to and my readers will need it to, and generally compose my life. I'm not writing the great American novel in these demonstrations. I am tackling the tasks that are part of my everyday existence.

Working on overhead transparencies, I wrote a letter to the editor of the *Boothbay Register* after another letter writer attacked my hairdresser (a long story). I wrote a review of Maureen Barbieri's *Sounds from the Heart* (1995). I wrote a memoir about the first time I met Laurel, one of my students. I wrote a short story about a girl who is rejected by her friends— something that happened to me in the eighth grade and to one of my seventh-grade girls. I wrote a eulogy for my dad. I wrote articles about teaching my students and guidelines for them about writing fiction, teaching poetry, and working in their artists' sketchbooks. Every year I write a birthday poem for Anne and a Mother's Day poem for Mom. I write letters of thanks, complaint, condolence, and recommendation, and I demonstrate responses to history and literature, the other subjects I teach.

I have almost overcome my anxiety about revealing to the world how hard and slow writing is for me, and how wildly off-base my first attempts can be. I learned that I only have to write a little bit better than my students for them to learn from my demonstrations. And afterward, in conferences, students believe I know what I'm talking about when I sit down with them and their writing. I can only become their mentor, someone whose advice carries weight and truth, because I know writing from the inside, and I've shown them I do.

The second edition of *In the Middle* describes the details of a writing workshop in which the teacher is as active intellectually as her students. The work is as hard as it ever was; the results ten years down the road are richer, more diverse, and more interesting to write and to read. I have moved from astonishment that kids could write at all, to an appreciation of how hard it is to write well, to an understanding that it's my responsibility to teach my students everything I can about writing well.

The epigraph to this chapter has been a favorite quote ever since I first read Glenda Bissex's *Gnys at Wrk* in 1980, just at the point when I had started to question the logic of my teaching. I knew that in writing workshop I had found a way to bridge the gap between how I teach and how kids learn, and today this feels truer than ever. What is different is my appreciation that I'll never fully arrive on the other side. I will always be arriving, and that feels more than okay.

In the Middle represents what I've come to understand about writing, teaching writing, and organizing a writing workshop at this point in my evolution. I know my students and I will continue to learn and be changed. I am resigned—happily—to be always beginning for the rest of my life as a teacher. As long as I write and read, pay attention to who my kids are, and keep in touch with each writer's needs and intentions, there's a good chance I can avoid the worst of the orthodoxies—the maxims that prevent me from teaching my students what they need to know. I can be less caught up in adhering to a program or curriculum and more concerned with responding to my kids, leading them, and helping them grow up.

2
Learning How to Teach Reading

My education was the liberty I had to read indiscriminately
and all the time, with my eyes hanging out.
Dylan Thomas

My sister called with the good news: their offer had been accepted. She, her husband, and my nephew Eric were about to move to a new house, one with a big yard, shade trees, and an above-ground pool. "Please," she asked. "Whatever you do when you visit us, promise you won't let on to Eric that Atwells don't swim."

Bonnie wants the Atwells to pretend that learning to swim is no big deal. Specifically, she wants to introduce Eric to their pool without any of his adult relatives betraying our long-standing panic about deep water. Bonnie remembers the swimming lessons of our childhoods—how our mother conveyed her own unease in the water, how her eyes worried, and how Bonnie and I kept our feet planted on the bottom and refused to put our faces in the water. We were no fools. We believed Mom when she showed us that swimming was going to be difficult and dangerous.

My sister knows that like all of us, her son will learn at least as much from the implicit as from the explicit. In defining the conditions necessary for learning to take place, Frank Smith refers to incidents of teaching, whether implicit or explicit, as "demonstrations." We are surrounded by demonstrations; everything anyone does "demonstrates not only what can be done and how it can be done, but what the person doing it feels about the act" (1982, 171–172). We learn by engaging with particular demonstrations, as I learned more from my parents' fear of deep water than from all their good, explicit advice about stroking, kicking, and breathing.

In the classroom, a teacher teaches and students learn. But the explicit advice that comes out of my mouth when I teach is at least equaled by implicit data. Every minute we're together I'm providing demonstrations with which my students may or may not engage. I'll never be able to account for everything that each of them learns from me in our time together.

The ways that middle and high school English teachers have traditionally approached literature in the classroom convey considerable tacit messages about reading—demonstrations about what, why, how, when, and for whom people read. Methods for teaching literature at the secondary level tend to be fairly standard across the country, with fairly standard results. Students learn from English teachers that they don't want to swim in our pool.

We select texts and assign them, one chapter or chunk at a time, to be read by the whole class as homework. We give tests to make sure kids did the homework, and we orchestrate discussions based on the questions in the teacher's manual or old lesson plans. We present lectures on literary topics and require students to memorize various literary information—the Roman equivalents of the Greek deities, characteristics of the New Criticism, Latin roots, Old English and Greek prefixes, characters in *Macbeth*, George Eliot's real name—followed by exams in which students report back what we said or assigned them to memorize. We talk a lot. We hold forth about the lives of writers, the symbols and meanings of literature, the legacies of our literary heritage. But we rarely make time in class for students to read or allow them any say in what they read. And students almost never see their English teachers reading.

Our students are learning from us. The question is, what are we teaching them? What implicit messages come across to kids through the standard approach to literature?

TWENTY-ONE LESSONS TEACHERS DEMONSTRATE ABOUT READING

1. Reading is serious, painful business.
2. Literature is even more serious and painful, not to mention boring.
3. Reading is a performance for an audience of one: the teacher.
4. There is one interpretation of a text: the teacher's (or the teacher's manual's).
5. "Errors" in comprehension or interpretation will not be tolerated.
6. Student readers aren't smart or trustworthy enough to choose their own texts.
7. Reading requires memorization and mastery of information, terms, definitions, and theories.
8. Reading is followed by a test (and writing often serves to test reading—book reports, critical papers, essays, and multiple-choice/fill-in-the-blank/short-answer assessments).
9. Reading involves drawing lines, filling in blanks, and circling.

10. Readers break whole, coherent, literary texts into pieces, to be read and dissected one fragment at a time.
11. It's wrong to become so interested in a text that you read more than the fragment the teacher assigned.
12. Reading is a solitary activity you perform as a member of a group.
13. Readers in a group may not collaborate; this is cheating.
14. Rereading a book is cheating; so are skimming, skipping, and looking ahead.
15. It's immoral to abandon a book you're not enjoying.
16. You learn about literature by listening to teachers talk about it.
17. Teachers talk a lot about literature, but teachers don't read.
18. Teachers are often bored by or tired of the literature they want you to read.
19. Reading is a waste of English class time.
20. There's another kind of reading, an enjoyable, secret, satisfying kind you can do on your free time or outside of school.
21. You can fail English yet still succeed at and love the other kind of reading.

In *Illiterate America* (1985), Jonathan Kozol estimates that sixty million Americans are at least functionally illiterate, and he quotes U.N. statistics to the effect that the United States ranks as low as forty-ninth in literacy levels among 158 U.N. countries. The latest National Assessment of Educational Progress shows a marked decline in inferential comprehension among secondary-level readers—and a marked lessening in the degree to which kids value and enjoy reading by the time they reach high school. At the same time, scholars note that the level of literacy required to function in American society and on the job is steadily increasing. Larry Mikulecky of Indiana University observes that "up through World War II newspapers were written at about the sixth grade level. Now wire service articles come out at the eleventh grade level, and even sports pages are around ninth or tenth" (in Fiske 1983). As the level of literacy defined as functional becomes increasingly more sophisticated, the activities schools sponsor and the demonstrations teachers provide are creating too many nonreaders—students who either cannot or do not read.

Rethinking Reading

Obviously, no one intends this outcome. English teachers do the best we can at what we learned teachers of literature are supposed to do—at what was done to us back in junior high and high school. But even the most conscientious version of the standard approach demonstrates some or all of the twenty-one lessons. Implicit is the conviction that there's a "proper" way to read; that done properly, reading is as difficult and unnatural an act for humans as swimming is for Atwells. The model of the good reader that we create is a stereotype few students can—or want to—emulate.

This good reader is a snob straight out of a *New Yorker* cartoon. Ensconced in a leather wing chair in his book-lined study, he's pedantic and dispassionate. He keeps his encounters with books free of messy personal associations and biases; instead he brings to bear a received body of literary theory and history. The good reader reads no text more contemporary than Hemingway. He finishes every book he starts. He reads every single word. He looks up any word he's not certain of, but only after applying his extensive knowledge of Greek and Latin roots, prefixes, and suffixes. *He is not us*.

Contrary to the portrait of an accomplished adult reader that we paint for our kids, we accomplished adult readers don't read this way. I think we're embarrassed about how we do read and believe that if only we can train them, our students won't inherit our sloppy habits—skipping or guessing at words we're not sure of, skimming passages of description when we get bored, abandoning books that don't grab us, are too hard, or, in my case, have paragraphs that are too long. They won't adopt our middlebrow tastes in contemporary popular fiction (or our lowbrow tastes for potboilers). They will become the good reader. And so we set our priorities for the secondary literature program. Discipline. Accuracy. Tradition. Mastery. And at the center of the curriculum are the Great Works of Literature.

Alan Purves set different priorities: "At the center of the curriculum are *not* the works of literature . . . but rather the mind as it meets the book. The response" (1972, 27). When we invite readers' minds to meet writers' books in our classrooms, we invite the messiness of human response—personal prejudices, tastes, habits, experiences. But we also invite personal meaning and the distinct possibility that our kids will grow up to become a different kind of good reader—an adult who sees reading as logical, personal, and habitual, someone who just plain loves to read. A new set of priorities for the secondary English curriculum emerges. Pleasure. Fluency. Involvement. Insight. Appreciation. Initiative. At the center are readers' responses—to the world of the book, to the worlds of other books, to their own worlds, to the meanings they make, to the choices the author made, to the literate community of which they automatically become members the minute they lose themselves in a book.

For a long time—more than three years—after my writing revolution, the same groups of students who sat at their own big desks each day in writing workshop returned to class when it came time for reading, which was scheduled as a separate class, to find me barricaded back behind my big desk. Writing was something students did, and literature was something I did to students. I passed out class sets of the literature anthology or a novel, wrote the vocabulary words on the board, lectured, assigned, spoon-fed, force-fed, then tested students to make sure they *really* read the material. Tom Newkirk came up from the University of New Hampshire for a visit and characterized my writing workshop—accurately—as a "writing ghetto"—the one period when kids made choices, took responsibility for their learning, and found their own meanings and purposes.

While admitting to problems with my writing program had hurt, owning up to problems with my reading curriculum promised pure heartache. Writing had been relatively virgin turf for me, but literature was my field. I became an English major, then an English teacher, in order to teach literature, and for years that's just what I did. I taught my middle school reading curriculum, not my middle school readers.

Four things happened.

First, on the heels of research showing that sustained silent-reading programs boosted students' fluency as readers, I began permitting my kids to read their own books one day each week, and my kids began to drive me crazy. Every day at least one student asked, "Are we having reading today?"

I didn't want to hear this. We had reading every day—at least that was my assessment of the situation from my vantage point at the front of the room. I felt pinpricks of conscience whenever someone voiced a desire for more time for self-selected reading. But there were too many wonderful selections in the literature anthology to cover and too many questions and activities I'd invested years in developing to waste valuable class time dallying with students' uninformed tastes. So I continued to cling each week to four days of curriculum and one day of reading.

Next, some Bread Loaf friends came to Maine for a weekend, and during dinner one night Toby discovered that one of our guests actually read and, better yet, appreciated his favorite author. Long after the table had been cleared, the dishes washed and dried, and everyone else had taken a long walk down to the beach and back, Nancy Martin and Toby sat at our dining room table gossiping by candlelight about the characters in Anthony Powell's series of novels *A Dance to the Music of Time*. This didn't help me appreciate Anthony Powell, but it did open my eyes to the wonders of our dining room table.

It is a literate environment. Around it, people talk in all the ways literate people discourse. We don't need assignments, lesson plans, lists, teacher's manuals, or handbooks. We need only another literate person. And our talk isn't sterile, grudging, or perfunctory. It's filled with jokes, arguments, stories, exchanges of bits of information, descriptions of what we love and hate and why. The way Toby and I and our friends—and Anne, who joined us when she was old enough—talk around the table was a way my kids and I could enter literature together. Somehow I had to get that table into my classroom and invite my students to pull up their chairs.

Next, I began to think back on finding my own seat at the dining room table—about how and when I had become a reader. I recalled a conversation with a teacher friend who sold encyclopedias as a summer job. When he remarked that some of his customers had never owned a book, I told him that a set of the *World Book* constituted the only volumes in my parents' house when I was growing up. They represented a huge investment for my family, and my brother and I read them over and over, cover to cover, as if they were novels. The teacher was surprised. "I guess I assumed your parents were English teachers," he explained, "from the way you talk about books."

My father was a postman; my mother waitressed at night. Although we had library cards, and used them, the turning point in my life as a reader came in fifth grade, when I contracted rheumatic fever. I spent most of the school year upstairs in bed. Books, the library, and my mother saved me.

Once a week, then twice a week, she scoured the library shelves, looking for something I might like to read. At first I read out of boredom. Then I began to fall in love—with Ellen Tibbetts, Henry Huggins, Beezus and Ramona, and the heroes and heroines from the Landmark biographies; Lotta Crabtree and Francis Marion, the Swamp Fox, were my particular favorites. The day Mom brought home *The Secret Garden* I wrinkled my nose at its old-fashioned cover and language and put it at the bottom of the pile. When I finally cracked it open, out of desperation, I practically inhaled it. I remember calling to my mother when I finished it and thanking her over and over again for the best book I had ever read. "Can you get me some more just like this one?" I begged. My poor mother tried, but there's only one *Secret Garden*. I became a fast, enthusiastic reader over that dark winter because all I had were time and books.

When I recovered, I kept on loving reading because of two teachers. In sixth grade Jack Edwards read to us, years after his colleagues had abandoned read-alouds as too childish. In his class we talked and laughed about the characters in the books and the authors who created them. He loved novels, and through Mr. Edwards I met E. B. White. I understood, for the first time, how reading could be a communal experience. Playground enemies forgot all about the playground when Mr. Edwards' voice took us to the Blue Hill fair and Wilbur's broken heart broke all of ours. Had my students ever laughed or cried together over literature? I couldn't remember one instance.

The other teacher is my husband; I was his student in a survey of world literature class during my sophomore year of college. Toby lives at the dining room table. I'd never met—I still haven't—anyone as knowledgeable about literature, or who finds in it more satisfaction and meaning. I know that part of my passion for literature came from my admiration for Toby, from wanting to be like him. Did my student readers want to be like me? Would any of them remember me as a teacher who helped them love literature? The questions began to nag at my conscience.

Finally, I did something I should have known to do long before. I matched my own processes as a reader against the process I enforced in my classroom. It was not a close fit.

I usually decide what I'll read, but my students seldom decided. Even when my reading isn't up to me, when the application has to be filled out the right way or I want dinner to be edible, at least I decide *how* I'll read. My students never decided. They read at the pace I set, usually fragments at a time—a chapter or assigned number of pages instead of a literary whole— in search of the answers I wanted to the questions I posed.

I read a lot, and I have routines, times I count on being able to read, like before I fall asleep at night and in the morning when Toby's in the shower. Too many of my students seldom read, and other than Friday's silent-reading time, I did nothing to encourage or accommodate the habits of readers.

Most significantly, there was that dining room table. I talk about books, authors, reading, and writing as a natural extension of a literate life. My students had few opportunities for congenial talk about literature.

While writing workshop had long begun to reflect what writers do and need, reading had continued to demonstrate my English-teacher assumptions about middle school students. What I did as an experienced, passionate reader of literature had nothing to do with what I asked of my kids—which, in truth, was not much. They were passive recipients of literature I selected and interpretations I devised. Four days every week I dosed them with my English-teacher notions of good literature, and on Fridays they were readers.

In response to their pleas for more days like Friday, I began a slow, painful dismantling of the wall around the writing ghetto. I started by adding another day of independent reading to the schedule. In January, I added another, the following September another, until finally the literature curriculum languished in my file cabinet. My kids became readers full-time. I was learning about teaching reading and, once again, students were my best teachers.

They taught me about adolescent literature, a genre that barely existed when I was in junior high. They introduced me to contemporary authors of juvenile fiction who write as well for adolescents as my favorite contemporary authors—Atwood, Berg, Erdrich, Hoffman, Atkinson, O'Brien, Munro, Weldon—write for me.

They taught me to fill the classroom with books—novels, but also short stories, plays, biographies, autobiographies, histories, humorous essays, and poetry. They showed me that if I gave them the chance they would devour books. The first year, when I scheduled reading workshop three days a week, my students read an average of twenty-four books. The next year, with four or five workshop days each week, they averaged thirty-five titles, from Blume to Brontë, Voigt to Verne. I never had enough books.

My students taught me that the context of books they choose is ripe for rich, dining room table talk about literature. We went deeper than I'd thought possible into such traditional teacher's-manual issues as theme, genre, technique, and character. We moved beyond the teacher's manual to new issues—reading process, analyses of authors' styles and techniques, relationships between reading and writing, between one text or author and others, between literature and our lives. This reader-to-reader dialogue was a far cry from empty lesson-plan questions and sterile book-report answers.

My students taught me that they loved to read. They showed me that in-school reading, like in-school writing, could actually do something for them; that the ability to read for pleasure and personal meaning, like writing ability, is not a gift or a talent. It comes with the ability to choose, books to choose among, time to read, and a teacher who is a reader. Finally, I learned that selecting one's own books and reading them in school is not a luxury. It is the wellspring of student literacy and literary appreciation.

Every September, in addition to establishing my classroom as a place for writing, I build a new dining room table, one where there's room for all stu-

dents of every ability to pull up their chairs and join me. In reading workshop I expect everyone will read and discover books they love. Together we'll enter the world of literature, become captivated, make connections to our lives, the world, and the worlds of other books, and find satisfaction. I expect these things will happen because, just as Bonnie asked me never to suggest that Eric might not learn to swim, I try to provide as few demonstrations as I can that my students might not read, or find books they love. I hope the literate environment I organize around an imaginary dining room table will demonstrate just the opposite.

I hope our dining room table will encourage the habit of reading and, with it, literacy, conjuring up a new, sensible image of the good reader that my students want to emulate. And I hope it places a reader's response in its rightful place—at the head of the table and the heart of the curriculum.

Making a Place for Reading

In establishing the structure of the reading workshop and organizing who would do what, when, and where, I looked to writing workshop for parallels. Writers had time in class to write, choices of topics and genres, access to materials, opportunities for peers to respond to their writing, and instruction and demonstrations from me in minilessons and conferences. I began to push the parallels across the curriculum, beginning with the right to choose one's own books.

I still remember when I finally chose *Pride and Prejudice*, in my late twenties. I was incredulous. This could not possibly be the same novel I suffered through my sophomore year of high school. A few summers ago I gathered my courage and reread *My Ántonia*, years after barely passing a multiple-choice test on the novel; it is an incredible book. My list of reconsidered readings goes on and on: *Anna Karenina, The Scarlet Letter, Crime and Punishment, The Mill on the Floss, Hamlet, The Great Gatsby, Moby Dick*, and *The Canterbury Tales* (which I discovered, when I finally got hold of a copy minus the standard high school ellipses, were bawdy).

Although I dutifully turned the pages, I never read, in any genuine sense of the word, most of the school-sponsored literature on which I fixed my teenaged eyes; I think Capote's *In Cold Blood* was the single exception. I was a good reader but a different reader—a different person—than I am today. When I was ready for complex, grown-up themes, language, and relationships, the literature was there, waiting for me to enter and enjoy it. That I did go back was in spite of, not because of, the high school teachers who had assigned the books. Making my own decision to live with the characters in these novels was my first step toward understanding and appreciating the literature.

If we want our students to grow to appreciate literature, we need to give them a say in decisions about the literature they will read. We begin by taking a giant step as readers and acknowledging that the term *literature* embraces more than the prescribed secondary-school canon of second-rate Dickens (*A Tale of Two Cities*), second-rate Steinbeck (*The Red Pony*), second-rate Twain (*The Prince and the Pauper*), and second-rate Hemingway (*The Old Man and the Sea*). The last thirty years have witnessed an explosion in the volume of novels and short stories written expressly for young adults, adolescent literature of breadth, depth, and power. Much of the writing—I'm thinking of Robert Cormier, Sharon Creech, Walter Dean Myers, Elizabeth Berg, Madeleine L'Engle—is both exquisite and profound. More importantly, much of the sentiment expressed in contemporary adolescent fiction mirrors and celebrates what Tom Newkirk terms the emerging power—that sense of independence and self—of the adolescent mind (1985, 119). As adults can turn to fiction for portrayals of the universalities of our condition, so our students can find their perspectives reflected and explored in a body of fiction of their own, books that can help them grow up and books that can help them love books.

The class average of thirty-five titles grew as much from students' power to choose as from the time I made for them to read. I heard again and again from students of every ability that the simple act of selecting their own books had turned them into readers. Jay commented, "This year I learned I could actually enjoy reading if I picked the kinds of books I wanted to read. Before I always thought it was totally boring." Teresa, who arrived in September calling herself "a hopeless case when it comes to books and reading," wrote to me in November:

> I've learned more from you already than from any other reading teacher I've had. The way my other reading teachers taught was, you read a story they tell you to read, then answer questions at the end. I never learned anything from it. Last year we did that, and we also *had* to read books like the *The Prince and the Pauper*, *The Mouse That Roared*, and *The Call of the Wild*. I could never get into those books because we HAD to read them. (Luckily I did finally get into *Call of the Wild*.) What I'm trying to say is that I'm happy with myself and what I'm doing as a reader, and I'm learning so much about books and authors.

Jay and Teresa's authors during reading workshop were among the best writing for adolescents. I have filled my classroom library with popular titles. Over the summers I read like crazy and add titles that aren't popular yet but deserve a chance. In minilessons I conduct book talks about new additions to the library as well as old favorites, and I schedule frequent "book shares": times for readers to go around the circle and describe their books to classmates. A classroom library invites students to browse, chat, make recommendations to each other, select, reject, and generally feel at home with literature. It also provides a crucial demonstration: supplying books for students to choose and read, creating a literary environment for them, are high priorities of their teacher and school.

Allowing readers to select their own books has a major impact on students' fluency, reading rate, and comprehension. For example, Sheri, a struggling reader, wrote:

> I think the reason I liked *Weetzie Bat* more than *The Island Keeper* was because I was more interested in it. It was so funny that it really kept me going, like I didn't want to stop. So I read faster so I could see what was going to happen next. I never moved my lips once.

Suzy, another student who diagnosed herself as a word-by-word reader, complained at the start of the year, "I guess from what people say, reading is a pretty good thing to do, but sometimes I read and I don't know what I read." By May, Suzy had read nineteen novels and wrote, "I really enjoy reading for pleasure. But I hate having books assigned. I just can't get into them as much." Allowing readers to choose virtually ensures that, eventually, everyone will "get into" books. Even the most reluctant readers can, with help, find that one good book that begins a turnaround in their attitudes toward reading and their abilities as readers.

And while the choices in a reading workshop can entice inexperienced readers to pull up a chair at the dining room table, experienced readers are given the opportunity to create literary environments of their own. Someone like Missy could become positively giddy about all the good books she was finding and choices she could make as a reader:

> Last weekend I started *Anywhere but Here* by Mona Simpson. I'm only 100 pages in, but I love it. The main character, Ann, is WONDER-FUL!! She has a great, strong voice. I am a little confused, though. She started out driving to California, but now I think she's telling me of *before* leaving, leading up to it, like a flashback. Maybe not. I'll find out.
>
> I've also started *My Posse Don't Do Homework* while reading *Anywhere but Here*. Since *Anywhere* is 538 pages, maybe I'll take some time out, but I want to finish it. I know I'll finish *My Posse* really soon. I'm more than halfway through it.
>
> *My Posse* is awesome. I don't think it matters that I read Johnson's second book first, because it isn't fiction. There isn't a main story; it's a bunch of little ones. I love how it's not the normal nonfiction. It's so good and exciting, you know? I'm afraid to see the movie now. It might be a letdown. Have you seen it? Is it good? Has LouAnne Johnson written anything besides these two books? I've heard of one about her Marine experiences, but I want another about her teaching. I love her!! Do you like her? I would have loved to be in her class.
>
> Wow, I wrote a lot! It must be because I am just ecstatic about my books! I love reading!

Expecting readers to choose their books also leads to surprises for me. On occasion these take the form of a book I think is unsuitable to be read in school. When this happens, when it's not a title I can defend, I have to level with the reader: "Please take this book home and read it there. It's not a book worth me risking my job over." This means I read or skim a lot of books and consider their merits and my own criteria, as a teacher of literature and of adolescents. For example, *Go Ask Alice*, which appears on banned-book lists, is a book worth me risking my job. As Janet Allen has observed, the anonymous diary gives kids the vicarious experience of experimenting with drugs, carried to its ultimate, deadly conclusion (1995). I can't think of a better cautionary tale—after being inside Alice's head, kids have already lived the consequences of drugs. They may never need to do so in real life.

More often, the ways that readers surprise me are wonderful, like Danny's discovery one day of "something different":

> I finished all of the seven westerns I bought. They were really great, but I'm a little bored with westerns right now, so I'm reading something different. The book is called *Waiting for Godot*. It is a book about a mess of people waiting for one guy and he never shows up! It's a really weird book and I can't wait to let you see it! It's written in play form and it seems quite funny. . . . This Godot might be a very high honored and respected man, or he might be evil and mean. I'm really not sure.

In Beckett's *Godot* Danny found a book he was ready and willing to read. Patrice was ready and willing to sample Shakespeare.

> I finished *Macbeth* today. . . . I found that the three witches were my favorite characters. Many movies have used takeoffs of these characters. *The Beast Master*, a movie I saw on cable, did. They used them differently, but they were used to tell the future.
>
> Macbeth himself was, overall, a very confused guy. His wife made him kill the king, and he was hearing voices that told him to "sleep no more." Putting one of Shakespeare's plays into movie form could almost be as bad as Stephen King, because of all the killing and walking around with people's heads.
>
> I truly enjoyed *The Comedy of Errors*. I enjoyed the way the two characters called Dromio spoke. Every time they opened their mouths they spoke in riddles. The overall idea was very good and funny. The reunions were like this: 2 father-son, 3 husband-wife, 2 brother, and 2 owner-slave. There is one wedding. Some of the reunions are *very* technical.

As part of selecting literature to read, students in the workshop develop their own theories about literature. Patrice's remark about "technical" reunions has its roots in a discussion about a poem that had taken place about a month before. We were talking about Hardy's poem "The Man He Killed" and Mike commented, "I really don't like this poem. I mean, why couldn't he just say it in regular language?"

Mike had been reading Robert Frost and Richard Wilbur. He loved E. E. Cummings. He wasn't asking for colloquial prose when he said "regular language." I said, "Show me what you mean," and he read Hardy's line, "We should have set us down to wet right many a nipperkin" (1984, 150–151)—a word I'd had to look up the night before and could find only in our *Oxford English Dictionary*.

I'd made a foolish assumption. I thought my kids understood that language changed over time, that English wasn't just American and contemporary. So we talked. Over the next weeks students collected and brought to class examples of prose and poetry from other times to share in minilessons. After Mary discovered Shakespeare's sonnets, I made copies of speeches from five of the plays and we looked at the language, then at how the language differed within the plays—how Romeo and Juliet spoke one way, Macbeth another, and why. We began to puzzle out what makes a tragedy a tragedy and a comedy a comedy. My classes decided that just about everyone dies in a tragedy and a new order begins. At the end of a comedy the characters are married, reinstated, or reunited. John said, "Yeah, just like on *Love Boat*." Kellie commented that the Capulets and Montagues were a lot like the two squabbling families on her favorite soap opera. And from there we talked about basic plot conventions through all of literature, and how and where Shakespeare had borrowed his story lines.

Opportunities for social interaction around literature is another component of a reading workshop. Literary talk with a teacher and peers is crucial to kids' development as readers. It is not enough to give them books and make time for independent reading. For too many students, sustained silent reading is just a pleasant study hall. When nothing happens before or after the reading, the context doesn't support or extend readers' interests or knowledge. Easy, obvious choices, such as series novels, come to set the literary tone, and reading and literary abilities don't develop. As Donald Fry observes, the reading teacher needs to intervene and keep the ball rolling, to be "resourceful and responsive to what (the student) does in order to maintain that interest and allow that process to bring about change and not stagnate" (1985, 29).

At Boothbay Region Elementary School re-creating my dining room table—being resourceful and responsive to what seventy-five readers were doing—presented problems of logistics. Class size averaged twenty-five, so one-to-one reading conferences during the workshop allowed individual students the chance to do little besides provide me with quick opinions and plot synopses. There wasn't enough time or teacher to go around. And I discovered that even when an opportunity arose for an extended discussion between a student and me, many readers had difficulty moving beyond telling what happens.

At the time I was struggling to figure out how to talk to my readers about their reading, Dixie Goswami pointed me toward Jana Staton's research with dialogue journals (1980, 1982). Staton studied the written dialogues that Leslee Reed, a sixth-grade teacher, sustained over every school year with each of her students, letters written back and forth in a bound journal. In these dialogues I recognized what I'd been looking for: a way all seventy-five students might pull up their chairs and join me at my dining room table. The following September I gave each reader a notebook with a letter from me inside inviting them to write back about books.

I initiated written dialogues about literature because I had some hunches about the possibilities in using writing as a way to reflect on reading, and about teacher-student correspondence as a way to extend and enrich kids' reflection through collaboration. I suspected their written responses to books would go deeper than their talk—that writing would give them time to consider their thinking and that thoughts captured would spark new insights. I also guessed that a written exchange between two readers, a student and an adult, would move kids deeper inside written texts, with the give-and-take of the dialogue helping them consider and develop their thoughts about the writing they were reading. Finally, I believed this special context—a teacher initiating and inviting first-draft chat—would provide a way for me to respond to every reader and create an occasion for them to write and reflect about books: a genuine, genuinely interested audience who was going to write back.

The dialogue journals between my kids and me confirmed my hunches. Over the years we have exchanged thousands of pages of letters. The correspondences go far beyond plot synopses and traditional teacher's-manual issues. We write accounts of our processes as readers, speculations on authors' processes as writers, and suggestions for revisions in what we've read. We make connections among published works, between published works and our own writing, and between books and our feelings and experiences. We troubleshoot difficult books together (I can't begin to count the letters devoted to *I Am the Cheese* by Robert Cormier and John Marsden's *Letters from the Inside*), try to build theories (why *don't* kids today like *The Catcher in the Rye* the way kids used to?), and recommend books and authors to each other nonstop. And we enjoy opportunities to engage in some serious, and not so serious, literary gossip.

For example, Jennifer read both *A Diary of a Young Girl* and the script of the stage version of the diary. In this exchange we're calling each other "Robert" because one week we read or talked about four works by authors with that first name. Jenn decided we'd substantially increase our chances of becoming published authors if we were white males called Robert, so she changed our names.

Ms. A. Robert,

Just to see what Anne Frank was going through was miserable. Her "growing up" with the same people every day. I think she got to know them a lot better than she would have if they weren't in hiding, her mother especially. That sudden change, going into hiding, must have been hard.

It amazed me how much more they went downstairs in the book than in the play version. And it seems so much bigger in the book. It also told a lot more of her feelings, right up until the end. It must have come suddenly—to see police come in and arrest them.

I'm going to read some Robert Frost poetry now.

J. J. Robert

P.S. I think she would have been a writer.

Dear J. J. R.,

I don't have any doubt—if she'd survived, she would have been a writer all her life. Her prose style is so lively, and her insights are so deep. And she loved to write.

We've talked about how movies alter (often for the worse) the books on which they're based. Plays can't help but do the same. All the inner stuff—reflections, reactions, dreams, and feelings—doesn't easily translate into stage action, although Hackett and Goodrich tried with Anne's between-act voice-overs.

If you're hungry for more information on Anne, please borrow my copy of Ernst Schnabel's *Anne Frank: Portrait in Courage* when Tom returns it to me.

Ms. Robert

When Jenn wrote to me again, it was the day after I returned from a conference. My lesson plan had called for the sub to read aloud, and kids were thrown by the difference in our read-aloud voices.

Ms. A. Robert,

We *missed* you! You get used to people's voice. The switch is hard for me.

Robert Frost's poems are really good. "The Witch of Coos" seemed to me somewhere between Stephen King and Ray Bradbury. Kind of weird, huh? I heard someone quote (kind of!) one of his poems. It was on *People's Court* (dumb show), and there was a fight about a fence. In the end the guy came out of the courtroom and was talking to the reporter. He said something like, "This goes to show—good fences don't make good neighbors." I almost freaked out.

Back to the books.

J. J. Robert

Dear J. J. R.,

They quoted Frost on *People's Court*? (You WATCHED *People's Court*?)

I need an aspirin.

N. A. R.

All of this is first-draft writing, unpolished and unrevised but still thoughtful, personal, and specific to literature and reading. Creating and maintaining a literary relationship with each of my students is one of my big goals as a teacher of reading. The informality of notes passed in class helps achieve that goal.

One January afternoon I actually caught two of my students, Jane and Arelitsa, passing notes in class during a reading workshop. When I asked, "What are you two doing back there?" Jane answered, "Oh, Ms. Atwell, you'll be interested in this." She was right.

Every year one of my students' favorite poems is Robert Frost's "Nothing Gold Can Stay." They like it because it's featured in S. E. Hinton's *The Outsiders* as the novel's leitmotiv, and they like it because it deals with the evanescence of youth and beauty. Sometimes they see themselves as golden, fated to join the world of adults just as dawn inevitably "goes down to day." Arelitsa was absent the day we glossed "Nothing Gold Can Stay" during a minilesson. Because kids requested I leave it on the blackboard so they could memorize it, the poem was still there when Arelee returned to school. The notes she and Jane passed were about the poem and what it meant to them, two exuberant thirteen-year-olds gossiping about poetry and forging meaning together.

Jane,

Did you guys talk about that poem on the board a while ago? I think I missed it. Could you PLEASE tell me what it meant and what she said about it. I really love that poem wicked. I got to know more about it.

Okay?

Arelitsa Kazakos

Dear Arelitsa,

She said it was like an apple was growing. First the bud is gold, then it has a blossom and the first and second lines of the poem are about how the buds on the tree can't stay gold. And the third and fourth lines are about how then the blossoms on the tree bloom. The fifth line is about how the leafs blow away in an hour. And the rest of the poem is about how the blossom turns into an apple.

Jane

Jane,

I don't get why it becomes an apple? So how could it be "Nothing gold can stay"?

Also, did she say anything about what it meant in real life. Ya know? WRITE.

Arelitsa

Arelitsa,

I don't know how the poem ends for the apple but the last line means you can't stay young for the rest of your life. And then it meant for Johnny and Ponyboy that they couldn't go back home to do all the things they did before, like look at the stars, because Johnny killed Bob.

Jane

Jane,

But I don't get "only so an hour"? I'm so confused with the poem that I'll probably ask Ms A.

Arelitsa

Arelitsa,

I don't know about the hour part. But the gold part meant that they don't do the things like they did before Johnny killed Bob. It meant that Ponyboy and Johnny couldn't act like 14 and 16, they had to act like adults.

Jane

So this whole poem is about how great it is to be a kid?

Arelitsa

Not really, but it's about how you have to go on with your life.

Jane

Clearly there were more audiences for dining room table talk than the teacher. It was time to change again. Jane and Arelitsa put their letters on overhead transparencies, and I shared them with my classes in the next day's minilesson, opening the door to student exchanges about literature. For the remainder of that school year, and ever since, my students have added congenial chat about books and authors to their social repertoires. Some of the letters in their reading journals are written to me; the rest are written to, and answered by, their friends. The seating arrangement around the dining room table changes day to day, but there are always enough chairs for everyone, and all the chairs are comfortable.

Cultivating the Garden: Reading Workshop Today

My kids were reading, collecting books, loving books, and talking and writing about them. I was buying them books, loving the books, and talking and writing about them. The dining room table was busy and crowded. But over time it began to seem like we were eating the same meal again and again. Here, as in writing workshop, new orthodoxies about teaching had come to define what I did and did not do as an English teacher.

Ownership reared its ugly head: thou shalt not assign reading. I was so conscious of never doing anything that might remotely smack of spoon-feeding, force-feeding, or the twenty-one demonstrations that had killed literature for me in high school, that I felt I could only talk about it generically—titles, leads, main characters, prologues and epilogues, conclusions, narrative voice, theme, characteristics of different genres—or in pieces—speeches from Shakespeare, individual poems, short stories or myths I read aloud to the group.

I saw that getting students to read well and love books was one thing. If they were to grow beyond enthusiasm and use literature as a prism for viewing and participating in the adult world, I had to figure out how to inspire them to higher, deeper purposes. It was time to think about literature: what it did in my life and could do in theirs, and why I had chosen English teaching as my profession in the first place.

In college I loved literature. I loved it so much that I decided I wanted to change kids' lives as mine had been changed—as it continues to be changed—because of what I read. I read the whole world differently because I have this nodding acquaintance with literature. I can understand my culture and participate in it. I can get allusions; I can even make my own.

When Russell Baker describes himself as a modern-day Miniver Cheevy in the *New York Times*, I understand what he means immediately; the persona and metaphor resonate for me. When a married couple in a movie are named Ulee (short for Ulysses) and Penelope, I groan because I get it. I can read a contemporary poem like Richard Wilbur's "Merlin Enthralled" and recognize the moment in Arthurian legend—and human history—he has captured. When politicians quote Shakespeare, badly or well, I recognize what they have done. And at home sometimes I feel as if Toby and I are speaking another language, it is so rich with references, literary and otherwise.

When a bird smashes against the bedroom window, we look at each other and intone, "I was the shadow of the waxwing slain by the false azure in the windowpane," lines from the poem in Nabokov's *Pale Fire*. When a television announcer, after Allen Ginsberg's death, talked about the influence of *Howl*, Toby and I recited the first lines, famous to us—and now to Anne, too, who wanted to know what we were talking about that was making us so happy. It made me even happier to be able to teach her.

Three years ago, when I returned to teaching, I began to look for ways to teach some of what matters to me in literature to my seventh and eighth graders. To rely on another metaphor (not to mention literary allusion), I began to cultivate the garden I planted in the first edition of *In the Middle*. I named what I love as an experienced reader, researched what I almost loved but didn't quite know enough about yet, and imagined how to convey my attachments to literature to my kids. I am trying to be an adult reader whose values are so passionate, so joyful, that students will want to apprentice themselves to me, trust that what they learn from me has significance, and love what they learn.

For a long time I had been reluctant to see myself as a teacher of literature; I preferred *teacher of reading*. But my seventh and eighth graders know how to read. While I certainly do teach lessons about comprehension, speed, and strategies, I am primarily a teacher of literature. I can't forsake the power of the literature and lore that changed me. So I have stretched the boundaries of reading workshop to embrace what I value and what I think my kids might value, too. Here, as in writing workshop, my goal is teaching that is based on knowledge—of literature, of young adolescents, of my students' tastes and needs—not teaching that follows the curriculum guide or the rules.

This is hard, satisfying work. I hadn't read Thoreau, the Bible, Homer, or Arthurian legend since college. I had never taught poetry by Wallace Stevens, Walt Whitman, Mary Oliver, Dylan Thomas, Sylvia Plath, Maya Angelou, Allen Ginsberg, Linda Pastan, Margaret Atwood, William Stafford, William Carlos Williams, or Alfred, Lord Tennyson. I had never read Anna Akhmatova, Rita Dove, Jane Kenyon, Seamus Heaney, Dwight Okita, Gary Snyder, Naomi Shihab Nye, or Ann Turner. I read literature, researched what others had to say about it, and figured out how to teach it so that there was a chance it would make my students as happy as it makes me.

Over the past three years whole classes and I have read and talked about *The Odyssey* and Greek mythology and written and performed one-acts based on the myths. We read and analyze about two hundred poems each year— grouped by author, subject, form, era, school, and devices the poets employed. We watched the videos of Zeffirelli's *Hamlet*, Luhrmann's *Romeo and Juliet*, and

Branagh's *Hamlet*, *Henry V*, and *Much Ado About Nothing*, and read scenes from all four; then small groups chose their favorites and mounted a production of scenes from the plays for the K–6 students. We studied Arthurian legend, selections from the Old and New Testaments, Thoreau's *Walden*, Tim O'Brien, the novels of Walter Dean Myers, the Rosetta stone, Whitman's Civil War ballads, *Bartlett's Familiar Quotations*, the classical (and other) sources of the vocabulary George Lucas developed for *Star Wars*. Everyone read S. E. Hinton's seminal novel for adolescents, *The Outsiders*, which she wrote at age sixteen. We set it in its historical and literary context, then, as writers attempting fiction of our own, analyzed what she did in the novel, how she did it, and the themes that emerged from the lives of her characters.

The rewards in teaching literature with a capital *L* are huge. Students in the reading workshop are acting both as readers, choosing and responding to literature, and as students of literature. As the teacher of the reading workshop, I'm both responding to my students and leading them.

Each June I ask my kids to assess their work of the year and describe their growth. Dylan, a seventh grader, reported that he had read twenty-five books, in genres including reportage, diary, memoir, war novel, contemporary realistic fiction, mystery, and fantasy. As the year progressed Dylan had moved from the popular mysteries of Lilian Braun and Lois Duncan to more literary works that reflected his interests and concerns as well as the fare I had highlighted in booktalks and minilessons: novels by Gary Soto, Walter Dean Myers, Tim O'Brien, and Robert McCammon. In June, Dylan listed some of his accomplishments as a reader:

- I tried new genres: war stories, reportage, memoir.
- I found out how to choose a poem and how to read it.
- I learned about literature and how it changed through the centuries.
- I learned how poems changed from no *I* voice to an *I* voice and who changed it (e.g., Walt Whitman).
- I learned different forms of poetry (e.g., sonnets, ballads) and who experimented with them.
- I learned about Greek gods and goddesses and mythology.
- I learned how allusions to Greek myths appear in books and life today.
- I learned about Shakespeare and his plays.
- I learned about the "Big Six" American poets and read their poetry and liked it.
- I found out about how different poets changed poetry.

Dylan's response was informed, specific, and different from anyone else's. *Every* response was informed, specific, and different. I learned that the more personal my teaching—the more it reflects my tastes, knowledge, and passions, coupled with my knowledge of middle school kids and sense of where they could be heading next—the richer and more personal their relationships with reading. Instead of diminishing or silencing their voices as readers, raising my literary voice has the effect of strengthening theirs—and of bringing us closer. I become someone whose ideas and obsessions identify me, in kids' minds, with the literature I teach in ways they see as worth emulating. Reading workshop becomes an invitation to grow up into an adult world that's cool.

One spring I gathered and taught poems about World War II, which my students were researching in history. I found some incredible poetry: Brecht's "A German War Primer"; "Mail Call" and "The Death of the Ball Turrett Gunner" by Randall Jarrell; "Redeployment" by Howard Nemerov; "Naming of Parts" by Henry Reed. I also researched the London blitz and taught about it; then we read "The Londoners" by Anna Akhmatova and Dylan Thomas' "A Refusal to Mourn the Death, by Fire, of a Child in London." The conversations in class about all of the poems were intense and worthwhile, but it's the discussion of the Thomas poem that stays with me, as one of many occasions when my kids felt the pull of a literary life.

"A Refusal to Mourn the Death, by Fire, of a Child in London" ends beautifully, movingly, with the line, "After the first death, there is no other." When I finished reading it aloud, I watched a tremor move through the group, as recognition dawned on the face of one kid after another: "That's where Cormier got his title! Now I get it!"

Many of them had read the novel *After the First Death* by Robert Cormier, about a bus hijacking in which the victims, as in the Thomas poem, are children. Their excitement—their pride—in making the connection was palpable. At that moment they were insiders, able to read and understand their culture through its literature. When I cultivate the garden of reading workshop, it's because I want to portray for my kids the most enticing version of that culture—of grown-upness—that I can imagine.

The second edition of *In the Middle* plants *and* cultivates the garden. I'm working out answers to the same practical questions about how to establish a reading workshop that I wrestled with the first time around, questions that I consider and reconsider every August:

- How do I help students find books that compel and satisfy them?
- How do we use the time available to us for maximum effect?
- What, how, and when do I teach about process, genre, craft, strategies, specific authors, and specific books?
- How do I talk with kids about their reading in ways that move them forward?
- How do I teach them to confer with each other about literature?
- How do I structure opportunities for them to be sociable around books?
- How do I help students go inside the texts they're reading and consider and critique the writing?
- What resources and materials will we need for them to grow as readers?
- How do we organize the physical space so it accommodates all the activities in which readers in a workshop engage?
- How do I organize myself? How do I arrange to keep track of each reader's activity, accomplishments, problems, pace, and growth, without killing myself?
- How do I provide models of the kinds of reading I want kids to engage in?
- How do I assess students' reading so it reflects what I ask of them as readers, doesn't put them in competition with each other, and makes sense to them and to their parents?

The second edition also reflects the new developments in my thinking as a teacher of literature:

- When do assigned readings, from a teacher who reads and loves it, help young readers engage and provide a platform for new selections and connections?
- What else can happen in minilessons besides me minilecturing?
- How do I teach about literary forms, traditions, and works without trotting out tired old English-teacher clichés that mute, distort, or deny the intensity of a literary experience?
- What behaviors do I want to see in the workshop? How do I encourage them? Which should be mandated?
- How and when do I demonstrate my experiences as a reader? To what ends?

One Sunday afternoon I was surprised by a visit from Eben. He was a student in my first reading workshop at Boothbay Region Elementary

School; today he's a carpenter, poet, and scholar. We sat at the dining room table in the sunshine, reminiscing about eighth grade and talking about what he's reading these days: Hermann Hesse, Ken Kesey, Kurt Vonnegut. Before he left he borrowed Michael Ondaatje's novel *In the Skin of a Lion*, and after he was gone I washed out our teacups and remembered a line from Vonnegut's *Slapstick*. In the novel Wilbur Daffodil-11 Swain becomes president of the United States on the strength of his pledge to provide every citizen with thousands of artificial relatives. His campaign slogan is "Lonesome no more!"

Every day at school I get to sit around my dining room table with readers who speak my language; many of them, like Eben, grow up to be adults who continue to speak it. For me one of the worst things about teaching literature in the old way was the loneliness. I'll never forget what it was like to stand by myself at the front of the classroom, rephrasing a question about the selection from the literary anthology again and again for a group of bored, polite kids, and praying that someone would come up with the right answer. One of the best things about teaching reading in a workshop, where I immerse myself and my kids in literature we love, is that teaching is lonesome no more.

3

Making the Best of Adolescence

You don't have to suffer to be a poet.
Adolescence is enough suffering for anyone.
John Ciardi

MY ROOM

My room
My haven
My block of peace
in a hectic world

My room
My own personal disaster area
of piled clothing and blaring music—
a comfortable chaos

My room
My harbor of fantasies
"Gee whiz, Ace, what kinda room is this?"
asked Ace detective's sidekick
"I don't know," Ace replied, "but I like it."

My room
My ongoing rationalization
Joe's brain: Joe's room is messy
Joe: What's new?

My room
My responsibility
the subject of many
"Go Clean Your's"

My room
My prison
the subject of many
"Go to Your's"

My room
My cubicle of terror
harborer of nightmares
sinister when dark
shelter of my angst

My room
My haven
My organized chaos
My ongoing rationalization
My responsibility
My harbor of fantasy
My prison
My terror
My block of peace
in a hectic world

—*Joe Powning*

When I read Joe's poem, I remembered my bedroom in my parents' house and the most complicated relationship I ever enjoyed with a physical space. I hid my cigarettes there, was banished there steaming with indignation whenever I mouthed off, lay there on my bed crying about my unfeeling parents, treacherous friends, embarrassing body, terrible clothes, and certain knowledge that not only was there something seriously wrong with me, but everybody knew it.

My bedroom was my haven. It was where I pretended I was adopted, wrote poetry and kept diaries, taught myself to play the guitar, applied sapphire blue mascara, listened in a trance to the Beatles and Dylan, ate candy, plucked my eyebrows, and lay on my bed fantasizing about boys I'd met and never met. Missy, one of my students, captured the yearnings of the romantic fantasies I indulged in up in my room.

CRUSH

You see him
walk past you
in the hall.
Your eyes lock.
Yours want to stay locked
forever.
His just bounce along
from one girl to the next.
How you long
to say one word to his beautiful face.

How you long
to touch his smooth hand.
Long to be able
to wrap your tired arms around
his lovely neck.
Long to be able
to say he's yours.
To say I love you,
and hear it back.
You wait for the day when
your eyes lock.

—*Melissa Raye Heselton*

And my bedroom was my solace. It was where I escaped to when the fantasies came crashing down—when a boy I loved asked someone I hated to go steady with him; when no boy approached me at my first junior high dance and I spent the night on the sidelines watching the mating ritual.

FIRST DANCE:

You knew when it was right,
and you knew much more when it was not.
Something clicked
              when a couple's feet
              moved together.
They couldn't tell.
              You could tell.
              You could tell
              who clicked.
See who's far away? The scared one?
                        You can't reach out to him.
See who's too close? The one that scares?
                        He scared you one time.
        Clicked with soul
              but only half—yours
              not his.
Do you know these changed little boys?
              They scare.
              They care.
        Do they care as much as you?
No.

—*Rachel Anne Schlein*

Surviving adolescence is no small matter; neither is surviving adolescents. It's a hard age to be and to teach. The worst things that ever happened to anybody happen every day. But some of the best things can happen, too, and they're more likely to happen when middle school teachers understand the nature of middle school kids and teach in ways that help them grow.

Most middle schools are structured to skirt the messiness—and exuberance—of these years, mostly by regimenting kids' behavior: academic tracking, busywork and seat work, tests and grades, tight deadlines, tons of homework, arcane systems of discipline, few opportunities for students to initiate activity or work together, and fewer opportunities for any demonstration of affect. Schools tell junior high kids that their active participation is too risky an enterprise. It's safer to keep them quiet, passive, and under control, to avoid any acknowledgment that our students' needs, tastes, and values are, alarmingly, not our own.

We won't get the best from middle school students until we stop blaming adolescents for their adolescent behavior and begin to invite their distinctive brand of middle school best. I think we make the best of adolescence when we recognize and act on three principles.

First, teachers have to accept the reality of middle school students. Confusion, bravado, restlessness, a preoccupation with peers, and the questioning of authority aren't manifestations of poor attitude; they are hallmarks of a particular time of life. By nature young adolescents are volatile and social. Our teaching can take advantage of this and help kids find meaningful ways to channel their energies and social needs instead of trying to legislate against them.

Next, we have to recognize that adolescence is as special and important a time in students' intellectual development as any other phase in a child's life. They might not be as charming in their attempts to learn as their little brothers and sisters, but adolescents, too, need to be seen as individuals and responded to as people who want to know.

Finally, middle school teaching should be organized so that it helps kids begin to understand and participate in adult reality. This means more independent activity, more say in what happens in the classroom, and more responsibility for their learning. It also means teachers who communicate the importance and usefulness in our own lives of the subjects we teach, who demonstrate our processes as learners and our personal knowledge of our fields, and who invite students inside academia by showing them that inside is a worthwhile, interesting place to be.

I've illustrated these themes with poetry written by seventh and eighth graders. When my students use writing to capture their feelings and give shape to their experience, poetry is the mode to which they most often turn. Their poetry is my best window on adolescents' hearts and minds.

THE GARDEN

It's a garden of roses—
Throwing their buds toward the sun,
Growing up, growing stronger,
Climbing up the supportive wall.
A little bud blooms
Throwing off its old petals
And leaving the wall.

It's a garden of thorns—
Slowly overtaking the delicate rose.
And as the rose climbs . . .
So climb the thorns.
Every so often
A thorn grows
Too close to the rose
Causing a tear . . .
A ruined petal.

It's a garden of roses—
It's a garden of thorns.

—*Amanda Crafts*

Adolescence

Adults are the supportive wall in Amanda's garden. One of the best things middle school teachers can do for our students is acknowledge that the thorns of adolescence are real and cause real pain. I'm not a counselor, but I can affirm that growing up is hard, and I can resolve to make it an exciting, confident, productive time. I begin by looking at my students as teachers who will instruct me about their lives.

I'll spend the rest of my years as a middle school teacher learning about the lives of middle school kids. I don't think there's a more unpredictable or fascinating age. Twelve-, thirteen-, and fourteen-year-olds, in the middle of everything, are especially in the middle of changes—emotional, physical, psychological, and intellectual. Their sense of themselves, the world, and the relationship between the two is challenged every day by their own needs and by the demands of new roles, and all of it is played out in public.

Because they respond to these changes in such varied ways, all I can predict with any certainty about any group of kids is a crazy range of abilities, problems, attitudes, and levels of maturity. My kids are boys who play tag at recess, and boys who grow mustaches. They're girls who slip and call me Mom in class, and girls who come to school with the straps of their black bras showing. Their looks constantly deceive me.

My kids pretty much look like adults. Most are taller than I am. When an eighth-grade girl lets me try on her new shoes, often they're too big. When the shoe does fit—when it's even a style I'd buy for myself—I forget for a minute that although my students' worlds and my world intersect, they are different. I have to keep relearning the ways young adolescents are like me, and the ways they aren't.

Every year I think my kids will drive me crazy over the Jim Morrison question. It goes like this: Do you think Jim Morrison is really dead? Morrison wrote lyrics and sang lead for the rock band The Doors. He is, in fact, really dead. I saved my old Doors albums from high school, and I still play them once in a while. I listen to "Light My Fire" and think, "Great song." Perfectly bright kids pass around beat-up copies of *No One Gets Out of Here Alive* and whisper, "Mystical Jim is alive, biding his time." They're less interested in music or truth than caught in the grip of communal intrigue. Somehow Jim has escaped the grave—the fervor of their belief will make it so.

Middle school students shuttle back and forth between naïveté and world-weariness. They shuttle back and forth between everything. They are self-confident and self-doubting; they think I'm funny and they think I'm pathetic; they take responsibility for the younger kids at our morning assembly, then run them over on the soccer field at recess. They never know—and I never know—what they'll be when.

One day in June when the temperature outside was in the nineties, it was even hotter in school. Jody asked me if we couldn't go outdoors for reading before we all fainted. I said fine, but first tell me what the procedures will be. The class proposed and agreed on rules: anyone who has to go to the bathroom, go now; once we get outside, sit together; read—and don't watch the little kids' phys ed class. They neglected "Don't throw acorns."

About five minutes into our retreat from the heat, acorns started flying. I had to round up the shooters, glare at their "but we didn't have a rule about acorns" excuses, and keep them by my side for the rest of class. They hadn't planned to misbehave. Their seriousness of purpose had flown the moment they discovered all those missiles on the forest floor. A poem Tim wrote exaggerating the specificity of his study hall teacher's rules rang true.

STUDY HALLS

Mr. Maxim always says,
"Now, in this study hall there is
NO
sleeping,
spitting,
swearing,
staring.
NO
singing,
slapping,
shouting,
scaring.
NO
saluting,
scaling,
scowling,
howling.
NO
escaping,
gaping,
taping,
hesitating,
(and, of course, no constipating.)
NO
talking,
taming,
taxing,
teaching.
NO
tearing,
telegraphing,
telephoning,
telling.
NO
testing,
trimming,
tenting,
bad-tempering.
NO
tonguing,
teething,
tipping,
time-watching.
NO

<pre>
tying,
        throwing,
                tracking,
                        trashing . . .
and
        NO
                talking.
</pre>
Is that understood?"
"Yes."
"I said NO talking. Is that understood?"
(Pause.)
"Good. Now get to work."

—*Tim McGrath*

Ken Maxim knows his kids. When it's time for study hall, where the point is managing a large group of adolescents, Ken isn't subtle. Physically and emotionally, adolescence can be a pretty unsubtle time of life. Physically, junior high students are antsy. They tap pens, jerk their legs and feet, squirm, gaze around the room and into space. Even when the teaching mode tries to decree that kids remain stationary—in rows, facing front, and silent—ripples of constant motion break the surface of the classroom. These kids cannot sit still.

Emotionally, junior high students experience wide swings of mood and deep extremes. When they like something they love it; when they dislike something they hate it. And the loves and hates are transient—friends speak only to each other or they don't speak to each other at all, couples go steady for two days, obsessions are fiercely defended until they give way to new obsessions. The same kids who scream at each other one day debating Phish versus Rage Against the Machine hatch a plan the next for a class Valentine's Day party to which they bring the stuffed toys they cuddled as babies; they pose for a group shot of themselves proudly hugging their doggies, bears, and bunnies.

Sometimes the loving and hating can be brutal. Adolescents see themselves and others through new, critical eyes. They measure themselves against the way they think they should be, and they seldom measure up; suddenly the world doesn't measure up either. My students can be sharp-tongued, even cruel, in their judgments, but often their criticisms of others begin with their own insecurities. They don't want to be weird; therefore, they see weirdness everywhere.

John laughs at the paucity of Brendan's vocabulary, then misuses three polysyllabic words in one sentence. During a field trip to Old Fort Western, Jay is so embarrassed by the tour guides' period costumes that he can't attend to what they're saying. A group of seventh and eighth graders rehearses the song "Here Comes the Sun" for the school talent show for two months, and when they take to the stage on the day of the performance, two girls sing and everyone else just stands there in mortification. When I take my camera to school, Jake puts up the hood on his sweatshirt and keeps it up all day. He also points out to me that my hairstyle makes me look like his grandmother.

When I started teaching, I took such comments straight to heart. If the remark were brutal enough—during my first year at Boothbay a boy told me his goal for the year was to make me cry in class—I would cry (but not in class). If the comment were a compliment—"Ms. Atwell, you're the best teacher in this school"—I'd take that to heart too. Now, even if it's in writing, I don't take it to heart. Young adolescents aren't insincere. They're trying to fit in, but the ground keeps shifting. With every mood swing, their whole world changes. They can be ecstatic for no reason; they can fall into the deepest of sulks for no reason. They can feel in love with everyone; they can feel friendless and utterly alone.

My students write poems about the tension between their private and public selves, about the unbidden feeling of isolation that lowers like a cloud bank out of a clear sky.

REMEMBER

If I
disappeared
from the earth—
would you miss me?

If you even realized I was gone,
would you
remember me?
How?

Would you remember
what I was like
or what
I liked?

Would you remember me—
how I think?
What I do?

I am here now.
I have not
disappeared from the earth—
Do you see me?

If you disappeared from the earth—
I would miss you.
I would remember you.

—*Rachel Anne Schlein*

ALONE AND BENEATH

She sits alone, looking outside—
No reason to run, or to hide.
Sitting, her head turns just to one side.
She sits before the window, looking
Outside.

She looks out and sees the bright, reddish sky.
She sees something little fly by.
She sits there as if something has died.
She is the only one who can see the
Sky.

There's no one there that she can hold.
She feels something gone, something she sold.
No one's there, so it can't be told.
There's no one left that she can
Hold.

She's gone somewhere; she's gone beneath.
She's out of breath; she cannot breathe.
She's the victim of a heartless thief.
Now she's gone, down,
Beneath.

Now she's gone, and there's nothing to hear.
She's all alone; no one's her peer.
Her face turns white, and down comes a tear.
But no one's there, her to
Hear.

—*Dede Reed*

The stirring up of dark feelings is balanced by the awakening of new intellectual powers. Adolescents begin to go deeper into ideas—political, moral, and artistic. They're powerfully attracted to metaphorical language and layers of meaning. They glimpse shades of gray amid all the black and white that surrounded their childhoods. They begin to see patterns and significances in what were once just events, like Curt's description of a shoot-out at a soccer game, or Martha's perspective on a family funeral.

SOCCER DREAMS

It all comes down to me
number five in our line-up
at the shoot out.

I place the ball on the white line
and stand back to wait for the ref's whistle.

The sun is low
shining across the field.
At this end
where the grass has died
the sun picks up the smallest mounds
giving them a shadow
an illusion of size.

Everything has a supernatural look
like I'm standing on another planet
my own shadow stretching
four times my height.

The ref blows his whistle
and I focus on the soccer ball.
It stands out starkly against the shadows
the white orb of a dream
against the sketchy black of incompletion.

My shot is drawn out in
black and white too—
make it and play on
miss it and go home.

I stand for an instant on my toes
then charge to strike
and my shadow lengthens.
I connect
and watch the ball silhouette itself

over the crossbar

like a moon
setting.

—*Curt Monaco*

NO TEARS

No tears were shed.

My back rigid
hard wooden chair identical
to the one on either side.
There weren't enough—
some people stood.

The minister spoke
solemnly
shared memories
cracked jokes.

Everyone became
a robot
laughing
when supposed to laugh
bowing heads
in prayer.

Leaves fell silently
from trees
seeming to share
in the sorrow.

Leaves of all colors
falling in place of
the tears we
never shed.

—*Martha Hutchins*

One lovely aspect of this deepening awareness is adolescents' humor. Middle school students discover they can be witty. They ad lib and understand puns and double entendres. They write parodies that cut right to the heart of the original. They imitate and caricature (including and especially their teachers), and their imitations and caricatures are dead-on. I admit it: a big reason I teach English at the middle school level is that middle school kids can be so funny.

Michael and Edie were captivated by the story of Jack Jouett, an obscure (to us) participant in the War for Independence, who saved the life of Thomas Jefferson. They decided to compare Jouett's rescue mission with Paul Revere's more famous ride, so they borrowed a rhyming dictionary and went off to an empty classroom to compose a song for their unsung hero.

JACK JOUETT'S LAMENT

I know I'm not as famous
as Mr. Paul Revere.
Nobody knows about me—
Why, I'd like to kick his rear.

I did considerably more
than that Bostonian fool.
I rode to Monticello and
saved Tom from Georgie's rule.

Cornwallis marched to capture
the future president.
In the darkening of the night
the trap wasn't evident.

So I rode across the barren fields
a feather in my cap,
long before the Old Dominion
had become a tourist trap.

I arrived at Monticello just
as Tom had finished his grub.
I said, "The redcoats are coming!"
Well, that caused a big hubbub.

Corny and Arnie were racing
with five thousand troops in their wake.
They had one thought in their brainpans:
arrest Thomas J. at daybreak.

So Jefferson hopped on his horse.
With a wave and a call he departed.
Away he went before the troops
with the news that I'd imparted.

Longfellow made Revere famous—
put his name on everyone's lips.
I'm stuck with the talents of Edie and Mike
to celebrate my citizenship—
what a gyp.

—*Michael Maxim and Edie Sperling*

Erin had had it with Wallace Stevens, and with me. We read Stevens'
poem "Thirteen Ways of Looking at a Blackbird" in class, and I talked
about the leaps of imagination that allowed Stevens to look at the blackbird from such diverse perspectives and cast it in so many roles. Because I

was trying to push my kids' poetry beyond the realm of pure description, I asked each of them to look at an ordinary object from a Stevens-like perspective. In the process I pushed a frustrated Erin right over the edge into parody.

RESPONSE TO WALLACE STEVENS: "BLACKBIRD"
VERSES 14, 15, AND 16

14

The blackbird stops
eyeing a piece of paper
it picks it up with its beak reading the name
    Wallace Stevens

15

I see the blackbird
but it is too late
the bird careens and hits the windshield
shattering the glass into a million pieces
an impossible jigsaw puzzle

16

the powerline is falling
the blackbird must be dead

—*Erin Arnold*

After a minilesson about sestinas, Jay saw the complicated elegance of the form as an opportunity to craft a fan letter to Michael Jordan.

A SESTINA FOR MICHAEL JORDAN

The NBA wasn't the same without Michael.
What was THE GAME
Became just a game.
I missed watching him in his hundred dollar shoes
Do his million dollar dunks
After pulling some of his million dollar moves.

Other people tried the same moves,
But they couldn't make them as smoothly as Michael.
They tried to copy his dunks,
To make it more of a GAME.
Some of them even wore his shoes.
But without him it was always, only, a game.

It got boring just watching a game,
Even if there were a few good moves,
And someone was wearing some really nice shoes.

In their hearts the fans knew that without Michael
There would never be another great GAME—
Just lay-ups and shots from outside, but no great dunks.

Sure, they all tried to do powerful dunks,
But they could never make it more than a game.
The only event that would make it a GAME
Again were the magnificent moves
Of the fabulous Michael—
With or without his hundred dollar shoes.

Some say it was the shoes,
And some say it was the dunks,
But all basketball fans loved to watch Michael.
Coaches don't like coaching a game.
They want steals, dunks, exciting moves—
They want a GAME.

The only way it could ever be a GAME
Again is him, wearing his hundred dollar shoes,
Pulling his million dollar moves,
Then going up for his million dollar dunks.
Without him on the starting five it was an amateur's game.
The playoffs, the steals, the fouls are nothing without Michael.

The plain truth is that before Michael there was no GAME.
It was just a predictable game played in boring shoes.
I'm relieved to have him back; I missed those dunks and moves.

—*Jay Spoon*

Every summer I look forward to the fall. I know I'll laugh a lot; I know I'll be surprised, perplexed, and interested; I know I'll learn. And I know, finally, that what I can take to heart about my kids is how they wear their hearts on their sleeves. They can be highly emotional—elated, confused, angry, afraid—but the high emotions are usually short-lived. Water flows over the dam in torrents in my classroom because I'm learning what to take seriously and seriously respond to, and what to wait out.

"This is boring." "This is stupid." "Why do we have to do this?" These are responses I've learned to take and respond to seriously. Adolescents question adult authority because they're trying to figure out adult reality. They're not trying to be obnoxious. They want answers. They expect the teacher to be a model—to make them work and be good and, most importantly, to make adult sense of the subject at hand. It took me a long time to discover that my adult authority didn't lie in my big desk, red pen, acid tongue, detention slips, seating charts, lesson plans, grade book, or any of the other trappings of the middle school status quo.

The Middle School Status Quo

When I listen hard to my students, their message is, "We like to find out about things we didn't know before. But make it accessible. Make it make sense. Let us learn together. And be involved and excited so we can be involved and excited." When I listen to the public perception of middle schools and what they should be, I hear a different message. My role is to keep the lid on, consolidate "basic skills" introduced in the elementary grades, and prepare students for high school by giving them grammar drills and homework.

If I look at my classroom as a holding tank, a place where kids pass their days reviewing old stuff and bracing for the famous martinets of the high school faculty, learning stops—theirs and mine. We mark time waiting for somebody's idea of the real thing. It's like the parting shot graduating eighth graders used to deliver: "Gee, Ms. Atwell. We're gonna miss you. Maybe some day you'll be smart enough to teach at the high school."

Too often America's junior highs function as holding tanks. We separate the big fish and little fish into their homogeneous groupings, and we provide the minimum environment necessary for survival. The tanks are drably furnished, the affect is flat, and the inhabitants have little say about what they'll do while they while away years of their lives. The status quo presents a bleak picture, revealing little evidence of the collaboration, involvement, and excitement in acquiring knowledge that our students crave—that all humans crave.

We have access to a sharply focused version of that picture, thanks to *A Place Called School*, John Goodlad's study of U.S. public schools and classrooms (1984). We know that young adolescents value school friendships and social relationships far more than school subjects and teachers. We know that junior high students have less say in how their education will proceed than elementary school children. And we know that tracking is still widespread by the seventh grade, despite repeated findings that homogeneous groupings don't lead to increased learning but rather to teachers'—and learners'—acceptance of poor performance.

In looking at adolescents' social needs and the social status quo, Goodlad turned up findings that are markedly similar to numbers of other studies of American adolescents. Junior high teachers won't be surprised: school is our students' social milieu. When asked, "What is the one best thing about this school?" more than a third of the junior high kids in Goodlad's study responded "my friends." Fifteen percent named sports activities, and 10 percent referred to good student attitudes. In other words, almost two-thirds most appreciated school as an occasion to meet and mix with other seventh and eighth graders. In fact, at 8 percent "nothing" outranked "classes I am taking" (7 percent) and "teachers" (5 percent) as the "one best thing about this school" (77). And when asked how they perceived the most popular students in their schools, 60 percent of junior high students identified good-looking or athletic peers. Only 14 percent named smart students (76).

It's easy for middle school teachers to respond to such hard truths about our kids as we usually do: remark on how shallow they are, harrumph about the mythical good old days when kids were serious about their studies, and impose even tighter regulations against students fraternizing in the classroom. But I'm willing to bet that in respect to kids' peer-group preoccupations, school most closely resembles the "life in the real world" we claim to be preparing them for. Ask any group of working adults, "What is the one best thing about this job?" and at least a third are sure to respond "my friends."

Middle school students look for in school what matters in life; they don't look at school as a place to *get ready for* what matters in life. Social relationships matter in life, and in spite of our view of adolescents' social needs as a distraction from our agendas as teachers, adolescents nonetheless figure out how to work out their needs in school (Goodlad, 80). In large part they come to school *in order* to work out their social needs.

Because the place where I teach is rural, families and kids are spread out over a wide area of many small towns. Students who live in the most remote reaches are happy when a weekend or vacation concludes. When they return to school, they'll use every means at their disposal to renew their social lives—catching minutes with friends before school and between classes, sitting together at lunch time, passing forbidden notes, scheduling rendezvous in the restrooms, maybe talking during art or phys ed, and definitely talking during writing and reading workshops, conferring with each other and me.

One year some former eighth graders made the mistake, as ninth graders, of believing that conferring about writing continued to be something that mattered in life. When they attempted to read their drafts to each other during the half hour their high school English teacher had given them to complete an assigned essay, she was aghast: "There'll be none of that in here. This isn't the eighth grade, and that kind of cheating will not be tolerated." So students became adept at passing a new kind of forbidden note, a draft to which they wanted a friend to write a response.

The status quo regards collaboration as cheating and learning as a solitary, competitive enterprise. Even though junior high students spend most of their school day sitting with groups of twenty-five peers, they spend most of their time working alone, either completing a seat assignment or listening to the teacher lecture or give instructions. Goodlad observed that American students spend at least 70 percent of class time listening to teachers talk. These are not conferences; it's not even conversation. As Goodlad points out, talking teachers "are not responding to students, in large part because students are not initiating anything" (229).

The listening-as-learning mode, complemented by varieties of seat work and busywork, wasn't arrived at haphazardly. I think that losing control looms as our greatest fear. Rather than risk overstimulation we choose not to stimulate. Better to limit the possibilities and keep a neutral tone than to risk a display of adolescents' strong feelings—the shared laughter, overt enthusiasm, and angry outbursts that Goodlad rarely observed. Better to limit the possibilities and keep students quiet and facing front than to risk big, adolescent bodies in motion. Better to blame kids for their exuberance than to help them figure out how to channel it in productive ways.

One result of a tightening-the-screws approach is that adolescents, who might reasonably be expected to assume more independence in the classroom as they approach adulthood, have less. While 55 percent of elementary school students in the Goodlad study felt they did not participate in any way in choosing what they did in class, *two-thirds* of secondary students reported having no say (109). When Goodlad looked closely at who made what decisions in junior high classrooms, he found that 90 percent of the observed classes were dominated by teachers, "with respect to seating, grouping, content, materials, use of space, time utilization, and learning activities" (229). What's left for students to decide? What ends can students legitimately call their own? When are middle school students' needs—social, personal, or intellectual—addressed in their classrooms?

The academic curriculum, a closed system, effectively shuts the classroom door on any ends that kids might call their own. When adolescents do find channels in school for their raging enthusiasms, the resulting projects generally take place outside the academic program. It comes as no surprise that the subjects best liked by the junior high students in Goodlad's study were the arts, vocational education, and physical education (116). Students chose as favorites the classes in which they routinely collaborate with other students and the teacher, have some say about the product, and take an active stance, classes in which whole-group listening and busywork are minor components. This is a finding teachers of academic subjects can't afford to dismiss. Goodlad's question wasn't "Which course is easiest? Most fun?" He asked students, "Which do you like best?"

Learning is more likely to happen when students like what they are doing. Learning is also more likely when students can be involved and active and when they can learn from and with other students.

When students are tracked according to ability levels, the possibilities for this kind of collaborative learning shut down. Too many U.S. school districts still view entrance to middle school as an occasion for identifying and sequestering "fast" and "slow" learners. The groupings established at the beginning of fifth, sixth, or seventh grade often proceed through the senior year—for those in the slow track who even make it to their senior year. Although low-tracked students obviously get the worst of it, both groups lose out.

Kids tracked into the top groups see their classmates as competitors; measuring themselves against their friends, they worry they're not smart enough and panic about grades. Kids tracked into the bottom groups are plenty smart enough to look around them the first week of school and catch on: "I'm in the dumb group, I'll be here forever, and I know what's expected of me." They also catch on to who's in the top groups when old friends from other sections describe the challenges of their courses and homework. The students placed in lower homogeneous sections most need interesting, challenging instruction. They most need school to enlighten and make sense. They most need individual conversations with a teacher. And they mostly get remedial work, low-level texts and low-level ideas, and teachers faced with a crazy situation: a whole class of kids who could benefit from one-to-one help, but mostly need to be disciplined and managed.

Worse than inappropriate, tracking denies lower-placed students' basic right to equality of educational opportunity. When Goodlad looked closely at tracked groupings, he found that the crucial difference between high and low groups constituted a "marked inequality in access to knowledge." Ability tracking creates an "instructionally disadvantaged" subclass of students in our schools (152), as teachers set a different course content, encourage different behaviors and attitudes, and relate and respond differently to their students.

When secondary teachers deal with higher-tracked kids, they're more organized, clear, and enthusiastic. In turn, high-track students perceive teachers as "more concerned about them and less punitive toward them," see their classmates as more friendly than lower-tracked students do, and seldom feel left out of class activities. Low-track students report the lowest levels of peer esteem and the highest levels of discord in the classroom; they view other students as unfriendly and feel left out of class activities; and they see their teachers as more punitive and less concerned about them. In short, students in the low tracks are "the least likely to experience the types of instruction most highly associated with achievement" (155).

When Goodlad looked at instruction of heterogeneous groupings, classes that include students achieving at all levels, he found that it did not sink to the lower levels associated with lower-ability students. Instead, classes containing a heterogeneous mixture of students "were *more like high than low track classes* [italics mine] in regard to what students were studying, how teachers were teaching, and how teachers and students were interacting in the classroom" (159).

Schools' justifications for tracking remain fairly constant across the country. Whatever terms it's couched in, the bottom line is the contention that the school is meeting individual students' academic needs by grouping homogeneously. We choose to believe this in spite of the body of research that shows tracking doesn't produce gains in achievement (Borg 1966; Borg et al 1970; Alexander et al 1978; Rosenbaum 1976). In fact, ability grouping makes the junior high status quo easier for teachers to maintain—one lecture and dittoed assignment for one group, another lecture and dittoed assignment for another. Tracking exists mostly for the benefit of teachers and the lecture/listen/busywork mode of instruction. It allows schools to blame students for failing to teach them well—all those low-tracked adolescents of whom less and less is asked or expected.

In many middle and high school language arts programs, the status quo combination of ability groupings, passivity, and solitary effort takes its own peculiar forms. "English" becomes a content course. For students it involves listening to teachers talk about English, writing themes about the English teacher's ideas, reading assigned literature texts one fragment at a time and answering the teacher's questions, memorizing definitions, correcting errors of usage and punctuation in English handbooks, and being drilled on assorted "facts" about static, inaccurate versions of English grammar (not to be confused with the complex systems that linguists invent, refine, and reinvent). Students in the lower tracks get a watered-down version of this content, consisting of "skills" (generally the same deadly skills, such as names of parts of speech, year after year) and "fundamentals" (workbooks and low-level readers). Goodlad found that the subject rated "interesting" by the fewest number of students at both junior and senior high levels was English (120).

It doesn't have to be this way. When the content of an English course is ideas—thinking and learning through writing, reading, listening, and talking—and when students in the course pursue their own ideas and purposes in the company of friends and their teacher, the middle school English classroom has the potential to become an extraordinarily interesting place. This place is a workshop, a way of teaching and learning uniquely suited to young adolescents of every ability. A workshop approach accommodates adolescents' needs, invites their independence, challenges them to grow up, and transforms the status quo.

Making the Best: The Workshop

When I first heard about the writing going on at Atkinson Academy, a workshop struck me as exactly the wrong approach to take in seventh and eighth grade English classes. It struck me as dangerous: all those big, unpredictable kids suddenly let loose to set their own agendas, move around my classroom, talk with their friends, and write about adolescent ideas and concerns. The prospect of twenty-seven thirteen-year-olds engaged in a writing workshop made the junior high status quo look pretty good.

Twenty years later I'm still learning about the ways a workshop approach is perfect for my kids. The behaviors I anticipated with such dismay are exactly those in which learners engage. And because they do engage, there's little danger. My students are busy going about the business of the workshop—writing, reading, observing, listening, thinking, and talking. As teachers let writers and readers assume control, they assume responsibility for the hard work of considering, shaping, and sharing their ideas.

A workshop is student-centered in the sense that individuals' rigorous pursuit of their ideas is the primary content of the course. In this environment, Murray says, "the student has no excuse for getting off the hook. He has the opportunity, the terrible freedom to learn" (1982, 133). A workshop grants me a terrible freedom, too. As the workshop leader, I can't hide up front. I have the opportunity to get out there and learn how to support and extend my students' learning.

At the beginning of this chapter I described its themes in terms of three principles teachers and schools might take into account in making the best of our adolescent students. In classrooms organized as workshops, middle school teachers transcend the status quo and act on these principles. We recognize and accommodate the realities of adolescence. We see our students as individuals and teach to the needs and intentions of each. And we begin to involve them as participants in adult reality.

In considering the realities of adolescence, if we know that social relationships come first, it makes sense to bring those relationships into the classroom and put them to work. In a workshop, social needs find a legitimate forum in students' conferences about their writing and reading. Here, kids talk about their ideas, and kids are the initiators of talk. And here genuine conversation occurs, not just between students but between students and me, too. One-to-one and in small groups, writers and readers socialize about the world of written language and teach each other what we know. This kind of on-the-job talk belongs in the classroom.

Within the structure of a writing workshop, students decide who can give the kind of help they need as they need it: if Joe knows about science fiction, ask him for help with your plot. If Michael the Resource Maven knows how to use a thesaurus, ask him to show you. If Rachel is famous for her poetry, ask her for a response to your poem. If Emily has mastered semicolons, ask her to help you edit for them. If the teacher knows about ways to organize raw data for an article, ask her. In the writing workshop small groups form and disband in the minutes it takes for a writer to approach another writer, move to a peer conference area, read a piece aloud or discuss a problem, and go back to work with a new perspective on the writing.

When Jay graduated from his local K–6 elementary school and entered the Center for Teaching and Learning as a seventh grader, he found himself surrounded by writers. He took the plunge—wrote a memoir, a play, and a book review—but hesitated when it came to poetry. He hadn't a sense of what it might do for him.

Then, one morning Laurel asked Jay to respond to a wrenching poem about her parents' divorce. Jay's floodgates opened. Laurel demonstrated to him that poetry was a genre made for adolescents' feelings. That day he wrote a poem about his parents' divorce; the next week he composed a poem as a birthday present for his childhood friend, Tyler, who had gone on to the consolidated junior high school when Jay had come to CTL.

FOREVER

I didn't want to go to school that morning.
Regretting the words I would have to say,
I entered my classroom
And walked straight to my desk.

Tyler came in a few minutes later.
I tried to avoid him
And I did pretty well until snack recess,
When he started walking toward me.
I tried to find someplace to escape to—
Too late.

Jay, is there something wrong?
I have something important to tell you, I replied,
Something I've been trying hard to ignore.
His face suddenly became as serious as mine,
And I was flooded with memories.

*   *   *

I remembered all the sleepovers
And how I felt as at home at his house
As I did at my own.
I remembered the endless games of basketball
On the cracked blacktop of the school playground.
I remembered when we sat together at a
School concert and got a detention for talking.
I remember the time he saved my butt—
When I forgot to do my science project
And he gave me the answers
And helped me get the A.
I remembered all the joking around.
I remembered a very special friend,
And I was afraid to lose him.

*   *   *

Now, I had to tell him the news.
I blurted it out:
I'm going to a private school next year.
We stood and stared at each other for a moment.
I wanted to go to that school too, he said,
But we don't have enough money.

Even though we won't see each other much
We can still be friends,
Right? I asked.
Right, he smiled.
Forever.

*   *   *

Forever is a long time.
Forever takes a lot of work.
I don't see him every day but
We still talk on the phone,
And whenever we can
We sleep over at each other's house.
I go to every one of his basketball games
To watch him play for his school.

I'm doing everything I can
To keep this friendship a part of me . . .
Forever.

—*Jay Spoon*

Because I know how adolescents can speak to each other if left to their own devices, I've learned I need to set the tone for talk in the workshop. Peer conferences won't work unless writers trust that their peers won't shoot them down. So I show my kids in minilessons how to confer with each other, and I watch my tongue. When I'm insulting, sarcastic, brusque, or gushing, I'm demonstrating that this is how they might respond to each other. When a response is brutal or hints at a best friend's empty flattery, I confer on the conferring: "How will that response help the writer?" And in order to maintain a volume level that won't interfere with the thinking of other writers, I insist on silence. Then I create places for kids to go to talk with each other, conference areas apart from the quiet areas for writing.

The workshop is filled with places to go. A reality of adolescence is that adolescents need to move; so do writers and readers. My students move purposefully among the areas of the room where they find what writers and readers need: books of every kind, new titles, recommended titles, materials for writing, word processors, resources and references, writing folders, places to publish, models of different kinds of writing, bulletin boards, response, solitude. When I organize my classroom as a workshop, the physical arrangement calls for motion. In turn, the organization of the workshop structures the motion and keeps it purposeful. With all these kids moving around the room I have many fewer discipline problems than in the old everybody-face-front days—less fidgeting, less restlessness, less boredom. And they have greater independence—more say in what they'll do, more self-regulation, and more involvement.

The workshop demands involvement because it exists to serve students' purposes. All the strong feelings and raging enthusiasms of adolescence get directed toward ends that are meaningful because students chose them.

When they can choose, middle school students will write for all the reasons literate people everywhere engage as writers. They recreate happy times, work through sad times, discover what they know about a subject and learn more, convey and request information, apply for jobs, parody, petition, play, explore, argue, apologize, advise, sympathize, express love, show gratitude, make money.

When they can choose, middle school students will read for all the reasons literate people everywhere engage as readers. They live other lives and learn about their own, see how other writers have written, acquire others' knowledge, escape, think, travel, ponder, love, laugh, cry.

The writing and reading workshop is a literate environment; by definition it is a place to become involved in writing and reading. And once they're involved, middle school students can become genuinely excited about finding out things they didn't know before, thinking about new ideas in new ways. Often they just need a "nudge"—Mary Ellen Giacobbe's word for the guidance that takes learners beyond where they are to where they might be.

In reading conferences I've learned to nudge students toward novels that give shape to adolescents' feelings and portray their emerging intelligence and understandings—*Durable Goods, Joy School, Jumping the Nail, The Chocolate War, Walk Two Moons, Boy's Life, Freak the Mighty, The Outsiders.* I nudge toward poets who describe the world in all its beauty and horror— Margaret Atwood, E. E. Cummings, Robert Frost, Langston Hughes, Pablo Neruda, Mary Oliver, Linda Pastan, Marge Piercy, William Stafford, Walt Whitman, William Carlos Williams. And I nudge toward books that explore the state of the world we live in—*I Am the Cheese, To Kill a Mockingbird, What Jamie Saw, At Risk, Reviving Ophelia, If I Should Die Before I Wake, Fallen Angels, The Things They Carried, Nothing but the Truth.*

In writing workshop I've learned to pose questions that ask kids to reflect on their lives. Dostoyevsky wrote, "One sacred memory from childhood is perhaps the best education," and I nudge writers to uncover and bring meaning to their own sacred memories of friendship and family. Missy said good-bye to her childhood in a poem that celebrates and memorializes a swing set that is, finally, too worn to be passed along to another family and another generation of children.

CEREMONY OF THE SWING SET

We trudged home
through the dark
each carrying a piece of it—
a swing, a ladder, a ring—
we brought home from
other children's yards.
No one would ever outgrow it again.
It was finally too old.
We tossed each piece into
the fire.

Crackle. Pop. It burned like mad,
giving off a smell we all recognized,
an aroma filled with memories.
Our eyes closed.
Smiles wrapped their way
around our faces.
We stood there
remembering the times.

The time I got stuck
on the top, screaming
for someone—anyone—
to *get me down.*

The time we tried to
flip over the seats and
everyone succeeded
except me.
My body came crashing
to the earth.
My wrist smashed.
My mouth tried to scream
but no sound came out.

The time we held
The Swing Olympics,
seeing who could
fly the highest or
land the farthest,
giving each other medals and
clapping and cheering for our swing skills.

The time we made up a routine
to "Chantilly Lace" for the
Fourth of July barbecue.
Everyone had a part—
swinging, flipping, singing—
everyone doing it perfectly
while our parents ate their
hot dogs and admired us,
until I fell and messed it up
for all of us.

But I especially remembered
the times—all the times—
we just sat and talked,
chipping off the

ugly green paint,
waiting for something
exciting to happen.

Now we stood there together
inhaling the memories,
remembering the times
we had in common and
the emotion we knew we
held in common.
Pure love.

—*Melissa Raye Heselton*

I nudge students to explore the social, political, and ethical issues that encircle personal experience. When they have avenues for considering the shape of the world around them, middle school students will take on the world in their writing, confronting such issues as civil rights, acid rain, animal rights, environmental protection, nuclear power, and peer pressure. Michael raised his voice by writing a song that our whole school learned and sang at morning assemblies.

DYING TREASURES

The world is made of so many treasures,
but we trash it and walk right on by.
We need to notice the mistakes that we make,
if we want our world to survive.

The earth depends on all of us helping.
We can't sit here, closing our eyes.
We need to stop and realize what we're doing,
or nature will shut down and die.

None of us ever pays much attention.
Mother Nature is saying good-bye.
We need to wake up and see the world whole—
Stand up and see eye to eye.

The world is made of so many treasures.
If we help, they won't fade and die.
We need to notice the mistakes that we make,
if we want our world to survive.
Let's help our earth to survive.

—*Michael Maxim*

Catharine raised her voice in a poem about the millions of land mines left behind in Vietnam, still maiming and killing children more than twenty years after the end of the war. The school recited it at an afternoon assembly; then we collected and donated money toward the demining effort.

ANOTHER SPRING

The war is not over yet.
Our explosive bulbs
are still planted
in the trampled
earth,
waiting to
burst
on some spring day.

Only these bulbs
won't burst into the
joy
that flowers
bring.
They will burst into
flames
and the screams
of the children
who will lose
arms and legs
because of them.

These bulbs will
burst on
some spring day in
Vietnam.

—*Catharine Hull*

These are individuals' genuine concerns, and the help I can offer my kids in writing and reading conferences is truly individualized instruction as I move within the group and stop to sit with one writer or reader at a time. Evaluation is individualized, too. When kids act on their intentions, rather than my one intention for the whole class, I have to look for individual changes and improvement: there is no basis for comparing one student against others. The context demands that I evaluate each student's growth over time, an important spur to learning for its own sake.

And students do grow and learn. Every day for a week Jason came into class waving his copy of David Eddings' fantasy novel *Pawn of Prophecy*, announcing in an awed voice, "This is a good book. I mean, this is a *really good* book." Every day for a week Andy came into class waving the drafts of his account of a typical baseball practice announcing in an awed voice, "This is a funny essay. I can't believe what a funny essay this is." One good book, one successful piece of writing, are enough to convince most middle school students of the challenges and satisfactions of written language. They want to find more good books, they want to write well again, and over the weeks or months of the workshop, they come to believe they can do both.

To convince students of their academic potential, we have to demonstrate our expectation that every student *has* an academic potential. Student-regulated activity, individualized instruction, and heterogeneous groupings are strong demonstrations—and more. Nontracked workshops work. Instead of accommodating one ability level and one level of instructional activity, heterogeneous workshops represent the whole range of middle school abilities, attitudes, and intentions. There are as many teachers in a workshop as there are students. Everyone learns from everybody, and our less able students may learn most and best of all.

Less able students need more able models; they need to be surrounded by other learners whose ideas will spark and charge the environment; and they generally need more response, advice, and collaboration. No matter how high my expectations, if I'm faced with a class of twenty-five low-tracked writers and readers, I'm hard put to provide the response each student needs. But if I have a handful of low ability or learning disabled students in each class, they can catch fire with the enthusiasm generated by other kids and I can give them the extra time they need as I circulate among all my students and confer. I can provide conditions favorable for everyone's learning because everyone has access to the same knowledge, and low-ability students can play an active role in interesting, complex activities.

Identified as a special education student, Laura could be mainstreamed for English instruction because my English course is a writing workshop. She brought her interests and abilities to the workshop, and I brought my expectation that she would write. Laura wrote a play, narratives, a profile, and letters, entered two essay contests (she came in second place in one of them), and composed pages and pages of poetry. Her favorite of her poems was written after the NASA shuttle disaster. She said, "I really liked that Christa McAuliffe. I was upset and mixed up, and this is the way I expressed my feelings."

ALL WE KNOW

All we know is that she lived in a small town called
    Concord,
That she had a family,
And that she was a social studies teacher.
All we know is that she had a dream to go to space,
That her dream almost came true,
That she was going to teach class while in space,
That she had a chance to explain to us about our outer
    world,
And that she took her son's teddybear to be the first in
    space.
All that we know is that she and six others boarded the
    shuttle with happiness and hope,
That they had a good lift-off,
That millions of people were watching the launch,
And that they will never come back to tell us about
    their discoveries.
All we know is that seven moons will be named after
    them,
That the families agree that life must go on,
And that they will be missed.
All we hope is that they went in peace.

When I asked Laura how she came up with the idea of the repeating line, she said, "I remember some of the poems you read to us that had a lot of repetition. And on the day of the explosion they kept saying on TV, 'All we know at this time is blah, blah.' I kept hearing it, and I knew I wanted to use it." I asked her if she wanted to send a copy to the *Boothbay Register*, the local weekly. I said, "I'm thinking about that because there was a poem in the *Register* about the shuttle disaster by one of their reporters, and I think yours is—" She interrupted me. "Mine is better. I thought so, too."

Laura learned about poetry by reading it, hearing it read by me and her friends, and writing her own. In turn, she nudged her friend Julie to try her hand at free verse and responded to Julie's drafts. When students are surrounded by poetry, they'll write poetry. When students aren't measured against each other, they'll feel free to take risks and give and accept help. When students aren't tracked, teachers are freed to expect and encourage each student's best, and our less able kids have a chance to see themselves as capable.

Barry saw himself as capable. He was another special ed student mainstreamed for English. When he came to the group meeting that ended one morning's writing workshop, it was with the language, information, and expectations of a writer. Before he read his piece to the class, Barry told them what he needed: "This is my second draft of a memoir about going squirrel hunting up to Back Narrows, but it's all dialogue. It ain't got no context. I'm looking for places to embed the context." Until class ended, Barry taught us what he knew about squirrel hunting, and we listened for places where we were confused or wanted to know more.

As exasperated as I get with the clocks that regulate my time with my kids, I know it's essential that Barry and his classmates pack up and travel to another classroom and teacher when it's time for math and science. Specialization in junior high is valid not just because adolescents need to move, but because they need teachers who know their fields. Goodlad found that teachers of the subjects for which kids expressed greatest liking and interest tended to be those who view themselves as adequately prepared (185). I know—and love—the humanities: language, history, and art. Middle school students are at an age when they still know they don't know everything (unlike high school, where kids start to assume they know it all). They're more likely to learn in cooperation with knowledgeable teachers who are enthusiastic about sharing what they know. They're more likely to get hooked.

My brother, a genealogist and historian, was hooked in the seventh grade by Miss Campbell, his social studies teacher. She belonged to all kinds of historical societies and professional groups, conducted her own research, showed kids how she went about studying local history, and engaged them in local research of their own. She hooked Glenn for life.

Nicholas Gage, former *New York Times* correspondent, is the author of *Eleni*, the story of his mother's execution for planning the escape of her children from their Greek village in 1948. Gage was hooked by his seventh-grade English teacher, Miss Hurd. She listened to the young immigrant struggle to tell his mother's story, then helped him find the English words to write it. Gage's composition won an award from the Freedoms Foundation; more importantly, he discovered that his writing gave him the power to make up for his mother's sacrifice and avenge her death. Miss Hurd gave Gage a voice—and hooked him for life.

David Halberstam, the author and Pulitzer Prize–winning journalist; John Bushnell, former chief of mission in the American Embassy in Buenos Aires; and Ralph Nader, the consumer advocate, were all in the same seventh grade social studies class and were all hooked by the same teacher, Miss Thompson. Halberstam wrote, "She taught with genuine passion . . . encouraging young people at a delicate moment to think that they could be anything they wanted" (1984). Miss Thompson opened her class-room door to a world rich with intriguing possibilities.

Adolescents are ripe to be hooked. With good teaching, this is the age when kids who are going to become interested and excited become interested and excited. When teachers demonstrate passion for our fields, we invite students to believe that learning is worthwhile. We answer the question, "Why do we have to do this?" with our own conviction and excitement, modeling the power we derive from knowledge and experience. We invite our students to join us in a compelling version of adult reality. In my writing and reading workshop I've cast off the trappings of the junior high English teacher status quo. I put my true authority on the line from the very first day of school: "I'm a writer and a reader. Writing and reading and teaching them to you are my life."

I write out loud in front of my students on overhead transparencies. I show them my drafts. I ask for their responses in writing conferences. I tell them that writing is a new habit for me, one I acquired later in life that has changed my life.

I read with my students. I show them what I'm reading, and I talk about and lend my books. I tell them that reading is an old habit, one that has shaped my life since childhood and gives it so much meaning I don't know if I could go on living if for some reason I suddenly couldn't read. I even write about my reading:

BIBLIOPHILE

I can't control them.
I can't seem to intercede.
My eyes have a mind all their own.
With me or without me, they read.
They need to fix
On print at all times:
Cereal boxes at the breakfast table,
Junk magazines on the checkout line.
But mostly my eyes
Are craving good stories—
Stories about my life and times,
Found in others' loves and worries—
Stories that take me inside myself,
Stories that take me away,
Luring me into other worlds
Where, whenever I can, I stay
And stay

Until it's distressingly late
(Until my eyes need that other world
Where they rest and anticipate)
Fixing and fixing and fixing again
On someone's words and ways,
Making those words belong to me, too,
Reeling in wonder and rage and dismay.
I couldn't live if I couldn't read.
It's nothing less: I'm hooked.
I know it sounds like a sales pitch
(YOUR ENGLISH TEACHER LOVES BOOKS)
But your English teacher loves books.

I'm demonstrating the truth. I love these things so much I can't imagine my students won't love them, too. From the first day of school I present myself as a writer and reader, and I expect my students will participate in written language as writers and readers do. I promise them that what we do together will make sense and bring satisfaction. Today my reputation as a teacher depends on the importance I place on writing and reading in my life, how my passion informs my teaching, and how I invite kids to share that passion.

The first day of school one September, I started the year as I always do, by surveying my kids about their writing and reading. I said, "This is for my information. I'm really interested in the truth. So please don't try to impress me or depress me. For this research to be valid and useful, I need you to be serious and honest." One question asked students to estimate how many books they'd read over the past twelve months. The average was surprisingly high: twenty books. In June I readministered the survey, then gave back the September surveys and asked kids to conduct some research of their own, by describing and analyzing any changes they noticed. What they did was burst out laughing.

"What's so funny?" I asked.

"We lied," they answered.

In September, three-quarters of my students exaggerated the number of books they'd read. Their dishonesty blew the validity of that particular piece of research but turned up something more interesting. I asked why they'd lied, and every answer was a variation on, "Because we'd heard about you. We came in here knowing you expected us to be readers, too."

My teaching has to make good on my expectations. While trusting that all my kids will become involved, I have to invite their involvement just as generously and sensibly as I can. My best invitation is the writing and reading workshop. Here, adolescents' social relationships can serve scholarly ends. Kids can be active, talking and moving as part of their activity as engaged writers and readers. They can capture and channel their ideas, feelings, and enthusiasms, have more say in their learning, and assume greater independence. Here, I can teach by example, in conversation, in collaboration, and in context. I can help my kids grow up by presenting as enticing a version as I can of what being grown up means. I can watch their faces shine like beacons when they and a new idea connect. I can help make school make sense.

Middle school teachers make the best of our students when we accept and build on the realities of middle school kids. We can't wish away, discipline away, or program away a time of life. We're there to help our students open a window on adulthood, on what really matters in life; we help by opening our curricula to young adolescents' preoccupations, perspectives, and growing pains.

In *School and Society*, first published in 1899, John Dewey wrote, "From the standpoint of the child, the great waste in school comes from his inability to utilize the experiences he gets outside of school in any complete and free way; while, on the other hand, he is unable to apply to daily life what he is learning at school."

When a middle school begins to reflect the nature of its kids, the great waste in our schools wanes, and great purpose waxes. School can be good for something. School and life can come to terms in practical, rigorous ways. We make the best of adolescence when we make the classroom the best context we can for the mercurial minds at work and play there.

II
Writing and Reading Workshop

It is not enough to be busy; the question is, what are we busy about?
Henry David Thoreau

4
Getting Ready

Be regular and ordinary in your life like a bourgeois so that you may be
violent and original in your work.
Gustave Flaubert

One spring day Donald Graves and Mary Ellen Giacobbe drove up from
New Hampshire to visit Boothbay Region Elementary School. My kids had
been hearing about Don and Mary Ellen for a long time, so this visit was a
special occasion. Bert happened to be passing through the front lobby when
they arrived. He took the stairs to the junior high wing three at a time, then
whipped down our corridor like some eighth-grade Paul Revere, shouting as
he passed each room, "The world's most famous writing teachers are here!
The world's most famous writing teachers are here!"

With Donald Graves in attendance during writing workshop, no one
moved off into one of the peer-conference corners—a first. Instead they sat
at their desks, writing away in absolute and eerie silence. Every now and
then one writer or another chanced a glance to locate Graves as he moved
among them conferring, all of them dying for him to drop by and whisper
the magic entrée, "Tell me about your writing." Bert's anticipation was rewarded. Don knelt by his desk for a long chat about Bert's passion for sci-fi
and Stephen King.

It was a good day. Taking themselves seriously as writers, the kids expected that Mary Ellen and Don would take them seriously, too. At the end
of the day Graves came and stood in my doorway with his coat on, smiling.
"What are you smiling about?" I asked.

"I'm smiling at you," he said. "You know what makes you such a good
writing teacher?"

Oh God, I thought. Here it comes: validation from one of the world's
most famous writing teachers. In a split second I flipped through the best
possibilities. Was he going to remark on the piercing intelligence of
my conferences? My commitment to the kids? My sensitivity to written
language?

"What?" I asked.

He answered, "You're so damned organized."

Then Don stopped smiling, probably in response to the way my face must have crumpled. "Look," he explained seriously. "You can't teach writing this way if you're not organized. This isn't an open-classroom approach, and you know it. It's people like you and Mary Ellen who make the best writing and reading teachers. You two always ran a tight ship and you still do, but it's a different kind of ship."

A workshop *is* a different kind of ship. From the beginning of my attempts to teach using a workshop approach, I've had to organize and reorganize my room and myself to support writing, reading, learning, and teaching. And as Graves suggested, I had to define *organization* in a new way. I don't mean neatness—a good thing, too, because meticulousness will never feature among my virtues. By organization I mean discovering what writers and readers need and providing plenty of it in a predictable setting.

Before any student comes anywhere near my classroom at the beginning of September, I need to get ready for our workshop. This means knowing exactly what I expect will happen, knowing how, where, and when I expect it will happen, and knowing who's expected to do it. I organize myself and the environment in August. My goal is to establish a context that invites and supports writing and reading so that when my students arrive they'll find what they need to begin to act as writers and readers: time, materials and texts, space, and ways for them, and for me, to monitor our activity, organize our work, and think about what writers and readers in a workshop might do.

Making Time

I pulled my chair up next to Amanda's, and she read her lead aloud. It was a new memoir, about attending Neil Diamond's concert in Portland Friday night with her parents and sister. It began:

> "Okay, you're here. Do you want Mrs. Cook's binoculars? If you do, there are three caps you can't lose. Be careful not to let anything happen to them because they're not ours. If you have to go to the bathroom go now, not during the intermission, so you won't get lost and it won't be so crowded. At the end, meet us by the place where the hockey players go in. Okay?"

I recognized Amanda's father's voice. When she finished reading his instructions, I asked her to go on. She had filled two pages with close descriptions of the events of Friday evening and verbatim dialogue—her family's as well as the chatter of the people in the seats around them. I laughed and shook my head. "Amanda, however did you remember all this in such detail?"

"Oh, I didn't," she answered. She pulled out a spiral-bound notebook and flipped through its pages. "I knew before we went that I'd want to write about it, so I brought this along and took notes all night on what was going on." Amanda thinks about her writing when she's not writing. She is a habitual writer.

Robbie was at home watching television one night, with school about the furthest thing from his mind. Out of nowhere came the perfect ending for his Maine humor story. He grabbed the only paper he could find and scribbled away. The next day he came to writing workshop armed with a brown paper supermarket bag bearing the perfect ending.

Karalee came to class the same week with the lead of a new narrative scrawled on tiny pieces of telephone-message paper. She explained, "The other night, when I was spending the night at Susan's, I thought up the whole beginning of my short story in my head. Luckily I remembered it until I got to paper." She reshuffled her tiny manuscript, frowned, squinted, and stared off into space. I recognized I'd been dismissed and moved on so she could pick up the threads of her story.

Robbie and Karalee think about their writing when they're not writing; they, too, are habitual writers. Writers need regular, frequent chunks of time they can count on, anticipate, and plan for. Only when I make time for writing in school, designating it a high-priority activity of the English program, will my students develop the habits of mind of writers—and the compulsions. Janet came into class one day and wailed, "Ms. A., my head is CONSTANTLY writing."

Graves (1983, 223) recommends allotting at least three class periods a week in order for students to be able to develop and refine their own ideas. When David said to me, "I think of things to write about just before I go to sleep—ideas seem to float into my head like hot air balloons," he is describing a ritual that could never evolve if he were a one-day-a-week writer. Without at least three writing workshops a week (preferably four or five), it will be hard for kids to conceive topics, sustain projects of their own, and behave as writers.

Regular, frequent time for writing also helps students write well. When they have sufficient time to consider and reconsider what they've written, they're more likely to achieve the clarity, logic, voice, conventionality, and grace of good writing. Sandy commented, "If a teacher says, 'Do a completed piece by the end of class and turn it in,' I answer not, 'Yes, I can,' but 'I guess I have no choice.' Having to rush my writing cuts down on thinking time and then on quality." Her friend Jennifer agreed. "When I get stuck, I take a little walk. Then I come back and try it again. I quit and come back and quit and come back because I know I won't write as well unless I give myself time to think."

I know exactly what they mean. I am not a good first-draft writer. In a typical morning's work on this book I produced two manuscript pages. I don't think I could pass a course in which writing was assigned to be completed in a single class period. Even if the requirement were extended to a piece a week, I might never compose anything I liked or cared about. But allow me time to think, rethink, wander around my garden, make a cup of tea, talk with others, reread, revise, and polish, and chances are I can produce something halfway coherent.

Sandy, Jenn, and I aren't alone. Hemingway revised the conclusion to *A Farewell to Arms* thirty-nine times. He had—he took—the time he needed to solve any writer's greatest problem: "Getting the words right" (Plimpton 1963, 122). Kurt Vonnegut writes about time as the great leveler. He claims that anyone willing to put in the sheer number of plodding hours it takes can make a go of it as an author:

> Novelists . . . have, on the average, about the same IQs as the cosmetic consultants at Bloomingdale's department store. Our power is patience. We have discovered that writing allows even a stupid person to seem halfway intelligent, if only that person will write the same thought over and over again, improving it just a little bit each time. It is a lot like inflating a blimp with a bicycle pump. Anybody can do it. All it takes is time. (1984)

Katherine Paterson, author of the Newbery award–winning *Bridge to Terabithia*, talked about the way a habitual writer's plodding days set the stage for the "good days":

> Those are the days you love. The days when somebody has to wake you up and tell you where you are. But there are a lot of days when you're just slogging along. And you're very conscious of your stuff and the typewriter is a machine and the paper is blank. You've got to be willing to put in those days in order to get the days when it's flowing like magic. (1981)

We need to acknowledge in our teaching of writing the reality of the act of writing. Good writers and writing don't take less time; they take more. Too many accounts of the practices of professional writers have been published—*Writers at Work: The Paris Review Interviews* is the best known series—for us to cling to school myths of polished first drafts or weekly deadlines. We need to acknowledge, once and for all, that writers and writing need time.

Even when students do write every day, growth in writing is slow. It seldom follows a linear movement, with each piece representing an improvement over the last. But regular, frequent time for writing also means regular, frequent occasions for teaching and learning about writing. In context, over a whole year, I teach one or two new conventions or techniques at a time; in context, over a whole year, my kids try out new styles, subjects, rules, genres, forms, devices, marks, and strategies. With adequate time to detour—to take risks and reflect on the results—writers learn how to consider what's working and what needs more work, to apply my teaching to their writing, and to take control.

I continue to learn this lesson. After a summer spent teaching teachers, advising them to be patient with their students because growth in writing takes time, I suffered a rude shock when I went back to the classroom and faced the worst writers who ever breathed air. That September I wrote one seriously depressed letter after another to Mary Ellen Giacobbe. My head was too filled with images of last year's students—writers who had grown a whole year by the time they left me in June—for me to recollect and consider my own good advice to other teachers. By November I was sending Mary Ellen ecstatic letters filled with anecdotes and writing samples; I didn't remember my own advice until I saw my kids begin to prove it by working hard, experimenting, producing, applying what I had taught them, and changing as writers.

When students have regular, frequent time set aside to write, writing can also play a crucial role in helping them grow up, making it possible for them to capture who they are, then come back and measure themselves against their earlier selves. Regular time for writing helps give students control over the distance between their pasts and presents. When they can count on time always being there, they learn how to use it—when to confront, and when to wait.

Jennipher waited. Jenn's father died when she was in seventh grade, and in early December of her eighth-grade year she began to write about him. She covered page after page of yellow newsprint.

Without reading or sharing what she'd written, Jenn tucked the yellow sheets away in a pocket of her daily writing folder. "It's too soon," she said.

"I'm not ready." She went on to other topics. Twice again, in January and February, she retrieved the yellow sheets, added more, then folded them up and slipped them back into her folder. In March Jenn said, "I think I'd like to write a formal piece about my dad, but not tell it first person. That's too close and too hard." So her formal piece told the story of a girl a lot like Jennipher, with a dad a lot like David Jones.

WHY?

"You're too old to cry," she thought as she forced back the tears and tried hard to listen to what the minister was saying.

"But I'm only thirteen," her thoughts interrupted. "This can't be happening to me." Some strong force was building up inside her now, and she wanted to scream. "I can't cry; I can't cry," she thought, holding tightly to her mother's hand. Her mother and brother were both crying.

When the ceremony was finally over, she was the last one to walk down the aisle and out of the church. Her cousin stood by the door. She burst into tears as she hugged her tightly. She was shaking as her cousin helped her down the steps where crowds of people were standing, talking. They were mostly her friends and family. She was hugged by an aunt and started to cry again. "Pull yourself together," she commanded herself, straightening up, wiping the tears from her face.

"It's funny all the time I've had to think in the last couple of days," she wondered, "even with all these people around." But she had thought. She'd thought about all the good times with her dad, about the stories her dad had told her.

He'd died of cancer three days earlier. When her aunt had told her she had cried and kept crying. "But now," she thought, "I can't cry again."

Then she was back at the house after the funeral, fighting through the crowds of *his* friends and family: that was who they really were. She had the chance to see a lot of people, and talk about him and them and herself.

She remembered again the stories he'd told. She loved the tale about the time he'd gone to Texas for treatment; had sat down on the curb waiting for his brother, who was checking the time of his appointment. A kid had come up to him to bum money for bus fare. Her father had asked him where he was from, and the boy replied, "Vermont." Her dad had teasingly responded, "I beat you; I'm from Maine." The boy had said something about his mother coming from a small town in Maine. And it happened that the boy's mother and her dad had grown up in the same town and had dated each other in high school.

Her dad was like that: he could make the whole world seem smaller and happier.

Now, the flowers around the house reminded her of the plants and flowers that had bloomed and blossomed under his green thumb. She snapped out of her reverie to realize someone was talking to her.

"He really was the greatest," the voice was saying.

She nodded, dazed, wanting to dwell on thoughts of all the good things about her father. "Why him?" she asked herself. "It's not fair!" The voices were screaming inside her now. It was pure fear.

She pushed the thoughts away and walked upstairs, where most of the kids were hanging out. She smiled and said "Hi" to everyone. And as they talked she forgot all her troubles. But later, when she went downstairs again, she heard someone say, "She has her father's looks, doesn't she?" and someone else replied, "Oh, yes."

"No!" she thought. But it was true. She had his eyes, his complexion, his hair.

Later in the day she'd once again forgotten everything that was wrong. She was laughing and talking with the others, playing games and watching TV. But in a moment a word triggered all those thoughts of her father, and they came crashing back down on her.

She was so scared—not like being-afraid-of-the-dark scared, but a really deep down, somebody's-dead scared. She knew she would live and keep on living. But she'd still be scared, and maybe she'd have to try hard not to cry sometimes. And maybe every time someone mentioned cancer, or she read the word in a book, there would be an empty space somewhere in her stomach. Maybe someday she'd forget, or maybe someday she wouldn't. But her heart held one, great hope: that when she grew up, she might be as good a person as her dad had been.

—Jennipher Jones

Jennipher benefited, academically and personally, from the steady availability of time in school to write—and to read. Over a long career of having to explain my teaching methods to parents and administrators, the daily time I made at Boothbay Elementary for students' independent reading was the most questioned of all my questionable practices. It looked as if nothing was happening. The principal even made the classic administrator's comment when he came in one day to observe and found me circulating among my reading students: "I'll come back when you're teaching," he whispered.

I responded to concerns about reading workshop by explaining my rationale for inviting students to sit (or, shudder, *lie*) around my classroom with their noses stuck in books. I cited research that indicates, study upon study, that the best readers are those who read a lot. I justified my practices by pointing to state and national progress reports that show that Maine and U.S. thirteen- and seventeen-year-olds read less than our nine-year-olds, both in school and out. And I explained about adolescents and the social upheaval in their lives that leads to fewer and fewer occasions for reading.

Reading takes a backseat in anyone's life when life becomes impossibly full. During the first two years of my daughter's life I didn't read a single novel. My students' lives are often similarly full—of sports, clubs, baby-sitting, homework, chores, music and dance and voice lessons, first jobs, first loves, and killer social lives. Amanda, a former student, anticipated April vacation of her freshman year of high school by informing me, "Ms. Atwell, I'm going to read six books this week. All of them are books I've been dying to read since Christmas. I just look at them and feel depressed. There's always something else I've got to do."

After the first year of reading workshop I could justify the provision of time to read in school by pointing to what my students accomplished as readers. At Boothbay, where reading was scheduled as a separate class and my kids read an average of thirty-five books, their scores on standardized tests averaged at the seventy-second percentile, up from an average at the fifty-fourth percentile. In June more than 90 percent of students indicated that they regularly read at home for pleasure—that they were taking home the books they read during the workshop. When I asked how many books they owned, the average figure they gave was ninety-eight, up from September's average of fifty-four. I have no way of knowing whether they did, in fact, own more books. I do know that they perceived themselves as the sort of people who acquire and collect libraries.

This is the kind of evidence that begins to convince doubting administrators and parents: students read more, comprehend better, and value books and reading to a greater degree when we make time in school for them to read.

Today I see my seventh and eighth graders four days a week for one ninety-minute language arts block that includes both writing and reading. Within the block I try to carve out time each day for a poem, a writing-reading minilesson, independent writing and conferring, a brief read-aloud from a novel or short story, and time for independent reading, usually fifteen to twenty minutes a day. In addition every student's baseline homework assignment every night is to read for at least another half hour: to create a routine—a time and place in their lives—for behaving as a reader at home.

Over the past three years at the Center for Teaching and Learning, between the seventy minutes a week I provide in class and the time I assign them to make at home, my students read an average of twenty-nine books,

September through June. Although briefer than I—and they—would like, the in-class time sets a tone and creates a milieu: a group of kids and a teacher who read together and talk about books. It's time enough to get students so hooked on their books that they want to take them home to find out what happens next. And it gives me time to circulate among my students, record what they're reading and how far they've gotten, find out what they think of it, and help them find books when they're stuck or when they don't understand it's okay to abandon a book they don't love.

When I sit down with my plan book in August, I write *Writing-Reading Workshop* every place on my schedule that it would otherwise say *English*. The workshop isn't an add-on; it is the English course—here, everything that can be described as language arts is taught as sensibly as it can be taught, in the context of whole pieces of students' writing and whole literary works.

If my schedule consisted of fifty-minute periods for English, writing and literature included, I'd continue to give over class time to writing and reading workshop. Below I've sketched two options for using the five periods and assigning homework, so that students can experience the sense of continuity and routine that writers and readers need. I would give the bulk of the fifty-minute periods to writing, because, of the two disciplines, it's where kids need the most hands-on help, teacher demonstrations, and structured time.

OPTION 1: WHEN A WORKSHOP APPROACH IS THE CURRICULUM

- Writing workshop on four regular, consecutive days (e.g., Monday–Thursday)
- Reading workshop on one regularly scheduled fifth day (e.g., Friday) but with booktalks and literary minilessons throughout the week
- A half hour's worth of independent reading as homework every night
- An hour's worth of writing as homework, done at the student's discretion between Thursday night and Monday morning

OPTION 2: WHEN A REQUIRED CURRICULUM MUST BE COVERED

- Writing workshop four days a week (e.g., Monday–Thursday) for one semester, with an hour's worth of writing as homework between Thursday night and Monday morning
- The required curriculum four days a week for the alternate semester
- Reading workshop on one regularly scheduled fifth day (e.g., Friday)

throughout the entire school year, and frequent booktalks and literary minilessons

- A half hour's worth of independent reading as homework every night.

Time for independent writing and reading isn't the icing on the cake, the reward we proffer the senior honors students who survived the English curriculum. Writing and reading *are* the cake. When we fight for time, giving students one of the basic conditions for writing and reading, we begin to make writers and readers.

Creating the Context

Donald Graves has compared a classroom organized as a workshop to an artist's studio (1981). The artist sets up her studio so it has everything she needs, arranged to suit her and her art. In the midst of the messy and unpredictable act of creating, the artist knows where to find the right palette knife, brush, or tube of color. The studio exists for the convenience of the artist at work, just as the writing-reading classroom should exist for the convenience—and productivity—of young writers and readers.

In August I start readying the studio by collecting and organizing materials for writing and reading. Beginning with writing, I fill two low bookcases. One holds utensils and supplies; the other contains standard references and other books I like about writing, publishing, and literature. Appendix A is the consummate wish list of materials, equipment, and references for a classroom organized as a writing-reading workshop.

The bare-bones materials for writing workshop are pencils and ballpoints, lined paper, colored pens for students to use to edit their writing, scissors and transparent tape for cut-and-paste revisions, a stapler and staples, paper clips, and correction fluid. In addition I provide pads of Post-it notes, stationery and envelopes, colored bond, rulers, colored pencils, markers, a three-hole punch, glue sticks, index cards in different sizes, and a crate of clipboards so we can write outside the classroom. I arrange the supplies in cups, baskets, and trays, and I police them zealously. Class time is so precious and limited that it makes me crazy when my kids or I have to waste time in pursuit of pencils, scissors, or the stapler.

The bare-bones references for a writing workshop are several college dictionaries, copies of *The New American Roget's College Thesaurus*, and, to help with issues of usage and format, *Writers INC* from the Write Source

and Kate Turabian's classic *The Student's Guide for Writing College Papers*. I also find it helpful to have on hand the one-volume *Columbia Encyclopedia* as well as *Bartlett's Familiar Quotations*, *The Scholastic Rhyming Dictionary* by Sue Young, *Write to Learn* by Donald M. Murray, *The I-Search Paper* by Ken Macrorie, *On Writing Well* by William Zinsser, and two books about poetry, X. J. Kennedy's *An Introduction to Poetry* and *Writing Poems* by Robert Wallace. Other references that I've collected and my kids and I have consulted are listed in Appendix A.

The reference bookcase also stores resources I create for my students. One is a crate of hanging files, each file containing samples of writing by students, professionals, and me, organized by genre. Examples of effective writing across the modes are an incredible help to my kids as writers and to me as their teacher. I can point them toward illustrations of what they're trying to do in their own writing, ask them to marinate themselves in a genre, or show them how another student or I approached or solved a writing problem. When I'm planning minilessons about qualities of good writing or characteristics of different genres, I grab the relevant file and make overheads of elements I want to highlight for my students.

The genres I've collected examples of in the files include book reviews, short stories, memoirs, historical fiction, feature articles, interviews, advertising, songs, cookbooks, fantasy/science fiction, parody, poetry, informational writing, cartoons, history, profiles, pieces of writing written as gifts for others, published student writing, surveys, opinion pieces, letters, pamphlets, petitions, and speeches. Whenever I read something I love or think is a noteworthy example of a kind of text, I try to remember to clip or copy it and add it to the files.

I created a second set of hanging files for information about authors. Here I include published interviews with writers and profiles about them, as well as promotional materials that publishers provide free to teachers. I collect author information at the conventions of the National Council of Teachers of English and by writing to the publishers of my kids' favorite authors and requesting any available materials. I also clip interviews, reviews, and articles from the *New York Times Book Review*, the daily *New York Times* and *Boston Globe*, *The New Yorker*, *The Nation*, *New Advocate*, *Voices from the Middle*, *Language Arts*, and *English Journal*. I refer kids to the files to learn how and why their favorite authors create, especially fiction, and I use this information, too, in minilessons about craft and genre.

A third homemade resource is a publication center to help writers enter contests and pursue other options for professional publication. It includes a bulletin board where I post the rules of writing competitions after I describe them in minilessons, a display of kids' writing that has been accepted for publication within the last year, a file of information about magazines and journals that publish middle school writing (see Appendix B), a copy of the *Market Guide for Young Writers* by Kathy Henderson, and back issues of our eighth-grade yearbook and *Acorns*, the school's literary magazine. I expect that every year every writer will attempt to be published professionally. I think they need the experience of raising their voices in the big world at the same time that they try to understand and meet its standards. Most of my students are published in the big world at least once by the time they leave eighth grade.

The supplies for reading workshop are books. I buy mostly paperbacks, because adolescents like the size, feel, cover art, and general format better than hardcovers. I shelve about a thousand volumes of novels and nonfiction literature alphabetically by the authors' last names; each is marked on the top of the spine with my initials in red ink. The collections of poetry are shelved in a bookcase all their own, and I make a separate place for drama. I also have two wooden stands, made by a parent, for displaying new titles after I introduce them in minilessons and for books students recommend to each other.

Throughout the year when kids finish—or abandon—books, they enter the titles in their individual reading records and rate each book on a scale of 1–10; in June they review the records and recommend the highest-rated titles for our annual lists of best-books, which I post in the classroom and use to restock the classroom library. The most recent best-book inventories appear as Appendixes L and M. I carry the lists with me all summer and refer to them when I browse at secondhand bookstores, garage and lawn sales, and flea markets, where I pick up a lot of my books. I also arranged to receive a 20 percent discount from Sherman's, our local bookstore, for purchases for the school. I make my classroom library a fiscal priority. Some years that means the funds will have to come from my own pocket. I bite the bullet and buy the books: my kids can't become readers without them.

I don't buy series novels. I think they rip off students by diminishing their pleasure in reading and lowering their expectations of contemporary fiction. The character development is so poor that kids can't feel close to or care about the characters. And the only next step after reading a Christopher Pike is another Christopher Pike. Adolescent readers who crave thrills, chills, and adventure need to know about Caroline B. Cooney, Lois Duncan, Arthur Roth, Robert Cormier, Tim O'Brien, Walter Dean Myers, S. E. Hinton, Stephen King, Gary Paulsen. My students find more thrills, chills, and adventure in the pages of Robert McCammon's *Boy's Life* than in all the Pikes put together—not to mention a main character they identify with, like, and care about.

When I began to get ready to return to middle school teaching in 1994, and encountered for the first time series novels for adolescents in the bookstores where I shopped, I caved. I picked up half a dozen titles by Pike and R. L. Stine. Three years later their spines still haven't been cracked by a student. The quality and attractions of the other books on the shelves, booktalks and minilessons, peers' recommendations and discussions around the circle, and constant, endless conversation about books, authors, characters, plots, themes, and our own responses create readers who have criteria and won't settle.

The basic equipment for a workshop is an overhead projector and access to a photocopier. I use the overhead almost every day—to demonstrate my writing in minilessons, show how a student solved a writing problem, present a poem to the group for discussion, or record information I want kids to copy into their writing-reading handbooks. I suspect there are a lot of overhead projectors moldering in a lot of schools' boiler rooms. We need to clean them up and put them back into action. Overhead transparencies focus the attention of the group and help make information immediate, concrete, and communal.

A photocopier creates opportunities for instant publication. Access to one is especially critical in situations where kids can't compose on word processors and use printers. Publication in a writing workshop must be a given: student writers need access to readers beyond the teacher if they're to understand what writing is good for, and if they're to write with care and conviction. Appendix B describes some of the ways my students have gone public with their writing, including individual pieces photocopied and passed along to a reader. In the past I labeled a stack tray "Writing to Be Photocopied," and kids placed in it the writing they wished me to copy for them. Today I give minilessons on the workings of the school photocopier, cross my fingers, and permit kids to make copies on their own.

More and more writing classrooms come equipped with computers networked to a printer. Through grants I've been able to acquire eight word processors and one laser printer. Probably two-thirds of my kids would do all their writing on the computers if I could assign one to them full time. Other students draft in longhand, then use the word processor as a publication tool. And some draft certain kinds of writing by hand—poems, for example—then format the writing on the computer at the very end. I schedule days for each student's access to the computer, but I also allow them to decline if they don't want it on a particular day or trade off with a writer who does.

Word processors have helped many of my kids produce more writing and mess around more with text—saving, rearranging, adding, deleting, experimenting, and correcting. Computers help all my students create clean, readable copy that goes straight out into the world beyond our classroom and makes a difference there.

Three pieces of furniture help me teach writing and reading. The first is a little pine footstool that I sit on during minilessons, when my kids are gathered around me on the floor in a circle. It puts me down on their level, but not all the way down on the floor, which, frankly, I can't do anymore.

The footstool goes with me when I confer with writers so I always have a place to sit as I move around the classroom. I also sit in a big pine rocker I bought at a secondhand furniture store; I roost there when I read aloud. And I have one of the low-to-the-ground wooden easels that Ken Maxim built for every classroom at the Center for Teaching and Learning. Made of scrap one-by-threes and plywood, it holds a 27 × 33" pad of easel paper that I use like a blackboard (we don't have any at the Center), except these notes are permanent and my kids and I can come back to them for reference or revision.

I copy poems onto the easel paper, make notes before or during minilessons, gather data from kids, and record instructions I want them to follow. Much of the data on minilessons in Chapter 6 was first captured on easel pads. When a pad is filled, I remove it from the easel rings and replace it, but keep it in the classroom so that we can refer to it if we need to. At the end of the year I page through all the pads and save the sheets that contain information and examples I don't want to lose.

I love teaching from an easel. While I appreciate the permanent record it gives me and the kids, I prize the intimacy it creates as it puts me into the circle with them. I would never go back to standing at a blackboard.

Getting the room ready for writing and reading means rethinking its physical arrangement. When students walk through the door the first day, I want them to enter a working environment—to take on the serious, productive affect of writers and readers in a workshop. The easel, overhead projector, and my footstool and rocker are at one end of the room (there is no teacher's desk). I've supplied a rug or, even better, pillows or whistle-shaped cushions for students to sit on when they gather in the circle. Quotes about writing, reading, literature, and life—the ones I live by—are displayed everywhere. (They're included here as Appendix N.) The publication center is ready and available to writers anxious to see their names in print. The low bookcases are packed with supplies and resources. Paperbacks and collections of poetry line a wall; computer stations line two others. The center of the room is filled with desks or small tables, separated to discourage conversation and distraction and to make it easy for me to move among them when I confer with writers.

While one writer can be called upon by another to provide a response to a piece of writing in progress, students' conferences won't take place at the desks or the computers. Figuring out how to accommodate a writer's need for quiet *and* need to talk presented one of my biggest headaches in moving to workshop-style teaching. At first, when students both wrote and conferred at their desks, I found myself having to stand up at least five times each class period to announce to the group, "It's too noisy in here. Knock it off." The volume always lowered for five minutes, after which I would have to stand and make the announcement again.

The solution was to give writers a place to go to talk with each other about their writing. Students who agree to confer with each other pick up their writing, pick up a clipboard that contains copies of the peer-conference record form (Appendix J), and move off to one of the several spaces I've identified as a conference area. In the past I've carved out space under tables, in corners and corridors and closets, and between lockers and coatracks. There are always just two or three conference areas, places I pass, or at least can keep an eye on, as I circulate around the room, which keeps a check on the volume of the conferences and keeps the talk on-task.

Keeping Track

Once I've established the physical environment of the workshop, I focus on management. In August I put serious hours into the forms and folders we'll use for keeping records and collecting students' work throughout the year. I spend time now so the kids and I can save it later.

When the school year starts, I'll be up to my ears—happily—in my kids, their writing and reading, and my plans for teaching them. I'll need to be able to be in touch, easily and thoroughly, with each student's activity and accomplishments. I won't have time or the inclination to chase kids down to find out what work they're doing or not doing. And, come evaluation time, I don't want surprises, for me, my students, or their parents. So August means refining old forms, creating new ones, and designing my kids' folders so that they and I can stay on top of their efforts, and so they can do most of the work of keeping track.

Each student needs six folders of different colors: three with grommets in the middle and inside pockets (for reading, spelling, and daily writing) and three with pockets only (for texts and lyrics, homework, and permanent writing).

The daily writing folder holds pieces of writing in progress and travels with students between the classroom, locker, and home. The permanent writing folder collects finished pieces of writing throughout the school year; these I store in hanging files in crates on the floor, along with students' reading folders, which contain the individual lists they make of the books they read during the year.

The spelling folder holds each student's individual spelling list, plus a copy of the procedures I want them to follow for word study. They use the homework folder to organize daily and weekly assignments, which they record on a weekly form. And the text and lyric folder is where they store their copies of samples of writing we read and discuss together in mini-lessons. Students keep these three folders—spelling, homework, and text and lyrics—in their possession and bring them to class each day.

I buy the folders, rather than ask students to purchase them, because I want uniformity of color. All the homework folders, for example, are always the brightest yellow I can find, so parents can pick them out easily if they're inclined to monitor their children's homework efforts. I also want to be certain of having enough folders, ready to go, on the first days of school.

In a letter home in the summer I ask every student to purchase two items before school starts and bring each to school the first day: a marbled composition notebook of at least one hundred pages, which will become a reading journal, and an $8\frac{1}{2}$-by-11-inch spiral- or glue-bound notebook, also of at least one hundred pages, to serve as a writing-reading handbook. I always buy an extra half dozen of each kind of notebook in case any student forgets. (Invariably someone forgets.)

Then I begin to run multiple copies of the forms students will use for record keeping in writing, reading, and spelling. I have a checklist in the front of my plan book that I pick away at as summer draws to a close. All but one of the forms listed below appear in the appendixes; the exception appears in Chapter 7.

_____ **WRITING SURVEY** (one each) for me to learn about each student's experiences and attitudes as a writer before we begin (Appendix D)

_____ **READING SURVEY** (one each) for me to learn about each student's experiences and attitudes as a reader before we begin (Appendix E)

_____ **STUDENT WRITING RECORD** (two each plus extras) for writers to keep track of finished pieces of writing throughout the year (Appendix F)

_____ **STUDENT READING RECORD** (two each plus extras) for readers to keep track of books finished and abandoned throughout the year (Appendix G)

_____ **INDIVIDUAL PROOFREADING LIST** (one each) for writers to record the conventions I teach them and for which they take responsibility in subsequent pieces of writing (Chapter 7, Figure 2)

_____ **EDITING CHECKSHEET** (many) to be completed by the writer and attached to each piece of writing submitted to me for teacher editing, to show me and the writer the conventions that were focused on during student editing (Appendix K)

_____ **PEER WRITING CONFERENCE RECORD** (many) for responders to use in capturing their reactions to other students' writing (Appendix J)

_____ **PERSONAL SPELLING LIST** (one each plus extras) for students to record the words they can't spell or aren't 100 percent certain of throughout the school year (Appendix H)

_____ **WEEKLY WORD STUDY SHEET** (many) for students to practice five spelling words they select each week from their personal spelling lists (Appendix I)

_____ **WEEKLY HOMEWORK ASSIGNMENT SHEET** (many) for students to record daily and weekly assignments (Appendix P)

The system of record keeping I've created puts major responsibility on individuals. It's especially important for teachers with large classes and many students to invest time in preparing the means for kids to keep their own records and, once school starts, to teach them how to use the forms. When students select their own books for reading and ideas for writing, when everyone is working on a different task, following the paper trail could become a teacher's full-time job. At the Center for Teaching and Learning, Nancy Tindal, the kindergarten teacher, starts turning over record keeping responsibilities to her kids just as soon as they have a sense of letter sounds.

As the teacher I have ultimate responsibility for what happens with my kids during our year together. This means that I keep records, too. For twenty years I've been working to streamline and simplify the information I chronicle. I ask myself again and again, as a teacher, _what do I really need to know?_

I need to know what each student is working on as a writer and reader at any given time. I need to know if they're staying on-task and finishing work, including their homework. I need to know what they need help with, when they're stuck or have made a breakthrough, where they've been—the patterns in their writing and reading over time—and where they might go next.

After juggling complicated systems of folders, notebooks, Post-it notes, self-adhesive labels, and three-ring binders, I finally settled on two clipboards of notes for each class. One holds a status-of-the-class record for a week of writing workshops, and the other a status-of-the-class record for a month or so of reading. Figures 4-1 and 4-2 illustrate examples of both.

On the writing record I note each student's plans for writing workshop: what they tell me each day when I call the role and take the status-of-the-class. I record topic, genre, and what the writer intends to do. The sample writing record shows students who are starting a new piece, continuing a work in progress or concluding one, editing, conferring with me or another student about problems they're having with content or craft, conferring with me about editorial issues I identified in a finished piece, brainstorming titles, proofreading, typing, developing a character for a short story, reading published models of a kind of writing, moving to a more appropriate genre, taking a break from a difficult project to whip off an easy one, collaborating with another writer, and abandoning a topic or genre that isn't working.

I also use the status-of-the-class form to keep track of which students are assigned to computers for writing each day. On Thursday at the end of class I record what everyone plans to work on during the assigned hour of at-home writing, and on Monday morning I look to see if it's done; if it's not, the student puts in writing time at lunch recess. When I think a writer needs to bull through a piece of writing that's taking too long, I ask him or her to set a deadline; then I note it on the writing record and help the writer follow up. After I edit a piece of student writing, which I do at night at home, I remind myself by making a note in the next day's column that tomorrow I'll return the piece to the writer and confer with him or her.

At the beginning of the school year I make a check mark whenever I confer with a writer, so I'm certain I'm seeing everyone in these crucial first days and helping each writer get off to a successful start. I also make a note to myself when I want to be sure to talk with students who seem to be struggling or stuck—not engaged, grounded, or knowledgeable enough about what they're attempting as writers. And I often cast my eyes back across the days or weeks of writing workshop to see what has been happening with each writer.

During writing workshop, as I move among my students and confer with them, I carry the writing-record clipboard and a pen, along with a pad of Post-it notes so I can leave reminders and records of our conversations with my kids. I jot down my observations of what kids are doing on the writing record, and note ad hoc assignments I might give individual writers.

HOMEWORK DONE?	2/5 (7th graders on computers)	2/6 (8th)	2/7 (7th)	2/8 (8th)	HOMEWORK
✓ LAUREL	Poem of CTL memory – 1st D.	→	CTL mem. poem; conf. w̄ Mike	Now a poem about memories for the yrbook	1 hr. poem
✓ MISSY	Poem – early childhood – swingset – conf. w̄ Rachel	ill	Edit "Ceremony of S."; I edit; type as a gift	Daisy Fay book review — See models —	Fin. b.r.
✓ MARGARET	Cont. leprechaun memoir →	Plus b'storm titles	Editing Conf. w̄ me Begin to type final of lep. ~~memoir~~	✓ Conf. w̄ me – Poem? (about climbing)	1 hr. poem
✓ MARTHA	New poem – response to Dead Man Walking	→	ill	Type D. 2. of poem Conf. w̄ Laurel	Edit
✓ MICHAEL	"Mexico in November" poem – start	Gathering notes / data for poem	Mex. poem – abandoned rhyme scheme that got in his way – free verse	Mex. poem: became a narrative (memoir)	1 hr. draft
✓ CURT	Book review: Twentieth Maine – start – look at models	✓ CTL web page w̄ Sam Conf. w̄ me	Web page w̄ Sam: interview Ron	Web page / Fin. book review	Edit
✓ JASON	Skiing memoir for Gould application	Try to complete D. 1 of memoir →		✓ Conclusion of memoir – See me – proofing issues	Edit
✓ JOE	Memoir of CTL – Jason's haircut?	Cont. working on mystery s. story	Cont. CTL memoir (Jason's hair)	Mystery / Revise poem	Fin. poem, edit
✓ JAY	✓ Cont. s. story (See me: is it working?)	Wants to cont. s. story Give it one more day?	Aban. s.s.: Poem about masonite missiles – became a narrative	Cont. masonite memoir for the yearbook	1 hr. draft
✓ SAM	Plan web page for Internet	✓ CTL web page w̄ Curt Conf. w̄ me	Web page: int. Ron in office	Rome poem / Web page	Fin. poem
✓ TOM	Finish hockey poem + edit	Editing Conf. w̄ me Final copy of poem	Mystery s.s. – char. int. and notes	Mys. s.s. Needs to reread A.C. Doyle	Notes on mys.
ERIN	ill	Civil War s.s. with Katy →		✓ Show me first 5 pages of s.s. Skim Dear Mr. Henshaw?	1 letter
0 ASA	New poem for "dark collection" IN AT RECESS	Cont. poem Conf. w̄ Matt	Fin. poem – B'storm titles Edit	Editing Conf. w̄ me Final poem + print others for dark collection ✓	new poem
✓ MATT	Short story: start new one (Work w̄ Curt)	New poem?	✓ Conf. w̄ me: is he stuck? Humor writing? Sports?	Essay on ESPN	1 hr. essay
✓ DYLAN	Look over expectations for 7-8. A book review?	Book review: The Things They Carried →		✓ Conf. w̄ me. Edit. Type review / cover letter?	s.s.?
✓ IZZIE	✓ S. story: begin drafting Confer w̄ me	Cont. s.s.	Thank-you letter (taking a break)	✓ Ed. Conf. w̄ me Final copy letter / char. int. w̄ Rachel	Fin. char. int.
✓ RACHEL	Type final of short story about runner	Type final of s.s. →		Too brief now that it's typed? Expand s.s.? Yes.	Add to s.s.
✓ KATY	Finish baby poem for the Arters; proof	Civil War s.s. w̄ Erin →		✓ Show me first five pages Skim D. Mr. H. – epistolary structure / style – all must be in the letters themselves	1 letter

FIGURE 4-1 Sample Status-of-the-Class Record for Writing

	TOM	ASA	MATT	DYLAN	IZZIE	RACHEL	TOBY	SARAH	CATHARINE
3/31	Airframe (251)	Red Storm Rising (REC MATT) ①	"Warn" (REC)	Others See Us (68)	Eng. Patient Screenplay ①	Johnny Got His Gun ①	Matineo	Cherokee Bat (REC) ①	Letters from the Inside (REC)
4/1	ill	" (37)	ill	Slaughterhouse Five (REC) (5)	" (57)	" (49)	" (200)	Ender the Miff (Carton)(REC)	Fin... Angel Factory (REC) (67)
4/2	Contagion (320)	" (53)	On Center (347)	" (80)	Eng. Patient (REC)	" (149)	" (228)	What Happ. to Janie? (REC)	"
4/3	" (341)	ill	Fin. O.C. Airframe (17)	" (213)	" (123)	" F.n. J.G. (211)	" (442)	Voice on the Radio ①	Serpent's Silver (243)
4/7	To Hong Kong w/ Monkey Chris	Red Storm... (123)	" (3/7)	Howl →	→ Howl	Lord of the Flies (21)	It (31)	Starching ?	Just Another Lie (134)
4/8	"	" (153)	Hunt for Red Oct. (3)	Slapstick ① (REC)	"	slow (29)	ill	Back Home ① (REC)	"
4/10	"	" (222)	" (101)	" (112)	Eng. Patient (47)	phil...int.byz char.net (9)	It (82)	Abandoned Angel Juan (REC)	Just Another Kid (213)
4/14	"	" (250)	" (200)	Welcome to Monkeyhouse (9)(REC)	" (151)	" (105)	" (124)	Shadows in the Water ①	Witch Baby (REC) ①
4/15	"	" (437)	" (245)	"	Letters from the Inside (REC) (48)	" (130)	" (161)	Fin... ① (147)	" (130)
4/16	Catch 22 (56)	Fin. R.S.R. Never Saw Another Butterfly (REC) (85)	Red Phoenix (29)	"	" (160)	" (21)	" (201)	Gallows Compass (REC) ①	Secret Diary (4) of A. Mole
4/17 VACATION	Kamikaze ① (REC)	Hiroshima ① (REC)	" (220)	Cat's Cradle ① (REC)	Back Home ① BRANDON (REC)	Fin. LOE Holocaust Poetry	" (262)	" (248)	Touching the Rock (14)
4/28	" (131)	" (60)	" (480)	" (90)	French Lt's ① Woman (REC)	" (165)	" (349)	" (316)	" (121)
4/29	Fin... " The Secret War (31) (REC)	" (90)	" (662)	Mother Night (67) (REC)	" (58)	Eva ①	" (382)	Missing (18) Angel Juan	If I Should Die... (REC)
4/30	" Catch 22 at home (40)	" (103)	Chickenhawk (34)	Cat's Cradle (130)	" (105)	" (145)	" (418)	" (60)	Class Picture (67)
5/5	Secret War (160)	" (160)	" (204)	" (191)	" (143)	Shake the Kaleidoscope	Bellmaker ① break	" (112)	" (105)
5/6	Fin... " Barracuda (52)	" (191)	Red Horseman ① (McCammon)	Night Beat ① (McCammon)	" (171)	Poems that Live Forever	" (29)	Fin... Beyond the Burning Time (REC)	If I Should Die... (103)
5/8	" (105)	Harris+ Me (REC)	Sum of All Fear (40)	" (84)	Torrington's Collected Poems	Shine On, Bright + Dang. Ob. ① (REC)	It (448)	" ①	Man Without A Face (12)
5/12	" (166)	ill	Red Horseman (290)	" (159)	F.L.W. (271)	" (116)	" (560)	Baby BeBop ① (REC)	" (64)
5/13	History of St. Paul's	Home (68)	Sum of All Fear (160)	" (247)	" (364)	Midsummer Night's Dream	" (614)	"	Cherokee Bat (12)

FIGURE 4-2 Sample Status-of-the-Class Record for Reading

All of the status-of-the-class records for a trimester of writing stay at-tached to the clipboard. At the end of the trimester some of my comments for parents about students' work and work habits will be based on these data.

In reading, the status-of-the-class record functions on the same princi-ple as the writing form. Here I divide a class in two and write their names across the tops of two grids; Figure 4-2 shows half the readers in a combined grades 7–8 group. Rather than calling the role, I move among readers while they're reading, confer with them quietly, and record on the form the title of the book each is reading and the page number the book is open to: I'm checking for the nightly half hour of homework reading by looking for read-ers to be at least twenty pages beyond where they were yesterday.

I also note kids who need, or who respond to, recommendations, read-ers who are abandoning too many books, readers who should be abandon-ing their books, patterns of authors or genres in students' selections, how they take breaks and what they choose when they go on a reading holiday, and the obsessions that begin to give each reader his or her identity: Matt and Tom Clancy, Izzie and *The English Patient*, Sarah and Patricia Wrede, Dylan and Kurt Vonnegut, Catharine's attraction to adolescent fiction with strong characters and relationships.

I fill out the reading record each time kids read in class. Often as I cir-culate I do nothing more than look over a reader's shoulder and note the page number. Other times I stop, confer, share an enthusiasm, extend one, or troubleshoot. Students know I'm coming, know I'm interested in their choices and responses, and know I will follow up to make sure they did the most important homework any English teacher can assign: reading.

Over a long history of experimentation with writing and reading records, I've come to understand how personal a decision it is when a teacher settles on a system of record keeping. We need to ask ourselves: What's useful to me as a teacher? What's manageable and convenient? What won't eat up my teaching time? What will help me know my students and be accountable to them? *What do I really need to know?*

Establishing Expectations

The longer I teach, the more I know what's possible and the less I'm willing to leave to chance. Although it would be nice some year to have perfect classes that intuited how to engage as writers and readers in a workshop, it hasn't happened yet, and I'm not holding my breath. I need to teach my students what I expect—often again and again, through the fall, until they get inside their new roles and responsibilities. But first I have to figure out what my expectations are. So I think on paper about what writers and readers do, about who my students are, about what I believe, what I know, and what my priorities should be as a teacher of writing and reading.

Right from the start I hope for rich, authentic, adult-like experiences for my students. I want them to use writing to know themselves and the world and to discover what writing is good for. They should experiment across four basic genres—fiction, memoir, poetry, and exposition—to learn the elements of each and explore what each can do for them. They should understand the importance of working from quantity, of producing a lot of writing and seeing where it takes them (and know that I won't accept the notion of blocked writers any more than their math teacher would sanction blocked mathematicians). I want them to develop criteria as writers, to step back and consider what is working and what needs more work in their texts, and to set realistic goals for their writing. I want them to finish pieces of writing and bring sufficient writing to final copy so they can experience the satisfaction of completed work, and so I can teach them how to edit and proofread. I expect them, always, to use what they know about conventions as they compose—to punctuate, capitalize, spell, choose words, and paragraph as they go, as adults do, rather than go back into reams of "sloppy copy" and try to impose conventionality after the fact. I want them to be considerate of other writers: to take care of shared materials and equipment and respond to others' writing in thoughtful, productive ways. And I expect them to try to make literature every time they write, to never be killing time by "doing another piece for the folder." We have just 175 days together as writers in a workshop. I want to make the most of every one of them. And so I try to set standards that are interesting, rigorous, and will give my kids diverse tastes of the real thing.

EXPECTATIONS FOR WRITING

Find topics and purposes for your writing that matter to you, to your life, to who you are and who you want to become.

Keep a list of your territories as a writer: topics, purposes, audiences, genres, forms, and techniques.

Try new topics, purposes, audiences, genres, forms, and techniques.

Make your own decisions about what is working and needs more work in pieces of your writing. Be the first responder to your writing.

Listen to, ask questions about, and comment on others' writing in ways that help them move the writing forward.

Create a handbook of writing and reading minilessons, recorded chronologically, with a table of contents.

Produce at least three to five pages of rough draft each week and bring at least two pieces of writing to completion every six weeks (Rief 1992).

Maintain a record of the pieces of writing you finish, and file finished writing chronologically in your permanent folder.

Sometime during this academic year produce a finished piece of writing in each of the following genres:

- a short story
- three to five poems or songs
- a profile of a local citizen based on original research, or an op-ed piece or essay about an issue that matters to you
- a book review
- a memoir

Attempt professional publication.

Recognize that readers' eyes and minds need your writing to be conventional in format, spelling, punctuation, and usage. Work toward conventionality and legibility, and use what you know about format, spelling, punctuation, and usage as you compose.

Keep an individualized proofreading list that you check your writing against when you edit and proofread.

Enter words you don't know how to spell, or aren't certain of, on the personal spelling list you keep in your spelling folder.

Take care of the materials, resources, and equipment I've provided for you.

Establish and work toward significant, relevant goals for yourself as a writer each trimester.

Take a *deliberate stance* (Harwayne 1992) toward writing well: try to make all of your writing literature.

Work as hard in writing workshop as I do. Re-create happy times from your life, work through sad times, discover what you know about a subject and learn more, convey information and request it, parody, petition, play, explore, argue, apologize, advise, sympathize, imagine, look and look again, express love, show gratitude, and make money.

In reading I want kids to use literature to know themselves and the world, to discover what reading is good for. I expect them to experiment across authors, subjects, and genres and begin to notice how they engage, disengage, connect, predict, participate, and pace themselves as readers. They should understand the importance of quantity, of reading a lot and seeing where it takes them. I want them to finish books and reflect on their literary experiences: to develop criteria as readers and choosers of books, step back and consider what works and what needs more work in other writers' texts, and set realistic goals for their reading and responses to literature. I want them to be considerate of other readers, to take care of our classroom library, and to respond to others' literary responses in thoughtful, productive ways. And I expect them to have a literary experience every time they read, to never be killing time with a book they don't appreciate or, even better, love. So in August I think on paper about standards for reading that will both stretch my kids and bring them satisfaction.

EXPECTATIONS FOR READING

Find books, authors, subjects, and themes that matter to you, to your life, to who you are and who you want to become.

Keep a list of your territories as a reader: authors, subjects, purposes, and genres.

Try new authors, subjects, purposes, and genres; expand your reading schemas.

Recognize that there are different modes of reading and different stances readers take in regard to different kinds of texts.

Develop and articulate your criteria for selecting and abandoning books.

Go *inside* your books and respond to the writing you are reading; decide what is working and needs more work in the books you read.

Write a letter at least once a week in your log about what you think and notice about the writing you are reading and in response to my and friends' letters to you; write to me at least once every two weeks and to friends whenever you wish to talk with them about your books.

Read as much as you can, as joyfully as you can.

Read for at least a half hour every night, seven nights a week.

Maintain a chronological record of the books you finish reading or abandon.

Create a handbook of writing and reading minilessons, recorded
chronologically, with a table of contents.

Take care of the books I have provided for you. Return each book you
borrow to the classroom library, shelving it alphabetically by the
author's last name.

Establish and work toward significant, relevant goals for yourself as a
reader each trimester.

Take a *deliberate stance* toward reading and responding with your whole
heart and mind.

Work as hard in reading workshop as I do. Live other lives and learn
about your own, see how other writers have written, acquire their
knowledge, escape, imagine, think, connect, contrast, travel,
ponder, laugh, cry, love, and grow up.

I type the two lists of expectations, make enough copies for every student, and hole-punch them so kids can insert them into the grommets of
their reading folders and daily writing folders as a source they can easily
consult, and to which I can send them easily when students need a reminder of what I expect them to accomplish. Then I think on paper one
more time about the real nitty-gritty: how I expect students to behave as
writers and readers.

Rules for a Workshop

I am always intrigued by the tension inherent in the act of writing, how it requires self-discipline and regularity yet thrives on the quirks of the individual writer. When I'm writing I write every day: I sit down at my table at 8:30
on a summer's morning and go at it until I drop or the rest of my life intrudes
in a major way. But a tight, consistent schedule is just about the only linear
feature of my writing behavior. I write notes to myself, make lists, stick Post-
its on the lampshade, doodle, churn it out, cross it out, reread, rearrange,
abandon, devise and revise outlines, proofread, and make piles on top of
piles until I don't know what I've got and have to stop and clear the decks,
mentally and physically. And all the while I'm still wearing my nightgown
and bathrobe, sometimes until 3:00 in the afternoon, and praying that no
one comes to the door. The structure has to be both tight and idiosyncratic if
I'm to produce writing that's any good or get any better as a writer.

At the conclusion of the groundbreaking study at Atkinson Academy,
Donald Graves wrote about this tension:

When all the data were in and the information brewed down to the most important finding, we recorded that:

WRITING IS A HIGHLY IDIOSYNCRATIC PROCESS THAT VARIES FROM DAY TO DAY.

Variance is the norm, not the exception.

Good teaching enhances even greater variation. The more risks a writer takes, and the more tools at a writer's disposal to carry out an audacious intention, the more the writing will vary in quality. (1983, 270)

Writing and reading can vary, and writers and readers can grow, when the teacher creates a reliable environment and pushes kids to use it. My students and I live together in a room for almost ten months, and every day for almost ten months I try to inspire them, teach them what I know, hold them accountable for their knowledge, help them develop new habits and hone their criteria, and show them how to discover their intentions, processes, and strengths as writers and readers. Predictable routines underpin all of this.

The rules for writing and reading workshop are designed to help kids develop habits of mind and action that will support them as they go out on limbs. They're based in part on what successful writers and readers do, and in part on common sense about how these things can be accomplished in a room occupied by twenty-some writers and readers and a teacher who needs to be able to monitor, evaluate, and report on their progress.

RULES FOR WRITING WORKSHOP

1. Save everything: it's all a part of the history of the piece of writing, and you never know when or where you might want to use it.
2. Date and label everything you write to help you keep track of what you've done (e.g., *notes, draft #1, brainstorming*).
3. When a piece of writing is finished, clip everything together, including the drafts, notes, lists, editing checksheet, and peer-conference form, and file it in your permanent writing folder.
4. Record every piece of writing you finish on the form in your permanent writing folder. Collect data about yourself as a writer, look for patterns, and take satisfaction in your accomplishments over time.
5. Write on one side of the paper only and always skip lines or type double-spaced. Both will make revision, polishing, and editing easier and more productive for you.

6. Draft your prose writing in sentences and paragraphs. Draft your poems in lines and stanzas. Don't go back into a mess of text and try to create order. Format as you go.

7. Get into the habit of punctuating and spelling as conventionally as you can *while* you're composing: this is what writers do.

8. When composing on the word processor, print at least every two days. Then read the text with a pen in your hand, away from the computer, and see and work with the whole, rather than a part at a time on the screen.

9. Get into the habit of beginning each workshop by reading what you've already written. Establish where you are in the piece and pick up the momentum.

10. Understand that writing is thinking. Do nothing to distract me or other writers. Don't put your words into our brains as we're struggling to find our own.

11. When you confer with me, use as soft a voice as I use when I talk to you: *whisper*.

12. When you need to confer with peers, use a conference area and record responses on a peer-conference form so the writer has a reminder of what happened.

13. Maintain your proofreading list and refer to it when you self-edit.

14. Self-edit in a color different from the print of your text and complete an editing checksheet to show what you know about conventions of writing.

15. Write as well and as much as you can.

RULES FOR READING WORKSHOP

1. You must read a book. Magazines, newspapers, and comic books don't have the chunks of text you need to develop fluency, and they won't help you discover who you are as a reader of literature.

2. Don't read a book you don't like. Don't waste time with a book you don't love when there are so many great ones out there waiting for you.

3. If you don't like your book, find another one. Browse, ask me or a friend for a recommendation, or check the "Favorite Books" list or display.

4. It's all right to reread a book you love. This is what readers do.

5. It's okay to skim or skip parts if you get bored or stuck; readers do this, too.

6. Record every book you finish or abandon on the form in your reading folder. Collect data about yourself as a reader, look for patterns, and take satisfaction in your accomplishments over time.

7. Understand that reading is thinking. Do nothing to distract me or other readers. Don't put your words into our brains as we're trying to escape into the worlds created by the authors of our books.

8. When you confer with me, use as soft a voice as I use when I talk to you: *whisper*.

9. Read (and write in your reading journal) the whole time.

10. Read as well and as much as you can.

I photocopy the lists of rules for writing and reading workshop and put these through the three-hole punch, too, for students to include with the lists of expectations in their reading and daily writing folders. We'll talk about all of the guidelines during the first days of school when they assemble their folders.

Then I breathe huge sighs of relief and start counting the hours until the kids come. Now I'm ready.

5

Getting Started

The compulsion to read and write . . . is a bit of mental wiring the
species has selected over time in order, as the life span increases, to
keep us interested in ourselves.
Lorrie Moore

The first week sets the tone. If students leave school on Friday afternoon
feeling serious and excited about themselves as writers and readers, and me
as their teacher, we're halfway there.

I plan the first days in more detail than any other week of the school
year. A lot has to happen. Kids will get to know each other and start to
come together as a corps of writers and readers. They'll become acquainted
with the space, how it's organized, and what it offers them in terms of materials, resources, equipment, and options. Many of the routines and procedures of the workshop are established during the first week; so is my role as
writer, reader, teacher, and learner. I'll begin to find out who my kids are—
what experiences they've had as writers and readers and how they perceive
writing and reading. I'll communicate my expectations and the rules of the
workshop. Students will organize themselves—put names on their new
folders and insert forms for writing, reading, and spelling into the grommets
of each. And I'll try to give my kids a strong enough taste of the satisfactions of writing and literature that they leave on Friday believing that this
class will be cool.

In a typical first week I plan drama games and interviews, to get kids
talking and listening to each other. I send off teams of students on a scav-
enger hunt to survey the classroom for the resources that writers and readers
will use (Figure 5-1). Each student receives a yellow homework folder and
completes a writing survey (Appendix D) and reading survey (Appendix E)
for homework; I collect them, read and highlight students' responses, and
start making notes about who my kids are. Students browse among the
books in the classroom library and make their initial selections. We read a
poem together each day of the first week and talk around the circle about
our favorite lines or how the poems make us feel; then students file copies
in their new texts and lyrics folders. I begin to read aloud—perhaps

FIGURE 5-1   Let's Play . . . Where Did Ms. Atwell Hide It?

_____   Poetry collections
_____   Ms. A.'s books, a.k.a., "The Teacher Shelf"
_____   Novels and other literature for independent reading
_____   Books about writing
_____   Permanent writing folders for your group
_____   Books about writing poetry
_____   Back issues of *Acorns*
_____   Plays
_____   Health and sexuality books
_____   Phonebook
_____   *Columbia Encyclopedia*
_____   New books
_____   Novels by Cynthia Rylant
_____   *Writers INC*
_____   Colored pens to be used for editing
_____   Reading folders for your group
_____   Peer-conference clipboards
_____   Atlas
_____   *Ode to Common Things* by Pablo Neruda
_____   Dictionaries, spellers, and thesauruses
_____   Publication options for middle school writers
_____   Box for recycling white paper
_____   *The New Yorker*
_____   Editing checksheets
_____   Novels by John Marsden
_____   *Bartlett's Familiar Quotations*
_____   Files of samples of different kinds of writing
_____   Files of about-the-author information
_____   *The Reader's Encyclopedia*
_____   Bookmarks
_____   Published writing by CTL students
_____   Computer disks for your group
_____   Reviews of books for middle schoolers published in *Voices from the Middle*
_____   Stack tray for writing ready for Ms. A. to edit
_____   Extra staples and tape
_____   Blank overhead transparencies
_____   Stationery and envelopes

Cynthia Rylant's autobiography *But I'll Be Back Again*, or the short story "Flowers for Algernon" by Daniel Keyes. And I launch the workshop.

I've initiated writing and reading workshop in many different ways, and I continue to tinker with the first lessons in search of methods that are generative—that help students produce substantive material to begin working with. I also want an introduction that suggests what is possible, in all its depth, breadth, and idiosyncrasy, and one that reveals me to my kids as a writer, reader, and grown-up who knows some things. I hope to construct a foundation that individual writers and readers can build on until June—and maybe for the rest of their lives.

I launch the workshop by exploring my spheres of interest as a writer and reader, out loud in minilessons, then inviting students to identify and lay claim to their own interests, concerns, and areas of expertise. I call these our *territories*. When I present my territories as a writer and reader to my students, I demonstrate, as explicitly as I can, all the ways that writing and reading matter in the life of their English teacher.

Writing Territories

Figure 5-2 shows the latest version of the running list I keep of my territories as a writer. These include subjects I've written about or might like to, genres I've written in or would like to try, and audiences for whom I write or would like to. The list of territories represents my self-portrait as a writer. Because I use it as a model for kids to learn from, I try to make it personal, specific, diverse, and unpretentious: ideas of mine that might generate ideas of theirs.

I reproduce the list on overhead transparencies and talk from it in the first writing minilesson of the school year. Students come to the circle with their new writing-reading handbooks, and we begin. Last fall I started like this:

> I'm ready to start. Make sure you can see the overhead from where you're sitting and also write in your new notebooks at the same time. You may want to write in your lap, or you can get a clipboard over here.
>
> To people who are new to the group this year, my students often take notes during minilessons. What you're creating with the notes you take during our time together at the start of class is your own writing-reading handbook. It's a place for both recording information that we create and keeping track of ideas you might want to use in your writing: dreams, topics, goals, projects, genres, audiences, places you might get

FIGURE 5-2   Ms. Atwell's Writing Territories

Topics:
- My students—what they do and what it means (*In the Middle*, second edition)
- My dog, Books, who died this year at age sixteen
- Anne—all the days and stages
- London—my special place; how I feel when I'm an ocean away from my life
- Adolescent girls and their relationships and dreams
- Toby—twenty-six years of adventures, being together, working things out, plus how we met
- Roman Catholic childhood—fainting at the Communion rail; picking a confirmation name; scapular medals; rosaries as jewelry
- Dreams of Grandma Lang—the comfort I derive from them
- Taking care of Grandpa Lang
- My namesake—Grandma Atwell—and her unhappiness in America
- My mother—the changes in our relationship and in her as she ages
- My father—who I am because of him
- Others' writing (e.g., Maureen Barbieri's book)
- Spring in Buffalo—the only thing I miss about western New York
- Books for teenagers
- Songs that speak to me and for me in pop music; the best play I ever saw in London: *Ferry 'cross the Mersey*
- Adult female friendships versus the friends of my youth
- CTL—its philosophy, history, methods, curriculum
- School business—grant proposals, parent handbook, reports on students, etc.
- Chocolate
- Motherhood
- Snow forts—the most creative collaborations of my childhood
- Making peace with Glenn, my brother, in our forties
- Ice-skating with Mom at Dieners' Pond—her free of her cares for once and figure-eighting backwards like a girl
- Exercise and why I HATE it
- How I read and write and why
- How I teach and why
- Pre-Raphaelite art and why I love it in spite of myself
- Writing
- Reading
- Literature
- Growing up and what that means to me
- My high school reunion—the cool clique was still a clique but not so cool
- Preschool dreams of teachers—the nightmares that begin every August 1
- Responses to American history—people, events, theories

Genres:
- Memoirs
- Book reviews
- Short stories
- Literary criticism

FIGURE 5-2, continued

- Poetry
- Gifts of writing
- Essays
- Parodies
- Letters to the editor
- Feature articles
- Research articles
- Letters to Anne at camp, friends, Mom, other relatives, my editor and publisher
- Letters to my students about their reading
- Notes to Ron
- Thank-yous
- Speeches
- Documents for my students about writing and reading
- Fan letters
- Sympathy notes
- Reactions to readings and other academic and artistic experiences
- Résumés and vitae
- Grant proposals and reports to foundations
- Guidelines and policy statements for CTL
- Letters of recommendation
- Lists of all sorts
- Lesson plans
- Evaluations of students

Audiences:
- Myself
- Toby
- Anne
- Mom
- My students
- Their parents
- Other teachers' students
- My friends
- Women my age
- Adolescent girls
- Niece and nephew
- Sister and brother
- Other relatives
- Ron
- Teachers at CTL
- Teachers in general
- Specific groups of teachers
- Readers of newspapers
- My community
- My elected representatives
- Other officials
- My editor and publisher
- Foundation officers and trustees

published. So it's both a personal notebook and a class notebook. Your first entry in your writing-reading handbook will be personal.

Maybe the most important thing for you to know about me is that I write. I write a lot and for lots of different reasons. I call the things I do as a writer my *territories*. They include genres that I write in or would like to try, subjects I've written about or would like to, and potential or real audiences for my writing.

Before school started this year I revised my profile of myself as a writer. The list of my writing territories appears here on overhead transparencies. This is how I'll ask you to begin your year of writing workshop, by brainstorming your own territories as writers.

My list gives me a window on who I am as a writer, person, woman, teacher, learner, mother, wife, and daughter. It also gives me a place to go when I'm trying to figure out what I'm going to write about next. It's my ideas bank. It's my big prompt, to remind myself, "Oh, yeah, I wanted to do that as a writer." And when I have an idea, and I know I'll lose it if I don't write it down, this is where I capture it.

I've been keeping a list like this one for the last couple of years, and it has helped me be more organized as a writer. It's my reminder of who I am and what I know and care about.

Here's what I'd like you to do. I'm going to talk from my list for ten minutes about the ideas, audience, and genres I come up with when I brainstorm my writing territories. I'm going to ask you to write that phrase—"My Writing Territories"—right now at the top of the third page of your writing-reading handbooks. Later on, the first two pages will become your table of contents.

While I'm describing some of my territories, if anything I say rings a bell and makes you think of something that's in your repertoire as a writer, or something you think you'd like to try someday, jot it down on the list in your handbook. When I'm done, you'll have ten minutes to continue your list and then interview each other, followed by time to write some more. I'll ask you to make these lists as long and complete as you can before you leave here today. Don't lose any germ of an idea that comes to you while I'm talking. Listen and write at the same time.

One of the things I write about a lot are my students, what you do and what I think it means. I wrote a book, *In the Middle*, in the 1980s, and now I'm writing a second edition about things I see and do differently as a teacher today. I started my data collection two years ago and I'm continuing it this year, because next summer I've got to finish writing the second edition. It will be a lot of work, but I like it. I am endlessly fascinated by what my students do, as writers, readers, and people. You guys have been a major topic on my territories list for almost twenty years now.

Right up there next to the major topic of my professional life is my dog Books and what she meant to me. She died in the spring at sixteen.

In many ways she was the best friend I ever had—the most accepting, loving, and loyal. Nobody looked in my eyes like my dog looked in my eyes. My relationship with her was one of the central ones of my life, and I dream about her all the time. Recently I read a poem in *The New Yorker* about a woman dreaming about her dead dog. I cried for half an hour, then realized I have a poem in me, about dreams of petting Books, when I wake up and my hand is still warm.

Last spring I met Rachel's twin-sister fifteen-year-old dogs. I couldn't believe it. I know what an effort it takes to keep one dog alive that long, and then I think about doing it for sister dogs . . . Rach, I hope you jotted down your girls on your list. Everyone? Your own pets?

My daughter, Anne, is on my list—all the days with her and all the stages she goes through and what it's like as a mom, watching her become this person.

London is on my list because in the world it's my special place, the place I can go and be absolutely free and myself. You know how I talked at morning meeting today about how at lunch time, when you're all outside—or are supposed to be—the teachers have this little twenty-minute window of opportunity when we can pretend we're not teachers, and just let down? London is my metaphor for forgetting the responsibilities of my teacher life and my principal life and just being. It also happens to be the best city in the world, with endless bookstores, gardens to walk in, and plays to see.

I'm also interested in the topic of adolescent girls, their relationships with each other, their dreams and goals, and their roles and voices in our culture. I've been trying to write a short story about this, which I've almost finished. It's my first attempt at short fiction. I expect it's a genre you'll attempt this year. I'm going to send my short story off to a magazine for girls like *New Moon* and try to get it published.

I'm interested in my husband, for all the obvious reasons. We've had twenty-six years of adventures, of being together and in love, of disagreeing and working things out. I like being married to him. I'd like to write about the experience of this marriage, but also tell the story of how we found each other in the first place. He was my teacher when I was in college in Buffalo; it's a romantic story—to have a crush on your teacher, then find out your teacher has a crush on you. Of course, we were both consenting adults, and I was no longer his student, so *don't panic*.

Another thing I'd like to write about is my Roman Catholic childhood, which was both devout and neurotic. When I grew up, the Catholic church was strict and complicated, in terms of its rules and rituals. For example—my brother just reminded me of this—I'd go to the rail at the front of the church to receive Communion and I'd be so wrought-up—and hungry, because we had to fast—that I would faint. He reminded me that the mother of a friend of his carried me out of the church on several occasions because I'd passed out again, through some combination of religious fervor and hunger.

I remember the thrill of picking my confirmation name. You can actually choose a third name when you're twelve or so, and the choices were great. It was all we talked about—a debate that went on among Catholic girls for a good six months or so. Would I become Teresa, Monica, Bernadette, Agnes, Veronica, Lucy, Magdalena, Beatrice? (I went with Mary, my mom's name.)

I also remember scapular medals, these cloth pictures that you had to wear all day under your clothing and when you went to bed at night. They were attached to long pieces of ribbon; you wore one picture in the front and the other one in the back. I was paranoid that I was going to be strangled in my sleep by my scapular medals, but I was equally paranoid that I'd die in my sleep without them and burn in hell forever—or at least suffer in limbo, which was God's waiting room.

And rosaries. Rosaries were like jewelry for Catholic girls: beads chained together, each representing a prayer. We collected rosaries in different gems, in our birthstones, and traded them.

So I have a series of anecdotes about the arcane rituals that are a big part of my memories of my early childhood. A lot of writers go back to early memories of their childhoods, the beliefs and rituals of the time, and explore this territory, for themselves and others, in memoirs. I hope you will, too.

One of the most important people in my life was my Grandmother Lang, who died when I was a senior in high school. I dream about her all the time. In my dreams we sit at her kitchen table and talk. That phenomenon, her coming back in comforting dreams, is something else I want to write a poem about. After she died I took care of my grandfather, who was a gruff bully, and pretty much deaf. I moved in with him during my freshman year in college and had to deal with him and cook for him, at the same time that I was sleeping in my grandmother's bedroom and missing her very much. That contrast is something else I'd like to explore.

I want to write about my mother, who I fought with for years. It was seriously bad: I was always grounded for life. When I turned twenty, it all changed. And now it's changing again as she ages. So there are these stages: intense love, intense hate, intense love, and now wondering how to take care. Relationships with parents—for you, too—are some of the crucial ones to explore in poems and memoirs and essays.

I also write about other writers' work. For example, I wrote a review of Maureen Barbieri's book, *Sounds from the Heart*, about her perspective on how teachers need to meet the needs of adolescent girls. I gave it a rave. I like to look at what other writers have done and think about it, and a book review is a genre that lets me do that. It so happens that Maureen co-edits *Voices from the Middle*, a journal for middle school teachers that publishes reviews of books for kids your age, written by kids your age. That's something you'll want to jot down as a potential territory: a review of a favorite book to submit to *Voices from the Middle*.

Another of my territories is books written for teenagers. I read a lot of adolescent novels, so I can introduce them to you in booktalks, but also because I write about them for teachers who are looking for good books for their students.

I'd like to write about springtime in Buffalo some day. Other than my family, the only thing I miss about western New York is the real springs they have there, unlike Maine. It's nice to go back to Buffalo during the first week of May, when everything is yellow and green and bright and it smells like spring should.

I'm really interested in popular music, by which I mean rock. I *wish* I were interested in classical music, and I have tried. I like rock because the songs speak for my life and my feelings. They resonate in ways that continue to surprise me. So I'm interested in writing about the songs that mean something to who I am and how I feel and figuring out why.

I'm interested in my adult female relationships, which seem to revolve around shopping—Nancy Tindal and I are going to Camden on Saturday to shop for shoes—versus the friendships I had with girls when I was young. In many ways my junior high and high school friendships were more intense than my marriage, I was so close to those girls. I'm interested in how a woman's relationships with other women change as she grows older.

I also write about CTL, its philosophy and history, the teaching methods we use here, and the curriculum for the school. It's part of my job as the director. You'd be amazed at how much writing people do at their jobs, every kind of job. In fact, in most cases, the more successful adults are, in terms of their work, the more writing they do.

Then I have this yucky writing. Part of my job-writing territories include grant proposals, the weekly newsletter, revising the parent handbook every summer, writing thank-you notes for donations to CTL, and filling out paperwork for the state.

But other territories can be things like chocolate. I need to write an ode to chocolate this year. It's my third favorite thing in the world. *Dark* chocolate. Although M&M's are also fine with me. Butterfingers—those are great, too. Godiva is obviously the best, but I really don't care. It is an extraordinary thing to live on a planet that includes chocolate.

Snow forts are on my list, too. In my childhood we didn't have a lot of money—the major creative outlet among my brother, sister, and me every winter was building snow forts on the front lawn. The whole Christmas vacation we built tunnels and towers and turrets, with places you could drop in and slide down, and compartments to hide in or stow a cache of snowballs.

Another topic will be my brother. He's a historian, two years older than me, and we competed with each other our whole lives up until about five years ago, when it stopped. Now he's one of my best friends. The intensity of my relationship with Glenn and how it has changed is another of my interests as a writer.

I told you we didn't have a lot of money when I was a kid. My father and mother worked hard and didn't have much leisure time. But one of the best memories I have of my mother is discovering that she was a wonderful ice-skater. She borrowed an old pair of skates from somebody one day, and she and I walked to Dieners' Pond, down our street. While I was skating she pulled on these borrowed skates, floated onto the pond, and started to do figure eights backwards, like this bird on the ice—my mother, who I mostly saw scrubbing floors. I couldn't believe it. She looked like a young girl, filled with such grace and energy. There's a poem there, I think—maybe a gift poem for her—about the contrast between the scrub woman that I always saw and this glimpse I suddenly had of what my mother must have been like as a girl.

I have a funny piece going about exercise, which I'm trying to do right now, again. I did ten sit-ups about two weeks ago, and I think I ruptured something. I *hate* exercise, but I know I have to do it. Your muscle becomes fat when you hit forty; you have to start exercising or you turn to jelly. One of the things I think I can do is make fun of it, now that I'm doing it every morning and trying to find diversions so I don't go crazy from the boredom of it.

I'm also interested in exploring how I read and write, as I'm doing right now, here, with you, and learning from that, so I can read and write better, with even more satisfaction, and teach better, too.

I'm interested in Pre-Raphaelite art. Of all the kinds or schools of art, this is what I like best, and it's pretty embarrassing. Remember last year we read "The Lady of Shalott" and looked at a copy of a painting by John Waterhouse? It's from the Pre-Raphaelite movement. Pre-Raphaelite art is very romantic—the colors are jewel-like and the subjects are usually women from mythology and legend, painted beautifully—and it's kind of hokey. This is something I'm interested in writing about: Where did the appeal for me of this style of art come from? The pictures of saints on holy cards? The illustrations from my favorite book of fairy tales? Why does it resonate for me as a grown-up? Where *do* our tastes in art come from?

I'm interested in the whole notion of growing up and what that means. When I went to my high school reunion, the dynamic I saw there amazed me. The kids who were cool in high school were still thinking they were cool, still hanging together, and still ignoring the people who they'd regarded as nerds in high school, who are now doctors and heads of departments at universities. I was unsettled because I had been on the fringes of the cool group, and I realized that there was much about us that was not cool.

Another thing I need to write about—because I've been conducting an informal survey—are the dreams teachers start having every year on August 1: nightmares about school. You know how sometimes, when you know you're going to do something that makes you anxious, you'll dream about it? Teachers begin to feel anxious on August 1, like clockwork. I dreamed one night last month that I had a pet elephant: I loved it dearly, but I spent all night nursing it, petting it, feeding it, washing it. I was exhausted when I woke up; I'm convinced the elephant's name was CTL. Another night I dreamed that you all came to school and the furniture was gone and we couldn't find it. I dreamed that the two wings of the building had fallen off overnight and we had to put seventy-six kids into two rooms. One of the things I'd like to try is a funny op-ed piece, for one of the teacher journals or maybe even a large-circulation newspaper, cataloging the ways that teachers' anxieties take shape as pre-September dreams. They're *way* worse than waitress dreams, something else I know about.

My writing about these subjects will take lots of different forms. The genres include memoirs, book reviews and literary criticism, poetry, short fiction, essays, articles, parodies, letters of all kinds, speeches, guidelines for you and CTL, grant proposals, reports, lists, and plans.

And I'll direct my writing to lots of different readers. My audiences include me, Toby and Anne, my mother and other relatives, you and your parents, other students, my friends, women my age, the teachers and staff here at CTL, the teachers who buy my books or hear my speeches or subscribe to the journals I write for, the whole midcoast community, people who read newspapers, elected and government officials. Something will happen with almost everything I write: I write to be read.

Now it's your turn. Will you take ten minutes to begin, or continue, a list of your territories? See how much you can capture. Go for quantity. What are the subjects you have explored? That you'd like to explore? What genres have you worked in? Which would you like to work in? Who do you write for? Who would you like to write for? Use the next ten minutes to sketch self-portraits of yourselves as writers.

After ten minutes, or when I see that enough wells have run dry, I ask students to partner up with another writer—if possible, someone who knows them—and read aloud what they have so far. The goals are for a friend to hear what may be missing from a writer's list and for writers to be inspired by the ideas their friends have captured.

For homework students select one of the ideas on their lists and start drafting: the assignment is to write for half an hour and see where it takes them. The first status-of-the-class conference, at the start of the next day's class, will be about these drafts.

Students add to their lists of writing territories throughout the school year, both independently, when an idea occurs to them that they might want to work with some day, and in response to prompts from me. For example, at the beginning of a new trimester I'll conduct a topic-search mini-lesson in which I ask the group questions to get the juices flowing about where they haven't been yet as writers, and they scribble additions to their list in response:

- What are your earliest memories?
- What have you seen that you can't forget?
- What do you have strong opinions about?
- What problems need solving in your life or the world you live in?
- Who might have solutions?
- What do you know about?
- What would you like to know more about?
- What are your tastes and preferences?
- What's a kind of writing you'd like to try?
- Who could you write for that you haven't yet?

Figure 5-3 (see pages 130–131) shows a seventh grader's list of writing territories for a whole school year. As with my list, each entry on Jonathan's is shorthand for an idea, genre, or audience that resonates for him. During seventh grade he completed thirty-two pieces of writing. A good three-quarters of these had their roots in his list of territories. Jonathan often had a hard time making the transition from a completed project and launching himself into a new piece of writing: "I don't know what to do now," was a frequent refrain. Each time I reminded him to sit quietly with the list in his writing-reading handbook and explore his territories, and most of the time he found new ground there that he wanted to cover.

I also show students, in minilessons, how some of their favorite authors discover and cover the ground of their territories. We look across a published writer's oeuvre, read interviews with the author, tease out links, patterns, and anomalies, and sometimes make additions to our own lists of territories. For example, one week we discussed some of the ways that author Cynthia Rylant draws on her experiences and imaginings:

FIGURE 5-3   Jonathan's Writing Territories

- Memoirs
- Short stories
- Squirrel Island
- Sebago Lake
- Traveling
- Sports
- Friends
- Family
- Boating
- Fishing
- Hunting
- My pets
- Poems
- Holidays
- Book reviews
- Marine life
- Animals
- Mom
- Dad
- School—coming to CTL
- Teachers
- Magazines
- Letters
- Postcards
- Letters to teachers about my reading
- Hobbies
- News articles
- Vinalhaven
- Other islands I've been to on the coast of Maine
- Clearcutting ban
- Science
- Peace
- TV
- Sleep
- Grandfather's death

FIGURE 5-3, continued

- Dog's death
- Dreams
- Technology
- Ollie
- Pool
- Florida
- Sailing
- Tennis
- Baseball
- Why I hate soccer
- Hockey
- Swimming—YMCA team
- Biking
- Basketball
- Lacrosse
- Lobstering
- Being in Europe for the first time
- Plane ride over the Atlantic
- Switzerland—memoir
- Driving
- Music—Smashing Pumpkins, Nada Surf, Rage Against the Machine
- Why I like the 7th–8th grade class
- How my sister and I get along better
- How my parents and I get along better
- Matterhorn—poem
- Skiing into Italy
- View of the Alps
- *Boy's Life* and other great novels—book review
- *Fallen Angels; Somewhere in the Darkness*—reviews
- Editorial—local channel preempts pro basketball games
- Maine Yankee
- Someone moving away that I liked
- Parents' stories about my birth
- My earliest memories
- Poem for the eighth graders for graduation

SOME OF CYNTHIA RYLANT'S WRITING TERRITORIES

Topics:

Growing up with grandparents in Beaver, West Virginia (*When I Was Young in the Mountains*)

The region in which she grew up (*Appalachia: The Voices of Sleeping Birds*)

A young child living with older relatives (*Missing May*)

Her neighbor in West Virginia, Miss Maggie Ziegler (*Miss Maggie*)

Visits from her family when she was a child (*The Relatives Came*)

Sounds of the night in the countryside (*Night in the Country*)

Her early religious experience (*A Fine White Dust*)

A girl who loses her father (*A Blue-eyed Daisy*)

Her son, Nate, and a big dog named Mudge that she used to know (Henry and Mudge series)

A teenager's observations of small-town life (*Soda Jerk*)

A friend's experience in World War II (*I Had Seen Castles*)

The first twenty years of her life and her love for the Beatles (*But I'll Be Back Again*)

Genres:

Picture book

Early reader

Novel

Poetry

Memoir

Autobiography

Reading Territories

Through discovering and naming who I am as a writer, I learned to articulate my identity as a reader, too, and demonstrate it to my students. In some ways my list of reading territories feels the more personal of the two: quirkier, more faceted, longer-lived. It gives me enormous pleasure to create and re-create it, to think with fondness about each of the writers or works that has shaped my imagination, politics, sense of language, sense of humor, perspective on the experiences of my life, memories, and relationships with other readers, including old friends and new ones, teachers and classmates at Bread Loaf, students in my classes over the years, colleagues at CTL, my mother, my sister-in-law, and, especially, Toby and Anne.

Figure 5-4 shows the latest version of my list of reading territories. In the first reading minilesson of the school year I talk it through, again from overhead transparencies, then invite kids to create reading self-portraits of their own.

The other day I talked about myself as a writer; today I'll look at my life as a reader. Turn to the *eighth* page in your writing-reading handbooks: we'll leave room for you to add to your writing territories throughout the year.

I didn't start out loving writing. It's a recent passion, one that began in my thirties. I've come to love writing because of what it does for me. It's the hardest work I know, and when it's done, if it's any good, it makes me incredibly happy and satisfied. But writing has nothing on reading.

For me reading is the equivalent of breathing chocolate air. It's pure, instantaneous pleasure. I get to go right into somebody else's world. If it's a good novel—vivid language and compelling situations and characters—I get to become a citizen of that world and another person.

I became an English major and an English teacher because of reading. In college I was an art major. During my freshman year I took only art courses, and by the end of my freshman year, I missed reading. So I signed up for a literature class.

In the second semester of my sophomore year I took two English courses. By my junior year I was an English major, because I realized that as much as I liked art—my goal was to become an illustrator—I loved the worlds of words, especially those created by poets and novelists. I couldn't imagine a better job—to spend my life reading and talking about it, surrounded by other people doing the same things, and inviting students to love reading and literature as much as I do. The whole direction of my life grew from a love of reading and a desire to be a citizen of the world of books forever.

I can't imagine anything worse than not being able to read. I read all the time, whenever and wherever I can. I never sit down by myself to a meal without something to read. I read the backs of cereal boxes. When I'm standing on the checkout line at Shop 'n Save, I read the headlines of all the *National Enquirers*, *Stars*, and *TV Guides*. I always have a book or newspaper in the car, in case I get stuck at the Southport Bridge or to fill the minutes in a theater while I'm waiting for the movie to start. I haven't gone to sleep without reading since I was in elementary school, even for five minutes when I'm dead tired. I read literature, and I read junk. I don't know if I could go on living if I couldn't read. And it's not because reading is good for me. It's because it makes me feel good: it makes me happy.

When I think about my territories as a reader, I realize they're huge—much bigger than my territories as a writer—because I've been

FIGURE 5-4   Ms. Atwell's Reading Territories

Favorite Authors of Fiction

Alice Hoffman	John Updike	John Cheever
Margaret Atwood	Amy Bloom	Isabel Allende
Tim O'Brien	Raymond Carver	Jane Austen
Jane Smiley	Anne Tyler	Virginia Woolf
Wallace Stegner	Charles Dickens	Alice Munro
Fay Weldon	Julian Barnes	Margaret Drabble
Rosellen Brown	E. L. Doctorow	A. S. Byatt
Michael Ondaatje	Carol Shields	Kate Atkinson
Roddy Doyle	Pat Barker	Louise Erdrich
Toni Morrison	Lorrie Moore	Elizabeth Berg

Favorite Poets

Mary Oliver	Elizabeth Bishop	Richard Wilbur
Emily Dickinson	Langston Hughes	Walt Whitman
Robert Frost	Eamon Grennan	McKeel McBride
Seamus Heaney	Wallace Stevens	John Updike
Marge Piercy	Katha Pollitt	William Carlos Williams
Linda Pastan	William Stafford	Michael Casey

Favorite Essayists and Columnists

Ellen Goodman	Frank Rich	Mary McGrory
Cynthia Heimel	Julian Barnes	Calvin Trillin
Alexander Cockburn	Katha Pollitt	Russell Baker

Favorite Playwrights

Tom Stoppard	David Hare	Harold Pinter
Wendy Wasserstein	Henrik Ibsen	William Shakespeare

Favorite Authors for Adolescents

Robert Cormier	S. E. Hinton	Wilson Rawls
Walter Dean Myers	Eve Bunting	J. D. Salinger
Lois Lowry	Robert Lipsyte	Sharon Creech
Han Nolan	Sue Townsend	Cynthia Voigt
Francesca Lia Block	John Marsden	Cynthia Rylant

Favorite Authors for Children

Faith Ringgold	Shirley Hughes	Janet and Allan Ahlberg
Barbara Cooney	Mairi Hedderwick	Charles E. Martin
Kevin Henkes	Chris Van Allsburg	William Steig
Mem Fox	Diane Stanley	Vera B. Williams
Robert McCloskey	Jon Scieszka	

FIGURE 5-4, continued

Favorite Rereads

French Lieutenant's Woman, John Fowles
A Charmed Life, Mary McCarthy
Collected Short Stories and the *Wapshot* books, John Cheever
Remains of the Day, Kazuo Ishiguro
To the Lighthouse, Virginia Woolf
Howard's End, E. M. Forster
Light Years, James Salter
Pride and Prejudice, Jane Austen
Lucky Jim, Kingsley Amis
Jane Eyre, Charlotte Brontë

Professional Reading

Donald Graves
Shelley Harwayne
Regie Routman
Maureen Barbieri
Donald Murray
Ellin Keene and Susan Zimmermann
Language Arts

Linda Rief
Stephen Pinker
Joanne Hindley
William Ayers
Alfie Kohn
Voices from the Middle
Teacher magazine

Literary and Political Journals

New Yorker
London Review of Books
Acorns
The New York Times

New York Review of Books
New York Times Book Review
The Nation
The Boston Globe

Guilty Pleasures

People
The International Express
Miss Manners
Nora Ephron
Clothing catalogs

Vanity Fair
Ann Landers
Boothbay Register
Carrie Fisher

Writing-in-Process

Book manuscripts   Student drafts   My drafts

Correspondence

Students' letters about their reading
Letters from friends and family
Inquiries from teachers and professional organizations
Letters from Anne in our home post office and from camp

Daily Life

Bills   Instructions   Warranties
Ingredients   Recipes   Prescriptions
Policies   Contracts

reading so long and because reading is so accessible: easy and convenient and inviting. I'm surprised at how much territory there is, and I'm intrigued by how the list captures who I am as a person, just as my writing territories do. Although here I'm considering writing that was written by other people, it shows at least as much about who I am.

As I go through my list on the overhead, would you begin to create a list of your own reading territories? If anything I say rings a bell, please capture it in your writing-reading handbook.

My favorite authors of fiction are mostly contemporary novelists who write about the lives of contemporary characters. I do have old favorites, authors who have been around for a while and whose works are referred to as the classics—Jane Austen, Charles Dickens, Virginia Woolf. Mostly I'm drawn to authors who are writing now about life now. Their books are the grown-up equivalent of the books back there on your shelves. Something wonderful for you to know, if you like authors like Sharon Creech, S. E. Hinton, Robert Cormier, and Walter Dean Myers, is that as you grow up you'll discover authors who write comparably for adults, about relationships, themes, and issues that matter to adults today. Some of my favorites are Alice Hoffman, Toni Morrison, John Updike, Wallace Stegner, Alice Munro, Margaret Atwood, Isabel Allende, and Elizabeth Berg. I love Tim O'Brien, who writes about the war in Vietnam and its aftermath. I love the great short-story writer Raymond Carver, whose death a few years ago was a loss I'm still mourning. I adore Fay Weldon, a feminist novelist who writes about relationships between men and women with a wicked wit, and Anne Tyler, who writes about ordinary people and their extraordinary lives. I like British novelists— Julian Barnes, Margaret Drabble, Roddy Doyle, and Pat Barker, whose trilogy of novels about World War I is astonishing. My new favorite novelist, Kate Atkinson, is British. I found her first novel when we were in London a few years ago, and it's the funniest sad book I ever read. I just bought her second one, and I can't wait to get started. I like E. L. Doctorow, who writes about America from a leftist perspective, and two Canadian novelists, Michael Ondaatje and Carol Shields. They write about men and women living and working in the twentieth century—their dreams, their problems, their relationships.

My favorite poets, too, are mostly contemporary. I have some old favorites, like Emily Dickinson and Langston Hughes, Walt Whitman and Robert Frost. But I'm especially drawn to poets who are writing for readers today—people who have dreams and disappointments, epiphanies and pain, who are falling in and out of love today, right this minute. They include Mary Oliver, who falls in love with nature, and William Stafford, who fell in love with humanity. Richard Wilbur is just about my favorite poet, because of the richness and complexity of his themes and languages—I like the way he makes me work, because the rewards are so great. Eamon Grennan and Seamus Heaney are two Irish poets whose work I read with amazement. I revisit William Carlos Williams, Wallace Stevens, and Elizabeth Bishop. I track down new volumes by Linda Pastan and John Updike. You'll see that some of my favorite writers show up more than once on my list. I love Updike's fiction, and I love his poetry, too.

I also read essays and columns in magazines and newspapers. When I want to know what someone in-the-know thinks about something that's going on in the world, I check out the op-ed pages of the newspapers: Ellen Goodman in the *Boston Globe*, Frank Rich, who writes on the op-ed page of the *New York Times*, Mary McGory in the *Washington Post*. They comment on what's going on, not relating an event but saying, "Here's the sense I make of the event. Here's my take on it." In the *Village Voice* I like Cynthia Heimel, who's crazy funny. She writes an advice column called "Problem Lady." People write to her with ridiculous problems, and she gives ridiculous answers. Julian Barnes writes about London, and Calvin Trillin writes about America. And I really appreciate Katha Pollitt, who writes about politics in *The Nation* and writes great poetry too.

One of the things that's interesting to me in looking at my reading territories is that there aren't many playwrights among the writers. I like Shakespeare and Ibsen, Harold Pinter and David Hare, Wendy Wasserstein and Tom Stoppard. Except for our trips to London I don't *see* a lot of plays; partly that's a function of living on Southport Island, Maine. So that's a short list.

I also have favorite authors for you guys. I love Cormier and Hinton, Wilson Rawls, who wrote *Where the Red Fern Grows*, and Walter Dean Myers, especially his *Fallen Angels*. I think Eve Bunting is good. I think J. D. Salinger is great. I'm a big fan of Sue Townsend's novels, which are written as if they're the diaries of a thirteen-year-old boy named Adrien Mole. I think John Marsden, Han Nolan, Sharon Creech, Lois Lowry, Robert Lipsyte, and the Mazers are all good writers for kids, and Francesca Lia Block and her punk fairy tales crack me up.

When Anne was little I rediscovered another genre, children's picture books, which I still read even though she's big now. That's because of authors like Faith Ringgold, Shirley Hughes, Kevin Henkes, Chris Van Allsburg, Jon Scieszka, and Vera B. Williams. I want to see what they're up to, always.

Another category of my territories is rereads. These are books I've read at least twice, some of them as many as half a dozen times. I love to go back into these worlds and be with the characters again, to experience the romance of *The French Lieutenant's Woman*, the wit of *A Charmed Life*, the humor of the *Wapshot* books by John Cheever. *Remains of the Day*, *To the Lighthouse*, *Howard's End*, *Light Years*, *Pride and*

Prejudice, *Lucky Jim*, and *Jane Eyre* are all favorites, because I know I'm going to have a predictable—great—experience when I return to each book. I want to be with the language again. I want to be with the characters again. I'd say a fair amount of my reading is rereading.

I also read professional literature by authors who write about teaching and from whom I learn about my students and the kind of teacher I want to be. I read about literature and politics in journals and magazines that arrive every week or two at our house: *The New Yorker*, *The New York Review of Books*, *The London Review of Books*, the *New York Times Book Review*, and *The Nation*. They're full of essays about and reviews of contemporary culture and literature. And every day I read the *New York Times* and the *Boston Globe*.

I have definite guilty pleasures. My husband saw this list and was appalled: "You're not going to tell people you read this stuff?" And I said, "Well, yeah, I am." It's part of who I am as a reader. A guilty pleasure is my polite term for junk. For example, the first thing I do when I get on an airplane is rifle through the magazines and look for a copy of *People*. When I travel by plane I have a hard time concentrating, I'm so afraid. I derive tremendous comfort from looking at glossy pictures and reading gossip. I read *Vanity Fair*, which is just a fat version of *People* with longer articles and tonier ads. I have to confess that when I read the *Boston Globe*, in addition to the news and commentaries, I read "Ann Landers" and "Miss Manners," to find out what problems people are having and what Ann Landers and Miss Manners advise people to do about them. I read the *Boothbay Register*, which has almost no news in it, ever, but I still stop at the store and buy it every Thursday morning and read it as soon as I get to school; I can't tell you why.

I read novelists like Nora Ephron and Carrie Fisher, who take the gossip from their own lives and turn it into fiction. I devour clothing catalogs. On Saturday morning I went back to bed with J. Crew, J. Jill, L. L. Bean, and Eddie Bauer and looked at clothes for half an hour. Again, these are my guilty pleasures; they have to go down on the list because they're part of what I consume as a reader.

I read a fair amount of writing that's in-process. Sometimes I read book manuscripts that people want me to comment on. I read your writing in draft; I read and reread my own writing in draft.

I read correspondence—letters from you about your reading and letters from my friends and family, since many of my friends and all of my family live out of state. I read letters from teachers and from professional organizations that have questions and queries. We have a post office at our house that Anne created, and one of the ways we communicate at home is through our four post office boxes: mine, Toby's, and Anne's, plus one for the dog. (Don't ask.) It's a nice way for us to talk as a mother and daughter—these conversations can be saved.

Finally, in my daily life, I read bills, instructions, warrantees, ingredients lists and recipes, prescriptions, policies, and contracts—all the stuff that's part of your life if you run a household, if you're a parent or a voter or a consumer.

That's a lot of reading. And for the most part, it's pure pleasure. The reason we have reading workshop at CTL, starting in kindergarten, is because we want reading to be pure pleasure for you, too. We've learned not to sponsor artificial "school" reading, with everybody working out of the same textbook, questions everybody has to answer at the end, and tests to prove that everybody read it and got what they were supposed to get. At CTL we want even five-year-olds to read with the richness, breadth, depth, and satisfaction that I know when I read. And that's my goal for you: bottom line, to love reading.

There's nothing better for you—not broccoli, not an apple a day, not aerobic exercise. In terms of the whole rest of your life, in terms of making you smart in all ways, there's nothing better. Top-ranking scientists and mathematicians are people who read a lot. Top-ranking historians and researchers are people who read a lot. It's like money in the bank in terms of the rest of your life, but it also helps you escape from the rest of your life and live experiences you can only dream of. Most importantly, along with writing, it's the best way I know to find out who you are, what you care about, and what kind of person you want to become.

So let's get started. Will you add to, or begin, your lists of your reading territories? Take the next ten minutes to sketch your self-portrait as a reader. You may use my categories, or come up with your own.

After ten or fifteen minutes of writing I ask kids to stop, review their lists, and star one or two items that surprised them or that they find interesting or revealing. We reconvene the circle, each reads aloud the starred items around the group, and we laugh, talk, and reminisce about the books in our lives.

Then it's time to browse among the books in the classroom library, talk about them, and make choices. Everyone should have a book by the end of class; tonight their homework assignment is to read for half an hour, as it will be every night from now on. I stand by the shelves with the kids, pull titles other students have loved, summarize plots and themes, and encourage kids to recommend to each other good books they're familiar with. Often there's enough time for students to curl up with their new books and read for a few minutes before the clock sends them on their way. I curl up with my book, too, glance around at all these kids absorbed in literature, and enjoy one of those moments when I know English teaching is the best job in the world.

First Workshop Routines

Everything is in place now for the first real workshop: students have writing to work on and books to read. The next class meeting will include all the elements of the daily ninety-minute meeting:

- reading and discussion of a poem, from the easel pad, an overhead transparency, or photocopies (five minutes)
- writing-reading minilesson (five to twenty minutes)
- status-of-the-class conference about individuals' plans for writing workshop (three minutes)
- independent writing and conferring (thirty-five to fifty minutes)
- read-aloud from a chapter book or short story (ten minutes)
- independent reading, including roving status-of-the-class record keeping while my students are reading (fifteen minutes)

The first day—the first weeks—I work hard to make sure every student has everything he or she needs at the start of class; this is a time for training. So I ask as they file in, "Do you have your daily writing folder? Spelling folder? Text and lyrics folder? Writing-reading handbook? Book for independent reading? If you don't, go back to your locker now. You need to check a mental list each day before you come to class. If you can't remember the list, please write it down and tape it inside your locker. These materials are your textbooks for this course."

I want routines to be crisp, and I want us to be able to move along smoothly—not waiting to start the minilesson, for example, until the students who forgot their handbooks have retrieved them from wherever they left them. So I grit my teeth and spend time teaching habits of self-monitoring.

The first poems are strong ones: poetry that's accessible and funny, moving, or compelling. They include "Maybe Dats Youwr Pwoblem Too" by Jim Hall, "Poop" by Gerald Locklin, "The Fish" by Elizabeth Bishop, "Autobiography in Five Short Chapters" by Portia Nelson, the anonymous "The Little Boy," and "The Summer Day" by Mary Oliver. I don't dissect the poems; just read them aloud and ask kids to go back into them to think and talk about favorite lines, hard lines, surprising lines, their feelings, what they imagine the poet was feeling. Chapter 13 looks in detail at some of the ways my kids and I select poems and write and talk about them together over a whole school year.

The minilesson in the first workshop is procedural, as most of my lessons will be at the start of the year. I teach my kids how to look at what they're doing as writers and identify it: I introduce the language of the status-of-the-class conference.

Each day, before you go your separate ways as writers, I'll ask you to tell me, quickly, what you're working on: what kind of writing it is, what it's about, and where you are. I'll write down your responses. This is called a status-of-the-class conference. It's how I keep track of what each of you is doing and begin to help you accomplish what you want to get done.

What will you be doing today? Perhaps you're continuing the first draft of the piece you started last night for homework. Maybe you're starting a second draft, a new version of this piece. You might be rereading it and revising—considering what you've written and making changes on your draft. You may have come up with an idea you like better, so you'll decide to abandon last night's writing and begin a new first draft. You might want to confer with me or a friend and get a response to what you've done so far. Take the next thirty seconds to look at what you have down on paper and decide what you'll be doing today as a writer . . .

Now, when I call your name, would you tell me your subject—not the title, because those usually come at the end, but what your writing is about? Would you also tell me what genre it is—poem, short story, essay, memoir, whatever? And would you tell me what you intend to do with it in today's workshop?

Please don't talk while others are reporting their plans. I want this to go quickly, so you can get down to work, and I want you to listen to other writers' plans, because they might inspire some new ones of your own.

Writers will need explicit instruction in what their options are before they can formulate and articulate plans. I use the language of writing right from the start, teaching the vocabulary of the workshop in context: *draft, revise, topic, genre, confer, response, abandon.* The last is a crucial concept to introduce early on, especially with students who haven't had experience selecting their own topics. They often make poor choices at the start: safe subjects they don't really care about or topics so broad it would take a book-length manuscript to do them justice. For all the grief teachers take over that chestnut of a writing assignment, "How I Spent My Summer Vacation," it's amazing how many students will bite this one off on their own— much too big, topic-wise, than they could hope to chew in a single piece of writing.

Another reason I introduce the language of writers is to speed up the status-of-the-class conference. Giving kids words means they can cut to the chase. But I need to cut to the chase, too. This isn't a time for me to engage in discussions with individual writers. The purpose of the conference is to make a record; if it takes longer than a few minutes, I'm wasting the group's writing time. So if a student hesitates or isn't sure, I leave a blank and come back once the others have started writing. If I have questions or qualms about a student's plan, I make a note to myself on the status-of-the-class record to go to that writer and confer with him or her first.

By the end of the status-of-the-class conference, each writer has made a verbal contract with me, one I can hold students to if they misbehave— *Excuse me, but you told me you were doing X today*—but also one I can help students revise if they reassess their work and decide they need to change course. Their responses aren't carved in stone, but students realize I will hold them accountable for working and producing.

Before students move off to their first session of independent writing and conferring, I ask them to turn to the list of rules for writing workshop, inside their daily folders, and we review them. Today I ask them to attend especially to two rules: write on one side of the paper only and skip lines or type double-spaced, to get in the habit of creating breathing space that will make it easier to make changes in text; and understand that writing is thinking—that conversations or other distractions make it impossible to think and write well. I refer to one of my favorite quotes as a teacher of writers in a workshop. Kafka wrote, "One can never be alone enough when one writes . . . there can never be enough silence around when one writes . . . even *night* is not *night* enough." I need to create the possibility of night for every writer—solitude and quiet, so students may listen to their own voices. From the first day I strictly enforce the rule against talking at the desks or computer stations, the two areas designated for writing. As soon as I hear a conversation begin, I get stern: "If you need to have a conference, pick yourself up and go to a conference corner. This space is for thinking and writing."

I also help keep the volume in the room low by keeping my own volume low as I circulate and confer with individual writers. I whisper and ask anyone who responds to me in a conversational tone to whisper, too. Some years I have even conducted procedural minilessons about whispering. If I am loud, the room becomes loud; it never fails. So I try not to provide a distraction to others when I pull my footstool next to a student's chair and whisper, "How's it coming?" "How can I help you?" "Where did this idea come from?" "Where are you headed with this?" "Tell me about your writing."

I have devoted all of Chapter 7 to writing conferences. What's important to me during the first week is to try to confer with everyone, however briefly, every day. I don't have time to help individuals solve major problems at this juncture, but I can make sure everyone has a topic he or she cares about, can articulate goals or plans for the piece, and is producing text. It's a busy time—an exhausting one—as the whole group requires the full force of my energy, enthusiasm, and curiosity to propel them as a workshop of writers. And it passes so quickly I can never believe it when I look at the clock and see we're about to encroach on reading time.

To end the writing time I ask writers to bring their daily folders and a pencil back to the circle. Once they're settled I instruct them:

> On some days we'll bring closure to writing time with a group meeting. The rules are: form a circle, sit with your bottoms on the floor, put your paper down if you're not reading, and look at and listen to the writer who is reading.
>
> Today I'll ask you to listen to leads. The lead of a piece of writing is its introduction. The lead section is probably the most important. It sets the tone and subject, introduces the style, and establishes the voice. Would you look at your draft-in-progress and lightly mark with your pencil what you consider your lead—the sentences or paragraphs that introduce your piece?
>
> Now, would you read your leads, one right after another, around the

circle? There's no discussion today—no critiques or congratulations. Let's just listen to and absorb what the writers in this group are doing. Watch the face of each writer as we go around the circle and listen to what he or she tells you.

It takes three or four minutes to read around the circle. At the end I summarize the range of genres and topics I heard, tell kids how excited I am about how smart, hardworking, and intentional they are, and let them know how much I'm looking forward to a year of their writing. Then it's time to tuck the drafts into their folders and settle back for the read-aloud.

For a long time I thought of reading aloud as something teachers in the elementary grades did to entertain young children. But from my students' responses to texts I read aloud in minilessons, I learned this wasn't at all true. Everyone is enthralled by a good read-aloud. Hearing literature brings it to life and fills the classroom with an author's language. The teacher's voice becomes a bridge for kids, taking them into territories they might never have explored because they don't yet have schemas for a genre, subject, author, or period. Read-alouds point kids toward new options in their choices of books and authors. They show kids how they might approach problems in their own writing. And they provide a communal reading experience in which we enter and love a book together.

My read-alouds have included *But I'll Be Back Again* and *I Had Seen Castles* by Cynthia Rylant (plus her picture books *When I Was Young in the Mountains*, *Appalachia*, and *The Relatives Came*); excerpts from Thoreau's *Walden* and the children's biography *A Man Named Thoreau* by Robert Burleigh; *King Arthur and the Knights of the Round Table* by Antonia Frasier and the ending of T. H. White's *The Sword in the Stone*; excerpts from *The Things They Carried* by Tim O'Brien; the novella *The Snow Goose* by Paul Gallico; *Walk Two Moons* by Sharon Creech (a major hit); *Bard of Avon: The Story of William Shakespeare* by Diane Stanley and Peter Vennema; *Walt Whitman* by Catherine Reef; Rosemary Sutcliffe's retelling of *The Odyssey*; collections of poems that tell a story, including *Baseball, Snakes, and Summer Squash* by Donald Graves, *I Am Wings* by Ralph Fletcher, *Been to Yesterdays* by Lee Bennett Hopkins, and *Waiting to Waltz* by Cynthia Rylant; most of Woody Allen's *Without Feathers*; *Nightjohn* by Gary Paulsen; *I Am the Cheese* (another major hit) and *The Chocolate War* by Robert Cormier; Robert Coles' *The Story of Ruby Bridges* and excerpts from Ellen Levine's *Freedom's Children*; *Polar Express* by Chris Van Allsburg (to contrast with the appalling—we thought—*Christmas Sonata* by Gary Paulsen); excerpts from *Great Expectations* by Charles Dickens and the children's biography

Charles Dickens: The Man Who Had Great Expectations by Diane Stanley and Peter Vennema; many short stories, some of which are listed in Chapter 12; and various memoirs, discussed in Chapter 11.

Whenever I attempt to read aloud from a book I haven't first read to myself, the result is a disaster. The meaning I bring to a text with my voice grows from my familiarity with an author's world. I've learned I shouldn't be discovering that world along with my kids, but guiding them as they discover it by enacting the story with my voice. As Daniel Pennac has noted, "He who reads aloud exposes himself absolutely. If he doesn't understand what he's reading, he betrays himself out loud. It's a shame, and you can hear it. If he's not as one with his book, the words will die on his tongue and leave a taste. . . . If he *really* reads, if he adds all his understanding to the act and masters his pleasure, if his reading becomes an act of empathy with the audience and the book and the author, if he can communicate the necessity of writing by touching our deepest need for stories, then books will open their doors, and those who felt excluded from reading will follow him inside" (1994, 204–205).

When reading aloud I go for it, changing my inflection for the different characters and moods of a text. I change my face, too—smile, frown, show anger or surprise or the effects of suspense or enlightenment—and I modulate the volume, louder or softer, to match the mood. I read slower than I speak, and I pause before and after parts I want to stress, to let things sink in. I ask questions: "What do you think might happen next? What do you already know about the main character? Is this character an antagonist or protagonist? What do you think the author is trying to get at here? Does this remind you of anything else you've read? Does it remind you of anything that's happened to you?" I show the illustrations. Before I read, I page ahead to get a sense of how much of a text I can read in ten or fifteen minutes, so the stopping point comes at a natural break. And I only read aloud from literature I like. The absolute worst thing I could demonstrate when reading to my kids is boredom. Literature I read with genuine pleasure is the only literature students will be able to listen to with genuine pleasure.

At the end of the first workshop's read-aloud, before I send students off to enter the worlds of their own books, we review the list of rules for reading. I remind students of the importance of being silent, out of consideration for other readers and so they may engage with their books. And I caution them: reading in a workshop takes some getting used to. Every September, after a summer of solitary reading, I relearn how distracting it is to read in a room full of people. It takes me, and many of my students, a while to adjust. At the end of the first few reading workshops we talk about what makes reading here different and note over several days how the workshop begins to feel more natural and comfortable.

Kids choose where they'll read—lying on the carpet, propped on pillows or whistle-shaped cushions, sitting in chairs at tables—just as long as they don't put their feet on the furniture. At Boothbay Elementary I taped a sign over the window in the door of my classroom (*Quiet, please—readers at work*) to cut down on criticisms from passers-by about what my students were doing lying all over the room with their noses in books. I want reading to be inviting and comfortable, and I want kids to develop habits and rituals—*this is what I do when I read*—in order to build personal identities as readers. But this largess doesn't extend to kids who sit together and fool around: I'm quick to separate talkers and remind them of the power of spoken words to distract attention from the pleasure of written ones.

Once kids are settled in, I circulate with the clipboard to which I've attached the reading records for the group and drop in alongside each reader. "What did you find?" I whisper. "What do you think of it so far?" I might ask, "Who's the author? Is she any good?" or "Where did you find your book?" or "What led you to choose this one?" I always ask "What page are you on?" or peek over the reader's shoulder, and I note the title and page number on the reading record.

My most important responsibility to my kids in the first days of reading workshop is to make sure nobody is reading a book he or she doesn't like. It's pretty unlikely that a student who is thirty pages into a book and still not enjoying it is ever going to love it. He or she is learning exactly what I don't want to teach: reading is a time-filler, or, worse, reading is boring. I escort the reader back to the shelves of the classroom library and pull five or six good paperbacks—novels that students from previous years agreed are among the best—then tell a little of the story of each book and ask the student to read the backs and beginnings to see if one of them strikes a chord. In the unlikely event that none does, I would pull another half dozen great books, tell their stories, and put them into the student's hands. Readers, as much as writers, need to begin the year feeling engaged, productive, and successful. I expend a lot of energy as a responder to kids' reading in the first week because it's important that they find their seats at the dining room table as quickly as they can, come to know and trust the satisfactions of reading, and begin to stretch and grow.

And they do, amazingly so. The workshop offers every student unlimited possibilities as a writer and reader. In each class meeting they see and experience an array of the uses of literacy. Reading becomes a whole, sense-making endeavor, and texts are open books—wide open to kids' opinions, questions, interpretations, and enjoyment. Writing becomes purposeful, personal, and world-changing—not the turf of the talented few but the domain of everyone who has something to say and someone to say it to.

The act of launching a writing-reading workshop each September, however exhausting, also feels like a blessing. I leave school at the end of our first week together with a sense of awe: they may not know it yet, but my students have already become members of a community of writers and readers.

6
Minilessons

Don't say the old lady screamed. Bring her on and let her scream.
Mark Twain

The first time I taught a graduate course, one of my students was a male elementary school principal. Fred confirmed all the worst stereotypes. He lectured and tried to intimidate female members of the class, stood up in the middle of sessions and pontificated, and talked about *his* teachers, *his* kids, and *his* school. One morning he stood up in the middle of a presentation and announced, "When I get back to my school, I'm going to fire all my third-grade teachers." I bit the insides of my cheeks and asked him why he'd want to do that.

Fred answered, "Because my art teacher tells me that kids in K, one, and two produce wonderful art. It's free, really creative and imaginative. Then the same kids hit third grade, and they lose it. Suddenly they don't like what they draw. Their spontaneity and self-confidence go right out the window. They produce these crabbed little pictures squeezed into the corner of the page. They erase until the paper rips. Something's going on with my third-grade teachers to undermine the kids, and I'm going to replace every one of them."

Fred is right. Something is going on. But it's going on with third graders, not their teachers. These children are on their way to adulthood and the stage Piaget termed sociocentricity. They're growing up, and their new maturity is reflected in their approaches to artwork—and to writing.

In the primary grades, playfulness dominates children's creative endeavors. They draw and write mostly to please themselves, and they generally like whatever they do. But students in the intermediate grades begin to seek reassurance that what they do is acceptable to others. They become aware of audience—of others' opinions—and realize that what they've done will be judged. And they develop new standards of their own, or at least recognize that standards exist. Donna Maxim, third- and fourth-grade teacher at the Center, calls these "the years of metamorphosis—when the safe cocoon of childhood begins to crumble" (1986).

In their art classes at Fred's school, third graders recognize that their stick figures don't look like real people. They see that their buildings and landscapes look flat and primitive. They understand that it's possible to draw accurately and realistically, but few have the natural talent to pull it off. When they leave the art room and return to their third-grade classroom, sociocentricity translates as a hesitation about putting words on paper and new doubts about the words that do go down.

Older writers—meaning all of us, aged eight through eighty-eight—can use some help in overcoming this self-consciousness, so we can take advantage of the new powers and perspectives that maturity brings. Teachers provide help by responding sensibly and sensitively to students' writing, demonstrating ways students might respond to each other, encouraging kids' choices, and giving enough time for writing so that writers can work through and solve their problems. And teachers help by teaching: by showing students how writers write and demonstrating techniques they can use to achieve their new standards.

By way of response to Fred's complaint I suggested, "Why not speak with the art teacher? Ask her if the kids might not need some simple lessons: how to use one- and two-point perspective to create the effect of three dimensions, how to use a light source to shade objects, then use shadows to give things depth, how to draw faces—how the human face is shaped like an upended egg . . ." and so on. With practical, teachable techniques at their disposal, kids can recapture and depict the worlds of their imaginations. These are minilessons for an artists' workshop.

In writing-reading workshop, minilessons serve similar ends. I use the presentations to introduce and highlight concepts, techniques, and information that will help writers and readers grow up. In the process students rediscover their earlier playfulness as they learn ways to control and shape it.

I know I was one of many teachers who welcomed the idea of minilessons with open arms. I began my career as a teacher of maxilessons, imparting wisdom to groups of silent students all day long. Then Donald Graves, Mary Ellen Giacobbe, and other teachers and researchers taught me how to let my students lead: how to come out from behind my big desk and let kids choose topic, purpose, genre, and pacing; how to move among them, observe their learning, and confer with them about what they're trying to do; and how to help them uncover their intentions as writers instead of acting on my one intention for the whole group. It was a heady time for many teachers as we discovered what our students could do. It was also, in those early days, pretty laissez-faire.

Teachers struggled: "Okay, if I don't lecture, assign topics and readings, collect dittos, give tests, come up with great, creative ideas for my kids to write about, and invent great, creative ways for them to respond to their reading, what *is* my role here? I'm learning about writing, reading, and literature all the time. As an experienced adult I know some things that would be useful to these writers and readers. Conferences reach just one writer or reader at a time. Is it still okay to teach the whole group? What's the forum that will allow me to reveal myself as an expert writer and reader and teach all my kids?"

Like many teachers I jumped at the idea of the minilesson. Initially I viewed it as an opportunity for me to impart my wisdom. Before kids headed off to work on their own projects, I presented a five-to-ten-minute, well-researched, well-rehearsed, pithy nugget of information to a silent audience of adoring students. I had a speech about show don't tell, a speech about focusing topics, a speech about the four kinds of narrative leads, a speech about the use of the caret in adding information. It was only after writing the first edition of *In the Middle* that I began to push to the edges of this practice—to consider what else the minilesson might do, aside from providing me a forum for delivering pieces of information like a life-size Pez dispenser. I began to reconceptualize the minilesson as a practice that serves many purposes.

The minilesson *is* a forum for sharing my authority—the things I know that will help writers and readers grow. I have experiences as an adult that my students have not had, and it's my responsibility to share the knowledge I do have—and seek the knowledge I don't—that will help them move forward.

The minilesson is also a forum for students to share what they know and for us to figure out collaboratively what we know—to think and produce knowledge together and lay claim to it as a community. It's an occasion for establishing a communal frame of reference, for us to develop vocabulary, criteria, and procedures together. It's when we organize or reorganize our space and figure out what materials we'll need. Minilessons are the ritual that bring us together as a community of writers and readers at the start of each workshop, when we come in from the rest of our lives—from lunch or science or the playground—and put on the cloaks of writers and readers. And the minilesson is the way the whole group gossips about the juicy stuff we love to discover about people who read and write for a living.

I am no longer talking about five-to-ten-minute scripted lectures. My new thinking is strongly influenced by Shelley Harwayne's book *Lasting Impressions* (1992). I am seeing some minilessons as *long*—twenty minutes—and *interactive*: teachers and students working together. In the past I relied too much on conferences with individuals as *the* forum for helping students reflect on and improve their writing, at the expense of discovering what we might accomplish together, and I put too much pressure on myself to try to confer with every single writer on every single day of every single week. Conferences remain a daily, crucial part of my teaching, but conferences reach one writer at a time. When my minilessons to the group are thoughtful, authentic, appropriate, and engaging, when they grow from what I see my kids do and need, they provide a powerful tool for teaching and learning, and they create invaluable frames of reference when I do confer with individual writers.

Where do minilesson topics come from? Most often from my analysis of what students need to know next, based on what's happening in their writing and reading, and from my experience of the kinds of information needed by this age group. Here is another instance when records of individuals' writing and reading activity come in handy, in pointing me toward lessons that address what's happening, or not happening, within the group. I keep an index card tucked into a flap in my lesson plan book, for jotting down ideas for minilessons that occur to me as I read pieces of kids' writing or respond to their letters about their reading. For example, when students are capitalizing the wrong words in a title, when all their poetry rhymes, when no one in the group has read any Robert Cormier, I'll make a note to myself to plan minilessons about capitals on first, last, and important words in a title, about what else poems do besides rhyme, about *The Chocolate War*.

Minilessons also come from my inside knowledge of writing and reading. I am an experienced reader and writer imparting practical information to a group of younger, less experienced readers and writers. I know the difference between recopying and revising; I know how to use the information on a copyright page to get a sense of a book's popularity. I teach my students what I know that so they can put the information to use in their writing and in their reading of literature.

Some minilessons tap literature representing genres I hope students will try or choices I want them to consider. I read aloud or show a text, then ask students to discuss with me what the author has done, and I record what we observe on an easel pad or overhead transparency for students to copy into their handbooks. The appendix of Ralph Fletcher's *What a Writer Needs* (1993) describes books, stories, and poems he finds useful in talking with kids about voice, settings, characters, leads, and conclusions. Harwayne's *Lasting Impressions* (1992) is another great resource for teachers of writing who wish to illustrate literary minilessons with literature. I also pull material from my files of samples of different kinds of writing and information about authors, and from the books in Appendix Q, which is a list of professional resources that feature accurate, practical, context-specific information about reading, literature, and writing.

Some minilessons feature pieces of my kids' writing, especially when a student has found a solution to a writing or reading problem or taken a "deliberate stance" in crafting or responding to a piece of literature. For all the obvious reasons, I'm reluctant to illustrate discussions of ineffective writing with examples written by students. Instead I highlight the good writing—interesting and effective choices, breakthroughs, changes, risks, experiments, and decisions that others can learn from. And I ask student writers and readers to conduct minilessons, and bring their techniques, strategies, and accomplishments before the group.

In other minilessons I demonstrate my processes as a reader and writer, so students can learn how I think, create, and respond to texts, make predictions and connections and decisions, establish criteria, change my mind, and go public as a writer and reader. In my current thinking these protocols are the most important minilessons of all—when I take off the top of my head and invite students to observe what I do and the choices I make. Chapter 10 is about the power of protocols in demonstrating to kids what writers do.

My minilessons are almost never based on commercial materials or language arts textbooks. Such "skills" as topic sentences, five-paragraph essays, the four kinds of sentences, main ideas, supporting details, and cause and effect don't exist in the real world of writing and reading. This doesn't mean I don't teach about conventions. Instead, I address the *functions* of marks, rules, and spellings in genuine pieces of writing: *how _____ helps readers make sense of a text*. Rather than conducting a lesson about sentence fragments, I shift the emphasis to show kids how to use a colon or dash to attach incomplete components to sentences, and I explain what these marks tell readers. Then I ask students to spend a little time looking for dashes and colons in their reading that day and to speculate about why the authors used them. In reading minilessons I teach what fluent readers actually do, based on the latest, best research, and in literary minilessons I draw on books written by novelists, reporters, poets, teachers, and critics, not textbook committees (again, see Appendix Q).

Some of my minilessons are mini: a five- to ten-minute lecture on a single, highly-focused topic. I'll spend five minutes on such issues as how to brainstorm titles and why title creation comes at the end, how to complete an editing checksheet, rules of a new writing contest, a literary definition, or a straightforward mark like the hyphen.

Other lessons are longer and interactive so students and I can generate ideas and build a theory together, or so I can demonstrate some of my understandings as a writer and reader. One day we'll spend twenty minutes reading an essay from the *New York Times Book Review* about the pleasures of memorizing poetry, then we'll memorize a poem together. Or I might read aloud the opening pages of a novel, and kids will discuss what the author did to introduce the main character. In longer minilessons we'll conduct a full frontal assault on pronoun case (*I* or *me*?), role-play good and bad writing conferences, or list on the easel pad the themes we found in S. E. Hinton's *The Outsiders*.

I'm learning a lot about the practical aspects of presenting minilessons. Sometimes they take shape as a course of study: a series of discussions and demonstrations over several days that explore different edges of a concept or convention. I've learned that overhead transparencies, easel pads, and handouts focus students' attention and make minilesson information accessible and concrete. Transparency film labeled for use in plain paper copiers (an important distinction, to avoid a meltdown) can be run through a photocopier, so a piece of writing becomes an instant overhead. I also create systems of folders to save minilesson notes, examples, overheads, and other materials from year to year. For a long time I thought this was cheating—that minilessons should be spontaneous responses to the moment. Now, if it worked, I want to save it and save myself the time of re-creating it another year when the need or occasion arises. And I learned from Linda Rief (1992) and her students that kids can create handbooks for themselves by recording and compiling materials generated or presented in minilessons. I haven't yet found the trade handbook that's as practical or appropriate as the one my students and I write together each year.

The topics I introduce in writing and reading minilessons fall into four broad categories. Some are procedural: the rules and routines of the workshop. Some relate to issues of literary craft: what authors consider when they create literature. Some address conventions of written language: the compacts or agreements between writers and readers that students need to know, the rules literate people follow so our writing will be taken seriously by others and understood as we intend it to be. And some minilessons focus on the strategies of good readers, of people who know how to choose, engage with, understand, and appreciate literature.

This chapter highlights the lessons I've conducted. Because my classes at CTL are combined groups of seventh and eighth graders and I teach each student for two years, I've described many more minilessons than anyone could teach in a single year. I hope the lists and examples suggest the range of what's possible.

Lessons About Workshop Procedures

At the beginning of the school year I invest my energy in procedural minilessons, at the expense of craft, conventions, and strategies. Writing-reading workshop does not come naturally to kids. They need to be taught its routines, sometimes over and over again, until they internalize the rhythms. But once they know what to do, usually by the first week of October, they can regulate how they use time in the workshop and stay on-task, and I can concentrate on showing them how to improve the quality and conventionality of their writing and the depth of their reading. The two lists below are pretty standard. They comprise September's procedural minilessons, designed to teach—or remind—students how to conduct themselves as writers and readers in a workshop environment.

MINILESSONS ABOUT PROCEDURES FOR WRITING IN A WORKSHOP

- Expectations for writing
- Rules for writing workshop
- Workshop routines: each day's schedule of poem, minilesson, status-of-the-class conference, independent writing and conferring, and sometimes a group meeting
- How the room is organized; how the space is to be used
- Status-of-the-class survey and typical writer responses
- Why the room is silent during writing: writing as thinking
- Where to find various writing resources in the classroom
- Daily writing folder and its purpose and organization
- Permanent writing folder and its purpose and organization
- Spelling folder and its purpose and organization
- Homework folder and weekly homework assignment sheet

- Writing-reading handbook and its purpose and organization
- Adding minilesson data to the writing-reading handbook
- Creating and updating a writing territories list
- Why we confer about writing
- Conferring with oneself about one's own writing
- Conferring with the teacher
- Conferring with peers: where, when, how
- How to whisper
- Response forms for recording what happens in peer conferences
- Procedures and agendas for group conferences
- Creating and updating an individual proofreading list of the conventions taught to each student in editing conferences
- What to do when a writer is "finished"
- How to use an editing checksheet
- Stack trays for filing student writing that is ready for teacher editing
- Procedures for writing final copies
- Possible modes of going public with finished pieces of writing
- Schedule for student use of the word processors
- How to run the photocopier
- Self-evaluation procedures and surveys at the end of each trimester
- Goal setting in writing at the end of each trimester
- Establishing a portfolio for the trimester: a collection of evidence that shows one's growth and goals as a writer
- Calls for manuscripts
- Writing contests

MINILESSONS ABOUT PROCEDURES FOR READING IN A WORKSHOP

- Expectations for reading
- Rules for reading workshop
- Workshop routines: each day's schedule of read-aloud and independent reading
- How the classroom libraries are organized
- Status-of-the-class survey and what the teacher will be looking for as she circulates and records
- Why the room is silent during reading: reading as thinking; Wallace Stevens's poem "The House Was Quiet and the World Was Calm"
- How the space and furniture may be used; the importance of comfort and solitude
- Classroom literary resources

- Using and revising the "Favorite Adolescent Literature" list of kids' recommended books
- Reading folder and keeping a record of books read (and abandoned)
- Rating books on a scale of 1–10
- Borrowing books and the importance of returning and shelving them
- Nightly homework reading assignment: why it's important; why homework reading for another course doesn't count
- Reading journals and how to write, pass, and answer letters about books
- Texts and lyrics folders and how to file materials chronologically
- Procedures for booktalks about recommended titles
- Self-evaluation procedures and surveys at the end of each trimester
- Goal setting in reading at the end of each trimester
- Establishing a portfolio for the trimester: a collection of evidence to show one's growth and goals as a reader
- Book-club offerings and deadlines

Procedural minilessons are usually brief. Here I do all or most of the talking, getting right to the point about how I expect something will be done, but I give time at the end for students to ask questions or voice concerns. The first lessons about procedures aren't meant to be definitive explanations. They serve as introductions, and the kids who are ready for the specific information I'm presenting will hear it best. I know I'll be reminding students about how to use the room and its resources all fall.

One of my early procedural minilessons with a group of inexperienced writers will outline a writer's activities. I'm careful never to talk about *the writing process*, because the phrase implies one series of steps through which everyone proceeds in creating a piece of writing. I can talk only in general ways about some of the things writers do, or in specific ways about what I or other writers have done on specific occasions. But I also know beginning writers need guidelines if they've never been asked for anything other than first-time-final writing. I make a poster that shows what writers in a workshop do:

WHAT AUTHORS DO

WRITERS:
- rehearse: develop an idea, perhaps make notes or lists or try different leads
  - draft one and read, revise, confer
    - (maybe) draft two and read, revise, confer . . .
      - decide the content is set
        - polish: final word choices, clarification, tightening
          - final, formal editing for conventions
            - peer editing, if you wish
              - submit to an outside editor (e.g., the teacher)
                - create a final copy
                  - proofread
                    - publish

I explain the poster and tell kids it suggests some of the things they'll do on their way to completing their first pieces of writing. Then, after three weeks, I take it down: once kids have an idea of the range of a writer's activity and some of the language of the workshop, I want them to make decisions about what to do next by considering their own texts. If they're consulting the poster after a month of writing workshop, they're not deciding.

Writing folders are another basis for presentations about procedural issues. I explain the difference between the two folders—one a portfolio of finished pieces, filed chronologically, which we'll keep in the classroom all year so that they and I can see and describe their growth; the other a working folder that comes to class each day with the writer and stores work-in-progress.

On another day I teach about the form attached inside the permanent folder and ask writers to record the titles and genres of finished pieces, so that they may see at a glance what they've accomplished and have another re-source for finding ideas and genres for new pieces of writing. I also explain the individual proofreading form, on which writers will list the conventions they learn from me in editing conferences and for which they're to take responsi-bility. I try to talk about each issue as it becomes an issue—for example, intro-ducing the proofreading list on the day of my first editing conferences with students who have completed drafts of writing, and addressing the writing record the first day writers in the group have finished pieces to enter there.

Explaining what students do with finished writing is another procedural minilesson. The final copy is photocopied before it goes wherever it's going. Then the drafts, notes, peer-conference records, and editing checksheet are stapled together, with the earliest work on the bottom and the photocopy of the finished piece on top. This is filed by the student in his or her perma-nent folder.

Another series of procedural minilessons deals with what happens dur-ing peer writing conferences. I talk a lot at the beginning of the year about responses that help writers and responses that don't. On the easel I list prin-ciples of conferring—how the writer explains what he or she wants, then reads the writing aloud, and how responders listen, ask questions about things they don't understand or would like to know more about, and give the writer the specific feedback he or she asked for. I also teach students how to use the peer writing conference record (Appendix J).

Then with kids' help I role-play successful and not-so-successful confer-ences. Two or three times during the first month of school I ask a writer to join me at the front of the room and read aloud a piece of writing for me to respond to; the rest of the class takes notes in their writing-reading hand-books under the heading *When a Conference Helps*. I model appropriate re-sponse by asking what the writer wants help with, looking at the writer, listening, jotting down notes, paraphrasing, and asking a few pointed ques-tions that help the writer reflect and make plans. I stick to business and make sure the conference takes no longer than ten minutes. I ask the rest of the class to describe what they saw and heard me do.

The next day I model an inappropriate, unhelpful response to the same piece of writing and, again, ask the class to take notes, this time under the heading *When a Conference Doesn't Help.* As the writer reads, I look over his or her shoulder, doodle, and gaze around the room. As soon as the student finishes reading, I jump in with an anecdote about a similar experience, idea, or piece of writing. I waste a lot of time. I make broad judgments: "That was boring," or "That was so great. Really great. Really, really great. Really." I tell the writer what should be in the piece. I make plans with him about what we'll do at noon recess.

At the end of the conference I ask kids to describe what went wrong. Peers need instruction, demonstrations, reminders, and time if they're to get better at responding to each other's writing, just as their teachers do. During the year I come back to role-play, for better or worse, what I hear as I pass the peer conference areas during writing workshop.

Other procedural minilessons involve announcements of interest to writers; these take place through the course of the school year. I take five minutes to read the rubric and submission rules for a magazine like *Merlin's Pen,* which publishes middle schoolers' writing, or an announcement about a new writing contest I discovered in my mail, on the teachers'-room bulletin board, or in the back pages of *Teacher* magazine. I describe to eighth graders the submissions they need to prepare for their yearbook: the class will and prophecy, each graduate's vital statistics, and memoirs of life at CTL. I remind kids of the deadlines for *Acorns,* the Center's literary magazine, published three or four times each year. I distribute and explain my own calls for manuscripts.

These are handouts that outline the requirements for in-class magazines. I explain the theme or genre, ask for legible, edited copy, and set a deadline. Everyone who submits a piece that meets the guidelines is published; the point is publishing a class magazine, not canonizing the best writers. Depending on the theme, between ten and forty-five writers have contributed to various class magazines, with poetry anthologies consistently the most popular. I've had good luck persuading parent volunteers to type the final copies. At Boothbay, high school business and work-study students also typed a lot of our magazine copy.

Four times a year I use procedural minilessons to discuss evaluation of writing and reading. The first time, in September, I describe general evaluation procedures and criteria, and the next three times I explain the questions students will answer as they evaluate themselves at the end of each trimester and set goals for themselves for the next twelve weeks. On overhead transparencies I list evaluation criteria, self-evaluation questions, and lists of materials students should include in their portfolios.

Other minilessons provide explanations of the classroom library and how it works: the poetry bookcases, displays of new titles and recommended books, fiction and nonfiction paperback literature, and drama, all filed alphabetically by authors' last names. There's no sign-out system because I don't have time to oversee one—it could become someone's full-time job. Instead, when I buy a new book I print my initials in red permanent marker across the top, put a green dot sticker on the spine, and add the book to the library. If a lost book gets found, chances are pretty good my initials and the green dot will be prominent enough for the finder to return it. All year I stress the need for students to return borrowed books. The only way others will have books to borrow is if readers use the system; the classroom library we start with in September has to last all year. I still lose books. I decided to accept the situation—paperback novels disappear no matter what system I devise—and minimize the time spent administering the classroom library and chasing after missing titles.

Throughout the year, as the monthly fliers arrive at school, I present minilessons on commercial school book-club offerings. I mention the books I think would be worth buying and owning, and the school gives kids a week to bring in orders and money. The advantages of book clubs continue to be their comparatively low prices and the bonus points teachers receive toward free books for the classroom library. The disadvantage, more so every year, is that fewer and fewer book-club offerings are books. Some months my students, confronted with choices of posters, Mad Libs, and software, order nothing.

In another procedural minilesson I instruct kids about their reading records. I begin by passing out the folders, two copies per student of the form for recording books, and a copy of the list of genres that appears later in this chapter, on page 178, under the heading "Minilessons About Literary Craft: What Readers Notice." The list of genres was created by students, and we revise it each year to reflect what they're reading with more exactness and insight than the broad categories of fiction, nonfiction, poetry, and drama allow. Then I explain what I expect and why:

> This year you'll be reading a lot. Readers often keep track of their reading and make records of the books and authors they encounter. It imparts a terrific sense of accomplishment to look back through a year's record, to see where you've been as a reader. Listing books and noting their genres also helps you spot trends in your reading: the kinds of books you like at different points in your history as a seventh and eighth grade reader. Listing books you didn't finish helps you begin to figure out and name your criteria for what makes a book interesting to you or

worth reading. And listing authors helps when you like a book: because you have the author's name, you can look for other good books by the same writer. Finally, it's interesting to see how long it takes to read certain books and whether the rate at which you read picks up through the year because you're reading so much or finding more books you like.

Each time you read a book, from now until June, record the title, genre, author, and the date you finish the book or abandon it. Keep good records—give yourself credit for everything you read. Please only number the ones you *finish*—in the far left-hand column with the # symbol at the top—so you have a quick reference at the end of the trimester, when I'll ask you to report how many books you read. Finally, in the far right-hand column, would you rate each book you finish or abandon? On a ten-point scale, with one the lowest and ten the highest, use this shorthand system to indicate what you loved, loathed, liked, or tolerated. During the year we'll add your nines and tens to the lists of favorite adolescent literature and poetry.

In Chapter 8 I reproduce the letter I write to students that invites them to correspond with me and their friends in reading journals. During the second week of school I give everyone a copy of the letter, to glue inside the covers of their journals, and I explain the procedures. Because the directions are complicated, I'm more than usually aware during this presentation that I'm providing background, not definitive instruction. In the opening minutes of other workshops I explain again when kids do the actual writing, how often they have to write and to whom, where the journals are kept, how letters are delivered, why it's necessary to date the correspondence and number the pages, and, most importantly, what to talk about when writing a letter about literature.

In helping kids with the content of their reading-journal entries, I review the second paragraph of my letter to the group: "Tell what you felt and why; what you noticed about how the author wrote; why you think he or she wrote this way; what you liked, didn't and why," etc. Then I show them what I mean on overhead transparencies, projecting a half dozen exchanges between previous years' students and between students and me. Nothing I tell kids about the letters has the same effect as their reading other students' words—now they see what I mean. Looking at and talking about how other students have written about books circumvents the worst problems connected with the letters—book-report plot synopses. Teachers who are considering dialogue journals about reading might start by making transparencies of letters in Chapter 8 to show their students what's possible.

The information I present in minilessons throughout September and early October covers the same kind of ground I used to attempt to conquer during the first week of school: all the basic information about how I expected everything to be done, which I then ended up reteaching all year. In procedural minilessons students are exposed to a specific expectation and have chances to ask questions about it. They still don't "get" everything the first time through, but the minilesson provides a practical forum for introducing guidelines and creating frames of reference. There's less student overload, a better sense of how and why things work, and greater independence earlier on.

Lessons About Literary Craft

Craft minilessons are those that address techniques, styles, genres, authors, and works of literature. These are my favorites, because I can explore tricks of the writing trade and insights about literature and authors. Some of the tricks are mine, lessons I learned through my own writing. Some are students', which they or I share as minilessons, and some come from the professional writers whose texts I learn from: Georgia Heard, X. J. Kennedy, Ken Macrorie, Donald Murray, Robert Wallace, E. B. White, and William Zinsser.

Showing students a writer's techniques has the same effects and benefits as demonstrating an artist's methods in the studio. Both help kids begin to develop a repertoire of approaches. As students discover when and how to apply what they learn, the strategies become second nature. Just as experienced artists don't have to contemplate principles of perspective every time they draw a vanishing point, the experienced writer turns naturally to techniques like brainstorming titles, cutting and taping to reorganize a draft, or finding transitional phrases for an essay. In minilessons I introduce information and examples, and in conferences I help students apply the lessons to their writing and intentions.

I've learned that when students don't revise their writing, it's usually because they don't know how. They don't have methods for manipulating the page—adding information, deleting it, changing it, or moving it around. In minilessons I teach techniques for revising by demonstrating with a draft of my writing or composing on a transparency. Below is a list of some basic revision devices I've taught.

- **Carets** (^) enable writers to insert new words, phrases, and lines.
- **Arrows** allow writers to extend writing into the empty space on the paper: in the margins or on the back.
- **Asterisks** and other codes are useful for inserting chunks, passages bigger than a caret or an arrow can accommodate. Often kids will

develop whole systems of symbols or numbers, insert them into the text where appropriate, then head up sheets of paper with the corresponding symbols and draft the additional material there.

- **Spider legs** are another method for adding. A writer drafts new material on strips of paper, then staples them to the original draft at appropriate points in the text.

- **Cut and tape** allows writers to insert new chunks of text and reorder existing sections. It saves a writer from having to recopy old material when moving to a new draft. Workable sections from an early version can be retrieved and inserted into subsequent drafts. And students can learn, in another context, that revising doesn't mean recopying.

- Writers can **highlight** sections of text in different colored inks as a way to reorganize. Especially when they're writing about ideas, students' drafts may jump from topic to topic and back again. When revising a draft to organize it, they use fine-point markers and circle in one color all references to one idea or topic, circle in another color all references to a second idea or topic, and so on. On the subsequent draft they combine each of the sections marked with a particular color.

- Writers **circle** to indicate what they'll keep in a given text. For beginning writers, deleting is often harder than adding. Once words are down on the page, they often become golden. I encourage reluctant deleters to circle what they like and want to keep.

Crossing out is tough—it still kills me to admit that a chunk of my text needs to go—but writers need to be tough-minded if they're to get better at writing. Sometimes crossing out is hard for kids because it messes up the page. Students who have never seen a revised draft are reluctant to cross out, write between lines or in the margins, make inserts with carets and arrows, or cut and tape their manuscripts. They need visual proof that this is what writers do. Teachers can provide it with demonstrations of our own writing. Students observe an experienced adult, who understands that writing is thinking, messing up the page in an effort to unscramble her thoughts.

Many of my minilessons about the craft of writing are demonstrations with my own manuscripts, in which I write out loud in front of students. When too many of the titles of students' compositions are descriptions ("My Ideas About the Clear-Cutting Ban," "Getting Lost on a Camping Trip," "Feelings About Spring"), I'll bring a piece of my writing to a minilesson and brainstorm titles in front of the group, as many as I can think of. Donald Murray advises writers to try for fifty—to push past the obvious, outwit the self-censors, and take a leap into the unknown. In a follow-up minilesson I ask students to name what they consider to be the characteristics of effective titles. I record their criteria, then type up the list as a document to return to them; they attach it inside the grommets of their daily writing folders as a reference.

GOOD TITLES . . .

- Catch a reader's attention
- Fit the big idea of the piece
- Are not mere descriptions (i.e., "The Day I Went Boating with Curt")
- Give a hint or a taste of the topic or idea
- Are often the result of brainstorming: writing down as many ideas you can think of on as many tangents as you can find
- Are the best possible combinations of words
- Are memorable
- Are usually decided on last, when the author can look back at the whole and get a sense of what the writing is about
- Can replace a working title that the writer uses while a composition is in progress (e.g., the working title of Paul McCartney's "Yesterday" was "Scrambled Eggs")

Some craft minilessons explore issues of style. Cutting adjectives and adverbs—showing rather than telling—is an example of a stylistic concern. One morning I took an apple to class to use as a prop in helping kids understand the difference between description that reveals and description that clutters. I copied onto the easel pad the advice from Mark Twain that provides the epigraph to this chapter: "Don't say the old lady screamed. Bring her on and let her scream." Then I began the lesson:

> I remember when I was in second grade, and we had writing on the last Friday of every month at the end of the day. My teacher brought in an object or picture, and we'd be asked to write a paragraph that described it. But first we'd have a lesson about adjectives and adverbs.
>
> Mrs. Perkins would hold up, say, an apple like this one and tell the class, "Now, boys and girls, let's see how many words you can think of to describe this apple." Role-play with me—I'll be Mrs. Perkins and you be my class. What words can you boys and girls come up with? I'll write your suggestions here on the easel.

When we were through providing descriptive words, Mrs. Perkins would say, "Very good. Now, I'd like each of you to write your own paragraphs with five sentences, using as many of these words as you can. These are called adjectives, and good writers use lots of them."

The problem is, good writers don't use lots of adjectives—or adverbs. Telling a lot, embedding the clutter of descriptive words, may be a teacher's idea of good writing, but it's not a writer's. Good writers *show* rather than tell. They let us see people and ideas in action rather than depend on qualifiers. They give us specifics: strong nouns, precise verbs, actions we can see and hear, reactions we can feel. An apple is big, red, round, crisp, shiny, and juicy. Unless this is a commercial for Macintosh apples, so what? Instead, a writer would try to show something about the apple only if there's something to be shown—if a quality of the apple reflects some meaning in the sentence or story. For example: *I gobbled the green apples I found in the clearing.* Now we have specifics: hunger, unripe apples, a forest setting; now the apple begins to have a significance we can understand.

The quote from Mark Twain points this lesson. He says a writer can tell readers that an old lady screamed, or the writer can bring her into the action and put the sound into her mouth so we can hear and feel that scream: "Arrrgggghhh!" You could describe a physical state in your writing with adjectives and adverbs: "I was really very hot." Or you could show it: "Sweat dripped off my glasses." You could describe embarrassment with adjectives and adverbs: "He turned bright pink." Or you could show it with a verb: "He blushed." Here's an example from a piece Heather wrote last week about when she fainted. In her first draft she wrote, "Daren's voice sounded really funny." She revised it as "Daren's voice echoed and boomed in my ears as if he were shouting at me through a megaphone." Now we begin to hear what Heather heard. You may want to read through your draft and mark in the margin anywhere you find yourself describing to the reader something that you could be showing instead.

I'll build another minilesson about style around Ken Macrorie's discussion of "The Really Bad Words" and his "Bad Word List" (1988, 208–215). He describes diminishers (little, slightly, rather, somewhat, sort of) and intensifiers (really, quite, very, even, actually) as bad words to use in writing because they weaken or overwhelm the nouns and verbs they modify; as Macrorie put it: "The lesser word draws energy away" (209). I show students Macrorie's examples of "before" and "after" sentences; then we write pairs of our own together:

BEFORE: The young boy ran really quickly down to the seashore and was so tired when he got there he actually lay down on the beach.
AFTER: The boy tore down to the shore, then collapsed in the sand.

Other style minilessons deal with narration; for example, the difference between first and third person and the need to keep a consistent narrative voice. Writers' first attempts at fiction often shift back and forth between first- (*I did it*) and third- (*She did it*) person narrators. I also talk with kids about maintaining an *I* voice in their memoirs. As soon as a writer slips into *we*, when describing an event he or she experienced as a member of a group, it becomes impossible to convey what the *I* was thinking and feeling, and there's no opportunity for reflection, no discovery of the significance of the memory or the writer's truth, and no one for a reader to be with in the story.

Minilessons frequently address ways writers can involve readers in the writing. A common problem in beginning writing is a lack of reflection. Students list facts or describe a string of events without discovering or describing the significance of their knowledge or experiences. I push hard for thoughts and feelings. Sometimes I show how I reflect in one of my essays or memoirs; sometimes I show an author reflecting—for example, I read aloud a passage from *Where the Red Fern Grows* where Wilson Rawls takes us inside the main character's heart and mind. I ask students to put a dot at the points in their drafts where they think a reader needs to know what the writer or narrator is thinking and feeling, then go back and add their reflections.

I also conduct lessons about verb tense and the need to keep a consistent tense, past or present. At the same time I discuss transitions between flashbacks, flash-forwards, and the present, because when writers start to experiment with sequence, they often lose control of the verbs.

Beginning writers need lessons about focusing the content of their writing. When writers start developing their own topics, they make broad choices—a whole week at camp rather than a significant episode, everything there is to know about motorcycles rather than the writer's perspective on helmet laws. Buried in the draft is the essence that drew the writer to the topic in the first place, but the reader can't tell why the writer cared enough to write about it—or why the reader should care. When beginning writers sacrifice depth for coverage, the result is sketchy information, a lack of specifics that makes it hard for a reader to engage with the writing, and no discovery or growth on the part of the writer.

Students need to know that writers select. I use the analogy of focusing a camera:

> Like a landscape photographer, a writer is confronted with a huge chunk of scenery; like the photographer, the writer chooses a focus—a section to narrow down to and depict with care and grace. Once the selection is made, the photographer begins to explore and sharpen the

details of the new scene he or she has framed, and the writer begins to explore and sharpen the specifics of the narrowed topic. The end result for a photographer is a precise view of one aspect of a landscape. For a writer it's a precise view of one area of knowledge, one feeling, one memory. So the writing starts big—everything about a topic. Then it shrinks—one piece of the whole. But it gets big again as the writer adds the actions, reactions, dialogue, thoughts, feelings, and specifics that bring the narrowed topic to life.

For new writers, focus is a revising technique, one they use to find the core ideas within rambling first drafts. I've found that as kids gain experience, they begin to select, reject, and sharpen focus in their heads, cutting to the heart of the matter before they ever put pen to paper.

Minilessons about first lines, leads, and conclusions help students internalize an awareness of these considerations. I read aloud good beginnings and endings from novels, short stories, essays, and feature articles, and we list their characteristics. I also demonstrate options: show students how writers create and consider alternatives rather than settle for the first introduction or conclusion that comes to mind. On overheads I experiment with different ways into and out of a given piece of writing.

In a minilesson on narrative leads I tell students:

> The lead is one of the crucial parts of a piece of writing. It's often the point when readers decide if they're going to continue reading. It's where the writer establishes topic, direction, tone, voice—just about everything. As writers, you'll want your leads to bring your readers into your writing by creating tension—some problem readers solve or question they answer by reading the rest of the writing. Later on you can embed the context and fill in the who-what-where-when-why that a reader will need as the text progresses.

Over several days I demonstrate on overhead transparencies four alternatives for kicking off a memoir: a lackluster lead that puts all the who-what-where-when-why information up front, followed by leads that show a character in action, reaction, and dialogue, so students can see how the alternatives might work in a given writing situation.

LEADS

Typical

It was a day at the end of June. My mom, dad, brother, and I were at our camp on Rangeley Lake. We had arrived the night before at 10:00, so it was dark when we got there and unpacked. We went straight to bed. The next morning, when I was eating breakfast, my dad started yelling for me from down at the dock at the top of his lungs. He said there was a car in the lake.

Action: A Main Character Doing Something

I gulped my milk, pushed away from the table, and bolted out of the kitchen, slamming the screen door behind me. I ran down to the dock as fast as my legs could carry me. My feet pounded on the old wood, hurrying me toward the sound of my dad's voice. "Scott!" he bellowed again.

"Coming, Dad!" I gasped. I couldn't see him yet—just the sails of the boats that had already put out into the lake for the day.

Dialogue: A Character or Characters Speaking

"Scott! Get down here on the double!" Dad bellowed. His voice sounded far away.

"Dad?" I hollered. "Where are you?" I squinted through the screen door but couldn't see him.

"I'm down on the dock. MOVE IT. You're not going to believe this," he replied.

Reaction: A Character Thinking

I couldn't imagine why my father was hollering for me at 7:00 in the morning. I thought fast about what I might have done to get him riled. Had he found out about the way I talked to my mother the night before, when we got to camp and she asked me to help unpack the car? Did he find the fishing reel I broke last week? Before I could consider a third possibility, his voice shattered my thoughts.

"Scott! Move it! You're not going to believe this!"

Some minilessons about craft explore the purposes and characteristics of different genres. I distribute copies of the list "Kinds of Writing That Emerge in Writing Workshop" (Appendix C), ask students to insert these in their daily writing folders, and teach about some of the different genres through the year. The third section of *In the Middle* focuses on the major areas of genre instruction—lessons I've taught and learned about memoir, fiction, poetry, and different modes of exposition and argument. Other genre lessons have addressed Web pages, young adult literature, letters of all kinds, plays and skits, book reviews, songs, standardized writing assessments, political ads, résumés and vitae, petitions, and parodies.

In minilessons on parody, a favorite genre of middle schoolers, for whom caricature is a way of life, I begin with a definition on the easel pad: *parody* is when a writer imitates a composition or an author and twists or plays with the structure or content. Then students volunteer examples of parody they know:

- Aal's poem "Hazel Tells Laverne" (*The Frog Prince*)
- Jon Scieszka (*Frog Prince*; *Three Little Pigs*; math textbooks in *Math Curse*; classic novels in *Time Warp Trio*)
- Weird Al Yankovic (Madonna and other singers)
- *Mad* magazine (everything and everyone)
- Paul Fleischman's *A Fate Totally Worse than Death* (Christopher Pike novels)
- Kenneth Koch's variations on "This Is Just to Say" (William Carlos Williams)

I add and read aloud others I know: Woody Allen's two-minute mysteries and mythological creatures in *Without Feathers* and the UFO sightings reported in *Side Effects*; Russell Baker's parodies of politicians in his *New York Times* column; Diane White's parodies of American popular culture, but especially Martha Stewart, in the *Boston Globe*; the Shouts and Murmurs page of *The New Yorker*; and parodies by students like B. J., who went after Robert Frost, and Jason, who messed around with William Carlos Williams.

NOTHING DULL CAN STAY (I HOPE)

School's first day is dull.
Teachers' talk rings in your skull.
Homework makes you sour,
But only so an hour.
Then class subsides to class.
You know you'll never pass.
The bell rings down the day.
Nothing dull can stay.

—B. J. Sherman

PARODIES OF "THE RED WHEELBARROW"
BY WILLIAM CARLOS WILLIAMS

So much depends
upon

whether a plane's gas
tank

is full or empty while
flying

over the Grand
Canyon.

So much depends
upon

whether the Coyote hits the
Road Runner

with the anvil or

it falls on
him

by accident.

                 *   *   *

So much depends
upon

whether the dishwasher
is

cleaned with Arm and Hammer
or

Lemon Scented
Tide.

—Jason Perry

In another genre minilesson I talked about differences among the various fictional forms:

- Short story: can be read (usually) in one sitting
- Novella: a short novel (i.e., eighty pages)
- Novel: a full-length work of fiction (i.e., a hundred pages or more)
- Chapter: a main division of a novel or novella
- Chapter book: for beginning readers; a shorter narrative divided into short chapters; a bridge between picture books and novels.

Joe asked, "What about a book that's based on a movie script? Is that a novel?" I explained that these were novelizations, added them to the list, and expressed my disdain for them. Joe agreed. He led the group in brainstorming alternatives to *novelization*: *desperization*, *dumbed-downer*, *twiceovercashmaker*.

Edie asked, "Then what do you call a book that's based on a movie script that was based on a book?"

"No such thing," I answered.

"Well, have you seen the paperback version of *Little Women* 'by' Laurie Lawlor?" she asked. Curt mentioned the paperback version of *Willow* he had just read that was "by" Wayland Drew. So we invented a genre: NAGA-TOBOETMBOTO—Not as good as the original book or even the movie based on the original.

A series of minilessons about young adult literature as a genre revolves around S. E. Hinton's novel *The Outsiders*. Written at Hinton's dining room table when she was a junior in high school, *The Outsiders*, published in April 1967, changed the world of books for teenagers forever. I buy enough paperback copies of the novel so that every student has one.

To start this series of minilessons I gather an armful of the books that were available to teenagers when I was in junior high—*The Hardy Boys* and *Nancy Drew*, Beverly Cleary's *Fifteen* and *Jean and Johnny*, *Seventeenth Summer* by Maureen Daley.

> Before S. E. Hinton, books for young adults either solved a mystery or asked the burning question, "Will I get to go to the prom?" In a speech at an English teacher's conference, Hinton once said, "There were no books that showed what was really going on with teenagers. I wrote *The Outsiders* because I wanted to read it." Her novel is packed with what is really going on with teenagers: peer pressure, concerns about social status, stereotyping, absent or even abusive parents, threats of violence, loneliness, the overwhelming importance of friends and friendships to kids your age. *The Outsiders* told the truth about life through a teenager's eyes. Its grassroots success—*The Outsiders* has sold millions and millions of copies—paved the way for other young adult writers, people like Robert Cormier, Walter Dean Myers, and Caroline Cooney.

I distribute a copy of the novel to each student and read aloud the first ten pages or so, while they follow along. I want to hook them with Hinton's style and my rendition of Ponyboy's voice, his fluid and compelling narration. Then I give each student three four-by-six-inch notecards and a homework assignment:

> Over the next five days read at least through page seventy-five of *The Outsiders*, when we'll stop to discuss Frost's poem "Nothing Gold Can Stay" and what it's doing here in the middle of this novel. Then you'll have five more days to finish the book. You can read it all tonight if you want—that's up to you. But in ten days I want us to be able to talk about what Hinton did in this novel as its author. The notecards are to tuck inside your copy of *The Outsiders* and make a record of your observations.

Please record the things you see her doing as a writer: how she develops the characters and advances the plot. Note your questions about what she did and why or how she did it. Note the themes that emerge for you—problems of and ideas about teenage life that Hinton explores through the characters' actions. Find the turning point in the action, when the world of the novel changes and nothing can go back to the way it was. And note relevant page numbers whenever you can.

Every year the richness of the conversations around *The Outsiders* amazes me. The poet X. J. Kennedy has said, "I would define literature generously, as memorable writing of any sort" (1984). For many of my students, S. E. Hinton is as memorable as they come. It's easy for secondary teachers to scoff at her novels, but she's important to adolescent readers—and writers—because they identify with and love what she did in this book. Part of it is Hinton's use of fiction to explore inequities in the social situation among kids in her hometown, but most of it is her style: the narrative voice and characters are direct and compelling, and the big ideas in the novel are both evident and important to my kids. They understand the concept of theme from the inside on the day that we gather for a minilesson to read aloud our notes and compile a list of the ideas we find in *The Outsiders*:

OUTSIDERS THEMES

- "Nothing gold can stay." But it is possible to find something like gold inside yourself. "In the country" is a place that exists inside each of us. It is:
    knowledge and self-knowledge
    compassion
    respect
    self-respect
    a personal voice
    memory
- "Family" isn't always relatives; everyone needs to belong to someone—to feel loved, wanted, and supported.
- Don't judge a book by its cover; don't judge people by their dress, style, looks, background, where they live. Underneath, everyone has the same needs as you do. Everyone dreams and yearns.
- Watch out for stereotypes. See every person as an individual. Find out who others are inside.
- Growing up is hard for everyone, rich or poor or in-between: "things are rough all over."

- Violence never solved anything.
- Nature can bring people together. Cherry and Pony's "communion of sunsets" means that the natural world belongs to everyone; it rises above the social rules and roles that people construct.

In other minilessons about literary craft I teach about resources and references that writers and readers use: rhyming dictionaries, *Bartlett's Familiar Quotations*, and *Roget's Thesaurus*:

A rhyming dictionary is a wonderful help when you're writing a rhymed poem, song, jingle, rap, or greeting-card message. Since rhyming sounds always begin with vowels, a rhyming dictionary lists words by the beginning vowel of the rhyming sound. *The Scholastic Rhyming Dictionary*, which is an easy one for kids to use, has six sections: A, E, I, O, U, Y. If I want to rhyme a word with *lice*, I look at the tops of the pages for *i to ice*, and I find this list of words I might use in an ode to our little friends:

dice	entice
ice	no dice
lice	precise
mice	sale price
nice	suffice
price	think twice
rice	merchandise
slice	paradise
spice	sacrifice
splice	three blind mice
twice	at any price
vice	fool's paradise
advice	legal advice
concise	self-sacrifice
device	sugar and spice

Another reference I love, because I adore quotes and epigraphs, is *Bartlett's Familiar Quotations*. An epigraph is a quotation at the beginning of a book, chapter, essay, poem, or play. *Bartlett's* is the granddaddy of quote collections. It was first published in 1855, when it consisted of 258 pages and quoted 168 authors. Now, in its sixteenth edition, it includes more than twenty thousand quotes and 2,550 authors.

What are your best guesses about the most heavily quoted authors? Well, they're Shakespeare and the Bible. But you'll also find John Lennon, Dr. Seuss, Elvis, Muhammed Ali, Arlo Guthrie, and Sesame Street.

Authors are included in the book in chronological order, from 2650 B.C. through 1985, in this edition. To find a quote by its subject, look in the index, which is six hundred pages long. Say I'm writing an antiwar essay and want to illustrate or illuminate it with a quote. So I flip to the *W* pages in the index and find *WAR*. The transparency shows all the war entries in the index of *Bartlett's*—four long columns of them. I skim the phrases down the columns, looking for one that fits with the meaning I'm trying to make.

This looks interesting: "peace not absence of w., 277:15." The numbers tell me to go to page 277 and look at quote number 15. When I do, I find:

Benedict [Baruch] Spinoza
1632–1677
Peace is not an absence of war, it is a virtue, a state of mind, a disposition for benevolence, confidence, justice.
Theological-Political Treatise [1670]

The entry tells me who said this and when he lived, and it provides the whole quote that was abridged in the index. It also gives me a source line: the title and date of the work in which the quote appears, in the event I'm going to cite the quote or want to learn more. You'll see the next Spinoza source line is given as *Ibid*. That's short for *ibidem*, and it means "from the same source as the quote listed above."

My minilessons about using a thesaurus are a combination of instructions, advice, and warnings:

You go to a dictionary when you know a word but you need its spelling or definition. You go to a thesaurus when you know the definition but you need a specific word. Peter Mark Roget prepared his first *Thesaurus of English Words and Phrases* in 1852. He was a physician and a *lexicographer*: that's a writer of dictionaries. How many of you have used a thesaurus? When do you use it? Brainstorm with me on the easel.

A THESAURUS IS . . .

- A way to nudge my memory—when the word is on the tip of my tongue
- A reminder of all the choices and not to settle for the first word that crosses my mind
- A way to avoid overuse of a word (e.g., *said*)
- A way to find out I don't have the right word, when I compare it with its synonyms
- A way to discover that finding the right word isn't my problem—it's my meaning that isn't clear yet
- A way to take a break and let another part of my brain work on the problem in my writing while I'm looking at synonyms
- A way to convey subtleties and shadings

- A place to find strong, precise verbs
- A place to find big words with lots of syllables to impress people with my vocabulary

The last entry on our list is *not* an acceptable use of a thesaurus in a writing workshop. This is another of the writing lessons from my own English teachers that I had to unlearn. I was sent to the thesaurus to find obscure, polysyllable words—mostly adjectives and adverbs—that I was supposed to use in my writing to make me sound intelligent. Long sentences with lots of phrases and clauses and no personal pronouns—no *I*—were other characteristics of "good" writing it took me years to expunge from my style. Polysyllabic vocabulary, long-winded sentences, and no actor, no *I* in the writing, are all ways to distance a writer from a reader. And they are excellent smoke screens for writers to hide behind when we don't know what we think or what we're talking about.

I'll ask you *not* to use the thesaurus to find big words, and I'll ask you *never* to use a word from the thesaurus when you're not certain of its meaning. The language of good writing is simple, direct, and active.

One way good writers use a thesaurus is to help them find simple, direct, active words—in other words, nouns and verbs. E. B. White advises us to "write with nouns and verbs." He argues, "It is nouns and verbs, not their assistants, that give good writing its toughness and color." I'll ask you to try to use the thesaurus this week as a source of strong verbs in your writing. Dylan worked with the thesaurus the other day to do just that. Take a look at this overhead of a draft of his review of *The Stand*:

The Stand	Penguin, 1978, $6.99
Stephen King	ISBN 0-451-17928-5

Imagine a plague that sweeps across the country, killing everything in its path—cities destroyed, people dead in their cars after they tried to get away from the terror of the plague. But there are survivors. They desperately try to find others and get away from the mysterious "dark man" and his evil followers, who are trying to eliminate them. Together they must fight to make the last stand.

The Stand, written by Stephen King, is a tremendous novel in every sense of the word. It's a huge 1,141 pages long, but it is worth it. If you like detailed plots, you will love this book.

Twice in the first paragraph Dylan used the weak verb phrase *get away from*. I haven't read *The Stand*, but I suspect the terror the characters feel isn't suggested by the words *get away from*. So Dyl and I consulted the thesaurus: no entry for *get away*, so we tried *escape*. The entry for *escape* is on the next transparency. Here we looked in the section headed *Verbs*, because that's the part of speech Dylan needs. What we found were lots of words that told us that escape wasn't the idea he was after. But among them was *evade* (*see* AVOIDANCE). So we flipped to AVOIDANCE, and the transparency shows you what we found. Some of the verbs are too mild (shun, sidestep, shirk, dodge, steer clear of) or don't sound like Dylan (circumvent, keep aloof, eschew). But others suggest what he means: evade, elude, flee. Whatever verb he settles on will help him punch up the meaning, plus avoid using the phrase *get away from* twice, which sounds awkward.

Again, the lists below, of lessons about literary craft and literature, represent a typical course of study in my workshop—they do not reflect everything I do, and I don't cover everything listed in one year. Because I work with students for two years, I teach some topics on an alternating cycle (e.g., profiles, Shakespeare, Greek mythology, and three of my "Big Six" poets one year; essays, *The Outsiders*, Arthurian legend, and three more poets the next) and some topics every year, either for introduction or review (e.g., writing and reading territories, revision techniques, book reviews, memoir, gifts of writing, elements of fiction). I hope the lists show how a teacher can lead students inside the worlds of writing and literature.

MINILESSONS ABOUT LITERARY CRAFT: WHAT AUTHORS DO

- Why we have writing workshop
- My own territories as a writer: subjects, genres, audiences
- Kids' writing territories: subjects, genres, audiences
- Professional authors' territories
- What writers do when they rehearse, draft, reread, revise, polish, edit, and proofread
- My demonstrations of my own writing across purposes, genres, and audiences
- Genres: what's possible and characteristics of each: memoir, poetry, short fiction, essay, profile, petition, parody, song, book review, drama, Web page, résumé, letters of thanks, condolence, complaint, etc.
- Purpose: the reasons that writers write
- Revising versus recopying and when to start a new draft
- Revision methods (carets, arrows, asterisks, spider legs, cut and tape, etc.)
- The importance of skipping lines or double-spacing when drafting to ease revision, polishing, and editing: this is what authors do
- Taking a "deliberate stance" and trying to create literature every time one writes

- Information: how to recognize when there's too little, too much, or if it's not organized, and what to do
- Focus: selecting and rejecting in order to narrow a topic, control information, and include specifics
- Embedding context after the lead rather than putting all the background information up front
- Drafting alternative leads and conclusions and choosing the best, rather than settling for the first
- Qualities of a good title
- Brainstorming titles: "Donald Murray's fifty" as a way to get beyond mere description
- Flashbacks, flash-forwards, and foreshadows in narratives
- Transitions and transitional words in narratives and essays
- The need for specific examples that *show* as opposed to general statements that *tell*
- Ways of generating specific examples for idea and opinion pieces
- Ways of organizing information and arguments
- Reflecting: putting oneself in the writing and giving the reader a place to be
- Finding the significances in memoirs (i.e., "So what?")
- Crafting realistic dialogue that reveals what the speakers are like
- The uses of dedications, epigraphs, epilogues, and prologues
- Poetic techniques: line and stanza breaks, using the white space, enjambment, figurative language (metaphor, simile, personification), rhyme schemes, sound patterns (assonance and alliteration), how to revise a poem, how to cut to the bone
- Rereading during drafting to maintain momentum and a sense of the whole
- Envisioning during drafting of narratives: close one's eyes; imagine the scene, action, people, and details; then find the words to describe the vision
- A fiction writer's decisions
- Why readers need a main character
- What makes a main character
- Developing a main character: questions to consider
- Theme in narrative and poetry
- Pace in narrative and poetry
- Plausibility in narrative
- Different narrative points of view

- Consulting resources and references that help a writer make decisions about meaning, word choice, and style: rhyming dictionaries, collections of quotations, thesauruses, lexicons, etc.
- Importance of strong nouns and precise verbs
- Eliminating adjectives and adverbs that don't add to the meaning
- Eliminating "Engfish" and "The Bad Words" (Macrorie 1988)
- Passive versus active constructions and why sentences with actors ("I did it" vs. "It was done") are more effective
- Gifts of writing for those we care about
- Collaborative projects: teacher and students creating writing together
- Professional authors' techniques and processes

MINILESSONS ABOUT LITERARY CRAFT: WHAT READERS NOTICE

Genres that readers will find on the shelves of the classroom library and some characteristics of each:

adventure/survival	memoir
antiwar	movie/TV tie-in or screenplay
autobiography	mystery
biography	mythology
classic	nature
comic	New Age
contemporary realistic fiction	new journalism
detective	parody
diary	philosophy
drama	poetry
epic poem	punk fairy tale
epistolary narrative	romance
essay	science
family saga	science fiction
fantasy	series novel
gothic	sports
historical fiction	spy
history	supernatural
horror	techno-thriller
humor	thriller
instructional guide	urban life
journalism	war
legend	western

- Individual authors and who they are, what they write, and how they write it: Maya Angelou, Aristotle, Avi, Dave Barry, Francesca Lia Block, Michael Casey, Michael Crichton, Robert Cormier, Sharon Creech, Charles Dickens, Fannie Flagg, Ralph Fletcher, Anne Frank, Allen Ginsberg, Ellen Goodman, Donald Graves, Thomas Hardy, Torey Haydon, Georgia Heard, Alice Hoffman, Homer, Lee Bennett Hopkins, LouAnne Johnson, Ann Landers, Harper Lee, Robert Lipsyte, Ken Macrorie, Walter Dean Myers, Tim O'Brien, Wilfred Owen, Gary Paulsen, Sylvia Plath, Plato, Edgar Allan Poe, Cynthia Rylant, J. D. Salinger, Siegfried Sassoon, Socrates, Tennyson, Elie Weisel, and the "Big Six" American poets: E. E. Cummings, Emily Dickinson, Robert Frost, Langston Hughes, Walt Whitman, William Carlos Williams, etc.
- Elements of fiction: character, problem, change, plot, pace, plausibility, voice, point of view, setting, first line, lead, conclusion, dialogue, theme, plan
- Approaches to character development in fiction: dialogue, interior monologue, anecdote, flashback, etc.
- What main characters do for readers
- Short stories, novellas, novels, and novelizations and the characteristics of each
- Sequels, trilogies, and series
- Three themes/conflicts in literature: people against people, against nature, and against themselves
- First editions, printings, remainders, advances, royalties, hardcover to paperback, jacket copy, blurbs, gutters, type faces, typos, cover art, literary awards (Newbery, Pulitzer, Nobel, American Book Critics, Maine State Book Awards)
- What copyright pages reveal to readers
- Literary allusions from text to text
- Selections of students' favorite books
- Selections of students' favorite authors
- What poems do
- Figurative language: personification, metaphor, simile, kenning
- Sound patterns in poetry: alliteration and assonance
- Rhythm in poetry: stresses, pauses, meter
- Forms in poetry: closed (blank verse, stanza, sonnet, haiku, sestina, couplet) versus open
- How to critique a poem

- Poets on audiotape reading their work (*In Their Own Voices: A Century of Recorded Poetry* (Presson and McLees) from Rhino Records)
- Selection of individual students' favorite poems
- Selection of individual students' favorite poets
- Students' presentations of favorite poems to the group
- How poets write about sports: "Ex-Basketball Player" John Updike; "Foul Shot" Edwin A. Hoey; "basketball" Nikki Giovanni; "Skier" Robert Francis; "The Sidewalk Racer" Lillian Morrison; "The Dancer" James Berry; "The Double Play" Robert Wallace; "The Base Stealer" Robert Francis; "Foul or Fair" Lillian Morrison; "Analysis of Baseball" May Swenson; "Elegy for a Diver" Peter Meinke; "To an Athlete Dying Young" A. E. Houseman; "A Pond Hockey Pledge" and "Rollerblading Along" Peter LaSalle; and poems by students: "The Game Point" Jenny Giles; "The Turnover" Luanne Bradley; "At Lunch We Play Basketball" Jason Perry; "Tennis Sestina" Michael Maxim
- How poets write about adolescence, childhood, siblings, mothers, fathers, objects, nature, dogs, death, memories, poetry itself

The Outsiders by S. E. Hinton

- Brief history of adolescent literature as a genre
- About S. E. Hinton and *The Outsiders*
- Read and discuss interviews with and articles about Hinton
- Use four-by-six-inch cards to take notes on what readers notice about how Hinton wrote
- Gloss the poem "Nothing Gold Can Stay" by Robert Frost
- S. E. Hinton on writing
- List and discuss themes of *The Outsiders*
- Discuss the techniques Hinton used in *The Outsiders*
- Write, perform, and critique poems in response to *The Outsiders*

Arthurian Legend

- What is a legend?
- Booktalks on assorted texts and picture books about the legend
- Key names in Arthurian legend and the relationships among the characters
- About Sir Thomas Malory and *Le Morte d'Arthur*

- About the Victorian Age and the revival of interest in Arthurian legend
- About Alfred, Lord Tennyson
- Read and discuss "The Lady of Shallot"; listen to Lorena McKennitt's song "The Lady of Shallot"
- Read and discuss the poem "Merlin Enthralled" by Richard Wilbur
- About the Holy Grail
- Brief history of England and the English language: old, middle, modern, and examples of individual words and how they have changed over time
- Discuss and try to translate a page from the original *Le Morte d'Arthur*

Shakespeare

- About Shakespeare's life and times
- About Shakespeare's oeuvre
- Characteristics of comedies, tragedies, and histories
- Shakespeare's plays available on videotape
- About *Romeo and Juliet, Hamlet, Much Ado About Nothing*, and *Henry V*
- Read scenes from and view performances on video of *Romeo and Juliet, Hamlet, Much Ado About Nothing*, and *Henry V*
- The claim of Henry V to the throne of France
- Shakespeare's language
- The sonnet form
- Read and discuss Shakespeare's sonnets 18, 29, 104, 116, 129, and 130
- Select scenes to perform from the four plays
- Abridge scenes for performance
- Block, rehearse, and perform scenes; critique them on video
- Write and present poems in response to Shakespeare

Greek Mythology and Philosophy

- Allusions to Greek mythology, culture, and history in contemporary society: a cumulative list on a poster
- Listen to, discuss, write scripts for, and perform ten well-known myths
- The epic poem as a genre

- Introduction to Homer, *The Iliad*, and *The Odyssey*
- Read-aloud of *Black Ships Before Troy: The Story of the Iliad* by Rosemary Sutcliffe and *The Wanderings of Odysseus: The Story of the Odyssey* by Rosemary Sutcliffe
- Read and discuss Richard Lattimore's translation of book 23 of *The Odyssey*
- Read and discuss poems that allude to the myths: "Hope Is the Thing with Feathers" by Emily Dickinson, "The Son" and "Argos" by Linda Pastan, "Down" and "Daphne and Laura and So Forth" by Margaret Atwood, "in just spring" by E. E. Cummings, "I, Icarus" by Alden Nowland, "Ithaca" by C. P. Cavafy, "Medusa" by Shel Silverstein, "Stop" by Richard Wilbur, and "You Are Odysseus" by Linda Pastan
- Greek stems in English words
- About philosophy
- The lives and philosophies of Socrates, Plato, and Aristotle

- About antiwar poetry and lyrics; read and discuss: "Dulce et Decorum Est" Wilfred Owen, "Does It Matter?" Siegfried Sassoon, From "A German War Primer" Bertolt Brecht, "A Refusal to Mourn the Death, by Fire, of a Child in London" Dylan Thomas, "The Londoners" Anna Akhmatova, "Army Reception Center" Raymond Souster, "Naming of Parts" Henry Reed, "Redeployment" Howard Nemerov, "In Response to Executive Order 9066" Dwight Okita, "The Nice Thing about Counting Stars" Dwight Okita, "An Argument" David Mura, "1945–85: Poem for the Anniversary" Mary Oliver, "First They Came for the Jews" Pastor Niemöller, "Never Shall I Forget" Elie Weisel, "Birdsong" Anonymous Child, "On a Sunny Evening" Anonymous Child, "The Butterfly" Pavel Friedmann, "Bummer" Michael Casey, "Alice's Restaurant" Arlo Guthrie, "What Were They Like" Denise Levertov, "To Whom It May Concern" Adrian Mitchell, "Two Villages" Grace Paley, "Vapor Trail Reflected in the Frog Pond" Galway Kinnell, "It Is Dangerous to Read Newspapers" Margaret Atwood, "The Man He Killed" Thomas Hardy, "Universal Soldier" Buffy St. Marie, "Goodnight Saigon" Billy Joel, "Born in the USA" Bruce Springsteen, "Masters of War" Bob Dylan, "Times Are a Changin'" Bob Dylan, "Eve of Destruction" Barry McGuire, "Fixin' to Die Rag" Country Joe McDonald, "Turn, Turn, Turn" Ecclesiastes 3:1-8/Pete Seeger, "Ohio" Neil Young, and "Long View from the Bell Tower" Paul Durgin.

- About E. E. Cummings' life and times
- Read and discuss Cummings' "loneliness," "Buffalo Bill's defunct," "anyone lived in a pretty how town," and "in just spring"

- About Emily Dickinson's life and times
- Read and discuss her poems "Autumn," "As Imperceptibly as Grief," "I'm Nobody! Who Are You?," "I Never Saw a Moor," "A Narrow Fellow in the Grass," "There's a Certain Slant of Light," "Because I Could Not Stop for Death," "The Soul Selects Her Own Society," "After Great Pain, a Formal Feeling Comes," "I Died for Beauty," and "I Heard a Fly Buzz When I Died."
- Read and discuss "Emily Dickinson" by Linda Pastan and "Altitudes" by Richard Wilbur

- About Robert Frost's life and times
- Read and discuss his poems "Stopping by Woods," "Dust of Snow," "The Road Not Taken," "The Pasture," "Fire and Ice," "The Mending Wall," and "The Need of Being Versed in Country Things"

- About Langston Hughes' life and times
- Read and discuss his poems "What Happens to a Dream Deferred?," "Aunt Sue's Stories," "Dreams," "Winter Moon," "Afro-American Fragment," "American Heartbreak," "The Dream Keeper," "I, Too," "Refugee in America," "Subway Rush Hour," "Lincoln Monument: Washington," and "April Rain Song."

- Mary Oliver's nature poetry: read it and tease out a list of the techniques and approaches she used in: "Hummingbird Pauses at the Trumpet Vine," "Goldfinches," "The Pond," "Finches," "Herons in Winter in the Frozen Marsh," "Egret," "When Death Comes," "Five A.M. in the Pinewoods," "Goldenrod," "Moccasin Flowers," "The Moths," "Picking Blueberries, Austerlitz, New York, 1957," "The Sun," "Landscape," "Gannets," "Hawk," and "The Summer Day."

- About E. A. Robinson's life and times and the Tilbury Town (really Gardiner, Maine) poems
- Read and discuss "Richard Cory," "Mr. Flood's Party," and "Miniver Cheevy"
- Listen to Paul Simon's song "Richard Cory" and read Glenna Johnson Smith's Robinson-like poem, "Summer Person"

- About William Stafford's life and times
- Read and discuss his poems "For You," "Coming to Know," "Some

Names," "In a Country Churchyard," "Fifteen," "Traveling through the Dark," "Dream of Now," "Brother Bob," "What's in My Journal," "Mother's Day," and "Vocation"

- About Wallace Stevens' life and times
- Read "If I Could Be Like Wallace Stevens" by William Stafford
- Read "Thirteen Ways of Looking at a Blackbird" and tease out the approach Stevens takes in each stanza
- Write and present "Thirteen Ways" poems à la Stevens

- About Walt Whitman's life and times
- Read and discuss excerpts from *Song of Myself*
- Listen to an audiotape of Whitman (maybe) reciting the opening lines of "America"
- The ballad form
- Read and discuss Whitman's Civil War ballads, "Bivouac on a Mountain Side," "Year That Trembled and Reel'd Beneath Me," "Wound Dresser," "A Sight in Camp in Daybreak Gray and Dim," "Beat! Beat! Drums!" "By the Bivouac's Fitful Flame," and "Song of the Banner at Daybreak"
- View Matthew Brady's Civil War photographs; write and present ballads à la Whitman

- About William Carlos Williams' life and times
- Read and discuss "This Is Just to Say," "The Red Wheelbarrow," "Nantucket," "To a Poor Old Woman," and "Burning the Christmas Greens"
- Read Kenneth Koch's parodies of "This Is Just to Say" from X. J. and Dorothy Kennedy's *Knock at a Star*

Lessons About Conventions of Writing

In writing, a convention is an agreement made over time between writers and readers about how something will be done in texts. Printing words left to right and top to bottom, spaces between words, periods at the ends of sentences, commas after items in a list, capital letters at the beginnings of sentences, indentations for new paragraphs, standardized spellings—these are all conventions in Western texts.

Teachers need to remember that conventions were invented by writers, not handed down by God or English teachers. Throughout history writers developed rules and forms so others would read their writing as they intended it to be read. We do our students a big favor by approaching rules and forms not as minutiae to be mastered, but as a means of helping them make their writing look and sound as they wish it to and in order that readers will engage with a text and take it seriously.

Readers' eyes and brains are well trained. We have definite expectations of written language. When a text doesn't meet our expectations, we are thrown. Ask students to remember their reactions when they've come across typographical errors in books. Usually they stop reading and focus on the typo. A book riddled with typos is so disconcerting, a reader may give up entirely. Our eyes and brains require that texts look a certain way; it's this predictable conventionality that makes reading possible. In my minilessons about conventions I level with my students:

> If your writing is misspelled—research shows that it takes as few as five or six errors in a text of three hundred words—readers will say, "There's something wrong with this writing," and they'll stop reading it. If your letter to your senator doesn't include a heading or date or inside address, the aide who opens the envelope is likely to say, "Oh, it's just some kid." If your short story consists of one long paragraph, a reader may never even start it—her mind will freeze up once she gets a look at the text and realizes there are no breathing spaces, no places to rest and regroup. If your essay doesn't have periods at the ends of sentences, a reader may start the piece but will abandon it posthaste: there's no indication of what he's supposed to do with his voice as he reads it. And if your poem looks like a prose paragraph, your reader will read it as a prose paragraph—so much for poetry.

Readers aren't snobs. And they aren't lazy. They need all the help they can get. They need *conventionality*: for a writer to hold up his end of the bargain and keep the pact. As readers we count on writers to follow rules and forms so we can act as readers. As writers we observe rules and forms so our writing will be read and understood as we intend it to be, so we'll be taken seriously, and bottom line, so we'll be viewed as intelligent and mature.

I know some teachers refer to spelling, capitalization, punctuation, and paragraphing as *skills*. But everything you do well as a writer is a writing skill. It's more useful, helpful, and accurate to call these areas *conventions*.

Convention comes from the Latin word for agreement. In our society, agreements or conventions govern our lives: we drive on the right-hand side of the road, put the fork to the left of the plate, say "Hello" when we answer the phone, answer "I do" when we marry. All this year in minilessons I'll teach you conventions of writing so that you'll be able to hold up your end of the bargain and be recognized and responded to in our society as a *writer*.

- What conventions are, what they do for readers, and why we need them in texts
- How and why writers edit as they go
- How to edit formally and why to use another color of ink, so the teacher can see what a writer can do as an editor
- How and why to proofread in preparation for one's readers
- Using dictionaries, spellers, and handheld spell checkers
- Using handbooks about conventions (punctuation, capitalization, word choice, indication of titles, permissible abbreviations, etc.): *Writers INC*, Turabian, etc.
- Prose margins, how they work, and what they should look like
- Paragraphing (and drafting in ¶s)
- Margins on poetry and indenting run-over lines
- Poetic formats
- Playwriting format: colons rather than quotes, how to indicate stage directions with parentheses, how to space between speakers
- Formats of other genres
- Keeping a consistent point of view: *I*, *you*, or *he/she*
- Keeping a consistent verb tense: past or present
- Capitalization of words in titles and of prepositions
- Treatment of titles (i.e., quoted, underlined, or merely capitalized)
- The difference between *grammar* and *usage*
- The need for end-stop punctuation to show readers where to drop and stop their voices
- Origins of various marks: in what cultures they originated and how they changed over time; Aristophanes, the inventor of punctuation
- Comma rules: highest priority rules in terms of frequency of use and violation, e.g., between independent clauses joined by *and*, *but*, or *or*; to separate a vocative from the rest of the sentence; to separate a quoted statement and an explanatory phrase; to separate an interjection or weak exclamation from the rest of the sentence; to separate words, phrases, or clauses in a series; before the *and* at the end of a series (i.e., the Harvard comma)
- Hyphens and what they do
- Dashes and what they do
- Double dashes to set off information

- Exclamation points (and why not: see Zinsser 1990)
- Colon before a list or explanation
- Comma splices and run-ons as errors
- Semicolons to avoid comma splices and to join two independent clauses when the writer wishes to show a relationship
- Semicolons to avoid confusion when items in a list already contain commas
- Appropriate use of contractions
- Apostrophes to show contraction
- Apostrophes to show possession with a singular noun; to form plurals of a letter, sign, number, or word discussed as a word; to show possession on one- and multi-syllable words ending in *s* and on plural possessives
- Punctuating conversation: putting spoken words within quotes, punctuating before and after a quoted remark, indicating quotes within quotes, and paragraphing for changes in speakers
- Splitting polysyllabic words between syllables at line breaks
- Writing numbers within texts: when to write a number as a numeral and when as a word
- Underlining, italicizing, and bolding
- When to use the articles *a* and *an*
- When to write *Dad* versus *dad*
- Easily confused verbs: *lie* and *lay*; *sit* and *set*; *rise* and *raise*; *take* and *bring*; etc.
- Friendly letter format
- Business letter format
- Addressing an envelope; how to fold a business letter and insert it into an envelope
- About Noah Webster and the first dictionary of American English (70,000 words versus today's 180,000)
- Parentheses
- Parentheses within parentheses (brackets)
- Subjective- and objective-case pronouns and how to test for which case is correct: *I* or *me*
- Permissible abbreviations in texts
- Spelling: why it matters; creating a personal word list; word study procedures; procedures for administrating a spelling review to a partner; personal survival words; personal demons; how to develop and use mnemonics; the history of the English language in terms of

influences on its spelling; how to proofread for spelling (read at the single word level, look at each word, and ask, "Does it look right?"; read a draft backwards and focus on each word without skipping; circle every word you're not sure of, then go back and look up each one; notice the *part* of the word that is misspelled); how to look up words in the dictionary; what makes a good dictionary; how to use the computer's spell checker; what to do if you've looked in a dictionary but can't find the word (ask an adult for help or look up a synonym for the word you want and see if your word is listed in its definition); good spellers versus poor spellers: spelling is a natural ability, but every writer can learn how to proofread; the importance while drafting of recording words you can't spell on your personal list, so you can work on them later in a word study; capitalization of school subjects (*science*, *English*); adding *-ing* or *-ed* to words that end in *c*; syllabication and splitting words between syllables; American versus British spellings (*judgment, judgement*); contractions; the prefixes *for-* and *fore-*; the prefixes *pre-, re-, dis-*, and *un-*; words that put *e* before *i*; dialect errors (would *have*, not would *of*); compound words; *a lot* and *all right* as two words; *than* and *then*; *wear, were*, and *where*; homonym pairs and trios; mispronunciations (*different, interest, favorite, February, probably, government*); dropping *y* and changing to *i* when adding *-ed*; adding *-ly* to a word that ends in *l; e.g., i.e.,* and other accepted abbreviations; common foreign words and phrases; dropping the silent *e* before adding a suffix that begins with a vowel (*experience/experiencing*); keeping the silent *e* when adding a suffix that begins with a consonant (*definite/definitely*); doubling the final consonant before adding a suffix that begins with a vowel (*get/getting*); doubling the final consonant of a multisyllable word that ends with a single consonant and is accented on the second syllable before adding *-ing, -ed*, or *-er* (*confer/conferring*).

Ideas for minilessons about conventions come directly from students' writing, from my analyses of the conventions they don't recognize or understand yet. When I edit pieces of writing, I note the one or two conventions I'll teach each writer the next day in class during an editing conference. I also jot down frequent problems and misunderstandings on the index card I keep in my plan book, and I begin to plan minilessons around these conventions. I consult handbooks such as *Writers INC* (1992), Weaver's *Teaching Grammar in Context* (1996), and Turabian's *The Student's Guide for Writing College Papers* (1976) to get a clearer understanding for myself of the function of a rule, form, or mark—exactly what it tells readers. Then I write explanations, examples, and sometimes even activities to help kids understand how a convention works.

Some minilessons about conventions address a small piece of a bigger pie, one we come back to and take slices from throughout the school year. Teaching all the comma rules together would take a month of minilessons and turn the workshop into a course in punctuation. I chip away, one at a time, at the ten or so conventions my kids violate most frequently.

ANOTHER COMMA RULE

A comma sets off an interjection or weak exclamation at the beginning of a sentence and shows a little break:
EXAMPLES:

- Hi, Sam.
- Hello, this is Martha.
- Hey, watcha doin'?
- No, they're not my sweatsocks.
- Please, can't you give us two weeks off?
- Well, okay.
- Good-bye, kids.

Can you invent two more? Then choose one to share around the circle.

Similarly, when addressing usage problems I tackle them one at a time, but I also try to help kids see patterns among them.

TO LIE OR TO LAY?

Lie = to recline

PRESENT	• I *lie* down when I read.
	• My grandmother *lies* down after every meal.
PAST	• Yesterday I *lay* down after lunch.
PAST PARTICIPLE	• I *have lain* down in the snow to make angels.

Lay = to put or place something

PRESENT	• I like to *lay* the M&M's in a pattern before I scarf them.
	• *Lay* those M&M's down here, mister.
PAST	• Yesterday I *laid* a bag of M&M's right here, and Dylan stole them.
PAST PARTICIPLE	• Unfortunately I *have laid* many bags of candy in places where Dylan could steal them.

Lie, sit, rise = verbs that describe an actor reclining or getting up
Lay, set, raise = verbs that involve something being acted upon; each
    requires an object

To address the eternal *I* versus *me* conundrum, I present a grammar minilesson that focuses on pronouns and case.

PRONOUN CASE

You know that a noun is a word that names a person, place, thing, or idea. A pronoun is a word that's used in place of a noun, like *I*, *you*, *it*, *her*. The *case* of a pronoun tells how it's related to other words. Nominative-case pronouns are used as actors, as the subjects of verbs: *I, you, he, she, we, they, it*. They usually come at the beginnings of sentences. Objective-case pronouns are words that receive the action: *me, you, him, her, us, them, it*. They usually come at the middle or end of a sentence.

Errors in case occur most often in your writing when the subject is compound and you confuse the nominative and objective cases. No one, except maybe George of the Jungle, writes, "Me rode my bike to the Harbor," but some of you are writing, "Danny and me rode to the Harbor." No one writes, "She gave M&M's to I," but I'm finding sentences in your drafts like, "She gave M&M's to my friends and I."

You can test for the correct case of a pronoun by determining if it's the subject of a verb or the recipient of an action. Or you can do the easy thing: test the pronoun all by itself with the verb. Drop the *Danny and* part and ask, is it *I* or *me*?

    [Danny and] _____ rode.
    She gave M&M's to [my friends and] _____ .

Would you take the next minute to write two sentences of your own? Give one sentence a compound subject, like *Danny and I*. Give the other a compound object, like *friends and me*. Then we'll go around the circle and hear them. And, yes, you can make them funny.

Another frequent grammatical error is the comma splice—two or more sentences mistakenly hooked together with commas. I target the error by presenting solutions; the semicolon is one of them.

COMMA SPLICES AND SEMICOLONS

A *comma splice* is the mistake a writer makes when two sentences are spliced or hooked together with a comma. A comma isn't strong enough to connect two independent clauses.

EXAMPLE:
The crowd had been waiting for Phish for two hours, many kids started to get rowdy.
SOLUTIONS:

- Make it two sentences: The crowd had been waiting for Phish for two hours. Many kids started to get rowdy.
- Keep the comma and insert *and*: The crowd had been waiting for Phish for two hours, and many kids started to get rowdy.
- Use a semicolon: The crowd had been waiting for Phish for two hours; many kids started to get rowdy.

A *semicolon* is used to join two (or more) sentences that aren't connected by *and*, when you want to show a relationship between them—a closeness in meaning, a cause or consequence. You can also use a semicolon if you have too many compound sentences and want to tighten the prose.
EXAMPLES:

- Once I had a '57 Chevy; it was the first car I ever owned and a classic.
- I adore dogs; English springer spaniels are my favorites.
- Ron bought ice cream and hot fudge for the teachers' meeting; he even provided whipped cream and chopped walnuts.
- The beast charged at Garth; this time he was ready.

A *semicolon* is also used to avoid confusion in lists that contain commas.
EXAMPLE:

- I read collections of poems that tell a story: *Waiting to Waltz, Soda Jerk,* and *I'll Be Back Again* by Cynthia Rylant; *Baseball, Snakes, and Summer Squash* by Donald Graves; and *Been to Yesterdays* by Lee Bennett Hopkins.

Other marks that give voice to writing are the colon and the dash. In minilessons about their use I focus on function—what they show readers and how they give voice to the writing.

COLONS

A *colon* indicates to readers that an explanation, clarification, example, list, or enumeration will follow. It tells readers to *pay attention:* the writer is going to fill you in.
EXAMPLES:

- Three students lost their notebooks: Jay, Jason, and Sam. Oy vay!
- He was tall, blond, and blue-eyed: the preppie type.
- Toby was happy: steak for dinner two nights running.
- My head just started to ache: it's going to rain.

A *colon* is also used after the salutation of a business letter or formal correspondence.

EXAMPLES:

- To the Editors:
- Dear Senator Snowe:
- Dear Sir or Madam:
- Dear Mr. Heyl:
- Dear Program Director:

And a colon is used between hours and minutes when you're writing time: 2:45.

TO HYPHEN (-) OR TO DASH (—), THAT IS THE QUESTION

The *hyphen* (-) shows *connection*. It's actually more of a spelling mark than a mark of punctuation.

- On a compound name: Atwell-McLeod
- On compound words: seven-year-old; son-in-law; good-bye
- When splitting a word of more than one syllable between two lines of text, to show the word will continue on the next line
- On numbers and fractions: twenty-two; four-fifths
- To indicate a span of time or pages or the score of a game: September–June; 1997–1998; pps. 17–31; 5–6

The *dash* (— or ---) shows *meaning*

- To indicate a sudden break or pause; a change in action, thought, or feeling
- To emphasize a meaning, to punch it
- To amplify or explain a thought that's stated in the first part of a sentence
- To show interruption in dialogue

EXAMPLES:

- "The writer is by nature a dreamer—a conscious dreamer." (Carson McCullers)
- He ran down the stairs—and his blood froze.

To create a dash on the school's computers:

1. press *shift* key and
2. *option* key (at the same time), then
3. *dash/hyphen* key.

Some marks involve rules that are so interrelated I've found it effective to teach them together in a brief series of lessons. We studied apostrophes over three days.

FUN WITH APOSTROPHES

Some styles use 's to form the plural (more than one) of a letter, number, sign, or word discussed as a word:
EXAMPLES:

- I got straight A's.
- You use too many and's.
- I loved the '60's.
- Let's play Crazy 8's.

To make a singular noun show possession, add 's:
EXAMPLES:

- JFK's assassination
- Matt's CD
- the kid's baseball glove
- the dog's breakfast
- year's end
- Communism's decline

When a singular noun ends in s already:

a. if it's a one-syllable word, some styles add 's:
EXAMPLES:

- lass's hair
- Kiss's last concert
- Graves's book
- boss's rules

b. if it's a word of more than one syllable, you can just add an apostrophe or you can add the apostrophe s:
EXAMPLES:

- Dallas' sports teams (or Dallas's sports teams)

When a noun is plural (more than one person, place, thing, or idea) and ends in s, just add an apostrophe to make it possessive:
EXAMPLES:

- The kids' CDs
- (many) dogs' breakfasts
- the Schleins' new kitty
- the Tindals' boat
- bosses' secretaries
- girls' basketball team
- boys' locker room

When a plural noun *doesn't* end in s, add 's to make it possessive:
EXAMPLES:

- children's mittens
- women's clothing
- men's room
- mice's homes

When possession is shared by more than one noun, use 's for the *last* noun in the series:
EXAMPLES:

- There's Katie, Ethan and Alison's mother.
- Katy, Jason, and Abby's pool is cool.

Some minilessons about conventions are so, well, *conventional* it's almost comical to teach them—to imagine the busy rulemakers who conceived the arcane agreements that govern such issues as how to indicate titles and which words may be abbreviated in texts.

INDICATING TITLES

Capitalize the first word of a title, the last word, and every word in between that conveys meaning. That means you won't capitalize articles (a, an, the), short prepositions (at, down, in, near, of, off, on, out, over, to, with, etc.), or short conjunctions (and, but, or, nor, for, yet, also, as, that) unless they come at the beginning or end of the title.

Underlined (or italicized in typed or published texts)	*Quoted*	*Just Caps*
WHOLE AND LONGER WORKS	PARTS AND SHORTER WORKS	SERIES
Novel	Poem	Belgariad
Book	Newspaper article	SACRED SCRIPTURES
Magazine	Magazine article	Bible
Movie	Song or piano piece	Torah
Long poem (Homer's *Iliad*)	Short story	Koran
Opera	Chapter	Talmud
Full-length play	One-act play	Book of Daniel
Musical	Speech	
Record, cassette, or CD	Essay	
Ballet	TV show	
Symphony	Reference to a piece of your own writing	
Newspaper		
Title of artwork (Van Gogh's *The Starry Night*)		
Name of a ship, aircraft, or spacecraft		

ABBREVIATIONS IN TEXTS

Acceptable
- Mr. (Master)
- Mrs. (Mistress)
- Dr. (Doctor)
- B.A. (bachelor of arts, usually four years of college)

No-Nos
- info (information)
- months (Sept.)
- days (Mon.)
- places (ME/Mass.)
- Numbers of *more than two words* are usually written as numerals:

- M.A. (master of arts, usually two years of graduate school)
- Ph.D. (doctor of philosophy, generally three to five more years of graduate school)
- Jr. (Junior) / III (the Third)
- St. (Saint)
- A.M. (ante meridiem)
- P.M. (post meridiem)
- B.C. (before Christ)
- A.D. (anno Domini)
- UNICEF
- UN
- USA
- CIA/IRS/FBI
- YMCA
- Inc. (Incorporated)
- e.g. (for example)
- i.e. (that is)

two (not 2)
nineteen (not 19)
twenty-three (not 23)
170
1997
2,367

Note: never start a sentence with a numeral. A number at the beginning of a sentence must be written as words:

One hundred and fifty years ago . . . (not *150 years ago . . .*)

Nineteen ninety-seven was a good year . . . (not *1997 was a good year . . .*)

Better: The year 1997 was a good one.

Sometimes I'll engage students in an activity as part of the minilesson— ask them to mess around with a particular convention or set of conventions and discover what they do and do not understand. Students messed around with the parody of a conversation, seen below. Independently, before the minilesson, they edited it as best they could. Then they took turns at the overhead projector, correcting a transparency of the conversation and playing teacher.

PUNCTUATING CONVERSATION

Please edit the following dialogue, which is a verbatim report of a conversation I swear I overheard this week:

Dylan said my favorite song is Everybody Hurts. Awesome Matt replied. That is a wicked groovy song Asa concurred. Will you sing it with me right now Dylan pleaded. Oh yes his friends exclaimed.

Lessons about spelling comprise a final category of convention mini-lessons. Misspellings seem to throw readers, not to mention disturb members of the general public, more than any other kind of error in texts. The challenge in learning spelling is that it takes a long time; in my forties, I am still learning. We need to make time for spelling instruction and practice, and we need to make sure that what we do in the name of teaching spelling is sensible and effective.

I've moved from teaching spelling solely through students' editing and correcting of drafts to a three-pronged approach that includes more opportunities for exploration of patterns and rules, as well as weekly, individualized, word studies. I still start, however, by teaching students how to proofread for and correct misspellings in their texts—with spelling in the context of writing:

> When you proofread read your final draft slowly with an editing pen in your hand. Draw a circle around any word that doesn't look right or any word you're not absolutely sure of. Good spellers are good proofreaders: they develop a sense of what words should look like. When you've analyzed the whole piece of writing for potential misspellings, get a dictionary or a hand-held spell checker and look up each of your circled words. If you weren't correct, see how close you were, notice *what part* of the word you didn't know, and write the correct spelling both on your draft *and on your personal spelling list*. No one can spell every word, but you should develop a sense of American spelling, of the ways words look. And you should have strategies to compensate for the fact that no one can spell every word. Do your serious best at identifying words you're not certain of; then look them up.

The personal spelling list (Appendix H) is a blank form with lines for students to record the words they don't know how to spell yet. The lists come from several sources: words writers realize they aren't sure of, as they're drafting; misspellings they find when they self-edit; words students notice in their reading; and words I find misspelled in their writing when I edit it, which I record on a student's editing checksheet (see Figure 1 in Chapter 7). Students only study the words they can't spell.

My spelling minilessons take place on Tuesdays. Although I don't necessarily conduct a spelling lesson every Tuesday, it is always the day my students prepare individual word studies for the week; and Thursday is always their spelling review day. In spelling minilessons I present information about the history of English, strategies of spellers, how to proofread, procedures for studying words, spelling resources, patterns, rules, and exceptions. As with all minilessons, I try to avoid instruction that isn't relevant to my kids. Then I check for correct spellings in the first column of each student's word study sheet: the list of five words he or she will study for homework, for the review test on Thursday. The weekly word study sheet and a completed example appear in Appendix I.

I adapted the procedures for word study and review from the work of Rebecca Sitton (1996). The guidelines are careful and specific. I direct them at helping each of my kids work with just a handful of words at a time (few enough to virtually guarantee retention), become intimately acquainted with each word, and acquire a strong visual sense, in long-term memory, of what a word should look like. Students tape the procedures for word study inside their spelling folders for their reference, and throughout the year I review the procedures in minilessons.

PROCEDURES FOR INDEPENDENT WORD STUDY

1. Copy no more than five words from your personal spelling list into the first column. Copy exactly as the words appear on your list: *don't learn misspellings*. And print, so you can see the individual letters.
2. Now, read the first word: look at it and say it.
3. Spell the word to yourself: touch each letter with your pencil and say each letter to yourself.
4. Close your eyes. See the word in your mind. Say each of the individual letters to yourself again.
5. Take a short break to give your long-term memory time to process the look of the word, its letters, and their order.
6. Now cover the correct spelling and print the word in the second column.
7. Proofread: check the word you just wrote, letter for letter, against the original.
8. If you spelled the word correctly, put a star in the third column and go on to the next word on your personal spelling list. If you misspelled it, repeat the process above, this time printing the word in the third column.

Completed independent word studies are due on Thursday morning. The first thing students do when they arrive in class is find a partner, exchange word study lists, and administer spelling reviews in pairs. Procedures for reviews, too, are taped inside their spelling folders.

PROCEDURES FOR SPELLING REVIEWS IN PAIRS

Tester: Say the word, use it in a sentence, and say it again.
Speller: Print the word.
Go through the whole list. Then:
Tester: Spell each word out loud, slowly.
Speller: Proofread by touching each letter of each word with your
    pencil. Circle any errors: *just the part you missed*. Then, with a star or
    checkmark highlight the words on your personal list that you
    spelled correctly in the review. Circle any words you missed, and
    study them again next week.

It's the student's responsibility to select words each week from his or
her personal spelling list. I limit the number because I want to maximize
the chance that they'll learn the words and, if they use the procedure as
I've outlined it, because it takes a while to work with each word. I don't
want to overload them or promote memorization-for-the-test; I do want
to acknowledge that retaining spellings is hard and time-consuming
work.

I am suprised—happily—at the impact of this system on student
spelling. Kids spell more conventionally in their reading journals and drafts
and edit and proofread better because they know they'll be accountable for
misspellings. When they do misspell, the time they spend with their personal word lists pays off. Colby remarked one day that he had been mis-
spelling *answer* for as long as he could remember and he had finally learned
how to spell it using our system.

EXAMPLES OF SPELLING STUDIES

Personal Survival Words: each student's first, last, and middle names;
    parents' first, last, and middle names; mother's maiden name;
    grandparents' and siblings' names; street address; town, county,
    and state; months of the year; teachers' last names; local
    communities and bodies of water; family car make(s) and
    manufacturer(s); allergies; place of birth; hospital of birth;
    physician's name; names to call in an emergency; names of
    references; etc.
Demons: a lot, all right, separate, stationery, stationary, tomorrow,
    weird, absence, presence, necessary, unnecessary, beautiful,

embarrass, beginning, cemetery, disappear, disappoint, occasion, occur, maybe, definitely, immediately, vacuum, psychology, dessert, desert, absolutely, skiing, skier, ninth, twelfth, eighth, forty, fortieth, recommend, character, genre, genres, etc.

School Subjects: science, history, social studies, drama, mathematics, algebra, prealgebra, English, geometry, biology, writing, literature, humanities, Spanish, recess, geology, physical education

Foreign Words and Phrases Used in English Texts: déjà vu, et cetera, cliché, résumé, vice versa, via, versus, ad infinitum, ad nauseam, ad hoc, à la carte, carte blanche, coup, laissez-faire, protégé

Contractions: let's, that's, don't, doesn't, it's, can't, won't, wouldn't, shouldn't, couldn't, I'm, I've, I'd, I'll, they're, they've, they'd, they'll, you're, you've, you'd, you'll, we're, we've, we'd, we'll, she's, she'd, she'll, could've, would've, should've

Words That Put E *Before* I: receive, deceive, perceive, receipt, sleigh, weigh, neighbor, freight, ceiling, sheik, seize, seine, heifer, weird

Fore *Words*:

- *before*: forecast, forethought, foreshadow, forebode, foretell, forecourt, forego, forehand
- *front part* or *superior*: forehead, forearm, foreleg, forecastle, foreman

For *Words*: forget, forgive, forbid, forever, forgo

Silent E:

- Drop the silent *e* when adding a suffix that begins with a vowel: confuse/confusing; ride/riding; achieve/achieving
- Keep the silent *e* when adding a suffix that begins with a consonant: careful, homely, tiresome, hopeless, resourceful, likeness, amusement, gracefully, movement, priceless

Exceptions: judgment, acknowledgment

Words Ending in y:

- If the word ends in *consonant -y*, change the y to *i* when adding a suffix: sunny/sunnier; party/parties; cry/cried; envy/envied; shy/shied; dry/drier; ally/allies; terrify/terrified
- If the word ends in *vowel -y*, don't change the y to *i*: play/played; annoy/annoyed; enjoy/enjoyed; delay/delayed

Exceptions: said, paid, laid

One-syllable words ending with a vowel consonant (e.g., *stop*) double the final consonant before taking a suffix that starts with a vowel: stopped, getting, dotted, tapped, begged, pitted, grinning, jogger, popped, blurred, shopping, wrapper

Note: panic/panicky; picnic/picnicked; traffic/trafficking

Words of more than one syllable ending with a vowel consonant (e.g., *gossip* or *confer*) double the final consonant *only* when the last syllable is accented (*gossiping* vs. *conferring*): permitted, referring, forbidden, controlling, occurred, transmitter, transferred, abhorred

But *not*: traveled, trumpeted, galloped, blanketed, deposited (because the accent isn't on the last syllable)

Note: *focused* and *focussed* are both acceptable

Homonyms are a focus of spelling minilessons throughout the year. In these minilessons I emphasize mnemonics: *What can you say to yourself or ask yourself each time you're not sure which word you want?*

COMMONLY MISSPELLED HOMONYMS

Homonyms are words that sound alike but mean and are spelled differently. Improper use of a homonym is considered a spelling error.

THEIR: Belonging to them (The teacher stole their M&M's.)
THERE: In that place; as an introductory adverb (There they are: on the teacher's desk./There are never enough M&M's.)
THEY'RE: They are (They're the world's best candy.)

TO: Preposition meaning TOWARD; also used with the infinitive of a verb (I'm going to M&M heaven./I'm going to eat many M&M's.)
TOO: In addition or also; more than enough (He, too, eats too many M&M's.)
TWO: The number (Two or three packs of M&M's provide a nutritious after-school snack.)

YOUR: Belonging to you (Your M&M's are my M&M's.)
YOU'RE: You are (You're in my power; hand over those M&M's.)

ITS: Belonging to it (The dog ate its M&M's and wanted more.)
IT'S: It is (It's the kind of day when I crave M&M's.)

KNOW: To have knowledge of (You know M&M's are superb.)
NOW: At the present time (Give me an M&M *now*.)
KNEW: Had knowledge (I knew she was hiding M&M's: I could smell them.)
NEW: Opposite of old (Happiness is a new bag of M&M's.)

On occasion the spelling minilesson is a chance for kids to try out what they're learning. One Tuesday they filled in the blanks below, then volunteers took turns correcting this "major test" on an overhead transparency, and everyone read his or her examples around the circle for others to groan and guess at.

A MAJOR TEST ON THEIR, THERE, AND THEY'RE

Fill in the blank with the correct homonym; use the mnemonics you've developed for each word.

1. _____ is no paper left on the roll.
2. They think _____ so cool.
3. _____ excited about the tofu dessert: I guess they don't get out much.
4. _____ is Molly, my favorite, fruit-eating dog.
5. I like _____ Lear jet; it's a cute little thing.
6. _____ hermit crab stomped my hermit crab.
7. _____ playing Ultimate Frisbee in Mrs. Maxim's van.
8. Don't go _____ without a bodyguard (i.e., Matt and Emily's house).
9. They think _____ going to get away with it, but _____ WRONG.
10. _____ is _____ pet rat, which _____ taking to Disney World.

Now, join the FUN and write two of your own:

1. _____
2. _____

Lessons About Strategies for Reading

Much of the advice students have heard about reading, by the time they hit middle school, is wrong. Telling readers to slow down, be careful, avoid mistakes, reread what they don't understand, read every word, find the main idea, locate supporting details, never skip, never skim, never look ahead, finish every book, look up unknown words, and sound out unfamiliar words, all make reading *hard*. The results of this bad advice are misconceptions, overload, an inability to remember what was read, boredom, frustration, and limited opportunities to experience what fluent, purposeful, *joyous* readers do. The work of reading researchers and scholars, as well as my own reading processes and those of my students, are teaching me about the kinds of advice that will invite kids to recognize and internalize the strategies of good readers.

- My own territories as a reader: favorite authors, poets, essayists, playwrights, authors for adolescents and children, rereads, professional reading, and journals; guilty pleasures; and work- and life-related texts
- Kids' reading territories
- Why people read
- Why we have reading workshop
- Choosing books and our criteria for selection
- Abandoning books and our criteria for rejection
- Why books (versus magazines, etc.)
- Students' and the teacher's individual reading rituals: when, how, and where we like to read
- Brief booktalks around the circle about the titles students are reading
- Daniel Pennac's "Reader's Bill of Rights" (1994)
- Why good readers have plans: a sense of where they want to go next, of what they want to read, and which author they want to experience
- Rereading and revisiting books and why this is more than okay
- Responding to literature: going beyond plot to think about how books affect us and how authors achieve their effects
- Tips for reading aloud
- How to perform a reading of a poem
- How and why to memorize poetry
- Pace: how readers decide to speed up, slow down, skim, skip, and look ahead
- Sociopsycholinguistic reading model: Frank Smith (1984) and Constance Weaver (1994)
- Schema theory
- Examples from Weaver's *Reading Process and Practice* (1994) of passages that activate different schemas and show different parts of words at work
- Short- and long-term memory
- Tests of hidden assumptions
- "Contentives," eye fixations, and peripheral vision
- Considerate and inconsiderate text
- Shannon's Game and cloze exercises to explore pattern, redundancy, and schemas

- Different approaches to monitoring comprehension during reading (Keene and Zimmermann 1997)
- Comprehension strategies (Keene and Zimmermann 1997)
- Individual readers' strategies in encountering unfamiliar words
- Individual readers' rates: how many rates a reader has, depending on the text and the purpose
- Timed reading tests: words per minute; pages per half hour
- How to take a standardized test of reading

Frank Smith (1986), Marie Clay (1991), Constance Weaver (1994), and Ellin Keene and Susan Zimmermann (1997) are the researchers who best inform me about what competent readers do. I read aloud or talk about excerpts from their work to help my kids understand reading as a *sociopsycholinguistic* process. It's not important that they remember the hundred dollar word, but it helps them to have basic knowledge of schema theory.

I conduct minilessons about schema theory and reading processes over three or four days in the fall; then, through the rest of the year, we talk about how to put the theory into practice. I begin by asking kids to tap their own theories and prior knowledge and make a collaborative list: why do we have reading workshop?

WHY WE HAVE READING WORKSHOP

- To become real readers for a lifetime
- To learn how to choose books
- To read new books
- To learn when and how to abandon books
- To learn new words and meanings
- To learn from other writers about how to improve our own writing
- To discover books we love
- To discover authors we love
- To discover genres we love
- To learn from each other about good books, authors, and genres
- To have vicarious experiences
- To escape

After the kids finish compiling their list, I add some rationales of my own:

- To learn what good readers do
- To become more fluent and proficient

- To unlearn bad habits
- To learn how and when to pace ourselves as readers
- To gain experience with new schemas
- To learn to read deliberately, with better understanding and insight
- To store experiences with texts in our long-term memories
- To read often
- To read a lot

These goals become the jumping-off point for my presentations about reading processes. To begin, I draw a diagram on a transparency (see Figure 6-1). Then I talk my kids through it.

Everyone who reads goes through the process I've depicted here. Your eye picks up "elements" from the world around you (also known as your *sensory store*); you pay attention to four or five elements at a time in your short-term memory; and about every five seconds or so, one element makes it into your long-term memory, where it stays permanently. For example, among the first bits of information you stored, when you were an infant, was your mother's face. Once you knew her face, you never had to learn it again.

As a reader you stored words like *and* or *the* in your long-term memory a long time ago. Once you did, you never had to learn to read them again. Long-term memory is like a file cabinet. Yours is much fuller than that of a beginning reader, who's storing such information as the difference between *b* and *d*. Right now you're probably storing words like *mnemonic* and *soliloquy*.

A good reader is someone who gets a lot of information through the short-term memory bottleneck into long-term memory. One difference is this: the size of the elements. A slow or beginning reader is trying to get four or five *letters* or *words* through short-term memory. The *fluent* reader (someone who reads well) is getting four or five rich, relevant *chunks of meaning* (phrases, for example) through the bottleneck. Again, only four or five elements will get through, but *each element* can be as large as a phrase or even a sentence.

So, while a slow or beginning reader is putting four or five words or parts of words into long-term memory, a fluent reader is putting four or five phrases or chunks of meaning into storage. And the fluent reader makes good use of all the information already stored in long-term memory to make guesses or *predictions* about the new information that's coming in.

The fluent reader also uses long-term memory of letter patterns and sound patterns. For example, a fluent reader understands that in word recognition, consonants are more important than vowels; be-

FIGURE 6-1   When a Reader Reads

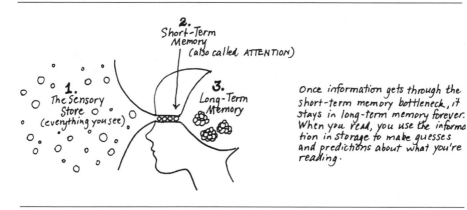

ginnings of words are more important than middles and ends; and ends are more important than middles. Nonproficient readers haven't yet learned to attend to the *parts of words* that contain the most information.

The important thing to realize is that the difference between long-term memory and short-term memory can be summed up in one word: *organization*. Short-term memory holds unrelated memories, while long-term memory is a network, a structure of knowledge, a way sense is made. Constance Weaver calls long-term memory a series of *schemas*. Only when we have adequate cognitive schemas, and only when the right schemas are activated, will we have understanding or recall of what we need.

For example, read this passage from *Reading Process and Practice* by Constance Weaver (1994, 22) once, and try to retell it in your own words.

Passage 1: *Cost or Other Basis* (on the topic of capital gains and losses)

In general, the cost or other basis is the cost of the property plus purchase commissions, improvements, and minus de-preciation, amortization, and depletion. If you inherited the property or got it as a gift, in a tax-free exchange, in-voluntary conversion, or "wash sale" of stock, you may not be able to use the actual cash cost as the basis. If you do not use cash cost, attach an explanation of your basis.
—Internal Revenue Service, 1985 booklet on *1040 Federal Income Tax Forms and Instructions*

Because we don't already know something about capital gains and losses, we can't understand much of what we've read here. There's not enough information in our long-term-memory file cabinets to support understanding; we have no cognitive schemas for this topic.

Try again with another passage from Weaver's book (1994, 23). Can you retell this one?

> The procedure is actually quite simple. First you arrange things into different groups. Of course one pile may be sufficient depending on how much there is to do. If you have to go somewhere else due to lack of facilities, that is the next step; otherwise you are pretty well set. It is important not to overdo things. That is, it is better to do too few things at once than too many. In the short run this may not seem important, but complications can easily arise. A mistake can be expensive as well. At first the whole procedure will seem complicated. Soon, however, it will just become another facet of life. It is difficult to foresee any end to the necessity for this task in the immediate future, but then one can never tell. After the procedure is completed one arranges the materials into different groups again. Then they can be put into their appropriate places. Eventually they will be used once more, and the whole cycle will then have to be repeated. However, that is a part of life.
>
> —John D. Bransford and Nancy S. McCarrell, 1974,
> "A Sketch of a Cognitive Approach to Comprehension"

What would your retelling be like if you knew this passage was about *washing clothes*? Even if we have a schema for a topic, if the schema isn't *activated*, it does us no good.

Let's shift gears and go back to look at the *physical side* of reading.

If you could closely watch people's eyes while they're reading, you'd notice their eyes make a number of brief, abrupt stops. The transparency shows an illustration of these stops—or *fixations*—as they might occur for different kinds of readers. The dots above the line show where a reader's eye would stop. It's during the stops that the actual reading is done. *The eye doesn't see when it is moving; only when it is stopped.* Stops typically last one-quarter of a second.

VERY SLOW READER

● ● ● ● ● ● ● ● ● ● ● ●

Some books are to be read only in parts, others to be read
(*Try to fix on each word: it's hard and it takes forever.*)

READER OF FAIR SPEED

● ● ● ● ● ●

Some books are to be read only in parts, others to be read
(*Try this one. Still too slow?*)

FAST READER

•   •   •

Some books are to be read only in parts, others to be read
(*How's this?*)

VERY FAST READER (Speed reader)

•

Some books are to be read only in parts, others to be read
(*This is what speed readers do: they've trained themselves to
stop at important words, stop less frequently, and see more at
each stop.*)

The fluent reader reads with fewer stops because he or she is able
to see more during each stop. Look back at the diagram of the reader
on the transparency. It's an illustration of a fixation. Research shows
that during a normal eye fixation of about one-quarter of a second,
we can identify four or five unrelated letters, or about ten or twelve
letters organized into two or three unrelated words, or about twenty
to twenty-five letters organized into a sequence of four or five related
words.

So, during a normal eye fixation, we might be able to identify a sequence like *jmbih*, or a sequence like *told her that*, or a sequence like *this
coffee is too hot*. Our perceptual span increases based on the relationships of the units we're identifying: we can identify more letters when
they're organized into words, and more words when they're organized
into a meaningful phrase or sentence.

Context helps you—the words and ideas around the words. In
phrases and sentences, we have two kinds of context, or schemas, in
our long-term memories to aid in word identification. *Syntactic context*
consists of the signals provided by word endings, function words, and
word order. *Semantic context* consists of the meaningful relations
among the words. In short, *syntax* means grammar, and *semantics*
means meaning.

To see how grammar and meaning help us identify and recall
words, look for a moment at the following four strings of words from
Weaver. Which string is the easiest to process? Which is the hardest?
Why?

1. Furry wildcats fight furious battles. (*Easiest: has grammar and meaning*)
2. Furry jewelers create distressed stains. (*Grammar only*)
3. Furry fight furious wildcats battles. (*Meaning only*)
4. Furry create distressed jewelers stains. (*Hardest: has neither grammar nor meaning*)

After these presentations, we start to draw implications. I begin by listing baseline suggestions for improving fluency:

GOALS FOR FLUENT READERS

1. Read more and often: get as many schemas into your long-term memory as possible. You need a ton of experience to be fast and good, as with any skill or art.
2. Read more during each stop. Try to pick up groups of words—chunks of meaning—rather than individual words.
3. Try to concentrate on key words that carry the meaning. Researchers call these *contentives*, and research shows that good readers fix longer on the words that carry meaning in a sentence.
4. Try to eliminate bad habits, like moving your lips or vocal cords while you're reading, or *regressing*: constantly going back to reread something you've already read. All of these slow down your reading. They overload short-term memory and force you to pick up single words instead of reading for meanings. Forge ahead: speed increases comprehension because it diminishes distractions. Count on the context that's built into texts to help you straighten things out.
5. Don't use a pencil or a card to "underline" each line you read. Syntactic and semantic context—chunking of meaning—is checked when you do this.

I ask kids to continue the list individually in their writing-reading handbooks. The prompt is: *Given what I know now, what are my personal goals as a reader?* Then, as they read their responses around the circle, I extend the list on the easel pad:

6. Read more genres: it creates more schemas in long-term memory.
7. Read more deliberately: where do your eyes stop? How much are you seeing at each stop?
8. Try to chunk meanings.
9. Try to recognize words by their shapes.
10. Time yourself as a reader: how many pages can you read in a half hour this month? Next month? By June?
11. Vary your reading rate: slow down when you don't have an adequate schema.
12. Read more often; read a lot.

We play games in other minilessons that reiterate the theories that kids are trying to get their minds around. I type passages from different kinds of books—a textbook, a novel, a collection of interviews—and delete every fifth word. In these cloze exercises, kids guess at the missing words. I ask them to be conscious of how they use semantic context, syntactic context, and prior knowledge to help them make predictions; then we discuss their observations.

We also play many rounds of Shannon's Game on overhead transparencies. Like its cousin Hangman, which uses the predictability of letter order in words, Shannon's Game taps long-term memory and the schemas we've stored there about word order in phrases and clauses. To play it I think of a sentence, then draw a line for each word. Starting with the first blank, kids call out the words they think comprise the sentence; I tick off the number of guesses it takes to identify each word. When they reach fifteen guesses, I give them that word and move on to the next one. At the end of the sentence we discuss the schemas that were activated, when they were activated, and how. (Some sentences, like one that taps my kids' schema about my obsession with chocolate, are easier than others.)

SHANNON'S GAME

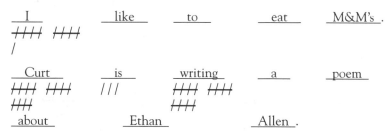

I also design quizzes that play on the assumptions that experienced readers have learned to make—when long-term memory switches into gear unbidden and supplies information that isn't on the page or doesn't fit the situation. Below are thirteen trick questions; the answers, as well as explanations about the features of the questions that trap fluent readers, appear at the end of the chapter.

THIRTEEN QUESTIONS

1. Two men played chess. They played five games, and each man won three. How do you explain this?
2. Answer this question within five seconds, and do not return to check your answer: How many animals of each species did Moses take aboard the ark with him? (*Note: the question is not how many pairs, but how many animals.*)
3. An archaeologist reported he had discovered two gold coins in the desert near Jerusalem dated 430 B.C. Many of his fellow scientists refused to take his claim seriously. Why?

4. If you have only one match and you entered a room to start a kerosene lamp, an oil heater, and a wood burning stove, which would you light first? Why?

5. Here's a question on international law: if an *international* airliner crashed exactly on the U.S.-Mexican border, where would they be required by law to bury the survivors?

6. Some months have thirty days; some have thirty-one. How many have twenty-eight?

7. A farmer had seventeen sheep; all but nine died. How many are left?

8. You have a dime in an empty wine bottle. The bottle is corked. Your job is to get the dime out of the bottle without taking the cork out. You must do this without damaging the bottle in any way. How do you do it?

9 Explain the following true boast: "In my bedroom, the nearest lamp that I usually keep turned on is twelve feet away from my bed. Alone in the room, without using wire, strings, or any other aids or contraptions, I can turn out the light on that lamp and get into bed before the room is dark."

10. If two U.S. coins total 55¢, and one is *not a nickel* (please keep this in mind) what are the two coins?

11. Is it legal in India for a man to marry his widow's sister?

12. Read this sentence aloud:

    FINISHED FILES ARE THE RE-
    SULT OF YEARS OF SCIENTIF-
    IC STUDY COMBINED WITH
    THE EXPERIENCE OF YEARS.

    Now, count aloud the letter *F*s in the sentence. Count them only once—don't go back and count again. How many *F*s are there?

13. Memorize the phrases below. As soon as you do this, turn the paper over and write them at the top of the back of this page. Don't look at the phrases again once you've turned your paper over.

PARIS	ONCE
IN THE	IN A
THE SPRING	A LIFETIME
BIRD	SLOW
IN THE	MEN AT
THE HAND	AT WORK

I have just started to work with the theory of reading comprehension described in *Mosaic of Thought: Teaching Comprehension in a Reader's*

Workshop by Keene and Zimmermann (1997). It draws on teachers' demonstrations of how literate adults think when we read as models for our students to learn strategies for engaging with texts. In comprehension demonstrations I read aloud a poem, short story, or article to my kids and weave in descriptions of what I think, do, and wonder about. Kids observe a range of mental activities—how I use schemas and connect with my general knowledge, life experiences, and experiences with other texts and authors; how I ask questions, make predictions, decide what's important, draw inferences, raise problems, attempt to solve problems, create visual images, synthesize ideas and language, draw conclusions, interpret, and monitor myself and the difficulty or ease—or sense—of the text.

We list the strategies I use on the easel pad; then the class reads a poem or short article independently and individuals record the strategies they use in their handbooks; afterward we come back together to discuss them. Students use Post-it notes two or three days a month during reading workshop to mark places in their books where they notice they used one of the comprehension strategies; at the end of the workshop they describe the strategies and connections around the circle.

I'm excited about this work because of the way it breathes life into the metaphor of the long-term-memory file cabinet. By using metacognition—by thinking about their thinking as they read—kids read more actively and analytically. They go deeper and get more. They become more connected to other readers and to the writers they're reading. They can better identify their confusions, and they have means to attempt to untangle them: they learn how and when to pause, consider, connect, and reflect. Of special relevance to teachers of students who can already read, Keene and Zimmermann's work shows how to help students read more deeply—how we can enhance comprehension without reverting to the made-up "skills" of commercial programs. Most exciting of all, this approach to enhancing students' reading depends on the teacher reading, too.

In other minilessons about reading strategies I teach simple speed-reading techniques—skimming, scanning, and skipping—and we discuss when and how readers use them. For example, fluent readers skim when they're looking for the answer to a specific question, reviewing material that's familiar, or deciding whether they're interested in reading a text. I teach kids that effective skimming depends on knowing that key information usually appears in the first and last sentences of a paragraph.

I don't teach formal systems of study skills. I remember rebelling in high school against SQ3R, PQ4R, REQUEST, and the other kid-proof study procedures because they made reading tedious. I had my own, underground system. Once, in a graduate course we taught, Mary Ellen Giacobbe and I asked our students, forty teachers, to describe their approaches to informational texts. Not one used a formal study procedure. They had their own underground systems, too. When we listed the strategies we employ when we read for information, we came up with the same techniques the proficient readers in my classes identify when I survey them:

WHAT I DO WHEN I READ FOR INFORMATION

- I look to see how long it will be.
- I do a quick scan of the whole thing.
- I read the conclusion first.
- I read the foreword or introduction.
- I read the first and last paragraphs.
- I read all the subheadings.
- I look at the illustrations or figures and read the captions.
- If I can, I underline, highlight, and write in the margins.
- I dog-ear the corners of important pages or put Post-its on them.

- I close the book when I'm done and write what I remember or think is important in my notebook.

These are the strategies I teach in minilessons about how to read textbooks and other kinds of informational writing. From the list each reader begins to develop his or her own repertoire of study strategies.

In the weeks before eighth graders take standardized reading assessments, minilessons become a context for teaching about the conventions of standardized tests. Students who recognize how assessments work are more confident going into a test situation and more adept at taking the test:

> Something you should know about standardized achievement tests in reading is that there are four basic kinds of questions. One group of questions asks for the best title, best topic sentence, main idea, or general idea. Whatever terminology the test makers use, all of these get at one thing: what the passage is mostly about.
>
> Then there are inference questions. These are meanings that are implied by the passage, rather than directly spelled out in black and white. Often, it's just plain common sense: what do you conclude based on the evidence they give you?
>
> There are always detail questions: these ask for specific information you can look up in the passage. I think these are the easiest, unless the test maker decides to get tricky and words a question ambiguously.
>
> Finally, test makers ask for the meaning of a word in context: what a word means in the sentence or passage in which it appears.
>
> I've photocopied a half dozen typical passages and sets of questions, the kind you'll find on the test next week. Let's take a look at the questions and analyze them in terms of what the test company is asking you to do in each one.

Then students and I look at selections and questions from old state and S.R.A. tests and analyze how they're constructed. In another minilesson I teach procedures for reading the test passages and answering the questions:

PROCEDURES FOR STANDARDIZED READING TESTS

1. Read the first couple of sentences, the last couple of sentences, and the questions. This way you'll have an idea of what you'll be reading about, plus what you'll be asked to decide about this passage.
2. Read the passage and look for answers to the questions—the general idea, supporting details, and so on.
3. When you answer the questions, start by eliminating the alternatives that show the least merit. Then reread the question and the remaining answers. Always use a process of elimination.

4. Return to the selection whenever you need to, using a skimming/
   scanning approach.
5. When a question asks for the meaning of a word, read the whole
   sentence or passage in which the word appears. You're not so much
   being tested on whether you already know the denotation as
   whether you can figure out a word's meaning from context by using
   the words around it as clues.
6. Avoid spending a lot of time coloring the dots. One big, deliberate
   mark is enough.

Other reading minilessons address more global strategies, like the rituals surrounding how, where, and when we read. I encourage students to read in bed at night as a tranquil way to end the day for a whole lifetime. Or we discuss the importance of rereading loved books—how it's never cheating or a waste of time to return to a favorite. I'm more convinced each year that rereading is one sign of a truly literate reader, one who understands what it means to appreciate a book. And we talk about abandoning books. Many of the students who don't like to read when they start seventh grade have never put aside a book: they stuck through to the bitter end every time. These kids need permission—and encouragement—to abandon books that don't satisfy them. In minilessons I describe my criteria for abandoning books and ask students to describe theirs. We talk about how many pages each of us gives a book, on average, to get good. Kids need to know that there are too many wonderful books out there, waiting to be read, to waste time on a book that doesn't satisfy them.

The reading lessons I can teach well are based on what I love of literature, understand about reading, and learn about my kids as readers. Some students won't trust that there is such a thing as a good book; their experiences of literature are so limited they don't yet know what they like to read. And I know that for some, inexperience with books will mean a delay in fluency; their reading will be awkward and slow. Some students come to reading workshop from homes where reading and talking about literature feel as natural as breathing; others have grown up without books and without adults who love books.

I also know my students' strengths as readers. Most can "decode" with some degree of proficiency; they don't have to be taught how to read. Many are on the threshold of analytic reading, ready to go beyond plot. Like all readers they have an innate desire for connection and meaning. They're willing to experiment, and they're uninhibited about showing wild enthusiasm when enthusiasm is warranted. They delight in quality. When they recognize that something is good, they acknowledge it. And they are generous. When something is good, they're more than willing to recommend it to others. In reading minilessons teachers can demonstrate and celebrate all the qualities of good readers, and more. We can teach the happiest lesson of all—how the mind of the good reader interacts with a text to create the good book.

ANSWERS TO THIRTEEN QUESTIONS

1. The two men didn't play the games with each other. Long-term memory supplies a word (*with*) and an assumption: if two men played chess, they must be each other's opponents.
2. Moses didn't build the ark; Noah did. Experience tells readers to assume that test questions provide correct information, and that we should direct our attention to instructions and italics.
3. The date "B.C." couldn't have been used before Christ: how could someone have foreseen the future birth of Christ? Our eyes have learned to skim over a commonplace like "B.C." without stopping each time to consider what it stands for.
4. You'd light the match first. Long-term memory automatically fills in the "missing" information that the match is already lit.
5. Survivors can't be buried. Again, prior experience with printed text tells us to focus on the words in italics. The emphasis on *international* shifts focus off the crucial word, *survivors*.
6. All of them. Here long-term memory inserts a word: *only*.
7. Nine. Experience with word problems in math tells us we should expect to perform an arithmetical operation—in this case, subtraction.
8. Push the cork into the bottle and shake the dime out. Experience tells us that corks are for pulling out of bottles, not for pushing in.
9. He does it in the daytime. Again, long-term memory supplies "missing" information: if darkness is mentioned, it must be night.
10. A nickel and a half-dollar. Long-term memory of how math problems are worded, plus the italics and special directions in parentheses, all misdirect our attention: maybe one coin can't be a nickel, but the *other* one can.
11. It may be legal, but it's not possible: the man is dead. Long-term memory is cued to anticipate a question about marriage law and a foreign culture.

12. There are six *F*s, not three. Reading the sentence aloud orients readers to the sound of the hard *F* in the first two words, *finished files*. When the word *scientific* is hyphenated at the hard *F* sound, it reinforces the pronunciation link. This makes it easy to miss the soft *F* of *of*.
13. Paris in *the the* spring. Bird in *the the* hand. Once in *a a* lifetime. Slow men *at at* work. Good readers see a chunk of meaning, and they focus on the words that carry the meaning, not on the articles and prepositions.

7
Responding to Writers and Writing

We'll spend a lifetime crafting our teaching in order
to allow children to be the authors of their own texts.
Donald Graves

Carolyn Chute is a Maine novelist. Her best-seller, *The Beans of Egypt, Maine*, is a favorite among my kids. A high school dropout, Chute started writing when she was eight years old, but she never wrote in school or took her stories to school to show her teachers. She explains:

> My stories were so precious to me. I didn't want my teachers to touch them, because everything I ever did in school was attacked by them. I even had a nightmare, when I was an adult, that my home economics teacher ripped all my stories up and threw them around. I think it's because she threatened my dignity while I was in school. (1985, 8–9)

Writers are vulnerable. That's the writer, there, on the page. Our essential selves are laid bare for the world to see. Writers want response that gives help without threatening our dignity. Every adult remembers at least one waking experience comparable to Chute's nightmare, when an English teacher's response took the form of an attack: red ink bled all over a piece of writing that represented the writer's level best.

But writers are also inquisitive and ambitious. We want to know how we can improve our essential selves. Writers want response that takes us seriously and moves us forward without condescension. Everyone can recall a time when something we did elicited a compliment that felt contrived. It didn't help, because our standards told us we could have done better, but we still didn't understand *how*.

Margaret Donaldson considered the conflict between rule-centered, "formal" education on the one hand and child-centered "progressive" education on the other, and concluded: "I can only see one way out of this dilemma: it is to exercise such control as is needful with a light touch and never to relish the need" (1978, 126). Donald Murray, writing about writing conferences, concurred: "I teach the student not the paper, but this doesn't mean I'm a 'like wow' teacher. I am critical and I certainly can be directive but I listen before I speak" (1982, 159).

Young writers want to be listened to. They also want honest, adult responses. They need teachers who will guide them to the meanings they don't know yet by showing them how to build on what they *do* know and *can* do. Student writers need response while the words are churning out, in the midst of the messy, tentative act of drafting meaning. And they need to be able to anticipate and predict how their teacher will approach them.

At the end of September, Sabrina started a new narrative. Sabrina's mother is Vietnamese, and she tells her children stories about growing up in Vietnam. One night she remembered a childhood dream, and Sabrina decided to write about it. She began her first draft the next day in class but stopped after a paragraph paraphrasing the mother's dream. The following day she started again, taking a different tack and putting the dream into direct quotes: her mother's words as Sabrina remembered them. Again she wrote only a paragraph or two before she bogged down.

Sabrina was busy making faces at her paper when I came along and parked my footstool next to her chair. "How's it going?" I asked, leaning on her desktop.

"Not good," she confessed.

"Tell me about it." I propped my chin on my folded arms and waited.

"Well, I'm trying to write about this dream of my mom's, that she told me and Mark about, but I can't get it to come out right. This is my second try, and it's just not working."

"What's the problem?"

She bit her lip and looked from her second draft to her first. "I don't know all the little details and stuff," she decided.

I sympathized and summarized: "You're having a hard time telling what's essentially your mother's story. It's her experience, so she knows the details you don't." Sabrina nodded. "That is a problem. What could you do about it?"

"Well . . ." she hesitated. "I could go home tonight and interview my mom about the details and write down what she says."

"That's an option," I agreed. But I suspected that Sabrina's lack of specifics, which was making it hard for her to write a prose narrative about this dream, wouldn't be solved by an interview: How could she ever ask enough, or the right, questions to be able to enter her mother's unconscious? Because I write and confer with writers, I knew another option: "Sometimes, when I have a glimpse of a situation, rather than the whole panorama and all its details, I write about it as a poem, where what I want is a condensed essence of the experience. That's something else I think you should consider here." Then I moved off to confer with another writer in another corner of the room.

Sabrina hadn't written poetry before. She went to the materials center, got more paper, and started her third draft as a poem. This genre did what Sabrina wanted. When it was finished she published "The Dream of the Dead" in the school literary magazine; in November's self-evaluation she said it was the best piece of her first trimester writing: "It's good because it's so mysterious, and because it's a poem," she concluded.

THE DREAM OF THE DEAD

We're sitting quietly on Mark's bed,
listening to the patter of the rain.
Mom begins to talk.
She begins with the story
of her grandfather's funeral in Vietnam.
(This is before she tells us of her dream.)
They pass before his body and
give the new widow gifts.
Mom does not look at him.
All are dressed in black
to ward off evil spirits.
When she goes home
to her own bed,
she dreams of a party
at her grandparents' house.
Her grandfather is there,
pale in color, strange looking.
Mom helps him cook a chicken.
It's crispy and brown on the outside.
When cut,
the inside is bloody and raw.
No one notices
except my mother.
Everything is quiet—
then everyone is gone!
Suddenly her grandfather becomes
a bat.
He starts to chase her.
She runs
and hurdles over a stool
into a void of darkness.

The void of darkness
turns into the soft bed of her parents.
And we—Mark, my mother and I—
are suddenly back on Mark's bed
in America.

—*Sabrina Lewis*

The before, during, and after of my conference with Sabrina is typical; its elements are present on the first day of writing workshop. The patterns of response become predictable so that writers may anticipate them, use them to meet their needs, and repeat them in their conferences with each other.

One constant in conferences is the immediacy of my response: students know I'll confer with them while they're writing, not after the writing is done. My job is to help kids develop as writers, not assign sink-or-swim tests of writing performance. After-the-fact response from a teacher comes too late; it assumes students will not only hold a teacher's advice in their heads until the next writing occasion and apply it to a new context, but that they actually read the teacher's written comments. Any English teacher who has ever spent a Sunday writing comments on class sets of compositions has harbored the unsettling suspicion that she is shouting down a hole. Donald Murray's suspicions were so strong he conducted an experiment one Sunday afternoon and wrote purposely bad advice all over his students' papers: "do this backward," "add adjectives and adverbs," "be general and abstract." When Murray passed back the papers, not one of his students questioned his comments (1982, 158). Writing workshop provides time in school for students to work on their writing, and it provides time in school for me to work with students on their writing.

Another constant of writing conferences is *where* I work with my students: I go to them. I move because I'm trying to control the length of the conferences and talk with many students each day. One fall I experimented with a conference table at the front of the room, where I sat for the duration of the workshop and met with writers one and two at a time. There were problems. I couldn't get students to leave once they joined me at the table: they had Ms. Atwell at their disposal until they decided to return to their seats, and they had me taking too much responsibility, as their audience and their fixer-upper. I conferred with just four or five writers during each workshop, and I was constantly distracted by what the kids on line for the seats at my table were up to, not to mention the behavior in the far corners of the classroom.

When I move I can keep conferences shorter, confer with more writers each day, and monitor classroom behavior in general. I move in a random fashion rather than from desk to desk: my kids always know I could be any-where in the room in a second. And I move carrying my three mandatory pieces of writing conference equipment: the status-of-the-class record on a clipboard, a pad of four-by-six-inch Post-it notes so I can show examples and help kids capture their ideas and plans, and my footstool. For the first two years of writing workshop I knelt alongside students' desks when I con-ferred with them. By the end of the second year my knees had given out. Now I carry my footstool, park it for each conference, look up into the writer's face, and begin.

My students can anticipate that I'll initiate the conference with one of the open-ended questions that are a writing teacher's stock in trade: "How's it com-ing?" (Calkins 1983, 132) "How can I help you?" "What have you done today?" "Where did this come from?" "Where are you headed?" By November I often don't have to say a word. When I pull up beside a writer, he or she starts right in, telling me how it's going, reading or showing the part that's causing diffi-culty, describing a section that's working well, or waving me off—politely—because the writer is on a roll. And the conference proceeds in a predictable fashion: I listen hard or read the draft, ask questions about things I don't under-stand or would like to know more about, talk with the writer about how he or she might solve a writing problem, offer the options and solutions I know that might work here, and ask what the writer plans to do next.

The purpose of my conferences is not to get writers to revise. I confer with kids about ideas, information, purpose, audience, language, and format so they can consider what's working, what needs more work, and what they can do next to make the writing work better. My goal is what Vygotsky termed "mediated" learning: "What the child can do in cooperation today he can do alone tomorrow" (1962, 104). Today I cooperate with Sabrina by pointing out that switching genres will serve her intentions; tomorrow Sab-rina can choose poetry on her own.

Waiting and listening are still the hardest parts of conferring for me. Mary Budd Rowe's work with teachers shows that we generally wait less than a full second before responding to what a student says (1974). I'm learning to relax, to use the predictable pattern of the conference to make room for deliberation, reflection, collaboration, and genuine conversation. When I listen hard, the writer and the writing become my focus. If I'm side-tracked, as I often was when I began responding to writing in conferences, I ask the writer to tell me about the writing again.

During the first years of writing workshop I was often struck by their responses when I asked my kids, "What could you do next?" The solutions

they developed on their own were the similar to—or better than—advice on the tip of my tongue. But just as often they had no idea what to do to solve a writing dilemma. The longer I write and confer with young writers, the deeper the pool of experience from which I can draw potential options for my kids. I tell and show what I know because this is my responsibility to the students in my care: to find out where they are and where they need to go next, and to demonstrate all the ways I know to arrive at the new place.

Conferences About Content and Craft

Arelitsa was tackling a new subject—God—and she was stuck. I settled my footstool beside her desk.

"Hi," she said. "I think I need some help. I'm pretty confused with this piece."

"What's up?"

She showed me her first draft. "You know how when you're little you have these funny ideas of how things work? Well, the other night I had a flashback. I remembered what I used to think about God. I used to have this picture of Him in my mind, like the Jolly Green Giant or something. And now I don't have a picture. He's just sort of everywhere."

I paraphrased. "So you're trying to write about two things here: first, how you used to see God, this specific image of Him when you were a little kid; then, how you perceive Him now that you're growing up, when there's no specific image. He's just all around you."

"Yeah," she agreed. "So it's really two parts? Like S. E. Hinton, that was then and this is now?"

"It sounds like it to me. What do you want to do now with this?"

"Umm . . ." she hesitated. "Probably a second draft, with two parts." Our conversation had served its purpose, helping Arelitsa get unstuck so she could proceed on her own.

THE GUY UPSTAIRS

When I was a kid,
I didn't have much of a brain:
I thought He was an engineer
(the kind that runs a train).

He wore overalls
with stripes down the sides.
He was as tall as a giant,
and Heaven is where He'd hide.

He was easy to make friends with,
although He'd never talk back.
Some people got responses
(I guessed they had the knack).

But now that I've grown older
He's harder to define.
I can't really explain Him—
He's just there, in my mind.

"Please no embarrassments!"
"Please don't let it hurt!"
I close my eyes and beg Him;
I stammer and I blurt.

When I am in trouble,
He is always there.
He guides me through my life—
I guess He really cares.

(Have you noticed through this poem
I've been calling Him a He?
For all I know He could be an It.
Hey— or maybe even a She.)

—*Arelitsa Kazakos*

The conference with Arelitsa follows the predictable pattern. I invite a writer to talk; she talks; I listen, paraphrase, ask clarifying questions, nudge toward or suggest options if the writer needs them, and ask the writer to articulate what he or she plans to do next. My purpose in conferences about content and craft is to help writers discover the meanings they don't know yet, name problems, attempt solutions, and make plans. The guidelines below help me make my conferences with students predictable and productive.

CONTENT CONFERENCE GUIDELINES

1. Keep an eye on the clock and remember you're responsible to all the writers in the room. At first, as a teacher gets the hang of conferring, conferences may run longer than you wish. But it's important to remember that you're not asking to hear every single word every student writes. Instead, ask kids to tell you about the writing—what it's about and what's happening. Ask them to read or talk to you about the lead, a section that's working well, or a part they need help with. Skim students' drafts—just be sure to focus on content and craft, not conventions. When teachers begin with long conferences, individual writers will come to count on this level of attention and won't learn how to identify and solve problems. Worse, the teacher will be able to meet with just a handful of kids each day.

2. Meet with as many writers as possible each day, and make notes on the status-of-the-class chart of who you didn't confer with; see those students first in the next workshop.

3. Go to to your students' desks, so you can control the length of conferences and the behavior in the classroom and see many writers. Circulate from one area of the room to another.

4. Make the conference personal and intimate. It should feel like a conversation. This means kneeling or sitting alongside writers as you talk, listen, and read their writing.

5. Whisper and ask students to whisper when they confer with you and each other. Writers won't be able to think, compose, or produce if the teacher's voice is filling their ears and your words are filling their minds. Try not to be a distraction to the other writers in the room, and try to set a tone of quiet concentration: if your volume goes up, the volume in the room will rise to match it.

6. Strive for a balance between listening to students discuss their writing; listening as they read aloud texts that are relatively brief (e.g., a letter or poem) or passages from longer works; and, after the writer has told you what he or she wants help with, reading their texts silently to yourself.

7. Some pieces of student writing are too long to listen to or read during class, especially in the upper elementary and secondary grades, as students begin to write extended prose. Ask the writer if you may take the draft home. Read it and jot down questions or suggestions on a Post-it. Return the writing to the writer in class the next day and confer about your response.

8. Build on what writers know and have done, rather than bemoaning what's not on the page or what's wrong with what is. Remember: kids usually write as well as they can. As you help them move forward, their best will get better. A piece of writing that isn't working yet *isn't working yet*; it's not bad.

9. At the other end of the spectrum, avoid generalized praise. It's a way many teachers were trained to talk—congratulating kids on their opinions, stroking verbally as a reward for desired behavior, deeming everything our kids do "Very good!"—and it's not a way human beings talk to each other. Praise by paying attention to the writer. Praise by becoming involved in the writing. Praise by congratulating writers who solve problems by dint of hard work. Praise by acknowledging writers who try something new. Praise by describing the effects of specific techniques on you as a reader: "Your lead brought me right into the essay" or "I like the way you built your argument: it anticipates the way someone who disagrees with you would argue back" or "The images are so concrete I can close my eyes and see this" or "I have goosebumps at the way you concluded this."

10. In questioning students about the content of their writing, ask about what you're curious about. Focus on meaning: What don't you understand? What doesn't make sense to you? What would you like to know more about? A string of inquisitions along the line of "When did you go there? Who did you go with? Did you have fun? What kind of day was it? Did you have anything to eat? What?" elicits a string of one- and two-word answers. But a more global question like "Tell me more about X" or "I don't understand Y" gets a writer thinking and talking.

11. Come prepared to take notes and make notes. You may want to travel, as I do, with a pad of Post-its. Or you might want to adapt the peer writing conference record (Appendix J) as a form for you to lean on as you get the hang of the rituals of face-to-face response. You'll need a place to jot down your questions and observations so you don't lose them; to demonstrate solutions to writing problems; and to transcribe for kids the ideas and plans they describe to you—to serve as recording secretary as they talk about what might happen next.

12. If an occasion arises for you to demonstrate a solution to a problem the writer can't solve, ask permission to draft on the draft. This calls for an especially delicate touch. Don't take over the piece of writing and make it your own; do confer with the writer about his or her intentions. If you think you understand them *and* believe you have something to teach, ask if you may demonstrate the technique, approach, or solution on the draft: "May I show you a way to do this?"

13. Be patient. Trust yourself and your students. Over a whole year of conferences, minilessons, and writing experiences, your students will improve as writers, and you will improve as a responder to writers.

Specific problems in student drafts call for more direct approaches. In the chart below I've identified situations that emerge in pieces of beginners' writing and examples of conference responses that have helped my kids address each problem.

QUESTIONS THAT CAN HELP

Situation	*Conference Approaches*
The teacher wants to open the conference, learn from the writer what he or she needs help with, and invite the writer to reflect on the draft.	• How's it coming? • What are you working on today? • How can I help you? • What part do you want help with?
The writing is unfocused: it covers several or many ideas, themes, days, events, etc.	• What's the most important thing you're trying to say? • What is this piece of writing really about?

- Do you have more than one point or story here?
- What parts are about something else? Can these be cut?
- Which example or illustration is the best one?
- What's your favorite part? How can you build on it?
- How can you cut to the chase?

There isn't enough information.

- I don't understand X. Put your draft aside and tell me about it.
- What else do you know about this topic? How could you find out more?
- You wrote X. Here's what I see or think when I hear X. Is that what you mean?
- What parts need to be explained better so a reader can see or understand them? Mark each with an *.
- Is the pace too fast here? Can you slow it down and expand the information in this part?
- Where and when did this happen? (Who are these people?) Where could you embed the contextual information?

The writing is a list of events, a list of facts, or all plot: there's no reflection, no voice, or no character for a reader to engage with.

- Why is X significant to you or others? Why does it matter?
- What do you think about X?
- How did you feel when X happened?

The lead holds the reader at arm's length, doesn't give direction to the writing, or puts all the details of background information up front.

- Can you put an * at every point in the draft where you could engage a reader by describing your thoughts and feelings, or the character's?
- Does this lead bring a reader right into the writing—right into the event, the idea, the life of the character?
- Would this lead invite a reader to continue reading?
- Your lead makes me feel X. Is this the tone you intend?
- Your lead makes me think X. Is this the impression you intend?
- Where does the writing really begin, really get going? Can you cut everything before that?
- On another sheet of paper can you rough out one or two new leads? I'll be back in fifteen minutes to see what you've come up with.

The conclusion is sudden, drags on, or doesn't give closure to the piece of writing.

- How do you want a reader to think and feel at the end? Will this conclusion do it?
- I'm confused at the end; I'm left wondering about X. How can you clear this up?
- The conclusion left me with a feeling of X. Is this how you want me to feel?

	• The conclusion left me thinking X. Is this the impression you intend?
	• Where does the piece of writing really end? Can you delete the rest of the draft and stop here?
	• On another sheet of paper can you rough out one or two new conclusions? I'll be back in fifteen minutes to see what you've come up with.
There are no or few direct quotes in a narrative.	• Did people talk here? Can you quote the words they said—let your reader hear how they spoke and use dialogue to reveal what they're like and how they feel?
The writer's purpose is unclear.	• Why are you writing about this? What makes this a subject you want to write about?
	• Do you know what you're talking about here?
	• Do you want to move on to a topic you know more about, care more about?
The teacher wants to close the conference, give the writer a chance to articulate a plan, and hear the plan.	• What will you do next?

These are typical responses to typical problems that crop up in writing workshop. The more I write, read about writing, respond to writers, and learn about each student, the more particular my conversations with my particular kids. I know that my conferences today are less ritualized and formulaic than when I began teaching writing in a workshop because my knowledge base has broadened and deepened. I've gone from acting as a mirror, someone who reflects back what I hear in the writing and gives a neutral response, to trying to act as a mentor to young writers. When what I know of writing and the writer will help a student learn something or meet his or her intentions, the conference becomes an occasion for student and teacher to collaborate on the writing.

My collaborations with kids take many forms. I ask leading questions, suggest options a writer might pursue, intervene when a writer moves off-track, point a new direction, demonstrate solutions to writing problems, show how to achieve an effect, even make brief assignments that invite students to engage as writers in ways they otherwise might not. My role as responder is more diverse these days, and more satisfying. I am teaching, and my students are producing writing they like, can learn from, and take pride in.

Asa is a blond, freckle-faced seventh grader. In a conference I intervened before he started to write, to refocus him and make it more likely he could succeed at what he wanted to do. Asa told me a story his mother had told him, about a pregnant girl, barely in her teens, who went off alone to deliver—then murder—her baby. He concluded, "I'd like to write a poem about it."

"What perspective are you thinking of taking here?" I wondered.

He replied, "First person. I'm going to be the girl who had her baby and killed it."

I gulped. "Asa, why do you want to write about this?"

"Well, I just think it's really sad and really cool. I can't get it out of my mind."

I asked him, "Does it strike you that to become this girl is going to require a pretty amazing leap of imagination?"

"Yeah, I guess so," he agreed. "But I really want to write about this." I wracked my brain for a way Asa could enter this occasion and imagine it.

"So . . . what if the girl has a brother?" I asked. "A little brother, who knows something is going on but doesn't quite know what. What if you looked at the situation through his eyes?"

"Oh, cool," he replied thoughtfully. "Yeah. Then I wouldn't have to deliver my own baby."

"Right," I agreed.

This is Asa's poem.

THE SISTER

When I was seven
my sister was always
gone
some people said she did
something bad or some guy
did something bad to her
something like that

The house seemed empty
without her
mama would sit in her rocking chair
and go back and forth
back and forth

I missed my sister
I remember she got big in the
belly
just like miss rorck who sat on her
porch, all lonely and sad

I wanted her to come home

then my sister did come
home
but when she pushed the frayed screen door open
with the slightest creak
mama was up and staring at
her colorless face
dripping with tears
and her dress
stained with blood
and all mama did was stare

I'm twelve now and my sister's eighteen
just yesterday I snuck up to the mountains
where I was told never to go
I found out why

I found the rock
the tiny bones
and an infant's soul

—Asa Kitfield

Collaborating with Asa before he began, by suggesting another focus, put him in a position to create literature. I know from my own attempts at fiction that there were limits to what I can imagine. Asa could close his eyes and become the boy; he could imagine his confusion and feel his sorrow. Asa loved the way the poem turned out; I do, too. The experience of writing it, in a voice close to his own, was one more springboard for him as he launched himself as a writer.

Other interventions take the form of assignments to the whole class. These are either prompted tasks that relate to a topic we're studying in history, reading, or art, or writing of a practical nature. I do the assignment, too. It's one of the most effective ways that I can collaborate with my students, when I show them how I identify and approach the constraints of a task.

A practical example are thank-you notes we wrote to parents who accompanied us on a field trip to the mountains and to the grandparents who loaned us their chalet as a bunkhouse. I wrote the thank-you to the grandparents in a demonstration lesson on an overhead transparency:

> Dear Mr. and Mrs. Cole,
>
> Thank you so much for giving us a perfect place to stay during our geology field trip this week. It was great to have a real house to come home to in the evening. There was just enough room, and we found everything we needed to be cozy and comfortable.
>
> Thanks again for your generosity and hospitality.

Along the way I talked about the challenge of thank-you notes—why people are tempted to buy preprinted cards. Once a writer says thanks, then what? Writing about the nature of the gift or favor and what it means to the recipient—that's the hard part. Then I started two more letters on transparencies, each with the same first line: "Thank you for everything you did to make our geology field trip a success"—in other words, the easy part. I sent the kids off in two groups to two overhead projectors to compose the hard parts.

> Dear John,
>
> Thank you for everything you did to make our geology field trip a success. Without your knowledge in geology, our trip wouldn't have been nearly so educational. We also appreciated your "in" at Perham's. If we hadn't been granted permission to visit the Perham's mine, we wouldn't have succeeded in finding so many rare minerals.
>
> The minilesson you gave us about cleavage planes was informative and easy to understand.
>
> Thank you for transporting us, for your expertise, and for being such a good friend to our school.

> Dear Gretchen,
>
> Thank you for everything you did to make our geology field trip a success. We had a lot of fun. Your geologic knowledge and expertise

helped us understand the world of minerals. We really appreciated the resources you brought along, so we could consult them as we made our finds.

Thanks, too, for driving. You're a good friend to our class.

I moved between the two projectors and conferred with the authors about specifics they might include and choices of words and phrases. The assignment took them away from their self-initiated writing for about fifteen minutes. I think it was time well spent as they experienced the conventions of a genre they'll write their whole lives.

Sometimes conferring with kids as a mentor means taking dictation from writers who are stuck, to help them get off the sticking point. Matt, writing an essay about what it's like to be the oldest sibling in a family of six children, was stuck. His essay began:

Believe me, you don't wanna be in a six-sibling family, let alone the eldest.

I'm not saying that you don't get attention. You get plenty of attention. It's just that most of the time shortly after, the words "Go to your room" are spoken.

It's worst in the car.

My youngest sister could make a living off the money she earns in there. For example, I'm sitting next to her in the back. I accidentally brush her trying to get my seat belt on. There's a scream to the front, and the next thing I know I'm down a dollar and my sister is up one. On a regular trip to Cook's Corner in Brunswick I'm fined at *least* two dollars.

What's worse is that my brothers are catching on.

Matt had a funny, specific lead, and then he lost it. His essay concluded:

There's only two things on the up-side: 1) I'm never bored, 2) when the day's done I'm tired enough to get to sleep.

When one of the little kids isn't home I swear I could stay up until midnight. There's no peace and quiet at all because by the time they get to sleep it's 9:30, and by then I'm tired because of them.

The way things are going I'm beginning to give up hope of a day of total peace until I'm in college.

I told Matt what I observed. "Matt, the essay begins with a specific occasion that your readers can participate in—I am there with you in that car. Then it becomes a series of general statements I can't engage or empathize with. Can we get back on track here, in terms of *your specific experience?*" I uncapped my pen and started a list. "Where else and when else could a reader engage? I know I've been at Shop 'n Save when you, your mother, and the other five come rolling in there. The reaction is *incredible*. People would pay to see this. I'm putting that one at the top of a list. So, when else is it interesting or wild?"

Matt thought for a minute. "Dinner time." I added *dinner time* to the list.

"When else?"

"Oh, God, at the movies."

"When else?"

"They invade my room. They take my stuff, my books, especially Natie. Going to Strawberries record store is bad, too. At the movie-rental shop it's like a horror movie."

I gave Matt the Post-it with the list he'd dictated to me. Now he had specific occasions he could play with. I also gave him something to read: *Dave Barry's Greatest Hits*. Matt needed examples of non-sequitur driven, off-the-wall humor essays—to know there are models out there for what he was trying to do. In his final draft he brought in three of the incidents he brainstormed to develop other points about life in his family. The essay concludes:

> It's a whole nother thing out in public. Walking into a grocery store on a good day the screams reach only 120 decibels. On an O.K. day, there will only be major fistfights. But on a bad day, the screams reach 150 decibels, accompanied by TKOs. It's interesting to watch, because before our crew enters a public place usually it's all chatty and business as usual. Then we walk in, and it turns all . . . hushed. It's weird.
>
> Dinner time . . . let's see. Where do I start?
>
> Basically there's a major food fight every night, but that's kind of boring to write about, so I'll give you some other scenarios: 1) My brothers and sisters don't like what we're having for dinner. 2) Sometimes they like it so much they'd rather have it decorating the walls and themselves than filling their stomachs. 3) Most of the time they're just plain bored.
>
> And then there's Natie, Mr. Chef Boyardee, always mixing and matching what's on his plate. It started out with him dipping his corn into his apple juice, but over the years it's grown into pouring his soda into his rice and charming stuff like that.
>
> Natie has also grown into a habit of breaking into my room and destroying it. Almost every day I come home from school to find my bookshelf on its side, books strewn all over creation, my desk upsidedown, and my chair on my bed.

I know it could have been any one of the five kids, but I have a hunch it was Natie. So the next day I fake being sick and sure enough, the second I take my eye off him he goes downstairs into my room. Of course I throw him out. From now on I lock my door with chains before I go to school.

Peace is a rarity at my house. If you're planning on coming over, bring your earplugs and helmet—oh, yeah, and pack your own dinner.

—Matt Miller

I had dog-eared four of Dave Barry's conclusions, which are often a variation on, "So, if you're ever. . . ." Matt modeled his ending on Barry's.

Sometimes in conferences I intervene when a writer doesn't have a direction—when there isn't anything to dictate because the writer can't envision his way out of the box he has built. Jay was drafting a short story about a teenaged boy named Paul who visits his cousin, Steve. They go fishing. Paul meets a pretty girl named Anna, but he's too shy to talk to her; then he goes home and has a fight with his little brother. Jay was doing a nice job of developing his character: Paul came off as a regular, well-meaning, insecure fourteen-year-old. The dialogue was effective, and I began to get a sense of exactly who Paul is—how he'd like to approach Anna, for example, but doesn't have the nerve and probably never will. I sat down with Jay, skimmed the five pages of the draft, and asked, "So, what's going to happen to Paul?"

"Well, that's the problem," he responded. "I don't know what the problem should be."

I reviewed some of what we'd discussed in minilessons about elements of fiction. "What's going to have to happen is a problem of some sort for your character. Look, let's go back together into your story so far and search for threads you could develop. Think in terms of what happens in the fiction for adolescents we've been reading. For example, here's what I see you've already got going here.

"One problem could be around guys' friendships: Paul and Steve. Maybe Anna comes between them? Another could be a first boy-girl relationship—Paul and Anna. Or you could develop something about the family—Paul and John, the little nasty brother, and their dad, the three of them. There could be a family crisis, a death or a divorce. Or maybe something happens to the cousin, Steve. You've established that he drives. Maybe when he comes to pick up Paul to go to the movies that night, there's an accident, and you could look at how Paul copes." All the while I brainstormed out loud, I listed the ideas on a Post-it note.

Jay said, "I *love* that. I want to use that, the accident thing—that would be good to develop Paul's character."

He picked up this thread and continued drafting for two or three days. Now, while Paul is waiting for Steve to pick him up, there's a horrible automobile accident. Steve is injured and falls into a coma. Paul goes to the hospital to see him; he obsesses: "This is my fault; I can't believe I did this to him." Finally Steve awakens from the coma. He begins physical therapy and gets a little better every day. Jay spun this much plot, then began to spin his wheels again: What was the point?

That night I took the story home and read it; the next day in class I asked, "Where are you going with this?"

Jay moaned, "I don't kno-o-ow." He put his head on the desk.

I said, "Look, let's go back to the point at which Steve woke up. Okay, Paul understands that Steve's going to need years of physical therapy, but he's alive. Close you eyes. If this is you, if you are Paul, *what are you thinking?*"

Jay replied, "Relief. I'm glad it's over. I can't believe it."

I agreed. "Okay, what else?" I prompted him.

"I don't know. I can't think."

"How about this?" I started taking notes again. "He's probably got a new perspective on how precious life is. Maybe the grass looks greener now, the sky looks bluer, all those clichés. Maybe he's thinking about what really matters; maybe he understands that getting your driver's license may not be completely great; maybe he's thinking everything's a risk. I don't know— you tell me. What else is he thinking?"

Jay took the list and added to it. "Well, he could die at any given time. He shouldn't take life for granted. You could die by just walking along the street. He should make more of life, should *do* more. Change somehow."

I responded, "Yes. Absolutely. These are ideas you could use to *direct* this short story, so it makes a point, has a theme, will resonate for your reader." I handed the draft back to Jay, and he went to work. The story concluded:

> I woke up at around three and watched T.V. for a while. Dad walked in and asked if I was feeling any better. He also told me that Aunt Mona had called: Steve had awakened. Finally. I was so excited to hear the good news. I felt better than I had in weeks. What Dad had said to me last night had got me thinking: it wasn't my fault about Steve's accident, even though I still felt bad about what happened to him. Now I was relieved he was alive—and I was alive.

While I sat there alone in the sunlit family room, I started thinking about my life. I wasn't going to live forever. I could die at any time—everything was a risk. It could happen while walking a dog or just strolling down the street or, like I'd learned these past few weeks, driving a car. So I made a decision, right then and there. I was going to do more with my life, to live it and love it.

I picked up the phone and called Anna.

—*Jay Spoon*

Because I read fiction, including young adult literature, I have a sense of how it works. I can give Jay my sense of how his story could work, then hand it over to him so he can make it work, so he can feel successful and learn from his success.

Sometimes an intervention in a conference involves teaching a writer about format. This is the first draft of a poem about running, by Joe, a member of our cross-country team.

> I am tense, a coiled spring,
>   Others next to me, we are one mind, one goal.
> The man says the commands, each word adding to
>   The tumult of tension, on your mark, set, *go*.
> We're off, all of us, the sound of feet breaking the hive-
>   mind.
>   Running
>   Running
>   Running
> Must keep going, must not walk, must run.
>   Pain, searing, hot, filling my lungs
> Must keep going, must not walk, must run.
>   The end lap is in sight,
> The cheers of my friends, a burst of speed
>   The finish, with it relief, anticipation
>   The final score, triumph, acceptance, a collage of
> feelings.
>   I have beaten my time.
>   JOY.

Joe read the poem to me, then I asked if I could read it again, to myself. I observed, "Joe, the *sound* of this is great, when you read it aloud to me. It's a poem that moves like running." Paraphrasing Robert Frost, I continued. "It has great *ear sense*, but does it have *eye sense*? It *sounds* like running, but does it *look* like running? How else could you use the white space and line breaks to arrange the words on the poem so that they look like running?"

I wrote on Post-it notes:

You could try:	I am
	tense
	a
	coiled
	spring

Or you could do:	I am
	tense
	a coiled spring

Or else:	I am tense
	a coiled spring

In his second draft Joe pulled the poem down so it looks like running, like one foot in front of another.

TWENTY-EIGHT SECONDS

I am
tense
a coiled
spring
each starting command
adds
to the tumult
of tension
ready
tension
set
tension
go

We're off
all of us
the sound
of stampeding feet
breaks the hive-mind
running
running
running
must
keep
going
must not walk
pain
searing my lungs

must
keep
going
the end
in sight
the cheers
of my friends
a burst
of speed
now the finish
with it
relief
and anticipation
the final score
triumph
acceptance
a collage of feelings
I have beaten my time
JOY

—*Joe Powning*

Joe observed, "The last lines are longer because the race is over, and I'm slowing my pace." In his subsequent open form poems Joe experimented with line breaks and the white space on the page independently.

In a series of conferences with Martha, I taught about essay format; I also helped by suggesting a unifying theme. Martha had decided to write in response to a contest announced in the *Boothbay Register*. The subject was "What Christmas Means to Me"; first prize was fifty dollars, cash. Because I had already shown in minilessons how expository writers begin by collecting ideas and information—generate data and see what emerges—Martha began by brainstorming everything she could think of about the meaning of Christmas.

IDEAS

Means more than opening presents
It doesn't mean just one thing
It's different for everyone
Family comes together
It's not always happy
~~Great grandparents aren't here~~
~~Time for remembering~~
Traveling to one grandparent

Traveling to the next
Opening presents Christmas Eve day
Like holding 2 Christmases
Christmas lights
One time I see all my relatives
One time we come together as a family

Martha began her first draft by trying to string the ideas into sentences:

WHAT CHRISTMAS MEANS TO ME

My family is more like a family of two than a family of four.

I can relate to my mom the best, my brother sort of, and my dad barely at all. As I grow older I grow less and less close to him. There is only one time of the year that we really are a family of four: Christmas. Christmas is when my family doesn't argue. It's when we agree and come together. It's when we help each other instead of make life more difficult.

We open our presents the 24th so we can have two days to come together.

That night at home Martha's essay drifted into my thoughts. She had ideas but lacked a thread to run through them, to connect them as a larger whole. I wondered, "What if she writes about Christmas as a time of miracles? What if she looks at an idea like getting along with her brother as, in fact, a kind of miracle?"

The next morning before school I passed Martha in the stairwell. "What if Christmas is a time of big and little miracles?" I asked. She called back over her shoulder, "Yes!" In writing workshop she began a second draft.

(1) Christmas is a time of miracles. *The big miracle, the greatest of all, is the birth of Jesus. But there are many smaller miracles that make this a time to wonder at the world.* ~~Not big miracles like the baby Jesus being born, but smaller ones like~~ / (2) ¶ My family comes together. Christmas is a time that my family acts like a family of four instead of a family of two or three. It's one of the few times that we sit down and eat a meal together. It's a time that my dad and I grow closer, it's a time that my loved ones relate to one another. / ¶ (3) Another Christmas miracle is that everyone is giving, we wait to see the looks of surprise on our loved ones faces when they open our gifts. / ¶ (4) I anticipate the time that we leave to go visit our relatives. Christmas is when we do things to help each other not do things to make life harder. / ¶ (5) Another Christmas miracle is the lights that light up Southport. They make

everything seem more real, they put everyone into the Christmas spirit. ¶ (6) Christmas to me is a time of miracles. It means that I can forget about my problems and just enjoy being who I am and who I'm with.

In our next conference I showed Martha how to isolate and identify the different ideas, number them, then separate each into its own paragraph and elaborate on it. For example, Martha talked to me about the lines we had marked with the number (2), about her parents and brother, and I took notes. I gave them to her, and she drafted a new paragraph:

> My family comes together. Christmas is a time when we act like a family of four, instead of pairing off, my mom and I going one way and my dad and brother going another. It's one of the few times that we sit down at the table together and enjoy a meal. Sometimes there are candles. There are always crackers. Christmas is a time when my dad and I grow closer and forget for a little while that we have a hard time talking to each other.

Martha took it from there. Now she made her own notes about each of the other numbered ideas and elaborated on it in its own paragraph. In another conference I showed her how to create transitions from one paragraph to the next and bring them together as a whole. Then she edited, I edited, she typed her final copy, and off it went to the *Boothbay Register*.

WHAT CHRISTMAS MEANS TO ME: A TIME OF MIRACLES

Christmas is a time of miracles. The big miracle, the greatest of all, is the birth of Jesus. But there are many smaller miracles that make this a time to wonder at the beauty of the world.

Christmas is a time my family comes together, when we act as a family of four instead of pairing off, my mom and I going one way, my dad and brother going the other. It is one of the few times we sit down around the table together and enjoy a meal. Sometimes there are candles, but there are always Christmas crackers with hats and surprises inside, and there is always laughter. Christmas is also a time when my dad and I grow closer and forget for a little while that I am growing up and we have a hard time talking to each other.

There are more miracles. My family gets bigger. On Christmas Day we travel to see my dad's parents and brothers and sisters, my mom's family, and my great-grandparents, too. It is a day packed with relatives, and it reminds me how many people's lives are connected to mine.

Another Christmas miracle is that everyone gets caught up in the spirit of giving. I can't wait to see the looks of surprise on my loved ones' faces when they open the gifts that I've bought or, even better, made with my own hands and heart. Christmas is the time I do things to help others and try to make them happy, not myself.

Living on Southport, I get to witness another Christmas miracle every evening at dusk. The town hall, the church, the fire station, the post office, and the school cast all the colors of Christmas over our little town. The lights remind us of how one person's generosity can lift everyone's spirits.

Christmas is a time of miracles. I forget all about my problems and enjoy being who I am and who I am with. And the most wonderful miracle of all is that Christmas will come again, next year and every year.

—*Martha Hutchins*

Martha won the contest and fifty dollars; she was also published in the *Register*. Later, when she worked on essays of application to high schools, she knew what she was doing because of our collaboration; she also showed the rest of the kids in her class what she had done in a minilesson.

Sometimes in conferences I intervene to nudge a writer to a place he or she hasn't been and needs to go in order to grow. Seventh grader Jonathan wrote three starts to a poem about seeing the Matterhorn on his family's first trip abroad. None contained a personal pronoun or went beyond five lines of description of the size of the mountain. It was consistent with other recent poems, which were also brief and distanced. When I approached his desk, he showed me the third draft:

> It rises
> above the clouds
> like the master
> of all mountains
> its shield of
> clouds surrounding it.

"I can't write any more today," he said. "I can't think of anything else to say. I think I need a picture from home."

"You mean one of the photographs you took on your trip?"

"Yeah, to help me with more details."

"Let me run something by you, J. T.," I responded. "My favorite nature poet is Mary Oliver. When she writes about the natural world, she captures how she relates to it. You can feel her presence, her intelligence, in every one of her poems about nature. It's a different kind of detail. What would happen if you put your presence into this poem? What if your next draft starts with *you*—what you see, think, feel, remember?"

"I'm not sure what you mean," he replied. In response, I wrote the pronoun *I* as the first word of his fourth draft. "See where this takes you," I suggested, "as a boy from rural Maine who got to see the Matterhorn."

In his next draft Jonathan broke through. He used poetry to find out what mattered to him in seeing the mountain for the first time, and to invite it to matter to others.

MATTERHORN

a veteran of the Camden Hills
I stare at it in
awe
the Camden Hills looked
big to me
now they're nothing but
a blemish on the
side of this
mountain
its ridges and ledges
jut deeper
farther and higher than
any other mountain
and I feel smaller than
I have felt
in my whole life

later
when I'm back on the Camden Hills
I'll remember this
I'll stand on
the side of a
mountain in Maine
and remember
awe

—*Jonathan Tindal*

Jason, another seventh grader, struggled that winter with his first piece of short fiction. He had little sense yet of his main character or how to develop one—how to work from the inside and invent a character's history, feelings, and reactions. To compound his problems, he chose, as the setting of his story, the Pacific Coast of Florida. Jason read his lead to me:

"Hey, Dad, when are we going to catch a big one?" Jack said sarcastically.
"I think they're farther off shore. I should have gotten some gas at South Miami while I was waiting for you," his dad replied.

The boat's gas was indeed running low, but they figured they had enough gas to get back, so they headed out.

"Okay this is far enough; let's throw out the lines," his dad said.

Shortly after Jack was not paying much attention to his rod, but it started to bend slowly up and down; then the line grew taut and yanked hard.

"Jack! You got a fish! Reel it in, reel it in," Jack's dad was screaming.

"I can't. It's too hard, it's a big one," Jack said.

I considered how to respond: Ask the dozens of questions Jason hadn't asked himself yet about Jack as a character? Try to salvage the lead by helping Jason embed information in it about Jack? Ask him to try one or two new leads?

I also considered Jason. I had learned he learned best when I showed him how to do something: when I paragraphed my writing in front of him in demonstration lessons on overhead transparencies, when I used scissors and tape to cut and paste a new section he had drafted into one of his memoirs, when I reconfigured one of his poems for him so that was a poem with lines and stanzas, not a prose paragraph. I decided to try a demonstration.

I found a fresh sheet of paper and asked Jason questions about Jack and his family. He talked about how old Jack was, his family, his relationship with his father. I wrote. I kept Jason's first sentence, then slowed down the pace to reveal specifics about Jack. I also asked Jason to set the story in a real place; he chose Maine's Monhegan Island.

"Hey, Dad, when are we going to catch a big one?" Jack said sarcastically.

"I think they're farther out," his dad replied. He looked worried.

"What's wrong?" Jack wondered.

"I think I should have gotten more gas while I was waiting for you," his dad answered. "We're running low."

Dad didn't usually worry about things like that. Now Jack was worried, too. They were out past Monhegan Island—at least an hour past—and this was no place to be running low on fuel.

Jack tried to push the bad thoughts away. He loved to go fishing with his dad, just the two of them without Wendy and Mom tagging along. Last year, when Jack had turned twelve, his dad had bought him a Mitchell rod, a really good one. Jack knew that meant his dad saw him as more of a grown-up and a real fisherman and less of a little kid along for the ride.

As I wrote I paused to push, listen, and make suggestions. After a page I said, "You have a character going here, a boy who has feelings, family, the details of a life. Take it away." Jason did. He continued onto the next page on his own.

> Now he was feeling impatient to catch a fish.
>
> "Dad, can we try the cove over there? There's not any fish here," Jack said while pointing toward the cove.
>
> "I don't know. We should be heading back," Jack's dad replied.
>
> "Oh, come on . . . please?" Jack begged.
>
> "I guess so, but only for a little while."
>
> Jack figured he had about twenty minutes of fishing left at the most, because it was getting dark and they still had to get back.
>
> "Well, let's start fishing."
>
> They pulled into the cove and threw out the lines. Just then the boat started slowing down, until they were drifting.
>
> "Hey, Dad, why are you slowing down? You're going to get the lines tangled," Jack said.
>
> "I'm not. I think we're out of gas!" Jack's father said.
>
> They were drifting. Jack could see the worry come back on his dad's face. He felt angry with himself for not going back in when his father had warned him. He also felt hopeless. All they could do now was wait for a boat to come by. Mom would tell the Coast Guard and put the word out. Or would she?

Jason's character had an inner life—reasons for acting and feeling as he does. And Jason had momentum. We picked up speed together; then I handed over the wheel so he could drive his vehicle by himself.

My students understand that I'll be active in our conferences about their writing. They know I'll help in any way I can and, afterward, that it's likely they'll be able to structure their writing for themselves. And they know that I do it, too—that I experiment, think and rethink my writing, and find my own purposes as a writer.

Intervention in students' writing—the collaboration and handover I've described here—are conference strategies for *after* the first weeks of school, when students are getting their bearings and learning to take initiative and I'm focusing on who they are as people and writers. Even then, handover works only because I write, because the teacher's interventions are perceived as valid and trustworthy. When I write and keep in touch with each writer's intentions, my responses to my kids can show them what they need to know. I can pay them the ultimate compliment of sitting side by side with them and teaching them what I have learned about composing a life.

Having a Writing Conference with Yourself

One morning in writing workshop I watched Jake. He wrote furiously for a half hour, put down his pen, picked up his draft, jumped up from his desk, and asked Brendan to respond to his writing in a peer conference. When I watched more closely, I observed the same sequence of events with other students. I was worried.

Writers were bypassing their most important readers: themselves. They weren't internalizing standards for effective writing, because they depended on other people to identify and solve the problems in their writing. And they weren't discovering the integral role of reading in writing.

Experienced writers spend at least as much time reading and rereading their texts as they do writing them. We cast an eye back over the writing to tinker, make adjustments, build patterns, extend arguments, find the holes in arguments, fix redundancies, clear up confusions, resolve contradictions, become more interesting, add specifics, untangle sentences, play with punctuation, pick up momentum, get distance, try to act as an objective "other," see if the writing hangs together and makes sense, grasp hold again of the big picture, and attempt to get back on the track where we want our writing to ride.

I wrote "Having a Writing Conference with Yourself" as a guide for my students, with their input. We based it on the questions I ask them in conferences and they ask each other; I also included questions I address when I read drafts of my own prose. The focus is on making decisions—about purpose, meaning, information, leads, conclusions, titles, language and stylistic considerations—and on acting deliberately, to write literature.

Each student receives a copy of the questions and attaches it inside his or her daily writing folder. In a series of minilessons I talk about the questions in three chunks: purpose and information; leads, conclusions, and titles; and style. At the end of each minilesson I ask students to highlight the questions they know represent problems in their writing—the questions they need to pay particular attention to as they read their writing to themselves. Handing kids the list and suggesting they ask every question every time they write would overwhelm them, and it would defeat the purpose. I want discriminating writers whose active readings of their own writing become a foundation for decisions they make in their drafts and in the nature of help they ask of others in conferences.

HAVING A WRITING CONFERENCE WITH YOURSELF

Read your writing to yourself, as you write and after you've written. The best writers spend a lot of time reading over and thinking about what they've written so far and considering where they might go next. They also let their writing "cool down": they come back to a text after a hiatus, read it with fresh eyes, and consider it from the perspective of a new day.

Your job, as a responder to your own writing, is to make decisions about what's on the paper: the weaknesses—parts that need more work or could be cut—and the strengths—parts that work so well you want to build on them.

A writer's basic questions are always, "What is it I'm trying to say here? *Why* am I writing this?" The particular questions below may help you find and shape your purposes as a writer.

QUESTIONS ABOUT PURPOSE

- Does the writing answer the question, "So what?"
- Do I have a big idea? Do I have enough specifics to support this theme, argument, or purpose?
- Is the writing honest?
- Will it make a reader think and feel?
- Do I know what I'm talking about?
- Will readers relate to the writing so strongly that I hold their attention the whole time?

QUESTIONS ABOUT INFORMATION

Is my information sufficient? Is it accurate?

- Have I told enough? Have I explained each part well enough that a reader will know what I mean, every step of the way?
- What's the strongest, most satisfying part, and how can I build on it?
- Have I described thoughts and feelings at the points where readers will wonder what I am, or what my main character is, thinking and feeling?
- Have I embedded the context: told where, when, how, what, and with whom?
- Have I described the scene with enough detail that a reader can see it happening—can envision people in action?
- Did people talk? Have I directly quoted the words they said? Does it sound the way these people would speak to each other? Can a reader hear what they're like?
- Have I created questions in a reader's mind about where the writing will lead?
- Have I included specifics that reveal my character, myself, my subject, or my argument?

- Is the pace too fast to hold someone's interest or convince a reader? Do I need to slow down and expand on any part?
- Is the writing plausible, or *believable*? Are the reasons for actions and reactions clear and compelling?
- Is the writing *true* in terms of history, science, mathematics, geography, contemporary social issues, etc.? Have I done the research that gives credence to what I'm saying?
- Is my information in the best order?

Do I have too much information?
- What parts aren't needed—don't add to my point, theme, character, or plot? Can I delete them?
- What is this piece of writing really about? Are there parts that are about something else? Can I cut them?
- Which is the one best example or illustration?
- Are there redundancies? Can I figure out the best way to say it *once*?
- Have I contradicted myself anywhere?
- Are there any places where the pace bogs down? Can I delete and compress information and speed things up?
- Is there too much conversation? Too many details? Too much description? Have I explained something too thoroughly?
- Is this a "bed-to-bed" memoir that describes every single event of one day? Can I focus on the important part of the experience and delete the rest?
- Have I cut to the chase?

QUESTIONS ABOUT LEADS

- Does the lead engage readers and bring them right into the theme, purpose, tone, action, or the mind of the main character?
- Does the lead give direction to the rest of the writing?
- Does the lead set the tone or create the first impression I want for my readers?
- Where does the piece really begin? Can I cut the first paragraph? The first two? The first page?

QUESTIONS ABOUT CONCLUSIONS

- How do I want my reader to feel and think at the end? Will this conclusion do it?
- Does my conclusion drop off and leave my reader wondering or confused?
- Does my conclusion feel tacked on?
- Does my conclusion go on and on?

- Does my conclusion give readers a sense of closure but also invite them to want to read this writing again?

QUESTIONS ABOUT TITLES

- Does the title fit the big idea of what the writing is about?
- Is the title a "grabber?" Would it make a reader want to read my writing? (Or is it merely a description of the topic?)
- Does the title give a hint or taste of the topic?
- Is the title memorable?

QUESTIONS ABOUT STYLE

- Is the imagery concrete? Can a reader see, hear, feel, smell, taste this?
- Is my choice of words simple, clear, and direct?
- Have I cluttered my writing with unnecessary adjectives and adverbs?
- Have I used strong, precise verbs?
- Have I used any of Macrorie's Bad Words (*really*, *very*, *so*, *all*)?
- Have I used any word(s) too often, especially in contiguous sentences?
- Are my sentences clear, direct, and to the point?
- Are my sentences active: *I did this*, not *It was done*?
- Are any sentences too long and tangled? Too brief and choppy?
- Have I used punctuation (: ; — . . .) that will give voice and meaning to my writing?
- Have I paragraphed often enough to give a reader's eyes some breaks?
- Have I broken the flow of my piece by paragraphing too often?
- Have I grouped together ideas related to each other?
- Is my information in order? Is this a logical sequence? Have I provided transitions for the reader from one idea to the next?
- Is there a voice, an actor?
- Does the voice stay the same—first-person participant (I did it) or third-person observer (he or she did it)?
- Does the verb tense stay the same—present (it's happening now or in general) or past (it happened before)?
- Does the writing sound like literature—does it flow—when I read it aloud to myself?

Conferences About Conventions

Charles Cooper wrote, "It's easier to persist with commas if you know you're engaged in some fundamentally important human activity that has very great consequences for your full development as a human being" (1984). It's my favorite quote about editorial issues, funny and true.

When students believe that what they have to say is important, both within their lives and beyond them, they care about how their words go down on the page. From our conversations in conferences and mini-lessons, my kids understand how conventionality contributes to a reader's appreciation of text. I think teachers do students a disservice if we represent reader response as an either/or proposition—that it's either "creativity" or correctness that makes a piece of writing good. Readers respond to both. If we teach simplistic formulas for good writing, we leave our students open to a reader's disdain or, worse, indifference. Other than a teacher, who is paid to do it, who would read an illegible or unpunctuated text? And what reader would read, very far anyway, a conventionally perfect text that says nothing? When teachers emphasize either creative writing or basic skills, we bypass a writer's sophisticated reasons for composing texts and a reader's equally sophisticated expectations of texts. Our job is to help students understand that content, craft, and conventions all matter. It's their job to make good decisions about what's appropriate, effective, and correct.

I ask my students to write as correctly as they can right from the start: to use what they know whenever they draft. An unfortunate legacy of the early days of writing workshop is the notion of "sloppy copies," a method that encouraged kids to ignore conventions when drafting and concentrate on content. Having edited—or tried to—enough sloppy copies for one lifetime, and having corrected the same errors time and again, I have learned to put conventions in perspective: it is reasonable and realistic for student writers to attend as they compose, to develop the habits of real writers. Adults do not go back when we've finished drafting and put in the periods; adults do use what we know of conventions to give our drafts voice and meaning. For example, marks like the colon, dash, double dash, and semicolon comprise a significant part of my drafting repertoire.

This doesn't mean that I don't edit and proofread myself at the end. When I'm as satisfied as I'm going to be with a text, I focus finally and formally on the issues that need my attention at this juncture, before a reader lays eyes on the product: spelling, sentence structure, punctuation, paragraph breaks and length, redundancies, verbs and tense, unnecessary modifiers, line and stanza breaks, active constructions, use/overuse of contractions, pronoun case, pronoun referents, commas to set off dependent clauses, correct placement of apostrophes on singular and plural possessives, and on and on. I ask my students to do the same: to become conscious of the conventions each of them needs to focus on and to attend to the errors and awkwardness that will distract their readers and interfere with meaning.

Students edit in a pen or pencil different in color from the text, to show what they know and can find on their own, before they submit writing to me for final copyediting. Because I want editing to be conscious and deliberate, I ask each writer to list the conventions he or she will focus on. Figure 7-1 shows an editing checksheet: a cover sheet that each writer completes before self-editing, then attaches to the edited copy before submitting it to me.

Laurel's individual proofreading list, which is attached inside her daily writing folder, is the source of the conventions she listed on her editing checksheet. Each time I copyedit a piece of student writing, I select between one and three conventions that the writer doesn't understand yet, and I note them in the last column of the editing checksheet. The next day, when I return the writing to the writer so he or she may make a final copy, I confer about these conventions; then the student adds them to his or her individual proofreading list. Figure 7-2 shows a seventh grader's proofreading list by the end of seventh grade. These are the conventions I taught Mike—one, two, or three at a time—in our editing conferences from September through June.

I teach no more than two conventions in a conference because I've learned that this is the most my students can digest. If there are ten kinds of errors in a piece of writing and I teach about all of them at once, chances are slim that the writer will understand or remember any of them. But when I teach about a couple of errors, marks, or rules at a time, a student builds understandings, and there's a pretty good chance that the new conventions will be retained and applied in future pieces of writing.

My copyediting is *editing* in the strict sense of the word: I mark up the text. In a third color of ink I correct or indicate every error I can identify. Figure 7-3 shows an example of an edited text. Here I'm giving Catharine what she asked me for—my expertise about conventions—so she may ready the writing for her readers' eyes and expectations. Because I'm marking up a paper the writer has already marked, there aren't any of the heartaches that students once associated with a teacher's red pen. As copy editor, I'm one of the last stops on a writer's way to an audience he or she cares about and wants to affect. My kids are counting on me—just as I'm counting on my copy editor at Heinemann to save me from embarrassment and make sure my ideas have the best possible presentation.

In the past I kept records of the conventions I taught each writer: after

FIGURE 7-1   Sample Editing Checksheet

Nancie Atwell
Center for Teaching and Learning

EDITING CHECKSHEET

TO BE PAPER CLIPPED TO THE TOP OF YOUR WRITING SUBMITTED FOR TEACHER EDITING

NAME   Laurel

TITLE OF PIECE   Follow Your Heart

DATE OF PIECE   1/2

CONVENTIONS	EDITED (√)	PEER EDITED (if you'd like) by Martha	TEACHER'S COMMENTS
Capitalize the first, last, and important words in title.	√	√	• When the words of a song or poem won't fit on a line, go down to the next line and indent the leftovers.
Circle every word you're not absolutely sure of.	√	√	
Use ‿ to join compound words	√	√	• Keep a consistent voice: I or he/she or (as here) you.
Use an apostrophe to show possession.	√	√	
The words between periods need to be able to stand alone.	√	✓	
Avoid exclamation points (except in dialogue).	√	√	
Apostrophes show missing letters.	√	√	WORDS TO ADD TO MY PERSONAL SPELLING LIST
Punctuate a song or poem like in a sentence — no extra commas.	√	✓	
An elipsis shows a long pause; it consists of just 3 dots.	√	√	• unusual • pressure

FIGURE 7-2 A Student's Individual Proofreading List

Mike's _____ 's Proofreading List

1. Circle every word you're not sure of and look it up.

2. Capitalize first, last, and important words in a title.

3. In a poem, let the line breaks and stanza breaks do the work of punctuation wherever possible.

4. Put a comma between a weak ~~interjection~~ exclamation or interjection and the rest of the sentence.

5. Must have punctuation between a quote and its explanatory phrase: , or ? or !

6. No abbreviations in the heading of a letter. A colon after the greeting of a business letter.

7. Never start a sentence with a numeral: Ten percent of kids, not 10% of kids.

8. Write out numbers of fewer than three words as words: ten, thirty-four, 306.

9. A list takes commas to separate the items: small, stylish, gray bird.

10. When a one-syl. word ends with a vowel-cons, double the consonant before adding a suffix: stop + stopped.

11. Use a dash to show an abrupt change or interruption.

12. Watch pronoun case on compound subjects: Alex and I or Alex and me. Test for which one.

13. Keep verb tense consistent: past or present.

14. Watch for comma splices. Put ; or and or start a new sentence.

FIGURE 7-3   Example of a Student Text After Self- and Teacher-Editing

to my desk and finish my homework, then ∅ get dressed
and sit down on the corner of my bed, wondering if
yesterday was a dream. Just to make sure ~~that yesterday~~ it
was real, I ~~go and~~ pull open the draw(er) of Jannie's desk.
Everything is still there, just ~~like~~ as it was yesterday.   I
look over at Jannie, still sleeping, as I ~~shut~~ shut the draw(er). She
looks perfectly normal, ~~there.~~   I tiptoe downstairs and
get some breakfast. It is only 7:00, which is pretty
early to be up on a Saturday morning.

   After a (wile) I go back upstairs, get out my book, and
start to read. About an hour later Jannie wakes up, tumbles out of bed,
starts to ~~go~~ head downstairs.

∅→ "Wait!" I ~~say~~ Say
∅→ "What?" she asks as she turns around.
   "I need to talk to you," I reply. "Yesterday," I began.
∅ "What's up?" Sue questions.
   "I was upstairs trying to do my homework, but I couldn't
find a pencil anywhere, so I looked in your desk. I
found one...but... How am I (souposed) to tell her this, I
wonder? And I almost tell her nothing, and ~~let her~~ try to
forget about it, But then I (realise) that ~~I will~~ I'll have to

---

I edited and noted on the editing checksheet the lessons I would teach in a
conference the next day, I also listed the conventions in my editing journals, which were three-ring binders with several pages for each student. After a couple of years, the duplication of effort wore me out. Since students
record on their individual proofreading lists the conventions teach them,
the proofreading lists can serve as a record for both of us. Students use their
proofreading lists when they self-edit by copying down the relevant con-

ventions onto an editing checksheet. At the end of each trimester they photocopy their proofreading lists, for us to use in evaluation. When I report to parents that I teach skills in the context of pieces of writing, I show them what this means. The proofreading lists demonstrate exactly what their children are learning about conventions over the weeks and months of a writing workshop.

The editorial issues I address in conferences run the gamut, from syntax to usage to spelling, punctuation, capitalization, word choice, format, and style. There isn't one set of conventions, no skills scope and sequence. There are individual writers with varying degrees of understanding. By teaching in context and one to one, I can go right to the heart of what an individual writer needs to know. It is surprisingly easy to make such judgments. As a reader I have expectations, and the ways a writer eases my way, or disconcerts me, jump off the page when I edit. Below I've listed conventions of texts that I've taught my students in conferences about editorial issues.

CONVENTIONS TAUGHT IN EDITING CONFERENCES
(TAKEN FROM STUDENTS' INDIVIDUAL PROOFREADING LISTS)

- Edit in a pen or pencil that's a different color from my piece, so I can show Ms. A. and myself what I found.
- Write on one side of the paper only, so I can cut and tape and use arrows to go onto the back of the page.
- Skip lines or type double-spaced, so I have room to revise and polish.
- Keep two left-hand margins on my prose pieces, one for regular lines and one for indents.
- Draft in paragraphs.
- Use the symbol ¶ to indicate where I think I need new paragraphs.
- Watch for paragraphs that are too long. Give readers more breaks and breathing space.
- Watch for too-short, choppy paragraphs: combine these.
- Use short (1–2 sentence) paragraphs to punch a point, idea, or turn of events.
- Circle every word I'm not absolutely sure of, then go back and look up its spelling.
- Write numbers of fewer than three words as words: e.g., one, twenty-six, 160.

- Never start a sentence with a numeral: *Ten percent of kids*, not *10 percent of kids*.
- Don't abbreviate in prose, except for the permissable words we listed in our handbooks.
- All right = two words. A lot = two words.
- Put capital letters at the beginnings of sentences.
- Capitalize *Mom* and *Dad* when they're names, but not when they're labels (*I asked Mom for a ride*, vs. *I asked my mom for a ride*).
- Capitalize names of countries and monuments.
- Put capital letters on the first, last, and important words in a title.
- Use *an* (not *a*) before nouns, adjectives, and adverbs that begin with vowels.
- Use brackets when I need parentheses within parentheses: ([ ]).
- Avoid parentheses in narratives.
- When I have to split words between lines, split them between syllables. See a dictionary to find out where a word splits.
- Never split a one-syllable word.
- Keep the voice of my narratives consistent: either *he/she* or *I*.
- Keep my pronouns clear so readers can tell who *he*, *she*, *we*, or *they* refers to.
- Keep my verb tense consistent: either *past* (it happened before) or *present* (it's happening now, or in general).
- Use _____ and *I* as a sentence subject (not _____ and *me*).
- Read my pieces softly to myself and put periods where I hear my voice drop and stop.
- Proofread softly to myself out loud and listen for missing words and missing sounds at the ends of words.
- Watch for comma splices, because a comma isn't strong enough to hold two sentences together. Use a period or semicolon, or insert *and* after the comma.
- Use a semicolon between two sentences where I want to show a relationship.
- Use apostrophe *s* to show something belongs to someone.
- Use an apostrophe to show a letter is missing: *let's*; *that's*; *don't*.
- Use ellipses to indicate a long, dramatic pause; an ellipsis is just three dots.
- To achieve a dash on the computer, hit *hyphen + option + shift*.
- Use a colon to show a list is coming.
- Use a colon to show an explanation is coming.

- Experiment with — and **:** to give my writing voice and power.
- On a list, put commas between items and use the serial or Harvard comma before the final *and*.
- Separate mild interjections from the rest of the sentence with a comma: *Wow, that's cool. Hi, how are you?*
- Separate vocatives from the rest of the sentence with a comma: *I told you, Mom, I'm coming. Ethan, wait for me.*
- Use a comma between two independent clauses joined by *and, or, but, nor, so,* or *because.*
- You're = you are. Your = belongs to you.
- It's = it is. Its = belongs to an it.
- There = a place or a sentence starter; their = belongs to them; they're = they are.
- Then = time; than = comparison.
- In a rhymed poem, the rhyming words go at the ends of lines.
- In a rhymed poem, keep one left-hand margin and no indents, except for run-overs that won't fit on the line where I want them: indent these.
- Use line breaks and white space to help punctuate a poem.
- Punctuate a song or poem as prose: no extra commas/comma at the end of each line.
- Use a deliberate, consistent format in an open-form poem, e.g., capitals and punctuation or no capitals and punctuation.
- Delete excess words in open-form poems: cut to the bone, until I can't cut another word.
- Put a comma after the closing of a letter: *Sincerely,*
- If the closing of a letter is more than one word, capitalize the first word only: *Your friend,*
- Don't indent the greeting of a letter.
- On every letter I write, use the same heading:
    my street address
    my town, state, and zip
    today's date
- On a business letter, include an inside address: the recipient's name, title, and address.
- Don't use abbreviations in the heading or inside address of a letter.
- On a business letter, put a colon after the greeting and print my name under my signature.
- Put quotation marks around the words people say out loud.

- When the *he said* or explanatory phrase comes after the quote, separate it with a comma, exclamation point, or question mark, never a period.
- When the explanatory phrase comes before the quote, it's followed by a comma.
- Unless the explanatory phrase begins the sentence, it's lower case: *"Okay," he said*.
- A quote and its explanatory phrase usually belong in the same paragraph.
- Start a new paragraph every time the speaker changes when writing dialogue.
- Use single quotes when quoting inside a quote.
- When proofreading, listen for too many *ands*.
- Proofread for the bad words: *really, very, so, a lot, just, sort of, kind of, little, big, all*.
- Avoid exclamation points except in dialogue. Let my choice of verbs and my sentence structure convey the excitement.
- People *lie down*; people *lay* things *down*.
- Check if I have the correct preposition (*in, for, from, about, of, to,* etc.) for the idiom I'm using.
- Avoid *you* unless I mean *you*.
- Watch for overuse of forms of *to be* (*were, was, is,* etc.) and strive for active verbs.
- Make sure my sentences have actors: *I did it* vs. *This was done by me*.
- Use a thesaurus to help find strong verbs.
- Avoid overuse of the thesaurus: keep my voice in the writing.
- Listen for redundancy: when I use a word more than once in close proximity.

Since I began teaching about conventions in the context of pieces of kids' writing, not only are students more correct and versatile, but I've become more knowledgeable about how conventions work. Because kids need rules and marks explained in terms of function, I have to understand how they work. So rather than parrot *Warriner's* rules about punctuation, I show my students why the different marks were invented—most often to cue readers about what to expect or what to do with their voices—and how different marks achieve their effects. Instead of reciting *Warriner's* seven models of paragraph formation—models seldom found in the real world of published prose—I explain how paragraphs were developed to give readers breaks. I show how the paragraph symbol was inserted in early illuminated texts, before indentation became a convention, to make breaks for readers and signal new themes or information, and I ask writers of unparagraphed drafts to decide where to break their prose so it's easier for a reader to take it in. The conference transcripts below illustrate ways of approaching basic conventions—end-stop punctuation, legibility, and paragraphing of dialogue in narratives—from the perspective of function.

Ms. A.: Sandi, there was one big problem I noticed last night when I edited this memoir; it had to do with periods and other end-stops. Can you tell me what a period does?

Sandi: It comes at the end of a complete sentence.

A: How can you tell if something is a complete sentence?

S: If you have a complete subject and a complete predicate.

A: Right. So . . . what does that mean?

S: (long pause) I'm not sure. It's a rule we learned in sixth grade.

A: Well, let's take a look at "Body in Gull Lake" and see if you can learn a convention you can apply. Punctuation shows people how to read a piece of writing—what to do with their voices. A period usually shows a reader where to drop and stop her voice. Do me a favor. Read this paragraph softly aloud and listen: Where does your voice drop and stop?

(Sandi reads.)

A: Can you hear the periods?

S: Yeah. I see what you mean.

A: Without periods what you have is a problem known as *run-on sentences*. Your reader's voice runs on and on. Periods are probably the single most important punctuation mark, because they signal the stops. Would you add this convention to your proofreading list, that from now on you'll proofread softly to yourself and make sure you've put periods where your voice drops and stops?

S: Sure.

Ms. A.: I had major difficulty editing this for you, Brian. Your handwriting had me stumped. It took me about three times as long to edit as the other drafts I read last night because I couldn't make out the words.

Brian: Everybody else can read my writing.

A: So I'm the first reader who's ever complained?

B: Yeah.

A: Well, let me tell you exactly what happened when I read this. The letters are so small I had to squint to see them. The *ms* and *ns* are written exactly alike, so I couldn't tell which is which. The letters with closed circles, like *o*, *a*, *d*, and *b*, weren't closed, so I couldn't figure out which letter you meant a lot of the time. All in all, I almost missed a great story because your cursive got in my way. Do you have any idea what you could do about this, so other readers won't be turned off and pass by what you have to say?

B: I could write neater.

A: Um-hmm.

B: Take my time.

A: You could. Can I suggest another alternative?

B: What?

A: Well, rather than retooling your cursive, which would take a tremendous amount of practice and steal time from your *writing* writing, why don't you print? How's your printing?

B: I think it's pretty good. But we're not supposed to print in school.

A: That's not a rule in my class. Let's face it. After all the time you spent on cursive in third and fourth grades, by the time you get to high school and college your teachers won't care whether you print or use cursive, just as long as they can read what you've written. The only thing you need cursive for is your signature. Would you be willing to print and see how it goes?

B: I guess so.

A: How are you going to add that to your proofreading list?

B: I'll say something like, "Print so other people can read what I've written."

A: Sounds good.

Ms. A.: I noticed you did an effective job here of using quotation marks around the words people said aloud. Every time someone speaks, you've indicated it's a direct quote by putting marks where they begin and marks where they stop.

Timmy: I finally got the hang of that.

A: Let me show you something else about writing dialogue. In this part, who's talking here, in this sentence?

T: Um . . . I am.

A: And who's talking here, in the next sentence?

T: David.

A: Besides starting a new set of quotation marks, do you know how writers usually show readers that one person has stopped talking and another has started?

T: Uh-uh.

A: Writers start new paragraphs whenever the speaker changes. That way readers have an easier time following the conversation. It's a way of signaling readers that one person has stopped talking and now another's about to start. You go down to the next line and indent each time there's a change.

T: And you leave all this space blank?

A: Right.

T: Doesn't that waste a lot of paper?

A: Well, I don't think it's a waste if it helps a reader. What book are you reading these days?

T: *Where the Red Fern Grows.*

A: May I see it? . . . Look, Rawls does here what I was talking about. See? The boy and his grandfather are talking, and as they converse back and forth each gets his own paragraph.

T: I never noticed that before.

A: It's probably one of those conventions that you never took particular notice of. It's always been there, helping you follow the story. So, could you add "new paragraphs when the speaker changes" as a convention on your proofreading list?

T: Okay.

For most teachers—and certainly it was true for me—conferences with individuals about works-in-progress are such a radical departure from what we used to do as English teachers that it takes a long time to get a sense of how they work, for us and for our kids. I know this time is worthwhile. Writing conferences work; they work for a lifetime of teaching; and their quality and effectiveness only improve with experience. Conferences don't require fancy equipment or expensive consumables. They demand teachers who care about kids and good writing, who make it our business to write and to read about writing. They call for teachers who know something worth saying after we sit down next to our kids and ask, "How can I help you?"

8

Responding to Readers and Reading

> Literature is no one's private ground, literature is common ground; let us trespass freely and fearlessly and find our own way for ourselves.
> *Virginia Woolf*

Dear Ms. A.,

I have a lot of poetry books now that I'm going to try this weekend. I'll definitely mark the poems that speak to me so I can photocopy them for you. One poem that I think we should read in class is "Bummer" by Michael Casey. I love that poem; it's one of my most favorites. I'm not sure why, but it definitely gives me goose bumps each time I read it, especially the last two lines.

In Cold Blood is good so far. I like how Truman Capote switches back and forth from chapter to chapter with different people's points of view. The first chapter was the hardest for me to get into because of all the description. But in a way that's good because the setting is pretty important to the story.

What genre is this anyway?

Love,
Martha

Dear Martha,

In Cold Blood is a nonfiction genre called *new journalism*. It's a famous book—a groundbreaker—because of the multiperspectives and imagination Capote brought to the narrative. The old journalism is just-the-facts, ma'am, and Capote broke the rules. *In Cold Blood* reads like a novel: the real-life people become characters, and it doesn't pretend to be objective. In its time it was a bold experiment. He blazed the trail for other new journalists like Tom Wolfe (*The Right Stuff*) and Michael Herr (*Dispatches*). Critics are still arguing about the merits of the genre.

When you guys start presenting poems to the group—probably in January—do you want to present "Bummer"?

Love,
Ms. A.

Nearly every day I receive a letter like Martha's—a message that reminds me how glad I am that I teach literature the way I do. Martha's plans for the weekend, her goose bumps over a poem, and her query about a genre demonstrate the involvement and initiative of kids who pursue their own interests as readers. In my response, I get to think and talk about literature. And I get to learn. Each year of letters about books teaches me about adolescent readers—their needs, concerns, and tastes. I learn the value of inviting kids to read as real readers do, to choose, skim, skip, abandon, reread. I learn about the books they love, the old favorites and the new ones. And I learn how to respond to what readers are trying to do without coming across like a teacher's guide or a test: how I can affirm, challenge, gossip, joke, argue, suggest, recommend, instruct, tell stories, and provide the information a reader needs.

Through our correspondence my students learn, too, about the worlds of writing and literature—what good writers do, what good readers do, how readers of literature think and talk, what books are good for, and how kids can get in on it. One June I asked my students to be specific about their knowledge of literature: to read through the journals and categorize the subjects we corresponded about over the course of the year. They named more than 150 topics related to literature, reading, books, and authors.

KINDS OF TALK ABOUT BOOKS

How the Author Wrote

- Topic: What was his or her subject? Why this topic?
- Plot: What happened; what were the events of the story?
- Pace: How quickly or slowly did the author move the plot? Was it gradual enough to be plausible and involving? Fast enough to hold a reader's interest? Was there too much action and not enough character development?
- Plausibility: Did the plot ring true? Would characters act and react this way? Were the circumstances believable? Did it matter?
- Description and detail: Could we see it happening? Feel it? Hear it? Too little description? Too many details?
- Dialogue: Was the talk realistic? Could we hear the individual characters' voices? Too much dialogue? Too little? What did the dialogue show about the moods, ages, intentions, and backgrounds of the characters?

- Flashbacks, flash-forwards, and foreshadows: How did the author use shifts in time, and why?
- Affect: Did the reader laugh? Cry? Why?
- Setting: What time and place did the author choose? Why? Was the setting integral to the story? Was it convincing? Confusing?
- Main characters: Who were they? What makes a main character a main character? How can a reader tell?
- Character development: How were characters introduced and developed? How were their actions, thoughts, and feelings depicted? Were they believable? Could the reader enter characters' hearts and minds and see through their eyes? Which characters did the reader relate to? Did the reader care about what happened to any of them? Did any of them remind the reader of characters from movies, plays, or other novels? Of people from the reader's real life?
- Titles: Did it fit? Was it a grabber? Did it give too much away?
- Theme: What ideas about life and living come through the story?
- Problem: What was the issue for the main character to try to resolve?
- Suspense: Did the reader wonder what would happen next? How did the author establish a suspenseful tone? Did the author surprise the reader?
- Formula: Could the reader predict too easily what was going to happen? Was it too much like other books by this author or from this genre?
- Conventions: Did a reader notice short paragraphs or chapters? Sentence fragments? British spellings? Why did the author write this way?
- Information: Were there enough specifics about character, action, background, and setting? Was there too much information? Irrelevant information?
- Specific information: What did the reader learn about the world—about history, art, politics, science, etc.—through the narrative?
- Length: Was this book too long? Too short?
- Point of view: Who told the story? What voice did the author choose: First person? Third person/anonymous? Single character, dual, multiple, or no character? Why did the author choose this point of view? What were the advantages and drawbacks for the

reader? Where did the reader stand in relation to the narrator?

- Grace of language: Did the sentences flow? Were they choppy? Did the reader savor particular phrases and sentences? Was there figurative language? Was there imagery: did the writing create pictures in the reader's mind? Were there sensory details?
- First sentence: How did the author bring the reader in?
- Lead: How did the author try to keep the reader there?
- Conclusion: How did the author leave a reader? Why this ending?
- Epigraphs and prologues: How were these special introductions used and to what effect?
- Epilogues: How was this special conclusion used and to what effect?
- Unusual or experimental narrative techniques: What did the reader think?
- In-jokes: Did the reader pick up on X?

The Author

- Speculations about, or references to published accounts of, an author's writing processes
- Titles of other books by an author, including sequels, trilogies, and series
- Comparisons with other books by an author
- Comparisons with other authors' styles
- Comparisons with similar books, in terms of topic, genre, or theme, by other authors
- Biographical information about an author or an author's published comments about his or her oeuvre
- Publishing-world gossip about an author
- How authors use elements of their own lives and experiences in their fiction
- Other ways authors might have researched their subjects (for example, reading a particular kind of fiction)
- Finding authors' addresses and initiating correspondence with them
- Published book reviews of an author's latest release
- News of a new release by an author

Concepts of Genre

- What are the elements of fiction?
- Novels: What makes a novel a novel?

- Short stories: What makes a short story a short story?
- Poetry: What makes a poem a poem? In what ways does it differ from prose? What are the elements of poetry? How do different poetic techniques affect a reader?
- Fiction and nonfiction: How do we classify books as one or the other?
- Classification of other books by genre:
  - Adventure/Survival
  - Antiwar
  - Autobiography
  - Biography
  - Classic
  - Contemporary realistic fiction
  - Diary
  - Drama
  - Epistolary novel
  - Family saga
  - History
  - Historical fiction
  - Horror
  - Humor or parody
  - Journalism
  - Legend and myth
  - Memoir
  - Movie/TV tie-in or screenplay
  - Mystery
  - Nature
  - New Age
  - New journalism
  - Romance
  - Science fiction
  - Series novel
  - Sports
  - Supernatural
  - Techno-thriller
  - Urban life
  - War and espionage
  - Western
  - Other kinds of writing one might like to read

The Reader's Strategies

- Choice: How does the reader decide what to read?
- Pace: Did the reader skim, skip, slow down, regress, speed up, look ahead? Why? When? To what effect?
- Abandoning: How and when does the reader make this decision?
- Rereading: Why does the reader reread a book? What differences are noted a second time through?
- Revisiting particular parts of a book: Why does the reader skim back? For pleasure? Clarification?
- Planning: Does the reader anticipate reading a particular book, author, or genre?
- Predicting: Did the reader imagine what would happen next? Was the guess confirmed?
- Revising: Did the reader consider other ways an author might have written?
- Connecting: Did the reader relate a book to another book? To a poem or song? To his or her experiences or feelings?
- Analyzing: What did the reader think the book was about?
- Length of time it took to read a book: Why so long or so quickly?
- Reading rate: How many pages did the reader read in a half hour? How does a reader vary his or her rate depending on the nature of the text?
- Reading "holiday" books: Why do readers need mindless breaks sometimes?
- Difficulty: What makes a book a challenge? What does the reader do when a book is difficult? Too difficult?
- Schema: Did the reader have adequate background experience to understand and appreciate the writing?
- Unknown vocabulary: What did the reader do when he or she came across an unfamiliar word?
- Contentives, eye fixations, and peripheral vision: What did the reader notice his or her eyes doing during reading?
- Rituals: When, how, and where does the reader read? Why?
- How did the reader learn to read?
- Does the reader buy, own, or collect books?

The Reader's Affect

- How did the book make the reader feel?
- What did the book make the reader think about?
- What does a reader think or understand that he or she didn't think or understand before?
- What was the reader's involvement with the characters?
- What did the reader learn about through the story?
- What did the reader like or dislike about a book?
- What were the best and worst features of a book?
- How does the reader rate books?

The Reader's Own Writing

- Comparisons with what the reader is writing and how it's coming
- Connections to ideas to use in current or future pieces of writing
- Ways the reader might use or has used elements of an author's writing in his or her own work
- Connections between an author's style or choice of subjects and the reader's style and writing territories

Recommendations

- Is a book worth recommending?
- Who might enjoy it?
- What reactions did other readers report?
- Who are good authors?
- What are titles of good books?
- What are titles of other good books by this author?
- What titles by other authors address a similar subject or theme?
- How will the reader arrange to borrow, lend, or return books?
- Where can the reader find a particular book in the:

  classroom library
  other classrooms
  other students' private collections
  teacher's private collection
  the town library (and its organization)
  the school library (and its organization)
  local bookstores (and their organization)?

Publishing

- Steps in how a book is published
- What agents do
- How advances and royalties work
- What editors do
- What copy editors do
- First editions
- Remainders
- How and when hardcovers become paperbacks
- Comparisons between movies and the books on which they're based
- Distinctions between screenplays, novelizations, and novels
- Sequels, trilogies, and series
- Format:
  - appropriateness of the jacket copy
  - appropriateness and effectiveness of the cover art or other illustrations
  - about-the-author information
  - copyright page
  - number of printings
  - style of typeface
  - size of type and gutters
  - typos
  - lengths of chapters
  - indexes, tables of contents, and appendixes

The Letter Writer's Style

- When necessary, comments about conventions that affect the readability of the letters:
  - legibility
  - punctuation
  - spelling
  - spacing of words and letters
  - how to indicate titles of books (capitals and an underline) and titles of stories and poems (capitals and quotes)
- When necessary, reminders about content:

- too "book-reportish" or too much recounting of plot: boring if the teacher has read the book and maddening if it's a book the teacher anticipates reading
- too brief to develop a point: a postcard rather than a letter
- confusing: unclear as to the reader's opinion or meaning
- off-topic: treating the letters too much as notes passed in class and not enough as vehicles for thinking and conversing about books, authors, writing, and reading.

Most of my written conversations with students about books are wide-ranging and touch on at least several of these topics. The letters sound like the discourse around my dining room table: chatty, engaged, reflective, and opinionated:

Dear Ms. A.,

I can't wait to read another Elizabeth Berg novel. She is an excellent writer. Is she new or are these old books?

I Am Wings was an awesome book. I like books that are told in poetry form, like *Been to Yesterdays*. That was good also.

Fletcher's *Fig Pudding* was younger than I expected. I don't know what I really expected, but it was different. The ending was weird. They start out with Josh having the fever, so you think he's going to die. Then, *bang!* Brad crashes his bike. Totally unexpectable, don't ya think?

I was thinking, remember all those short stories you read to us early this year? Like "The Metaphor?" I'd like to borrow that book if you still have it. What was the author's name?

Love,
Raye

Dear Raye,

The Budge Wilson collection (she wrote "The Metaphor") is called *The Leaving*. If there isn't a copy on the bookshelves, I'll loan you my PERSONAL, PRIVATE VOLUME. Ooooooo—lucky you.

I just finished a collection of short stories that I borrowed from Erin. There were a half dozen *great* ones. The editor, Don Gallo, asked prominent writers of novels for teenagers to experiment with the short form; then he chose the most successful for inclusion in the collection. Would you like me to ask Erin if I may pass it along to you next?

Elizabeth Berg is a new novelist, first published in 1990. *Durable Goods* is her only kid-as-main-character novel so far, but I've heard rumors of a sequel. *Range of Motion* is about a young wife whose husband is in a coma, and *Talk Before Sleep* is about a long-standing friendship between two women, one of whom is dying of breast cancer. The last is, believe it or not, extremely funny. My friend Maureen Barbieri turned me on to Berg, and I'm forever in her debt: I thought I was too old for a new favorite novelist.

Love,
Ms. A.

Dear Rachel,

Watcha reading? I'm reading *The Gathering* by Isobelle Carmody. Have you read it? I love it. It isn't that fast paced, but there are so many creepy things that tie together in the chapter that follows that you have to read on. You should try it sometime if you haven't read it.

Did you like the Shakespeare read-aloud, *Bard of Avon*? It was okay but a little *too* informational. I will say I learned a lot though.

I loved watching the videos of the plays. My favorite was *Much Ado About Nothing*. I thought it was funny and well written. I noticed that some of the jokes were hard to get unless you thought about them a lot. Hamlet was just too sad and weird for me. I'm glad it ended the way it did, except for the fact that Hamlet died. I did really like him.

Y.F.,
Michael
Maxter
Mic

Dear Maxter,

I just finished Voigt's *Dicey's Song*! I loved it! If you haven't read it, I definitely recommend it. I've decided that the reason I liked it so much is because I liked Dicey so much. At the beginning of the story there were a lot of things I didn't like that she did, but toward the end she changed and opened up more. Also I liked the grandmother a lot. Sort of the same thing that Dicey goes through happens to her. There's so much going on in this novel. The only thing is, a lot of it doesn't get resolved. That's why I want to read the rest of the trilogy.

You finished *The Gathering*, didn't you? If so, did you like it? You should definitely read *Anne Frank*. I brought in my copy, if Izzie and you still need one so you can read it together.

Happy Reading!

Love,
Rachel

Dear Rachel,

I haven't read *Dicey's Song*, but it sounds good. Maybe I'll try it. I did finish Carmody's *The Gathering*. It was *really* good. I loved the characters and how everything fit together at the end. It has a great theme, about peer pressure. Have you read it yet? If not, I think you would like it, even though you don't like mysteries. It's a mix of thriller and mystery, which makes it even better.

Izzie and I are reading *Anne Frank* together. Thank you for bringing that copy of yours in. Well, see ya lata, Alligata!

Love,
Michael

Dear Ms. A.,

I'm having a hard time with *if i should die before i wake* (yes, I did mean to not capitalize that). What I think is happening is that Hillary is the teenager who got in the motorcycle accident and is in a Jewish hospital, in a room with Chana, an old lady who is Jewish. Chana somehow knows that Hillary doesn't like Jews and is trying to show Hillary what it was like to live when Chana was growing up. Is this correct? An author who switches points of view always confuses me.

I don't understand why Hillary can't talk, and why her mother keeps reading from the Bible. Do Hillary and Chana have some kind of mental telepathy thing going?

I also picked up, from Catharine, *The Voice on the Radio*. It's really good. Reeve is still telling Janie's story. I'm glad you bought a copy at that conference where you heard Caroline B. Cooney.

I like how my Empire State Building memoir is going, but I am not quite sure how to end it. I am up to the part when I went down the elevator. I think using *I* instead of *we* or *us* makes it more personal. Thanks.

I am also happy with my memoir/poem about the barn. I really like the ending to it, about the children's eyes.

Sincerely,
Katherine

Dear Miss Katherine,

Hillary is in a coma. Han Nolan combined science fiction and historical fiction so that (yes, you guessed it) Chana is "giving" her experience of the Holocaust to this young neo-Nazi, putting her inside the heart and mind of a Jew in Poland in the 1930s and 40s. It's one of the most powerful books I know about the evils of anti-Semitism, especially because the ending (I won't give it away) is so strong.

I like the poem about the barn, too. The ending gives it a "so what?" Keep this in mind as you shape endings for the E.S.B. memoir: what does it mean to you that you did this? What could it mean to others?

Have you read B. Cooney's other books about Janie? Now, there's an author who gives her readers what they want: *endless* sequels, in case anyone anywhere ever wonders what happens next. I'm not sure how I feel about that. There's something to be said for ambiguity, for asking the reader to chew on the characters at the end of a book—to keep on writing the story in our heads after we turn that last page.

Love,
Ms. A.

Readers often use the letters in their journals to connect the lives of the characters to their own feelings and experiences. I think this empathy is one of the surest signs of a reader's involvement. Jon responded personally and intensely to the loyalty of the roommates in *The Lords of Discipline*.

> Pat Conroy puts four boys in a room, changes them into men, and then pits them against the world. But there is a traitor amongst them, which is a startling blow because there is so much love in that room. That is another thing that I liked. Conroy put an incredible amount of feeling in this book. The roommates love each other an incredible amount. When the main character exposes a secret organization, you have an immense feeling of joy for that character because he succeeded in doing the right thing; he put himself against men in power and he won. I just can't stop thinking about how much love there was floating in that room. It isn't like they are gay, they just care an incredible amount for each other, and Conroy illustrates this excellently. Normally I would have dropped a book like this, but this book has changed my way of thinking. I don't think that one boy caring for another boy is weird now.

Jon's personal connections with books ran the gamut. In the same week he connected fiction and real life as only an eighth grader can.

> I have an uncanny experience to tell you about. I was going up to Sugarloaf/USA and I took *Live and Let Die* with me. I came back on Sunday (I went up on Friday), the book finished. On Sunday, *Live and Let Die* was on ABC-TV!! I really couldn't believe it!!

In their letters students also reflect on themselves as readers. They describe how they learned to read; their reading rituals, strategies, and habits; and their needs and desires in encounters with literature.

> When I read it's a special time for me to be alone. I sit on my bed with a pillow leaning against the wall and another one on my lap so I don't have to hold my arms up. I get completely relaxed. Also, after I finish reading, I just sit for a while thinking about the book. . . . The only thing that bothers me is when I get a phone call or if it's time for dinner and I'm right in the middle of a good book. I try to get the interruption over with so I can get back to reading. How about you?

> Whenever I read a book more than once, and don't like how it ends, I'm always hoping for a different ending. Especially with *No One Here Gets Out Alive*. I think most people do that sometimes without even realizing they're doing it. Not just in books either, but also in dreams and even real life.

Right now I've really changed my reading rate. I started out mostly skimming Clancy, and on the good parts slowed down to normal speed. But I think now I've moved to "savor" speed, especially on the good parts. These seem to be happening all the time now—the good parts, I mean. I really hate the end of a book that is good. Except it means you can read it all over again.

While I was reading *About David*, I could imagine what David looked like. I could picture the town, the houses, the school, everything. Like in *The Language of Goldfish*, at the end the author lets you think about what is going to happen. I like that, it makes me part of the book. You have to let the reader do some of the writing. Let them be a part of the book they're reading. That way they will like the book more.

In their letters students frequently critique the writing they're reading. As authors themselves they have something to say about the choices other authors have made. These excerpts, which touch on plausibility, titles, character development, style, and format, show readers' emerging criteria for good writing:

I think that some of Auel's situations were a bit silly. One thing that bugged me was how Ayla discovered things, like building a fire with flint, riding Whinney, etc. You could predict exactly what she was going to do next. When she gets on Whinney, you know that's going to lead to riding her, then using her to chase animals, then to hunt. Auel makes it too obvious.

I just finished the sequel to *The Cat Ate My Gymsuit*, you know, *There's a Bat in Bunk Five*. I think the titles of both of these books were stupid. They have nothing to do with the major plot, and I was sort of lost by how the title and story differed. I don't think Danziger wanted me to spend time being confused by that.

I finished *Dead Poet's Society* yesterday. I think it was okay considering it was based on a movie. If I had written it I would have picked a main character though. That way the book would have had some thoughts and feelings. I think that would have helped a lot when Neil committed suicide. If I could pick a character to go inside, I would have picked Todd because he's so quiet and to himself and you're always wondering what's going through his head.

I love the way King puts thoughts in italics and parentheses and sometimes runs all the thoughts together into one sentence. It gives you a feeling of what's running through a person's mind. Have you noticed him doing this?

I like your copy of *Macbeth* a lot better than the library's. The synopsis in the front helps a lot, and the type is easier to read. I can really get the gist of the line lengths and poetry quality with the larger book. In the smaller one it did things like:

> Double, double, toil and
> > [trouble]

and that was confusing.

The letters that compare books and authors or discover connections among them are among the most exciting for me to read, since here my students are bringing their literary experience to bear on the act of reading.

I just finished *I Am the Cheese*. I liked it but it was weird. I still don't quite get it. I think I'll keep it over the vacation and reread at least the ending, if not the whole thing. Reading Cormier was a lot different than Eddings and better I think. Eddings weaves a good story, but it is all straightforward with almost no thinking involved. Whereas Cormier wove an interesting story but it was harder to decipher. I had fun reading Cormier. I think having to think made it a better book.

I finished *Yellow Raft in Blue Water* by Michael Dorris. I really, really liked it. At first I wasn't sure if I was going to like the mother and grandmother parts, because I thought that they were going to be about their present lives as adult women. I was glad when they were about their teenage years too. I loved how everything came together at the end, like in *Walk Two Moons*. There were a lot of connections between the three generations. And I liked where it ended—not too soon, and not too late.

I started the new O'Brien, *If I Die in a Combat Zone*. It is written somewhat the same way as *The Things They Carried*, but it is more of a narrative. It doesn't have the abstract connection between chapters; it goes on an event-to-event basis so it is a lot easier to read. It is also nonfiction, so there are none of his "writings" that you don't find out are "writings" until after. That drove me crazy reading *The Things They Carried*. I'm used to a plot line and it didn't really have one. He wrote short pieces of fiction inside a story; it really broke all the ground rules I'm used to in writing. I definitely think I should have read *If I Die in a Combat Zone* first to get used to O'Brien's style.

I think people are wrong when they say all books are better than the movies they're made into. I have read a couple of books where they've stunk. For example, *My Posse Don't Do Homework* wasn't as good as the movie *Dangerous Minds*. (I saw that today: really good.) I think the reason I didn't like *My Posse Don't Do Homework* was because each

chapter was about a different student and they weren't really connected. But the movie script gives you a main character to be with.

References to themes, and connections among books by theme, are an important sign of literary maturity. After living the novel, students step outside of it and ponder its big ideas.

> I really loved *Johnny Got His Gun* by Dalton Trumbo. It was one of the most powerful books I've ever read. There was this one part that really spoke to me. It happened to be marked in this copy, so it must have spoken to someone else, too. If I ever knew anyone who was really for war, I would make them read this novel and then see how they felt about war.
>
> When I read the book I kept thinking about one of my favorite poems, "Bummer" by Michael Casey. Didn't you say that he wrote a whole book of poetry about Vietnam? If he did, I would really like to read it.
>
> This may sound strange, but when I was reading *Johnny Got His Gun*, it seemed to remind me of "Flowers for Algernon." Probably because both stories were mostly opinions of one person, and both authors had very strong themes that they tried to get across (which I think they did). And there also seemed to be a lot of strong emotion in both—anger and sadness, and most important they both felt helpless in the end. They both made me cry in parts, especially at the end, and want to do something to help.

The book *The Ancient One* was written to make you want to stop defor-
estation. The writer wrote to make your heartstrings stretch at the situation of reckless foresting. It is about a twelve-year-old girl who is
invited to her aunt's house. The aunt is trying to save a mystical redwood forest from reckless loggers. The girl and the aunt try to stop
them, and in the process the girl is sent back in time with a magical
staff to save the forest from a similar ordeal by an ancient redwood. I
cried because the redwood was cut down in the end. It was wonderful
to read a novel with an ecology theme.

Kids also use their letters to identify books by genre and to consider
their favorite genres. Michael discovered diaries.

It Happened to Nancy is so good. I could hardly put it down last night
and today. You could tell that "Collin" was such a bad character. It
made me feel sad that she didn't understand he was just making her feel
good and like she could trust him. The whole section building up to
the part about HIV is all so good. You get a hint that something is
wrong from the beginning. I like this genre, or diary-type form. It
makes the story more real for me and like I'm there, talking, eating,
and sleeping at the same time they are. I really like this book! Do you
know any other books in diary-like form I might like?

In letters in her journal Sandy defined the differences between gothic
romances and novels about relationships, both of which she was reading
and enjoying, but for different reasons.

My analysis of a romance is: a book with a simple plot, not much you
have to go by in terms of who the characters are, and the same book as
a lot of others only the title is changed. A novel is: a book you enjoy
reading because of an interesting, different plot, where the characters
are different and each has a quality (whether good or bad): themselves.
It's a book you don't know the ending to just by reading the first couple
of pages or chapter. It's something that has substance, that you can grip
onto rather than fall through; a surprise ending. Also, not a book that
has 100–150 pages so that you zip through it. Something longer, with a
problem or theme that keeps you interested.

I have shed most of my anxiety about adolescent readers' attraction to
formula because I've seen so many kids grow out of this stage in the pages of
their journals. Amanda discovered the formula of her teen mysteries, and
Jenn discovered the Sweet Valley recipe.

This book was a lot like a Nancy Drew. I saw them in a magazine and
the ad said "Getting tired of Nancy Drews from your mother's time?"
Well, the Susan Sands are almost exactly alike. And every single

Nancy Drew is the same. When I was reading them a lot, I could tell exactly when things would happen, like when she would be captured near the end, etc., etc., etc. It drove me crazy. The girls are *so* perfect. Then the author makes them have dead parents or something so it won't be so perfect, but the girls don't even care. It's dumb.

I have read many, probably just about all, the books in the "Sweet Valley" series. It used to be all I ever read. As I kept on reading so many, I realized that basically they're all the same. I'm surprised with myself lately. I haven't been reading *any*. I've read other books I enjoy more, stories with more of a plot than: a boy and a girl fall in love, have some problems, and at the end get together again. They are so boring. My mother is happy I'm getting over my love stories and into interesting novels. Although I don't know why, she usually reads Harlequins.

A big piece of kids' dissatisfaction with formulaic fiction grows from their new awareness of point of view in novels and their sense of what a good main character does for a reader. They want to believe in, trust, feel close to, *be with* a central character.

I've decided I like a book that has a one-person point of view. *Killing Mr. Griffin* would have been better if a character involved had told the story from his or her view. I like a book with more feelings; I like to know what a character is thinking rather than just his or her actions.

I'm having a hard time with *Catcher in the Rye* because I don't like Holden. I can't sympathize with his feelings. It seems like he's whining through the whole book, and I'm finding him hard to take.

After I read Plath's biography in the back of *Bell Jar*, my happy feelings about the recovery of the main character soured. "The bell jar descended again" and Plath succeeded in killing herself. Well, maybe Esther did too. How are you supposed to read an autobiographical novel? If Plath died can Esther live?

Many of our letters are about good books: which ones are they, who wrote them, and who's got them. Jason advised me about Gary Paulsen.

No, I don't think you should read *The Winter Room*. It was boring. It didn't have much action, and like you said, "Don't waste your time reading a book you don't like." I really liked *The River*. It was fast-paced and very exciting. Within the first twenty-five pages they were already in the wilderness. I suggest you read *The River*, not *The Winter Room*.

And Izzie advised Rachel about John Grisham:

> You have *got* to read *The Firm*. I absolutely loved it because it was so different. I know you don't want to read it because it's not your type, and you "don't like John Grisham," but you *have* to give it a try. It's all action and suspense, and, although it's confusing, if you see the movie with me, it's not too bad.
>
> So, how'd you like *Weetzie Bat*? I thought it was really fun because it had the modern and the fantasy combined. I liked too that everything was fairly realistic—in her wishes and stuff, and how everything was literal, like her boyfriend's name.
>
> What are you reading now? You'll have to fill me in, and if you're not reading anything, just try *The Firm*, if not for a change, for me. I need someone to discuss it with, and even if you don't like it, I think you need a "mindless" book as opposed to Plath and all the depressing suicide ones.

The ways my students write to each other are different from the ways they write to me—not better or worse, but different in the same ways their conversations differ from talk with a teacher. The conventions are less careful as kids adjust handwriting, spelling, and punctuation to a different audience's expectations. They doodle, attach stickers, invent pen names, and postscript into tomorrow. These letters look like notes passed in class.

There is also more description of affect when students write to each other about their books. They write about crying, laughing out loud, screaming with surprise, slamming down a book in anger. The question they ask each other most frequently begins, "How did you feel when . . . ?" There's more description of character and plot and more relating of "the good parts." Peer correspondents ask more questions about what to read, and they make and follow up on more recommendations. However widely and sympathetically I've read their books, kids need and trust each other's advice. They're more playful with each other, joking and teasing as they couldn't with an adult. And they write more and longer letters than when I'm the sole audience.

Their correspondences with each other about literature and reading put my students' social relationships to work in the classroom. Kids like to talk to their friends, and reading journals enable them to go even deeper into the literate life by talking with their friends about their books. This exchange between Martha (aka Super Depp) and Laurel (aka Super Leo) is as much about literature as it is who the two girls are, who they want to be, and what their friendship is like.

Dear Super Leo,

(I'm talking into my microphone.)

I'm waiting to start *A Mid-Summer Night's Dream* until I have time to get into it. I'm going to read *Hamlet* again, too.

So, did you ever finish *Mists of Avalon*? If you did, did you like it? I'm going to read that during April vacation.

Are you almost done with *Range of Motion*?

I'm really enjoying the Shakespeare scenes we're doing. I'm hoping in high school I'll be able to do a whole play. You'll have to come see me star as Ophelia (or maybe Hamlet!). I'm glad we'll have some background in Shakespeare for when we get to high school.

Love,
Super Depp
(Hee, hee)

Dear Super Depp (Hee, hee),

(I don't have my mike, but I'll pretend anyway.)

I read the beginning of *Mists*, then skimmed. Some parts are really good, and other parts are really boring. It's really detailed in some parts. No, I didn't finish it. I wish I had though!! My mom and Edie read it, and they both loved it. I hope you finish it. Ms. A. said I could skim the boring parts, so you can, too.

No, I'm not done with Berg but I will be soon. We're going to Cape Elizabeth, and that's two hours altogether both ways, so I hope I'll finish in the car.

I know I really love Shakespeare, too, especially the movie of *Hamlet*. The actors were so good and brought the whole thing to life. It really stuck with me, especially Ophelia. It's amazing how some characters just stay in your mind. They connect in some way. Do you know what I mean?

I'm sure in high school we will talk about Shakespeare. We'll already know and feel all smart and everything. Cool! I bet we'll do scenes from Shakespeare's *Romeo and Juliet*. That's what they all seem to do. That's okay. As long as I get to be Juliet. Ha, ha. If we did *Hamlet*, then both of us would already have done Ophelia so we'd have a better chance at playing that role.

I love Shakespeare's language and the stuff he wrote about.

Oh, yeah, I wanna see if you felt the same way. Okay. When we watched *Hamlet*, then watched *Much Ado About Nothing*, did you feel really strong connections with *Hamlet*, then nothing for *Much Ado*? I didn't feel anything for *Much Ado*. It was really weird. It's hard to explain, but do you know what I mean?

Love ya,
Super Leo

Dear Super Leo,

I know exactly what you mean about *Hamlet* sticking with you and *Much Ado* not doing anything. I know that Ophelia and Hamlet will be some of those characters that will always stay with me, like Scout or Juniper or Torey Haydon. There weren't any characters in *Much Ado* that spoke to me. Maybe it has something to do with the genre, comedies vs. tragedies?

After I'm finished writing this letter I have to go over my Shakespeare lines. I don't really want to do the Benedict and Beatrice scene, but, oh well.

I just read a *really* good book. It was called *Yellow Raft in Blue Water*. It has three parts. The first one is about the daughter Rayona, the second is about the mother Christine, and the third part's about the grandmother Ida. At first I wasn't sure, but it was really good. The characters were well developed and it was really cool how there were all these connections between the three of them. My mom's reading it now. If you want you can read it when she's done.

Well, gotta fly.

Love,
Super Depp

P.S. Did you finish *Range of Motion*? I want it next!

There's no guarantee that readers' letters to each other won't get out of hand or that they'll stay confined to literary topics. When peer correspondence exceeds reasonable boundaries, either one of the correspondents puts on the brakes, or I intervene. Since I have access to their correspondence, I know what and how they're writing to each other and can step in if the letters are consistently inappropriate. Dan and Kevin, for example, started out in September trading some information and many insults.

Dear (Tramp) Kevin,

This book I am reading, *Gulliver's Travels*, is getting better. Gulliver the adventurer was just attacked by a giant creature, sort of like me to you. The big man is probably thirty feet tall, while Gulliver is about six feet tall. How is your book going? I hope it takes you two years to finish it. Ha! Ha! What is it called? What is your main character's name?

I'm thinking about reading The Earthsea Trilogy. Jon says it's great. Or I might read that series that you're on. Give me your opinion on the series. Thanks, vegetable.

Sincerely, Yeah! All right!
Yahoo! Excellent!
Dan #1

Dear (Doilly) Dan,

It sounds as though you aren't actually reading the book but are remembering it from the cartoon movie they had on cable last year.

My book's main character's name is Garion, although through circumstances he is now called Belgarion. I guess that's where Eddings got the name *The Belgariad* for the series. In my opinion you should read this series (although words like *to*, *it*, and *we* are awfully tough for you.)

Are you sure your brain can handle all this information in one letter?

Unsincerely,
Kevin

When the insults overwhelmed the information ("My dog is better looking than you *when* your hair is brushed." "Oh yeah? Concerning your hair, have you ever seen a Medusa?"), I intervened. I wrote to Dan and asked him to talk about books more and trade taunts less; I reminded him that literary dialogue was the purpose of the journal. He and Kev complied and still maintained the playfulness of their previous exchanges.

Kev,

How is *The Enchanter's End Game* going? I'm beginning to get more interested in my book, *The Lord of the Rings*. It's beginning to get more exciting. Anyhow, I haven't been having too much trouble understanding it. Any trouble I have had would be understanding some of the words Tolkien uses, like *unintelligible*.

After I finish this I'm going to read some of Mike's books, then I will probably go back to the series.

Ms. A. says I have to stop insulting people so much instead of telling about my books.

I hope you enjoyed this letter.

Dan

Dan,

Let's have a peace treaty. (Letters only!)

What is your new book about, anyway? Mine is going well, although Ms A. says I should read more at home.

Kev

Kev,

Sign the peace treaty:

I *Kevin Ames* will write letters about books and books only in my log and in Dan's log.

My book is about this guy named Frodo Baggins . . .

Writing Back

There isn't one set of questions for a teacher to ask students in their reading journals. Instead there are all of these individual readers with their own strategies, questions, tastes, needs, opinions, backgrounds, and experiences. Nor is there one way to approach or interpret a work of literature. Instead there are all of these individual readers' responses. The letters I write to my kids about their reading and mine are *personal* and *contextual*: what I say in my half of the dialogue comes from my knowledge of how a student reads and thinks, of what a student understands or needs to know. My responses also grow from my own experiences as a reader. When I categorize my letters to kids, they seem to do three things: *affirm*, *challenge*, or *extend* a reader's responses.

Like the writing conference, responding to readers requires a delicate touch. While I've learned to respond personally to each student, the first principle of writing back is not to become too personal. Toby Fulwiler reminds teachers that academic "journals exist somewhere on a continuum between diaries and class notebooks. . . . Like the diary, the journal is written in the first person; like the class notebook, the journal focuses on academic subjects the writer would like to learn more about" (1990, 257). The subject of an academic journal isn't "I," as in a diary, but "I-it": the relationship between a student and a subject. In their reading journals the subjects of my kids' letters should be books, authors, reading, and writing. The purpose of our correspondence isn't for me to invite kids' personal problems or offer counsel about them.

Neither is the purpose to test writing. The correspondence is first-draft chat; these aren't polished pieces of writing. I don't make corrections on students' letters, but I do comment when I have trouble reading them or if a reader hasn't followed basic conventions and needs instruction or a reminder.

Nor is the purpose of the letters to test reading. Kids' most perfunctory notes are written in response to letters from me that read like a teacher's manual. When I bombard kids with teacher questions, I turn our correspondence into a test. One good, thoughtful question is more than enough. I receive the most insightful letters from my students when I ask about something I want to know, but also when I level with readers about my own experiences, tastes, and opinions as a reader, sharing freely and frankly, agreeing and disagreeing.

Teachers have asked me, "How do you ever read all the books your kids are reading?" I do read a lot of adolescent and adult fiction, but no one has read every book. I have conversations all the time with my friends about books I haven't read in which they teach me about their responses and help me decide whether I want to read a book, too. It helps to look at the journals not just as a vehicle for teaching my kids, but as a forum for me to learn from them about their reading, then help them decide what they'll do next.

I also know I don't learn about adolescent literature solely by reading it or reading letters about it. I learn at least as much through the responses I write in the journals. Some of my best letters to students are the ones that teach me something I didn't know I knew. In my worst responses I'm going through the motions, and I cringe when I reread them. In hindsight I see myself asking questions I know the answers to ("Who are the main characters in *The Outsiders*?"), making dumb assumptions about what kids are or aren't doing ("You're not finishing books because you'd rather fool around than read"), pretending to be interested in something I'm not ("I'm a big fan of Tom Clancy, too"), and congratulating kids for having an opinion ("What a great letter. I love it when you share your thoughts with me. They're so interesting")—which doesn't mean I never think it's appropriate to congratulate kids on their letters. When I do I tell them what fascinates me about their reactions to books or describe what they have taught me.

Looking back through the reading journals, I think the responses that were most useful to kids echo the ways I talk with my friends. This is opinionated, engaged, comfortable chat. When I ask questions, they're sparked by curiosity, not a sense of obligation. If we really want to take kids inside books, our one good question will probably be some variation on the questions that are implicit or explicit in our conversations with friends about literature: How did you feel about the book? Why? What did you think of the writing? What was the author up to?

When we help kids focus on craft and their own responses—on how a book was written and how it affected them—we encourage an active, critical stance as readers. We teach them how to go beyond plot, stop letting stories happen to them, and start making decisions about what is and isn't working in pieces of their reading. Asking "What do you think of the writing, of how the author wrote this?" invites kids inside a text, where they can engage, analyze, and interpret it, instead of synopsizing plot. We show them the way to come inside, to pull up a chair at the dining room table.

At the start of the school year Libby stayed on the outside in her letters to me. She gave blow-by-blow accounts of plot, of what the characters were up to, as in this letter about June Foley's *Love by Any Other Name*.

Dear Ms. Atwell,

Billie is getting restricted because of Bubba and his friends mostly, and partly herself. First she was restricted for being late. And then she got restricted for sitting with Bubba's friends (the day before they got a lecture on food fights), and a girl (a friend of hers) brought in a table cloth, wine glasses, china plates, napkins, and champagne, for them and the table! And so they all got detention for a week. But why would they get a detention? Because of the champagne? Probably.

Your friend,
Libby

P.S. Have a nice day!

Every time I wrote back to Libby, I wrote back about the author. I used the author's name and speculated about why he or she decided to have characters behave as they did.

Dear Libby,

Well, I do think champagne is a bit much for a school cafeteria lunch, but it's a good example of what Foley is trying to do here. Can you see how she's trying to show how far and foolishly Billie is willing to go, to be in with the in crowd? And can you guess what's going to happen to Billie by the novel's end, how Foley is going to have Billie end up? I can see it coming.

Ms. A.

I directed and redirected Libby throughout the first two months of school, demonstrating author talk in every letter I wrote to her. At the end of October, Libby began to come inside.

Dear Ms. Atwell,

I have started reading *That Was Then, This Is Now* by S. E. Hinton. It is a pretty good book. I didn't know that she had Ponyboy Curtis in the book as a character. That surprised me!

I like the way she writes. It's like you are there in the book. You can picture what it is like and stuff.

Sincerely,
Libby

P.S. Have a nice day!

Dear Lib,

I know what you mean. Hinton is good at putting us inside the characters. She tells so much about what they're thinking and feeling that we see things through their eyes and feel with their hearts. In *The Outsiders*, with Ponyboy as her narrator, she really puts us there, in the world of the novel.

I loved it that Pony showed up in *That Was Then, This Is Now*. It was like an in-joke. You had to know *The Outsiders* to pick up on the reference: be a member of the Hinton Club.

Ms. A.

P.S. I'll be anxious to know what you think of how Hinton decided to conclude this one. She shook me up, but I think she was right.

My role as correspondent strikes a balance between experienced reader, mentor, and teacher responsible to her adolescent students. This means sharing what I've learned about reading and literature, offering my advice and expertise, and nudging—sometimes hard—when I think a student needs it. Dan needed a nudge to set aside a book he wasn't enjoying; I let him off the hook.

Dear Dan,

Is *Watership Down* feeling too long to you? You aren't making much progress. It's okay—more than okay—to abandon a book you're not enjoying. I know I recommended *Watership Down* to you, but that doesn't obligate you to finish it. If it's feeling overwhelming, please put it back. Does this make sense?

Ms. A.

Dear Ms. A.,

Yes, I think it does make sense. Yes, even though I liked *Watership Down* it got too long for me, and I was getting pretty discouraged. I put it back and found this other book I really like by Farley Mowat, *Never Cry Wolf.*

Thanks.

Dan

I nudge kids who are going through the motions to push their responses beyond book reports. After two months of my one or two good questions, not to mention the demonstrations of my own letters, Keith's were still book reports, and there was no dialogue in our correspondence.

Dear Ms. A.,

I have just finished two books, *The Beast* by R. L. Stine, and *Carrie* by Stephen King. Now I am reading *House of Stairs* by William Sleator. It is about these five orphan teenagers that are brought to this place that is only stairs. Inside there is this machine that gives them a whole lot of food.

Your friend,
Keith

Dear Keith,

I'm going to be frank. I'm practically killing myself trying to write to you the kind of letters I want you to write to me, so we can get a conversation going here like two real readers.

Please write to me about the writing you're reading. What do you like about what the authors have done? What do you notice? How does the writing make you feel? Think?

I'm also curious about your reactions to the new read-aloud (*Nightjohn*) and the series of minilessons about what the eye and brain do when a good reader reads. Did it ring any bells?

In short, please *think* in your letters to me. These are all topics you might think about. You're so smart, Keith. Dive below the surface of what you're reading and see what you can find there. I think you'll surprise yourself.

Love,
Ms. A.

Dear Ms. A.,

I don't like Sleator's *The House of Stairs*. It's moving too slow for me. I think I'm going to abandon it.

I like *Nightjohn* by Gary Paulsen. It has a lot of description in it. It makes me think a lot of how slaves were really treated back then. I'm glad I wasn't a black slave back then.

I think I will start reading *Christine* by you know who, Stephen King. I am really liking his books. They have a lot of action and a lot more scary suspense. I have seen the movie of *Christine* and I liked it. I think I'll enjoy the book.

Keith

Dear Keith,

I agree with you about King: he is the King of Action. I think his high-energy plots have a lot to do with his popularity. They move so quickly they pull readers in immediately, so that people who might not have the patience for a thick book or a story that unwinds slowly are hooked by King's narratives right from the start . . .

Some of my letters remind readers of what they can write about in response to literature—of the kinds of ideas and topics they can consider in their letters. Jay needed to stretch his thinking, and he knew it.

Dear Ms. Atwell,

I have just finished *Shades of Gray*. It was a pretty good book. I am going to start reading *Fallen Angels* after vacation, meanwhile I am going to read *Hoops* over vacation at my dad's. On Saturday, before I go to Dad's, I am trying out for the AAU Maine Hawks basketball team.

I think I'm finally getting the idea of using less dialogue in my short story. This is a short letter. I'm sorry but I can't think of anything else to write.

Jay

Dear Jay,

I can sense you're struggling to figure out what to say about your books. Take a look again at the second paragraph of my letter that appears on the inside cover of your reading journal. It's a reminder of ideas to consider when you write.

As your teacher, and as somebody else who reads, I'm most interested in how you felt and thought as you read and what the author did (in terms of characters, etc.) to make you feel that way. Right now you're on the outside, and the book is happening to you. I want you to go *inside* the book and think about what the author has done—the choices he or she has made.

For example, when you write to me about *Fallen Angels* and *Hoops*, can you focus on Walter Dean Myers? Write letters about him, about what he did as the author of these books you are loving?

This is a harder kind of letter to write. But it's also more important and grown-up, and it might even help you think about your own writing from new perspectives—like your realization that you need more description and less dialogue in your pigeon racing story.

Have a great time at your dad's.

Love,
Ms. A.

Dear Ms. Atwell,

Walter Dean Myers has really explained how Lonnie dealt with his basketball and how he felt about being some, in Lonnie's words, "loser." *Hoops* started out slow but now it is really starting to speed up as it gets close to the basketball championship. Myers is showing all the different attitudes Lonnie is having towards certain friends. I am still a little foggy about why Lonnie and his mom don't get along very well. I'm trusting Myers to clear it up for me.

Jay

Some of my letters to kids are attempts to untangle their confusions or answer their questions. Sandy was confused about the conclusion of *Z for Zachariah* by Robert O'Brien.

Dear Ms. Atwell,

I'm trying to decide whether this book was too deep and whether it was written for kids my age. I'm trying to think if maybe there is something there, like the answers to my questions, and I just don't realize it. I was really disappointed by the ending. I felt she gave up what was rightfully hers. I felt she could have had more guts. Also, I didn't like, to me, an unanswered ending.

Sandy

Dear Sandy,

Sometimes I think: is there something wrong with me or something wrong with this book? This most often happens when I read something I don't understand. I'm tempted to write to an author and say, "Would you mind revising this? I don't get it, the way you've done it here," or even "I don't like how it came out: change it, please."

I did like the resolution of Z—the fact that it didn't become a futuristic version of Adam and Eve. The girl and the man didn't live happily ever after because they couldn't. Even just two human beings couldn't live amicably; the man had to initiate his own, private war after the big one had managed to wipe out (probably) the rest of humanity. For me, O'Brien's theme is human nature, about how our instincts lead us to suspicion and competition, rather than harmony and cooperation. I think he's essentially pessimistic, like William Golding in *Lord of the Flies*. And although I'm interested in this theme, I don't think I agree with him.

Ms. A.

Ms. Atwell,

I agree with you. I'm awfully glad they didn't make the story out to be a happily-ever-after book, because life isn't like that. Also they get boring after reading so many of them.

The book was different from any other book I've read. I decided finally that I like that. I like the change. Your statement makes a lot of sense to me. I guess I really didn't try to look at what he was getting at until now. Your opinions helped me a little more to understand the confusing parts.

Sandy

Some of my responses supply background information, filling readers in about an author's life, sources, or ideas.

Dear Ms. A.,

I've just finished Lois Duncan's *A Gift of Magic*. It was really good. You know what? I have a little bit of ESP myself. I used to have it a wicked lot when I was little. (My mother told me, from experiences with me back then.) But now I get it only once in a while. I wonder how Duncan knows about this.

The book's really good. It sounds like it could happen in real life, too, except when Brendon and Greg made the boat and it floated. I really don't think that could happen.

Kristen

Dear Kristen,

In a speech she gave at an NCTE convention, Duncan said she gets hundreds of letters from kids who've read *A Gift of Magic* who also experienced astral projections and that, like you, they seemed to gradually lose the gift as they matured. Duncan based the novel on research into children's ESP conducted at Stanford University in California. If you're interested in following up on this, you might want to write to her for more information, or for the name of the Stanford study.

Ms. A.

Sometimes students want me to tell a novel's story—to whet their appetites about a book they're flirting with. Catharine saw a TV listing for the movie of *To Kill a Mockingbird* and wondered what the novel was about. I wrote:

> It's about so many things: love, honor, family, magic, growing up, life in the Deep South before integration, murder, and racism. The main character (and narrator) is a girl named Scout; she's one of the best characters in all of contemporary American fiction—a great observer, reactor, *and* actor. Just thinking about the book makes me feel happy. Boy, is it ever a great, satisfying read—not to mention reread. (The movie of *Mockingbird* isn't bad, especially given what Hollywood does to great stories, e.g., the current *Scarlet Letter*, with *Demi Moore* as Hester Prynne.)

And sometimes kids have technical questions that only an English teacher can answer.

> Dear Ms. Atwell,
>   Why, thank you for that oh-so-touching comment about the twisted nature of my abundant imagination.
>   David Eddings is good. I'm reading book three of the Belgariad,* and I've never had my emotions so manipulated. Each book in this series is so good I can only address them as a group and not as individuals. I fear, though, that all of the books beyond the first rely heavily on the hope that a reader had read the books before it.
>
> Joe
> *What do I do with this? Do I have to underline it or just capitalize?

> Dear Joe,
>   Kate Turabian says series take caps only—no quotes; no underline/ italics. What I want to know is, who decides stuff like this? And how do I apply for the job? Can you imagine the power?
>   Next week's minilessons and homework will focus on dozens of obscure word choices and points of correct usage. My goal is to turn all of you into Usage Police: junior English teachers who prowl the earth protecting the language and punishing those who would seek to corrupt it. We shall prevail. (Pause for mad laughter.)

Write to me when you've finished the fifth book in the Belgariad. Curt felt manipulated by this point—as if he could see through Edding's plot machinations. I'm wondering how you'll react.

Love,
William Safire

Sometimes my teaching letters are about strategies of proficient readers. Missy wrote to ask if it was okay to read *Fried Green Tomatoes* again in reading workshop.

Dear Missy,

Yes. Rereading loved books—or even favorite passages from loved books—is for me one of the best parts of the whole act of reading. To be with great characters again—to feel their feelings and my own, again—gives me incredible pleasure. Wait until you're my age and you have a whole lifetime of reading experiences and favorite books behind you and favorite rereads ahead of you. (Mine start with *A Wrinkle in Time* and *Charlotte's Web*.)

Love,
Ms. A.

Jason and I corresponded about his reading rate, which was so slow it was affecting his fluency. He wrote to me that he had set a goal of adding three pages to the number he could read in a half hour. I responded:

Dear Jason,

I'm glad you're trying to pick up the pace of your reading. Continue to push yourself. I'll never give you a test on a novel, so you should remember that you're reading just for *you*, and you should feel free to experiment: to skim, to skip, to read ahead, to come back. As long as you're getting meaning out of the story, however you read is okay. I hope you'll play around with different *styles* of fast reading.

Love,
Ms. Atwell .

Some of my teaching letters are about the diversity of our tastes as readers. For example, I reassure students that there isn't something wrong with them if they don't like a book. When Jenn wrote that she was worried about being the only kid she knew who hadn't enjoyed *A Wrinkle in Time* "because it was very confusing and, well, boring," I responded:

It's interesting to me that people's reactions as readers are so varied— that everyone's tastes are at least slightly different and sometimes wildly so. One thing this means is there's no such thing as A Good Book. Since a book becomes good only in interaction with a reader, and since there's always at least one reader who'll disagree (e.g., you not liking *Wrinkle*), maybe the best we can do as readers is work hard at developing criteria for what we mean when each of us says "X is a good book."

For me *Wrinkle* was a good book because it was the first novel I read in which I was aware of theme. I was in fifth grade, and I remember being amazed: the book was about Meg, Charles Wallace, Calvin, etc. But it was *also* about good vs. evil and using the power of love as a weapon to fight the darkness. I was awestruck. So, *Wrinkle* is on my list of Good Books because it was a benchmark experience in my growing up as a reader—and also because I love Meg, Charles Wallace, Calvin, and the Missesees. You probably have a similar benchmark book of your own.

Reading is amazingly personal, yes?

Because I teach reading and writing, some of my letters ask my students to draw lessons and inspiration from the work of other authors.

Dear Ms. Atwell,

I have always wanted to read Avi's *Something Upstairs*. I have it on my bookshelf at home. I think I will try it, when I finish *Hoops*.

I'm enjoying *Hoops*. Walter Dean Myers is such a *great* writer. He knows where to put everything. I have noticed that a lot of his books are about basketball or not having a dad in the house and living in Harlem. I wonder if any of these things happened to him as a teenager?

When I was reading the part where Lonnie shot himself, I could imagine myself being there and shooting myself. Myers can make you feel like the character just as much as Avi. I think I might read some more of Myers' work. *Scorpions* sounds good. What was your favorite Walter Dean Myers book?

Love,
Michael

P.S. I must tool off in my white convertible to N.H. with Laurel! (What a dream!)

Dear Michael,

My favorite Walter Dean Myers is *Fast Sam, Cool Clyde, and Stuff*. It's one of the best novels I know about kids' friendships. I also found *Fallen Angels* interesting, moving, and *powerful*.

I always assumed that Myers lived—or closely observed—the kinds of experiences he writes about. I agree that he works hard and to good effect at creating characters so real a reader can become the character. This combination—of specific details and the characters' emotion—brings the people he creates to life for me.

In your own short story, about Brad, can you try to write like Myers? Close your eyes and "see" Brad; feel his feelings and what it's like to be doing what he's doing. Then open your eyes (duh) and use lots of words to describe what you saw and felt, so your readers think Brad is real, too.

And stay away from white convertibles.

Love,
Ms. A.

When I see a change in my kids' reading, I write to them about it. This ongoing assessment helps students become aware of their growth and build on their accomplishments.

My friend Don Graves once said to me that you can judge a student's strengths as a reader based on whether he or she has plans (i.e., of what book to read next). A big change I see since September is that you have become that kind of strong reader: a planner. In the fall you had a panic attack at the end of each book: "Oh my God! What will I read next?" Now I look at your list of books you're dying to read, and I see a reader.

About a third of the contents of my letters to readers are recommendations of books. For me this is the real headwork of the journals: to balance what I know about plots, characters, authors, genres, and levels of difficulty against the needs and abilities of each reader. Joe, a fan of fantasy, was feeling "narrow genred" and asked for some titles outside his domain. It is one thing for a teacher to ask a genre-challenged reader to branch out; it's another to help the reader by extending some new branches.

Dear Joe,
What about another S. E. Hinton (*That Was Then, This Is Now*) or Robert Cormier (*After the First Death, I Am the Cheese, Fade*, or the sequel to *The Chocolate War*)? Have you read J. D. Salinger's *Catcher in the Rye*? Golding's *Lord of the Flies*? Lee's *To Kill a Mockingbird*? McCammon's *Boy's Life*?

All are *great* stories with *great* characters. Missy and I also recommend her favorite author, Fannie Flagg, and her books *Fried Green Tomatoes* and *Daisy Fay and the Miracle Man*. You might also take a look at *Cold Sassy Tree* by Olive Ann Burns.

Whew. Dog-ear this page and refer to it when you're on the prowl for a non-sci-fi-thriller-fantasy opus.

Love,
Ms. A.

Dear Ms. A.,
Whew is right. I'll never need another recommendation ever again! I think I'll try an S. E. Hinton and get back to an old familiar. Reading

a different book by a familiar author is like trying foreign food, like Italian, for example—I've tried pizza (*The Outsiders*), now I can try the gnocchi. Sometimes (you're not going to believe this) I get tired of my normal sci-fi-thriller-fantasy mold, and this is one of those times. Thank you for that *long* list, and may the hair on your toes flourish.

Joe

Dear Joe,

May your ears grow mold.

I believe even *you* can tire of a genre, and I see it as a good stage in your development. The readers who worry me are kids who get hooked on, say, R. L. Stine or Francine Pascal, Inc., and perceive reading only in terms of ingesting the latest, formulaic piece of fluff/garbage by the author. They don't grow.

Reading should serve a bunch of human needs. Your imagination requires a lot of care and feeding, God knows, but there are other parts of your psyche that need fertilizer, too. I hope Hinton fills the bill in exploring teen angst.

When I finish *Daisy Fay*, I will MAKE YOU read it. It's long, fast, and funny (so far—Missy says it gets sad).

Love,
Ms. A.

Finally, some of my letters to kids comment on the letters themselves. In September Katy's correspondence with me and her friends was consistently off-topic, and I intervened:

> I need to remind you about the purpose of the letters to me, Katy, and to your friends. The reading log is a way to comment on and analyze the writing you're reading, and I'm afraid you're drifting off into another kind of correspondence. As much fun as it is—you are one lively letter writer—I don't see it helping you as a responder to literature.
>
> Please review the second paragraph of my first letter to you—the one that's glued on the inside cover of this journal. It will help you write letters that push your thinking and, along the way, maybe even give you insights to help you solve your own writing problems.
>
> I can't wait to hear about Monica Furlong: fill me in, okay?

Several letters in a row from Michael were indecipherable. I asked him to attend to his handwriting; he did; then we got back to the good business of books, authors, reading, and writing.

Dear Michael,

No offense, but your last letter was rather, shall we say, *unusual* in its appearance. Did you write it in a moving vehicle? Perhaps a dump truck on a mountain road?

Are you stuck for your next book, or am I reading between the lines? I have some recommendations if you're not sure where to go next.

Love,
Nancie the Neat

Dear N.T.N.,

I did write that letter in a moving vehicle. Sorry.

I'm really liking *Jumping the Nail* by Eve Bunting. I can tell what's going to happen next. You'd think after someone got hurt from jumping, nobody would do it again. Someone has to die in order for them to stop jumping.

I didn't like Paulsen's ending in *Tilt-A-Whirl John*. It *did* come too quickly, and it didn't have enough information about what happened to the characters after they got split up.

The Snow Goose is fabulous. He does a great job with description. He doesn't have too much, but he doesn't have too little. I have a feeling the snow goose will be shot, and the hunchback (name?) will be so sad he dies from sorrow. Or the war might tie in with the story. That will probably happen soon.

Read on!

The trying to be neater and succeeding,
Michael

Dear Attempting to Be Neater Michael,

I think Bunting knew she had to make the plot of *Jumping the Nail* extreme and striking—to drive home her theme about the danger of teenage conformity. Adolescence is a time when fitting in can mean everything. Being like other people—or, at least, not unlike them—will never matter again as much in the rest of your life. So some adolescents go too far in doing stupid things in order to be accepted. Saying no can be incredibly difficult, in spite of the simplistic advice kids get from politicians to "just say no." I think Bunting was issuing a warning that it's more than okay to resist peer pressure, more than okay to think for yourself and decide what's right for you. *Nail* is just about the best novel I know about teen peer pressure.

I love *The Snow Goose*, too. When you think about it, there's barely a plot: a crippled painter and a girl help a bird. But Gallico's language is like a dream, like a wave you ride on and on. I can picture him considering every single word—more like a poet than a writer of prose.

Your second prediction may come true, HINT, HINT.

Love,
Ms. A.

Procedures for Reading Journals

It took me a while and some major revisions to get straight the mechanics of dialogue journals—what they would look like, who would write when, how letters would be exchanged, and where the journals would be kept when no one was writing in them. I ask my students to buy marbled composition notebooks because they're sturdy, permanent, and can function as a bound book, in which we turn and number the pages; they also contain enough paper for nine months of correspondence.

On the day in September that I introduce the reading journals in a minilesson, I deliver to each reader a copy of my first letter of the school year. It spells out the purposes and procedures I expect students to follow. I trim the margins with a paper cutter, so the instructions will fit neatly inside the cover of the notebook. My letter is reproduced below.

Dear _____,

Your reading journal is a place for you, me, and your friends to talk this year about books, reading, authors, and writing. You'll think about literature in letters to me and friends; we'll write letters back to you. Our letters will become a record of the thinking, learning, and reading we did together.

Letters should be at least a page long. In your letters tell what you felt when you read a book and why. Tell what you noticed about how the author wrote. Tell why you think he or she wrote this way. Tell what you liked and didn't and why. Tell how you read a book and why. Tell what a book said and meant to you. Tell what it reminded you of— what other books or experiences from your own life. Tell what surprised you. Ask questions or for help. And write back about our ideas, feelings, experiences, and questions.

As a bare minimum you must write a letter to me or a friend in your own journal at least once a week, due by Friday morning. I need a letter from you at least once every two weeks. This is only a minimum requirement. You may pass a literary letter to me or to a friend as often as you wish.

When you write a letter, give your journal to the person to whom the letter is addressed; if that's me, put your journal in my rocking chair. When a friend gives you his or her journal, *you must answer within twenty-four hours.* After you've written back, deliver your friend's notebook directly to him or her. You may not lose or damage another's reading journal.

You may write and respond to letters both during and outside reading workshop.

Number the pages of your reading journal, as in a book. Date your letters in the upper right-hand corner. Use a greeting and closing, just as you would in any friendly letter. Mention the name of the author of the book you're talking about and its title, and indicate the title by capitalizing and underlining it (e.g., *The Outsiders*).

I can't wait for us to begin reading together. And I can't wait for your letters—for the chance to learn from you, learn with you, and help you learn more.

Love,
Ms. A.

My letter doesn't leave much to chance. Although I know it will take kids a while to get the hang of the system, its rules and regulations are in place from the beginning; so are my expectations. Our letters will be a vehicle for me to teach them and for them to teach themselves. Few students ignore the minimum requirement, especially after they lose a lunch recess or, at Boothbay, received their first quarterly grades. They recognize that I am serious: the letters are more than a nice thing to do. They are a yardstick for measuring a reader's achievements.

Readers date their letters so we have a record of when they wrote to whom and so I can observe patterns in their growth over time. They number the pages because this is data I report to their parents at the end of each grading period, along with the number of books read and the range of genres represented.

Students write and answer letters both during the workshop and for homework. This means that at any given time in reading workshop some students will be reading, some will be writing letters in their own journals, some will be answering letters in others' journals, and some will be retrieving or delivering notebooks. All of this happens silently. The twenty-four-hour rule about writing back ensures that letters answered outside of class are back in time for the next day's workshop, and that students don't lose track of each other's journals.

I write back in journals for up to an hour after school, before I go home. If the volume is heavy on a given day, I keep my responses brief. Once my students get beyond plot synopses, usually by November, I'm eager to read what they have written about their reading, and I can't wait to crack open the journals. I also write letters during the workshop—it's a workshop for me, too—after I make the rounds to see what everyone is reading.

Margaret Meek wrote, "For all the reading research we have financed, we are certain only that good readers pick their own way to literacy in the company of friends who encourage and sustain them and that . . . the enthusiasm of a trusted adult can make the difference" (1982, 34). I love to read and respond to my kids' letters. I never know what I'll find when I turn to the last entry. I remember suffering through piles of junior high book reports, the dullest writing I've ever read. By contrast, the letters are a constant source of surprise, pleasure, and stimulation. And what they replaced—book reports, worksheets, quizzes, and tests—ate up more time than keeping up with my correspondents ever will. Best of all, our letters allow me to be on the inside, too, and to act and react as another reader in the workshop.

9
Valuing and Evaluating

The days that make us happy make us wise.
John Masefield

Rachel never marked time as a writer. It seemed to me she was always writing or planning writing—gathering ideas, phrases, words, lines, and images, often in the little notebooks she carried with her everywhere. She attended hungrily to minilessons about techniques and conventions. She was also the most intentional writer in her class. In September we locked horns right away over what Rachel felt like doing and not doing. I had to insist, and I had to work hard to earn her trust that my expectations and advice could help her meet her intentions, discover new ones, and use writing workshop as a jumping-off place to adulthood instead of an occasion for composing more of the exquisite but distanced nature poetry that had been her claim to fame since fifth grade.

In June, at the end of our first year together, Rachel described her growth as a seventh-grade writer and the reasons for it in a final self-evaluation:

> Last year I almost always got stuck between pieces, but this year I was always writing something. I don't think I've ever written as many pieces as I did this year, and I'm very happy with most of them.
>
> I developed a style in my poetry, one that's always there. Last year I only wrote poems about a subject from a distance. None had my voice in them; they didn't have *I*. But this whole year almost every single poem of mine has my voice, not just metaphors. I learned that I no longer need to think of topics to write poems about, but that I'm always inspired to write poems. That's one reason why I've been so productive.
>
> I think I wrote a better short story this year than last because I started with my character, not the plot. I was having a hard time with that last year. I also tried to make my theme and characters a little more everyday. The "Elements of Fiction" helped me focus in on the character and what needs to be in him/her. That's really what helped me have a more successful short story.

At the beginning of the school year I was discouraged about the amount of writing I was expected to write, and also the different genres I had to try. I'd never written half of them. But now, at the end of the year, I've been able to do all the expected things, and I didn't have to struggle as much as I thought I would. I wrote more in general. I almost never wrote at home in the past, but now I do all the time. That's how I get a lot of poetry started. I don't let my ideas go anymore. Even though the expectations intimidated me at first, I wouldn't have written as much if I wasn't pushed at the beginning.

I never thought about putting a collection of poems together to form a story, like *I Am Wings* and *Been to Yesterdays*. I'm definitely going to try that genre soon. And Stevens' "Thirteen Ways of Looking at a Blackbird" and Walt Whitman's Civil War ballads were two new genres for me, too, and if we weren't assigned to write them, I probably never would have known they existed. "Ways" poems are a genre I have continued to use. Since I've gotten more assignments to write specific poems, I have widened my genres and increased quantity.

I have learned so many spelling and comma rules. It makes me more nervous when I write, because I try to be so aware of putting them in, but at the same time I can be more confident about my writing because people can focus on the meaning in my writing, and not my mistakes. The spelling workshops and comma minilessons were a direct help in this.

Of my twenty-seven pieces of finished writing, my most effective were my bat mitzvah speech and the profile that was published in the *Wiscasset Newspaper*. From writing these I really learned how to write about people, including myself, so I can make people I care about and the community aware of them. In my speech my subjects were myself, my feelings, and God; and in the profile, it was Georgi Thompson, a very important woman in our community.

Reading Don Murray's chapter from *Write to Learn* helped me start my profile. That was definitely the hardest part for me. These pieces of writing took so much work, and I got to learn all the techniques while writing them, like different ways of starting and outlining with Murray.

No one knows Rachel's writing like Rachel knows it. As Linda Rief has observed, "Until we realize that the student is the best evaluator of his or her own learning, we will never know what our students really know or are able to do" (1992, 131). Because they write and read in a workshop, Rachel and her seventh and eighth grade classmates are in a constant state of self-evaluation.

Self-assessment begins in writing conferences. It manifests itself in the choices students make as writers and revisers of writing. And it drives kids' analyses of literature, and themselves as readers of literature, in the pages of their reading journals. When I ask kids, "How's it coming?", when they conduct writing conferences with themselves about their own drafts, when they tell a friend what they want help with in a peer conference, when they identify what an author has done in creating a book they love or one they hate—they have stepped back from engagement to become evaluators. In the day-to-day workings of a workshop, kids ask for help, make decisions, set plans and goals, and form judgments. They learn how to look at what they've done and what they need to do next. They learn how to articulate what they understand and recognize where they're still on shaky ground.

Whether I'm teaching in a system that requires letter grades, number grades, or doesn't grade; whether I have 125 students or 25; whether there are standardized tests, local assessments, final exams, teacher narratives, or portfolios; if I'm teaching in a workshop, I have to figure out how to put students' appraisals of their work at the heart of the evaluation process. At the Center for Teaching and Learning, self-assessment comprises a major chunk of our approach to evaluation.

The formal evaluation scheme at the Center features three components: students' portfolios and self-assessment questionnaires, teachers' written comments, and student-led conferences with their parents and the teacher. Throughout the year, teachers keep records of observations of each student's daily work in math, writing, and reading; and children keep their own records of activities and accomplishments. The work our students produce stays at the Center for the duration of the school year, in folders, so we and our kids can observe signs of growth over time and establish appropriate goals.

At the end of each trimester students select representative work for inclusion in their portfolios. These are three-ring binders with plastic sleeves inside to hold photographs, record-keeping forms, samples of work, and other two-dimensional materials that illustrate the efforts of the trimester. There's no standard list of what a portfolio includes. At the same time, in order for portfolios to represent the activities of a trimester and our school's program, students collect lists of books read and pieces written, personal spelling lists, individual proofreading lists, individual math computation records, photos that the teachers have taken of students at work and of the work itself, examples of work produced in each discipline and each major unit of study, and students' self-evaluation questionnaires.

Our goal in using portfolios is to collect evidence that documents what a student has worked on and produced and how he or she has grown. The portfolios are personal, but not idiosyncratic; representative, but not standardized. At the end of a trimester, each subject area class becomes a self-assessment/portfolio workshop, as students draft answers to the questions that teachers pose in the self-evaluation questionnaires, and as they compile and photocopy the contents of their binders.

Teachers write notes about each student's achievements and the goals we determine should be our kids' next steps. We also create lists of the minilessons, discussions, read-alouds, activities, topics, and concepts of the trimester in each subject area. Both documents become part of a student's permanent record, and parents receive copies of the notes and lists at the evaluation conferences.

The student leads the evaluation conference and talks parents and teachers through the work collected in the portfolio. Then teachers describe our observations of the student's progress and achievements in writing, reading, history, science, and math, and we explain the goals the student needs to work toward in the subsequent trimester. We invite parents to discuss their impressions of what's working for the child or their concerns about the child's program or progress; the teacher adds any parent comments to the evaluation notes.

In June each student and his or her teachers coauthor a final report that's intended to provide a portrait of the child, as a learner and person, at the completion of a school year. The student portion of the report consists of a summative self-evaluation questionnaire. The teacher portion takes a semi-narrative form—descriptive phrases rather than prose paragraphs. It details a student's strengths and accomplishments and the goals the child needs to work toward.

We've revised or adapted our evaluation scheme almost every year since the school opened, striving always for a balanced reporting system that gives the fullest possible picture of a student's abilities, reflects what happens in our classrooms, involves parents, doesn't exhaust the teachers (not totally, anyway), and relies on students' assessments of what they know, can do, have done, and need to do next. Throughout the history of our school, in every subject and at every grade level, evaluation has always begun with self-evaluation.

Self-Evaluation

Three times a year I compose a list of questions I want my students to consider in assessing where they've been and where they'll go next. I type these up as two questionnaires, one for writing and one for reading. My questions ask kids to collect and record data about their accomplishments, articulate their criteria for good work, describe their growth and new knowledge and activity, set goals, and assess the progress they made toward the goals of the previous trimester. The questions I ask them to think about fall roughly into four categories.

Some ask for hard data: the quantity of books read and pieces written, the genres represented, the number of pages written in a student's reading journal. Some ask for definitions of criteria: most effective pieces of writing and why; favorite books, read-alouds, authors, poems, poets, and minilessons and why. Some of my questions review the work of the trimester and ask kids about the topics we emphasized in minilessons and literature studies. And some invite writers and readers to assess their habits, progress, and growth, then consider what they need or want to work on next.

Each questionnaire is two pages long and includes between six and ten questions, with lines and blank spaces for students' answers. Figures 9-1 and 9-2 show two examples of self-evaluation questionnaires, one for the first trimester of writing and the other for the second trimester of reading. As a trimester draws to a close, I spend part of a Sunday afternoon reviewing my plan book from the previous twelve weeks and setting the questions I hope will help my kids do two things: reflect on the trimester that has passed and look ahead to the next one.

The writing and reading questionnaires always begin by asking for hard data:

- How many pieces of writing did you finish this trimester?
- What genres are represented among these pieces?
- How many books did you finish this trimester?
- What genres are represented among these titles?
- How many pages of letters have we written in your reading journal?

These represent the important numbers in a workshop—to parents, who recognize quantity as one measure of achievement; to me, so I can see who met the course expectations and the individual goals of the previous trimester; to students, who get perspective on what they have accomplished as writers and readers over the weeks and months of the trimester.

The questions below, which appear regularly in self-evaluations, ask students to choose their most effective work and decide what makes it

FIGURE 9-1   Sample Seventh Grade Writing Self-Evaluation

WRITING SELF-EVALUATION: TRIMESTER 1

NAME _Michael_   DATE _11/27_

1. How many pieces of writing did you finish? _7_
   What genres are represented among these pieces?

   Poetry   _Book review_   _____

   Debate   _Cover letter_   _____

2. Which piece of writing do you consider your most effective? _"Fiery Sparks"_

   Why? What did you do as the author?

   Throughout the piece I used metaphors, something
   new for me. Also something new was using a simile.
   The lines were what I wanted them to be; they gave the
   right meaning. The linebreaks were also very pleasing to
   me. The image in this poem was made stronger by the
   fact that this really did happen to me, in Rangeley.

3. How did you use your territories list this trimester?

   I used it as a source of ideas for writing poems. If
   I was going to start a new piece and had no ideas, I
   would refer to it. I used it many times for ideas, and
   I added little ideas onto it. It was a list to always
   fall back on.

4. What new things did you try as a writer?

   ① To write a piece of fiction on a subject that
   had never happened to me and I knew little about
   and to research it by reading other fiction about the
   subject.

   ② Writing a poem as a gift to my grandmother.

FIGURE 9-1, continued

5. What have you learned about the elements of fiction and writing short stories?

Learning about character, problem, and pace:

Character is one of the most important parts of fiction. If I don't have a strong, main character, the reader won't want to read my story.

Problem is something I have trouble with. There has to be a problem in order for the main character to change. It can be a major theme in a story. It also can really help you think about what is going to happen and what <u>needs</u> to happen.

Pace can be very slow or quite fast. The pace can help the writer with setting the mood, and what the characters are feeling.

6. What would you do differently if you could rewrite the trimester?

Start with a memoir, so I could get into the mood of writing the short narrative form.

Although I did write a lot of poetry, starting with poetry was not good for me.

7. What are your goals for the second trimester?

① To finish my short story

② Start a memoir about CTL

effective—to define the criteria they bring to bear as writers and readers of texts.

- Which piece of writing do you consider your most effective?
- Why? What did you do as the author?
- How did you come up with the idea for this piece?
- What was your favorite book among those you read on your own?
- What makes it the best? What did the author do?
- How did you find or choose this book?
- What was your favorite poem? Why?
- What was your favorite read-aloud? Why?

Other questions about criteria reflect the particular focus of a trimester's work. In connection with specific studies, I have asked my students:

- What are the elements of fiction you consider most important in a short story or novel? Why?
- What's the most important or useful information about conventions of written English you learned this trimester? Why?

FIGURE 9-2   Sample Seventh Grade Reading Self-Evaluation

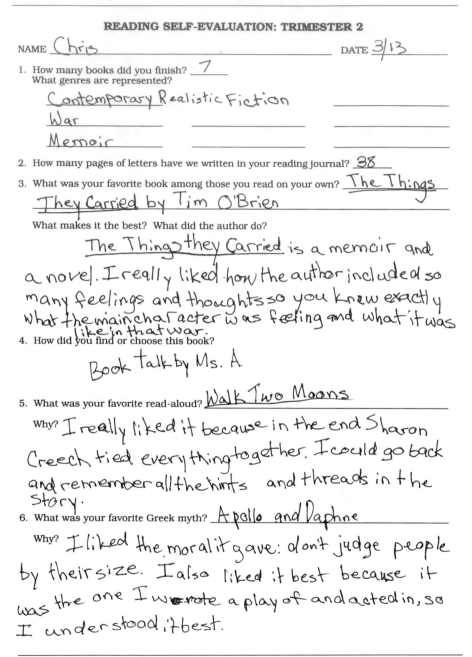

READING SELF-EVALUATION: TRIMESTER 2

NAME Chris   DATE 3/13

1. How many books did you finish? __7__
   What genres are represented?

   Contemporary Realistic Fiction   _____
   War   _____   _____
   Memoir   _____   _____

2. How many pages of letters have we written in your reading journal? 38

3. What was your favorite book among those you read on your own? The Things
   They Carried by Tim O'Brien

   What makes it the best? What did the author do?

   The Things they Carried is a memoir and
   a novel. I really liked how the author included so
   many feelings and thoughts so you knew exactly
   what the main character was feeling and what it was
   like in that war.

4. How did you find or choose this book?

   Book Talk by Ms. A.

5. What was your favorite read-aloud? Walk Two Moons

   Why? I really liked it because in the end Sharon
   Creech tied everything together. I could go back
   and remember all the hints and threads in the
   story.

6. What was your favorite Greek myth? Apollo and Daphne

   Why? I liked the moral it gave: don't judge people
   by their size. I also liked it best because it
   was the one I wrote a play of and acted in, so
   I understood it best.

FIGURE 9-2, continued

7. What will you take away from our study of Greek mythology and culture?

I learned about how the Greeks explained every day things by making up a story or myth. Also how many Greek words show up today, like panic from Pan.

8. Evaluate the process of finding a poem that resonates for you, preparing a presentation, and actually presenting it. What were the problems? How did you solve them? What was enjoyable or satisfying? What did you learn?

① Find a poem you love: a poem where you love the language and the images it gives you, and the description.
② Find things about the poet: little tidbits of information. Then think about what you want people to do with the poem and how they can enjoy it.
③ It was enjoyable to share William Stafford with other people and difficult to choose just one poem.

9. What were your reading goals at the start of the trimester?

① Read a new genre, not a mystery or thriller.
② Read at least 6 books.
③ Write deeper letters in my journal.

What progress did you make toward meeting them?

I read 7 books. I didn't read any mysteries. The Things... was a new genre and I'm reading another O'Brien. I think I'm talking more about the author and my feelings in my letters.

10. What are your goals for yourself as a reader during the final trimester?

① Read more than 7 books.
② Try to read an autobiography or biography, something non-fiction.

- Who are the writers who influence your writing? What do you learn from each of them?
- Who is a new favorite novelist you discovered this trimester? What appeals to you about this writer's style?
- Who is your favorite poet? What appeals to you about this poet's style?
- What is your favorite Greek myth? Why?
- Of the Shakespearean plays you know, which is your favorite? Why?

Sometimes, in my questions that review the work of a trimester, I ask students to articulate what they remember and will take away. I've discovered the importance, if their learning is to last, of creating formal occasions for students to put things into words—to sum up and capture a learning experience and not let it melt away into hazy recollection.

- Evaluate the process of writing a profile (or play, essay, memoir, short story, etc.). What were the problems? How did you solve them? What was enjoyable or satisfying? What did you learn about writing this genre?
- List the conventions we discussed this trimester that you use these days in your writing—or, at least, of which you're extra aware.
- What have you learned about writing a poem?
- What have you learned about reading a poem?
- Evaluate the process of finding a poem that resonates for you, preparing a presentation, and presenting it. What were the problems? How did you solve them? What was enjoyable or satisfying? What did you learn?
- What will you take away from our study of Greek mythology and culture?
- What will you take away from our study of Shakespeare's life and times, from the plays and sonnets?
- What will you take away from our reading and study of Hinton's *The Outsiders*?
- What will you take away from our study of Walt Whitman (or any of the other poets whose life and work I asked students to look at in depth)?
- What were the most meaningful minilessons and discussions of the trimester: which ones helped and will stay with you?

The most important questions are the true self-evaluators. These nudge students to look inward, take stock, reflect, make plans, and set goals. I ask six constants every trimester:

- What were your writing goals at the start of the trimester?
- What progress did you make toward meeting them?
- What are your goals as a writer for the next trimester?

- What were your reading goals at the start of the trimester?
- What progress did you make toward meeting them?
- What are your goals as a reader for the next trimester?

Similar questions I've posed, to invite students to reflect on who they are as writers and readers, have included:

- What did you learn about yourself as a writer this trimester?
- What have I/we done in writing workshop that helped you?
- What helped you most as a writer of literature?
- What new things did you try as a writer?
- How did you use your writing territories list?
- What would you do differently as a writer, if you could rewrite the trimester?
- What do you do outside of school, as a writer, that I don't know about?

- What did you learn about yourself as a reader this trimester?
- What have I/we done in reading workshop that helped you?
- What helped you most as a reader?
- What helped you most as a reader of literature?
- What new things did you try as a reader?
- What would you do differently as a reader, if you could rewrite the trimester?
- What do you do outside of school, as a reader, that I don't know about?

Students draft answers to the questions in class and as homework during the self-assessment/portfolio workshops of late November, early March, and June. I circulate among them, confer about their answers, and edit the drafts of the questionnaires. Students produce a final copy for homework, then insert these in their portfolios.

Every June, as I understand more each year about how well students can judge and what exactly they might be judging, I revise and reformat the final self-evaluation questionnaire. For example, one year the questions I posed in the final questionnaire focused narrowly:

- What did you read this year that helped your writing? Name the authors and texts that influenced you and tell a little bit about what you took away from each.

- What was your favorite read-aloud of the school year? Why?
- What new things did you try as a poet?
- What effect, if any, did demonstrations of my writing have on your writing?
- Where did the ideas for your best pieces of writing come from? List your sources of inspiration.

Kids' responses were interesting from a research standpoint but not comprehensive. The questions didn't invite them to look at the big picture of themselves as writers and readers. So the next year I went with more global queries, to which students responded by composing narratives (à la the excerpt from Rachel's that opens this chapter):

- How have you grown as a writer during this school year? Describe all the changes you can think of.
- What changed you? Describe the experiences, expectations, and kinds of help you received: in short, how did you get to be so smart as a writer?
- How have you grown as a reader during this school year? Describe all the changes you can think of.
- What changed you? Describe the experiences, expectations, and kinds of help you received: in short, how did you get to be so smart as a reader?

Although some students' responses to the broader questions were eloquent and specific, others were brief or not particularly insightful. Kids left out a lot when I didn't provide a prompt that helped them retrieve experiences and discover their meanings.

Last June I tried to strike a balance between picky little questions and more global queries; the result is the questionnaire that became my students' half of the final report to their parents. It asks students to recount hard data, name their favorites, define criteria, summarize changes in their use of conventions, assess strengths and weaknesses, and relate their accomplishments as writers and readers. Figure 9-3 shows an eighth grade boy's final self-evaluation. It reveals who he is as a writer and reader in his own voice; it also gives him a platform to show what he knows, formally lay claim to his knowledge, and recognize what he doesn't know.

Appendix O provides a slightly revised (I will never stop fiddling with it) version of a final self-evaluation questionnaire for students who write and read in a workshop. If I were teaching today in a different setting—if

FIGURE 9-3 Sample Eighth Grade Final Self-Evaluation Questionnaire

Final Self-Evaluation

General (Personal and Social Development)

What is your favorite subject? _Reading_

What is something you've accomplished this year at school, apart from academics?

Strong friendships that I hope will last throughout my life.

What is something you wish you had done differently? _Planned ahead and worked harder towards my goals._

Writing and Spelling

How many pieces of writing did you finish this year? _26_

What genres are represented?

Response to a film		_Thank-you letter_
Poetry	_Parody_	_Research report_
Short Story	_Essay_	_Speech_
Memoir	_Letter of Complaint_	_Play_

What are your favorite genres to write? _Poetry_

Which pieces of writing are your most effective? Why? (What did you do as the author?)

I think my short story was the most effective because of the response I got from my peers. Personally I don't know what I did that made it the most effective — probably because of the believeable and realistic dialogue and a strong theme.

What writing rules and conventions have you mastered? _Colon before a list; Semi-colon to connect two related sentences; when to capitalize titles; dash to emphasize; keep a consistent verb tense; Harvard comma; business letter format; apostrophes to show possession._

What changes have you made in your approaches to spelling? _Take apart the word; use mnemonics to help me; try alternative versions of an unknown word._

I had 100+ students and was required to put grades on report cards—I would adapt the final self-evaluation questionnaire further and leave a space at the bottom of the last page for brief teacher comments about the areas in which a student made gains and the areas where there was still work to be done.

FIGURE 9-3, continued

What are your strengths as a writer? Metaphors; common punctuation; Harvard comma; realistic dialogue; character development; poetry; when to start a new paragraph; having a good lead that grabs the reader and pulls them into the story; creating a character that people like.

What are the areas in which you can improve? I need to set my mind to it and just write; I need to work on pacing the action, use all the elements of fiction, and avoid comma splices.

Reading

How many books did you finish this year? 25

What genres are represented?

Contemporary realistic fiction	War Story
	Diary
Anti-war novel	Mystery
Science fiction	

What are your favorite genres to read? C.R. fiction

Which books were the best? Why? (What did the authors do?) I really liked Kurt Vonnegut's Slapstick. I liked the way he introduced the main character and the point of view he chose. The whole story was a flashback, and there were ten different themes.

Who are your favorite authors? Kurt Vonnegut, Robert McCammon

Who are your favorite poets? William Stafford

Which poems were the best? "Bummer", "Digging for China", "The Fish", "Autobiography in 5 short Chapters", "Local Events"

What literary techniques can you identify and appreciate in the texts you read?
Metaphors, flashbacks, Personification, strong character development, simile, alliteration, emerging themes in fiction, suspenseful twists in plot.

FIGURE 9-3, continued

What are your strengths as a reader? I have schemas for lots of different kinds of writing. I understand books by authors. I know when to skip and skim. I know what I like. I can Identify good books by authors. I have a good reading vocabulary. I know how to choose books. I know different authors' styles.

What are the areas in which you can improve? I need to analyze more what the writer has done, take a break from the same writer and read easy books, and get better at abandoning.

Teacher Evaluation

In evaluating my students, I know whatever system I use has to take into account the range of abilities that come into play when anyone writes or reads. Writing, by way of example, involves experimenting, planning, choosing, questioning, anticipating, putting words on paper legibly, analyzing, organizing, reading, listening, assessing, reviewing, spelling, formatting, punctuating, using other conventions, editing, proofreading. I also know one piece of writing can't provide an accurate picture of a student's abilities but represents a step in a writer's growth.

So reliability—fairness to my students and my understandings of writing and reading—becomes one of my criteria as an evaluator. Validity is another. My system for grading should reflect the expectations I communicate to my kids, day in and out, in the workshop. For evaluation to be valid, I can't turn around at the end of nine or twelve weeks and impose "objective" standards for "good" writing on the collections in the folders, or for "good" reading on the response journals and lists of finished books, and rank them accordingly. When Melissa tries her hand at a letter to the editor, attempting to persuade readers of the local paper to vote to close Maine Yankee, the local nuclear power plant, it's the attempt I value first. As a writer she's trying a new genre, persuasion, and risking a wide, critical audience. I'll help her research and organize her information. I'll ask her to consider the attitudes and needs of her readers, many of whom count on the plant for employment and property tax breaks. But when the letter isn't particularly well argued, I won't punish the attempt in my grade book or view it as a failure. My own writing and my students' have taught me that

growth in writing isn't a linear progress, with each piece representing an improvement over the last. I know it's hard to write well when I'm trying new genres or chancing complex topics.

Teacher evaluation in the workshop must focus on the big picture: who a student is becoming—and who he or she might become—as a writer and reader. But teachers must also draw close to the canvas and look and look again at as many of its features as we can observe. Our responsibilities as evaluators involve collecting and sifting through the evidence that reveals what a student can do and can't do, understands and doesn't understand, has accomplished and needs to accomplish.

I gather this evidence at the end of each trimester, beginning with the contents of the portfolios. These include my students' self-evaluation questionnaires and photocopies of their personal spelling lists, individual proofreading lists, records of books read and pieces written, the entries from their writing-reading handbooks that they chose as most useful, their favorite in-class poems, one or two pieces of their best writing of the trimester, including all drafts and notes, and one or two favorite or representative letters from their reading journals. I add my status-of-the-class records to the evidence. Then, based on these data, I write notes for the parent-teacher-student conference.

Figure 9-4 shows my writing and reading evaluations of two seventh

FIGURE 9-4a   Teacher Evaluation of Jess

1st Trimester Progress Report

Student: _Jess_   Grade: _7_ Teacher: _Nancie Atwell_   Date: _11/30_

ACCOMPLISHMENTS AND STRENGTHS	GOALS
Writing • Finished 8 pieces of writing representing 4 genres: business letter, poetry, collaborative poem, + memoir. Only the last was self-initiated; remainder were projects I assigned/suggested. Is many pages into a s.story + feeling discouraged. Content and style-wise, trying to get her feet under her: learn new habits of mind + apply new techniques • Experimented with brainstorming titles to find the best + with line and stanza breaks; is consulting a thesaurus; picked up speed at the keyboard; is beginning to understand drafting/revision. • Highly conventional prose: excellent, adult-like spelling; correct punctuation, apart from overuse of commas; and appropriate paragraphing. • Her writer's voice shows in her reading journal: fluent and funny here. How to get this Jess into her narratives + poetry?	• Understand in-school writing as an opportunity for self-expression and exploration; use her territories list to help her develop projects she cares about. • Continue to add ideas, feelings, relationships, experiences, objects, people, problems that matter to her to her territories list. • Finish a short story; more poetry.
Reading • Finished 14 books representing 4 genres: fantasy, supernatural, mystery, and contemporary realistic fiction. Favorite was <u>The Juniper Game</u> by Sherryl Jordan; favorite poem was Updike's "Dog's Death." • Gives, seeks, and responds to others' recommendations; has lively, literary relationships with Alice + Emily in particular. • Is drawn to novels with extreme plots: a safe way to experience the dark side. Has also pushed off into young adult literature (e.g., John Neufeld + Robert Cormier). • Excellent comprehension: a fast, fluent reader. • Becoming an adept reader of poetry: thoughtful contributions to discussions of poems. • Reading journal responses are insightful; is making connections between texts, as well as observations about character development that draw directly on mini-lessons about fiction.	• Try Sherryl Jordan's other two novels. • Try more novels about adolescents and their feelings and experiences. • Continue to push in her reading journal to explore how the author wrote, why, and to what effect.

graders at the end of the first trimester. (I also comment on my students' progress in history, the other subject I teach; the math and science teachers write notes of their own; and we combine these as one report.) Jess transferred to the Center as a seventh grader and was new to a workshop approach; Alice had been choosing her own books and topics since first grade. In my notes I summarize a student's accomplishments in terms of quantity and range, note the new things he or she attempted, describe strengths and areas of concerns, analyze progress made toward previous goals, and set new ones. The objectives I list are a combination: some represent goals identified by students in their self-evaluation questionnaires, and others are the areas I identify in my observations of a student at work or in the work itself.

I limit myself to setting two or three high-priority goals because the student has already set goals, and because I know kids can only work on so much at one time. If they're overwhelmed by objectives, it's unlikely they'll be able to attend to or accomplish any of them.

In class on the day after I've written up my notes, I loan them to the stu-

FIGURE 9-4b   Teacher Evaluation of Alice

1st Trimester Progress Report

Student: *Alice*   Grade: 7   Teacher: *Nancie Atwell*   Date: *12·1*

ACCOMPLISHMENTS AND STRENGTHS	GOALS
Writing	
• Finished 10 pieces of writing representing 6 genres: poetry, essay, parody (of a political ad), speech, memoir, collaborative poem. Also made progress on a L-O-N-G short story. Identified her letter-to-an-author essay (submitted to *Read* contest) as most effective: developed a planning sheet to generate & order ideas and stretched, hard, in taking on a non-narrative genre. A productive trimester.	• Finish her short story and try to get it published; a book review; perhaps another parody?
• Other stretches were the parody, campaign speech, & attempts to develop a rounded main character.	• Get frequently mis-spelled words (we've identified about 20 of them) under control: break these habits now.
• Quick to experiment; spends considerable time reading, revising, and polishing her writing. The results (e.g., ω the letter to author LouAnne Johnson) can be stunning.	
• Her wide reading is apparent in her prose: it flows.	• Experiment with new marks (: ; —) to give her writing greater voice.
• Spelling issues and comma splices are conventions she hasn't conquered yet; #ing & sentence structure good.	
Reading	
• Finished 9 books representing 3 genres: short stories, memoirs, and contemporary realistic fiction. Favorite was Torey Hayden's *Ghost Girl*; also loved L. Johnson's memoirs of teaching in L.A. Favorite poem was Margaret Atwood's "Bored."	• Read more books (She says, "Read more than nine.").
• Attends hungrily to mini-lessons about poets & poetry, as well as booktalks by peers and me.	• Take a more analytic stance in the letters in her reading journal: describe connections & teach herself by exploring her thoughts about the writing she reads.
• At a crossroads: moving into a young adult identity and looking for lit. with strong emotions that explores extremes of experience.	
• Is learning how to skim.	
• Fast, fluent, motivated reader; excellent comprehension and reading vocabulary.	• Try some contemporary poetry on her own: Oliver? Pastan? Stafford?
• Reading journal entries are mostly reports ("I finished that; now I'm reading this") or plot synopses.	

dent and direct him or her to copy the goals onto two index cards—one for writing and one for reading—and staple them to the inside pockets of the writing and reading folders. I want students to have prominent, daily reminders of what they're supposed to concentrate on over the subsequent twelve weeks. These goals run the gamut—from conventions and work habits to techniques, strategies, procedures, genre experimentation, and book and topic selection. The lists below illustrate the range and specificity of the objectives I've established for my kids or they've established for themselves.

SAMPLE GOALS FOR WRITERS

- Confer with yourself. Read your writing as an *other* and decide for yourself what works and what needs more work.
- Draw on personal knowledge in your short fiction and essays: problems you care about or know about.
- Push off into genres that will stretch you intellectually: parody, essays, poetry.

- View writing less as a performance and more as an opportunity to explore, experiment, look inward, and discover what matters.
- Write more prose: discover how memoirs, short fiction, and essays can explore your feelings, experiences, and perspective.
- Try at least two new genres next trimester. Check out the list of kinds of writing in your daily folder.
- Update and refer to your territories list, so you can become accustomed to thinking and planning as a writer.
- Use writing more as an occasion for personal reflection: push yourself to name and examine your thoughts and feelings.
- Focus: stick to one memory, topic, or big idea in each piece of writing.
- Tell more in your writing. Provide the details that will help readers see, hear, and feel your narratives, essays, and profiles.
- Work from quantity: experiment with alternatives—several different leads, passages, sections, examples, conclusions, titles— then choose and work with the best.
- In your prose, focus on coherence: moving logically from point A to B to C and anticipating a reader's questions and need for information along the way.
- Write more prose: concentrate on putting sentences and paragraphs together to build coherent prose texts.
- Write a sustained piece of short fiction: a character who changes, a problem, setting, plot, theme, the works.
- Begin your next piece of short fiction by developing a character, and use the main character questionnaire to help you.
- Finish your short story.
- Finish your profile of X and try to get it published.
- Write a book review and submit it to *Voices from the Middle*.
- Try parody.
- Try some open-form poetry.
- Try a poem that uses a given form (e.g., sestina, sonnet, cinquain).
- Try a feature article or piece of original research: investigate a topic or person of special interest to you.
- Work on embedding context in your narratives: weave in the who-what-where-when-and-why amid the dialogue and action.
- Include more of your reflections in your prose—your thoughts and feelings about why events or ideas are significant to you. Give your readers a way in, a person to be with.

- Work on succinctness, or at least deletion after the fact. What don't you need? What doesn't add to the character, plot, tone, theme, idea?
- When you read fiction, begin to notice how authors begin and conclude their novels and short stories and develop their main characters.
- Ask for group response to problems in your drafts—or at least response beyond me and the same one friend.
- Spend less time conferring with peers. Pull through difficulty with more independence, push for closure, finish a draft, then seek others' responses.
- Ask a serious writer/friend to interview you when you're stuck for your next topic or genre.
- Work at a faster pace when attempting short fiction.
- Finish more pieces of writing. Bull things through and try not to abandon so much or soon.
- Produce three to five pages of rough draft each week.
- Bring at least two pieces of writing to final copy every six weeks.
- Be more scrupulous about record keeping: record titles of finished pieces and file them chronologically, with all drafts, in your permanent writing folder.
- Organize yourself. Take time at the end of each workshop to straighten your folder and file your drafts. Make a special place in your locker to store your daily writing folder.
- Record new conventions on your proofreading list immediately after each editing conference with me.
- Slow down your handwriting.
- Abandon cursive, except for your signature, and print your texts.
- Spend more time on final copies. When you're finished, proofread them with a pen in your hand.
- Proofread for sense: for missing words and missing word endings (e.g., s and ed).
- Attend to conventions while drafting: punctuate, capitalize, and paragraph as well as you can, right from the start.
- Spell as conventionally as you can in your drafts.
- Draft your poems in lines and stanzas.
- Draft your prose in paragraphs.
- Watch for too many paragraphs.

- Self-edit for spelling by circling, then looking up, every word you're not absolutely sure of.
- Proofread for spelling at the single word level; try proofing your writing backwards for misspellings.
- Use our word-study procedure deliberately to master a handful of spellings at a time.
- Use the spell check on the computer before you edit by hand and eye.
- Get homonyms (especially *your/you're*, *their/they're/there*, and *it's/its*) under control.
- Listen for periods: for where your voice drops and stops.
- Try new marks to give your writing greater voice, e.g., ; : and — .
- Learn the basic conventions governing commas; delete unnecessary commas.
- Recognize and keep a consistent verb tense in narratives.
- Avoid passive voice. Use active constructions: *I.*
- Make more use of direct quotes: bring speakers' words to life rather than paraphrasing them.
- Develop a style of rough-draft-handwriting that's more consistently legible.
- Capitalize only when you intend to.
- Work on legibility: close your *os*, *as*, *ds*, etc. and extend the tails of *ts*, *fs*, *ps*, etc.
- Watch for comma splices. Connect independent clauses with *and*, start a new sentence, or use a semicolon.
- Put punctuation—! or ? or ,—between a quote and its explanatory phrase (never a period).
- Use apostrophes on contractions to show missing letters: don't, let's, that's, etc.
- Eliminate the qualifiers and diminishers that can clutter writing: *so*, *really*, *very*, *sort of*, *kind of*.
- Watch out for convoluted sentences: too many phrases and clauses hooked together with commas and conjunctions can lose a reader and the thread of sense.
- Work toward conciseness in your poetry: cut to the bone.
- Practice keyboarding some of your final copies, especially the shorter texts (e.g., poems).

SAMPLE GOALS FOR READERS

- Read with a finger on your lips to prevent lipreading, which slows your reading rate and prevents chunking of text.
- Read with a finger on your throat to prevent word-by-word inner vocalizing.
- Read as fast as you can, trying to see "chunks" instead of one word at a time. Read for the meaning of a text, not to say the words. Push distractions away and forge ahead.
- Get out of the habit of using a card or bookmark to underline your reading: it checks peripheral vision and slows you down.
- Experiment with pushing your reading rate: skip, skim, and scan.
- When you get to an uninteresting section of text, try skimming or skipping it: what happens?
- Read as much as you can: the more books and experiences under your belt, the greater your fluency.
- Time yourself: how many pages do you read in a half hour? Can you increase the average number of pages?
- Read more at home: at least a half hour every night.
- Ask your parents for a bedside lamp.
- Develop consistent reading habits: times and places you can expect you'll get lost in a book.
- Read just one book at a time so your experiences with books are literary and coherent and so you can respond in literary, coherent ways.
- Don't stick with a book you're not enjoying. Give the author [some number of pages or chapters] and if you aren't happy with the writing, abandon the book.
- Try a longer novel (e.g., more than 150 pages).
- Try to finish two more books than last trimester.
- Begin to identify authors you love, and follow through with more of their books.
- Ask for recommendations of good books from me and your friends.
- Insist on authors, books, and genres that compel you, so you are never marking time or trying to satisfy someone else's tastes in literature.
- Try new authors who write about your interests: Arthur Roth? Will Hobbs? Mary Oliver? Robert Frost?
- Try at least one book that represents a different kind of writing than you've been reading.

- Expand your range of genres/schemas.
- Try some popular fiction that's more literary, e.g., Doctorow, Vonnegut, Kesey, Updike, Ondaatje.
- Try some contemporary poetry. Stick Post-it notes to, photocopy, and collect your favorites.
- Try one of Shakespeare's plays on your own.
- Try a classic: *Jane Eyre? Great Expectations?*
- Begin to explore young adult literature about peer relationships.
- Give Caroline Cooney another try; look at Sheryl Jordan's other novels.
- Begin to identify authors of adult fiction to whom you can look for satisfying reading experiences, e.g., Lamott, Hoffman, Atwood, Atkinson, Colwin, Kingsolver, Plath.
- Give a booktalk to the group about Fannie Flagg's novels.
- In your journal, synopsize plot less and analyze writing more: tell what you think of how a book is written.
- Push yourself to interpret and analyze more: What has the author done? Why? How? To what effect?
- Describe what you thought about and felt as you read a book.
- When you like a book, try to name the techniques and features you're responding to.
- When dissatisfied with a novel's conclusion (e.g., an ambiguous or unhappy ending), consider why the author had characters make these choices. What theme is he or she pointing?
- Read my letters to you in your reading journal, and respond to what I've written.
- Write letters at least a page long in response to your reading.
- Stay on-topic in your reading journal (i.e., books, authors, reading, and writing).
- Remember to bring a book to class with you every day.
- Remember to write regularly in your journal: once a week, and to me at least every two weeks.
- Return books you borrow to the shelves.

This evaluation scheme—student self-assessment and goal setting combined with teacher description, analysis, and goal setting—fits my school, its philosophy and curriculum. Teachers do not assign grades at the Center. A student's incentive is the work itself—improving as a writer and reader, accomplishing goals, experiencing the increasing power and pleasure that writing and reading can bring to one's life. But no matter where I have taught English—suburban middle school, rural elementary school, or private demonstration school—I have never graded individual pieces of writing as part of my evaluation scheme. If I'm to do justice to what I know of writing and writers, I can't. A student writing about the death of his coonhound, expertise as a lobsterman, anger over the principal's decision banning junior high dances, or love for her grandfather, isn't writing for a grade.

If I were responsible for assigning grades to my students, I would base them on students' level of participation in the workshop and the degree of progress they made toward the goals we had set at the beginning of the trimester. At Boothbay, where it was my responsibility four times a year to record letter grades for English and reading on my students' report cards, this is just what I did.

The challenge in grading is to make sure that the grades reflect as closely as we can what our writing and reading programs ask students to do. My writing program at Boothbay asked writers to demonstrate growth in topic selection, level of involvement and intentionality, clarity and grace of language, degree of effort and initiative, completeness and organization of content, and consistency in conventionality, editing, and proofreading. To look for growth I worked from each student's whole collection of writing, always a writing teacher's most reliable basis for evaluation.

I experimented with different formats for grading that would include both student self-assessment and teacher assessment. As a beginning teacher of writing in a workshop, I needed to hear my students' voices and get as close as I could to their thinking. I was also aware that self-evaluation wasn't yet part of their repertoires as beginning writers in a workshop. Rather than give them questionnaires to complete, I conducted brief evaluation interviews with each writer.

During the last week of each grading period I conducted the status-of-the-class conference, then put my other writing teacher roles on hold, asked students to rely on each other for response to works-in-progress, and spent five days of class time conferring with individual writers on their efforts of the previous nine weeks. A week before the close of the grading period I decided on the four or five questions I would pose this time around. Many are the same as those I include today in students' self-evaluation questionnaires, which are listed in the previous section. My final question was always, "What are your goals for the next quarter? What do you want to try to do as a writer?" Students' responses to this question became one of the bases for their grades in writing.

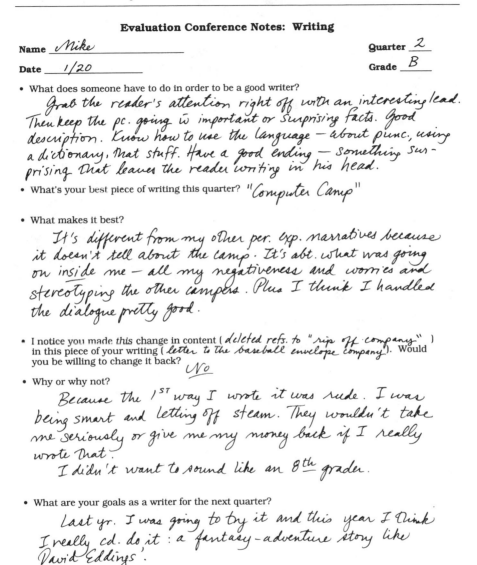

Evaluation Conference Notes: Writing

Name *Mike* Quarter 2

Date *1/20* Grade B

- What does someone have to do in order to be a good writer?

  Grab the reader's attention right off with an interesting lead. Then keep the pc. going w̄ important or surprising facts. Good description. Know how to use the language — about punc., using a dictionary, that stuff. Have a good ending — something surprising that leaves the reader writing in his head.

- What's your best piece of writing this quarter? *"Computer Camp"*

- What makes it best?

  It's different from my other per. exp. narratives because it doesn't tell about the camp. It's abt. what was going on inside me — all my negativeness and worries and stereotyping the other campers. Plus I think I handled the dialogue pretty good.

- I notice you made this change in content (*deleted refs. to "rip off company"*) in this piece of your writing (*letter to the baseball envelope company*). Would you be willing to change it back? *No*

- Why or why not?

  Because the 1ˢᵗ way I wrote it was rude. I was being smart and letting off steam. They wouldn't take me seriously or give me my money back if I really wrote that.
  I didn't want to sound like an 8ᵗʰ grader.

- What are your goals as a writer for the next quarter?

  Last yr. I was going to try it and this year I think I really cd. do it: a fantasy-adventure story like David Eddings'.

Before beginning evaluation conferences I conducted a minilesson about the questions I would be posing in the interviews, then tacked them to the bulletin board. I instructed kids, "You're responsible between now and your conference with me to think about the questions and consider how you'll answer them." Because of the thoughtfulness and seriousness of their responses when they had advance notice of the questions, I'm convinced it's crucial that students rehearse for evaluation conferences and are given responsibility to come prepared to talk.

In the first half of the evaluation conference I asked my four or five questions, working from a preprinted form, and wrote down students' answers; one of the forms appears as Figure 9-5 (see page 323). I learned after trial and error to take dictation during the conference rather than tape-record and transcribe later. By writing as kids spoke, I slowed down the conference and gave a writer a chance to continue thinking and talking while I wrote; I gave myself a chance to continue thinking, too, about follow-up questions. (The one time I tape-recorded conferences and took everything home, I discovered it took me ten hours to transcribe one hour of tape.)

When the interview was concluded, the student and I set goals for the next nine weeks. Prior to the conference I had noted two or three specific things the writer needed to work on; I based the goals on my observations of the student's writing and behavior during the quarter. Again, I limited myself to two or three high-priority goals because at least one more goal would be set by the student in response to the final question and, again, because I know kids can only work on so much at one time.

I came to each conference with a half sheet of paper headed "_____ Quarter Writing Goals for _____" on which I had written down my two or three areas of concern; I also brought a pile of blank copies. At the end of the conference the writer made a copy of the goals for his or her records, returned the original to me, and stapled the copy inside the cover of the daily writing folder.

At the end of the next quarter I based a writer's grade on the progress he or she had made toward the goals we established in the previous evaluation conference. Prior to the new conference I reviewed the goals from last time around, then assigned a letter grade reflecting what I observed in the student's work of the intervening nine weeks. If a student had accomplished his or her goals, I gave a grade of A; if there was good or more than adequate progress, a B. Adequate or fair work received a C; students who did little received Ds; and if a student did nothing—or lost everything—I gave a failing grade (this happened one time in my history as a teacher at Boothbay).

At the close of the evaluation conferences I told students their grades for writing and explained how had I arrived at them in terms of progress made toward goals. The conclusion of my conference with Mike, the boy interviewed in Figure 9-5, illustrates how I set a grade and communicated it to the writer.

Ms. A.: Mike, your goals for this past quarter were to try some new kinds of writing—to go beyond personal-experience narrative—and to work on proofreading finals so you didn't end up making a lot of new mistakes on the published copy.

MIKE: I really spent a lot of time on that.

A: Believe me, I noticed. I appreciate it. When I read your stuff—at the end, when I can read it as a reader, not an editor—I didn't find myself distracted the way I did last quarter. Mistakes didn't get in my way.

M: Yeah, my mother noticed that, too.

A: So, that's a goal you've conquered. That's something you can do. What about the other goal, trying something new?

M: I really didn't do too much on that. Except for my letters, my pieces are still mostly stories about me. But I am going to try fiction this quarter.

A: Your David Eddings–type story?

M: Yeah. And I also think I'm going to write two more letters. One to that guy who invented Logo. . .

A: Seymour Papert?

M: Yeah. And one to the company where I got this last program. They totally screwed up on Logo.

A: Sounds good. So, looking back again, I'd call this solid progress. It's B work. You accomplished one goal and did some work toward the other, with your letters to the baseball company. Let's see what you can do this coming quarter toward your new goals, and toward an A for next time around.

M: Okay.

One of the new goals Mike established was to write a fantasy-adventure short story. A week into the quarter he read a magazine article about Halley's comet that moved him to abandon the short story and conduct and report research into the comet's history and trajectory. I can't penalize a writer for taking this kind of initiative. In a quick conference we changed the evaluation goal to reflect Mike's new project. The goals aren't carved in stone, and if something happens that they require alteration, the writer and I alter them.

At the end of the first quarter I couldn't base grades on progress toward goals because there hadn't yet been time or an occasion to set them. So in this first round of grade setting I looked for what Tom Romano has called "good faith participation" (1987, 113, 126–128) in the expectations and routines of the workshop, as well as growth over time in the basic activities in which writers engage, as defined by Donald Murray and Donald Graves in an unpublished manuscript:

- finding a subject
- collecting specific information on the subject
- ordering the information
- presenting the information with clarity and grace
- following the customs of spelling, mechanics, and usage.

To these I added three criteria of my own:

- amount of time and effort spent on writing
- degree of initiative and thoughtfulness
- daily preparedness.

I copied the criteria onto an overhead transparency, and during the second week of school presented a minilesson in which I explained that progress during the first quarter would be measured by these criteria. Every writer started the school year with the same goals.

In grading reading, too, the system for rating students' progress should match what we ask of them each day in the workshop. At Boothbay I asked my students to come to class every day with a book, read every day in school and at home, follow the rules for reading workshop, and write at least a letter a week in their reading journals. I asked them to go beyond plot in their letters, to analyze and evaluate what they read. And I asked them to grow in the directions I emphasized in my teaching of reading: fluency, pacing and speed, rate adjustment, personal involvement, connections to other texts and to personal experience, recognition of good writing and analysis of what effective writers do, establishment of criteria for selecting and abandoning books, awareness of genres and authors.

I based half of a student's reading grade on the degree to which he or she conformed to workshop procedures and expectations, including the writing in the reading journal, where I looked for quantity—the number of entries and pages—and growth in the depth of a student's responses. I based the other half on the progress a student made toward two or three goals we established in conference at the end of each quarter. In the first quarter, when I didn't know readers well enough to establish individual goals, I figured their grades by averaging adherence to workshop procedures and the quality and quantity of the thinking in their letters.

My reading-evaluation conferences with kids proceeded along the same lines as the quarterly meetings about writing. I asked questions and recorded students' answers; then we evaluated progress toward the goals from the previous quarter and set new ones. In interviewing readers I modeled my questions on those I asked when evaluating writing. "What does someone have to do in order to be a good reader?" explored changing notions of reading. "What's the best book you read this quarter and what makes it the best?" revealed criteria for good writing. And "What do you want to do as a reader during the next nine weeks?" helped students consider strengths, needs, and new directions. Again, many of my questions for students about their reading appear in the previous section as questions readers can ask themselves. Prior to the evaluation conferences I reviewed the questions I'd be asking in a minilesson, so readers could begin to plan their responses. During the conference week I didn't circulate, read, or answer letters, but met briefly with each reader instead.

To each reading evaluation conference I brought a form with my interview questions, a slip of paper on which I had my written goals for the reader, and a blank slip for the student to copy the goals for his or her reference. The sample goals for reading that I listed earlier in this chapter include many of the goals I set for my Boothbay students and they set for themselves.

Tom Romano has observed about evaluation, "Our responses and grades should nurture" (1987, 125). Evaluation of writing and reading in the workshop should focus on young writers and readers and the ways an adult can promote their development by supporting and encouraging kids' efforts and teaching them how to do better next time. Evaluation that nurtures takes time. I think the time is worth it.

When we transform English class into a workshop, when our language arts programs are based on what writers and readers do and need, we give students unmistakable signals about the importance of experience, practice, effort, and self-assessment to their growth and progress. Making evaluation an occasion for a student and teacher to analyze the work together, set goals, and assess progress, extends and enriches students' development. It provides another opportunity for us to learn more about our kids, their writing, and their reading. And it strengthens what happens in the workshop across the days and weeks of a school year. To paraphrase Linda Rief (1992), the better our students become as evaluators of their writing and reading, the better their writing and reading will be.

III
Teaching with a Capital *T*

The work of the world is common as mud.
Botched, it smears the hands, crumbles to dust.
But the one thing worth doing well done
has a shape that satisfies, clean and evident.

· · · · · · · · · · · · · ·

The pitcher cries for water to carry
and a person for work that is real.
Marge Piercy
"To Be of Use"

10
Taking Off the Top of My Head

> Good writing occurs because a writer passionately desires to say
> something. . . . Students do not need more abstract advice about how
> to write. They need somehow to have their feelings kindled.
> X. J. Kennedy

Over the past twenty-five years the notion of the writing-teacher-as-writer became a commonplace—a welcome one—in our profession. I'm still learning about what this title means, still thinking about the kind of resource I might become for my students-as-writers.

Right from the time I established my classroom as a workshop, I wrote with my kids whenever I could. Once they settled in to the routines of the workshop and their own writing, I found stray moments when they didn't need me, when I could sit down at an empty desk and write for a few minutes. I wrote among my kids in order to provide a role model: here's an adult who writes. Sometimes I published a story or poem in a class magazine, or brought a finished draft to the group for their response, or showed them a piece of my writing that had been professionally published. I did these things with one agenda in mind: to play the role of writer for their benefit and to try to lend adult credibility to the act of writing. I performed writing.

I want to contrast the performances I gave at school for my students with the demonstrations I conduct at home, with my daughter. For example, I can't imagine myself casually plopping down next to her on the sofa with a loaded toothbrush in my hand, brushing away, and hoping oral hygiene will rub off on her as a worthwhile human activity. Instead I *make* her come into the bathroom with me. I say, "Okay, Anne, watch me. This is how much toothpaste I use. You can squeeze from the top of the tube, but I'm warning you your father won't like it. Then I make little circles on my teeth with the bristles, and I brush for a long time, maybe two whole minutes. When I think I'm done, I run my tongue over my teeth to see if any of them is still wearing mittens. Now you try it." Then she tries it, and we talk about her attempts.

I can't think of anything I do in my life as a parent that I stage for Anne's benefit. I never think about being her role model. Instead I teach her, directly, how an adult does things—things that have purpose and meaning to me, so I do them as best I can.

This is a mundane analogy, but the ordinary, hard work of writing requires ordinary examples. Some days writing is like dental hygiene. It's like my brain is wearing mittens, and I'm trying to scrape off the fuzz. Writing, like taking care of my teeth, requires perseverance, purpose, love, and a commitment over the long haul. It means false starts, page after page that goes nowhere, enough bravado to confront a blank piece of paper, enough self-confidence to fill the page with writing that is stupid, pompous, or off-the-wall, and enough patience to go back and think about it, again and again, and try to revise toward something like intelligence and maybe, if I'm lucky, grace—or else to slash and burn when I recognize that it's pointless, hopeless claptrap. It means constant rereading of what I've written to maintain a sense of what has come before, and endless fiddling and polishing. It means surprises that come out of nowhere in the midst of doing something else. It means the word or phrase that's *perfect*, the idea that makes me laugh out loud, the rare times when I burn through the pages, the insight, comparison, observation, or hook that makes me feel brilliant for two seconds. It means days when I can't bear to tear myself away, when I want everyone to shut up and leave me alone so I can write.

And when the writing is done, if it's good, it brings me more satisfaction than almost anything else in my life.

This is just a sampling of what my students don't see when I sit among them and perform as a role model. But when I stand at the front of the classroom, take off the top of my head, turn on the overhead projector, and invite them to hear my thinking and see what I do as an adult writer, they learn about purpose, patience, and love. They begin to understand the hundreds of choices I make every time I write. They see that almost nothing is accidental, that whenever I write I try deliberately to write well, to *create literature* about something that matters to me, not merely do another piece for the folder. I show them how I plan, confront problems, weigh options, change my mind, read and reread my own writing as I'm writing it, use conventions to make my writing sound and look the way I want it to or my readers will need it to, and consider questions of audience, intention, craft, and coherence every step of the way.

For years Donald Murray composed on overhead transparencies at professional meetings. When I watched his demonstrations, I always learned from what he did as a writer. An important lesson to me was how much of his writing process was ordinary hard work. I never saw anything come to Murray on the wings of a dove, and I found this very encouraging.

Several years ago, before I had a class of my own, I experimented with demonstration lessons by writing in front of Susan Benedict's fifth and sixth graders at the Center. I had read Harwayne's *Lasting Impressions* (1992) and was itching to work with her idea of taking a deliberate stance. For a week Susan let me teach the minilesson to the writers in her workshop. I worked on a memoir about the first time I lied to my mother, something I wanted to think about in relation to five-year-old Anne's first lie to me—what it felt like and what it might mean that my mother hadn't punished me, as I hadn't punished Anne. Before I started I told the kids I would be trying to write well—taking a deliberate stance—and asked them to act as researchers and take notes about anything they saw me do that surprised them or anything I did as a memoirist that seemed to work.

I told them the basic story, brainstormed the various points at which I might enter the narrative, chose one and explained why I thought this lead had merit, and began to write. As I wrote I talked it through, word by phrase by sentence, in terms of what I was aiming for. Throughout the week I drafted in front of Susan's students and at home; I made transparencies of the at-home writing, showed them what I'd done, and explained my choices. I revised and polished in front of them and brainstormed a title with them. When the memoir was finished, I asked them to bring the notes of their observations to a minilesson, so we could begin a group document that listed some of the things a writer does when he or she is trying hard to write well.

The kids described sixteen behaviors. Some were familiar techniques that their teachers and I had taught them in minilessons: "You start new paragraphs to give yourself and your reader a rest"; "You look for a grabbing lead that's also a logical place to begin"; "You flash back and forward in the action and move around in time." But nine were techniques I had never explicitly addressed in twenty years of teaching about narrative. The kids told me that:

1. I close my eyes when I'm writing a narrative and see a scene, then try to find words to capture the people, setting, and action—a kind of movie behind my eyelids—so my readers might see it, too.
2. I give hints that I hope will create questions in a reader's mind about what will happen next.
3. I try to create rhythms, patterns of words or phrases to move the action along.

4. Where it's appropriate, I attempt humor to break the tension.
5. When I write dialogue, I try to capture how the different people in a situation would really speak.
6. When I'm not sure of how to say something, I draw a line, keep going, and come back later to fill the hole.
7. I like to put surprising combinations of ideas or words together, e.g., an "exquisite lump of clay."
8. I invent details that didn't happen but that fit with the spirit and truth of the memory and make the memoir feel more real.
9. I continually stop writing, go back into my text, and reread it in order to get a sense of the writing so far and to jump-start the next piece of text. I spend more time reading than I do writing when I compose.

One of the benefits of demonstrating writing is the element of surprise. I wasn't aware I did these things when I write, and my kids weren't aware these were things a writer could do. I had never taught any of the strategies in conferences or minilessons; they were hidden from us until I took off the top of my head. The demonstrations made them explicit and gave us new ways of talking about what writers do—and about what students might do as writers.

During each of the last three years, I've written at least twenty pieces of writing with my seventh and eighth graders. When I looked back and counted, the quantity was a surprise. The writing felt natural and easy, part of who I am as a learner, teacher, mother, daughter, reader, writer, researcher, and citizen.

In this chapter I'll look at examples of some of this writing and describe the lessons it taught my students and me. The big, bottom-line lesson is this: as a parent I won't take the chance that Anne won't learn all there is to know about caring for her teeth, so I show her as much as I know. As a writing teacher I'm not willing to take the chance that my students will intuit coherence, technique, convention, and, especially, purpose. In the time they're with me I show them just as much as I can about literacy, including my own.

On occasion I've written badly on purpose for my students. I won't use examples of students' work to show what isn't working in their writing. Instead, since I know from long experience what such writing looks and sounds like—I read it in my dreams—it doesn't take much imagination to create comparable pieces of my own.

In September I wrote a bad memoir about Laurel, one of my students, and the first time we met. I had three agendas in the Laurel story: to figure out why the memory of our first meeting, when she was a second grader, stuck with me; to help kids understand that memoir is a way to figure out what the events of our lives *mean*, to find the significances, not record the facts; and to introduce the notion that because memoir is narrative, and narratives have characters, the main character of a memoir is the first person. Student memoirists should be discovering and describing their own reactions and reflections, just as they should work at ascribing thoughts and feelings to main characters in their fiction.

I started the minilesson by explaining that I was writing a memoir about meeting Laurel; I asked who they thought the main character would be. "Laurel," was the consensus.

"I figured you might say that," I responded. "But I think the main character is me. It's my memory; it's my story. I'm inviting you inside my head and heart as I try to figure out why meeting Laurel for the first time sticks with me and feels worth writing about. Last night I drafted a way the memory could be written if I *weren't* thinking about trying to find the significances, if I *didn't* consider myself to be the main character in a story from my own life."

FIRST DRAFT OF "LESSONS FROM LAUREL"

"Knock, knock." [This is a classic seventh-grade lead, right up there with "Ring, ring."]

"Who is it?" I asked.

"Hi, I'm Susanna, Laurel's mother. I've come to talk about your new school."

She came into my study: Laurel wasn't with her. "Laurel fell asleep in the car," her mother said. "Shall I wake her up?"

"Yes. I'd like to meet her," I answered.

Laurel came in rubbing her eyes. I took her up to use our bathroom. Then Laurel, her mother, and I talked, and we decided that CTL would be a good school for Laurel. She was awake by now and smiling. We were all smiling.

Sam didn't think the bad first draft was that bad. "It's even got a conclusion," he observed. I flipped a blank transparency on the overhead, uncapped a fine-line permanent marker, and said, "Let me try to show you the difference I'm talking about; let me create myself as the main character in the next draft, so you can be with me. That's how we're going to begin to define a main character this year: as the person the reader will be with in the story." I began to write, out loud and on the transparency, getting as far as Laurel's parents' decision to send her to CTL (Figure 10-1).

In the next day's minilesson I wrestled with my other problem as a memoirist. I'd met Laurel. So what? What did it mean? I like this girl—I love her. What does our first meeting say about me, her, and our relationship? I continued drafting on the projector, struggling now with the paragraphs in which I tried to find the deeper meaning.

LESSONS FROM LAUREL

It was a sticky day in late August. I stood with my face pressed against the screen door, trying to catch a whiff of breeze and worrying. School was to open in a week—the school, my school, for the first time ever—and I was still talking with parents, still meeting kids, still trying to get enough students to begin the year and have a real school. The worry consumed my days and nights.

When the car finally pulled into our driveway, I backed away, not wanting to appear as eager as I felt. A woman was behind the wheel—the mother? I couldn't see anyone else. She got out, walked up the sidewalk, and knocked on the door frame. There was no child. Yet. I opened the door and smiled. "Hi. I'm Nancie Atwell."

The woman shook my hand. "I'm Susanna Card. I'm afraid Laurel's fallen asleep. It was a long drive."

"Please, come in," I urged. She sat down on the sofa in my study; I picked a chair that faced the screen door and, as we talked, kept my eyes peeled for Laurel. In about five minutes my vigilance was rewarded. A sleepy kitten of a girl with a halo of black curls stumbled up the sidewalk rubbing her eyes, her face red from napping in a warm car.

"Mom?" She hesitated outside the door. I jumped up, put on my biggest smile, and let her in.

"Hi, Laurel. I'm Nancie." I extended my cool right hand, and she extended her warm left one, so that we were holding hands instead of shaking them. She squinted up at me.

"Will you please take me to the bathroom?" she asked.

"Sure." I gave her fingers a squeeze. This was nice.

As Laurel and I walked hand in hand through the house and up the stairs to the bathroom, she tried to wake up and I tried to imagine my daughter Anne, then in nursery school, as a second grader. I wondered if she'd still hold my hand when we went walking together, if she'd be this same combination of big girl and little girl. I waited outside the bathroom, liking Laurel.

We went back downstairs together, hand in hand again. She squeezed next to her mother on the sofa and listened to the adults talk. I talked fast—I wanted Laurel.

I got her. I got enough students to open the Center for Teaching and

FIGURE 10-1   Second Draft of "Lessons from Laurel"

Version 2   9/29

It was a sticky day in late August. I stood with my face pressed against the ~~front of the~~ screen door, trying to catch a whiff of breeze, and worrying. School was to open in a week — *the* school, my school — and I was still ~~the~~ talking with parents, still meeting kids, ~~and~~ still trying to get enough students to ^begin the year and have a real school. ~~The worry weighed I was never not worrying I felt a weight on me all the time.~~ The worry consumed my days and my ~~sleeps~~ nights. When a car the finally pulled into the driveway, ~~and~~ I backed away, not wanting to appear ~~too~~ as eager ~~as~~ as I felt. A woman was behind the wheel — ~~&~~ the mother? I couldn't see anyone else. ~~She~~

She got out, ~~of the car~~ walked up our sidewalk, and ~~approached the screen door~~ knocked on the screen door. There was no child. Yet.

Learning that September. Then, from September to September, I got to know Laurel—as a third grader adjusting to a new school, as a fourth-grade teenager, as an infinitely powerful fifth grader, as a sixth grader testing the limits of her power, as a seventh grader learning to channel her energy to give voice to her life and change the world, as an eighth grader whose heart practically burst with compassion for others.

All the time I watched her, I learned how children change and stay the same, how they are their essential selves right from the start. I learned about Anne and how she might grow up. I learned how much I liked bigmouthed girls—and boys—who would still hold a grown-up's hand. I learned how lucky I am to have CTL—my own school and a good place to work, yes, but, more importantly, a place to watch all these lives unfold and find their purpose, to look with love and wonder at many children as time transforms them from sleepy kittens to young adults. It is a privilege. It took me by surprise. I didn't understand that there would be dozens of Laurels, hundreds of stories to tell, and so many hands to hold.

Five autumns after Laurel and I first met, I was helping the photographer from the school photo company line up the eighth graders for their portraits. She did a double take when she came to Laurel and looked back and forth between us, at our dark curls and light eyes. "Is this your daughter?" she asked.

"No," I replied. "But I wish."

—Nancie Atwell

After the series of demonstrations, many students came to their next attempts at memoir with a new sense of purpose and the awareness that memoir is a genre that serves to ask the big questions: What experiences of my life are worth capturing? Which stick with me? What do they *mean*?

Laurel started a new piece of writing, a memoir about the day she learned the truth about Santa Claus. She said, "I want this to be big—about an important thing that happened to me in my life—and I want to work on making me the main character. I want people to really be with me in the story." The memoir became a piece of Laurel's childhood, captured forever, in a way that helps her recognize and understand what happened and how the experience is part of the adult she is becoming.

GROWING UP

It was a cold December day, the snow pure and fluffy, the ice-covered trees bare. It was close to Christmas, and I was excited—except for something that I'd been wondering. I tried to block it from my mind, but whenever I thought of Christmas it came back. It was the question all children ask. "IS THERE REALLY A SANTA?" I didn't want to have to consider the question because I wanted there to be a Santa always—a Santa with a red suit and a beard as white as snow, whose belly shakes like a bowlful of jelly, who drives reindeer and a sleigh. Everything about Santa was so magical and so right.

On this day I couldn't stand it any more. I needed to ask someone. When my dad was driving me home, I decided to ask him. "Dad . . . is there really a Santa?" I whispered. He just sat there for a minute. Then he looked deep into my seven-year-old eyes with his sad adult eyes. He looked like he was going to say something, but no words came out. I was puzzled. Finally he spoke.

"No, Laurel . . . there isn't . . . a . . . Santa. . . . I'm sorry." He paused a lot, not wanting to tell me, not wanting me to grow up—wanting me to stay his little girl.

"There isn't? Why, Daddy? Why?" I had felt certain he would say, "Yes, of course, there's a Santa." All I'd been asking for was for some reassurance. Instead, I got the truth.

I was also mad that my parents had lied to me. They had never lied to me before about anything. How could they have done this to me? I felt betrayed.

But as I thought about it more, it came clear why they had lied. They only wanted there to be something magical for me to believe in, to have fun with. When I looked over at my dad again, he looked like he was going to cry. But he didn't.

I did. I cried for Santa, and I cried for me.

When we finally got to my mom's house, he leaned toward me and kissed me. "Santa is still alive," he said. "He's alive in the hearts of all. You and I need to keep Santa's spirit alive for our family and for all the children. Can you do that?"

I nodded.

That night, as I lay in bed, I thought about what had happened. I concluded there is a Santa—not some old guy who brings presents, but, like my dad said, a spirit that lives in the hearts and minds of people who believe in caring for and loving others. And that is what Santa is all about.

—*Laurel Card*

Another lesson I demonstrate throughout the year is the value of gifts of writing as a natural, practical purpose of composition. Since my daughter was six, I've written a poem for her every year on her birthday. I tell my students, "I know the bike I give Anne will rust or become too small for her. I understand that the Barbies' heads will fall off and they'll end up at the Boothbay dump. But the things I write for her—my words about her, me, and us—will last forever. These are the best gifts of all for the people we care about."

The year of Anne's ninth birthday I wrote under the influence of William Carlos Williams. That week we had read one of his poems at the start of class each day and looked at how he celebrated the rituals that give meaning to middle-class lives. He made me think about the rituals that connect my childhood to Anne's. One is a mother teaching her daughter how to ride a bicycle, that delicate balance between holding on and letting go at almost the same time.

At the start of a minilesson, I told students, "Teaching Anne how to ride her bike, and connecting it with my mother teaching me, are experiences I want to use as a prism for thinking about Anne's birthday. Help me figure out a way into the poem." I wanted to hear them consider and articulate the ways a writer could craft a poem around a memory. They made suggestions, which I wrote on a transparency:

POSSIBLE FORMATS FOR ANNE'S POEM

- Do you remember when . . . ? (a direct address)
- Begin with a quick synopsis of other memories, then move to the bike
- Start with recent memories, then flash back to the bike
- Start with the philosophy: holding on is easy; letting go is hard
- I remember when . . . (a dramatic monologue)
- A three-parter:
  1. Memory of my mother and me and the bike
  2. Memory of Anne and me and the bike, then
  3. *So what?*

The brainstorming led to a structure that worked for me: the memory of my mother and me, then the memory of me and Anne, then a reflection on what it might mean. I didn't write the poem in front of them; the minilesson had gone on long enough. They went off to work on their writing and so did I, messing around with the parallel narratives.

At the end of the workshop, when I had enough going, I came back to the kids in group meeting and said, "What I'm trying to do is develop a parallel structure: two stories told similarly, so that Anne will put the two next to each other in her mind. Some of the words, images, and ideas will be alike, and some will contrast, when I want to make a point about the differences. This is one of those projects where I'll spend serious time going back into my text and reading what I've written so far. I need to take cues from what's come before and echo myself."

Over the next three days I worked in and out of class on the poem. I copied the third draft in my best semi-calligraphy and showed it to my students on the overhead. A discussion about the parallels led to one of those serendipitous discussions that emerge from the demonstrations, this time about how hard it is to achieve textual coherence, including parallel structure, when you write on a word processor and don't print out: writers who don't glance back and get a sense of the whole text have a hard time looking forward.

Then I gave the poem to Anne, and she gave me the joy of watching her face as she read it.

FOR ANNE ON HER NINTH BIRTHDAY

My mother—your grammy—
held on to the seat of my bike.
Tar bubbles made sticky sounds
as she wheeled me down our street
past the porches where neighbors sat after supper
drinking their coffee in the
waning sunlight.

"Shift your weight right. Shift it left. Just a little.
Can you feel it? Feel the balance?" she panted.
Mostly I felt her not letting me fall
as I tried to do too many things at one time—
steer, pedal, stay upright, watch where I was going,
not wear her out as she ran beside me
holding on.

One night after supper, gripping my handle bars
as the neighborhood whirled past,
I turned to say something to her
and she wasn't there.
I was there alone, riding my bike.
At some delicate moment
she had let go.

Last summer I held on to the seat of your bike.
We went back and forth in front of our house
past birches and balsams
listening for the cars of summer people
as you tried to do too many things at one time.

"Shift your weight right. Shift it left. Just a little.
Can you feel it? Feel the balance?" I panted.
I thought my heart would burst
from holding you up and running beside you and
never letting you fall.

One night after dinner, gripping your bicycle seat
as the woods whirled past,
I could feel it—feel the balance.
In that split second I knew
it was time to let you go.

You pedaled on without me
all the way to the curve in the road
when you finally slowed and turned
and I wasn't there.

I stood alone back at our house
clapping and cheering for my fabulous girl.

Which is harder? Holding on or letting go?
Maybe it's the knowing when to do what.
We'll learn to hold on to each other
and let go of each other
for the rest of our two lives
as you turn into your grown-up self and I stand here
clapping and cheering for my fabulous girl.

Kids wanted to try this. Over the year all but one of my students wrote gifts for people they loved and appreciated—moms, dads, grandparents, aunts, siblings, friends, coaches. Edie experimented with parallel structure in a birthday poem for her sister Abby.

A POEM FOR ABBY

"You wanna come? Well, too bad."
    "No kidding you don't understand. You never do!"
      "*I'm* not the stupid one!"
        "Look who's talking!"
These are some of the insults we throw
          back and forth—
every other sentence makes one of us feel like
        yelling—
      Can't we just be friends?

"You wanna come? Okay, let's go."
    "You don't understand? I'll explain."
      "I know I act stupid sometimes."
      "Let's talk."
This is what I wish we could say
      to each other—
every other sentence one that makes us proud,
        makes us feel like yelling—
    I love you.

—*Edie Sperling*

Mike wrote a poem as his birthday present to his grandmother, who is famous for her love of hummingbirds.

Hovering at your feeder
they sip the sweet, sugary syrup.
You sit in your chair watching,
admiring their shining, ruby-colored throats.

Another hummer appears in the corner of your eye.
It hesitates over the bright red flowers in your garden.
You watch the needle-like bill disappear into the flower
while the bird's wings shine transparent in the wind.

The hummer flies away into the pine trees.
It nestles in its tiny nest, resting on top of the two white eggs.
Soon the eggs will hatch, and you'll clutch your binoculars,
watching out the window, waiting for those babies to fly.

When the new hummers hatch, they'll be happy.
They'll be lucky to have a garden as sweet as yours.
In this way, I am like the hummingbirds.
I'm lucky to have you, and your beautiful birds, too.

You really can make beautiful things love you, can't you?

—*Michael Maxim*

Below is another of my poems, written for Mother's Day. In the demonstration I told kids I was trying to propel myself beyond bland Hallmark-
card sentiments by centering the poem on something concrete: a memory
of my mother ice skating. Izzie, who was searching for an approach for a
poem for her mother, drew inspiration from mine and went cross-country
skiing with her mom.

ICE

A Saturday morning in January
Your voice freezes me
Wait a minute, Sister
One mittened hand turning the backdoor knob
The other dragging my skates by their laces
I pause
Itching to be down at Dieners' on the ice
Now what?

I'm coming with you
You brush past me and
Splash a bucket of gray washwater on the snow
Wring out rags between red fingers
Fetch your coat and hat
Scarf and mittens
And the ice skates you borrowed from Rose
I'll probably kill myself
You laugh

Bank Street lies snow packed
Our boots scrunch as we march
Down the middle
I tie my skates together and
Sling them over my shoulder
Like yours
Your eyes are gray ice

At Dieners' boys on skates
Push shovels and call to us
We park on the bench
Toss our boots on the pile and
Wedge our toes into stiff leather
You groan when you lean over to lace up
A sound like reaching down for steaming laundry
To peg to a frozen line

I don't wait—I can't
I wobble down the bank
Pick up speed
And burst onto the ice
Perfect ice
I push left, push right, never fall
To the other side
Then turn back to see if you saw me

Instead I see you
Alight on the ice
Spin and
Back to me
Spread your wings
And carve a lazy figure eight
On Dieners' Pond

Ice is your element
You clasp your hands behind you
And waltz with yourself
You spray shavings of ice
And whistle
Like some wild ice bird
Like a girl
Out for a skate on a Saturday morning
I see you
Perfectly
Happy

—*Nancie Atwell*

THE PATH THROUGH THE SNOW

I follow
Your figure
Silhouetted against the ebony sky
And the field
Snow glowing iridescent purple
As it reflects the dangling crescent moon

I follow
Your track
The path
You have set for me
My path in life
Your path though the snow

I follow
Feeling I could take off
Soar across the field
And break free of this rhythm of life, of ski packing snow
Knowing reality and destiny hold me back
Knowing I will be grateful

I follow
But become cold
Lose my energy, my will to continue
Feel I could lie in the wet snow
Pause and forget all that is around me
But you will keep me going

I follow
Yet I stumble
The path
Is not always smooth
And often
Holds surprises

I follow
At times
Longing to stand beside you
In this beautiful clearing
Where all is peaceful and perfect
And stop, not change a thing

I follow
Knowing you
Have a path to follow too

For paths are made
To be taken
And explored

I follow
For you
Are the trail I travel
The stars that guide me
And the moon that lights my soul
You are the peace in my mind
And the warmth in my heart

And I shall follow

—*Isabeall Quella*

Some lessons I demonstrate focus on conventions. For example, I show an overhead of a draft in which skipping lines or double-spacing gave me room to fiddle, maneuver, and change my writing for the better; with a colored marker, I highlight everything that was added or changed between the lines so kids can see it. Or I show how I take notes on a reading or film and ask kids to tease out and name what I did as a notetaker, instead of ordering kids to take better notes and feeling frustrated when they don't.

I conduct some of my social correspondence in front of my students, to make explicit the etiquette of the epistolary form. Below is an entry from a student's writing-reading handbook, her notes from a minilesson about social correspondence.

> Etiquette = conventions of *social* behavior
> *Miss Manners* (Judith Martin) = an expert who interprets rules of etiquette in her newspaper column and books. According to Miss Manners:
>   1) Sympathy letter: written when someone you know suffers the loss of someone they love. The note should be written on plain paper (white, cream-colored, or gray); a purchased sympathy card with a preprinted message won't do.
>   2) Thank-you letter: written *whenever* you get a gift. It should be written on plain paper or a decorated, blank-inside note card, not a preprinted thank-you card.

I talked about conventions of letters of condolence in this minilesson because one of my student's grandparents had died; I wrote my sympathy note to her out loud on a transparency (see Figure 10-2).

As I wrote in front of the class, I talked:

> I'm not going to include my address in the heading because Izzie is somebody I know well; this is going to be a less formal note. And I

won't use a printed sympathy card. I need to use a plain piece of paper—cream-colored, gray, or white—and write my own personal expression of sympathy.

When I write, "Dear Izzie," I'll attend to convention: I won't indent the greeting, and I'll follow it with a comma. Could I use a colon here? Why not? Now, where do I start the body of the letter?

Can I say "death," or do I say "passed away"? No, I'm not going to use a euphemism—he died. *I was so sorry to hear about the death of your grandfather.*

What do I know about Izzie and her grandfather? I know she went to Vermont to see him, and that they had a lot of good times together. How about *I know how much you loved him and how special your times together in Vermont were for both of you?*

I've said I'm sorry. My next job in this letter—here's the *real* challenge in sympathy letters—is to try to make Izzie feel better. How do I do that? . . . *He was fortunate to have such a loving grandchild. I know your good memories of him will live on in your heart.*

How shall I sign it? I'll close it, *Your friend,* because I want her to know I'm thinking of her this way. I've got to line up the Y in *your* with the beginning of the date, so I'll draw an imaginary internal margin down the page to help me do that. And I've got to remember to capitalize the *your* but not the *friend* on the closing.

I worked out in front of my students how to proceed after I say I'm sorry, because that's the part of condolence letters that trips people up—just as in

FIGURE 10-2 Condolence Letter for Izzie

25 October

Dear Izzie,

•——→ I was sorry to hear about the death of your grandfather. I know how much you loved him and how special your times together in Vermont were for both of you. He was fortunate to have such a loving grandchild. I know your good memories of him will live on in your heart.

Your friend,
Nancie Atwell

(Sincerely yours,
Nancie)

---

thank-you notes, the struggle for the writer is with what comes after the thank-you. It's talking about the significance of what we've been given that's difficult.

That day in class Elizabeth said, "Jenna's grandfather just died. Could I write her a note? Is this the sort of thing people do?"

I said, "Absolutely." Elizabeth borrowed whole chunks of my sympathy letter, trying on the language I'd provided.

Dear Jenna,
I am sorry about your grandfather. I know how much you loved him. We will all miss him. He was a very special person to everybody who

knew him. He was very lucky to have you as a grandchild. I know your memories of him will live forever.

Your friend,
Elizabeth

Because Elizabeth is learning from me, I'm choosing to see this as an example of intertextuality, not plagiarism. I'm happy for her to view a condolence note as something she can do as a writer and for her to borrow from me in order to try on how writers use words on occasions of solace, so that later she can try to console others on her own. The payback for me came when my dog died that spring and I received half a dozen letters of sympathy from writers who have more than mastered the conventions of sympathizing in writing. Laurel's was a favorite:

Dear Ms. A.,

I'm so sorry about Books. It's hard to lose an animal that you love so dearly. I know by the things you've told me and by the way she looked that she had a wonderful life with you and was a very happy dog. It's better off for her to go when she can still be happy instead of in pain or crippled. You can also remember her this way instead of later on when she's worse. I think you made the right decision and you shouldn't regret it.

I hope you're feeling better. If you're not, you know the cure: M&M's (ha, ha).

Here is a little quote from a song I sing in voice lessons. It's so beautiful and true I thought I'd share it with you.

> Mama whispered softly,
> "Time will ease your pain.
> Life's about changing.
> Nothing ever stays the same."
> And she said, "How can I
> help you to say good-bye?
> It's okay to hurt
> and it's okay to cry.
> Come let me hold you
> and I will try.
> How can I help you
> to say good-bye?"

Love,
Laurel

Some of the writing I demonstrate for students is *collaborative*: the class and I compose a piece together in the minilesson. One day Matt had presented William Stafford's wonderful poem "What's in My Journal" to the group:

Taking Off the Top of My Head   **349**

WHAT'S IN MY JOURNAL

Odd things, like a button drawer. Mean
things, fishhooks, barbs in your hand.
But marbles too. A genius for being agreeable.
Junkyard crucifixes, voluptuous
discards. Space for knickknacks, and for
Alaska. Evidence to hang me, or beatify.
Clues that lead nowhere, that never connected
anyway. Deliberate obfuscation, the kind
that takes genius. Chasms in character.
Loud omissions. Mornings that yawn above
a new grave. Pages you know exist
but you can't find them. Someone's terribly
inevitable life story, maybe mine.

—*William Stafford*

After Matt led the discussion—about how the poem mixed physical objects, metaphors, and character traits to create a portrait of the speaker—I asked the class to try something similar. Each of us wrote two lines about what's in our own journals. Then, borrowing together from Stafford, we created a portrait of us. Students read their lines around the circle, and I transcribed them on the overhead as an instant poem.

WHAT'S IN OUR JOURNALS

The brown pools of a dog's eyes
a talent for hiding behind a joke
cards and dice spilling out in confusion
dark places where I'm sure I'll find what I'm looking for
pucks, skates, and sticks
many cracks on a pond I wish were smooth
music and CDs
words that I can't describe
cold steel, a silvery crankshaft, and chrome tools
a misfired bullet ricocheting off an unintentional target
springs from a spiral notebook
rain on a cloudless day
a baseball glove
a roller coaster out of control
a blank piece of paper and a pencil
a clear pool of ideas waiting for someone with the courage to break
    the surface
basketballs and poems
clues that could kill me hiding in dark corners

carabiners worn to retirement but saved under a crumpled sheet
    of music
black caves never explored and roads never traveled
greasy bike chains
a twisting ball of yarn that I'm pretending isn't me
baseballs
doodles that mean nothing
mysterious gadgets that would do it all if I knew how to use
    them
books of poetry
photographs of ended dreams
memories long lost and forgotten
a tennis ball hitting the line
words drifting, waiting to be found
feathers floating over empty pages
secrets whispered between the words like wind sweeping across a
    butterfly's wing
"Little Earthquakes" trembling my words
a weeping willow swaying in the breeze
the sounds of Phish echoing throughout my body
optimistic thoughts lost in a pool of words

— *Tom Allen, Erin Arnold, Nancie Atwell, Laurel Card, Missy Heselton,*
  Martha Hutchins, Asa Kitfield, Michael Maxim, Matt Miller,
  Dylan Nickerson, Jason Perry, Joe Powning, Izzie Quella, Rachel Schlein,
  Katy Seiders, Jay Spoon, Sam Stewart

My students and I also collaborate in producing documents for their use as writers and readers: criteria for an effective book review, elements of fiction and examples of each element, qualities of a good title, how to read a poem. They talk, I talk, I record the ideas, then I craft the document—organize, order, and format it—in front of them on transparencies so they can see how I manipulate the information in order to create a lucid presentation of the ideas.

Sometimes I ask for student collaboration on some of the documents I create in my professional life—book reviews, articles, correspondence—so they can see how exposition unfolds differently from fiction, memoir, and poetry. For example, a substitute teacher who was a frequent presence at the Center applied for a position elsewhere and asked me for a letter of recommendation. In a minilesson I divided a transparency into three parts and headed them *Attributes, Roles at CTL,* and *Specific Projects.* I explained I was creating a planning sheet to help me do two things: generate everything I might say about the teacher so I could build the recommendation on specific examples of his abilities (and do a better job of selling him), and figure out the best way of organizing and presenting the information, so it felt logical to the reader and had maximum impact.

Again, kids talked, I talked, and I wrote, recording our data under the four headings. That night I took the transparency home and worked from it as I drafted, using a code of numbers and letters as I decided how to order the information we generated and crossing off items as I incorporated them into the draft (Figure 10-3).

The next day I reproduced the draft as a transparency and talked kids through the letter: the ordering of the raw material and how I used the planning sheet to organize my presentation, as well as format considerations: the inside address and a colon after the greeting, introductory paragraph, separation of the groups of ideas as paragraphs, transitional words and phrases at the beginnings of paragraphs, concluding remarks, closing, and my signature above my typed name.

Another kind of collaboration involves parallel writing, when I'm one of the writers in a group who takes on a task individually. As homework I asked students to write poems in response to the experience of watching films of Shakespeare's plays. Curt could not write this poem. He loved the plays, but intellectually; the history—and the swordplay—appealed to him more than the relationships among the characters. He came to school with no poem, and was well and truly stumped. Only after the rest of the kids and I read our drafts around the circle was Curt able to write, too. He needed my poem and perspective to help him find his way in.

AMONG THE GROUNDLINGS

Claudius, you doofus!
Beatrice is great.
That Claudio is a wimp.
Hamlet switched the letters!
I am an ass.
Nancie, did Hamlet really love Ophelia?
There's poison in the cup.
There's poison on the blade.
Is that guy Fortinbras?
Joe, can I have some popcorn?
Boo! Hiss! Don John!
I love Shakespeare.

I didn't love Shakespeare.
I learned he was hard and not for me.

FIGURE 10-3   Brainstorming Data for a Letter of Recommendation

ATTRIBUTES ②

d ~~Goes from child to child and really pays attention —~~ to individuals + to everyone

a ~~Talks to students as if they're artists, not kids~~

e ~~Understands kids' struggles because he's an artist, too — encouraging~~

~~Good disciplinarian —~~
b ~~keeps people on task but not too strict~~

c ~~Encourages kids to experiment, try new things, discover their best~~

① **ROLES AT CTL**

- Guest artist
- Sub. teacher
- Music teacher (K)
- Co-taught K
- Recess supervisor
- Song writing teacher

③ **SPECIFIC PROJECTS**

landscapes at his studio
Still life values experiment
Block printing
Song about great white shark
Self-portraits
"Moody's Diner" song
Color + design still lifes
Brought W. Guthrie to a.m. meeting
Came to CTL as Van Gogh
Journals and poems

I learned to take apart the language,
take the tests, write the essays,
get my facts straight.
I learned to feel properly awed,
daunted, and unworthy.

I never laughed,
hissed,
felt goose bumps rise,
turned to a friend to meet eyes at a good part,
wished I had Beatrice's tongue,
fell in love with Hamlet,
wept at the loss of Ophelia,
wanted to rewind.

I love it here
in the cheap seats
surrounded by the groundlings.
Shakespeare wrote for the Queen
but he wrote for you, too—
and never for the professors.
You live the plays,
breathe the words,
fill your ears and eyes,
your heads,
your hearts.

The rest is silence.

—Nancie Atwell

SHAKESPEARE FEELINGS

"Stab him!"
"Watch out for the poison sword!"
"Nice hit, Hamlet!"
"Now, get Claudius!"
"Yeah! Good work, Hamlet."

From this to—

"Ha, ha, ha, ha!"
"I can't believe it—Benedict fell for that!"
"And Beatrice, too. Ha, ha!"
"This is just too much."

And then to—

"Villain!"
"Traitor!"

"Only you would think of poison, Claudius."
"Cowardly scum!"
"Hamlet will give you your just deserts."

Feelings so true and tangible,
they reverberate
through crowds everywhere,
from groundlings to queens
to audiences four hundred years later.

—*Curt Monaco*

A major writing demonstation is a short story I worked on with my kids for two years. I attempted to use fiction to explore a topic that matters to me—when girls reject other girls—because it happened to me in the eighth grade and to one of my seventh-grade girls. I wanted to write about this kind of rejection in a way that would help resolve the situation for a fictional character and, in so doing, maybe help resolve the situation for real girls who read the story. I also wanted to let girls know this *happens*. It has *always* happened. And weirdly enough, although it feels like the most personal thing in the world, it's not even personal; I think it's part of the age and gender. The only work of literature I know that describes the phenomenon is *Cat's Eye*, a Margaret Atwood novel. Otherwise, girls rejecting girls is the dirty little secret of growing up female in America. Finally, I wanted to try to develop a character in a narrative who wasn't me, to write my first serious piece of short fiction and experience firsthand the demands and satisfactions of the genre.

I struggled with the story at every juncture, but I especially grappled with the lead (Figure 10-4). I still hadn't figured out where I stood in relation to the particulars of my own experience—my memories of eighth grade—and the situation of the fictional main character. Was I Leah, or not Leah? Was I grown-up Nancie, or an eighth grader? This is the sort of writing that curls my toes when I reread it:

> I look back at that spring with unaccountable shame. Although I had done nothing wrong, it was the first time in my life that I was ashamed of myself—aware of who I was to other people and embarrassed to be me, Leah. It was as if someone drew a curtain between one day and the next. On the other side the sun shone on my old, easy life with my circle of girl friends. On this side I stood abandoned in the dark, numb except for the pain of a piercing question: what was wrong with me? The sun would never shine on me in the old way again. The kingdom of my childhood—of unguarded, unself-conscious *Leah*ness—was gone.

FIGURE 10.4 First Draft of Short Story Lead

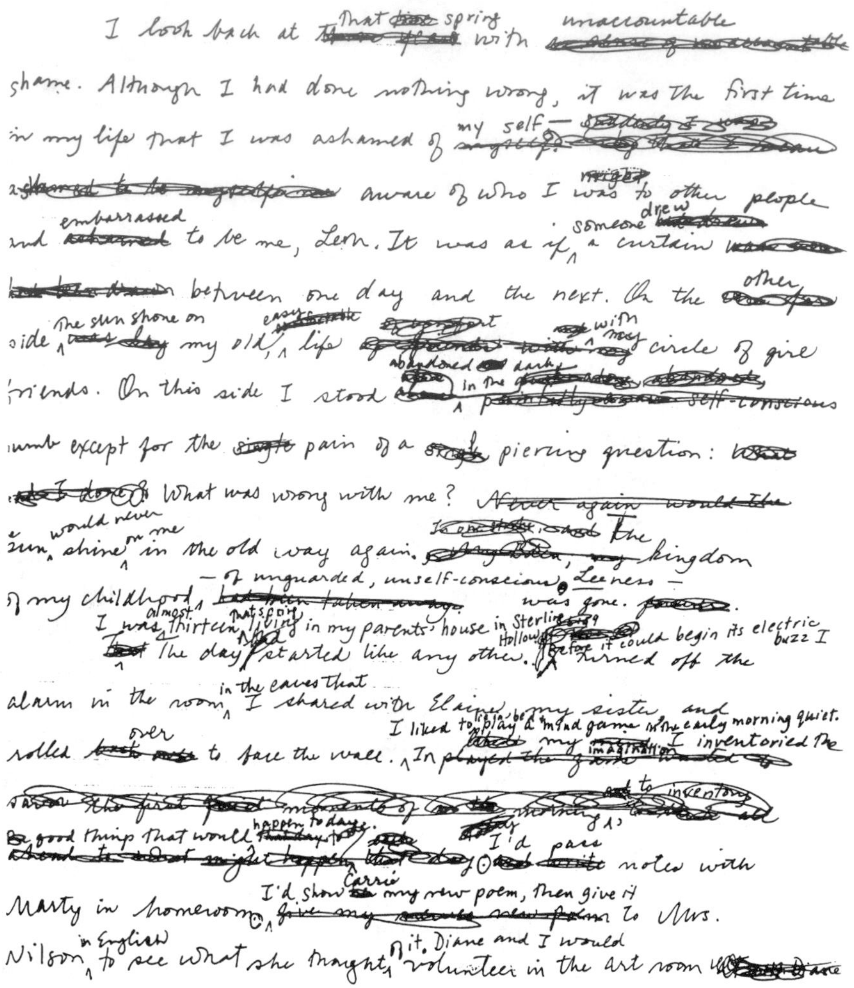

I had to write *pages* like this before I got it out of my system—to write badly as a prelude to, perhaps, writing well. I started again, pushing myself beyond the particulars of my own experience (and the trauma I discovered I was still feeling). I shifted to third person and talked with my students about how this decision made the writing both harder and easier. It was less immediate, but it became more a work of my imagination, more one I could control. The new version took shape:

Leah loved to beat the clock. Any morning she could wake up before the alarm's electric buzz shattered the silence was a good one This was one of the good mornings. She punched the alarm button and rolled over to face the wall of the room in the eaves she shared with Evie. Leah began to play the game, her favorite morning ritual. In her mind she listed everything great that would happen to her today.

In homeroom she and Marty, her best friend since second grade, would pass notes. She'd show her new poem to Carrie, who wrote poetry, too. It was about war and how adults never listen to kids, the ones who end up fighting and dying. Then in English she'd give the poem to Ms. Voight, to see what she thought. Since it was Monday, Leah and Dee planned to volunteer in the art room during study hall and hang out with the student teacher, who was weird but interesting—her pierced nostril had everybody talking. Leah had third period lunch on Monday, which meant she could sit with Marty, Dee, and Carrie in the cafeteria. She had finished her homework in study hall on Friday, and no tests loomed on the horizon. It was shaping up to be a great Monday.

She flopped onto her back and watched the rainbows that Evie's crystals cast across their ceiling. Out of the corner of her eye she noticed her sister was awake, up on one elbow, and staring at her from her bed on the other side of the room.

"Mommy said you're supposed to wash your hair today," Evie sniffed. She was eight, the baby of the family. More than anything, Leah hated sharing a bedroom with her. There was no time or place to be alone, to daydream, write in her journal, or become lost in a book. Evie was either in their room already and had turned the floor into a housing development for Barbies, or she was threatening to come in, threatening to tell Mom, threatening to make Leah's life just as miserable as possible.

"M.Y.O.B., you little pain," Leah yawned. She struggled out from under the weight of covers, swung her legs over the side of the bed, and tested the bare floor with her feet. It was freezing. None of the second floor rooms were heated. Leah, Evie, the twins, and their parents slept under layers of blankets from fall to spring. She wished she hadn't decided she was too old to wear slippers, as she sat contemplating the trip to the bathroom. "I'll tell her I forgot. It's too cold to wash my hair. Besides, it's late. It'll never dry before the bus comes," she shivered.

These were familiar excuses. The truth was, Leah hated to stand under the shower with her eyes squeezed shut as she groped around for the shampoo and tried not to breath soapy water. She hated the blast of cold air when she drew back the shower curtain, and she hated hopping around on the tile floor as she tried to pull on her clothes over wet skin. Ripping a brush through wet snarls was even worse. "I'll do it tomorrow morning," she concluded.

"I'm telling," Evie warned.

"Go ahead, Miss Perfect. Go wake up Mom and see what happens to you." Leah knew Evie wouldn't call her bluff. Now that all four kids were old enough to make their own breakfasts, their mother got up at 5:30 with their father, counted out lunch money and left it on the dining room table, then went back to bed after Dad left for the plant. Evie wouldn't dare disturb her.

Leah tiptoed across the icy floor to her chest of drawers and pulled out a pair of jeans and her favorite sweatshirt, the one Marty got her at Disney World. From another drawer she grabbed clean underwear and socks, which she bundled inside her jeans. Evie was pretending to be asleep; Leah could see her eyelids quivering. "You'd better be up by the time I get back," she said as she gripped the doorknob. "I'm not going to make the bus driver wait for you again."

From the look of the bathroom, she guessed that Joe and Jamie were already up and showered. She kicked aside their wet towels and changed out of her pajamas and into her clothes. Then she wiped the steam from the mirror over the sink and sighed. Her hair was dirty; it hung together in clumps. She found her mother's comb and tried to smooth her bangs off her face, but they fell down onto her forehead in strings. "Nobody's going to be looking at your hair anyway," she lectured herself in the mirror.

She checked on Evie—who was finally up and getting dressed— then headed downstairs to find her shoes. The twins were already gone; they rode the high school bus. Leah hoped they hadn't finished the good granola. She was in luck. She filled a bowl and added milk, then read the back of the box for the twentieth time while she gobbled spoonfuls of cold cereal. She loved breakfast—cereal was one of her favorite meals. Comfort food, their mother called it. While she was rinsing her dish, Evie clattered into the kitchen, singing at the top of her lungs. "Peace is the world smiling. Peace is a gentle dove . . ."

"Give me a break," Leah cringed. She escaped to the bathroom to brush her teeth.

The school bus met the sisters at the end of their driveway. Evie and the other elementary school kids were dropped off first; then the bus chugged up the hill to the junior high. When the school came into sight, Leah searched for her friends among the mobs of kids streaming along the sidewalk—no sign of them yet. She stepped down off the bus and waded through the crowd to the gym door, where she always waited for Marty and Dee so they could walk to homeroom together.

Leah brushed her bangs off her face one last time and checked her watch. She was going to be late for homeroom. Where were they? She clutched her books against her sweatshirt and tapped her foot. "C'mon, guys," she muttered. When the first warning bell rang, she sighed. Were they both out sick? Bummer. She looked up and down the sidewalk one last time then headed for homeroom, disappointed that the plans she had hatched that morning wouldn't come true. School felt totally different when her friends weren't there, like a color movie shown in black and white.

Leah entered homeroom just as the second bell—the real one—sounded. The first thing she saw as she walked through the door were Marty and Dee, sitting next to each other in the front row. She felt surprised, then hurt. They were whispering with their heads together and didn't look up when she came in.

"Take a seat, Leah," Mrs. Orr said when the bell stopped ringing. "You're late. Well, almost late." Marty and Dee still hadn't looked her way, but Leah could see that Marty was blushing as she stumbled to an empty desk two rows behind them. She felt her own face getting hot. Were they ganging up on her about something? Great.

She leaned forward and whispered, "You guys, where were you? I was waiting. Guys? *Guys?*"

Instead of answering they kept their heads together, Marty's red hair against Dee's blonde. "You *guys*," she demanded, not bothering to whisper this time. "What's going on?" The back of Marty's neck glowed bright red, but still she didn't turn around.

"That's enough, Leah," Mrs. Orr warned. "It's almost time for announcements."

She sat back in a daze. Now Marty and Dee broke apart and sat rigidly, eyes facing front, as the voice of the vice-principal boomed from the intercom. They were acting as if she were invisible. She tried to remember Friday, the last time they had been together. What had she done to make them so mad at her?

"Marty," she whispered, when the intercom clicked off. "What's wrong?" The only reply was the straight line of Marty's back. Suddenly Leah realized that the boys on either side of her were watching this show with interest. She opened her math book and pretended to read. She could feel tears starting behind her eyes. "Don't cry," she commanded herself. "Don't let them see you cry."

When the bell rang to end homeroom, Marty and Dee bolted through the door as if they had been shot from a cannon. Leah got to her feet slowly and picked up her books. Her face felt as if it were on fire. She spied a crumpled piece of paper on the floor at the front of the room and recognized Marty's handwriting. It looked like a note. She hesitated, then scooped it up and jammed it into her jeans pocket.

She practically ran to the first-floor girls' bathroom, where she locked herself inside one of the stalls, leaned against the door, and pulled the note from her pocket. Her hands shook as she unfolded it.

Dee—

Did you see her HAIR today? How about that sweatshirt. B.O. or what? She is *so* weird.

W.B.S.

Marty

Marty—

I can't believe we ever hung out with her. Run for it when the bell rings or else she'll keep on bugging us.

Leah started to cry. Huge tears, baby tears like Evie's, rolled down her cheeks. This couldn't be happening. It had to be a bad dream, one of those just-before-the-alarm nightmares. She and Marty and Dee had had plenty of arguments, but nothing like this—this humiliation. Because of what? Her hair? Her sweatshirt? It was so stupid and unfair. Did they expect her to go home and shower and change her clothes or something? Would they be happy then?

Then it hit her. They had planned this. They hadn't met her before school because over the weekend they had talked about her and made a decision. It wouldn't have mattered if she had washed her hair that morning, or worn a different shirt. They had already decided not to be friends with her anymore. Leah ripped the note into pieces and threw them in the toilet. She flushed it again and again until every scrap was whirled away. Then she banged the door of the stall open and, avoiding her face in the mirror, hurried from the bathroom. She had to find Carrie. She had to know if Carrie was in on this, too.

She slipped into her first period class, English with Ms. Voight, after the bell rang. The teacher shot her a look but didn't say anything. Usually Leah was on time; this was her favorite teacher and favorite class. She sat down next to Carrie, whose face was hidden behind a copy of *Lord of the Flies*. "Hi," she whispered, as Ms. Voight began to take attendance. "Do you know what's going on with Marty and Dee?"

Carrie's lips moved as she silently mouthed the words in her book. "Carrie?" she tried again. Leah's heart sank. No response, except for total fascination with a novel she knew Carrie hated. She could feel herself shrinking. She was two feet tall, she was two inches tall, she was nothing. She had read about how soldiers were shell-shocked during wars. That was how she felt now—shocked beyond numb. She tried to concentrate on Ms. Voight's face and voice, to find something solid and reliable to focus on as her world—of friends and fun and liking who she was—blew apart.

Somehow she endured walking the corridors alone between classes. She sat by herself at lunch and managed not to cry and didn't do anything stupid, like try to talk with them again or sit at their table. She stood at her locker next to theirs at the end of the day and remembered her combination and didn't look up to see what they were snickering at. Somehow she held it together during the bus ride home, through the walk up the driveway, through the climb to the second floor. Then she lost it, completely.

Evie had arrived home half an hour before, and she and the Barbie army already occupied every square inch of the bedroom floor. Leah burst into the room sobbing. "Get out!" she wailed. "Get out of here, you little brat."

Evie gaped at her sister's tear-streaked face. "What's wrong?" she asked. "What's the matter?"

"Nothing. Just get out of here. I mean it. *Now.*" Leah collapsed across her bed and buried her face in her pillow.

"I'm not going. You can't make me. I was here first," Evie pouted.

The emotions Leah had hidden in her heart all day surged through her body. Without thinking she charged over to Evie, where she sat playing on the floor, and slapped her across the face. Time stopped. Evie stared at her with huge eyes. Leah couldn't believe what she had just done. She felt sick as she watched a red splotch in the shape of her hand begin to glow on Evie's cheek.

"Mommy! Mommy!" Evie exploded. "Leah hit me, really hard, on my face. Mommy-y-y-y-!"

Leah could hear her mother taking the stairs two at a time. She came into the bedroom drying her hands on a dish towel. "Now what?" she sighed. She sat down on the edge of Evie's bed and held out her arms. Evie climbed onto their mother's lap and cried hard as Mom rocked her. "Honestly, Leah, you haven't been home two seconds and you're already picking on her. Shhh, it's all right. Shhh, Evie, Mommy's here. It's all over." Finally she looked over at Leah. "I'm ashamed of . . ." she started, then stopped. Leah was slumped across her bed again and crying at least as hard as Evie. "What is it?" she asked. "Leah?"

Leah wanted to crawl onto her mother's lap right alongside Evie and be rocked, too. "I wish I were eight," she sobbed. "I wish I didn't have to care about all this stupid stuff."

"What stuff? What happened, sweetie? Tell me."

"I can't. It's too awful. I just want to be left alone. Could you all just leave me alone?" She felt exhausted, as tired as she had ever felt in her whole life. She scrunched her pillow into a ball and lay down facing the wall. In a second she felt Mom's cool hand on her forehead.

"You're hot," she said. "Do you want some juice?"

"No, Mom, please. I just want to be left alone. Please take Evie and go away."

"Okay," her mother answered. "Sleep now. We'll talk later. Maybe I can help you with this. You know whatever it is, I love you." She heard her mother whisper to Evie, who sniffled something in response. In another moment the bedroom door clicked shut.

She closed her eyes and played the events of the day over and over again in her mind like a horror movie. How could they do this to her? What had she done to them? Didn't they understand this was killing her? She prayed for sleep—anything to stop the hurt. Leah curled up with her knees against her chest and drifted.

When she opened her eyes again the room was dark. She could make out the sound of plates and cutlery clattering in the kitchen: dinner must be over and the twins were washing the dishes. There was a soft knock on the door. "Leah? It's Mom. I have some dinner for you. May I come in?"

"Okay," she moaned. She turned on the bedside light and sat up, blinking. Her mother entered carrying a tray on which she had arranged a bowl of mashed potatoes swimming in butter, an orange cut into sections, a glass of milk, and a piece of apple pie.

"I figured you needed some serious comfort food tonight," her mother smiled. She settled the tray on Leah's lap. Leah returned the smile—her first of this long, terrible day. She loved her mother so much. Why couldn't she stay home with her and never go back to school again? She felt new tears gather in the corners of her eyes. Her mother sat down at the end of the bed, rested a hand on Leah's ankle, and gave it a squeeze. "Do you want to tell me about it?" she questioned.

A wave of relief swept over her. "Oh, Mom. It was terrible. It was the worst day of my life . . ." And between sobs and spoonfuls of mashed potatoes she told about her friends, the note, the long, lonely day—all the hurt and humiliation came tumbling out.

I had run up against the "so what?" of my short story. Leah's mother will comfort and sustain her. The mother's words will be the part of the story that provides its meaning and resolution and, I hope, helps girls who read it. I worked for weeks on this conversation and produced five attempts that went nowhere. Finally I put all the drafts away, fetched a fresh pad of paper, and brainstormed a list of everything the mother might say. This was a tactic I'd never tried before—generating potential solutions to a problem in the middle of a piece of writing (Figure 10-5).

In a nutshell, the mother's response has to be just right, in terms of consoling girls who read this story:

- she should be soothing, physically affectionate, and warm
- she has to stay calm and not blame
- she has to show her strength and reassure Leah with it.

I conducted research at this point and skimmed two books about adolescent girls, Mary Pipher's *Reviving Ophelia* and *Mother Daughter Revolution*

FIGURE 10-5   Brainstorming Solutions to a Writing Problem

Finding Solutions to the Problem

The mother's response needs to be perfect: just right in terms of helping girls who read the story:
- soothing – physically affectionate & warm
- she stays calm & doesn't blame
- she shows her strength, & reassures ~~Leah~~ with it

- Your friends ~~aren't evil~~ monsters. They're typical adolescent girls – this happens all the ~~time~~. They aren't ~~well adjusted~~, and they're struggling to ~~find~~ define themselves – basing their ~~popularity~~ identities on popularity
- ~~Something like that happened~~ to me in 8th grade. It was very hard – the dirty ~~secret~~ of female adolescence / coming of age (Atwood's novel Cat's Eye).
- What ~~can you do~~? (Who can you Reach out to ~~other~~ ~~kids~~ boys + girls, people not in your clique or ~~class~~? ~~Who can you~~ ask for a sleepover? Can you get ~~involved~~ in other people +/or helping them – babysitting, coaching, sports?
- What can you learn from this experience? (Don't learn mistrust.) What are you willing to change / to balance a healthy appearance + your own values? about yourself
- Maybe camp this summer to meet new kids?
- ~~Family can do more together~~ – ~~you~~ I cd. take guitar lessons ~~or read to each other the way we used to~~
- Nobody is liked by everybody. But there are people who'll like you
- What are the good things about you?   for you. Let's work on
- You are smart, funny, artistic, creative.   finding them.
- I love you. I love who you are.
- Jr. high isn't LIFE. There are other places, people, + times. You won't be trapped here forever. It will get better.
- Tomorrow is a new day – a new chance to start over.
- I know friends are all important at your age – this must really hurt.
- I'll be strong with you + for you.
- Let's keep talking about how this feels – write in your diary. Draw?

Reviving Ophelia
Mother Daughter Revolution

by Debold, Wilson, and Malave. I noted everything Leah's mother might say, for example, how these girls are typical adolescents and she can't take their rejection personally, or how junior high isn't LIFE, or that nobody is liked by everybody, or how maybe Leah, with her mother's help, could identify girls who would like her for who she is and reach out to them.

I kept the planning sheet at the side of my desk. Then, as I continued to draft the short story, I went back to the plan and worked from it—adding, revising, eliminating—instead of sitting there stuck at this juncture in the story and trying to craft the perfect speech, word by word, from thin air.

I transferred the planning sheet to a transparency and demonstrated to the kids how I had generated a highly focused *quantity* of ideas and language to get me unstuck and move the character and narrative forward. We added this technique to the classroom repertoire of things writers might try when they were stymied: to put everything away, clear their minds and desks except for a fresh sheet of paper, and concentrate narrowly on the one problem at hand.

While I was struggling with the resolution to my short story, Dylan was trying to figure out how his short story would end. The plot involved a boy who became lost in the wilderness after an argument with his parents during a family camping trip. Dylan borrowed my brainstorming strategy and listed everything that might happen next. He then eliminated some of the possibilities, asking himself, "What's realistic? What's appropriate to the big ideas of my story?" I was relieved when he recognized that in this first-person account, it would be pretty hard for the narrator to die.

DYLAN'S IDEAS FOR THE ENDING

~~Parents ground him.~~
~~Parents get mad.~~
~~He dies.~~
He dies ~~but someone~~ finds him.
~~Parents forgive him but he doesn't them.~~
(1) Parents forgive him and he does too.
~~He forgives them but they don't.~~
He learns his lesson.
~~Never comes back to civilization.~~
~~Suicide.~~
(3) They live like the family he sees across the stream.
(2) They share their problems then get everything resolved.

Last year, to commemorate Anne's eleventh birthday, I tried a sestina. It was a new form for me as a poet, one based on the power of repetition; after five years of birthday poems I was stretching to find new approaches and perspectives. The six words I worked with in the sestina were *hand, rings, promise, mommy, eleven,* and *girl.*

By the end of the third stanza I was well and truly stuck. In a minilesson I showed my kids what my desperation by stanza four looked like (Figure 10-6) and debated out loud about whether the sestina form was worth this level of frustration. I talked myself into seeing it through—to use the constraints of the repeating pattern like a shifting kaleidoscope for viewing Anne.

A SESTINA FOR ANNE'S ELEVENTH BIRTHDAY

I take your hand,
slender fingers in silver rings.
I want to ask you to promise
that I'll always be your mommy.
But you are eleven.
You're your own girl.

When you were my baby girl,
it was always my hand in your hand.
In the times before eleven,
when you sat in my lap and played with my rings,
you asked, "Are you my real mommy?"
Yes. Forever. That is a promise.

I love your grown-up ways. You never break a promise.
You're a loyal friend, a compassionate girl.
You'll be a great mommy.
I see you and your baby, hand in hand,
our love growing, rings within rings . . .
But now, you're still eleven.

Compared with other ages, eleven
may not seem to hold a lot of promise.
But just as a young tree's years add rings,
each year of Anne adds to the girl.
Some day you'll look down at your hand
and see the hand of your mommy.

My life's great joy is to be your mommy—
to watch you each year get smarter and stronger, straight on
        through to eleven,
and know I had a hand

FIGURE 10-6 Draft of Stanzas Four Through Six of "A Sestina for Anne"

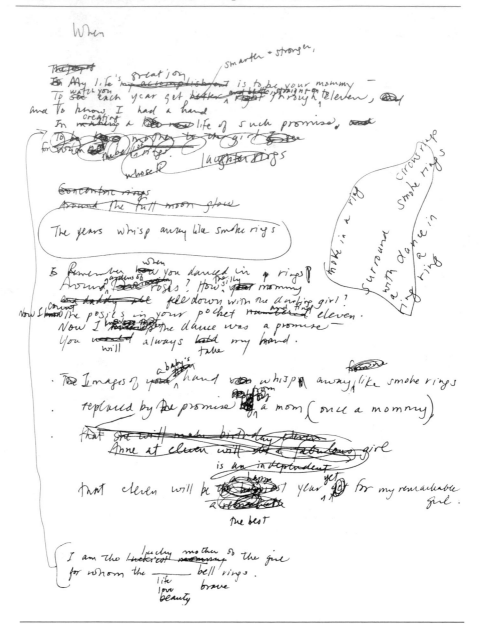

in creating a life of such promise.
I'm the lucky mother of the girl
for whom the bright bell rings.

Remember when we danced in rings
around gardens of roses? How daddy and mommy
all fell down with the darling girl?
Now I count the posies in your pocket and find eleven.
Now I know the dance was a promise—
you will always hold my hand.

Images of a baby's hand whisp away like smoke rings,
replaced by a promise from a mom (once a mommy),
that eleven will be the best year yet for my growing-up girl.

Nancie Atwell

Again, many of my students were intrigued. They wrote sestinas about Michael Jordan, reading, New York City, tennis, a best friend. Tom composed a sestina about his passion for hockey. It ends:

The feeling of skating is smooth,
a strong push,
maybe an ice-biting fall,
always a glide.
My nerves are on edge
loving the cold, gray ice.

Life can be like ice—cold, hard, not always smooth.
All it takes to go over the edge is one push.
But don't push too hard. Glide. Be ready for the fall.

Tom Allen

Be ready. A teacher's demonstrations help kids *be ready* as they watch how an adult pushes off and works to make the sharp edges smooth.

At the end of the first year of demonstrating writing to my students, I asked them what effects, if any, my demonstrations had had on their writing. Every response was different. Joe observed how I drafted my prose in paragraphs and my poems in lines—how I didn't go back into reams of text after drafting and try to impose form. He said he got the knack of doing both things in first drafts by watching me on the overhead. Sam learned shortcuts—ways of cutting to the chase and making the process simpler, more manageable, and more straightforward. Jay learned to skip lines when he was drafting because it left room for him to make revisions. Edie took away ideas for pieces of her own writing, including a play based on my short story about Leah. Laurel took heart from big changes I was willing to make in poems and narratives that weren't doing what I intended—especially major deletions, when I scrapped seven pages of text and started all over rather than trying to salvage my investment and turn seven bad pages around. Curt learned how to draft more recklessly; he stopped weighing every word, burned through pages, and brought significantly more writing to final draft. Michael learned about pace—when to slow down and reflect and when to speed up and delete writing that didn't reveal character or develop a point. Martha, struggling to write fiction that sounded real, noticed character development: "I learned from the way you went back and reread and added to and changed Leah. It helped me remember how detailed you need to be with character."

I learned, too. I understand now that English teachers don't have to be published poets, novelists, or essayists in order to have lessons to teach our students about writing. Again, we only have to write *a little bit better* than they do for them to take something away from our demonstrations. While Jason learned—finally—about indenting and lining up the left-hand margins in prose writing, everyone learned how a piece of writing can be a treasure to give to people we love.

I learned that although I may have one overarching agenda when I plan a demonstration lesson, I can never account for what each student will take away or what will come up in the discussion, which makes this mode of teaching particularly rich.

I learned the difference between role-modeling writing and taking off the top of my head, between performing and demonstrating. Everything I wrote in front of my kids was true, it all mattered to me in my life, and none of it was an exercise done for their benefit. Because of that, I'm convinced, it benefited them enormously.

It's one thing to have success orchestrating the mechanics of writing workshop and the student activity it promotes: it can look impressive as the students draft away and the folders fill up. But it's another to look at who we are to our students and how our activity as writers promotes their engagement, their sense of purpose, and the chance they'll achieve excellence as writers.

In taking responsibility for teaching writing, in acknowledging and accommodating the processes in which writers engage, many English teachers took a huge step: we invited students into the real world, where the memorized minutiae of scope and sequence convey few lessons of lasting value to writers. But we need to keep taking huge steps as teachers if the new lessons of writing process are to bear fruit that can nurture young writers for a lifetime.

We need to find ways to reveal to students what adult, experienced writers do—to reclaim the tradition of demonstration that allows young people to apprentice themselves to grown-ups. Observing adults as they work is an activity of enormous worth and power when it illumines what is possible. When we, as English teachers, demonstrate the uses of writing in our lives, we answer the most important question of all about writing: *Why would anyone want to write?* We give our students another taste of the complexities and satisfactions of composing a life.

11
Call Home the Child: Memoir

Call home the child, whose credulous first hours
Burn at the heart of living, and surprise
The better reason with unbidden truth.
David McCord

Personal-experience narratives provided a welcome jumping-off point for writers in the early days of the writing workshop. I asked my Boothbay kids to write about events from their lives and to measure their drafts against reality— or, at least, memory. I taught revision as the process of changing a narrative to reflect ever more accurate versions of the events a writer had experienced. Before literature became integral to the workshop, before I demonstrated my writing, I depended on the constraints inherent in real-life experience to support my kids' efforts to write with confidence, control, and information.

But for many students, my nudges toward the ubiquitous personal experience narrative began, like a slow leak, to sap their pleasure in writing. They grew bored telling what happened to them and bored listening to stories about other kids' experiences. I tried to rejuvenate the environment by issuing calls for manuscripts for in-house magazines that I themed around categories of adventures (times with friends, sports exploits, first memories), and by presenting minilessons about features of narrative: how to compose better leads, dialogue, and conclusions; how to write with active verbs in an active voice; how to come up with catchy titles. After I left my classroom at Boothbay, and while I watched the children at the Center make their way through the elementary grades, the dissatisfaction of young writers with the personal experience narrative was a bone I gnawed on.

I realize now that what I viewed as the easiest jumping-off point for a beginning writer was, in fact, the easiest place for a beginning teacher of writing to jump from. If I didn't yet know how to teach the features of genres—how to identify, name, exemplify, demonstrate, and respond to the elements of different literary forms—I stood on safe ground when kids and I focused on little stories about moments from their lives. Then I could reach into the bag of tricks I had gleaned about writing workshop and employ proven de-

vices for improving narratives: minilessons and conferences about finding a focus, avoiding bed-to-bed storylines, composing grabbing titles and inviting leads, grafting on satisfying conclusions, creating realistic dialogue, and inserting the writer's thoughts and feelings at critical junctures in the plot. The approach feels mechanical to me now, but it made the workshop possible. It gave me a scaffold to lean against as I began to learn about the craft of writing and how to teach it to kids.

Bringing fiction and nonfiction literature into the writing workshop—reading it aloud, reading it together with my kids, reacting to it with them, and naming what we noticed—changed me, changed us, and changed the workshop. We pushed off, genre by genre. As I shared examples with kids, tried the genres myself, and asked kids to help me tease out their elements, the personal-experience narrative was squeezed tighter and tighter into a corner of the workshop, where my kids tiptoed around it. What they did as poets, parodists, essayists, reporters, dramatists, petitioners, and short story writers felt more interesting, satisfying, and *grown-up* than chronicling more of their experiences. No longer the workhorse of the workshop, personal-experience narratives almost disappeared from my kids' writing repertoires.

I'll be honest: I did not miss them. Sometimes I felt the work that went into crafting them—both the writer's and mine as the teacher—wasn't justified in the finished writing. Sometimes there was no significance to be found in an experience; it was just one topic on a writer's list. He or she couldn't say why this experience was important, interesting, or worth writing about, and the ordeal of trying to turn a casual choice into a meaningful expression of something almost killed both of us.

Three years ago I took stock. I began to read a new genre, to myself and to my students: it is *memoir*. I wrote memoirs in search of the genre and my own past; I wrote them to try to open windows into my life. These were not personal experience narratives about how I did this, then I did that, and it was all so much fun. In memoir I discovered a genre that helps me live my life.

Memoir is how writers look for the past and make sense of it. We figure out who we are, who we have become, and what it means to us and to the lives of others: a memoir puts the events of a life in perspective for the writer *and* for those who read it. It is a way to validate to others the events of our lives—our choices, perspectives, decisions, responses.

Memoir recognizes and explores moments on the way to growing up and becoming oneself, the good moments and the bad ones. It distills the essence of an experience through what a writer includes and, more importantly, through what a writer excludes. Memoir celebrates people and places no one else has ever heard of. And memoir allows us to discover and tell our own truths as writers.

Katy knows this. She used memoir to dig into her heart and excavate her own truth about a famous incident in the life of CTL: the day a bunch of girls ate berries they found on the playground, berries none of us teachers could identify.

POISON FRUIT

It was a warm, December day at C.T.L., and a typical noon recess was about to start. There wasn't much snow on the ground yet; red berries covered the shrubs along the bottom of the hill. I remember it was the day of Rachel's birthday party. She was turning eight; I was seven. As we walked out the door onto the playground, Rachel suggested that we play house. Of course, we had to agree with her: it was her birthday.

"With animals?" someone asked.

"Yeah. Let's go down to the bottom of the hill." We ran down the slope, Meggie and I in the lead. At the bottom Rachel noticed the red wintergreen berries.

"We can eat the berries and pretend they're food and medicine."

"They're okay to eat?" Izzie questioned.

"Sure. My mom said so," Rachel replied.

"Okay," Meggie said. "Let's start." If Meggie thought they were all right, I guessed I'd eat them, too. They looked fine, and Rachel had said they were edible. I never doubted Rachel.

"Let's go over there first," I said. "It looks like a better spot to play."

"Yeah," Izzie agreed. "We could make a snow fort."

"Great idea!" Rachel exclaimed.

"I'm the baby," Martha said.

"Rachel, are you going to be the mother?" I questioned. I claimed my role: "I'm the older sister."

"Of course, I'm the mother. I always am." Rachel the mother again? I thought. I wished some time I could choose first but, of course, it was her birthday.

"Mommy," Martha cried, "I'm sick." She was already in character.

"Here." Rachel handed Martha some wintergreen berries, and she promptly ate them.

The sun shone brightly. It glistened on the snow. The berries were even redder on the backdrop of white. The scent of snow about to fall filled the air. We all ate the wintergreen berries, except Izzie. The leaves were green. Their scent smelled like wintergreen, but their taste didn't have much flavor.

Clang, clang! The bell on top of the school pealed, so we charged up the hill. We had writing next, and I had something good to write about. Changing our shoes quickly, Meggie and I walked upstairs, almost running. There we were stopped by Mrs. Maxim, our teacher. Rachel came up behind us.

"What have you been eating?" Mrs. Maxim asked.

Rachel was quick to respond. "Red berries—wintergreen berries." Then I noticed my friends' faces. Their mouths were red. The teachers know we've been eating berries, I thought. I knew they would yell—or would they? Well, at least we had told the truth.

Ms. Atwell ran down to the kitchen and called someone on the telephone; I don't know who. Then she left in her car. Mrs. Maxim said she would be back and to wait there. She wasn't gone long. When Ms. A. returned, she made five phone calls. Later I found out the calls were to our parents.

Ms. A. said that the poison control center told her the berries we ate could be bad for us, we would have to take ipecac, which is a medicine that makes people throw up. I began to cry. I didn't want to throw up. I hate throwing up. We knew the berries were safe. Well, that's what Rachel had said.

I looked at the staring faces of my group. I wanted to run away from all this. Ms. A. came downstairs again. She gave each of us a spoonful of the grossest thing I've ever tasted. To top it off, we each had to drink a whole glass of orange juice. I almost threw up just from the taste of orange juice and ipecac combined. Mrs. Maxim directed me to the writing room bathroom.

"I don't want to go in the bathroom," I cried.

"Come on," she said.

"No."

"Come with me," Ms. Atwell said. She was speaking so strictly and looking so scared I didn't dare disobey. Meggie and I went into the bathroom with her and stood over the sink and the toilet. We stood there and stood there. Then Rachel came into our bathroom, and as soon as she entered, she threw up. I started to cry again. Five or ten minutes passed.

"Should we give them another dose?" Ms. A. asked Mrs. Maxim. She was talking about Meggie and me. We got another taste of ipecac and orange juice and went back to the bathroom again, we hoped for the last time that day. Then it happened: I threw up, and so did Meggie.

"There's nothing there," one of the teachers remarked. "No berries." I thought, how could they make us take this and then throw up for nothing? I wondered if Meggie felt the same way. I still felt sick.

Rachel's mom drove into the school parking lot. We ran to the car, and Rachel and Martha crowded into the front. Still feeling sick I got in, with Meggie in the middle. Why? I thought again. Why did I eat the berries? They were fine to eat, weren't they? On the way to Rachel's, riding along the newly built road, Meggie started screaming.

"I'm going to throw up!" Oh, my gosh! Not again, I thought. Mona stopped the car, but it was too late. Meggie had thrown up. I hate to watch people throw up, almost as much as I hate to throw up. I got out of the car while Mona tried to clean up. Suddenly I threw up, too. I didn't even know it was coming. I never considered that the double dose of ipecac might make me throw up more than usual.

I called my mom from Rachel's: I didn't want to spend the night. She said she'd come pick me up. Meggie threw up the whole time I was waiting. I felt sorry for her, but I was glad it wasn't me.

"You're sure they were fine to eat?" Martha asked Rachel.

"I told you they were. If you don't believe me, ask my mom," Rachel replied.

"That's okay. I believe you," Martha responded.

I knew the berries were safe, too. I'll always look back on that day with anger and a sense of truth. We had told the truth. They asked us, and we did not lie. A new rule was passed at school that week about eating vegetation on the playground. No teacher will ever forget its cause, and I won't either.

—Katy Seiders

We began to define memoir as the writer's truth and to explore its uses and occasions. What could this genre do for us as writers? Some kids considered the good days of their lives as a reason for memoir: to describe growing up on the coast of Maine. In a day spent hauling lobster with a friend and her father, Meghan found a memoir.

A DAY OF LOBSTERING

Whoosh! A wave comes up and splashes us. "Kathryn, thanks again for inviting me to come out with you and your dad. I'm having a great time," I say.

Kathryn and I have been friends since third grade. Her dad, Gordon, is a lobsterman. When she called and asked me along for a day on his boat, I said yes right away. I love to be out on the sea; I love to be with Kathryn and Gordon.

Now the boat slows down. "Buoy ahead!" Gordon yells.

"I wonder how many lobsters will be in this trap," Kathryn comments. We pull up alongside the buoy, and Gordon hauls the trap aboard, saying, "Looks like four or five 'keepers,' girls." He cleans out the leftover bait, rebaits the trap, and slides it over into the deep, translucent waters. We swiftly, gently place the lobsters in one of the two holding barrels.

A bit later Kathryn announces that all this fresh air is making us hungry. Gordon agrees and proceeds to put three cans of Campbell's soup into brand new bait bags, one can per bag. He drops these into a pot of boiling water, leaving the strings of the net out over the edge of the pot.

Several minutes later we hear him holler, "Lunch is ready!" I never thought canned soup could taste so delicious as it does this day, served with fresh salt air and such good company. I am impressed with Gordon's method of serving a hot lunch on board ship.

Each time we approach a buoy, Kathryn and I become excited at the prospect of finding a full trap. Occasionally there are a couple of shorts that we throw back to grow bigger. As the day wears on, the barrel fills to overflowing and, with each trap pulled, Kathryn and I help by putting a thick blue rubber band on each lobster's crunch and scissor claws. This is fun; it feels good knowing I am really working on a lobster boat, not just tagging along as a passenger.

Now the sun begins to drop in the west, and Gordon turns the boat and heads for shore and the docks he knows so well. Tired but happy, we help unload the catch, clean the boat, and ready it for another day's work.

—Meghan Kennedy

Elizabeth said good-bye to her childhood in a memoir. In "Leprechauns" she becomes a growing-up girl, one who can measure the distance between herself and the little kids at our school and use her imagination to make magic for them now.

LEPRECHAUNS

"Look, leprechauns!" Small feet pounded up the stairs, and a small hand pushed a scrap of paper and a tiny clay cup in my face.

"Neat," I replied.

"See?" Ryan said shoving it closer to my nose. I nodded.

"Where did you find it?"

"In the field." He pointed excitedly in the direction of the sloping hill, covered with grass the color of spring thanks to the March rains. Ryan ran off to show someone else. Rachel looked at me.

"I was wondering where I'd lost those," she said. Rachel's famous hedgehog collection, I thought. Rachel loved hedgehogs and had tons of small accessories for her tiny stuffed toys. I thought I had seen that cup before.

"Ryan thinks they were left by leprechauns," I told her. Rachel smiled.

"Hedgehog leprechauns?" she suggested. "We should leave more stuff out for the little kids to find, like build little houses for them and things." She looked over at Ryan, who was talking excitedly to his friend Ethan.

"They'd be even more excited." I looked over my shoulder at Ryan. "If that's possible." Our teacher, Ms. Benedict, came up behind us in time to hear our last sentence.

"We should do that!" she exclaimed.

"Do what?" Rachel and I turned to face her.

"Make leprechaun houses," she replied. She turned to make sure Ryan had left the room.

"The whole class?" Rachel looked doubtful.

"Just the people who want to," Ms. B. replied.

"It might be kind of fun," I said to Rachel.

"Why not?" Rachel said. "Sure, that would be neat."

"We'll talk about it in writing class," our teacher told us. I sighed: this was going to be interesting. It would be fun to surprise the little kids. Only we would know. I grabbed my coat and ran out to recess.

". . . So if you want to build a leprechaun house or bring in accessories . . . ?" Ms. Benedict talked on. I looked at my feet and followed the pattern of my shoelaces. They were dirty and falling apart. I would have to ask for new ones for my birthday.

"Bring them in tomorrow," the teacher continued. "SO LAUREL, what do you think of *A Wrinkle in Time?*" she demanded, trying to sound impatient but not succeeding. Finally Ethan trotted down the stairs, letting the door bang behind him.

"Sorry," Ms. Benedict apologized to Laurel. "I didn't want Ethan to hear."

"Uh, yeah," Laurel replied.

"As I was saying, bring the stuff in for the leprechauns tomorrow. You can get your lunches now." We dashed down the stairs; I was in the middle. Someone stepped on the heel of my shoe. I turned around and glared at Curt. He grinned and stepped on the other shoe. I kicked backwards, missed, and jumped down the rest of the stairs.

What does a leprechaun house look like? I asked myself. On my desk was a pile of twigs that were shedding bark all over the place. I had dug through the drawers in our house and come up with two spools, which should do for leprechaun tables, and a scrap of cloth for a bed. Now all I needed was the house.

I began to make a frame. When I was done, I had more glue on my hands and the desk than was left in the bottle. After the glue dried I tied sticks onto the frame and lashed down pine bows for the roof. The sticks were slightly crooked, with spaces in between them. The house stood there unsure of itself, like a colt just learning to walk. I packed moss between the cracks, and with more glue I attached small sticks to a scrap of cardboard and tied it to the space I had left open for the door. I pushed it with my finger. It creaked back and forth. I placed two spools inside, put the house in a plastic bag, and set it beside my backpack.

I looked at the books behind me on the shelves in the reading room, trying to choose one to read. Morning meeting was boring me.

"I found this on the floor," I heard Ms. Atwell announce from her chair at the front. All eyes below fourth grade looked up at her. She held a small piece of paper. Our class had composed the note, and Curt had written it in his smallest handwriting.

"Dear Sean," she read. "Greeting! Yesterday I went and explored the giant structure. I found some boards with rounded ends. I was going to bring them out to build my house, but I was scared by a big rabbit. I was so frightened that I kept on running after I got out of the structure. I lost several of my belongings. If you are here, look for them. Patrick." Now all eyes were on her.

"It must be from the leprechaun!" Ryan shouted.

"Did you see the leprechaun stuff I found!" Ethan yelled. Patrick must've dropped it!" Now almost everyone was talking. I looked over at the rest of our class; they were sitting quietly in the back row, trying to look bored.

Rachel spent snack recess planting small cups and plates on different shelves in the math/science room. Little kids quickly found them and showed everybody. No one seemed to mind that outside it was a bleak, cold, March day. After snack Rachel and I slipped outside to put out my leprechaun house. Everyone else was still in the school. I shivered and wrapped my arms around me tighter.

"Here, put these in," Rachel said. She dumped two tiny cups and a carefully stitched green hat no bigger than my thumb into my hands.

"Cool," I replied. I knelt down beside the small house, now tucked between the thick roots of the old oak. I placed the cups on a spool, then put the spool as far inside the house as I could reach through the small door. The wind blew my hair in my face. I stood up, brushed the dirt from my pants, and jogged back inside.

It was still windy at noon recess; I brushed the hair out of my face. When the soccer ball came whizzing toward me, I drew my leg back, and it settled on the ground in front of me.

"Over here!" Curt yelled, waving his arms. I kicked the ball to him. Rachel ran after him.

"Rachel!" Ethan cried. "Come look!" He ran onto the soccer field and tugged on Rachel's hand.

"What?" she asked.

"Look!" Ethan pointed to where Ryan and a bunch of other kids were standing. "There's a leprechaun house by the oak tree! It has things in it, too!" I bit my lip to stop the smile. Rachel had been right: the leprechaun things really had them excited.

The kids believed. When they lived in the magic we had created, I found myself wanting to believe in it, too: not in the leprechauns, but in the magic itself.

After a week outside in the March wind and rain, which seemed to come more often than not, the leprechaun house by the oak collapsed. Rain moistened the glue, and wind scattered the carefully collected twigs. The small dishes were blown away to be found another year, when the snow would finally melt. It dissolved the way a dream dissolves after dawn—slowly, leaving fragments of memories and magic behind.

None of us ever told. I don't think the younger kids ever knew. For most, I think, it was the magic of the leprechauns, like the magic of the coming spring.

Some memoirs explore the dark corners of a life. Laurel wrote "Painful Parting" about her parents' decision to divorce; she published it, with their permission, in *Acorns*. Laurel explained, "I think it will help kids who might go through this some day, plus kids who will never have to, to know what it feels like."

PAINFUL PARTING

We were all in the TV room, Mom and I both in tears, my brother trying to be strong, and my dad staring into space with sad, glazed eyes, trying not to cry.

"I'm sorry, but people just fall out of love," my mom kept trying to explain. No one was listening. I never thought anything like this could happen to me. It felt like someone was grinding a knife into my heart it was so painful. I buried my face in my dad's chest; his arms wrapped around me. I wanted to hold on to him and never let go.

"My parents are happy together. They are in love," I repeated to myself. I was trying to change the story, hoping this was a dream. Whatever my mom was saying couldn't be, wouldn't be, true.

"You both will be living with me," she said between sobs.

"What?" I jumped up. "What about Dad?" By then I couldn't control myself. "Dad, don't you want me anymore?" I yelled. My dad's sad eyes looked up at me.

"Yes, Laurel, I want you and Stephen more than anything. But the judge said for you two to be with your mom. I'm sorry." I saw one tear trickle down his face. It made the pain worse.

I looked over at my mom. I could see she had hurt in her eyes too, like "What about me?" But I thought it was her fault this was happening: she was the one who was leaving. Then I looked over at Stephen. He just sat there, frozen, stunned, with Mom's arm around him.

The picture froze in my mind. When I close my eyes, I see the day repeating itself, endlessly. It was the worst day of my life.

Looking back on it now, I can see the good that came of it. I'm partly glad it happened, because my parents are happy, and I have two families. But my other feeling of sadness remains. I'm still sad that I can't have *them*.

—*Laurel Card*

Izzie and Toby explored even darker corners in memoirs. In the process they celebrated two lives that would otherwise have gone unsung: a grandfather with a long life behind him, and a baby brother whose life had just begun.

JACK

We sat gathered in a circle at the edge of the pond. I looked around at everyone. Their faces were somber and tear stained. As we sat and were carried away by the words in the poems being read, my mind floated.

Faces, pictures, and memories were projected in my head, and I was surprised at the depth of sadness they brought me. Today was the day I had been scared of for the past year. Today I had to say the final good-bye to my grandfather, Jack. For eleven years I had admired him, loved him and everything about him—his stories, his comments, his sense of humor. And I loved that no matter what I talked to him about, he always understood.

I remembered last summer coming down here to the pond to pick blueberries.

"Did you get that bush?" he asked.

"Yup," I said. He gave a slight nod of satisfaction and continued to fill the tin pail with what looked like crumpled blue velvet.

We talked about the heat, the gardens, the berries, and the pond. I don't think I realized then how much I would treasure this time with him.

I remembered the last time I saw him. As he lay in his bed and held my hand, I never even considered I was seeing him for the last time. Now that I thought about it, as he lay there, enveloped in the white covers surrounding him, he looked like an angel or a cloud—beautiful but sad.

Of all the people who have touched my life, few have I missed this much.

Now, I looked over at my grandmother, her hair blowing in the soft breeze. She untied a bag, which she passed around. I watched as everyone took a handful, then held it like gold. I was nervous—even scared—but I reached in and took out a handful of rough, crumbled earth. I stood up, my mind spinning. I held close to my mother, confused, sad, and overwhelmed that I was holding part of my grandfather in my hand. I walked slowly, tears burning my face.

"Put them somewhere you can always come back to, where you can talk to him whenever you need to," my mom told me. I walked toward the blueberry bushes. At the base of the patch we had picked from together, I knelt and sprinkled a few ashes onto the ground. Then I walked over to the willow tree that hangs so gracefully over the water and sprinkled ashes under it, too. I took the rest and blew them into the rippling water. Oddly, I felt calm now, relaxed, as if it were a comfort to know he was safe. I walked back and sat again in the circle, the tension released.

Next summer, when I go down to pick blueberries, he will be there with me. He might never hold my hand again, but he'll be there—in the berries, the pond, the willow tree, and me.

—*Isabeall Quella*

SHIPPY

When my aunt called and told me my brother was being born, I was surprised and happy because I had four sisters, and he was my first brother.

My parents were divorced when I was three or four and both remarried soon after. I have one sister from before my parents got divorced, who is a year older. My mom had two kids after, so I have two half-sisters. Then my stepmom, Sas, gave me another half-sister. That makes four sisters and no brothers, and that brings me to June 3, 1995.

I couldn't wait, so I found my mom and told her the news. She drove my sister and me to the Maine Medical Center. When we got there, my aunt and cousin were sitting in the waiting room, my grandparents were walking the halls with my little sister, my stepmom Sas was in the delivery room giving birth, and my dad was running back and forth between the waiting room and the delivery room. He gave us reports of the latest news like, "The baby's head is coming out, now," or "You can see the baby in half an hour."

Whenever he made an announcement, I'd get just as excited as he was and stay that way for a couple of minutes. Then I'd relax again and enjoy the thought of having a brother and teaching him the sports I love. I took a deep breath and inhaled that hospital smell. It seemed distinct to me because I was always there for some reason, like sisters who went for speech therapy and I would be dragged along while I could be playing with my friends, or the smell of illness and sadness when I visited sick relatives. But this time it smelled like baby. Each time there seemed to be a feeling that went long with the smell. This time the feeling was happiness.

Before I knew it, it was time to see him. My cousin Maya, Tookie my sister, and I went in together. As we entered, we heard the baby crying. Finally I had a brother. I got to hold him first, which was hard because one of my arms was in a cast; I had broken it playing keep-away. I had to ask my dad to help me. I looked into my brother's eyes, and he looked back at me. Then he yawned and put his fist in his face as if he were trying to suck his thumb. I felt as if I were dreaming, and I wanted to remember this moment forever. "Say cheese," a voice commanded, and I looked up as someone took a picture of us. Now everyone else had a chance to hold the baby, and I sat down. Then he went to the nursery, and my mom drove us home.

Over the next couple of weeks I talked with my dad and visited on the weekends. Before I knew it, school was out and I went to my dad's for the six weeks of summer I always spend with him. I recall seeing a story on Sudden Infant Death Syndrome on the news during those weeks. I hadn't thought much of it at the time. Later, I wished I had.

Soon it was time for me to go back to my mom's and start school again. I talked with my dad still, and I visited every other weekend. The baby was getting big and learning how to crawl. I looked forward to the weekends I went to Dad's so I could see what my brother was up to.

It was about 4:00 in the afternoon on October 6th, the day after

Tookie's birthday. We were about to go to the movies; she was taking some friends. We were in the basement and my sister and I were fighting about something, when my mom yelled, "Tookie! Toby! Could you come up here for a sec?"

I thought we were in trouble. Instead my mom had us pick up phones on the same line. Suddenly I heard my dad's voice. "I have some tragic news," he said. I could tell it was bad, and thoughts raced through my mind: was there a car accident? Did Sas hurt herself? I had no idea that my worst nightmare had come true.

Baby Shippy had died. I was stunned. Pain shot through my spine like lightning coming out of nowhere. After I was done talking I went up to my room, lay on my bed, and thought. I blocked out all other sounds. All my dreams of a brother and our life together went down the drain. Memories flooded me. I remembered a time in the car, when we found out early that the baby would be a boy. Then I remembered the story about SIDS on the news. My dad had said they weren't sure how Shippy died, that they thought it might be SIDS.

We went to the movies that night. I couldn't pay attention to the movie. I kept thinking. I would look up and watch the movie, but then I would think again.

I skipped the couple days of school left in the week so I could visit my dad and Sas. It was awkward and painful going to their house after the baby died. They had found out the cause was SIDS, like I'd thought. Lots of people were at the house, mostly aunts, uncles, and grandparents. My cousins and I hung out together and did nothing. I could tell they were as sad as I was. We tried to get our minds off Shippy by playing cards, but that went over like a lead balloon. We tried a lot of other diversions we thought would work, but none did. We thought each idea was a sure fire plan, but instead it was like the Titanic. When we hit the iceberg of Shippy's death, it sank like a stone.

Soon it was time for the services in memory of Shippy. First we had a morning candlelight service. We lit candles in the early, early morning, walked out into our field, stood in a circle, and dropped the stones we had given everyone earlier. Each of us planted a bulb, which formed his memorial. Later, during the church service, the church was so full of people from the community, some we didn't even know, that people had to stand in the halls. I was an acolyte in the service, which meant a lot to me, to be part of remembering my brother.

Sas and my dad had Shippy cremated. They sprinkled his ashes in the ocean. My cousins, my sisters, and I took balloons as gifts for him, and we let them float up over the clouds. Mine had a hole in it, but it still managed to climb over the clouds when I let it go. I believe my love for Shippy was what helped make it over.

—*Toby Bright*

Other memoirists distilled experiences for themselves and their readers. During school winter vacations Duncan travels with his family to exotic climes. In a memoir he gave his readers—his classmates and his teacher, stuck in the frozen north—a taste of the tourist lifestyle in Costa Rica.

TOAD MOTEL

It was a sunny afternoon when we reached the Sugar Beach Motel. As we pulled into a small parking lot, a three-legged dog hobbled over to greet us. After the dog lost interest in us, we unpacked our bags from the rented van, checked in, and settled into our rooms.

My parents were reading, the twins were checking the place out, and I was searching for something in my bag. Suddenly I stopped.

Something had caught my eye. I turned my head to where I had seen the image. My eyes widened as I backed off. I had spotted a scorpion.

I tiptoed over to my dad. "Dad? There's a scorpion on the wall!"

"Sure, Dunc," he replied with a smile.

"Really, there is."

"Okay, okay, I'll come over," he replied with another smile, and a sigh.

Then I pointed to it, and sure enough, it was a scorpion climbing up our bedroom wall. My dad picked up a sandal and gave it one big WHACK! I ran outside. My brother and sister were already running up from the beach. My mom said, in a small, hard voice, "I heard."

Dad walked out on the small porch and told Mom a story about how he thought it was one of the plastic bugs we had brought with us, because one happened to be a scorpion. Mom's response was, "We are leaving here tomorrow, no matter what." That night we were awake until we were convinced there weren't any scorpions in our beds.

The next morning Brooks and my dad went out in search of a new motel. At around noon they came back, and Dad reported that they had found a cheap motel with a pool, a beach, and a restaurant. So we packed up and left our scorpion-infested getaway.

On the way I was still thinking about the scorpion. I said, "Mom, you never told me there were scorpions in Costa Rica."

"We never knew either," she replied.

When we pulled into the next motel parking lot there was no hobbling dog, but there was an open restaurant, a beach, and a pool. We began to unpack the van again, while my mom went to the office to get a room. I thought to myself how this was going to be a better motel—much better than one filled with killer bugs and crippled dogs.

Once we got everything into the new room, the twins wanted to go for a swim, so my dad took them swimming, and my mom and I stayed in the room to unpack the bags. All of a sudden the twins came running back into the room; they told us a woman at the pool had unfolded her towel and a scorpion had crawled out.

"Not another one," Mom said. But this time it was just a hard voice. From that moment I was careful wherever I stepped.

The twins didn't get out of the pool until later that afternoon, when Fiona came in, yelling again. "There are toads coming out of the pool and hopping around everywhere!"

Mom put her head in her hands. "OK, that's just great."

That night Dad went to the restaurant ahead of us because we weren't ready yet. A minute or so after he left we heard this scratching and tapping at the door. I walked over slowly and opened the door a crack. There was the most humungous land crab I'd ever seen, sitting there, waving its claws at me. My first thought was that Dad had put it there as a joke. But there weren't any places he could have hidden in time. Just as we'd scared it away, Dad came back to the room. "Come on. What are you waiting for?" he asked.

"There was a giant crab at the door that scared us half to death," my mom said, glaring at him.

"Dad, did you put it there?" I asked, smiling.

"No. I've been waiting in the restaurant the whole time. I saw a couple more toads, Brooks," he said, smiling at my brother. Brooks was terrified of the giant things ever since he had seen their size and learned they spit stuff.

That night while we ate our dinners, giant toads hopped around our feet and peed on the floor. On the way to the bathroom I saw three of them. Once I got to the door I peered in, didn't see one, and shut the door behind me. Suddenly there was one sitting there, in the bathroom. It hopped once and looked at me like it was ready to spit. I opened the door and ran back out, leaving the bathroom to my new friend.

We were in the pool the next day when Mom came out with an unhappy look on her face. We stopped playing and looked at her with surprised expressions. "Guess what?" she asked. "I found a baby scorpion on my shirt when I went to get dressed."

"Well, I guess that means we have to search through the bags and turn all the clothes inside out, because where there's one baby, there are probably more of them," my dad said with a sigh. Mom and Dad spent most of the afternoon going through the contents of suitcases.

Since our itinerary listed three nights at Sugar Beach, we stayed at the toad motel for another night and didn't bother to search for another. The next morning, after we packed our stuff back into the bags, the twins wanted to go for one more swim; so did I.

"It will have to be a short one," Dad said, "because we have a long drive ahead of us."

We jumped in one last time, then we left the toad motel forever. I didn't look back.

—*Duncan Kerr*

Other memoirists wrote on formal occasions of looking back and creating closure. The Center's annual eighth-grade yearbook includes a memoir by each student of a memorable corner of his or her life at the school. The restlessness, exuberance, and emerging self-awareness of adolescence are themes in Tom's memoir about playing King of the Mountain and Sam's memoir about the secret hideout in the elevator shaft.

KING OF THE MOUNTAIN

It was the day we had been waiting for: no parent had volunteered for recess duty, so Pam was alone in the daunting task of watching over eighty balls of energy at noon recess. Joe and I noticed at once that Pam was alone, and we began to round up kids of all ages to join a game (translation: savage contest) we had been playing sporadically for the past week: King of the Mountain.

For those of you who don't know, King of the Mountain has one rule: knock (shove) the person (King) standing on the mountain (hill, mound, or lump) off the mountain (ibid.). If you manage to do so, you are now the King and inherit the crown (solely imaginary), only to lose it seconds later. Yes, it is great fun but, as you can guess, a game that involves intense physical contact, which is a clear playground no-no, which, of course, accounts for most of the pleasure (savagery) we take in playing it. With the task of rounding up kids complete, we set off for the venue.

Our game was played on and around the long-jump pit (large litter box) near the woods. One of the benefits of using the pit was its location at the bottom of the big hill (eroded mudslide). Kids would stride along to the summit, looking as innocent as possible, scan for prying adult eyes (infrared), decide on the unsuspecting target, and take off— look out below!

Now, sometimes the person running (falling) down the hill might be seen by someone on the mountain. Prepared (sort of) for the on-rushing person (blur), we stood there casually, not seeming to notice until the very last second. Then we stepped aside, clearing the way for the human bullet to trip on something like the sand (preferably a foot) and go somersaulting into the woods at a little under Mach five (human chainsaw).

On this particular day we were grouped at the bottom of the hill and ready to go. We played with a wide range of combatants, from macho Curt, Sam, Jay, and Jason (no surprise), to fearless Nutty, Nick, and Chris (no surprise). Now, in a battle between Jay and second grader David Nutt, who do you think would win? I thought so, too—but I thought wrong (no surprise).

I was striding up the hill for one of my innocent runs (charges) when I heard an agonized, "AAAH, get away from me you weirdo! Leggo my leg!!" I recognized Jay's voice and turned to see what the commotion was about. Nutty had adopted his favorite take-down maneuver—latching on to people's legs—and was about to topple Jay. Then I heard the patented giggle (contagious cackle) that could only come from Nutty, and I knew that Jay had eaten sand. Nutty, smiling a smile that floated off his face, targeted another "big kid," Curt, and went to work with the same results.

I continued my own trek to the top and headed (stumbled) down. Unfortunately, Nutty and Chris saw me and, just at the right moment, dove at my feet, sending me smack into the sand, face first. The sand tasted fine, just a bit crunchy (overcooked).

Then came the inevitable Pam visit. "Pam's coming!" someone yelled, and we started to walk up the hill (innocently, don't forget). After she moved on, our group held a quick council of war and decided that conditions were too risky to continue King of the Mountain today.

The next day Pam did have help at recess, which almost caused us to put the game on hold again. However, much to our delight, one of our spies monitoring adult movements tipped us off that Pam and the parent volunteer were both involved in cooling down an ugly dispute concerning fort territory around the pond (frog bowl). We knew that the kindergartners brandishing clubs (twigs) wouldn't soon be sorted out, so we ran to the pit and started to rumble.

Five minutes later Pam came into view from around the school and ended the game with an abrupt, "Hold it right there." She gave us the patented talk (speech) that teachers give in situations of intense physical contact (ZZZZ). I won't even go into it—you know what I mean—and told us it was the last time we would play the game or we would be in trouble. We nodded and walked away (innocently).

We gave the game a rest for a week or so, but finally couldn't cope without it any longer (withdrawal symptoms). So, once again, Nutty tackled everybody in sight, people flew into the woods (seen by Hubble), and Pam put another grinding halt to it all. However this time we didn't get a Pam talk (not so bad); we got a full blown Ms. A. talk (off the scale bad), which put a permanent end to King of the Mountain (semipermanently).

This memoir was written in the interest of happy childhood memories (savage to the bone). No children were harmed or mistreated. The author, Tom Allen, is in no way responsible for any action taken by any of the subjects of this memoir. He is, and, always will be . . .

(Innocent).

—*Tom Allen*

THE PERFECT HIDEOUT

There were two months left in my last year at CTL, and Jay and I were itching to get into some kind of trouble. We had been friends ever since he came to the school two years ago. It felt like we had been in and out of trouble pretty much every other day the entire time.

Today was a mild day in March. There was still snow on the ground, but it was rapidly melting. It was around 12:30 and everybody was down in the new barn playing games. The teachers had just headed up to the writing room to eat their lunch.

"The room is clear," Jay called as he closed the door, blocking off the Play Place. "Now, what did you want me for?" he asked, curious about what kind of trouble I was contemplating.

"I'd like to introduce you to our new get-out-of-afternoon-meeting hideout," I announced, removing the flimsy aluminum door that led to the elevator shaft.

"Looks cozy, but . . . why the elevator shaft?" Jay asked.

"No one could ever find us here, and when you talk it sounds like you're a million miles away," I answered.

The elevator shaft itself was only one part of the hideout. Directly behind the aluminum door is a room not very big and crowded with about two hundred paint cans. To the right is a small opening just big enough to fit into. After squeezing through this passage, it's a six-foot drop into the main shaft.

These were the directions I gave Jay. "Cool," he said. "So, I'll meet you here at 2:30, then?"

"Sure. We might as well put it to use today," I answered.

The rest of the day went as usual: the occasional note and flying paper clip, ending with the hypnotic tone of Kinne's voice—until 2:30. When he left for meeting, Jay and I stalled for a while, then hid in the stairwell until we couldn't hear him anymore. No sooner had we opened the door into the lab than Jason and Curt appeared from *their* hideout in the bathroom. Since they were here, we included them in our hideout.

"Open the door quick, Jason. I think I hear footsteps." We piled into the tiny room, and I pulled the door into place behind us.

"Jees, it's dark in here," Curt whispered.

"Wow, this place is awesome," Jason said.

"So, who's going in the shaft first?" I asked.

We made Curt go first and tell us what it was like. He edged over in front of the door, looked down, and described it as a bottomless pit. With a quick push from Jay and me, Curt was on his way down. He went tumbling to the bottom of the shaft, followed by an echoing slap.

"This place is weird," Curt called up.

I crawled down the board that leaned on the side of the wall and checked it out. Around me was nothing but white wall topped by a ceiling thirty-five feet high.

"Do we have any power down here?" I asked Curt. He bent down and fooled around with the pump. It started with a jolt. "Great! That means we can string some lights. Come on down, guys." Jay and Jason crawled down the side of the shaft.

"What should we do now?" Jay asked. Everybody just looked at each other. Then we heard footsteps entering the room.

"Be quiet," I said. "No one will find us if we just keep quiet." We heard the footsteps stop, then the sound of something dropping, then the start-up of a vacuum cleaner.

"That was a close one," Jay said, "I could have sworn it was Ms. A."

"Yeah, me too. Well," I said, looking at my watch, "two forty-five. I've got to get going."

"See you tomorrow?" Jay said.

"See you tomorrow," I answered.

The next day was Friday. Soon it was 2:30: another fifteen minutes, and we'd be home free for the weekend. Kinne headed up to the meeting and left us alone. Quickly, Jason, Curt, and I ran to the elevator shaft and dove in; Jay wasn't with us today because he was sick.

"Yes! We are free!" Jason cried.

Curt was trying to pull himself through the door.

"You know what we should do? We should decorate the walls of the shaft," Jason said.

"You are an idiot, Jason," I called back to him.

"No, listen to me. I could download pictures off the Internet, then print them out," Jason replied.

"Whatever," Curt remarked.

"If we do anything it'll be to string Christmas lights along the walls up and down the shaft," I decided.

"Maybe," Curt added. As he spoke, we were interrupted by the sound of footsteps again. Curt was down in the shaft, and Jason and I were sitting on some old paint cans.

"Nothing to worry about," I said. "It's only Conny cleaning again." But now there was the sound of another set of footsteps coming from the opposite doorway.

"Don't worry, guys. No one can ever find us in here," I said, trying to reassure them. The two sets of footsteps merged, and out came the sound of Ms. A.'s voice. She moved straight for the aluminum door.

"Brace yourselves, boys," I whispered.

Ms. Atwell tore off the door and commanded, *"Come out, now."* We climbed out and stood in a line. She looked at us, speechless for a moment, then told us to get upstairs. We ran up the stairs and sat through the rest of another painful afternoon meeting.

Before we left school that afternoon Ms. A. did talk to us, but she wasn't half as ticked off as we imagined she would be. She talked about supporting our peers and being part of the school and what a stupid place to hide and how scared she had been when she couldn't find us. The truth is, I wasn't really listening. I was wondering how to get the chairs out of there before they installed the elevator.

—*Sam Stewart*

In teaching about the art of memoir, I ask kids to look at good memoirs and bad ones. The bad ones are mine. I present them in minilessons, prewritten on overhead transparencies. This was a good bad one, in terms of the discussion it evoked:

MS. A.'S B-A-A-A-D MEMOIR

We were going ice skating at Dieners' Pond.

"Will you wait for me?" Mom said.

"How come?" we asked.

"I want to go skating with you."

"But you never go skating," we replied.

"I have borrowed Rose's skates," she said.

Then we walked down to Dieners' Pond. When we got there, we changed into our skates. When Mom skated, she was really good. She did figure eights backwards. We had never seen our mother skate before. It was a big surprise.

After about two hours we went home and had hot chocolate. It was a great day.

I left the transparency of the memoir projected on the wall, moved to the easel pad, uncapped a marker, and asked, "Okay, okay, I know it's terrible, but what makes it terrible? What doesn't work here?" I wanted kids to consider their criteria as writers and readers of memoirs and to articulate what they know about effective ones. Together we made a list, which I recorded on the pad.

WHAT DOESN'T WORK IN MS. A.'S MEMOIR?

- It's all plot: just the bare facts about what happened.
- There are no thoughts or feelings of the memoirist.
- There is no memoirist: it's a *we* voice instead of first-person-singular *I*.
- The reader doesn't know who the main character is because there's no voice, no person to be with in the story.
- The reader doesn't know any of the characters, who they are or what they're like.
- There's no description of people or actions: a reader can't see it happening.

- The dialogue doesn't reveal what the people are like, how they sound, or what they might be feeling.
- There's too much dialogue, in relation to action and reflection.
- The pace is too fast. It's over before it starts.
- The setting isn't clear: when and where did this happen?
- The ending doesn't leave the reader with a feeling.
- There's no sense of why the writer wanted to write about the event in the first place.
- There's no *so what?* for the writer: no point, discovery, or significance.
- There's no *so what?* for the reader: no point, discovery, or significance.

To teach about features of good memoirs, I tried to write a good one in a series of demonstration lessons; "Lessons from Laurel," which appears in Chapter 10, was the result. I also read aloud published memoirs, either short works or chapters from longer ones, and made a list of the memoirs in our classroom library that my kids could look to for inspiration:

MEMOIRS TO READ, READ ALOUD, OR EXCERPT IN MINILESSONS

- *I Know Why the Caged Bird Sings*, Maya Angelou
- *Growing Up*, Russell Baker
- "A Christmas Memory," Truman Capote
- *Having Our Say*, Sarah and Elizabeth Delany with Amy Hill Heath
- *Dispatches*, Michael Herr
- *All Creatures Great and Small*, James Herriot
- *Dangerous Minds* and *The Girls in the Back of the Class*, LouAnne Johnson
- *The Liars' Club*, Mary Karr
- *The Woman Warrior*, Maxine Hong Kingston
- *Surprised by Joy*, C. S. Lewis
- *Autobiography of Malcolm X*
- *Never Cry Wolf; The Boat That Wouldn't Float; The Dog Who Wouldn't Be*, Farley Mowat
- *The Things They Carried*, Tim O'Brien (a judgment call and an interesting one to discuss with kids: what nature of truth is O'Brien exploring?)

- *When I Was Young in the Mountains* and *But I'll Be Back Again*, Cynthia Rylant
- "A Child's Christmas in Wales," Dylan Thomas
- *Walden*, Henry David Thoreau
- *Mama Makes Up Her Mind*, Bailey White
- *Night*, Elie Wiesel
- *This Boy's Life*, Tobias Woolf
- *Black Boy*, Richard Wright

From these good examples, we teased out a new list, which we added to throughout the year:

QUALITIES OF MEMOIRS THAT WORK FOR US

- The voice is first-person singular: *I*, not *we*, *one*, or *you*.
- The memoirist is the main character, the someone for readers to be with in the story.
- The writer's thoughts and feelings, reactions and reflections, are revealed.
- There's enough context—background information—to understand the events of the story.
- The context is woven into the story.
- A reader can envision the action—can see it happening.
- A reader can imagine the setting—where and when the memoir is unfolding.
- A reader can imagine the relationships among the characters.
- The dialogue sounds like these people talking, both what they would say and how they would say it: *Boy, you're gonna be sorry* versus *You will be sorry.*
- The pace is slowed down so a reader can enter the story and live it, moment to moment, with the characters.
- There isn't unnecessary information: the writer leaves out what a reader doesn't need to know.
- The lead invites a reader into the world of the memory.
- The conclusion is deliberate: it represents a writer's decision about how to leave his or her readers.
- The writer isn't acting like a reporter: the writing is subjective, the writer's truth.
- The writer invents details that fit with the specific memory and the writer's theme or purpose.

- The memoir sounds and feels like literature, not like reportage.
- The memoir leads to a *so what?* for both the writer and the reader: a discovery of some significance in the memory.
- A reader learns something about LIFE by reading about *a life*.

In minilessons and conferences I teach about memoir as *literary nonfiction*. Memoir is not autobiography, not a diary or chronicle of one's days; it is an art. Like fiction, it's fashioned deliberately. *Walden* may read like this great, cool life that unwinds naturally as literature, but Thoreau wrote seven drafts of *Walden* over eight years. The possibilities of the genre lie in how a memoirist decides to fashion a portion of his or her life.

Memoir calls for strong language; for metaphors and similes; for characters in action and a good story; for problems and themes; for humor and voice; for rich specifics; for rhythm and repetition; for the telling detail. Bottom line, memoir calls for selection: the writer edits his or her life for a reader.

I would like to say I've returned to the memoir with a new sense of appreciation. But in truth, I'm exploring memoir for the first time. The personal-experience narrative, which I've come to think of as a school genre, has disappeared from my classroom. My kids and I don't need it anymore. We do need to call home the child, to surprise ourselves and our readers with unbidden truths, to reinvent our pasts, to become *memoirists*.

12

Hanging with Big Sis: Fiction

Fiction is truth's older sister.
Rudyard Kipling

Seventh and eighth graders long for the Real Thing. They want algebra, the truth about U.S. government policies, science experiments with chemicals, poetry that grapples with the extremes of the human experience. In writing workshop they want fiction. Adolescents are primed to hang out with memoir's big sister. They want to write what they love to read.

Fortunately they love to read S. E. Hinton, Walter Dean Myers, Tim O'Brien, and Alice Hoffman. And, unfortunately, they love to read S. E. Hinton, Walter Dean Myers, Tim O'Brien, and Alice Hoffman. These novelists inspire my kids to write fiction, with styles so lucid and seamless that the prose is transparent. Kids—adult readers, too—see straight through the writing: as readers we jump into the world of a novel and live there with the characters. The paradox of good fiction is how easy it is to enter a fictional world as a reader, and how hard it is to create one as a writer.

For a long time my advice to students who aspired to fiction was *please don't*. Their fiction overwhelmed me. It was so bad I didn't know where to begin by way of response: bereft of plausibility, specificity, theme, coherence, and, especially, characters even remotely convincing or motivated. Novice fiction writers defined fiction as a daydream on paper: "My new story is about a ballet dancer who lives in Hawaii." Their plots went wherever they took them and ended with the inevitable punchline *Then he woke up and realized it was all a dream*. Kids had no concept of pace—enough plot happened in a page and a half to fill several novels. Often I couldn't tell who the main character was. When I could, I knew his or her hair color, eye color, birthday, and height to the half inch, but I didn't understand one thing about the character's needs, problems, feelings, or dreams. And theme was negligible. At best the conclusion presented a crude moral: *Erik learned that might doesn't make right, but he was still glad he killed the evil wizard*.

During the years I taught at Boothbay Elementary and conducted the

research that became the first edition of *In the Middle*, I mostly steered writers away from fictional narratives and toward their own lives. It was here they could learn about the processes of writing, manipulate and focus information, and begin to write confidently and well—with conviction, voice, and involvement. Personal-experience narratives held up the mirror of real life and helped students draft and revise toward what they meant, what was significant, what was true. Some students—those who read novels for breakfast and had narrative in their blood—broke into fiction by the end of our year together.

When the student population at CTL finally reached seventh grade, I was ecstatic to return to classroom teaching. But I was also challenged in a way I hadn't anticipated. Writing had gained a serious foothold at my school, and I encountered a new breed of middle school writer. These students had been writing for years. They clamored to write "fiction pieces," and there was no reason to nudge students toward memoir as a way of learning about narrative. They needed advice—concrete information about fiction and how it works—to combine with the old lessons about narrative in order to develop expertise with a new genre. This meant I had to discover practical, accessible ways of talking about the considerations and decisions of writers of fiction.

So I hit the books. I read about fiction, about writing it and teaching it. I reread favorite fiction, this time taking the stance Frank Smith calls "*reading* like a writer to *write* like a writer" (1988, 25), and I made notes about different authors' techniques for introducing main characters, using dialogue to reveal character, employing one narrative voice or another, embedding information, creating and resolving conflict, establishing theme. In minilessons, I read aloud leads and other passages from young adult novels, and the kids and I researched what the authors had done to develop characters. Walter Dean Myers was an especially good source for studying character development:

HOW AN AUTHOR INTRODUCES HIS MAIN CHARACTERS:
WALTER DEAN MYERS

Hoops (pp. 1–7)

First-person voice: Lonnie Jackson
> Growing up in Harlem
> Father split; lives with his mother
> Confused about his future
> Great at basketball
> 17 or 18 years old

Three little stories that reveal character:
- Flashback of a conversation with his father
- Teabag incident
- Case of Scotch

What we know already in terms of theme:
- Lonnie's getting older
- He's not getting along with his mom or taking responsibility at home
- He's looking for easy money

Fast Sam, Cool Clyde, and Stuff (pp. 7–15)

First person voice: Francis/Stuff
> Has parents and a sister
> $12\frac{1}{2}$ during the events of the story, but 18 when he's telling it
> Lives in Harlem on 116th St.
> Cautious

Wants to be accepted
Notices everything
Doesn't like violence

Style:

- Written like a memoir
- Uses a prologue to set the scene and introduce the characters
- Is exploring friendship and setting up the reader to feel like a friend of these characters

Scorpions (pp. 3–9)

Third-person voice: He = Jamal. Narrator knows and reveals only what the main character (Jamal) is thinking and feeling.

His brother (Randy) is in jail, probably for 7 years
Has an 8-year-old sister, Sassy
Has a typical sibling relationship with Sassy
Lives with his mom—no dad
Is 12$\frac{1}{2}$
There's not much money
The Scorpions gang is trouble—it's why Randy's in jail

Style:

- Embeds information in the dialogue
- Embeds information in Jamal's thoughts
- Embeds information in Jamal's actions

Next, I looked for short fiction to read aloud to my students because short stories, not novels, were what they would be writing in the workshop. They needed to hear how writers used the short form, not to mention identify their own attempts at fiction as short stories (not "fiction pieces"). I chose stories because I liked them in terms of character, problem, theme, and structure, and thought kids would like them, too:

SHORT STORY READ-ALOUDS

Angell, Judie. 1984. "Turmoil in a Blue and Beige Bedroom." In *Sixteen: Short Stories by Outstanding Writers for Young Adults*, edited by Donald R. Gallo. New York: Bantam Doubleday Dell.

Brancato, Robin F. 1984. "Fourth of July." In *Sixteen: Short Stories by Outstanding Writers for Young Adults*, edited by Donald R. Gallo. New York: Bantam Doubleday Dell.

Cormier, Robert. 1980. "Guess What? I Almost Kissed My Father Goodnight." In *8 Plus 1: Stories by Robert Cormier*. New York: Dell.

Kottemann, Molly Hallgren. 1995. "Danse du Luc." In *Merlyn's Pen*, Middle School Edition. Vol. XI, No. 1, Oct./Nov.

Lipsyte, Robert. 1984. "Future Tense." In *Sixteen: Short Stories by Outstanding Writers for Young Adults*, edited by Donald R. Gallo. New York: Bantam Doubleday Dell.

Pfeffer, Susan Beth. 1984. "Pigeon Humor." In *Sixteen: Short Stories by Outstanding Writers for Young Adults*, edited by Donald R. Gallo. New York: Bantam Doubleday Dell.

Soto, Gary. 1990. "No Guitar Blues," "Seventh Grade," and "Growing Up." In *Baseball in April*. New York: Harcourt Brace.

Strasser, Todd. 1987. "On the Bridge." In *Visions: Nineteen Short Stories by Outstanding Writers for Young Adults*, edited by Donald R. Gallo. New York: Bantam Doubleday Dell.

Wilson, Budge. 1990. "The Metaphor" and "Lysandra." In *The Leaving*. New York: Philomel.

Finally, I began to write my first short fiction: the story about Leah that is excerpted in Chapter 10. It almost killed me. I grappled with voice (*first or third?*), perspective (*near or distant past?*), main character (*is she me, or is she not me, and if she isn't me, then who is she?*), plus her family background, the invention of her friends and teachers and school, how much or how little to tell about every aspect of her life, the lead, and, especially, the conversation between the girl and her mother that suggests how a resolution might be achieved. I did much of this writing and thinking out loud, in front of my students on overhead transparencies during minilessons. I took them inside my head in order to demonstrate the questions I wanted them to ask themselves as writers of fiction.

Together my students and I learned a lot about fiction. Two documents emerged from the writing, reading, demonstrations, and discussions. The first is a set of guidelines for writing fiction. This mini-handbook undergoes revision whenever students or I encounter another example, make a new discovery, or change our minds. Students keep a marked-up copy of the latest version in their daily writing folders and consult it before and as they compose short stories. In June, two-thirds of my kids identified the minilessons about elements of fiction as among the most valuable and lasting lessons of the school year.

SOME ELEMENTS OF FICTION: A WRITER'S DECISIONS

1. Character

The main character is someone for *the reader to be with*. We go inside this person's head and heart, use his or her thoughts and feelings as a prism for living in the story, and come to understand the individual's reasons for acting as he or she does.

Sometimes the character is a composite of real people, as Henry Huggins is based on boys Beverly Cleary knew when she was growing up. Sometimes the main character is drawn from a specific person the author knows: Robert Cormier based Jerry in *The Chocolate War* on his own son. Sometimes the author uses himself or herself as the basis for the main character: Meg in *A Wrinkle in Time* is Madeleine L'Engle. And sometimes the characters are mostly imaginary.

The writer of fiction begins by creating a character: Who is she? What is her name? How old is she? What does she look like? Where does she live? What is her family background? What does she like to do? What is different about her? What does she care about? What does she fear? What are her dreams? Who are the important people in her life? What are the important things? What is the problem she's facing? How will she change? What will she understand about herself and her world at the end of the story?

These are questions you can ask yourself, or give to a partner to interview you about as if you are the main character, to help you flesh out the details of the person you're trying to bring to life.

Don Graves writes, "The involvement of a strong character seems to produce the most plausible plots, which seem to result in the best stories" (1989, 70). Develop strong characters, then see what they will do. Remember Rosemary Sutcliff's comment: "The characters grow and change as I write. When I start off I've just written down color of hair, color of eyes, likes and dislikes, family backgrounds, and so on. As I go on writing I get to know them as real people, and if I make them do something that is out of character, I think instantly: 'No, they wouldn't do that. They wouldn't react in that way'" (in Lloyd 1987, 84). Keep your characters true to themselves.

2. Problem

What is the problem—in terms of his relationship with others, himself, or the world—that the main character must resolve? What is the challenge he will confront?

The problem is the *so what?* of fiction: the reason the writer is writing the story, the reason the main character is acting in it, and the reason the reader will keep on reading it. Involving stories revolve around compelling problems.

3. Change

What is the main character's outlook, knowledge, or self-image at the beginning of the story? What events will change the character? What is the character's outlook, knowledge, or self-image at the end of the story? Why has it changed? It may be a big change (learning how to survive in the wilderness in Gary Paulsen's *Hatchet*) or a small one (staying home alone for the first time and realizing it's lonely without parents in "Growing Up" by Gary Soto).

4. Plot

Plot is the characters in action; what the characters make happen. Plot is the beginning-middle-end of the work of fiction. The keys to a successful plot are pace, plausibility, and character.

Plot follows character. Madeleine L'Engle put it this way: "My characters are constantly doing or saying things that surprise me. And when that happens, then I know that the writing is going well" (in Lloyd 1987, 77). Robert Cormier said, "I know where my story is going to, but I'm not quite sure what's going to happen along the way. I let my characters take me toward the climax of the story" (in Lloyd 1987, 61).

5. Pace

How quickly or slowly does the writer move the plot? Pace involves keeping a balance between *too fast* to be involving or plausible and *too slow* to hold a reader's interest.

Writers don't let the events of the story happen too quickly, with few details or little character development. If the plot takes over the characters, the writer loses plausibility.

On the other hand, writers don't drag out the events of the story, going on for pages of dialogue and description without anything significant happening, so that the plot disappears and the reader loses the thread of the meaning.

As Kurt Vonnegut Jr. said, "Don't put anything in a story that does not reveal character or advance the action" (in Murray 1990, 155). You can *add* information about your character's actions, thoughts, and feelings to slow down the pace of your writing. Or you can *delete* or *compress* dialogue and description to quicken the pace.

6. Plausibility

Plausibility means having the appearance of truth. In fiction we ask, does the plot ring true? Would the characters act and react this way in real life? Are there clear and compelling reasons for the characters to behave as they do? Are the circumstances of the story believable? Are there enough details to give the writing the texture of real life, to make it seem as if this is really happening?

This is where *visualization* helps. Close your eyes and put your imagination to work. See, hear, and feel the scene unfold at the pace of real life. Make a movie behind your eyelids. Then open your eyes and find the words to re-create the scene in words on paper, so that your reader can see, hear, and feel it, too.

Remember Rudyard Kipling's comment about what it takes to create a fictional world, as opposed to recalling real life in a memoir: "Fiction is truth's older sister." You're going to have to work hard at plausibility if you want to hang with big sis. Consider what novelist Anne Tyler said, "Mostly it's lies, writing novels. You set out to tell an untrue story and you try to make it believable, even to yourself. Which calls for details; any good lie does. I'm quicker to believe I was once a circus aerialist if I remember that just before every performance, I used to dip my hands into a box of chalk powder that smelled like clean, dry cloth being torn" (in Murray 1990, 155).

7. Voice or Point of View

The author of a fictional narrative decides who will tell the story. When he or she chooses a narrative voice, it both limits and focuses the vantage point: the reader's way of perceiving the events of the story. Writers of fiction have to decide how much a narrator will know about the thoughts and feelings of the different characters. The writer weighs the advantages and disadvantages of the possibilities for points of view:

FIRST PERSON—I

- Interior monologue: the narrator is speaking to himself or herself, thinking aloud; it's like a soliloquy in the theater (*Johnny Got His Gun* by Dalton Trumbo).
- Dramatic monologue: the narrator is speaking out loud to someone else and telling his or her story, mostly without interruption (Anne Rice's *Vampire Chronicles*; *The Princess Bride* by William Goldman).
- Diary narration: the narrator writes on successive dates about events and his or her state of mind; there's no particular audience ("Flowers for Algernon" by Daniel Keyes; *Daisy Fay and the Miracle Man* by Fannie Flagg; *Ever After* by Rachel Vail; *The Secret Diary of Adrian Mole, Aged 13³/₄* by Sue Townsend; *Catherine, Called Birdy* by Karen Cushman).
- Subjective narration: a fictional speaker addresses us, the general public, shortly after the conclusion of the events of a story in which he or she was involved (Ponyboy Curtis in *The Outsiders* by S. E. Hinton; Sarny in *Nightjohn* by Gary Paulsen; Sal in *Walk Two Moons* by Sharon Creech; Cory in *Boy's Life* by Robert McCammon; Charlotte in "The Metaphor" and Elaine in "Lysandra's Poem" from *The Leaving* by Budge Wilson; Charlotte in Avi's *The True Confessions of Charlotte Doyle*).

- Single-character point of view: the author takes us only where a certain character goes and permits the reader to know only this character's thoughts and feelings (Brian in *Hatchet* by Gary Paulsen; Jonathan in *The Fighting Ground* by Avi; Fausto in "The No-Guitar Blues" and Victor in "Seventh Grade" in Gary Soto's *Baseball in April* collection; Jamal in *Scorpions* by Walter Dean Myers).

- Dual-character point of view: the author alternates between the inner lives of two different characters. This is particularly challenging. (Chana and Hillary in *If I Should Die Before I Wake* by Han Nolan; David Eddings' novels, in which the protagonist and antagonist alternate; Morning Girl and Star Boy in *Morning Girl* by Michael Dorris; the man and the dog in Jack London's "To Build a Fire").

- Multiple-character point of view: the author leads the reader among several characters' points of view. This is even more challenging. (*The Chocolate War* and *Beyond the Chocolate War* by Robert Cormier; *Fair Game* by Erika Tamar; Brian Jacques' Redwall series).

- No-character point of view: the writer stays outside the minds of all the characters. The narrator is like an eyewitness who reports the events without commentary, as in a summary ("The Lottery" by Shirley Jackson; *King Arthur and the Knights of the Round Table* by Antonia Frasier; most fairy tales, myths, and legends).

8. Setting

The setting gives the reader a specific *place and time to be* in imagining the events of the story. The writer decides the particular time and particular place the main character is at any given moment (inner-city Tulsa in the 1960s in Hinton's *The Outsiders*; a sanitarium in the present in *I Am the Cheese* by Robert Cormier; the Essex Coast and Dunkirk in the late 1930s–1940 in *The Snow Goose* by Paul Gallico; Vietnam during the war in *Fallen Angels* by Walter Dean Myers; Stephen King's novels set in rural Maine; *If I Should Die Before I Wake* by Han Nolan, set in Poland during the Holocaust and in a Jewish hospital in the 1990s).

Writers need to know their settings, either through personal experience or research, so that readers can know them, too—can sense them and fully believe in them. Madeleine L'Engle notes, "The writing of fiction is very sensory. I have to know what a place smells like, what it feels like, what it sounds like. All of my settings for my stories are places I've been in. I might exaggerate it—take a bit out, make it bigger or smaller, or move it around—but the setting still has to be some place that I'm familiar with with all my five senses" (in Lloyd 1987, 78).

9. First Line

Donald Graves calls the first sentence "a window to the entire work" (1989, 17) for both the writer and the reader. It's probably the most important sentence in the whole story. The first line sets the tone, introduces the style of the writing, establishes the voice, and piques the reader's interest—and the writer's. Elie Wiesel wrote, "With novels it's the first line that's important. If I have that, the novel comes easily. The first line determines the form of the whole novel. The first line sets the tone, the melody. If I hear the tone, the melody, then I have the book" (in Murray 1990, 125).

MEMORABLE FIRST LINES:

"They murdered him." (*The Chocolate War*)

"It was a bright cold day in April and the clocks were striking thirteen." (*1984*)

" 'Where's Papa going with that ax?' said Fern to her mother as they were setting the table for breakfast." (*Charlotte's Web*)

"When I stepped out into the bright sunlight from the darkness of the movie house, I had only two things on my mind: Paul Newman and a ride home." (*The Outsiders*)

10. Lead

The lead is the beginning section of a story: the first paragraphs or pages. Writers of fiction usually introduce their characters in the lead and often hint at the problem or theme, which makes it a crucial section of the story in terms of character development. The lead provides the reader's first glimpse of the main characters—and first chance to decide whether he or she wants to be with these characters and read the rest of their story.

11. Conclusion and Last Line

In the conclusion the writer sets the tone for how a reader feels when he or she finishes reading the story. These lines deserve as much thought as the first sentences. The conclusion shouldn't go on and on, but it shouldn't come too fast and leave a reader confused and unsatisfied.

In shaping the ending, the writer decides where and how he or she wishes to leave the reader (hopeful? *The Outsiders*; alarmed and wondering? *I Am the Cheese*; inspired? *Nightjohn*).

12. Dialogue

Dialogue is one of the fiction writer's most useful tools in creating character. Talk shows the reader what a character is like in terms of mood, age, educational or ethnic background, and intention. It reveals the relationships between and among characters. Dialogue helps to vary the structure of the story, to break up passages of description and make the writing more lively for the reader. It allows the characters as well as the narrator to tell the story. Dialogue also helps the characters seem real, and it moves the action forward. Sometimes authors use their characters' spoken words to state the themes of their fiction (e.g., S. E. Hinton's "Stay gold" and "Things are rough all over" in *The Outsiders*).

13. Theme

A theme is an idea about life that comes through the story. The richer the characters and changes in the character, the deeper and more interesting the themes. Often authors aren't aware of all the themes threading through their stories until the writing is over. But generally they do have a concept or big idea they want to explore by writing a story about it (the tragedy of kid-to-kid violence, based on social class, in *The Outsiders*; the danger of blindly following leaders in *The Chocolate War*; the horror of war in *The Fighting Ground* and *Fallen Angels*; prejudice and its consequences in *The Drowning of Stephan Jones* by Bette Greene; teen peer pressure in *Jumping the Nail* by Eve Bunting; fear of big government in *I Am the Cheese*). Cynthia Voigt calls theme " 'long-line' thoughts—ideas that I want to run through the whole story" (in Lloyd 1987, 62).

14. A Plan

Creating and keeping track of a fictional world is a complicated business. Many authors take notes before and while they write, to help them generate, organize, and remember their ideas. They may jot down details about their characters or the setting, draft snatches of dialogue, describe scenes, make character grids or webs, draw a map of the plot, list the things that might happen, invent names and characteristics, or brainstorm solutions to various writing problems as they occur.

This is not the same as writing using a strict outline, in which there is no room for surprise. The writer of fiction makes many plans and even more revisions as the characters come to life and take over their story. Cynthia Voigt keeps a notebook with chapter plans for her novels. She says, "My notebook is a kind of living document, growing as I'm writing the book" (in Lloyd 1987, 62).

The second document I developed is a questionnaire to help writers invent, develop, and reinvent their characters. Even with all the information we generated about fiction, too many students still jumped into their first stories by spinning plot. To help them break an old habit, I asked fiction writers to start by interviewing themselves, or asking a peer to conduct an interview, *as if the writer were the main character*. The character questionnaire forces writers to back off, slow down, and attend to building a person that their readers can be with through the events of the story.

MAIN-CHARACTER QUESTIONNAIRE

Consider the questions below on your own, or ask a partner to interview you as if you are the character, to help you begin to create your main character and flesh out the details.

1. What's your name?
2. How old are you?
3. What do you look like?
4. Where do you live?
5. What is your family background?
6. What do you like to do?
7. What is different about you?
8. What do you care about?
9. What do you fear?
10. What are your dreams?
11. How would a friend describe you? As the kind of person who . . .
12. Who are the important people in your life?
13. What are the important things in your life?
14. What is the problem you're facing?
15. How will you change? Possibilities:
16. What will you understand about yourself and your world at the end of the story? Possibilities:

The fiction handbook and main character questionnaire don't make fiction easier to write, but they do make good fiction more likely to be written. Students can better articulate what makes a short story or novel work for them as readers. As writers they can better articulate for themselves, and for each other in peer conferences, what needs to be done to improve their stories, because they share a language for talking about elements of fiction.

I discovered that it takes considerable time, reflection, and response to learn how to write a short story—just like learning to write memoir did—and that it takes even more time to write a good one. My students spend anywhere from four to twelve weeks on one short story. The results justify the time that they and I devote. Not only is the fiction character-driven, plausible, thought provoking, and moving, but every story has at least one passage of what I call book language—chunks of prose that flow so clearly they assume the transparency and lucidity of the writers whose books my kids love to read. Most importantly, the fiction they write teaches my students at least as much about their own lives as memoir does. The themes of their stories reflect adolescents' problems and concerns, but from a distance so generous that students can use fiction to invent resolutions.

Sam wrote about Keith, a high school prankster who finds himself in such serious trouble that he damages his ego and his reputation; having pushed too far, he's forced to confront himself and decide what kind of person he wishes to become. Laurel told the story of a girl's close relationship with her mother, which is threatened when she becomes a teenager and feels the pull to disconnect from home and connect with the rest of the world. Elizabeth wrote about two girls whose friendship is destroyed when their parents feud and the girls, caught in the middle, must choose between family and friendship; an unfinished tree house they were constructing becomes the symbol of their powerlessness. Curt's fantasy, inspired by the novels of David Eddings, took a surprising twist as he discovered, through envisioning the actions of his main character, that he hated violence. Dylan and Michael wrote survival stories in which boys are accidentally separated from parents who are driving them crazy; both main characters figure out how to survive in the wilderness and eventually reunite with their parents, but with a new sense of understanding and appreciation.

Matt used short fiction to put a character in the middle of a situation he had experienced, as a child of divorce, and resolve it:

TWO WINS

I grabbed my bags and bolted out the door. The bell had finally rung, and the weekend was here. I usually liked English, but today was my first day of high school football practice, and boy was I nervous: I had already made the team; today they decided the starters. I was pretty sure I'd make it because I was the only receiver who never missed a pass that hit my hands.

I jumped on my bike and sped by the students walking home. After my parents had divorced, my dad decided to move to the other side of town. Since he had won custody, I had to move with him, but I didn't want to leave my school. So now I have to bike three and a half miles each day to school and back. Here's where the real problem occurs: I was the only one on the team who didn't get a locker because there weren't enough for everyone. Now, school ends at around 2:45, and we have to be on the field in uniform by 4:00 sharp. You're probably thinking an hour and fifteen minutes is a lot of time, but it takes about twenty minutes to get home even when I'm pedaling fast, plus I have to get my gear, and I don't think you know how long it takes to put on football equipment. All in all, I have to haul butt.

When I finally reached my house, I jumped off my bike, ran inside, and bombed down the stairs into my room. I failed to notice my father's car parked in the garage. After I grabbed my equipment and jumped back up the stairs, I nearly ran into my dad in the process.

"Oh, hi, Dad. You're home early," I said, once I looked up. In fact he's only about an inch taller than me, but I was down a step.

"Yep, got off work early today so I could have a little chat with you," he answered.

"Can it wait until after I get back from practice? As you know, Coach is gonna pick the starters today."

"I don't think so. It's kind of important. Here, sit down," he said quietly, pointing toward the couch in the living room.

I looked at my watch. I was still ten minutes ahead of schedule, so I figured I had time for a quick talk. I sat on the couch, and Dad took a chair across from me.

"Today at the university," he started, "I received a letter from Baylor, in Texas. They offered me a job as chairman of the English Department at the college—"

"And you didn't take it, right?" I interrupted.

"Well, that's what we need to talk about. You see, I think I'm probably going to accept it," he said quietly.

"WHAT!" I yelled as I stood up.

"Listen. The job pays better and it's more important. I'll get much more recognition for what I do."

"I don't care. I'm not leaving Arizona, let alone Tempe, and that's final!" I said, then barged out the door in a wild rage. I jumped on my bike and sped off toward the practice field.

When the practice began, I couldn't keep my mind off my dad's announcement. My mind was racing. I didn't want to move and leave my mom and friends behind. I decided to see if I could find somewhere to spend the night, then go talk things over with my mother.

Somehow I managed to impress the coach enough that he assigned me to the starting lineup. It was 6:00 by now. I asked my friend Neil, the starting running back on the team, if I could stay at his house for the night. He said it was okay; I told him I'd be over at 7:00.

I rode my bike over to Mom's house, pulled into her driveway, got off the bike, and walked to the door. I prayed she was home, because I really needed to talk to her about what was going on. When I knocked on the door and she answered, I sighed with relief.

"Hi, Trevor. What's up?" she said when she saw me. Her smile stretched ear to ear.

"Well . . . can I come in?" I answered.

"Sure."

I walked in and plopped down on a couch. I thought for a minute about what I should say and how to start. I decided to begin with a question.

"Do know that Dad wants to move to Texas and take me with him?" I asked, hoping she had heard the bad news already.

She had. "Yeah. I was planning on talking to you about it tomorrow when you came over for our weekend together," she said, rubbing her eyes. She had been working the late shift at the hospital as of late. "I decided I'm going to fight it all the way."

"I hope you win, because I really want to stay here," I said truthfully.

"You do?" She seemed surprised.

"Yeah, I like it here a lot. Why would I want to leave?" I asked.

"I don't know. I guess I thought you'd want to stay with your dad. Wait!"

"What?" I asked.

"What do you say about testifying in court? If you do, you might be able to stay here in Arizona with me." She sounded hopeful.

I looked at my watch: 6:20. "I don't know. I don't want Dad to be mad at me, but I don't want to leave either. I'll think about it," I concluded. And I really would. I decided I should take off and have some time to think before I went over to Neil's for the night.

"Well, I'd better get going. See you tomorrow," I said as I stood up and hugged her.

"Bye, Trevor." She hugged me back.

I got on my bike and rode to the outskirts of Tempe. I stopped at the park where I used to play when I was little. What my mom had suggested was a good idea and might even work. The thing was, no matter what I decided, the other parent would be upset. On the one hand I didn't want to ditch my mother and my friends and my life and leave for Texas. On the other hand I didn't want to have Dad mad at me for the rest of my life. I came to the conclusion that I had to find out what Neil thought. Neil was my best friend; he knew me better than anyone.

When I got to his house, he was the only one home. "What's up?" he said happily. He was obviously in a good mood.

"You seem happy. What happened?" I wondered. I dropped my backpack on the floor and followed him into his room. The walls were covered with posters of rap "artists," as he referred to them: they were one of the few things we didn't have in common.

"Guess what?"

"I don't know," I answered.

"You know who Gloria is, right?"

"Yeah." Gloria was a girl in my English class that Neil had liked since we were ten but never had the guts to ask on a date.

"Well, I asked her out. We're going to the movies on Friday. Cool, huh?" He sounded excited, and I couldn't blame him.

"Cool," I managed.

"Hey, man, what's up? You're really dampening my mood." He sounded concerned, so I decided to spit it out, even though I'd been trying to wait until later.

"Well, you know my parents are divorced, right?"

"Really, man? When did this happen?" Neil burst out laughing.

"Shut up. This is serious!" I was getting a little angry with him.

"Sorry, man. Go on," he said, while he pulled himself together.

"Thank you. Well, my dad got an offer from Baylor University in Texas, and he wants to take the offer, and me, to Baylor."

"What? You can't leave me here by myself! How we gonna win any football games without our star receiver?" He was obviously not happy with the whole idea, which was good, considering he was my best friend.

"Is that all you can think about, football? Hey, I don't like it one bit either, but I have to go. He does have custody, you know." I was getting more depressed by the minute.

"Can't you do something about it?"

"Well, my mom said if I went to court and told the judge I didn't want to go, I could probably stay with her. But then my dad would get real mad at me, and I don't want that to happen," I said, knowing already from the look on his face that this was what Neil wanted me to do.

"Come on, man, you got to go to court. Who cares what happens with your dad? He's leaving no matter what happens," he said angrily. "Oh, man, this sucks!"

"Tell me about it."

The next weeks passed like a bad dream. A court date, to determine who would get custody now that Dad was leaving, was set. I couldn't believe the timing—it was the same afternoon as the championship game. I would have to miss the game, the biggest of the whole year.

The night before the hearing I couldn't get to sleep. It was twelve o' clock and in thirteen hours I would go to court, instead of the big game, and find out what the future would hold. Even worse, Dad didn't know I was thinking of testifying at the hearing. I'd been trying to find a way to bring it up, but it was too hard to tell him that I wanted to stay in Tempe with Mom. I hadn't told Mom I'd testify either. I kept putting off the decision. I didn't want to disappoint anyone.

When I woke up I was tired. Dad had left for work already. I had some breakfast, then biked to Mom's house.

When I got there she was just getting home from work. I parked my bike and said hello.

"Hi, Trevor, what's up?"

"I'm going to come with you to the courthouse and tell the judge I want to stay here," I answered.

"You are?" She was very happy.

"Yes." She hugged me tight, which helped a little.

When we got to the courthouse my dad was already there, standing by his car. When I stepped out of Mom's car, he saw me immediately. I didn't know what to do. I tried not to make eye contact. I was scared. I started walking with my head down. When I got halfway to the building, he stopped me and pulled me aside.

"What are you doing here, Trevor? I thought you had a big game today," he said, confused.

"I do. I came here to tell the judge that I don't want to leave Arizona and I don't want to leave Tempe and I don't want to leave period," I answered. I was angry and messed up, didn't know what to say, and felt like crying. So I did.

"Come on, Trevor, pull yourself together." Dad put his arm around my shoulder. "I was a kid once. I may be an English professor, but I know what your friends mean to you. I also know football is your life. When you skip the championship game, I know you're serious about this." He hesitated. There were tears in his eyes. "I realize how much you want to stay, so I'm going to hand custody over to your mother. You have to learn to trust me, though, and tell me these things. When I do leave, you have to call me every day, and you're going to visit me every month, at least. Now clean yourself up and get to that game."

"Thanks, Dad." I couldn't believe it. I should have known better— should have known him, and myself, better. I would miss him a lot, but I knew this decision was for the best. I hugged him, hugged Mom, then turned in the direction of the high school. I was going to have to haul major butt if I wanted to suit up in time for the game.

Oh, yeah, we won the championship.

—*Matt Miller*

Erin and Katy worked together on an epistolary short story. Their main characters were sisters; one disguised herself and enlisted as a Union soldier during the Civil War. The girls researched the background by reading *The Twentieth Maine* by John Pullen. They worked hard on the language, on making the two sisters, Louisa and Elizabeth, sound like small-town girls of the nineteenth century.

LETTERS HOME: A CIVIL WAR STORY

August 28, 1862

Dear Elizabeth,

By the time you find this letter, I will be miles away. I have gone to enlist in the Union Army. The 20th of Maine will leave tomorrow, so this is my final chance. Please do not tell Mother and Father where I have gone until evening, because I know Father will try to stop me. Tell everyone I am sorry, but I want some sort of adventure in my life. Here in Wiscasset nothing exciting ever seems to happen. Also, I feel I must go and serve our country because Mama and Papa have no sons, and Papa cannot go because of his leg.

Don't worry about me. I borrowed some of Father's old clothes and cut off my hair, so I am now disguised as a boy.

Take care and send my best regards to everyone. I will write as soon as I am able.

> Your loving sister,
> Louisa

September 7, 1862

Dear Elizabeth,

We have arrived in Washington! No one has seen through my disguise. I suppose the army has such a great need for volunteers they cannot be particular. Everything we own we carry on our backs. They have given us knapsacks to carry our necessities, such as wool blankets, a canteen, a great coat and uniform, a dipper, a piece of canvas to use as a tent, brogan shoes, a rifle, and a bayonet. Gloves are not permitted, so our hands may be kept free to use our weapons. We must fold down the cuffs of our coats instead. We only get towels if we are lucky.

I hope this letter finds you in good health. I miss you terribly. How is Father faring? Say hello to Mama and the little ones for me. Tell Mama and Papa not to worry about me. I am doing fine.

I had better get some rest because tomorrow we leave bright and early on a march to Fort Craig on Arlington Heights.

Give my love to everyone.

> Your loving sister,
> Louisa

September 10, 1862

Dear Louisa,

We are all doing well here in Maine. I hope the same is true for you. At first Mother and Father were angry that you had gone without telling them. Father threatened to find you and bring you home, but I told them you had your heart set on being a soldier and that you thought they would be proud having one of their own fight for the Union cause, because of Father's bad leg and their not having any sons to fight. Then I think most of their anger turned to worry. They were a little reassured after reading your letter.

We miss you with our whole hearts. Please write soon!

> Your loving sister,
> Beth

Mama was devastated when she heard you cut off your beautiful hair. Papa told her not to be silly; it would grow back soon enough.

September 12, 1862

Dear Beth,

Since I last wrote to you we spent a restless night in a vacant lot next to the U.S. Arsenal. The next morning we gathered muskets and ammunition from the arsenal, then started marching on to Fort Craig on Arlington Heights.

I am sitting on the side of the road, resting while writing this letter. We have already started our next march—to the Antietam River. Although my feet are sore, I am in good health and have met many soldiers here. Do you remember William Davis, the blacksmith's son? He is here in my regiment. I have to be careful for fear he will recognize me through my disguise.

How are you? I miss everyone in Wiscasset, but at least now I am having a true adventure.

We are ready to resume marching, so I must go—I am sorry this letter is so short. I will write more later . . .

Please write back soon. I love you all.

Your devoted sister,
Louisa

September 14, 1862

My Dearest Beth,

I have seen my first Confederates! They were taken as prisoners after the battle at Turner's Gap. But now, dear Beth, I am so confused. I had expected to hate them. After all, they are the enemy. But Beth, they looked so pitiful standing there in their dirty gray uniforms. One was merely a boy of sixteen, my age. Tell me, Beth, am I wrong not to hate him? True, he is a traitor to our country. But he is only a boy, playing at being a soldier, with tear streaks running down his dirty face. Am I just as much a traitor as he, to think of him this way? To pity the enemy?

No. I must not think this way. I must remember why I am here, to have an adventure and to fight for my country, not to question its reasons. Is that not the right thing to do?

You must not take this the wrong way. I am seeing the world, and Beth, there is so much of it to see!

We are starting up the march again, so I fear I must go. I miss you all and do so wish to hear from you.

Your loving sister,
Louisa

September 14, 1862

Dear Louisa,

Do you remember little Charlotte Barter? She was a few years younger than I? Well, she has up and married Robert Carver. But I am afraid their happiness is shattered. You know the "raffle," where men are "volunteered" to serve the Union army? Robert was volunteered! You should have seen their faces when the announcement was made. At first I did not think it could be real. How could something so terrible happen to someone at the peak of their happiness? Robert cannot possibly pay the $300 to get out of going to war, so I asked Charlotte to stay with us. It was the least I could do. Imagine if Robert does not come back.

Mother is happy to have Charlotte stay here. I think she reminds her of you.

Mama worries about you all the time, and Papa and I miss you with all our hearts.

Your devoted sister,
Beth

September 16, 1862

Dear Beth,

As I write this letter, the 20th Maine is atop South Mountain near Sharpsburg. There is fear in the air, for we know there is a battle brewing. From here we can see clear across Antietam Creek and out to Sharpsburg, where the army of Bobby Lee is encamped. We have been working on drills all day, with hardly a moment's rest. Tomorrow, after defending South Mountain, we will join forces with more Federal troops.

We have to do more drills. My feet are on fire. Sorry such a short letter. I will write more later . . .

Send my love to everyone.

Your devoted sister,
Louisa

September 20, 1862

Dear Louisa,

A group of wounded soldiers has come to Wiscasset to be tended at a temporary hospital at the old jail. Mother and I are going to see what we can do to help them this afternoon. Mother is not making Charlotte go with us, for fear she will become upset about Robert again.

Father's leg is getting worse, so in order to have a man in the family when he is gone, he is trying to arrange a marriage for me. I will have none of it.

We all miss you, and Mother worries about you all the time. Take care of yourself and pray for the best.

Your devoted sister,
Beth

September 24, 1862

Dearest Louisa,

Why did you not write back? I guess I should not dwell on it. Your letter might have been lost in the mails. Father says the postal service is not as efficient as it was before the war.

Mother and I go regularly to see the wounded soldiers. I have befriended one of them. His name is John Brady. Robert writes to Charlotte constantly. I do hope nothing happens to him.

Please write soon, so we know you are well. There is a list in the post office of men killed or missing. Every time I go in I hope not to see your name.

Has anyone seen through your disguise yet? What will happen if they do?

I miss you terribly. Everyone does. Take care of yourself and pray for the war to be over soon.

Your loving sister,
Beth

October 4, 1862

Dearest Beth,

I am coming home. The army has released me. I was shot in my right leg at Sharpsburg. The wound is serious. The pain is horrific. I hope not to lose my leg. I want to go home.

Whoever said battle was glorious was wrong. It is horrible. So many die, and for what? The clear water of Antietam Creek was red with blood by the end of the day. Bodies were strewn across the field. I could hardly tell the dead from the living. And the cries . . . they were the worst. Wounded men cried for water. Cried for help. Cried for a kind soul to talk to them, to hear their last words.

When they took me to the hospital, I was hoisted onto a wagon with many other wounded soldiers. It was an old farm cart, and the ride was bumpy. Men screamed at every jolt. I confess that I did, too.

All I want is to come home. I never want to experience another battle, hear another Rebel yell, see another patch of ground stained with blood.

How could I have expected war to be an adventure? It all started so innocently, like a fairy tale: ". . . she ran away from home to see the world." How could a dream like that end so badly?

I am sorry if my going away caused you grief. I love you all so much. Tell Mother and Father not to worry any more. I am coming home!

Your loving sister,
Louisa

*   *   *

June 6, 1996

Dear Grammy,

Hi, how are you? I'm fine. School will be out in twelve days! Pretty cool, huh? Well, anyway, to get to the point, my friend Ashley and I found some old letters in the attic. They date back to the time of the Civil War and were written from a sister at home to a sister who fought in the war and was injured. Do you know what happened to her? I'm really interested in the rest of the story.

Love,
Lizzie

P.S. The girls' names are Louisa and Beth. Beth is short for Elizabeth, I suppose.

June 14, 1996

Dear Lizzie,

I am fine, thank you. I was overjoyed to get your letter. I can't believe you found the letters. I thought they were lost long ago. But look here, I'm already rambling on, and you must be wondering about the mystery.

The two girls in the letters are relatives of ours. Beth was my great-great-grandmother. She eventually married John Brady, the soldier she met at the makeshift hospital in Wiscasset. They had four children; the youngest was my great-grandmother.

Louisa was not so fortunate. She returned home after being wounded at the battle at Sharpsburg, and after only one week the wound became infected. She refused to have her leg amputated, and three weeks later she died.

Enclosed is a family tree I keep in my old Bible. I thought it might help you understand how you're related to Beth and Louisa.

Please save the letters until I visit you this summer. We can read them together, and I'll answer your questions then.

Love,
Grammy

—Katy Seiders and Erin Arnold

My students have fallen in love with the big sister. She is a wonderful teacher about life, history, feelings, changes, problems, and resolutions. Rubbing shoulders with fiction has, more than anything else they do as writers, helped them grow up and made them feel like authors.

13
Finding Poetry Everywhere

The French critic Joseph Joubert once said "You will find
poetry nowhere unless you bring some of it with you."
To which might be added that if you do bring some of it
with you, you will find it everywhere.
Karla Kuskin

June Oakes is a Boothbay grandmother and one of my daughter's first friends. She took care of Anne in the months after her birth, when I returned to the classroom to finish the school year. One still, hot afternoon Anne and I dropped by to visit, and the three of us sat talking around June's kitchen table. I was despairing over Anne's refusal to accept that the summer sun could be bright at bedtime, and June recited the first stanza of "Bed in Summer":

> In winter I get up at night
> And dress by yellow candle-light.
> In summer, quite the other way,
> I have to go to bed by day.

I said, "I haven't thought of that poem in a long time," and June explained, "That was my primer, you know, when I was a grammar school girl. I learned to read from the poems in *A Child's Garden of Verses*." I thought it must have been a sweet prescription. June brought Robert Louis Stevenson's verse with her for seventy years. She found poetry in our kitchen conversation because poetry was the written language of her one-room schoolhouse.

Poetry is also one of the written languages of English majors. I majored in English, and I thought poetry was the ultimate genre to read and write. But for all my passion about poems, it took me a long time to discover how to be a teacher of poetry. I barely taught it at all. When I did, it was in the form of line-by-line critical analysis of the handful of poems in the Scott, Foresman anthology and contrived writing exercises. My students seldom found poetry, because as much as I loved it, I didn't know how to help kids look for it.

Other teachers I knew avoided teaching poetry because they felt intimidated by it. They perceived poetry as difficult to read, difficult to understand, and, especially, difficult to talk about. They stopped reading it the moment it stopped being required. The junior year in college marked the end of their histories as readers of poetry—and what a relief. Never again to have to invent and support a thesis statement about a poem, never again to feel thick and incompetent as the professor of English rattled off the correct interpretation.

Tom Newkirk has written about the method of critical analysis that hides the process of reading a poem and concentrates instead on products, on the teacher's full-blown interpretation, without ever revealing the messy business of how the teacher got there (1990). When students don't have a sense of how a teacher *gets there*—of how a teacher reads a poem and grasps a meaning—it's unlikely that they'll ever develop a sense of themselves as readers of poetry. These are the students who stop poems just as soon as they can at the end of their junior year. Some become teachers—but not of poetry.

Seventy years ago, when June Oakes was a grammar school girl, fully half the literature taught to fourth graders in the United States was poetry. Today, it's 97 percent prose and just 3 percent poetry. It would be easy to criticize the committees that compile literature anthologies for virtually ignoring poetry, among their other sins of omission and commission. But I think the problem cuts deeper, that it's more a matter of our own experiences with poetry. Either we read it and love it, as I did, but can't imagine how to begin to help students experience it—and end up lecturing or assigning cute formulas for kids to write to—or we don't read it, don't love it, and relegate it to the enrichment unit we'll assign in June if we don't run out of time.

Poetry deserves better, and kids deserve better. In his essay "The Noble Rider and the Sound of Words," the poet Wallace Stevens writes that the poet's role "is to help people to live their lives" (1951, 29). The poet Marge Piercy speaks of her desire that her poems *work* for others. The title of one of her favorites of her own poems (and my own favorite Piercy) is "To Be of Use." Poetry itself should be of use, Piercy writes:

> What I mean by useful is simply that readers will find poems that speak to and for them, will take those poems into their lives and say them to each other and put them up on the bathroom wall and remember bits and pieces of them in stressful or quiet moments. That the poems may give voice to something in the experience of a life has been my inten-

tion. To find ourselves spoken for in art gives dignity to our pain, our anger, our lust, our losses. We can hear what we hope for and what we most fear, in the small release of cadenced utterance. We have few rituals that function for us in the ordinary chaos of our lives. (1982, xii).

My K–12 school experience wasn't rich in poetry—my love of poems came later, through my husband—but two poems are the memorable pieces of literature of my adolescence. In 1968 or 1969, articles in *Life* magazine about the Vietnam War and U.S. race relations featured two contemporary poems as sidebars. One was "What Were They Like?" by Denise Levertov, a poem about the Vietnamese, written as a series of questions a student might ask an anthropologist about a vanished race. The other was "What Happens to a Dream Deferred?" by Langston Hughes. I carried these scraps of poetry with me through twenty years of moves, they meant so much to me, struck so deep with me. My anguish over the state of my country—its foreign affairs and policies at home—was spoken for in the poems. They were rituals that functioned for me in my ordinary life, talismans clipped from *Life* magazine that gave me a glimpse of how poetry could work for people in their lives.

When I finally became a teacher of poetry, I saw my middle school students take poems into their lives in the same way—not the dry-as-dust selections in the literature anthology, but contemporary poetry that gave voice to their feelings and experiences. I watched as students realized that poetic topics were not limited to love, seasons, flowers, and rainbows. Poetry could be about anything—any subject, any theme, in any voice. You could write a poem about McDonald's; you could write one as if you were a neurotic Peter Parker, aka Spiderman.

"YOU CAN'T WRITE A POEM ABOUT MCDONALD'S"

Noon. Hunger is the only thing
singing in my belly.
I walk through the blossoming cherry trees
on the library mall,
past the young couples coupling,
by the crazy fanatic
screaming doom and salvation
at a sensation-hungry crowd,
to the Lake Street McDonald's.
It is crowded, the lines long and sluggish.
I wait in the greasy air.
All around me people are eating—

the sizzle of conversation,
the salty odor of sweat,
the warm flesh pressing out of
hip huggers and halter tops.
When I finally reach the cash register,
the counter girl is crisp as a pickle,
her fingers thin as french fries,
her face brown as a bun.
Suddenly I understand cannibalism.
As I reach for her,
she breaks into pieces
wrapped neat and packaged for takeout.
I'm thinking, how amazing it is
to live in this country, how easy
it is to be filled.
We leave together, her warm aroma
close at my side.
I walk back through the cherry trees
blossoming up into pies,
the young couple frying in
the hot, oily sun,
the crowd eating up the fanatic,
singing, my ear, eye, and tongue
fat with the wonder
of this hungry world.

—*Ronald Wallace*

MAYBE DATS YOUWR PWOBLEM TOO

All my pwoblems
who knows, maybe evwybody's pwoblems
is due to da fact, due to da awful twuth
dat I am SPIDERMAN.

I know, I know. All da dumb jokes:
No flies on you, ha ha,
and da ones about what do I do wit all
doze extwa legs in bed. Well, dat's funny yeah.
But you twy being
SPIDERMAN for a month or two. Go ahead.

You get doze cwazy calls fwom da
Gubbener askin you to twap some booglar who's
only twying to wip off color TV sets.
Now, what do I cawre about TV sets?
But I pull on da suit, da stinkin suit,

wit da sucker cups on da fingers,
and get my wopes and wittle bundle of
equipment and den I go flying like cwazy
acwoss da town fwom woof top to woof top.
Till der he is, some poor dumb color TV slob
and I fall on him and we westle a widdle
until I get him all woped. So big deal.

You tink when you SPIDERMAN
der's sometin big going to happen to you.
Well, I tell you what. It don't happen dat way.
Nuttin happens. Gubbener calls, I go.
Bwing him to pwice. Gubbener calls again,
like dat over and over.

I tink I twy sometin diffunt. I tink I twy
sometin excitin like wacing cawrs. Sometin to make
my heart beat at a difwent wate.
But den you just can't quit being sometin like
SPIDERMAN.
You SPIDERMAN for life. Fowever. I can't even
buin my suit. It won't buin. It's fwame wesistent.
So maybe dat's youwr pwoblem too, who knows.
So maybe dat's da whole pwoblem wif evwytin.
Nobody can buin der suits, day all fwame wesistent.
Who knows?

—*Jim Hall*

My students discover that poetry doesn't have to rhyme. Poets do play
with rhyme, but they also play with forms, sound and language patterns,
with feelings and symbols, words and images. Poets play with the rules and
bend them to suit their subjects and themselves. Nikki Giovanni and E. E.
Cummings play with punctuation—or, rather, they play without it. Robert
Francis plays with repetition in "While I Slept," a poem about a mother and
child that my students love the sound of.

WHILE I SLEPT

While I slept, while I slept and the night grew colder
She would come to my room, stepping softly
And draw a blanket about my shoulder
While I slept.

While I slept, while I slept in the dark, still heat
She would come to my bedside, stepping coolly

And smooth the twisted, troubled sheet
While I slept.

Now she sleeps, sleeps under quiet rain
While nights grow warm or nights grow colder.
And I wake, and sleep, and wake again
While she sleeps.

Jonathan played with figurative language in his poem about swimming in a YMCA meet. He is on fire in the water:

SWIMMING IN FIRE

The burning grows in my lungs
I thrust feverish arms through cool water
Now my legs burn
The tension in my head grows—
until I'm relieved by a fresh breath of air
and ignite again
in the blaze I am making

—*Jonathan Tindal*

What else does poetry do? Like a telegram, it doesn't waste words. It conveys the essence of the thing. In Jason's miniature poem, its power lies in the beauty *and* the economy of the language.

HAIKU FOR A BONSAI

Hardy ancient dwarf
you are a Japanese art
American born

—*Jason Perry*

Poetry can comment on literature itself. Martha's response to Jim Carroll's *Basketball Diaries* was a poem for Jim Carroll.

JIM

Flying
soared he did—
hand touched ball touched rim
kept moving
didn't stop
never stopped.
His hand
flew over the page
scribbling the words.

Hand stopped—
snorted once, twice,
once more.
Then hand flew again.
Higher and higher he soared
seeming lost in a world
confused, but understood.
Many things he understood—
death was one.
Death became an old friend,
taking everyone else—
friends, loved ones, never him.
Flying he did
'til one day
he came
crashing
down.

—*Martha Hutchins*

Poems make us laugh—as their readers and as their writers. Matt, the master procrastinator, poked fun at his homework dilemma.

HOMEWORK

Aarrgghh!
Time's running out.
I hear the clock's
tick, tick, tick . . .
I turn on the radio.
Great—bad song.
I go for my CDs.
Ugh, left them at Asa's.
Inertia sets in.
No excuses now . . .
I doodle.

Tick, tick, tick . . .
The minutes pass
like seconds.
The hours pass
like minutes.
No excuses now.
I'm
      dead
            meat.

—*Matt Miller*

And poems give shape to deeper feelings. Donald Murray writes that "Poets remind us not to preach, but merely to reveal" (1986, 427). For me the most effective writing about the war in Vietnam wasn't an essay or speech but *Obscenities*, a collection of poems by Michael Casey. The best writing about being a parent is the poetry of Eamon Grennan; the best writing about women's personal relationships is the poetry of Linda Pastan and Margaret Atwood; the best writing about relationships between people and the natural world is by Mary Oliver, Emily Dickinson, and Robert Frost. These writers never preach. They open up the world of feelings by showing it to us. In her poem "English as a Second Language," Lisel Mueller reveals the struggle of immigrants to understand our language and become Americans.

ENGLISH AS A SECOND LANGUAGE

The underpaid young teacher
prints the letters t, r, e, e
on the blackboard and imagines
forests and gardens springing up
in the tired heads of her students.

But they see only four letters;
a vertical beam weighed down
by a crushing crossbar
and followed by a hook,
and after the hook, two squiggles,
arcane identical twins
which could be spying eyes
or ready fists, could be handles,
could be curled seedlings, could take root,
could develop leaves.

—Lisel Mueller

Reading Poetry

There's only one requirement for the teacher who wants to teach poetry. Read it. Read it and be amazed at what contemporary poetry does: this is the poetry we never got to in high school and college. Read it and understand how contemporary poetry means, how it reflects and resonates our lives and feelings. Read it for yourself first, to fall in love with it. Then begin to collect the poems you love to share with your students.

Teachers new to poetry or intimidated by it might want to start with

Writing Poems by Robert Wallace, which is both an anthology of great poetry and a text for writing poetry of one's own. Wallace is a poet, and *Writing Poems* is clear, forthright, and inviting. A similar book is X. J. Kennedy's *An Introduction to Poetry*, which is rich with definitions of the vocabulary of a poet and reader of poems and even richer with examples. I also like *Knock at a Star: A Child's Introduction to Poetry* by X. J. Kennedy and Dorothy Kennedy; this one is directed at eight-to-twelve-year-olds and their teachers. The Kennedys combine superb poetry with down-to-earth advice about reading it. And I love two books by the poet and teacher Georgia Heard: *For the Good of the Earth and Sun* and *Writing Toward Home: Tales and Lessons to Find Your Way*, which invites adults to write poetry of our own.

One impediment to the reading and teaching of poetry is that it's not that easy to spot in libraries. In the Dewey system, poetry is buried in the 800s, far away from the novels that are our and our kids' more accustomed source of pleasure reading. When I tracked down the poetry shelves at Boothbay's school library, after teaching there for almost ten years, I discovered a trove of books to read to myself and then to my kids, and for my kids to borrow to read to themselves.

In Appendix M I list the poetry collections that my kids and I identified as the sources of the poems we liked best over three years of daily poetry presentations by me, presentations to the group by students, and students' independent immersion in the collections they picked up, after poetry presentations and booktalks, to read on their own.

Jack Wilde has observed that we need to treat poetry "like architecture; we've got to let kids get inside of it and walk around for a while" (1989, 47). By the end of June my students have spent ten months walking around inside some breathtaking architecture. Choosing poems that might take their breath away is a high priority for me. As I read books of poetry to myself, I mark the poems I like and think kids might like with Post-it notes. Then I photocopy each marked poem and fill folders with them by subject, theme, form, school, and poet. I only present poems I like, so my invitations to kids to become poetry readers—and lovers—will be as genuine as I can make them.

After a few seriously bungled readings, I learned never to read a poem cold. I practice. I mark up my copy to indicate pauses and stresses so my voice can give meaning to a poem, express the speaker's or poet's feelings, and mediate the poem for my students. I try to read in a normal voice, to follow the rhythm of the poem, but naturally, as though I'm telling kids about a new car or a TV program (Hopkins 1987). And I devise ways to show students the poems they're hearing. In a genre in which both form and content matter, kids need to know what poetry looks like and see how a poet uses the white spaces on the page to create rhyme, rhythm, emphasis, deemphasis, shape, flow, pauses, and stops. I make class sets of copies of a poem, reproduce poems on transparencies, or copy them on chart paper or the easel pad. As kids follow along, they observe how I use my voice to make my own sense of a poem. I tell them, "Please ride on my voice."

I also tell and show in minilessons how these performances aren't my first readings. I describe the problems I had in deciding how to read a poem. I tell why I chose to read a poem—what in the work spoke to me. I point out things I noticed about the poem in my first and second—and third and fourth—readings. Together each year my students and I compile, then add to, a list of what we do when we read poetry:

HOW TO READ A POEM

- Slow down and savor the language; it's meant to be savored.
- Read it more than once.
- Read parts of it more than once.
- Read it out loud.
- Notice how you feel and how words and images create feelings.
- Notice images, the pictures the poem puts in your mind.
- Notice other sensory language, the phrases and lines you can taste, touch, hear, and smell.
- Notice words and phrases you like.
- Notice metaphoric language you like.
- Notice sound patterns, like alliteration or assonance, rhyme or rhythm.
- Notice how a poet uses punctuation and the white space, breaks lines, breaks stanzas, and locates the words on the page.
- Notice how the poem begins and ends.
- Think about the poet's big idea: why he or she might have written this poem.
- Think about who's speaking in the poem.
- Mark the lines you love, that tell you something about yourself, the power of language, or the human condition.
- Mark the lines you need to talk about—because they fill you up, move you, make you laugh, confuse you, create images, give you goose bumps.

Before I read a poem aloud, I ask questions to help kids relate it to their experiences: Who remembers . . . ? Who has ever . . . ? Who has seen . . . ? Who has read . . . ? Who wonders about . . . ? I tell how I relate it to my experiences. Or I provide background that helps students enter the world of a poem—information about a person, place, event, painting, historical period, novel, or myth alluded to in the poem. Sometimes I tell stories about the poet's life and other poems, show their photographs or reproductions of portraits, or display their books and biographies of their lives.

Every June I ask my kids to name their favorite poems of the year. Some day, if the cost of permission fees isn't too onerous, we'll edit and publish a poetry anthology of our own. It would surely include the anonymous "The Little Boy," "The Fish" by Elizabeth Bishop, "Bummer" by Michael Casey, Frost's "Nothing Gold Can Stay," "Digging" by Seamus Heaney, "Icicle" by David Huddle, Peter Meinke's "Elegy for a Diver," "Autobiography in Five Short Chapters" by Portia Nelson, "Famous" by Naomi Shihab Nye, "Tecumseh" by Mary Oliver, "Sestina at 3 A.M." by Linda Pastan, Henry Reed's "Naming of Parts," "Richard Cory" by E. A. Robinson, "Summer Person" by Glenna Johnson Smith, "Fifteen" by William Stafford, "Thirteen Ways of Looking at a Blackbird" by Wallace Stevens, "Digging for China" by Richard Wilbur, "This Is Just to Say" by William Carlos Williams, and Updike's "Dog's Death." These are poems my students have plenty to think and say about: poems that have become, for them, Piercy's rituals in the ordinary chaos of their lives.

At the same time that students name favorite poems, they step back and name what's going on in the poems they select. I ask, "What makes each poem a good one for you? What makes it *resonate?*" Students' responses have the specificity of language of people who know how to walk around inside the architecture of a poem—who are architects of poems themselves.

WHAT MAKES A POEM RESONATE FOR ME?

- It describes a situation or experience similar to something from my own life or past.
- It describes feelings like I have sometimes.
- It describes feelings I've never had but that I could try on when I read the poem.
- The language is simple and direct.
- It's the poet's personal experience of something.

- It's funny.
- The format is interesting or unusual or fits what the poem is about.
- It has a good ending.
- It's honest.
- It uses metaphors and other figurative language.
- It puts images in my mind.
- I can feel, hear, taste, or smell it.
- There's a strong message, moral, or theme.
- It uses repetition.
- It uses rhyme in a cool way.
- It uses (or doesn't use) punctuation in a cool way.
- It has mysterious language and deep meanings.
- It weaves in information, for example, about history, mythology, art, geology.
- It tells a good story.
- I agree with the moral or message or philosophy.
- It's "elegant shorthand": brief but packed.
- It makes me think, really *think*.
- It seems to come right from the poet's heart.
- It makes me wish I'd written it.
- I can read it over and over and never get tired of it.

I try hard to demystify the process of reading poetry so my students can understand—and experience—how a reader can relish unraveling its difficulties. I continue to learn about the difference between talking a poem to death and inviting readers to walk around inside it. I have abandoned line-by-line analysis, finding a main idea and supporting details, and those inane "creative" responses it makes me blush to remember: What color is this poem? What season does this poem remind you of? Can you draw this poem? Instead I plan invitations for response that match the mood, subject, theme, or language of the poem and help my kids meet the poet halfway.

OPTIONS FOR GROUP RESPONSE TO A POEM

- Just sit quietly for a minute and savor the poem before we move on to today's minilesson.
- Read the poem again with me.
- Read aloud certain lines (stanzas, or dialogue) with me.
- Read aloud the stanzas/lines I assign to you (as individuals, in pairs, or small groups).

- Underline your favorite lines and write a sentence about why; then we'll read these around the circle.
- How does this poem make you feel? Write a sentence or two to share around the circle.
- What do you notice about this poem? What do you like?
- How do you think the speaker feels? Write one or two sentences that we'll share around the circle.
- How do you think the poet feels? Why? Write a sentence or two.
- Why do you think the poet wrote this poem? Write a sentence or two to share.
- What else could this poem be titled?
- Write in your own words what you think the poem is saying.
- Mark the lines you can see, hear, taste, touch, or smell—that create concrete images in your mind. Remember what William Carlos Williams wrote: "No ideas but in things" (1963, 6).
- Mark the lines that give you goose bumps.
- Mark the hard lines—the ones that confuse you, are hard to understand, need to be read many times.
- Mark the metaphors. Mark your favorite metaphor.
- Mark what you think is the most important line in the poem.
- Mark the lines that make you want to read more of this poet's poetry.
- Memorize the poem together with me.
- Write a collaborative poem with me in response to the poem.

Writing Poetry

My students started to write good poetry when they started to read good poetry, learned how to walk around inside it, learned that they *wanted* to walk around inside it. In this environment, poetry is abundant, alive, and attractive to young writers. Each year students become accomplished poets, but first they become accomplished readers of poetry who have observed what the genre is good for and what it might do for them.

WHAT POETRY DOES

- Poetry expresses our feelings, dreams, and needs: no other genre does it so well.
- It gives shape, focus, and resonance to our ideas and experiences.
- It puts into words things that are hard to say.

- It teaches us that "every living thing . . . is sacred" (Georgia Heard, 1995).
- Poetry changes us: it makes us think, look, hear, and wonder in ways we never would have otherwise.
- Because it speaks of things and feelings as if they are something else, it gives us new ways of perceiving our worlds.
- It makes us laugh and brings us joy.
- It makes us cry, and it comforts us.
- It connects us with other humans at the most basic level—one heart touching another heart, one mind touching another mind.
- Poetry is infinitely rereadable and different with every rereading.
- Poems and lines we have memorized go with us wherever we go as part of the rhythm of our breathing, as prisms for viewing the experiences of our lives.

My students take ideas for poems from many sources: experiences they want to capture and distill, stages in their lives they want to reflect on, their feelings about themselves, friendships and families, family pets, beloved objects, memories of their early childhoods, daydreams and memories of night dreams, loves, fears, quirks and idiosyncrasies, novels they read, other poets' poems, historical figures they read about, political and ethical dilemmas, family photographs, the impulse to express how they feel about someone and bestow the expression as a gift, songs they want to sing, and poetry minilessons about all of these possibilities, about kinds of poems, about how poems look, and about the techniques and forms poets use.

The experiences of their lives that become the subjects of poems reveal as much about who my kids are as photographs or fingerprints. Jonathan, the lobsterman, celebrates his summer roles and rituals.

LOBSTERING

The thick fog blankets Boothbay Harbor.
With the nasty smell of bait and a full tank of gas
I head out to Squirrel, stalking the ferry in my skiff.
The water is smooth as glass.
The fog lifts quickly and I bypass the ferry.
I round the point heading into the cove
At Squirrel Island.

I putt-putt alongside one of my buoys and begin the task.
The trap gets closer and closer 'til suddenly it's in the boat.
Flapping of the lobsters' tails delights me.
Measuring and banding begin.
At the end of the day I head back in to the harbor,
Joining the parade of tour boats
With a nasty smell of bait,
Half a tank of gas,
And five keepers.

—*Jonathan Tindal*

Sarah, the scientist, celebrates the lunar eclipse.

LUNAR ECLIPSE

Slowly
slowly
the moon is covered by the shadow.

You look at the moon
through binoculars
like a deer
frozen
in front of headlights
not with fear
but amazed
at how beautiful it is.

Pink, yellow, gray, and midnight blue
all around,
you are
alone
on the top of a shed
shrouded in a deep, deep, midnight blue.

And you like the blue.
And you like the mystery.
And you like being alone
with the shadow.

—*Sarah Duggan*

Asa, the dreamer, celebrates the mystery of a flock of crows outside his window.

THE VELVET, THE DARKNESS, THE CLOUD

I turn toward the mantelpiece and fire
In search of warmth I spy a cluster of black velvet from the
corner of
my eye
I do a slow but greedy double-take turning
turning back to the velvet
to discover the source of this flock of darkness so I may
satisfy my yearning
mind
A flock of crows I tell myself
eating at their pleasure
I take myself to the closest couch
and sit
and gaze away at this enormous sight
at least four dozen
Then the dusky cloud evaporates at the sound of barking

in the background
The velvet, the darkness, the cloud is spread across the sky
like black
butter
The party is over, the barking dies down, the wind screams of
loneliness
in my head
and the seeds feel abandoned until a single crow starts the
trend again

—Asa Kitfield

My students' poems can take them where memory can't—to the hazy rec-
ollections of their earliest memories, where there isn't enough information to
craft the complete experience, but there's more than enough feeling to distill
it. Matt captured the time long ago when he's certain he saw a coyote.

FACT

I sat there, staring out on the golf course,
my young eyes still, trying to
focus on the gray object.
When my vision cleared I realized
I was looking at something like a dog.
But it wasn't.
My brain started to register what I was seeing,
and I remembered my dad reading to me about them.
This looked exactly like the pictures in the book—
the patchwork coat,
pointy ears, bushy tail,
and long snout were all familiar to my eyes.
It made its way across the fairway,
down the side of the green, into the woods,
and out of my sight.
Later I told Dad of my sighting
but he never believed me.
I always knew that what I saw was a real, live
coyote.

—Matthew Miller

Dylan's first memory is of standing with his father as they watched
earthmovers make a playground for the local elementary school, and Dylan
was the lord of all machinery.

ENCOUNTER

the steam rises off the hot rocks
i stand intrigued

at the big machines performing
just for me
a dance it seems
shovel, roll, shovel
i stand above it all
the conductor of
the orchestra of noise
i am in charge
they are making something
for me
for me
to play trucks, play ball
up here i am safe from the monsters
rolling, dumping, loading
now i open my small fist
to reveal mini trucks
steamrollers and back hoes
they are tiny and helpless
i am big, a giant
the noise stops
the gulls call
i walk

—*Dylan Patrick Nickerson*

A series of sports poems that we read in class gave rise to memories and celebrations of physical efforts, of kids exploring what their young, strong bodies can do.

BODY RHYTHMS

Anxious faces everywhere.
Girls in black leotards chatter.
A woman enters the room . . .
Silence.
A sea of pink legs
makes its way to the bar
and begins to move in time
with the music that fills the space.

My teacher's voice echoes through the room.
Concentration takes over.
"Demi-plié, demi-plié, grande-plié, stretch."
My head,
my feet,
my arms
begin to move.

Freedom envelopes me.
My whole body lets go—
all doubts,
worries,
thoughts of homework,
thoughts of everything,
escape me.

Now the music changes
but my teacher's voice remains.
Freed from the bar
the real dancing begins.
Run and leap, and then repeat . . .
run and leap, and then repeat.
I fly high
and something lifts me
invisible.
Could it come from inside me?
I am part of the music.
My body moves without thought—
pure instinct.

When the music stops
I feel my body again.
Room in my mind for only one thought—
I am a dancer.

—*Emily Miller*

AT LUNCH WE PLAY BASKETBALL

At lunch we play basketball.
The court doesn't even have a three point line.
It's just a small piece of black tar
    floating on a gravel driveway.
We only have one hoop at one end,
But we still have fun.

At lunch we play basketball.
There may only be three people on a team.
Sometimes we don't exactly follow the rules.
Nobody wears a jersey, or the right shoes,
But we still have fun.

At lunch we play basketball.
We aren't seven feet tall, and we can't dunk.
We're just a bunch of seventh graders shooting hoops.

Most times we don't even keep score,
But we still have fun.

At lunch we play basketball.

—Jason Perry

When we read protest poems and lyrics—about American wars, racial prejudice, and the decimation of the American Indian—students were inspired to reveal and shape their feelings about U.S. history and its consequences.

THE BRIDGE

We built a bridge of soldiers
across the sea to 'Nam.
Strong and sturdy
defending peace
the bridge grew high,
the war grew long,
no end in sight.
They fought
holding steady the bridge.
Months turned to years,
years turned to a decade.
Lives lost, hearts shattered,
and the bridge weakened.
The people asking "Why?"
ignored the soldiers coming home.
No end in sight,
no way to win.
So home they came
across the bridge.
One war lost
many lessons learned
one bridge collapsed.

—Meghan Kennedy

SKIN DEEP

Once upon a time
there was a little boy.
He liked to play with
paper dolls.
He would dress them up
in different outfits,

but underneath they
were still the same.

One day the little boy grew
bored with his dolls.
He took out his paint set
and painted them all different colors.
He gave them races and religions.
But underneath they
were still the same.

Now some dolls decided they didn't
like other dolls.
White dolls decided
they didn't like black dolls,
so the black dolls had to work
for the white dolls all day.
And the German dolls decided
they didn't like the Jewish dolls,
so they killed millions of them.
But what the paper dolls didn't
understand is
underneath they
were still the same.

And lots of paper dolls were killed
before the little boy realized
what he had done.
So he scraped off the paint,
and they had no races and no religions,
and they stopped fighting.

What the dolls didn't understand is
nothing ever changed.
They were all always paper dolls.
Underneath they were—
we are—
always
still the same.

—*Luke Peavey*

THE BLASTED LAND

We had to move.
We had no choice.
We moved on
while the whites rejoiced.

Our lives or our land
and we chose life—
white musket against
Iroquois knife.

Our lives or our land
and we chose life—
a land not ours to trade or sell.
Now we're living in a white man's hell.

Our lives or our land
and we chose life—
white man's musket against
Iroquois knife.

—Joe Powning

Many of their poems are inspired by other works of literature: kids' imitations of what we found, through class discussions, in the poems they loved. Catharine and Rachel wove together all that we discovered about Mary Oliver. When they found "Mary Oliver moments" in the natural world, they recognized them.

BLUE HERON

She stands in the water
her sleek head pointed straight ahead,
motionless
against the dark pool
that surrounds her.

Then, in one
swift motion
the gray statue
snatches a shiny
fish out of the water
and
snaps her head back
to swallow the wriggling
silver animal.

She looks up
to see me
sitting in a
yellow boat
the oars resting in the rippling water.
She tenses watching me
watching her.

Her graceful wings brush the water.
Then it is as quiet
as if she were never there.

—Catharine Hull

SUMAC

You make the dye
to turn me to blood red.
Furry cocoons mask
the zealous color
you are leaking
into your own arrow leaves,
your leaves like ruby slippers.
As I look to you,
you bleed into me.
Make me do the crimson dance—
think the crimson thoughts.

—Rachel Anne Schlein

Sam was inspired by Thomas Hardy's antiwar poem, "The Man He Killed."

TRAGEDY

Our men stand together on one side of the field,
Our foes bide time on the other.
Waiting . . . waiting for what? To kill and be killed?

Yes. Then it begins—bombs bursting in air—
As our men and theirs fall like lead soldiers off a mantle,
Fall to the earth already running red with blood.

We stand again on each side of the field,
Only a few of us now, foes on opposite sides,
Picking up what remains of what used to be our friends,

For this brief moment, working together.

—Sam Stewart

Luke borrowed from William Carlos Williams, a poet he loves, some of the techniques we noted in our readings of Williams: the domestic moment, the title as part of the first line, and the directness of language.

THE BROWN AND WHITE CAT

lies on his back
in the warm chair by the fire,
his front legs stretched up over his head,

revealing his soft, white stomach.
Sound asleep.
Trusting me.

—*Luke Peavey*

Many writers borrowed from the Wallace Stevens masterpiece "Thirteen Ways of Looking at a Blackbird." In our discussions of the poem we characterized what was going on in each of the stanzas: one sounded like a fairy tale, another like folk wisdom from the *Farmer's Almanac*, others like a math problem, lines from a sermon or scriptures, a mystery, a myth. Students found their own ordinary objects—spoons, curtains, eyes, pens, television sets—and looked at them in Stevens' ways. Curt looked at the engine he was overhauling—or trying to.

SIX WAYS OF LOOKING AT AN ENGINE

One step into the cellar
and the obvious comes into focus:
A hulking, 1956, 40hp Evinrude.
One hunk of junk.
One mass of dead weight
with low compression.

Catch
(this monolithic excuse
for an engine
knows 2 + 2
does not equal
    4)
22.

The silent lurking
of now contrasts
with the hoped-for
overpowering roar,
which contrasts again
with the future: guaranteed
omnipresent silence:
The engine's thanks
to its benefactor.

I found new depths of hatred
when I pulled the ripcord
and the engine froze.

In the Bible
Goliath never ruled David.
But this is the real world,
and antique engines
run on borrowed legs.

When the sky went black
at 12:00 noon
the impossible happened.
My engine started.

—*Curt Monaco*

A whole class and I collaborated on a poem inspired by Charles Simic's poem "Soup," in which the poet creates a recipe for his life from metaphorical ingredients. We brainstormed cooking verbs, then I asked each student to write one or two Simic-like lines for homework; the next day we put the lines together and wrote the recipe for "us."

CTL SOUP

Begin by sprinkling in the stars
from a winter night in Maine
Add a drop of blood
from the month of your birth
Stir in the pages of a book
you turn with your own hands
Instead of sugar
bake a piece of your smile
Leave the darkness for later
Add the comfort of your mother
Frost it with a cloud
for each year you've lived
Fold in the fear of monsters
under your bed
Take the calluses on your hands
Blanch green grass from the day
you saw the rainbow and the full moon
together
Take a snip of happiness
Bake it in the early morning sun
Toss in the comfort
of your favorite quilt
Stir in the color
of your dog's eyes
Boil a cup of the sadness

you feel too often
Whip in moonlight
Sift in love
Then, as it simmers
a simmer of a hundred years,
throw in knowledge
and sprinkle in memories
Stir some more
Stare into the pot and
watch the soup swirl by you
in the maelstrom of images
that are you.

Other poems with literary roots were students' reactions to works of literature they read in the workshop. Rachel wrote poetry after reading Sylvia Plath's poetic novel *The Bell Jar*.

AFTER READING PLATH

The melancholia of Sylvia.
Her life
trying to climb its way
out of the black holes
over and over.

Over.

Do we pray for phoenix girls?
When can they rise?
When will the ashes blow away?

—*Rachel Anne Schlein*

Katy and Tom wrote poems about *Hamlet* and *The Outsiders*.

FLOWERS FOR OPHELIA

Only dead stalks of grass
only old bones
only a rusty nail
tied together with string
but to her they are more
rosemary for remembrance

running through the field
her hair no longer braided
a bouquet in hand

the last
a song in the air
the last to roam
the pond
so calm
the water
even more peaceful than her life
a perfect match

floating she is found
       her last
         bouquet
         on her breast
her last note echoes

Not only dead stalks of grass
not only old bones
not only a rusty nail
lie by her grave
       but
daisies for innocence
lavender for distrust
       and
rosemary
       for
remembrance

—*Katy Seiders*

OUTSIDERS POEMS

1.
There was a shaky gold bridge
       held together by a fraying rope.
Johnny and I crossed it
       one day . . .
Then came the Socs, the fountain,
       the murder . . .
The gold bridge fell and splintered
       on the rocks below.

Turning back was not an option.

2.
I look up through water.
       Drunken hands hold me under.
Blood rushing,
       lungs burning,

stomach churning,
        there's no turning.

Back.

Robert Frost was right.

    —Tom Allen

As a poetry assignment students wrote Civil War ballads, after marinating themselves in Walt Whitman's ballads about the war and in response to photographs taken by Matthew Brady.

WAITING . . .
THE FIFTH VERMONT REGIMENT,
CAMP GRIFFIN, 1861

Waiting for the battle
apprehension stalks the lines
pulled up in formation
the soldiers mass to fight

Waiting for the cannons' roar
to decimate the ranks
as the sickle reaps the wheat
the soldiers mass to fight

Waiting for the battle
bayonets glint in the sun
rifles at the ready
the soldiers mass to fight

Waiting for the rifles' roar
the whiz of flying shells
the cries of wounded men
the soldiers mass to fight

Waiting for the battle
they say their silent prayers
they'll see their next tomorrow
the soldiers mass to fight

Waiting for the order
to be pounded out on drum
the bugles call the charge
the soldiers move to fight

    —Tom Allen, Curt Monaco, and Joe Powning

Besides the ballad, other forms I introduced through our daily poems or in minilessons about poetry included haiku, sestinas, sonnets, poems for two voices, soliloquies, and songs.

The haiku consists of three lines, of five syllables, seven syllables, and five again. Meghan loved the challenge of the form.

HAIKU

Watch trembling whispers
fall hard through grace and let the
night silence be heard.

—*Meghan Kennedy*

We look at the forms of songs every day at the Center, where every day begins with a meeting of everyone at the school: we come together to make and hear announcements, hatch plans, discuss current events, and sing. The other teachers and I print the lyrics on oak chart paper; we taught Laurel and Martha the traditional structure of verse, chorus, bridge, and repeating verse.

PEOPLE SAY

1) Love can be as big as an ocean
   or as small as a grain of sand.
   Just as long as you have love
   you'll never, ever feel alone.

chorus:
   People say love will break your heart.
   People say love will leave you standing alone.
   I say it's the greatest gift of all,
   'cause there's no life without love.

2) Love is what's going to get us somewhere.
   Hatred, you know, starts the wars.
   Maybe someday the future will be brighter.
   All we need to do is love.

chorus

bridge:
   Without love, your heart is bleeding,
   and your soul cannot take flight.
   Without love, you're never free to dream—
   your day's an endless night.

chorus

repeat 1

chorus:

    People say love will break your heart.
    People say love will leave you standing alone.
    I say it's the greatest gift of all,
    'cause there's no life without love.
    'cause there's no life without love.

—Laurel Card and Martha Hutchins

Paul Fleischman's *Joyful Noise: Poems for Two Voices* and Georgia Heard's poems "Fishes" and "Frog Serenade" inspired several poems for multiple voices, among them Meghan's playful exploration of the dispute between her and the couple who lives next door. They love the birds that come to their feeders; Meghan has cats.

A POEM FOR THREE VOICES: A NEIGHBORLY DISPUTE

I hear tiny footsteps pattering.	We hear tiny footsteps pattering.
Birds belong on posters.	
	Cats belong in stories.
I think of my cats. I think of an adorable, fuzzy kitty.	We think of our birds.
	We think of vicious little pests.
I think of cats as poetry in motion, catching mice.	
	We think of birds as flying music, singing beautifully.
I cuddle up with them at night, admire their delicate features.	
	We listen to them in the daytime, admire their delicate features.
Thinking of my cats I smile.	
	Thinking of our birds we smile.

But I don't blame you.

I love my cats.

But we don't blame you.

We love our birds.

—*Meghan Kennedy*

Other dramatic forms include the soliloquy and dramatic monologue: poems with one speaker talking aloud. In the soliloquy the speaker talks to himself or herself, in the dramatic monologue to a silent listener. Jason took on the persona of an old salt in a dramatic monologue.

FISHIN'

I wake up
put on my draws
grab my rod
and leave
"there ain't no fish out here"
I sez to myself
as I'm walkin'
down to the crick
I plunk da line in and
whoa Nellie
I got me a keepa
she pulled so hard
I swear da rod was
bent in a loop
I hauled her out and
put her in a bucket
she just sat there lookin'
like this here world
were comin' to an end
I don't blame her
seein' she was gonna
be my dinna
for a minute there
she almost
looked human
kinda like my wife's
fishy eyed look
"shoot"
I sez to myself
"you're getting soft"
with dat in mind
I fire up da grill

—*Jason Perry*

Rachel experimented with the English sonnet form: three quatrains and a couplet. She was the only writer, including her teacher, to brave it.

SONNET I

My mind a hole closed always to the new.
Deep solemn faces, ones that keel.
Grinding in my mind a photograph of you.
Your eyes in mine full of sharp zeal.
Caught in the back of my eyes wanting to flow
Sour salt tears holding your cold.
Small mind—never would know
Trapped psychedelic light I hold.
The sweet enchanted words I wanted came.
All my joy flew through happy-cruel.
Fast it came, serious, only a game.
The sickly sad faded to harsh ridicule.
In my mind quick eons of solemn love
Flew from my heart at dusk—mirth far above.

—*Rachel Anne Schlein*

A sestina is a repetitive form invented by the troubadour poet Arnaut Daniel and consisting of seven stanzas. The lines in each of the first six stanzas end in one of six words, repeated in the order below. The seventh stanza of three lines, called the *envoy*, includes two of the six words in each of its lines.

Stanza	1	2	3	4	5	6	7
	1	6	3	5	4	2	1–2
	2	1	6	3	5	4	3–4
	3	5	4	2	1	6	5–6
	4	2	1	6	3	5	
	5	4	2	1	6	3	
	6	3	5	4	2	1	

We read sestinas by Linda Pastan, Julia Alvarez, Elizabeth Bishop, and Bruce Bennett, and a bunch of kids tried them. Izzie's was a present for her father, written after they spent a weekend in Manhattan.

NEW YORK CITY SESTINA

I look out across the city
Fascinated by a swarm of lights
And the sea of yellow taxis
Below my window. I wonder
And I watch in amazement the endless faces,
And I hope someday, in the glorious crowd, one of the faces will
    be me.

Imagine me,
In this huge and lavish city,
Looking out an apartment window that faces
Times Square, watching a ball covered in lights
Fall from the sky to a crowd gazing in wonder
And filling the streets, where for once there are more people
   than taxis.

I leave the window, and we walk out through the streets,
   avoiding the speeding taxis.
The buildings that never end tower above me
And I look up and wonder
How anyone could build such a city
And power so many lights
And still find room for so many faces.

Ten chimes ring from all the clock faces
And ten cents is added to the fare of the taxis.
We are guided through darkness by bright, shining lights
In every store and office window around me.
So many objects of beauty, unique to the city—
Things I can only dream and wonder

At. From the wonder-
ful buildings and parks, to the empty, lonely faces,
I am learning the city.
From restaurants, to streets, to taxis,
To skyscrapers that melt to clouds, subways tunneling through
   darkness below me,
And the countless, flashing, rainbow billboards made of a
   million tiny lights.

I will always love the lights
And how they make this city a wonder-
land. It's amazing to me
How looking at things from a distance masks all the pain and the
   fearful faces
That lurk inside the buildings and taxis—
That which we don't look to see, hiding in the city.

I will miss the city, and dream of the lights,
The elegant limos, the smell of perfume and leather in the
   taxis, all a part of my world of wonder—
And our two faces, you and me, surrounded by the glow of New
   York City.

—Isabeall Quella

My fattest file of poems by students is labeled *gifts of writing*. Kids discover in poetry a vehicle to express their feelings about the people they love—this genre is made for feelings. Laurel loves her grandfather and showed him how in this Christmas present.

THE *GIVER*

i look into his eyes
they're deep
and
tell a thousand stories
i look deeper
i see the
wisdom
the love
i see his life
play before me
the wars
the hunger
the deaths
he has lost
so much
still he *Gives*
enjoys life
his life my life
all he has been through
doesn't show
hidden by
the laughter
he embraces
everything he has
loved and
experienced
he *Gives*
to me
he is my
grandfather
he is my
friend
he is my
teacher
and my
Giver
i love him

i want to
be his
Giver

—*Laurel Card*

When family friends had their first baby, Katy's present for the new parents was a poem.

BABY

small
fragile
lying next to you
mini feet
miniature hands
like a toy
a baby doll
sleeping
so peaceful
so perfect
so noisy
crying
such a loud noise
for such a little doll
your treasure
waiting
for
first
word
first
smile
first
steps
your first baby
almost a kitten
almost a puppy
but
your love for it is greater
bigger
then any you've ever known
your
most prized possession
fragile
small

and
growing
already

—*Katy Seiders*

In May, as Mother's Day drew near, I asked the group to brainstorm how they might approach a poem for their moms that would avoid cliché (*thanks for being there, Mom*) and get at the feelings they have for their mothers underneath the day-to-day traumas of the charged relationships that develop between parents and children during adolescence. In a minilesson we made a list:

POSSIBILITIES FOR POEMS FOR MOTHER'S DAY

- A list of thank-yous for specific favors, qualities, and gifts
- A straightforward, heartfelt expression of love
- A story of you and her doing something together that captures the relationship
- A physical attribute of your mother
- Your mother and a loved object or possession
- A story of you and your mother in action, doing something that's a metaphor for your relationship
- A "Ways" poem à la Wallace Stevens
- A setting that reveals her—a favorite or typical place

Students who took up the challenge wrote poems that made me wish I were their mothers. Missy's mother loves lilacs; she wrote a poem for her in the style of Wallace Stevens.

LILAC BUSH

1
The perfume creeps
through the cracked window.

2
She walked down the aisle
with a wreath of lilac
in her hair.

3
The storm hurled its way
through the town,
but the lilac bush stood
alone and untouched.

4
You hear the tapping
at the window.
The shadow of the lilac
fades away.

5
One lilac bush
plus love
equals happiness.

6
The sky was a light purple.
The old lady looked out
and saw her husband's ghost.

7
There's a hole
in the ground
and no trace of
the lilac robbers.

8
The flowers are wilting,
my mother is missing.

9
I know what it
means to you—
the sparkle in your eye
when its name is mentioned.

10
The field was barren.
The only living things
were the lilac bush
and you.

—*Melissa R. Heselton*

Jonathan put his mother in the setting that reveals her best: on an island off the Gulf Coast, combing a beach.

THE SHELLS YOU FIND

Walking down the beach behind you
I watch as
you pick through the shells
pulling out the beautiful ones
as if by magic

I follow your
footprints in the sand
trying
trying as hard as I can
to find a beautiful one
never succeeding

Only wishing to find
some of the beauty
you always discover

Thank you for all the beauty

—*Jonathan Tindal*

Rachel centered her poem on familiar physical objects—her mom's two boats—and used a new technique for her, personification.

FOR MY MOTHER AND HER BOATS

They are sleeping on their river
of ice and snow,
dreaming of making you happy
on their summer Kennebec.
They imagine the tarps around them
are the never ending blue water
that you could ride forever.

You have given them an identity,
a home.
You make them fly.

But for now,
the water in your dreams
will carry the three of you
through spring.
And that is almost enough.

—*Rachel Anne Schlein*

Students learned about other poetic techniques and approaches in minilessons. In a series of lessons about figurative language—metaphors, similes, and personification—we read poems from Wallace's *Writing Poems* and Kennedy's *An Introduction to Poetry* that illustrate how poets depart from denotation. One morning in late April, snowflakes the size of fists began to fall outside the classroom windows. I told the kids to meet me in the parking lot, and we ran around in the oddest spring snowfall I can recall. Then I rounded them up, brought them back inside to the circle, and said, "What was it *like*? Write a simile or three." They wrote, read their favorites to me, and I transcribed them as a collaborative poem.

APRIL SNOW

It's snowing like a shower of pussywillows,
like dandelion puffs floating down,
like cotton balls tumbling, tumbling off a shelf.

It's snowing like flour pouring endlessly into a bowl,
like hundreds of silky parachutes drifting to earth,
like thousands of petals falling from the blossoms of a tree
    somewhere where it's really spring.

It tastes like thick fog,
like the coldest cotton candy,
like April disappointment.

It feels like cold, wet feathers from angel wings,
like I'm engulfed in a sea of gray,
like God's dandruff.

It's snowing like a television channel that won't come in,
like God's idea of an April Fool's joke,
like winter is having its revenge on spring.

Katy, a runner on the cross-county and track-and-field teams, began a new poem by asking herself, What is running *like*?

WINGS OF WIND

Like a lonely ghost
    The wind blew
        As the hurricane rose

Like a bird on wing
    The soft breeze blew
        In early morning

Like an electric fan
    The cool ocean air blew
        In summer heat

Like a shot of winter
    The cold wind blew
        And colored leaves fell

> Like a jolt of hope
> > The puff of wind
> > > A spurt of energy I run on
>
> And on
>
> *—Katy Seiders*

These poems evolved in a setting where kids went inside poetry every day—read it, talked about it, learned how it works, wanted to make it work for them. Each poem grew from a moment, a need, an itch, and a sense that only this genre could scratch it. And each poem went through multiple drafts and revisions before the poet said *yes*.

Rachel lost track of the number of drafts of her sonnet. Izzie spent at least twenty hours on her sestina. The first version of Jonathan's poem about the YMCA swim meet is unrecognizable in "Swimming in Fire." Poems evolve from hard work. There's a myth about writing poetry, that it's an exquisite experience that comes on the wings of a dove and requires a kid-gloves response from the teacher. *Good* poetry is hard to write. Student poets revise toward their sense of what a good poem is. Eventually, over days and months of reading poetry, they carry inside them a wealth of experiences with poems and a wealth of connections between poetry and their lives.

Poetry is useful to my kids. The joy of it for me, as their teacher, is my conviction that seventh and eighth grade won't be an isolated moment. I believe they'll live other poems without me. Poems won't keep them safe, ensure them a happy life, heal their pain, or make them rich. But poetry will give voice to the experiences of their lives. This seems enough to ask of it.

14
Taking Care of Business

Problems make good subjects.
Donald Murray

My students slammed into the classroom at full tilt one November morning. Fingers jabbed the air, and adolescent voices squeaked in indignation.

"Can you believe it?"

"I kept changing the channel. Every one did exactly the same thing."

"Yeah. *Nothing.*"

"What a waste. They must think everyone who watches television is as big a moron as they are."

"*My right hand is on my left shoulder,*" I shouted over the din. I continued to give the school signal for kids to be quiet and pay attention until everyone finally grabbed a pillow and settled into the circle for the mini-lesson.

I already knew what they were upset about. I had fumed all night, too, over the local television stations' coverage of the fall elections, especially the presidential race. In history class we spent weeks researching electoral politics, following the campaigns, debating, polling, and voting in the state student election. On election eve everyone took home blank maps of the United States so we could track the electoral vote as it was tallied. But the local coverage sabotaged any attempt to conduct serious research about the national scene.

After kids had sounded off around the circle, I asked, "So what should we do about it?"

"Letters," Jonathan offered. "To all of them, telling them what jerks they are."

"Jonathan," I laughed, "a letter is an appropriate response. But let's see if we can write one in which we don't come off as even bigger jerks. So, how would you begin to compose this kind of writing? What's always a first step in generating nonfiction prose?"

"Brainstorm the ideas," Tom responded. I handed him a marker and flipped to a clean page on the easel chart. Tom listed while we talked:

- way too many local reporters waiting around in hallways to interview local candidates
- way too many interviews with local campaign staff
- hardly ever showed an electoral map
- showed it too fast
- local coverage kept interrupting national reports
- local reporters not very smart about politics
- electoral map was too small to see
- almost no national results of a national election
- Channel 6 citizen advisory panel added nothing

When no one had any new complaints to add, I tore the list off the pad, taped it to the wall, and used it to help the class compose a collaborative letter to the local news programmers. I asked them to think in terms of four parts: an introduction that establishes the context, examples that show the problem, suggestions of solutions to the problem, and a conclusion, followed by the standard two-word closing paragraph, *Thank you*. Along the way we talked about business-letter format, language, paragraphing, transitional phrases, and tact. After school I called the stations and asked for the names and addresses of the directors of news programming. The next day in writing workshop Dylan typed the letters, and everyone signed them.

November 6

WCSH-TV, Channel 6
Mr. Mike Curry
Director of News Programming
1 Congress Square
Portland, Maine 04101

Dear Mr. Curry:

We are a group of students who have been studying the campaign/election process since September. Last night we eagerly tuned in to your election coverage so we could learn the results of the electoral vote, which we know to be the most crucial in selecting a president of the United States.

We were disappointed and frustrated at the lack of a national perspective and national election coverage. Specifically, a map of the electoral votes was seldom shown; when it was, it either flashed by so quickly or was so small we couldn't determine which state went for which candidate.

In addition there was too much local coverage. It was disorganized, repetitive, and empty of content. We needed more national coverage, more of the big picture, and fewer scenes of reporters waiting in corridors for local candidates to appear or interviews with their staff. The citizens' advisory panel added little to the analysis of the results and seemed a shocking waste of time, because it revealed nothing about either the local or the national scene.

In the next national election, may we suggest that the local affiliate cut back to brief up-dates and leave the bulk of the reporting to the networks? We wanted the election news last night; we didn't get it.

Thank you.

Sincerely yours,

I would love to be able to say the kids received thoughtful, encouraging responses from all three affiliates. In fact no one wrote back to them, and, in fact, students did not seem particularly bothered by this. The experience of crafting an argument out of inchoate anger—*of doing something about it*—gave them perspective, a voice to raise, a sense of purposefulness, and the satisfaction of closure.

Writing about ideas may well be the hardest genre to sponsor in school, especially at the middle- and high-school level, where the English teacher teaches English only. It's easy and obvious to ask students in an English class to write what they read: narratives and poetry, which invite them to examine their own experiences or imagine others'. It takes a different kind of effort to push out into the world of ideas—social, moral, ethical, political—and pull it back into the writing workshop. I think we need to make the effort. Argument, opinion, and persuasion should be nurtured as part of every writing workshop and every life. Writing teachers need to plant the seeds for those moments of change, when a student stops being a victim or allowing others to be victimized and writes as an agent, someone who uses written language to *act*.

This chapter describes some of the ways my students have used written language to take care of the business of ideas, sometimes at my invitation and sometimes on their own initiative. In their letters, essays, petitions, speeches, editorials, interviews, profiles, and résumés, kids learn how to collect and work from evidence, discover what they believe, bring order to their arguments, and apply the lessons they've learned about craft to new, nonfiction genres. They learn to write with a critical reader in mind, someone who wants information, needs sense, and has questions the writer must anticipate. They learn how to identify problems that need solving and give voice to solutons. And they learn how to be brave—to send ideas and evidence out into the world and try to have an influence there.

Petitions are one of my students' most direct routes to influencing others. When I conduct minilessons to help kids add to their lists of writing territories, I often ask them to consider this question: "What problems need solving—in your life, others' lives, this school, community, state, country, world?" Their answers have led to petitions about cafeteria food, proposed legislation to limit the Endangered Species Act, and distribution of potassium iodide to citizens who live or work in the plume area of the local nuclear-energy plant. When students at Boothbay wanted the option to attend away basketball games, Catherine wrote a petition to the principal that was signed by sixty eighth graders:

> We the undersigned feel the need for a student bus to go to sports events at other schools. We all agree that riders on the bus will pay a fee of two or three dollars per head for gasoline and the driver's fee. We also agree that this student or spectator bus would only make a run if twenty-five people sign up in advance to use the bus. There would be a sign-up sheet in the office for students who wish to register to ride the bus to a given event. We look forward to your response. Thank you.

They got the bus. At the Center, as its quasiprincipal, now I'm the one on the receiving end of student petitions, where it's not so comfortable sometimes. Several years ago the Center's faculty instituted a buddy program to help bring kindergartners into the life of the school: each child was assigned a seventh grader to help him or her navigate the K–8 meetings that begin and end each school day. In January I received a petition written by Joe and signed by all the seventh graders, who were weary of baby-sitting:

> We the undersigned feel the K-and-7th buddy system is no longer needed. Nancy Tindal, Nancie Atwell, and the other teachers established this program saying that the kindergarten kids needed to be taught what to do during the meeting. We who have signed feel that the kindergartners have learned what to do at both afternoon and morning meetings. Therefore all who have signed below ask that the buddy system henceforth come to an end.

The teachers and I talked, agreed with the seventh graders that the K's were acclimated, and let them off the hook. Later we reexamined the buddy system and revised it so the age group that would adore acting as buddies to younger children—our fourth graders—could take on the role. They did; they shone with the new responsibility; and the K's adjusted better and were just plain happier with custodians closer to their own ages.

One of the most important petitions my kids wrote began in a discussion at a K–8 morning meeting. It was the day after an all-school science field trip to a state park located on the shoreline. We hadn't been the only school there that day, and some of the behaviors our kids witnessed had upset them. I asked for volunteers from my class to take on the problem as a writing task, and during morning meeting on two days Laurel and Martha asked the rest of the school to generate data: specifics about what we observed at the park and potential solutions. Then the two girls crafted the notes as a petition to the park manager.

> We, the undersigned, feel strongly about some things that happened on Tuesday, October 11, at Reid State Park. We observed student groups from another school behaving in a reckless and irresponsible manner. They took every living creature from the tidal pool area and filled many buckets with plants and animals. It made our school feel sad that living organisms were taken from their natural habitats. Specifically, we observed that:
> - Students took dozens—if not hundreds—of creatures out of their habitats.
> - Students grabbed up dozens—if not hundreds—of creatures and threw them into buckets; the water in the buckets became hot in the sun, and the animals died.
> - Teachers put live organisms on picnic tables for students to study and draw; these also died in the hot sun.
> - Students were running recklessly in the rocky shore area, not looking at what they were stepping on.

- Students stomped on mussels on purpose.
- Students pulled mussels off rocks and threw them into the water.
- Students picked up crabs by one leg and threw them into the open ocean.
- Someone threw a rock at a seagull and injured it.
- An adult chaperone commented, "Oh, look, a starfish! I've always wanted one. I think I'll take it home." And she did.
- Students pulled seaweed from the rocks and did not put it back into place.
- Students left trash behind, including rubber gloves they had brought with them.

We hope that you will consider taking some steps to help school groups that are going to Reid State Park understand their responsibilities to this special environment. We suggest the following policies for school groups:

- Take only pictures; leave only footprints.
- All critters need to be put back with care. Visitors need to leave things exactly where and as they found them, including rocks and seaweed.
- Respect all wildlife and take responsibility for sea life.
- Be considerate of other school groups visiting the park and their desire to view the natural habitats in a pristine state.
- Don't walk in the tide pools.
- Take home trash: all of it.

We also suggest that the park take the following steps:

- Send written materials about the rules to schools before they visit the park.
- Post rules and guidelines at the front gate.
- Consider instituting fines for people who don't follow the rules.

Thank you.

The petition brought our students a letter of thanks from the park manager for their concern and commitment; it also initiated policy changes at the park.

I am always looking for opportunities for my kids to write about ideas and information. I haunt the school's junk mail and spend time every month grazing in the back pages of *Teacher* magazine in the "For Your Students" section, highlighting writing contests my seventh and eighth graders are eligible to enter, which usually call for essays in various guises. Izzie was one of several kids who entered a contest I found there, to write a letter to an author of a favorite book. She began at the beginning: by generating ideas and information and working from quantity. Her notes about *Fallen Angels*, a novel about the Vietnam War by Walter Dean Myers, formed two columns:

FEELINGS, THOUGHTS, PERSONAL CONNECTIONS, ETC.	INFORMATION, FACTS, DATA, ETC.
He told the reasons why people go to war.	U.S. involvement ended in 1973.
He described the setting— what Vietnam was like.	Direct U.S. involvement 1961–72, more than 58,000 U.S. dead; South Vietnamese: 400,000; Viet Cong/North Vietnamese: 900,000.
He told the real horrors of that war (torture, prisoners, etc.)	
The soldiers were young like me and scared like I would be.	By 1966, 190,000 U.S. troops in Vietnam.
No more wars!	U.S. sided with South Vietnam; Russia and China with North Vietnam.
It must have been painful to write (dedication to his brother).	Presidents Johnson and Nixon lied.
Now I've read other books about the Vietnam War.	Source: *Columbia Encyclopedia*

Izzie used the page of notes as a planning sheet as she drafted and revised—numbered the items on the list and covered them with arrows and other symbols. She made the letter an occasion to learn more about the war and more about the reasons for the intensity of her reaction to the novel—as Catharine learned about inequities in U.S. schools and society from LouAnne Johnson's *My Posse Don't Do Homework*, Emily empathized with Torey Hayden's struggles to reach abused children, and Martha, who won the contest and was published in the book *Dear Author* (Conari Press, 1995), confronted the stigma of HIV and AIDS by writing about *It Happened to Nancy*. Izzie typed a final version of her letter, addressed the envelope, bought a stamp, crossed her fingers, and sent herself out into the world:

Dear Walter Dean Myers,

Your Vietnam war novel, *Fallen Angels*, introduced a whole new experience into my life, one different from mine but through an individual I could identify with.

Until I read *Fallen Angels*, I had never understood why anyone would choose to go to war, especially those as young as Richie—just seventeen and eighteen years old.

I had known facts of the war in Vietnam—about the 58,000 American soldiers who died there and the 1,300,000 Vietnamese deaths—but I hadn't understood the lies and torture of those years. Or perhaps I didn't want to know.

Fallen Angels taught me not only about the war; I learned, too, how much I am like the people who fought there. I realize now they were just as frightened as I would be and disliked the war as much as I do. Because of *Fallen Angels* I have read other books about the Vietnam War, not because I like the topic, but because I feel I understand it so much better now. I want to appreciate and know what so many young people had to go through, and I want to do whatever I can to make sure our country doesn't involve young men and women in such a needless war ever again.

I realize that were the war going on today, by the time it ended, many of the boys—and girls—in my class would have been sent to fight, which puts the events of *Fallen Angels* into a personal perspective that I find harrowing.

I know you dedicated the book to your brother who died in Vietnam, and I'm sure it must have been painful to write. But I want to thank you for it, because I can't think of a more powerful way I could have learned about the war and come to appreciate the people, such as your brother, who fought and died there.

Sincerely,
Isabeall Quella

In addition to helping kids submit their essays to contests, I ask them to publish in-house in *Acorns*, the school literary magazine, which I edit three or four times a year. My students mostly write to be read, but it's especially important that their opinions and ideas find audiences. Students have also written letters to the editors of regional and local papers, point-counterpoint features (Edie and Michael's debate in the *Boothbay Register* about the legalization of marijuana for clinical use drew some interesting local response), and, during the fall elections, guest editorials. Matt's guest editorial in the *Wiscasset Newspaper* was his attempt to explain to local voters a complicated referendum on the November ballot and, in the process, argue his own position.

YOUR GUIDE TO THE CLEAR-CUTTING REFERENDUM
by Matt Miller

To clear-cut or not clear-cut, that is the question. Or both? What about partial cuts? Well, you'll have three choices in November: 1) The Forest Practices Act, which is already in place; 2) The Ban Clear-Cutting Bill; or 3) The Forest Compact, created by Governor King and various organizations with an interest in the forest.

Let me bring you up to speed on what each means. First, the Forest Practices Act is the one the loggers like. It says there is no limit on the amount of wood cut, that the maximum size per cut is 250 acres, and that there should be buffer zones of 250 to 500 feet between cuts. This applies statewide. I realize this sounds like lumber companies are ruining the environment, but we must need all this wood or we wouldn't be cutting it. On the other hand, I do have to point out that nearly half of our state is owned by paper companies.

Then there's the Ban Clear-Cutting Referendum, initiated by the Green Party. It says that any clear-cutting in a 10.5 million acre area in the unorganized towns of northern Maine is completely prohibited. It also says that landowners cannot cut more than one-third of their wood per acre over a span of fifteen years, trees must be de-limbed where they are felled, and no openings of clear-cuts greater than one-half acre are allowed.

Personally, I think this is a little harsh on the paper companies and the people who work for them. The Green Party does have a lot of good points, however, such as the number of species of trees and animals declining in northern Maine—though there are a couple of species of trees that are actually on the rise.

I know that this is confusing, but bear with me. We're almost done.

Last but not least is the Forest Compact, recently added to the November ballot by the Maine legislature at the request of Governor King. It would apply state-wide, except for forests used for research. It says the maximum size is seventy-five acres per clear-cut, all of which would require a permit, and that large landowners are subject to limits on the total land clear-cut each year. Each town must hire a licensed forester to write a local ordinance about clear-cutting. The compact also creates the possibility of an ecological reserve of around 13,000 acres on public land, to study the effects of logging. My choice (if I could vote) would be the Forest Compact, because not as many jobs would be lost and it lays stricter laws on the loggers.

Probably by the time you read this there will be new facts to consider. Try to stay informed, so your vote counts in setting a thoughtful course for our state.

Rachel disagreed with Matt wholeheartedly and wrote an essay in response.

HERE'S YOUR CHANCE
by Rachel Schlein

Everyone says he or she wants to change the world, and here is your chance to do just that. Vote to ban clear-cutting in the woods of Northern Maine.

The trees have existed for a long time, and they know so much we do not. They give us much we can't live without: oxygen, shelter, and heat, to name a few. If we keep cutting trees at the rate we are now, soon they will be gone. The paper companies are cutting trees twice as fast as they can grow back. Some trees, like the red spruce, are cut more than five times faster than they can grow. Does that sound like healthy forest management to you?

And what about the animals? They're hurt by clear-cutting, too. The heavy machinery used by the paper companies compresses the soil and pushes the oxygen out of the ground; it takes oxygen away from the worms and insects that need it to live. The trees shade the ground, and when they are clear-cut, the sun dries up the soil and destroys animals' homes and the animals themselves. Silt goes into streams that fish live in and ruins their spawning. Deer yards are destroyed, too. Proponents of the Governor's compromise argue that clear-cutting provides animal habitats that wouldn't exist otherwise. What science is behind this claim? Open spaces are made naturally, by fires, insect infestations, and hurricanes. We don't need man-made disasters.

Fears about the economy seem to be a major reason voters are being urged to support 2B, the compromise written by the King administration. How exactly would 2A, the citizens' referendum, take away jobs? "No trees = No jobs" says the 2A bumper sticker, and I agree. At one paper company's woods operation only three people run the clear-cutting/harvesting equipment. But if there were selective cutting, the industry would need to hire more individuals to select and cut more individual trees. After clear-cutting, many of the trees the paper companies harvest are turned into paper pulp, which involves another mechanical job, rather than one that requires human labor. A large number of trees aren't being used for purposes like furniture and high-quality lumber production, both jobs that require more employees.

Once land is clear-cut, it takes sixty to seventy years to grow back. There will be no more jobs in that same place again in your lifetime. Right now, under the old Forest Practices Act, the forest industry is clear-cutting an average of thirty-three acres per woodlot. The Governor's compact would allow 74.9 acres to be clear-cut. This is NOT helping to solve the clear-cutting problem.

A final contribution the trees make to our lives is their incredible beauty. We can't afford to lose that, either. Jonathan Carter, author of the citizens' referendum, calls the Northern woods "an emerald dream." This helps our economy. Tourists want to come to Maine to see its beauty. They don't want to see clear-cuts from the top of Mt. Katahdin or on the boundaries of Baxter State Park.

For me the most important issue is that trees are living things. We can't wipe them out. Trees have voices and rights, too. And although we may not understand what they are saying to us now, when their voices are silenced we will be sorry we didn't support them by banning clear-cutting. I strongly urge you to vote yes on 2A.

Rachel's response to Matt came too late to be published in the local papers but just in time to establish a new tradition at the Center: guest editorials by students included in our weekly newsletter to parents. Here was a built-in, easily accessible, responsive audience for kids' takes on problems they recognized or encountered in the world around them. Meghan wrote an editorial about her experience as a new student at the Center. Tom advocated for the deactivation of Maine Yankee. Dylan's editorial railed against inflated salaries in the NBA and the joylessness for young fans of a game that was mostly about money. Jonathan, another sports fan, urged newsletter readers to write to the NBC affiliate in Portland to complain about basketball games that were preempted by reruns of "Dr. Quinn, Medicine Woman." Asa expended his energies on a *hot* topic among the members of the school community, the exorbitant prices at the new cineplex in Brunswick.

THE CANDY CRUNCH
by Asa Kitfield

You walk into a Hoyt's movie theater and read the sign by the ticket booth: $6.50 a person. Three people in your group? That's $19.50. On some days, like Super Tuesdays when discount tickets are available, it's not that bad. But $6.50 is the going rate for a ticket, nowadays.

After you purchase your tickets, it's on to snack central: rows and rows and towers and towers of candy. They now offer something called movie bytes—nuggets of chocolate-covered vanilla ice cream—as well as soft serve, giant Cokes, popcorn, you name it, they've got it. But if you name it, it's going to cost you a pretty penny.

What—$7.14 a pound? THAT'S ABOUT TWELVE GUMMY BEARS FOR A BUCK! "Though you have to include the variety factor," some people say. Hoyt's offers Milk Duds, Sour Patch Kids, gummy worms, chocolate covered peanuts, and on and on. But no matter what Hoyt's you go to, I can promise there's a gas station or mini-mart nearby where you can bypass the "candy crunch." Same candy, lower prices. (Just be sure to sneak it into the theater.)

For example, one of the best money savers is Sather's, which costs only one dollar for two bags of candy. Sather's offers just about the same variety as Hoyt's, except for the rare line of Sour Fruit Salad.

Another price issue is the popcorn. As I said before, there's always a gas station nearby, but the problem is that not all gas stations sell popcorn, and sometimes it's not cheap. That's why I suggest bringing your own from home. At grocery stores or wholesale warehouses you can purchase microwaveable popcorn at very low prices. Pre-pop it and bring two bags, if you want.

One more thing: soda. And the obvious answer is . . . bring it from home. Now, after playing your cards right, the cost of your movie excursion should be reduced to a reasonable amount for an evening out.

Before:

Tickets: $6.50 for three people	$19.50
Candy: $7.14 a lb. for three people (1.5 lbs)	10.71
Popcorn: medium-sized box	4.59
Total:	$34.80

After:

Tickets: $5.45 (at discount) for three people	$16.35
Candy (Sather's): $1.06 for 2 bags for 3 people	3.18
Popcorn: microwave bags for three people	1.20
Total:	$20.73

And there you have it: saving more than fourteen bucks and avoiding the candy crunch is the way to go.

In another, more sober, guest editorial, Asa explained to parents about the efforts of kids at the school to help remove the land mines that the United States and other countries left behind in Vietnam.

MINES ON MY MIND
by Asa Kitfield

Today, every twenty minutes, a child or adult is maimed or killed by a land mine that was planted long before the child was born. Because of the 120 million live mines scattered across seventy-one countries, thousands of acres of perfectly fine land are unusable, not to mention lethal.

Around two million mines are planted each year, and only 100,000 are removed. When will these barbaric weapons be stopped? Finally, action is being taken. Many countries around the world are no longer supporting land mine warfare, which means the ban of use and manufacture of these weapons.

"The cry of land mine victims rings out from Nicaragua to Cambodia. No country that calls itself civilized can continue to allow these weapons," Canadian Foreign Minister Lloyd Axworthy said. "A global ban is within our reach." Since the mid-1920s, this is the first time the world has come together to try to ban one weapon, one that has been used by almost every country.

Right now Canada is pushing the pact and wants completion by December. They want an international treaty, but many of the superpowers, including the U.S., are uneasy and aren't supporting the pact. They're not thrilled about scrapping the millions of dollars they invested in the latest technology in land mines. Other military superpowers that won't budge are Russia, France, and Britain. They need to be pressured into signing the global ban, and, if Canada gets enough smaller countries to sign by December, that is just what will happen.

But what about us? What can we do? In the last year a new program was founded called PeaceTrees Vietnam. This organization is collecting as much money as possible so they can travel to Vietnam, to the Quang Tri Providence, to conduct a three-phase project to begin to remove the 3.5 million land mines still buried in the country of Vietnam.

Phase One: Experts will find and remove the old mines, then, in their place, plant "peace trees." This phase will cost more than a hundred thousand dollars because of the expense of the process of removing mines—it costs a hundred dollars for experts to remove a single mine. And, as you know, there a lot of them out there.

Phase Two: In late November volunteers will officially open the Friendship Forest Park, made up of all the trees planted in place of the mines: almost 1,700 trees comprising thirty-seven indigenous species on eighteen acres of freshly de-mined land.

Phase Three: Architectural plans for a children's center for land mine education were unveiled last December, and construction should be finished in late fall. This operation is going to cost $45,000. Tax-deductible contributions are being accepted now and can be sent to:

> Earthstewards Network
> PO Box 10697
> Bainbridge Island, WA 98110

The students of CTL recently received a thank-you card from PeaceTrees Vietnam, written to acknowledge our donation of a hundred dollars. Thank you to all who helped us achieve our goal. Now we can say that CTL removed one mine, planted one tree, and saved one life.

All of this writing was responded to by the parents of the authors, other kids' parents, other kids, and teachers. People knew my students for their opinions and arguments. This can be a heady kind of recognition for twelve- and thirteen-year-olds, but sometimes it can be a challenge, too, as their ideas go out into the world and meet with disagreement. It can be scary for writers of any age to put ourselves out there. I give students the best, most accurate advice I can to help them write essays that have something to say, that say it logically and with conviction, and that rely on evidence.

To teach about essays, I collect them. Every year I clip timely editorials and columns from the *New York Times*, *Boston Globe*, and the Portland paper; I photocopy them or put them on overhead transparencies, and the kids and I name the conventions we find. We never find five paragraphs—the essay form still taught in many schools—and we seldom find topic sentences, thesis statements, compare-contrast essays, before-after essays, or developmental paragraphs. Our lists provide us with new definitions of the essay genre.

WHAT WE FIND IN GOOD ESSAYS

- A short, grabbing title: funny, a play on words, a question, alliteration, an allusion, a connection to something else
- A lead that brings the reader right in to the issue or problem
- Examples that show what the writer is talking about
- Quotes
- Statistics
- Humor
- Sarcasm
- A voice—a person behind the writing
- A sense that the writer really cares about the subject
- Personal pronouns—*I* and *we*
- Simple language
- Big words defined: in context or explained directly
- Simple sentences
- Short paragraphs
- Some paragraphs made up of only one sentence, to punch a point
- Transitional words that connect paragraphs and ideas
- Evidence and information woven in
- Anecdotes—little stories about the writer and/or other people that help make a point
- Anticipation of a reader's questions
- Direct questions to the reader
- Ideas that move from point to point in an order that seems logical
- Surprising combinations of words or ideas
- A conclusion that resonates—that gives readers something to think about when we're done reading

In other minilessons I teach about the importance of generating quantities of information and ways to do it: brainstorming, webs, lists, columns. Murray's *Write to Learn* is particularly helpful in demonstrating alternatives to the traditional outline, which presumes that the information a writer needs preexists in his or her head and marches out single file on command. Kids need to start with quantity, work from wealth, and organize later.

In other lessons I teach about organization, simplifying, using paragraphs to help and cue readers, and the importance of transitions. I assigned students to skim newspaper columns for a week in search of transitional words, to see how essayists cement their paragraphs together when meaning alone doesn't do it; they generated a long list:

TRANSITIONAL WORDS AND PHRASES WE FOUND

According to	Meanwhile
After	Most important
Again	Next
Although	Nonetheless
And	Now
Another	Of course
As soon as	Oh, sure (Dave Barry)
As a (girl, etc.)	On the one hand
At the same time	On the other side
At this point	Or consider
But	Perhaps
Finally	Questions:
For years/months	When . . . ?
Fortunately	How . . . ?
However	Where . . . ?
Immediately	So
In any case	Somehow
In other words	Sometimes
In short	Soon
In the meantime	Still
It's obvious/clear that	Then
Just consider	This
Like	True
Maybe	When

One lesson to emerge from essay writing was significant because it's so familiar to my students: writing—all writing in any genre—is a series of decisions. Nothing is accidental, and no decision is too small, especially in an essay, when the right decision means not losing, confusing, or boring a reader, or, even better, when it moves a reader to a new perspective.

Book reviews are another occasion for persuasion: a writer tries to convince readers of his or her literary opinions. Toby and I love reviews, sometimes, I admit, as much as we enjoy reading the books themselves; our mail is flooded with literary journals. But nothing we read about literature in those stacks of magazines bears any resemblance to the only writing about literature that shows up in most elementary and middle school classrooms: the book report.

The book report is a school genre contrived for school purposes: make kids read, make them prove they read, make them practice a prescribed format. No one writes book reports except students in school; no one reads them except teachers. But the book review, a genre that exists in the real world, invites students to discover their passions—and their prejudices—as readers and to teach others what they find in a book so engagingly that others will want to look for it, too.

To help students write book reviews, I made transparencies of some of the student reviews that appear in the NCTE journal *Voices from the Middle*. My students took notes about what they observed, and then we compiled a group list on the easel pad:

QUALITIES OF AN EFFECTIVE BOOK REVIEW

- First-person voice: semiformal, between a book report and a letter in the reading journal
- A plot summary that doesn't reveal too much (i.e., the ending) and tells just enough for a reader to decide if it's the kind of book he or she likes; an invitation or hint of things to come
- Quotes from the book that reveal character, plot, or theme
- A brief description of the main character(s)
- Where and when the story is set
- What genre it is
- Descriptions of good things the author did (e.g., flashbacks, realistic details, fast pace, hopeful ending, etc.)
- A description of the problem or theme
- How the book fits in a larger context—political, historical, social
- A suggestion of who would like the book and why

- Comparisons with other books and genres
- What's different about this book, contrasting it with others of the same genre
- Comparisons with works by other authors
- Comments about the author's style or use of language, metaphors, etc.
- The reviewer's feelings about the book: his or her specific reactions
- The reviewer's reading process: how he or she read the book
- A grabbing lead and an emphatic conclusion

On another day we looked again at reviews published in *Voices from the Middle* and teased out a list of the techniques writers used in their leads: how did the authors of reviews accepted for publication whet a reader's appetite?

POSSIBLE LEADS FOR A BOOK REVIEW

- Plot synopsis:
    This book is about _____ or
    This book tells the story of _____ .
- Synopsis of the problem or theme:
    This book is a powerful look at _____ .
- Identification of the main character and his or her problem:
    Duncan never knew that _____ .
- Invitation to the reader to engage with the topic:
    Imagine a story about _____ , and you've got _____ .
- Question to the reader:
    When was the last time a book made you laugh out loud?
- Quoted dialogue from the book:
    "I am here now, Ehland," Sparhawk murmured. "Somehow I'll make everything right again."
- Description of an action from the book:
    "Swish! Ten perfect shots in a row."

Each year my students are required to write at least one book review, compose a cover letter, and submit it to *Voices from the Middle* or one of the regional teachers' association journals; I'm sure there are other markets for reviews by students that I haven't come across yet, and I continue to look. Matt and Izzie were among the students who received the tell-tale fat envelope from NCTE that informs a reader a book review has been accepted for publication in *Voices*.

Catch-22   Dell, 1955, 455 pp., $7.50
Joseph Heller   ISBN 0-440-20439-9

"The Allies won the war!" "Hurrah, we beat the Nazis!" This was the mind set following World War Two. Everyone was cheering over our victory in the "good war"—everyone except Joseph Heller. Heller knew there was no such thing as a "good war" and wrote about it in a genre known as black comedy, which takes something awful, something that wouldn't normally be funny, and makes it darkly hilarious.

Catch-22 takes place on an island off Italy, called Pianosa, and in Rome. The main character is Captain John Yossarian, a lead bombardier, who spends most of his time trying to get out of the war in a lot of zany ways. He can't because his superior officer keeps raising the number of required missions using something called catch-22 . . . but I've already said too much.

Catch-22 is an antiwar war novel. It is magnificently funny, brutally sad, and has the best characters of any book I've ever read.

—Matthew Miller

Practical Magic   Putnam, 1995, 244 pp., $22.95
Alice Hoffman   ISBN 0-399-14055-7

For more than two hundred years, everything bad that happened in town had been blamed on the Owens women. Gillian and Sally Owens live in the big dark house on Magnolia Street with their elderly aunts, who are known for their witchcraft. As Gillian and Sally grow up, they grow apart, until through Sally's children and Gillian's escapades the women learn the value of family and understand that even practical magic won't solve everything.

I loved this book because of the modern mystery and the magic it's filled with. The characters are intriguing, yet always believable. The plot is captivating from the first page. I've read many of Alice Hoffman's books (*At Risk*, *Illumination Night*, *Second Nature*, and *Turtle Moon*) and of them all, *Practical Magic* is my favorite. I would recommend it to anyone who likes fantasy, family, love, lies, or magic.

—Isabeall Quella

The résumé, another persuasive genre, has particular relevance to my eighth graders who are fast approaching fourteen, the age at which Maine kids can obtain work permits. In a minilesson I show them to begin, once again, by generating data, this time about their own experiences and qualifications. Since most of them don't have formal job experience, I encourage them to list school activities, honors and awards, responsibilities at home, odd jobs, and education. I make transparencies of other students' job applications; then I explain:

Résumés have two important functions: to obtain an interview with a prospective employer and to demonstrate how your experience, knowledge, and attitudes can satisfy their needs. A résumé isn't your autobiography. It's selected information, designed to introduce information that will get you an interview.

A good résumé can go a long way in helping you get a job you want. You'll want to make sure it reflects your strongest assets. Tell the contribution you can make. Indicate the position you're applying for and the reasons you think you can do the job well. Be brief. Use simple, direct language. Organize and present your information just as clearly as you can. Then make sure the final copy makes a good impression—that it's neat, correctly spelled and punctuated, and follows a consistent format.

There are two kinds of job application letters. One is an independent letter, like Darren's. He didn't feel he had enough experience to list it on a résumé, so he decided to tell his prospective employer about his assets in a letter.

> Box 77, Route 27
> Boothbay Harbor, Maine 04538
> April 26

Mr. George Werner
McKown Point
West Boothbay Harbor, Maine

Dear Mr. Werner:

I am a fourteen-year-old native of Boothbay, and I'm interested in doing all your yard work at your summer home. Chris Paine told me about the job and told you about me. I am a hard worker and responsible, too. Other jobs I have held include lawn mowing (for Lorraine Smally and my father) and snow shoveling for various local people.

I think I could handle the responsibility of your big lawn. At the end of last summer Chris showed me how your tractor and weed whacker work and how to mow all sections of your lawn.

I am very interested in the job and in your reply. I can be reached to set up an interview at the address above or by calling 555-4602 after 3:00 P.M.

I look forward to hearing from you.

Thank you.

> Sincerely yours,
> Darren Winslow

Darren gave Mr. Werner four important pieces of information. He explained that he could do the job, told about his work habits and other job experiences, asked for an interview, and let Mr. Werner know where, when, and how he could be reached.

Luanne decided to write a résumé—a formal series of statements about herself, her history, and her job experience. She started with her name, address, and phone number, along with her job objective and a summary of her qualifications. Then she described her education, experience, and assets, and generally tried to make a case for herself as someone who is responsible and cooperative.

Luanne Bradley
Eastern Avenue
Boothbay Harbor, Maine
555-1161

Seeking position as part time summer ice cream waitress

Offering: a sense of responsibility; the willingness to learn any assigned task; energy; and a cheerful outlook.

EDUCATION	Will graduate in four years from Boothbay Region High School. Best grades and most enjoyed classes: reading and algebra. Honors and mostly As throughout the year.
SUMMER AND PART TIME EMPLOYMENT	Last summer helped with pogie fishing around Boothbay; the previous summer assisted as a sternman, lobstering. All employers were complimentary about the quality of my work and general helpfulness.
RELATED EXPERIENCE	Only experience serving food is at home, when I sometimes make dinner. Occasionally serve at bake sales.
OTHER ACCOMPLISHMENTS AND ASSETS	Since I was little have been in both Brownies and Girl Scouts where I learned many responsibilities . . . Most enjoy myself when busy . . . Teachers say I'm a fast learner . . . Have always made friends easily . . . Missed days of school only because of dentist appointments . . . In late November appeared at the Rotary Club to make a presentation about the Boothbay Writing Project . . . In January participated in an assembly program honoring the B.R.E.S. Special Olympians.
PERSONAL DATA	Fourteen years old. Excellent health. Well-groomed. Enjoy reading, downhill skiing, basketball, tennis, softball, and music.

Finally, a job applicant sends a cover letter along with the résumé. It should be addressed to the specific person in the company who does the hiring, not to "Dear Sir or Madam" *and never* to "To Whom It May

Concern." Be sure to spell his or her name correctly. Your letter should be short and to the point, emphasize the skills you could bring, refer to your enclosed résumé, and ask for an interview. You can see how Carol handled this in her cover letter.

Seaview Road
West Boothbay Harbor, Maine 04575
March 23

Mrs. Linda B. Kerns, Personnel Manager
Patterson's Wharf, Inc.
Southport, Maine 04576

Dear Mrs. Kerns:

I am writing in order to apply for a job at Patterson's Wharf as a part time summer ice cream waitress. I am willing to do any job assigned to me, cheerfully and enthusiastically. I would appreciate it if you would seriously consider me for this position.

My updated résumé is enclosed with more information.

I will look forward to you contacting me concerning possible employment. I can be reached at 555-2404 weekends and after 4:00 P.M. on weekdays.

Thank you.

Sincerely,
Carol Creaser

My kids who write résumés almost always get the jobs they seek. A lot of homework goes into writing a good letter of application. Kids who take the trouble to learn the conventions, research the job, and figure out how to best present themselves are impressive to prospective employers. And my students get the chance to impress themselves—to take on a practical, adult writing task and succeed at it.

The most grown-up of the writing tasks I have asked my kids to take on is the profile. I assigned profiles because I wanted students to learn that they're surrounded by interesting adults who lead worthwhile lives. I wanted them to become curious about the life of another, ask questions, inform themselves, and inform others. And I wanted them to experience reportage: to learn how to observe, interview, research, write with information, and discover Donald Murray's "revealing specifics" (1993) among the information they generate.

We started by reading profiles from *The New Yorker*, *Vanity Fair*, and *Rolling Stone*. I asked students to make notes about how the profiles worked, then in minilessons we created group documents that listed the elements we decided were important. For example, after students read a profile of me by Tom Quinn that appeared in *Esquire* (1984), they created a group list of their observations:

WHAT WE NOTICED IN THE NANCIE ATWELL PROFILE BY TOM QUINN

- The lead sets the scene—the place; an exact location.
- The leads points the direction and sets the tone for the rest of the profile—*it will be a story.*
- Quinn establishes a theme, then allows it to resonate throughout the profile.
- He interviews Toby and students, too.
- He pays attention to the other people in N.A.'s surroundings; puts her in a context.
- The movement is present → past → present, etc. He messes around with the chronology.
- He weaves in a lot of quotes from N.A. throughout the narrative.
- He uses quotes to convey information, instead of just giving information to the reader in his reporter's voice.
- He uses a poem to suggest a theme for a person's life.
- He uses imagery: details that make a scene visible.
- The physical descriptions and details are woven in and presented in a context.
- He includes humor.
- He describes N.A. at work and the details of her day.
- The profile is 40 percent background; 60 percent N.A. at work.
- He includes N.A.'s dreams and memories.
- He includes small, personal details (e.g., a pear for lunch).
- The piece moves as a circle, back to the poem that is the lead.
- He uses a pithy, one-line conclusion.

The next step was for kids to choose local subjects to profile. I asked them to choose women. I realize that rural Maine is not the only place in America where the political and cultural agendas are set by men, but I think there is particular difficulty here in recognizing the work of women and the contribution it makes to the life of the community. I also know that women will talk more freely and make it easier for my kids, as novice reporters, to capture and identify Murray's revealing specifics.

For homework students came up with the names of three to five local women they might like to observe and interview; I explained these couldn't be their teachers, mothers, or other relatives because the kids need distance from their subjects in order to generate fresh specifics and craft a revealing portrait. They identified artists, physicians, dancers, lawyers, travel agents, teachers, authors, scientists, reporters, and all manner of business entrepreneurs, from the founder of Sarah's Pizza to the owner of the Bunny Barracks. On the easel pad I listed each student's name and his or her choices, and we began a process of elimination and negotiation. By the end of class each student had decided who he or she would profile, and they began to plan the interviews.

Zinsser's *On Writing Well* (1990) features a specific, helpful chapter about how to conduct an interview. In a minilesson I read aloud an abridged version of his advice and asked kids to take notes: good practice for the interview itself. As I read aloud, Michael captured the essence of Zinsser in his notes:

INTERVIEWS, ACCORDING TO ZINSSER

- Get people talking.
- Ask questions about important things in life.
- Their words are always more important than yours.
- The writing comes alive when quotes are woven into it.
- Pretend you're writing for publication (we really are).
- Choose someone interesting, important, unusual.
- Choose someone who would touch some corner of people's lives.
- Have basic tools: paper, 2–3 sharpened pencils, pens that flow very well.
- Keep notebook out of sight 'til you need it.
- Take a little while to chat and get to know each other so they trust you.
- Do your homework: find out information about them before you go.
- Make a list of likely questions.
- Better questions might come to you.
- Questions are a guide, but not a guide you have to stick with.
- Don't use a tape recorder: it's not writing.
- If writing, you're getting the meaning.
- People talk faster than people can write—tell person to stop and write 'til you catch up ("Hold it a minute, please").
- Develop some shorthand—omit the small words (and, of, the, with).

- Write first letter of a word, leave rest blank, then once interview is over, fill it in right away.
- At home type your notes.

On another day kids drew classmates' names and designed and conducted practice interviews with each other. I told them to be sure to choose a focus for their questions: to select an angle for the interview appropriate to the subject. Katy interviewed Jay about his experience as a basketball player, then typed up her notes:

INTERVIEW WITH JAY

Q: How long have you been playing basketball?
A: Six years. **1.**
Q: What positions do you play?
A: Power forward. **2.**
Q: How many points do you average a game?
A: Ten points a game. **3.**
Q: Do you want to continue to play basketball in high school and college?
A: Yes, and in the NBA. **4.**
Q: Do you have any player in college basketball or the NBA that inspires you or you like?
A: Scottie Pippen, Michael Jordan, and Dennis Rodman. **5.**

The results of the practice interviews gave students rich opportunities for discussing, then practicing, follow-up questions. I asked interviewers to put a number after any answer that might have prompted another question about feelings, opinions, or experiences. The numbers that appear in Katy's interview with Jay signal her potential follow-up questions:

1. What grade were you in when you started? Where did you play basketball during those six years? What is it about the game that you like so much?
2. Why only power forward? How do you feel when you play this position?
3. How do you feel about your point average?
4. Where will you play high school basketball? What's their team like? Will you look at colleges that have strong teams? Where do you think you might apply?
5. What is it about these guys that makes them special to you?

Then it was time for kids to approach their potential real subjects and request interviews. They were nervous wrecks about making the phone calls, so we wrote a sample script together on an overhead transparency. Most of them read it verbatim when they contacted the women they had chosen.

SCRIPT FOR REQUESTING AN INTERVIEW

Hi, my name is _____ . I'm in a writing class at the Center for Teaching and Learning in Edgecomb. I think your work is important and interesting, and I'd like to write a profile of you. If you agree, I'll attempt to get it published in _____ . Would you consent to a profile?

NO—Thank you very much for your time. Good-bye.

YES—That's great. Thank you. I'd like to schedule a day that I can both meet with you for an hour or so and talk one-to-one about your work, and spend the rest of the time observing you at work. Is this okay? _____ .

The best days for me are _____ . What's best for you? _____ .

That's great. Again, I'd like to spend the whole day with you, so where and when shall we plan on meeting? That's _____ _____ . I'll see you then. Thank you very much. Good-bye.

Every woman they contacted said yes, and kids began their final preparations. They arranged with parents for rides to their subjects' homes or places of business and wrote and finalized the principal questions they wanted to ask. In a minilesson we listed other revealing specifics they needed to be sure to capture, beyond the women's words.

OBSERVATIONS TO BE SURE TO NOTE

- Details of the physical environment—the space/studio/room(s), etc.
- Details about the appearance of the subject; her habits, manner of speaking, gestures, expressions
- Details about the subject in action: her actual work, her process as a worker
- Details about other people in the subject's environment and/or life
- Details about how the subject interacts with others in her environment: voice, eye contact, touch, conversational tone
- **If you don't write it down, you don't have it to use!**

The individual interviews were spread out over a month. During writing workshop students worked on the profiles as well as their other projects, and I conducted minilessons about what to do with the data once the first writer had completed the interview and observation. Murray's *Write to Learn* became an invaluable resource. His advice about techniques for ordering writing, creating effective leads and titles and closings, asking a reader's questions, and outlining information—he describes ten different approaches—all helped my kids develop a focus and find ways to structure their pages of notes into coherent profiles. In a final checklist I asked students to answer a reader's questions:

FINAL PROFILE CHECKLIST

- Is the lead quick, simple, and packed with information?
- Does it set the tone for the rest of the profile?
- Does the end connect with the beginning?
- Can we see the woman: her physical appearance and at work?
- Can we see her work environment?
- Do we hear her voice throughout the profile, directly quoted?
- Do we see her as she's speaking?
- Do we know why she does what she does?
- Do we know how she got here?
- Do we understand how she feels about it—what it means to her?

The final products were as different as the subjects and the authors. Joe spent a day with wildlife rehabilitator Justine Logan and her bats, hawks, eagles, and other critters.

PROFILE OF JUSTINE LOGAN
by Joe Powning

It's Monday, and that means cage cleaning day at Chewonki Foundation on Chewonki Neck Road in Wiscasset. I'm greeted by the sound of newsprint being trashed as I walk into one of the buildings with Justine Logan. Logan is Chewonki's Director of Outreach Programs. She is based in a small office, when not working with rehab animals. The room outside her office is reminiscent of a high school biology classroom, except the animals are alive, not skeletal. There are turtles, bats, a snake, and a baby alligator in various cages or bins. All seem content to live in human care.

"Chewonki is the only place in Maine that deals with bat rehabilitation and is the first to set up successful bathouses," Justine explains. "Our focus is on bats, birds, and reptiles, but we work more with bats for that reason."

Her days are anything but idle, yet she takes time to joke with her coworkers. Justine is a confident woman with a sunny disposition and a fondness for vigorous hand motions. She wears a blue sweater and black jeans. Her casual manner puts the people around her at ease. It takes a special person to teach both people and animals, and Justine does both with grace and skill.

She smiles as she recounts a story about a crazy foundling duck. "One day we spied this duckling waddling down the middle of Route One, like she had a business meeting or something. We picked her up and my daughter named her Milly and raised her. Milly sees my child as her sister and goes ballistic any time she sees her. One day she just took off. I was frantic, looking for her. It was winter, and Milly's such an airhead I was sure a fox would get her. On the third day I was out with the cows and saw a speck on the horizon. It was Milly. When she saw me she dive-bombed, honking the whole time. Then she landed and began following the cows around as if she'd never left."

A large part of Justine's job involves scheduling visits to area schools to teach students about Maine's creatures. "I feel like I'm making a difference," she says, "through the fact that we've reached so many kids and dispelled so many myths about bats. I believe the fate of the plant lies in the next generation. We reach thousands of children a year, and I believe that's worth its weight in gold."

Born in Manhattan, Logan moved many times because of her father's job in textiles. She considers Middlebury, Vermont, her home because she lived there the longest. She attended College of the Atlantic, Bar Harbor. Logan started working for Chewonki in 1989, when she was hired as a consultant to train a bald eagle for education purposes. She explains why she stayed on: "I took this job because I love working with animals and it gives me the chance to teach children, too. I've been the outreach director for four years now." When asked how her job affected her personal life she replies, "I'm pretty much on call twenty-four hours a day, seven days a week. We just have to pick up and go. My daughter's gotten used to it and has begun to enjoy it. Not every kid gets to keep seal pups in her bathtub, so it's not all that bad."

Logan smiles and jokes as she feeds and weighs the bats in her care. She's familiar with each of their personalities. Later in the day a gauss hawk that has been shot is delivered. "I hate to see a bird in a cage, but if it can't fly, in the long run it's doing so much for education that it's worth it for us to keep it here," she says. She watches reverently as the hawk eats mice, then coaxes it to drink Gatorade. "It's mostly a matter of trust. If wild animals don't feel they can trust you, they won't work with you. If they know you're a friend and won't hurt them, you can work with them. It's no good if they're not happy," Justine explains.

The affection and respect she feels toward the animals in her care is evident in the way she handles them, talks to them, and tries to solve the problems involved in their welfare. As I prepare to leave Justine Logan, she is back behind her slightly cluttered desk. It's been a long day and it isn't over yet, by a long shot. I say good-bye with a new perspective on the natural world—and new hope.

Curt tore his hair as he tried to organize thirty pages of notes and craft a profile of Marcia Stewart and her three professions.

PROFILE OF MARCIA STEWART
by Curt Monaco

Although plants grow slowly, keeping them alive is a nonstop occupation. Add a florist shop and orders for flowers, greenhouse orders, waiting on customers, supervising employees, making and mailing ads, and training to become a florist, and things become downright hectic. But this is only part of what Marcia Stewart has taken on. She also runs an art gallery single-handedly. This makes for eleven- to twelve-hour days, seven days a week, but she says she doesn't mind. This high-energy existence is the life this hard working woman has carved for herself, and it is a life she loves.

Marcia Stewart is the owner of Gallery House on Route One in Nobleboro. With her husband, John, she runs Holly Hill Nursery, also in Nobleboro, and Cottage Gardens on Church Street in Damariscotta. She's tiny—only four feet eleven inches—but she projects energy wherever she goes. It's impossible to miss her as she charges through her day in a loose sweater, baggy corduroys, and hiking boots.

Stewart conducts all three businesses with high efficiency, even Cottage Gardens, the florist shop she and John bought just three months ago. Today is Tuesday, and she is holding her weekly conference with employees in the back room.

"Monday's a cut day, so does it make sense to keep the daytime help lean, then come in in the evening and green-up?" she asks her three employees.

"It makes more sense to have people come in on the off day to green-up," one of them answers.

"Does it matter? That's what I want to know," Stewart responds.

When that problem is solved, it's on to the next. And the problems are numerous. They are preparing for their first Mother's Day, which is the second busiest holiday in the floral business. There are only a couple of days to prepare because the flower arrangements are cut, and cut flowers only stay fresh for a day or two.

This is one of the major problems Stewart has encountered in running a florist shop. "All the plants here are perishable," she notes. "Nursery plants aren't. The difference is here they have to be turned over to the customer earlier."

The florist business may be new to Marcia, but she is tackling it with characteristic gusto. She has hired a consultant to help her learn about cut flowers. "With my experience," she says, "I feel confident, but anyone can put flowers together. They may die. I need the technicals." To get those technical skills, she is also going back to school to learn how to run yet another successful business.

Marcia Stewart graduated college as an art major. She taught art at the high school level, then stopped when she and John moved to South Bristol. John started a landscaping business, and Marcia went to work as an art director. After three years John's landscaping business was big enough that it needed a nursery. So they bought the house that is now Holly Hill. It was perfect in all respects. Marcia Stewart could set up an art gallery inside the house, and John could have a nursery outside. "People tell me what a wonderful idea it is to have the two together, but it really came from necessity," she comments.

As Stewart was getting her gallery off the ground, she found she was also doing a lot of work in the nursery but didn't always know what she was doing. Just as she is doing now, she went back to school to become a trained horticulturist. As soon as she walks into a greenhouse, she's in her element. And that step into a greenhouse is a big one: it's like plunging into a jungle. The heat is constantly at or above eighty-five degrees, and the air drips with moisture. Two rows of hanging baskets and four rows of flats, each holding a myriad of plants and flowers, run the length of the greenhouse. Each flower has its own fragrance to add to the already laden atmosphere. The hum of fans permeates the area.

Marcia moves around the greenhouse as if it is her natural environment, checking plants, moving some outside, and watering others. At this time of year the plants need all the attention they can get. Spring is one of the hardest times of the year, Stewart says, "because the plants have to be outside for the customers to see, but the weather might turn sour and kill them all."

Marcia Stewart loves all three of her businesses, but if she had to choose one, it would be Gallery House. "It's where my heart lies," she says. Looking around the gallery the eye is assaulted by a pleasing collage of Maine art. Stewart notes that 90 percent of the art she features is created by Maine artists, and the rest has something to do with Maine, for example, a Scottish sculptor she's featuring this summer who makes maritime sculptures.

Stewart's natural talent is in the graphic arts, but she doesn't draw any more. She doesn't need to, she says. "I get my pleasure from the diversity of the artists. If I drew myself, I would end up with a certain style, but selling art I get all the different artists' styles. I can say I like the picturesque quality of this drawing; I like the colors of that painting. I have it all."

The gallery isn't all that big—only two medium-sized rooms. Stewart calls it a collector's gallery, because, as she says, "People have to decide to come here. It's not a tourist business." She moves art through the gallery quickly, changing the display every month. She also does other projects on the side.

As one of her special projects she purchased 150 goose eggs. "For Christmas," she says, "I try to find something unique, something besides large paintings, because they're so expensive. I'll give each artist three blown eggs and ask them to paint them as Christmas ornaments. These will be professional artists, so the eggs will be valuable."

The gallery is open in the summer, when people are in the mood to buy art. During the winter, when both the nursery and gallery are closed, Stewart has a bit of spare time. That's one of the reasons she and John decided to buy Cottage Gardens, because its primary season is winter. She also does freelance consulting, which she likes, she explains, because "I might suggest a painting to someone at the gallery and they'll be lukewarm about it. Then I go to their house and I find I'm all wrong. It really helps me to know my clients a little better."

Right now it is May, and she has bigger things on her mind. On top of worrying about the nursery, the florist shop, and preparations for Mother's Day, she has to ready her gallery. The newest exhibit opens on Sunday. Stewart has designed the invitation, which she will send to two thousand people. She has to go to Camden to have the cards printed, then to a copy shop to get them reproduced. That's the easy part. Finally she will hand-address every one of the cards. She confesses, "I don't know how I'm going to get through this."

But she will. She'll work hard and make it through the week. She's not only going to do it—she's going to have fun in the process.

I found homes for all the profiles in community newspapers. Most of the editors sent photographers to take pictures of the women my kids had sketched, and for the remainder of the school year we paged through the local weeklies in search of their bylines. I never saw students as excited about finished writing as they were with the published profiles. And I heard again and again from the profiled women about community members who had approached them to say, "I never knew this about you." Feature articles written by students helped some great women become more visible in their communities.

When Donald Murray writes, "Problems make good subjects" (1993), I can almost hear the pleasure he takes in the word *problems*. For the writer a good problem is an adventure—a chance to feel curious and anxious, to hang suspended in time and space between one idea and the glimmer of the next, to use writing to solve new problems that the writing creates, to understand, again, what inspiration feels like.

Problems make good teaching, too. The power of teaching in a workshop grows from making a place where students and a teacher can say "I don't know" and feel "I think I can find out." The tension of knowing and not knowing—writing, reading, my students, myself—becomes a continuous adventure and a source of inspiration for a lifetime.

Appendix A
Materials for Writing, Reading, and Publishing

I.   Paper of different sizes, weights, and colors:

    Pads of narrow-ruled lined paper
    White and colored construction paper
    White and colored letter-size copy paper
    Stationery and envelopes
    Index cards ($3 \times 5''$, $4 \times 6''$, and $5 \times 8''$)
    Post-it notes
    Poster board

II. Writing implements of various sizes, colors, and styles:

    Regular pencils
    Colored pencils
    Pens in blue or black
    Pens in colors (e.g., turquoise, red, etc.) for editing
    Markers (broad-tipped, fine-tipped, and italic)

III. Supplies and equipment:

    Erasers
    White correction liquid
    Postage stamps
    Staplers and staple removers
    Paper clips
    Scissors
    Transparent and masking tape
    White glue and glue sticks
    Rulers and a yardstick
    Three-hole punch
    A crate of clipboards
    Bulletin board
    Collections of literature (See Appendixes L and M for a list of recommended titles for middle schoolers)
    Book display stands or bookcases

Easel stand and pads of lined easel paper
Overhead projector, transparencies, and markers
Word processors networked to a printer
Photocopier
Tape recorder and blank tapes

IV. Resources and references:

College dictionaries

The New American Roget's College Thesaurus, revised edition by Philip D. Morehead (Signet Books)

The Complete Rhyming Dictionary edited by Clement Wood, revised by Ronald Bogus (Doubleday)

The Scholastic Rhyming Dictionary by Sue Young (Scholastic)

Spellex spellers (Curriculum Associates, Inc.)

Bartlett's Familiar Quotations by John Bartlett, edited by Justin Kaplan (Little, Brown)

The Columbia Encyclopedia, 5th ed. 1 vol. (Columbia University Press)

How Writers Write by Pamela Lloyd (Heinemann)

On Writing Well: An Informal Guide to Writing Non-Fiction by William Zinsser (HarperCollins)

Inventing the Truth: The Art and Craft of Memoir, edited by William Zinsser (Houghton Mifflin)

The Student's Guide for Writing College Papers by Kate L. Turabian (University of Chicago Press)

Market Guide for Young Writers by Kathy Henderson (Writer's Digest Books)

Nuts and Bolts: A Practical Guide to Teaching College Composition, edited by Thomas Newkirk (Boynton/Cook)

Shoptalk: Learning to Write with Writers by Donald M. Murray (Boynton/Cook)

The Teachers and Writers Handbook of Poetic Forms, edited by Ron Padgett (Teachers & Writers Collaborative)

The I-Search Paper by Ken Macrorie (Boynton/Cook)

Writers INC, by Patrick Sebranek, et al. 3d. ed. (Write Source)

The Elements of Style by William Strunk Jr. and E. B. White (Macmillan)

Write to Learn by Donald M. Murray (Holt, Rinehart and Winston)

A Writer Teaches Writing by Donald M. Murray (Houghton Mifflin)

A Writer's Notebook: Unlocking the Writer Within You by Ralph Fletcher (Avon Camelot)

The Writer's Quotation Book, edited by James Charlton (Penguin)

An Introduction to Poetry by X. J. Kennedy (Addison-Wesley)

Knock at a Star by X. J. Kennedy and Dorothy Kennedy (Little, Brown)

Writing Poems by Robert Wallace (Little, Brown)

Masterpieces of World Literature in Digest Form, edited by Frank Magill (HarperCollins)

A Century of Recorded Poetry (audiotapes from Rhino Records)

Dear Author: Students Write About the Books That Changed Their Lives (Conari Press)

The Reader's Encyclopedia, edited by William Rose Benét (Thomas Y. Crowell)

The Friendly Shakespeare by Norrie Epstein (Viking Penguin)

Recent issues of *The New Yorker*

A crate with hanging files containing samples of writing by students, professionals, and the teacher, organized according to genre: book reviews, short stories, memoirs, historical fiction, feature articles, interviews, plays, letters, editorials and opinions, advertising, songs, cookbooks, fantasy/science fiction, parodies, poetry, informational writing, cartoons, history, profiles, gifts of writing, surveys, letters, pamphlets, petitions, speeches, published student writing

A crate with hanging files containing interviews, press releases, and other published information about authors popular with adolescents, organized alphabetically

Displays of students' published writing

A file folder and a display of professional publications that feature student writing

A bulletin board to post announcements of writing contests

V. Materials for organizing writing, reading, and homework:

Folders with pockets and grommets, three per student, one to serve as a daily writing folder, one for spelling, and one for reading. In the grommets of each student's daily writing folder:

1. A proofreading list of the conventions the writer has been taught by the teacher, one or two conventions at a time
2. "Expectations for Writing Workshop"
3. "Rules for Writing Workshop"

4. "Having a Writing Conference with Yourself"
5. A list of kinds of writing students might try (Appendix C)
6. A list of ways to go public with writing (Appendix B)

In the grommets of each student's reading folder:

1. Two copies of the Student Reading Record (Appendix G)
2. "Expectations for Reading Workshop"
3. "Rules for Reading Workshop"

In the grommets of each student's spelling folder:

1. Two copies of the Personal Spelling List (Appendix H)

Folders with pockets only, three per student, for collecting and storing finished writing, texts and lyrics, and weekly homework assignment sheets

Stapled inside each student's permanent writing folder: a form to record pieces of writing finished over the course of the school year (Appendix F)

One marbled composition notebook per student, to serve as a reading journal, with a letter of instructions from the teacher glued inside the cover

One spiral notebook per student, to serve as a writing-reading handbook

Two clipboards, each containing multiple copies of the Peer Writing Conference Record form (Appendix J)

Multiple copies of the Editing Checksheet form (Appendix K)

Multiple copies of the Weekly Homework Assignment Sheet form (Appendix P)

A file cabinet, or crates with hanging files, for storing students' permanent writing folders

A file cabinet, or crates with hanging files, for storing students' reading folders

Trays or boxes to collect writing ready for photocopying and teacher editing

A rug or pillows for students to sit on together during minilessons and read-alouds

For the teacher's records:

1. A status-of-the-class record sheet for each group of writers, attached to a clipboard
2. A status-of-the-class record sheet for each group of readers, attached to a clipboard

Appendix B
Ways Student Writers
Can Go Public

A sense of audience—the knowledge that someone will read what they have written—is crucial to young writers. Kids write with purpose and passion when they know that people they care about reaching will read what they have to say. More importantly, through using writing to reach out to the world, students learn what writing is good for. Writing workshop isn't a method for filling up folders with "pieces." It is a daily occasion for students to discover why writing matters in their lives and in others' and what it can do for them and the world.

In this context, publication takes many forms and includes all the ways a writer might connect with a reader. Sometimes the idea for a piece of writing comes first, and later an author or I will recognize a publication possibility. Sometimes the idea of publication comes first: after learning about a new option in a minilesson, a student will decide to pursue it. One of the writing teacher's roles is to help writers go public and connect with readers. We need to show students how to recognize potential audiences for given pieces of writing, and we need to look for, create, and demonstrate opportunities for writers to be read and heard.

Publication in the writing workshop should be a given—frequent and ongoing—and not an award bestowed on what teachers decide is the "good" writing. When class and school magazines are juried, the students who most need responses to their finished writing will never be published, and the same "good" writers will be published time and again.

1. Individual bound books of memoirs, short stories, content area research, poetry, lyrics, etc. Mary Ellen Giacobbe's bookbinding technique, described in Rief (1992), requires only cardboard, wallpaper, glue, and dental floss, and the results are sturdy and attractive. Students can make their own.
2. Individual pieces handwritten or typed, then printed or photocopied and shared with friends and families. The result is instant publication. It helps to provide a tray or box in the classroom labeled "Writing to Be Photocopied." The teacher or students can take responsibility for making the copies.

3. Individual pieces of writing intended as gifts for people who writers care about: poems, stories, memoirs, letters, and opinions to be presented to someone special. These can be written on cards, posters, or bookmarks; mounted or matted; illustrated; printed in beautiful fonts or on special printer paper; or rendered in calligraphy.

4. Submissions to class magazines: collaborations and collections about one theme or exploring one genre. Everyone who meets the guidelines of the call-for-manuscripts is published in the magazine.

5. Submissions to a school literary magazine.

6. Submissions to a middle school yearbook, which includes feature articles, reminiscences, and poetry.

7. Submissions to local newspapers, including letters to the editor, editorials, feature articles, profiles, and poetry.

8. Submissions to magazines that publish student writing, including *Blue Jean* (P. O. Box 90856, Rochester, NY 14609), *Merlyn's Pen* (P. O. Box 1058, East Greenwich, RI 02818), *Read* (245 Long Hill Road, Middletown, CT 06457), *Stone Soup* (P. O. Box 83, Santa Cruz, CA 95063), *Writes of Passage* (817 Broadway, New York, NY 10003), *Writing* (245 Long Hill Road, Middletown, CT 06457), and *Voices from the Middle* (NCTE, 1111 Kenyon Road, Urbana, IL 61801).

9. Submissions to writing contests—local, regional, state, and national. My students have won books, plaques, subscriptions, scholarships, a computer, publication in magazines and trade books, and hundreds of dollars.

10. Intercom or assembly announcements: notices, poems, songs, and stories written by students and shared with the school community.

11. Submissions to the principal's weekly newsletter: announcements, anecdotes, poetry, and guest editorials.

12. Posters—poetry, research, announcements, handbills, jokes and riddles, and advertisements—for classroom bulletin boards and school corridors.

13. Classroom bulletin board and school corridor displays, changed frequently. I purchased twenty Plexiglas box frames for students' writing and art, to hang on twenty nails along the stairwell outside my classroom. Students can pop old work out and new work in in about thirty seconds, and it looks finished and professional.

14. Displays at public events (e.g., projects featuring writing presented at local fairs and festivals and at the school's open house).
15. Enactments and recitations of scripts, speeches, and awards. These include tape-recorded radio plays, videotaped scenes and commercials, skits and plays, puppet shows, readers' theater performances, assembly presentations, and graduation speeches.
16. Petitions—to the principal, school board, local board of selectmen, YMCA, etc.
17. Correspondence—pen pal letters, letters of inquiry, thank-you letters, complaints, postcards, fan letters, letters of condolence, cover letters, messages in bottles, time-capsule lists, etc.
18. Writing read aloud to students in other classes.
19. Writing read aloud to classmates in conferences and during group meetings.

Appendix C
Kinds of Writing That Emerge in Writing Workshop

The list below describes the range of writing produced by my students since I began asking them to develop their own ideas and choose the appropriate genres. When students read different kinds of writing, when teachers introduce new genres in conferences and minilessons and encourage students to try them, and when teachers demonstrate what's possible for writers as we explore ideas and genres relevant to our own lives and experiences, students learn about purpose. They begin to understand that writing connects with real life in myriad ways. Teaching about topic development and genre takes on new depth and significance as we help writers make sophisticated decisions about the appropriateness of particular genres to particular purposes, ideas, themes, and occasions that matter in their lives.

Memoirs
Short Stories and Novellas
    (tall tale, sci-fi, fantasy,
    historical, romance, fairy
    tale, contemporary realism,
    myth, mystery, etc.)
Biographies
Profiles
Essays, Editorials, and
    Opinions
Reports of Research
Pamphlets and Brochures
Textbooks
Reviews of Books, CDs, Plays,
    Magazines, Movies, and TV Shows
Reports of Current Events
Reports of Sports Events
Feature Articles
Books for Younger Children
Coloring Books with Text
Cartoons
Annotated Calendars

Advertisements
Poetry
    Ballads and Other Narrative
      Formats
    Rhyming Formats
    Counted-Syllable Formats
    Sestinas
    Free Verse
Correspondence
    Friendly Letters (to pen
      pals, teachers, friends,
      relatives, etc.)
    Invitations
    Letters to the Editor
    Holiday Greetings
    Special Occasion Wishes
    Permission Requests
    Fan Letters
    Cover Letters
    Letters of Thanks, Complaint,
      Love, Application, Sympathy,
      Inquiry, Farewell, Protest,

Advice, Apology,
Congratulation
Parodies
Speeches
Eulogies
Tributes
Graduation Speeches
Scripts
  Skits
  Plays
  Slide Shows
  Radio Plays
  Puppet Shows
  TV Commercials
  Soliloquies
  Dramatic Monologues
Posters

Memoranda and Messages
Interviews
Oral Histories
Instructions and Advice
Rules and Regulations
Lists and Notes
Mottoes and Slogans
Bookmarks
Greeting Cards
Contest Entries
Awards and Inscriptions
Surveys and Forms (for others
  to complete)
Computer Programs
Web Pages
Résumés and Cover Letters
Cookbooks

APPENDIX D
WRITING SURVEY

NAME _____ DATE ____

1. Are you a writer? _____
   (If your answer is YES, answer question 2a. If your answer is NO, answer 2b.)

2a. How did **you** learn to write?

2b. How do **people** learn to write?

3. Why do people write? List as many reasons as you can think of.

4. What does someone have to do or know in order to write well?

5. What kinds of writing do you like to write?

6. How do you decide what you'll write about? Where do your ideas come from?

7. What kinds of response help you most as a writer?

8. How often do you write at home?

9. In general, how do you feel about what you write?

APPENDIX E
READING SURVEY

NAME _____ DATE _____

1. If you had to guess . . .

   How many books would you say you owned? _____

   How many books would you say there are in your house? _____

   How many books would you say you've read in the last twelve months? _____

2. How did you learn to read?

3. Why do people read? List as many reasons as you can think of.

4. What does someone have to do or know in order to be a good reader?

5. What kinds of books do you like to read?

6. How do you decide which books you'll read?

7. Who are your favorite authors? (List as many as you'd like.)

8. Have you ever reread a book? _____ If so, can you name it/them here?

9. How often do you read at home?

10. In general, how do you feel about reading?

Appendix F
Student Writing Record

Pieces of Writing Finished by _____ during _____

#	TITLE	GENRE	DATE COMPLETED

Pieces of Writing Finished by __Matt__ during 1996-97

#	TITLE	GENRE	DATE COMPLETED
1.	"Your Guide to the Clear-cutting Bill"	Essay	9/18/96
2.	"Perfect Spot"	Poem	9/17/96
3.	Cover Letter to Kid's Ink	Letter	9/14/96
4.	"Writing"	Poem	9/26/96
5.	Bio-Poem	Poem	9/30/96
6.	"Glancing Back"	Poem	10/7/96
7.	"For Our Grandparents"	Collaborative Poem	10/30/96
8.	"Loretta Lawry LeSuer"	poem	10/30/96
9.	Letter to Ch. Six	Letter of complaint	11/6/96
10.	Commercial for Matt's Campaign	Parody	11/15/96
11.	Trevor: "Two Wins"	Short story	11/96
12.	All-American Thanksgiving Play		11/8/96
13.	"What's Wrong with Sports"	Opinion	12/14/96
14.	"Mission: Impossible"	Poem	1/20/97
15.	"ESPN"	Poem	2/15/97
16.	"Holiday Soup"	Col. Poem	12/5/96
17.	"The Outsiders"	Poem	2/20/97
18.	"Response to Platoon"	Essay	3/1/97
19.	"Vietnam"	Poem	3/10/97
20.	"Coyotes-Fact"	Poem	3/13/97
21.	"Catch-22"	Book Review	4/8/97
22.	Letter to Marge Kilkelly	Letter	4/8/97
23.	"Phil vs. Pittsburgh"	article-sports	4/18/97
24.	"Angels"	Poem	5/10/97
25.	"Floor Hockey"	Memoir	5/19/97
26.	"Tree Swallow"	Poem	6/3/97
27.	"Leaving CTL"	Speech	6/18/97

Appendix G
Student Reading Record

Books Read by _____ during _____

#	TITLE	GENRE	AUTHOR	DATE FINISHED	DATE ABANDONED

Reading Record for _Missy_

Nancie Atwell
Center for Teaching and Learning

#	TITLE	GENRE	AUTHOR	DATE FINISHED	DATE ABANDONED	RATING
1	No One Here Gets Out Alive	Biography	Jerry Hopkins + Danny Sugarman	9/20	/	8
2	To Kill a Mockingbird	Cont. Rea. Fic.	Harper Lee	10/5	/	10
3	Go Ask Alice	Diary	Anonymous	10/16	/	6
4	Daisy Fay + the Miracle Man	con. r.f.	Fannie Flagg	10/21	/	10
5	Ever After	Diary Nar.	Rachel Vail	10/25	/	5
6	At Risk	c.r.f.	Alice Hoffman	11/12	/	9
	Illumination Night	c.r.f.	" "	/	11/15	3
7	Practical Magic	Fantasy	" "	11/18	/	9
	Searching for Caleb	c.r.f.	Anne Tyler	/	12/3	4
8	A Fate Totally Worse Than Death	Parody	Paul Fleischman	12/5	/	6
9	Walk Two Moons	c.r.f.	Sharon Creech	12/23	/	9
10	God on a Harley	New Age	Joan Brady	12/27	/	5
11	Happy All the Time	c.r.f.	Laurie Colwin	1/15	/	7
12	Farenheit 451	Sci-fi	Ray Bradbury	1/17	/	6
13	It Happened to Nancy	Diary	Anonymous	1/19	/	7
14	Shine on, Bright + Dangerous Object	c.r.f.	Laurie Colwin	1/30	/	7
15	Sophie's World	Philosophy	Jostein Gaarder	2/6	/	5
16	And Still I Rise	Poetry	Maya Angelou	2/8	/	8
17	Collected Poetry of Maya A.	Poetry	Maya Angelou	2/8	/	9
18	Playboy Interview w John Lennon + Yoko Ono	Interview	David Sheff	3/1	/	10
19	Shout !! (Beatles)	Biography	Phillip Norman	3/3	/	8
20	Talk Before Sleep	c.r.f.	Elizabeth Berg	3/10	/	10
21	Hanging out w Cici	c.r.f.	Francine Pascal	3/11	/	5
22	My First ♡ + Other Disasters	c.r.f.	" "	3/13	/	5

Reading Record for _Missy_

Nancie Atwell
Center for Teaching and Learning

#	TITLE	GENRE	AUTHOR	DATE FINISHED	DATE ABANDONED	RATING
23	Anywhere but Here	c.r.f.	Mona Simpson	4/8		7
	Catcher in the Rye	" "	J.D. Salinger		4/30	3
24	Girls in the Back of The Class	Memoir	LouAnne Johnson	4/12		8
25	My Posse Dont Do Homework	Memoir	" "	4/28		8
26	Range of Motion	c.r.f.	Elizabeth Berg	5/10		9
27	Wolf Rider	"	Avi	5/20		7
28	Durable Goods	c.r.f.	Elizabeth Berg	6/3		9

APPENDIX H
PERSONAL SPELLING LIST

PERSONAL SPELLING LIST

hatchet ✓	weapon ✓	would've ✓
sequel ✓	natural ✓	could've ✓
recommend ✓	different ✓	collaborative ✓
beginning ✓	usually ✓	true/truly ✓
should ✓	carefully ✓	against ✓
teenager ✓	tempera ✓	African ✓
maybe ✓	definitely ✓	article ✓
raspberries ✓	separate ✓	speech ✓
scorpion ✓	description ✓	different ✓
personal ✓	character ✓	nuclear ✓
campaign ✓	interesting ✓	stories ✓
senator ✓	wouldn't ✓	board/bored ✓
representative ✓	restaurant ✓	fascinated ✓
Democratic ✓	disappear ✓	women ✓
Republican ✓	disappoint ✓	tried ✓
Independent ✓	locally ✓	remarked ✓
register ✓	conferring ✓	within ✓
ballot ✓	legend ✓	tomorrow ✓
poll ✓	especially ✓	which/witch ✓
candidate ✓	author ✓	series
incumbent ✓	Arthur ✓	excitedly
trouble ✓	genres ✓	approach
	chipped ✓	voice
		smirk
		loosened

APPENDIX I
WEEKLY WORD STUDY

NAME _____ DATE _____

	COPY	SPELL	SPELL AGAIN OR ★
1.	_____	_____	_____
2.	_____	_____	_____
3.	_____	_____	_____
4.	_____	_____	_____
5.	_____	_____	_____

Adapted from Rebecca Sitton's *Spelling Sourcebook 1*

Weekly Word Study

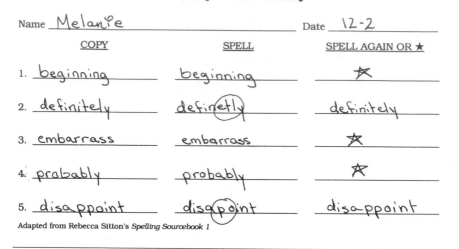

Name _Melanie_   Date _12-2_

COPY	SPELL	SPELL AGAIN OR ★
1. beginning	beginning	★
2. definitely	definetly	definitely
3. embarrass	embarrass	★
4. probably	probably	★
5. disappoint	disappoint	disappoint

Adapted from Rebecca Sitton's *Spelling Sourcebook 1*

APPENDIX J
PEER WRITING CONFERENCE RECORD

Writer's Name _____ Date _____

Responder _____ Topic/Genre _____

Writer, before you ask for a conference, your job is to consider what you want help with: ideas, language, images, organization, coherence, a part of the piece, a sense of the whole? Tell the responder what you want response to:

Responder, when you agree to confer with a writer, your job is to help the writer think and make decisions about the writing:

- Ask what he or she needs help with.
- Listen as the writer reads, try to understand the writing, then tell what you heard.
- If there are parts that confuse you, you don't understand, or you'd like to know more about, ask the writer about them. It will help you—and the writer—if you jot down your questions during and after the reading in the space below.
- Ask the writer what he or she plans to do next.
- Give this record of the conference to the writer.

Writer, jot down your plans before you forget them:

Appendix K
Editing Checksheet

To Be Paper Clipped to the Top of Your Writing
Submitted for Teacher Editing

Name _____ Date ____

Title of Piece _____

CONVENTION	EDITED (√)	PEER EDITED (if you'd like) by____	TEACHER'S COMMENTS
			WORDS TO ADD TO MY PERSONAL SPELLING LIST

Appendix L
Favorite Adolescent Literature

Each June my students look back over the books they read during seventh or eighth grade and rate them for a final time, using a scale of 1–10. When I restock the classroom library over the summer, I use their ratings as the basis for my shopping list. The following books received high ratings from at least three students. If I were setting up a classroom paperback library, I'd start with as many of these titles as I could afford or persuade my school to order in lieu of expensive sets of literature anthologies.

Adams, Douglas. 1994. *The Hitchhiker's Guide to the Galaxy*. Series. New York: Crown Publishing Group.

Adams, Richard. 1976. *Watership Down*. New York: Avon Books.

Angelou, Maya. 1971. *I Know Why the Caged Bird Sings*. New York: Bantam Books.

Anonymous. 1976. *Go Ask Alice*. New York: Avon Books.

Anonymous. 1994. *It Happened to Nancy*. New York: Avon Books.

Asimov, Isaac. 1988. *The Fantastic Voyage*. New York: Bantam Books.

Atwood, Margaret. 1986. *The Handmaid's Tale*. New York: Bantam Books.

———. 1989. *Cat's Eye*. New York: Doubleday.

Auel, Jean M. 1980. *Clan of the Cave Bear*. New York: Crown Publishing Group.

———. 1984. *The Valley of Horses*. New York: Bantam Books.

———. 1986. *The Mammoth Hunters*. New York: Bantam Books.

Avi. 1984. *The Fighting Ground*. New York: HarperCollins Children's Books.

———. 1990a. *Something Upstairs*. New York: Avon Books.

———. 1990b. *The True Confessions of Charlotte Doyle*. New York: Orchard Books.

———. 1993a. *City of Light, City of Dark*. New York: Orchard Books.

———. 1993b. *Nothing but the Truth*. New York: Avon Books.

Baker, Mark. 1987. *Nam*. New York: Berkley Publishing Group.

Barron, T. A. 1994a. *The Ancient One*. New York: Tor Books.

———. 1994b. *The Merlin Effect*. New York: Putnam Publishing Group.

Barry, Dave. 1991. *Dave Barry Turns Forty*. New York: Fawcett.

———. 1996. *Dave Barry's Guide to Guys*. New York: Fawcett.

Bellairs, John. 1991. *The Face in the Frost*. New York: Macmillan Children's Book Group.

———. 1993. *The Ghost in the Mirror*. New York: Dial Books for Young Readers.

Berg, Elizabeth. 1993. *Durable Goods*. New York: Random House.

———. 1994. *Talk Before Sleep*. New York: Random House.

———. 1997. *Joy School*. New York: Random House.

Block, Francesca Lia. 1991. *Weetzie Bat*. New York: HarperCollins Children's Books.

———. 1992. *Witch Baby*. New York: HarperCollins Children's Books.

———. 1993. *Cherokee Bat and the Goat Guys*. New York: HarperCollins Children's Books.

———. 1995. *Missing Angel Juan*. New York: HarperCollins Children's Books.

Blume, Judy. 1971. *Then Again, Maybe I Won't*. New York: Macmillan Children's Group.

———. 1981. *Tiger Eyes*. New York: Macmillan Children's Group.

———. 1987. *Just as Long as We're Together*. New York: Orchard Books.

———. 1992. *Deenie*. New York: Macmillan Children's Group.

———. 1993. *Here's to You, Rachel Robinson*. New York: Orchard Books.

Boatright, Lori. 1982. *Out of Bounds*. New York: Fawcett.

Bonham, Frank. 1971. *Cool Cat*. New York: Dutton.

———. 1972. *Durango Street*. New York: Dell Publishing.

Bradley, Marion Zimmer. 1985. *The Mists of Avalon*. New York: Ballantine.

———. 1996. *Lady of the Trillium*. New York: Bantam Books.

Brooks, Caryl. 1993. *The Empty Summer*. New York: Scholastic.

Brooks, Terry. 1982. *Elfstones of Shannara*. New York: Ballantine.

———. 1986. *Magic Kingdom for Sale Sold*. New York: Ballantine.

———. 1988. *Wishsong of Shannara*. New York: Ballantine.

———. 1991. *Sword of Shannara*. New York: Ballantine.

———. 1994. *The Tangle Box*. New York: Ballantine.

Bunting, Eve. 1991a. *The Hideout*. New York: Harcourt Brace Jovanovich.

———. 1991b. *Jumping the Nail*. New York: Harcourt Brace Jovanovich.

Card, Orson. 1985. *Ender's Game*. New York: Tor Books.

Carmody, Isobelle. 1994. *The Gathering*. New York: Doubleday.

Carr, Caleb. 1994. *The Alienist*. New York: Random House.

Chute, Carolyn. 1984. *The Beans of Egypt, Maine*. New York: Ticknor and Fields.

Clancy, Tom. 1985. *The Hunt for Red October*. New York: Berkley Publishing Group.

———. 1987a. *Patriot Games*. New York: Putnam Publishing Group.

———. 1987b. *Red Storm Rising*. New York: Berkley Publishing Group.

Clancy, Tom, and Steve Pieczenik. 1997. *Tom Clancy's Op-Center: Acts of War*. New York: Berkley Publishing Group.

Colwin, Laurie. 1984. *Shine On, Bright and Dangerous Object*. New York: Viking Penguin.

———. 1985. *Happy All the Time*. New York: Viking Penguin.

Coman, Carolyn. 1997. *What Jamie Saw*. New York: Viking Penguin.

Conroy, Pat. 1986. *The Lords of Discipline*. New York: Bantam.

Cooney, Caroline B. 1991. *The Face on the Milk Carton*. New York: Dell.

———. 1993. *Whatever Happened to Janie?* New York: Delacorte.

———. 1994a. *Driver's Ed*. New York: Delacorte.

———. 1994b. *Emergency Room*. New York: Scholastic.

———. 1994c. *Unforgettable*. New York: Scholastic.

———. 1995. *Both Sides of Time*. New York: Delacorte.

———. 1996a. *Out of Time*. New York: Bantam Doubleday Dell Books for Young Readers.

———. 1996b. *The Voice on the Radio*. New York: Delacorte.

Cormier, Robert. 1977. *I Am the Cheese*. New York: Pantheon.

———. 1986a. *Beyond the Chocolate War*. New York: Dell.

———. 1986b. *The Chocolate War*. New York: Dell.

———. 1991a. *After the First Death*. New York: Dell.

———. 1991b. *We All Fall Down*. New York: Bantam Doubleday Dell.

———. 1992. *Tunes for Bears to Dance to*. New York: Bantam Doubleday Dell.

Creech, Sharon. 1995. *Walk Two Moons*. New York: HarperCollins Children's Books.

Crichton, Michael. 1969. *Andromeda Strain*. New York: Alfred A. Knopf.

———. 1987. *Sphere*. New York: Alfred A. Knopf.

———. 1990. *Jurassic Park*. New York: Alfred A. Knopf.

———. 1996a. *Airframe*. New York: Alfred A. Knopf.

———. 1996b. *The Lost World*. New York: Ballantine.

Cushman, Karen. 1994. *Catherine, Called Birdy*. Boston: Houghton Mifflin.

Dahl, Roald. 1988a. *Boy*. New York: Viking Penguin.

———. 1988b. *Going Solo*. New York: Viking Penguin.

Dank, Milton. 1986. *Game's End*. New York: Dell.

Delany Sarah, and Elizabeth Delany, with Amy Hill Heath. 1994. *Having Our Say*. New York: Dell.

Dorris, Michael. 1987. *Yellow Raft in Blue Water*. New York: Henry Holt.

Draper, Sharon M. 1994. *Tears of a Tiger*. New York: Macmillan Children's Book Group.

Duncan, Lois. 1974. *Down a Dark Hall*. New York: Little, Brown.

———. 1977. *Summer of Fear*. New York: Dell.

———. 1981. *Stranger with My Face*. New York: Little, Brown.

———. 1982. *Chapters*. New York: Little, Brown.

———. 1984. *The Third Eye*. New York: Little, Brown.

———. 1990a. *A Gift of Magic*. New York: Pocket Books.

———. 1990b. *Killing Mr. Griffin*. New York: Dell.

———. 1990c. *Ransom*. New York: Dell.

———. 1990d. *They Never Came Home*. New York: Dell.

———. 1992. *Who Killed My Daughter?* New York: Delacorte.

Dygard, Thomas J. 1994. *The Rebounder*. New York: Morrow Junior Books.

Eddings, David. 1985. *Castle of Wizardry*. New York: Ballantine.

———. 1986a. *Enchanter's End Game*. New York: Ballantine.

———. 1986b. *Magician's Gambit*. New York: Ballantine.

———. 1986c. *Pawn of Prophecy*. New York: Ballantine.

———. 1986d. *Queen of Sorcery*. New York: Ballantine.

———. 1988. *Guardians of the West*. New York: Ballantine.

———. 1989a. *Demon Lord of Karanda*. New York: Ballantine.

———. 1989b. *King of the Murgos*. New York: Ballantine.

———. 1990a. *The Diamond Throne*. New York: Ballantine.

———. 1990b. *Sorceress of Darshiva*. New York: Ballantine.

———. 1991. *The Ruby Knight*. New York: Ballantine.

———. 1992a. *The Sapphire Rose*. New York: Ballantine.

———. 1992b. *The Seeress of Kell*. New York: Ballantine.

———. 1993. *The Losers*. New York: Ballantine.

Filipovic, Zlata. 1994. *Zlata's Diary*. New York: Viking Penguin.

Flagg, Fannie. 1987. *Fried Green Tomatoes at the Whistle Stop Cafe*. New York: Random House.

———. 1992. *Daisy Fay and the Miracle Man*. New York: Warner Books.

Fleischman, Paul. 1997. *A Fate Totally Worse Than Death*. Cambridge, MA: Candlewick Press.

Fowles, John. 1969. *The French Lieutenant's Woman*. New York: Little, Brown.

Frank, Anne. 1967. *The Diary of a Young Girl*. New York: Doubleday.

Furlong, Monica. 1987. *Wise Child*. New York: Alfred A. Knopf Books for Young Readers.

———. 1991. *Juniper*. New York: Alfred A. Knopf Books for Young Readers.

Gallico, Paul. 1941. *The Snow Goose*. New York: Alfred A. Knopf Books for Young Readers.

Golding, William. 1959. *Lord of the Flies*. New York: Berkley Publishing Group.

Goldman, William. 1987. *The Princess Bride*. New York: Ballantine.

Green, Hannah. 1964. *I Never Promised You a Rose Garden*. New York: Henry Holt.

Greene, Bette. 1984. *The Summer of My German Soldier*. New York: Bantam Books.

———. 1991. *The Drowning of Stephan Jones*. New York: Bantam Books.

Greene, Shep. 1980. *The Boy Who Drank Too Much*. New York: Dell.

Grisham, John. 1991. *The Firm*. New York: Doubleday.

———. 1994. *The Client*. New York: Dell.

Guest, Judith. 1993. *Ordinary People*. New York: Viking Penguin.

Hahn, Mary Downing. 1993. *The Wind Blows Backwards*. Boston: Houghton Mifflin.

Hart, Bruce, and Carole Hart. 1978. *Sooner or Later*. New York: Avon Books.

Hayden, Torey L. 1981. *One Child*. New York: Avon Books.

———. 1983. *Murphy's Boy*. New York: Avon Books.

———. 1992. *Ghost Girl*. New York: Avon Books.

Hayes, Daniel. 1992. *The Trouble with Lemons*. New York: Fawcett.

Head, Ann. 1968. *Mr. and Mrs. Bo Jo Jones*. New York: NAL-Dutton.

Heller, Joseph. 1985. *Catch 22*. New York: Dell.

Herriot, James. 1972. *All Creatures Great and Small*. New York: St. Martin's Press.

Hersey, John. 1989. *Hiroshima*. New York: Random House.

Hesse, Karen. 1994. *Phoenix Rising*. New York: Henry Holt.

Hinton, S. E. 1968. *The Outsiders*. New York: Dell.

———. 1975. *Rumble Fish*. New York: Delacorte.

———. 1988. *Taming the Starrunner*. New York: Delacorte.

———. 1989a. *Tex*. New York: Dell.

———. 1989b. *That Was Then, This Is Now*. New York: Dell.

Hobbs, Will. 1992. *Down River*. New York: Bantam Books.

Hoffman, Alice. 1988. *Illumination Night*. New York: Fawcett.

———. 1989. *At Risk*. New York: Berkley Publishing Group.

———. 1993. *Turtle Moon*. New York: Berkley Publishing Group.

———. 1994. *Second Nature*. New York: Putnam Publishing Group.

———. 1996. *Practical Magic*. New York: Berkley Publishing Group.

Holland, Isabelle. 1987. *The Man Without a Face*. New York: HarperCollins Children's Books.

Hunt, Irene. 1987a. *The Lottery Rose*. New York: Berkley Publishing Group.

———. 1987b. *No Promises in the Wind*. New York: Berkley Publishing Group.

Jacques, Brian. 1990a. *Mossflower*. New York: Avon Books.

———. 1990b. *Redwall*. New York: Avon Books.

———. 1991. *Mattiemeo*. New York: Avon Books.

———. 1993. *Mariel of Redwall*. New York: Avon Books.

———. 1994a. *The Bellmaker*. New York: Putnam Publishing Group.

———. 1994b. *Salamadastron*. New York: Ace Books.

———. 1997a. *The Outcast of Redwall*. New York: Ace Books.

———. 1997b. *Pearls of Lutra*. New York: Putnam Publishing Group.

Johnson, LouAnne. 1995. *Dangerous Minds*. New York: St. Martin's Press.

———. 1996. *The Girls in the Back of the Class*. New York: St. Martin's Press.

Jordan, Sherryl. 1993. *Winter of Fire*. New York: Scholastic.

———. 1994. *The Juniper Game*. New York: Scholastic.

Karr, Mary. 1996. *The Liars' Club*. New York: Viking Penguin.

Kerr, M. E. 1982. *Gentlehands*. New York: Bantam Books.

Keyes, Daniel. 1966. *Flowers for Algernon*. New York: Harcourt Brace.

Kingsolver, Barbara. 1989. *The Bean Trees*. New York: HarperCollins.

Klass, David. 1994. *California Blue*. New York: Scholastic.

Lamott, Anne. 1997. *Crooked Little Heart*. New York: Pantheon.

Lasky, Kathryn. 1992. *Shadows in the Water*. New York: Harcourt Brace.

———. 1993. *A Voice in the Wind*. New York: Harcourt Brace.

———. 1994. *Beyond the Burning Ground*. New York: Scholastic.

Lee, Harper. 1988. *To Kill a Mockingbird*. New York: Warner Books.

LeGuin, Ursula K. 1968. *The Wizard of Earthsea*. New York: Bantam Books.

———. 1970. *The Tombs of Atwan*. New York: Bantam Books.

———. 1972. *The Farthest Shore*. New York: Bantam Books.

———. 1990. *Tehanu*. New York: Bantam Books.

L'Engle, Madeleine. 1976. *A Wind at the Door*. New York: Dell.

———. 1976. *A Wrinkle in Time*. New York: Dell.

———. 1979. *A Swiftly Tilting Planet*. New York: Dell.

———. 1980. *The Arm of the Starfish*. New York: Dell.

———. 1981a. *Meet the Austins*. New York: Dell.

———. 1981b. *The Moon by Night*. New York: Dell.

———. 1981c. *A Ring of Endless Light*. New York: Dell.

Lipsyte, Robert. 1967. *The Contender*. New York: HarperCollins Children's Books.

———. 1981. *Summer Rules*. New York: HarperCollins Children's Books.

———. 1984. *Summer Boy*. New York: Bantam Books.

———. 1991. *One Fat Summer*. New York: HarperCollins Children's Books.

London, Jack. 1964a. *Call of the Wild*. New York: Airmont.

———. 1964b. *Sea-Wolf and Other Stories*. New York: NAL-Dutton.

———. 1964c. *White Fang*. New York: Airmont.

Lowry, Lois. 1978. *Find a Stranger, Say Good-bye*. Boston: Houghton Mifflin.

———. 1979. *A Summer to Die*. New York: Bantam Books.

———. 1992. *Number the Stars*. New York: Dell.

———. 1993. *The Giver*. Boston: Houghton Mifflin.

Lunn, Janet. 1983. *The Root Cellar*. New York: Macmillan Children's Book Group.

MacCracken, Mary. 1975. *A Circle of Children*. New York: NAL-Dutton.

———. 1977. *Lovey*. New York: NAL-Dutton.

Magorian, Michelle. 1992. *Back Home*. New York: HarperCollins Children's Books.

Major, Kevin. 1980. *Hold Fast*. New York: Delacorte.

Marino, Jan. 1992. *Like Some Kind of Hero*. New York: Little, Brown.

Marsden, John. 1989. *So Much to Tell You*. New York: Little, Brown.

———. 1994. *Letters from the Inside*. Boston: Houghton Mifflin.

Mason, Robert. 1984. *Chicken Hawk*. New York: Viking Penguin.

McCaffrey, Anne. 1996. *Black Horses for the King*. New York: Harcourt Brace.

McCammon, Robert. 1992. *Boy's Life*. New York: Pocket Books.

Michener, James. 1953. *Bridges at Toko-Ri*. New York: Random House.

Mitchell, Margaret. 1975. *Gone with the Wind*. New York: Macmillan Children's Book Group.

Mazer, Harry. 1975. *Snowbound*. New York: Dell.

———. 1981. *The Last Mission*. New York: Dell.

Mazer, Harry, and Norma Fox Mazer. 1982. *The Island Keeper*. New York: Dell.

———. 1989. *Heartbeat*. New York: Bantam Books.

Mazer, Norma Fox. 1983. *Taking Terri Mueller*. New York: Morrow Junior Books.

———. 1988. *Silver*. New York: Morrow Junior Books.

Mowat, Farley. 1956. *Lost in the Barrens*. New York: Little, Brown.

———. 1963. *Never Cry Wolf*. New York: Little, Brown.

Murphy, Jim. 1990. *The Boys' War*. Boston: Houghton Mifflin.

Myers, Walter Dean. 1981. *Hoops*. New York: Delacorte.

———. 1987. *The Outside Shot*. New York: Dell.

———. 1988a. *Fallen Angels*. New York: Scholastic.

———. 1988b. *Fast Sam, Cool Clyde, and Stuff*. New York: Puffin Books.

———. 1988c. *Scorpions*. New York: HarperCollins Children's Books.

———. 1988d. *Won't Know Till I Get There*. New York: Puffin Books.

———. 1992. *Somewhere in the Darkness*. New York: Scholastic.

———. 1994. *Glory Field*. New York: Scholastic.

Neufeld, John. 1970. *Lisa, Bright and Dark*. New York: NAL-Dutton.

———. 1996. *A Small Civil War*. New York: Simon and Schuster Children's Books.

Nolan, Han. 1994. *If I Should Die Before I Wake*. New York: Harcourt Brace.

O'Brien, Robert C. 1974. *Z for Zachariah*. New York: Macmillan Children's Book Group.

O'Brien, Tim. 1989. *If I Die in a Combat Zone.* New York: Dell.
————. 1991. *The Things They Carried.* New York: Viking Penguin.
Oneal, Zibby. 1990. *The Language of Goldfish.* New York: Puffin Books.
Orenstein, Peggy. 1994. *School Girls: Young Women, Self-Esteem, and the Confidence Gap.* New York: Doubleday.
Pascal, Francine. 1985. *Hanging Out with CiCi.* New York: Dell.
————. 1986. *My First Love and Other Disasters.* New York: Dell.
Paulsen, Gary. 1986. *Hatchet.* New York: Macmillan Children's Book Group.
————. 1989. *The Winter Room.* New York: Orchard Books.
————. 1990a. *Tilt-a-Whirl John.* New York: Puffin Books.
————. 1990b. *Woodsong.* New York: Macmillan Children's Book Group.
————. 1991a. *The Monument.* New York: Delacorte.
————. 1991b. *The River.* New York: Doubleday.
————. 1993a. *Harris and Me.* New York: Harcourt Brace.
————. 1993b. *Nightjohn.* New York: Doubleday.
————. 1994. *The Car.* New York: Harcourt Brace.
Pevsner, Stella. 1989. *And You Give Me a Pain, Elaine.* New York: Pocket Books.
Pfeffer, Susan Beth. 1980. *About David.* New York: Delacorte.
Philbrick, Rodman. 1993. *Freak the Mighty.* New York: Scholastic.
Pipher, Mary. 1994. *Reviving Ophelia.* New York: Putnam.
Plath, Sylvia. 1975. *The Bell Jar.* New York: Bantam Books.
Prejean, Sister Helen. 1993. *Dead Man Walking.* New York: Random House.
Pullman, Philip. 1996. *His Dark Materials, Book I.* New York: Alfred A. Knopf.
————. 1997. *His Dark Materials, Book II.* New York: Alfred A. Knopf.
Rawls, Wilson. 1961. *Where the Red Fern Grows.* New York: Doubleday.
————. 1989. *Summer of the Monkeys.* New York: Doubleday.
Read, Piers Paul. 1979. *Alive.* New York: Avon Books.
Reeder, Carolyn. 1989. *Shades of Gray.* New York: Macmillan Children's Book Group.
Rice, Anne O. 1993. *The Vampire Chronicles: Interview with the Vampire, The Vampire Lestat, Queen of the Damned, and Tale of the Body Thief.* New York: Ballantine.
Rinaldi, Ann. 1990. *The Last Silk Dress.* New York: Bantam Books.
Roth, Arthur. 1989. *The Iceberg Hermit.* New York: Scholastic.
Rylant, Cynthia. 1993a. *But I'll Be Back Again.* New York: Morrow.
————. 1993b. *I Had Seen Castles.* New York: Harcourt Brace.
Sachs, Marilyn. 1982. *Class Pictures.* New York: Avon Books.
Salinger, J. D. 1951. *The Catcher in the Rye.* New York: Little, Brown.
Scott, Michael. 1994. *Gemini Game.* New York: Holiday House.
Shakespeare, William. 1960. *Romeo and Juliet.* New York: Viking Penguin.
————. 1981a. *Hamlet.* New York: Viking Penguin.
————. 1981b. *A Midsummer Night's Dream.* New York: Viking Penguin.
————. 1981c. *Much Ado About Nothing.* New York: Viking Penguin.
Simpson, Mona. 1987. *Anywhere But Here.* New York: Random House.
Sleator, William. 1979. *Into the Dream.* New York: Dutton.

————. 1985. *House of Stairs*. New York: Dutton.

Soto, Gary. 1990. *Baseball in April and Other Stories*. New York: Harcourt Brace.

————. 1991. *Taking Sides*. New York: Harcourt Brace.

Strasser, Todd. 1990. *The Accident*. New York: Dell.

Sutcliffe, Rosemary. 1993. *Black Ships Before Troy: The Story of the Iliad*. New York: Delacorte.

————. 1995. *The Wanderings of Odysseus: The Story of the Odyssey*. New York: Delacorte.

Tamar, Erika. 1993. *Fair Game*. New York: Harcourt Brace.

Tan, Amy. 1989. *Joy Luck Club*. New York: Putnam Publishing Group.

Temple, Frances. 1994. *The Ramsay Scallop*. New York: Orchard Books.

Thesman, Jean. 1992. *The Rain Catchers*. New York: Avon Books.

————. 1994. *Cattail Moon*. New York: Avon Books.

Tolkien, J. R. R. 1974. *The Lord of the Rings*. Boston: Houghton Mifflin.

————. 1986. *The Hobbit*. Boston: Houghton Mifflin.

Townsend, Sue. 1984. *The Secret Diary of Adrian Mole, Aged 13$^3/_4$*. New York: Avon Books.

————. 1987. *The Growing Pains of Adrian Mole*. New York: Avon Books.

Trumbo, Dalton. 1970. *Johnny Got His Gun*. New York: Carol Publishing Group.

Twain, Mark. 1967. *Huckleberry Finn*. New York: Macmillan Children's Book Group.

————. 1983. *Tom Sawyer*. New York: Puffin Books.

Vail, Rachel. 1993. *Ever After*. New York: Orchard Books.

van der Rol, Ruud, and Rian Verhoeven. 1993. *Anne Frank: Beyond the Diary*. New York: Viking Children's Books.

Voigt, Cynthia. 1981. *Homecoming*. New York: Macmillan Children's Book Group.

————. 1982a. *Dicey's Song*. New York: Macmillan Children's Book Group.

————. 1982b. *Tell Me if the Lovers Are Losers*. New York: Macmillan Children's Book Group.

————. 1983. *Solitary Blue*. New York: Macmillan Children's Book Group.

————. 1984. *Building Blocks*. New York: Macmillan Children's Book Group.

————. 1985. *Jackaroo*. New York: Macmillan Children's Book Group.

————. 1987. *Izzy Willy Nilly*. New York: Fawcett.

————. 1994. *When She Hollers*. New York: Macmillan Children's Book Group.

Vonnegut, Kurt. 1970. *Slaughterhouse-Five*. New York: Dell.

————. 1972. *Mother Night*. New York: Dell.

————. 1978. *Slapstick*. New York: Dell.

Walker, Alice. 1982. *The Color Purple*. New York: Harcourt Brace.

Waugh, Sylvia. 1994. *The Mennyms*. New York: Greenwillow.

————. 1995. *Mennyms in the Wilderness*. New York: Greenwillow.

————. 1996. *Mennyms Under Siege*. New York: Greenwillow.

White, Ellen Emerson. 1984. *The President's Daughter*. New York: Avon Books.

————. 1989. *Long Live the Queen*. New York: Scholastic.

White, Rob. 1973. *Deathwatch*. New York: Dell.

White, T. H. 1996. *The Once and Future King*. New York: Ace Books.

Wiesel, Elie. 1982. *Night*. New York: Bantam Books.

Wilson, Budge. 1992. *The Leaving*. New York: Putnam Publishing Group.

Wolfe, Tom. 1983. *The Right Stuff*. New York: Bantam Books.

Zindel, Paul. 1983. *The Pigman*. New York: Bantam Books.

———. 1984. *The Pigman's Legacy*. New York: Bantam Books.

———. 1992. *The Pigman and Me*. New York: HarperCollins Children's Books.

———. 1993. *David and Della*. New York: HarperCollins Children's Books.

———. 1994. *Loch*. New York: HarperCollins Children's Books.

Appendix M
Favorite Collections of Poetry

Adoff, Arnold. 1989. *Chocolate Dreams*. New York: Lothrop, Lee and Shepard.

Akhmatova, Anna. 1985. *Selected Poems*. New York: Penguin Books.

Alfred, Lord Tennyson. 1992. *Selected Poems*. New York: Dover Publications.

Angelou, Maya. 1990. *I Shall Not Be Moved*. New York: Bantam Books.

———. 1994. *The Complete Collected Poems of Maya Angelou*. New York: Random House.

Atwood, Margaret. 1995. *Morning in the Burned House*. Boston: Houghton Mifflin.

Berry, James. 1991. *When I Dance*. San Diego: Harcourt Brace Jovanovich.

Bishop, Elizabeth. 1979. *The Complete Poems: 1927–1979*. New York: Farrar, Straus and Giroux.

Booth, David, ed. 1989. *Til All the Stars Have Fallen: Canadian Poems for Children*. Markham, Ontario: Houghton Mifflin.

Burns, Robert. 1991. *Poems and Songs*. New York: Dover Publications.

Cummings, E. E. 1944. *Selected Poems*. New York: Liveright.

Dickinson, Emily. 1960. *The Complete Poems of Emily Dickinson*, edited by Thomas H. Johnson. Boston: Little, Brown.

Dunning, Stephen, Edward Lueders, Naomi Shihab Nye, Kieth Gilyard, and Demetrice A. Worley, eds. 1995. *Reflections on a Gift of Watermelon Pickle . . . And Other Modern Verse*. 2d ed. Glenview, IL: Scott, Foresman.

Espada, Martin, ed. 1994. *Poetry Like Bread: Poets of the Political Imagination*. Willimantic, CT: Curbstone Press.

Farrell, Kate, ed. 1995. *Art and Nature: An Illustrated Anthology of Nature Poetry*. New York: Metropolitan Museum of Art; Boston: Little, Brown.

Fleischman, Paul. 1985. *I Am Phoenix: Poems for Two Voices*. New York: Harper and Row.

———. 1988. *Joyful Noise: Poems for Two Voices*. New York: Harper and Row.

Fletcher, Ralph. 1991. *Water Planet*. Paramus, NJ: Arrowhead Books.

———. 1994. *I Am Wings*. New York: Bradbury Press.

———. 1996. *Buried Alive: The Elements of Love*. New York: Atheneum.

Florian, Douglas. 1994. *Bing Bang Boing*. San Diego: Harcourt Brace Jovanovich.

Frost, Robert. 1971. *Robert Frost's Poems*. New York: Washington Square Press.

———. 1975. *You Come Too: Favorite Poems for Young Readers*. New York: Scholastic.

———. 1994. *Poetry for Young People*. New York: Sterling Publishing.

Gillan, Maria Mazziotti, ed. 1994. *Unsettling America: An Anthology of Contemporary Multicultural Poetry*. New York: Penguin.

Ginsberg, Allen. 1956. *Howl and Other Poems*. San Francisco: City Lights.

Giovanni, Nikki. 1975. *The Women and the Men*. New York: William Morrow.

———. 1978. *Cotton Candy on a Rainy Day*. New York: Quill.

Graves, Donald. 1996. *Baseball, Snakes, and Summer Squash: Poems About Growing Up*. Honesdale, PA: Boyds Mills Press.

Heaney, Seamus. 1990. *Selected Poems: 1966–1987*. New York: Farrar, Straus and Giroux.

Heard, Georgia. 1992. *Creatures of Earth, Sea, and Sky*. Honesdale, PA: Boyds Mills Press.

———. 1995. *Writing Toward Home: Tales and Lessons to Find Your Way*. Portsmouth, NH: Heinemann.

Hopkins, Lee Bennett. 1995. *Been to Yesterdays: Poems of a Life*. Honesdale, PA: Boyds Mills Press.

Hughes, Langston. 1987. *Selected Poems of Langston Hughes*. New York: Random House.

Janeczko, Paul B., ed. 1983. *Poetspeak: In Their Work, About Their Work*. New York: Bradbury Press.

———, ed. 1984. *Strings: A Gathering of Family Poems*. New York: Bradbury Press.

———, ed. 1987a. *Going Over to Your Place: Poems for Each Other*. New York: Bradbury Press.

———, ed. 1987b. *This Delicious Day*. New York: Orchard Books.

———, ed. 1990. *The Place My Words Are Looking For: What Poets Say About and Through Their Work*. New York: Bradbury Press.

Kenyon, Jane. 1990. *Let Evening Come*. St. Paul: Graywolf Press.

———. 1996. *Otherwise: New and Selected Poems*. St. Paul: Graywolf Press.

Lerner, Andrea, ed. 1990. *Dancing on the Rim of the World: An Anthology of Contemporary Northwest Native American Writing*. Tucson, AZ: Sun Tracks and the University of Arizona Press.

Levin, Gail, ed. 1995. *The Poetry of Solitude: A Tribute to Edward Hopper*. New York: Universe.

Longfellow, Henry Wadsworth. 1992. *Favorite Poems*. New York: Dover Publications.

Neruda, Pablo. 1994. *Ode to Common Things*. Boston: Little, Brown.

Nye, Naomi Shihab. 1980. *Different Ways to Pray*. Portland, OR: Breitenbush Publications.

———, ed. 1992. *This Same Sky*. New York: Macmillan.

———, ed. 1995. *The Tree Is Older Than You Are: A Bilingual Gathering of Poems and Stories from Mexico*. New York: Simon and Schuster.

Nye, Naomi Shihab, and Paul B. Janeczko, eds. 1996. *I Feel a Little Jumpy Around You*. New York: Simon and Schuster.

Oliver, Mary. 1990. *House of Light*. Boston: Beacon Press.

———. 1992. *New and Selected Poems*. Boston: Beacon Press.

———. 1996. *West Wind*. Boston: Houghton Mifflin.

Pack, Robert, and Jay Parini, eds. 1993. *Poems for a Small Planet: Contemporary American Nature Poetry*. Hanover, NH: University Press of New England.

Pastan, Linda. 1982. *PM/AM: New and Selected Poems*. New York: W. W. Norton.

———. 1988. *The Imperfect Paradise*. New York: W. W. Norton.

———. 1995. *An Early Afterlife*. New York: W. W. Norton.

Piercy, Marge. 1985. *Circles on the Water*. New York: Alfred A. Knopf.

Plath, Sylvia. 1969. *Ariel*. New York: HarperPerennial.

Rylant, Cynthia. 1984. *Waiting to Waltz: A Childhood*. New York: Bradbury Press.

———. 1990. *Soda Jerk*. New York: Orchard Books.

Sandburg, Carl. 1994. *Carl Sandburg: Chicago Poems*. New York: Dover Publications.

Schiff, Hilda. 1995. *Holocaust Poetry*. New York: St. Martin's Press.

Shakespeare, William. 1995. *Shakespeare's Sonnets*. New York: Simon and Schuster.

Shange, Ntozake. 1994. *I Live in Music*. New York: Stewart, Tabori, and Chang.

Stafford, William. 1991. *Passwords*. New York: HarperCollins.

———. 1992. *My Name Is William Tell*. Lewiston, ID: Confluence Press.

———. 1993. *The Darkness Around Us Is Deep: Selected Poems*. New York: Harper-Collins.

———. 1996. *Even in Quiet Places*. Lewiston, ID: Confluence Press.

Stallworthy, Jon, ed. 1984. *The Oxford Book of War Poetry*. London: Oxford University Press.

Steele, Susanna, ed. 1991. *Mother Gave a Shout: Poems by Women and Girls*. Volcano, CA: Volcano Press.

Stevens, Wallace. 1990. *The Collected Poems*. New York: Vintage Books.

Sullivan, Charles, ed. 1993. *American Beauties*. New York: Harry N. Abrams.

Thoreau, Henry David. 1990. *Walden*. New York: Philomel.

———. 1992. *The Poet's Delay*. New York: Rizzoli.

Turner, Ann. 1993. *Grass Songs: Poems of Women's Journey West*. San Diego: Harcourt Brace Jovanovich.

Whitman, Walt. 1988. *Voyages*. San Diego: Harcourt Brace Jovanovich.

———. 1991. *Selected Poems*. New York: Dover Publications.

———. 1995. *Leaves of Grass*. Amherst, NY: Prometheus Books.

Wilbur, Richard. 1963. *The Poems of Richard Wilbur*. New York: Harcourt, Brace and World.

Williams, William Carlos. 1986. *The Collected Poems of William Carlos Williams, Volume I*. New York: New Directions.

———. 1988. *The Collected Poems of William Carlos Williams, Volume II*. New York: New Directions.

Appendix N
Quotes for the Walls of a Writing-Reading Workshop

Nulla díes síne línea [Never a day without a line.]
> —*Anonymous*

Most of the basic material a writer works with is acquired before the age of fifteen.
> —*Willa Cather*

Be happy. It's one way of being wise.
> —*Colette*

If you have a minimum of talent, but you sit at that typewriter long enough, something will emerge. All I had was this burning desire to be a writer and all these emotions.
> —*Robert Cormier*

The hardest battle is to be nobody but yourself in a world that is doing its best, night and day, to make you like everybody else.
> —*E. E. Cummings*

Anyone who has begun to think places some portion of the world in jeopardy.
> —*John Dewey*

If I feel physically as if the top of my head were taken off, I know that is poetry.
> —*Emily Dickinson*

One sacred memory from childhood is perhaps the best education.
> —*Feodor Dostoyevsky*

If there is no struggle there can be no progress.
> —*Frederick Douglass*

The important thing is not to stop questioning.
> —*Albert Einstein*

A thread runs through all things: all worlds are strung on it as beads: and men, and events, and life, come to us, only because of that thread.
> —*Emerson*

'Tis the good reader that makes the good book.
> —*Emerson*

The best way out is always through.
> —*Robert Frost*

You must be the change you wish to see in the world.
—*Mahatma Gandhi*

There were no books that showed what was really going on with teenagers. I wrote *The Outsiders* because I wanted to read it.
—*S. E. Hinton*

Experience is not what happens to you; it is what you do with what happens to you.
—*Aldous Huxley*

And the trouble is, if you don't risk anything you risk even more.
—*Erica Jong*

One can never be alone enough when one writes . . . there can never be enough silence around when one writes . . . even *night* is not *night* enough.
—*Franz Kafka*

I know a poem is finished when I can't find another word to cut.
—*Bobbi Katz*

Fiction is truth's older sister.
—*Rudyard Kipling*

I try to leave out the parts that people skip.
—*Elmore Leonard*

That is what learning is. You suddenly understand something you've understood all your life, but in a new way.
—*Doris Lessing*

We are the ones we've been waiting for.
—*Audre Lord*

No one remains quite what he was when he recognizes himself.
—*Thomas Mann*

The days that make us happy make us wise.
—*John Masefield*

The difficulty in life is the choice.
—*George Moore*

Write what makes you happy.
—*O. Henry*

Tell me, what is it you plan to do
with your one wild and precious life?
—*Mary Oliver*

The real voyage of discovery lies not in seeking new landscapes but in having new eyes.

—*Marcel Proust*

If I were to begin life again, I should want it as it were. I would only open my eyes a little more.

—*Jules Renard*

The moment of change is the only poem.

—*Adrienne Rich*

Be patient toward all that is unsolved in your heart and try to love the questions themselves.

—*Rainer Maria Rilke*

You must do the thing you think you cannot do.

—*Eleanor Roosevelt*

Writing stories has given me the power to change things I could not change as a child. I can make boys into doctors. I can make fathers stop drinking. I can make mothers stay.

—*Cynthia Rylant*

A life spent in making mistakes is not only more honorable but more useful than a life spent in doing nothing.

—*George Bernard Shaw*

My education was the liberty I had to read indiscriminately and all the time, with my eyes hanging out.

—*Dylan Thomas*

Don't say the old lady screamed. Bring her on and let her scream.

—*Mark Twain*

Reader and writer, we wish each other well. Don't we want and don't we understand the same thing? A story of beauty and passion, some fresh approximation of human truth?

—*Eudora Welty*

Say it, no ideas but in things.

—*William Carlos Williams*

Literature is no one's private ground, literature is common ground; let us trespass freely and fearlessly and find our own way for ourselves.

—*Virginia Woolf*

APPENDIX O
FINAL SELF-EVALUATION OF
WRITING AND READING

NAME _____ DATE _____

General (Personal and Social Development)

What is your favorite subject? _____

What is something you've accomplished this year at school, apart from academics? _____

_____

What is something you wish you had done differently? _____

_____

_____

Writing and Spelling

How many pieces of writing did you finish this year? _____

What genres are represented?

_____   _____   _____

_____   _____   _____

_____   _____   _____

What are your favorite genres to write?_____

Which pieces of writing are your most effective? Why? (What did you do as

the author?) _____

_____

_____

_____

_____

_____

_____

What were your major accomplishments this year as a writer?

_____

_____

_____

What are your strengths as a writer? _____

_____

_____

_____

What are the areas in which you can improve?_____

_____

_____

_____

What rules and conventions have you mastered?_____

_____

_____

_____

What changes have you made in your approaches to spelling?_____

_____

_____

_____

Reading

How many books did you finish this year? _____

What genres are represented?

_____   _____   _____

_____   _____   _____

_____   _____   _____

What are your favorite genres to read? _____

_____

_____

Which books were the best? Why? (What did the authors do?)

_____

_____

_____

_____

Who are your favorite authors? _____

Who are your favorite poets?_____

Which poems were the best?_____

_____

_____

What were your major accomplishments this year as a reader?

_____

_____

_____

_____

What are your strengths as a reader?_____

_____

_____

_____

_____

What are the areas in which you can improve?_____

_____

_____

_____

_____

What literary techniques do you identify and appreciate in the texts you read?_____

_____

_____

_____

Appendix P
Weekly Homework
Assignment Sheet

HOMEWORK FOR THE WEEK OF _____

DUE MONDAY
- Read a book for at least a half hour
- One hour's worth of writing
  (My plan: _____)

DUE TUESDAY
- Read a book for at least a half hour
- Spelling: five new words, copied from your personal spelling list onto a word study sheet

DUE WEDNESDAY
- Read a book for at least a half hour

DUE THURSDAY
- Read a book for at least a half hour
- Spelling: word study on your five words

DUE FRIDAY
- Letter in your reading journal due by today to Ms. A. or a friend
- Read a book for at least a half hour

APPENDIX Q
RECOMMENDED RESOURCES FOR TEACHERS OF MIDDLE SCHOOL WRITING, READING, AND LITERATURE

Writing

Atwell, Nancie, ed. 1989. *Workshop 1: Writing and Literature*. Portsmouth, NH: Heinemann.

———. 1991. *Side by Side: Essays on Teaching to Learn*. Portsmouth, NH: Heinemann.

Charlton, James, ed. 1985. *The Writer's Quotation Book: A Literary Companion*. New York: Penguin.

Fletcher, Ralph. 1993. *What a Writer Needs*. Portsmouth, NH: Heinemann.

———. 1996. *A Writer's Notebook: Unlocking the Writer Within You*. New York: Avon Books.

Graves, Donald H. 1989a. *Experiment with Fiction: The Reading/Writing Teacher's Companion*. Portsmouth, NH: Heinemann.

———. 1989b. *Investigate Nonfiction: The Reading/Writing Teacher's Companion*. Portsmouth, NH: Heinemann.

———. 1991. *Build a Literate Classroom: The Reading/Writing Teacher's Companion*. Portsmouth, NH: Heinemann.

———. 1994. *A Fresh Look at Writing*. Portsmouth, NH: Heinemann.

Harwayne, Shelley. 1992. *Lasting Impressions: Weaving Literature into the Writing Workshop*. Portsmouth, NH: Heinemann.

Henderson, Kathy. 1993. *Market Guide for Young Writers: Where and How to Sell What You Write*. 4th ed. Cincinnati: Writer's Digest Books.

Hindley, Joanne. 1996. *In the Company of Children*. York, ME: Stenhouse.

Lloyd, Pamela. 1987. *How Writers Write*. Portsmouth, NH: Heinemann.

Macrorie, Ken. 1988. *The I-Search Paper*. Portsmouth, NH: Boynton/Cook.

Murray, Donald M. 1990. *Shoptalk: Learning to Write with Writers*. Portsmouth, NH: Boynton/Cook.

———. 1991. *The Craft of Revision*. Fort Worth, TX: Holt, Rinehart, and Winston.

———. 1993. *Write to Learn*. 4th ed. Fort Worth, TX: Holt, Rinehart, and Winston.

Newkirk, Thomas. 1990. *To Compose: Teaching Writing in High School and College*. 2d ed. Portsmouth, NH: Heinemann.

———, ed. 1993. *Nuts and Bolts: A Practical Guide to Teaching College Composition*. Portsmouth, NH: Boynton/Cook.

Rief, Linda. 1992. *Seeking Diversity: Language Arts with Adolescents*. Portsmouth, NH: Heinemann.

Rief, Linda, and Maureen Barbieri, eds. 1995. *All That Matters: What Is It We Value in School and Beyond?* Portsmouth, NH: Heinemann.

Romano, Tom. 1987. *Clearing the Way: Working with Teenage Writers.* Portsmouth, NH: Heinemann.

Wilde, Jack. 1993. *A Door Opens: Writing in Fifth Grade.* Portsmouth, NH: Heinemann.

Zinsser, William, ed. 1987. *The Writer's Craft: Inventing the Truth: The Art and Craft of Memoir.* Boston: Houghton Mifflin.

———. 1990a. *On Writing Well: An Informal Guide to Writing Nonfiction.* 4th ed. New York: HarperCollins.

———, ed. 1990b. *The Writer's Craft: Worlds of Childhood: The Art and Craft of Writing for Children.* Boston: Houghton Mifflin.

Reading: Process, Strategies, and Comprehension

Clay, Marie M. 1991. *Becoming Literate: The Construction of Inner Control.* Portsmouth, NH: Heinemann.

Keene, Ellin Oliver, and Susan Zimmermann. 1997. *Mosaic of Thought: Teaching Comprehension in a Reader's Workshop.* Portsmouth, NH: Heinemann.

Ohlhausen, Marilyn M., and Mary Jepsen. 1992. "Lessons from Goldilocks: 'Somebody's Been Choosing My Books But I Can Make My Own Choices Now!'" *The New Advocate* 5 (winter): 31–46.

Padgett, Ron. 1997. *Creative Reading: What It Is, How to Do It, and Why.* Urbana, IL: National Council of Teachers of English.

Pennac, Daniel. 1994. *Better Than Life.* Toronto, Ontario: Couch House Press.

Smith, Frank. 1984. *Reading Without Nonsense.* New York: Teachers College Press.

———. 1986. *Insult to Intelligence.* Portsmouth, NH: Heinemann.

Weaver, Constance. 1994. *Reading Process and Practice: From Socio-Psycholinguistics to Whole Language.* 2d ed. Portsmouth, NH: Heinemann.

Reading: Literature

Allen, Janet. 1995. *It's Never Too Late: Leading Adolescents to Lifelong Literacy.* Portsmouth, NH: Heinemann.

Atwell, Nancie, ed. 1990. *Workshop 2: Beyond the Basal.* Portsmouth, NH: Heinemann.

Beckson, Karl, and Arthur Ganz. 1960. *A Reader's Guide to Literary Terms: A Dictionary.* New York: Noonday Press.

Benét, William Rose, ed. 1965. *The Reader's Encyclopedia.* Vols. 1–2. New York: Thomas Y. Crowell.

Campbell, Oscar James, and Edward G. Quinn, eds. 1966. *The Reader's Encyclopedia of Shakespeare.* New York: Thomas Y. Crowell.

Donelson, Kenneth, and Alleen Pace Nilsen. 1989. *Literature for Today's Young Adults.* Glenview, IL: Scott, Foresman.

Epstein, Norrie. 1993. *The Friendly Shakespeare: A Thoroughly Painless Guide to the Best of the Bard.* New York: Viking Penguin.

Harwayne, Shelley. 1992. *Lasting Impressions: Weaving Literature into the Writing Workshop*. Portsmouth, NH: Heinemann.

Hindley, Joanne. 1996. *In the Company of Children*. York, ME: Stenhouse.

Kleyn, Howard. 1996. *The Play's the Thing*. Wisbech, England: Howard's Corner.

Magill, Frank N., ed. 1991. *Masterpieces of World Literature*. New York: Harper-Collins.

Rief, Linda. 1992. *Seeking Diversity: Language Arts with Adolescents*. Portsmouth, NH: Heinemann.

Rief, Linda, and Maureen Barbieri, eds. 1995. *All That Matters: What Is It We Value in School and Beyond?* Portsmouth, NH: Heinemann.

Rosenblatt, Louise M. 1983. *Literature as Exploration*. 4th ed. New York: Modern Language.

Weekly Reader Corp. 1995. *Dear Author: Students Write About the Books that Changed Their Lives*. Collected by Weekly Reader's *Read* Magazine. Berkeley, CA: Conari Press.

Poetry

Collom, Jack, and Sheryl Noethe. 1994. *Poetry Everywhere*. New York: Teachers and Writers Collaborative.

Heard, Georgia. 1989. *For the Good of the Earth and Sun: Teaching Poetry*. Portsmouth, NH: Heinemann.

———. 1995. *Writing Toward Home: Tales and Lessons to Find Your Way*. Portsmouth, NH: Heinemann.

Kennedy, X. J. 1993. *An Introduction to Poetry*. 7th ed. Reading, MA: Addison-Wesley.

Kennedy, X. J., and Dorothy M. Kennedy. 1982. *Knock at a Star: A Child's Introduction to Poetry*. Boston: Little, Brown.

Padgett, Ron, ed. 1987. *The Teachers and Writers Handbook of Poetic Forms*. New York: Teachers and Writers Collaborative.

Presson, Rebekah, and David McLees, comps. 1996. *In Their Own Voices: A Century of Recorded Poetry*. Los Angeles: Rhino Records. Audiocassettes.

Wallace, Robert. 1995. *Writing Poems*. 3d ed. Boston: Little, Brown.

Wilson, Lorraine. 1994. *Write Me a Poem: Reading, Writing, and Performing Poetry*. Portsmouth, NH: Heinemann.

Young, Sue. 1994. *The Scholastic Rhyming Dictionary*. New York: Scholastic.

Spelling, Usage, and Other Conventions

Henderson, Edmund H. 1990. *Teaching Spelling*. 2d ed. Boston: Houghton Mifflin.

Hughes, Margaret, and Dennis Searle. 1997. *The Violent E and Other Tricky Sounds*. York, ME: Stenhouse.

Routman, Regie. 1991. *Invitations: Changing as Teachers and Learners K–12*. Portsmouth, NH: Heinemann.

Sebranek, Patrick, Verne Meyer, and Dave Kemper, eds. 1992. *Writers INC.* Burlington, WI: Write Source Educational Publishing House.

Strunk, William Jr., and E. B. White. 1979. *The Elements of Style.* 3d ed. New York: Macmillan.

Turabian, Kate L. 1976. *The Student's Guide for Writing College Papers.* 3d ed. Chicago: University of Chicago Press.

Weaver, Constance. 1996. *Teaching Grammar in Context.* Portsmouth, NH: Boynton/Cook.

BIBLIOGRAPHY

Alexander, K. L., M. Cook, and E. L. McDill. 1978. "Curriculum Tracking and Educational Stratification: Some Further Evidence." *American Sociological Review* 43: 47–66.

Allen, Janet. 1995. *It's Never Too Late: Leading Adolescents to Lifelong Literacy*. Portsmouth, NH: Heinemann.

Barbieri, Maureen. 1995. *Sounds from the Heart*. Portsmouth, NH: Heinemann.

Bartlett, John. 1992. *Bartlett's Familiar Quotations*. New York: Little, Brown.

Bissex, Glenda. 1980. *GNYS AT WRK: A Child Learns to Write and Read*. Cambridge, MA: Harvard University Press.

Borg, W. R. 1966. "Ability Grouping in Public Schools." Madison, WI: Dembar Educational Research Services.

Borg, W. R., M. Findley, and M. Bryan. 1970. "Ability Grouping." ERIC, ED 048382.

Bruner, Jerome. 1986. *Actual Minds, Possible Worlds*. Cambridge, MA: Harvard University Press.

Calkins, Lucy McCormick. 1983. *Lessons from a Child*. Portsmouth, NH: Heinemann.

Chute, Carolyn. 1985. Interview in *Bittersweet* 8 (5): 7–12.

Clay, Marie. 1991. *Becoming Literate*. Portsmouth, NH: Heinemann.

Cooper, Charles R. 1984. "The Contributions of Writing to Thinking and Learning." *English Record* 34 (1): 176–190.

Cormier, Robert. 1986. *The Chocolate War*. New York: Dell.

Dewey, John. 1899. *School and Society*. New York: Norton.

Donaldson, Margaret. 1978. *Children's Minds*. New York: Norton.

Fiske, Edward B. 1983. "Americans in Electronic Era Are Reading as Much as Ever." *New York Times*, 8 September, p. 1.

Fletcher, Ralph. 1993. *What a Writer Needs*. Portsmouth, NH: Heinemann.

Francis, Robert. 1976. "While I Slept." From *Robert Francis: Collected Poems, 1936–1976*. Boston: University of Massachusetts Press.

Frost, Robert. 1969. "Nothing Gold Can Stay." From *The Poetry of Robert Frost*. New York: Henry Holt.

Fry, Donald. 1985. *Children Talk About Books: Seeing Themselves as Readers*. Philadelphia: Milton Keynes.

Fulwiler, Toby. 1990. "Journals Across the Disciplines." In *To Compose: Teaching Writing in High School and College*. 2d ed, edited by Thomas Newkirk. Portsmouth, NH: Heinemann.

Goodlad, John. 1984. *A Place Called School*. New York: McGraw-Hill.

Graves, Donald H. 1975. "The Child, the Writing Process, and the Role of the Professional." In *The Writing Processes of Students*, edited by Walter Petty. Buffalo: State University of New York.

———. 1978. *Balance the Basics: Let Them Write*. New York: Ford Foundation.

———. 1981. Presentation at the National Council of Teachers of English Annual Convention, November, Boston, MA.

———. 1983. *Writing: Teachers and Children at Work*. Portsmouth, NH: Heinemann.

———. 1984. "The Enemy Is Orthodoxy." In *A Researcher Learns to Write: Selected Articles and Monographs*. Portsmouth, NH: Heinemann.

———. 1989. *Experiment with Fiction*. Portsmouth, NH: Heinemann.

———. 1994. *A Fresh Look at Writing*. Portsmouth, NH: Heinemann.

Halberstam, David. 1984. "Teachers with Class." *Boston Globe*, 14 October, p. 83.

Hall, Jim. 1980. "Maybe Dats Youwr Pwoblem Too." From *The Mating Reflex*. Pittsburgh: Carnegie-Mellon University Press.

Hardy, Thomas. 1984. "The Man He Killed." In *The Oxford Book of War Poetry*, edited by Jon Stallworthy. London: Oxford University Press.

Harwayne, Shelley. 1992. *Lasting Impressions: Weaving Literature into the Writing Workshop*. Portsmouth, NH: Heinemann.

Heard, Georgia. 1995. *The Words of True Poems: Poems by Children*. Portsmouth, NH: Heinemann.

Hinton, S. E. 1968. *The Outsiders*. New York: Dell.

Hopkins, Lee Bennett. 1987. *Pass the Poetry Please*. New York: Harper and Row.

Keene, Ellin Oliver, and Susan Zimmermann. 1997. *Mosaic of Thought: Teaching Comprehension in a Reader's Workshop*. Portsmouth, NH: Heinemann.

Kennedy, X. J. 1984. Presentation to the National Council of Teachers of English Annual Convention, November, Detroit, MI.

Kozol, Jonathan. 1985. *Illiterate America*. New York: Doubleday.

Lloyd, Pamela. 1987. *How Writers Write*. Portsmouth, NH: Heinemann.

Macrorie, Ken. 1988. *The I-Search Paper*. Portsmouth, NH: Boynton/Cook.

Maxim, Donna. 1986. Presentation at the Wiscasset Primary School, April, Wiscasset, ME.

Meek, Margaret. 1982. *Learning to Read*. London: Bodley Head.

Moffett, James, and Betty Jane Wagner. 1976. *Student-Centered Language Arts and Reading, K–13*. 2d ed. Boston: Houghton Mifflin.

Mueller, Lisel. 1986. "English as a Second Language." In "Your Tired, Your Poor" from *Second Language: Poems* by Lisel Mueller. Baton Rouge: Louisiana State University Press.

Murray, Donald M. 1982. *Learning by Teaching*. Portsmouth, NH: Boynton/Cook.

———. 1983. "First Silence, Then Paper." In *Fforum: Essays on Theory and Practice in the Teaching of Writing*, edited by Patricia Stock. Portsmouth, NH: Boynton/Cook.

———. 1985. *A Writer Teaches Writing*. 2d ed. Boston: Houghton Mifflin.

———. 1986. *Read to Write*. Fort Worth, TX: Holt, Rinehart, and Winston.

———. 1990. *Shoptalk: Learning to Write with Writers*. Portsmouth, NH: Boynton/Cook.

———. 1993. *Write to Learn*. 4th ed. Fort Worth, TX: Holt, Rinehart, and Winston.

Nabokov, Vladimir. 1989. *Pale Fire*. New York: Random House.

Newkirk, Thomas. 1985. "On the Inside Where It Counts." In *Breaking Ground: Teachers Relate Reading and Writing in the Elementary School*, edited by Jane Hansen, Thomas Newkirk, and Donald Graves. Portsmouth, NH: Heinemann.

———. 1990. "Looking for Trouble: A Way to Unmask Our Readings." In *To Compose: Teaching Writing in High School and College*. 2d ed, edited by Thomas Newkirk. Portsmouth, NH: Heinemann.

Orwell, George. 1950. *Nineteen Eighty-Four*. New York: NAL-Dutton.

Paterson, Katherine. 1981. *FLB Newsletter* 3 (3). Chicago: Follett Library Book Company.

Pennac, Daniel. 1994. *Better Than Life*. Toronto, Ontario: CouchHouse Press.

Piercy, Marge. 1982. *Circles on the Water: Selected Poems of Marge Piercy*. New York: Alfred A. Knopf.

Plimpton, George, ed. 1963. *Writers at Work: The Paris Review Interviews*. Second Series. New York: Viking Press.

Purves, Alan. 1972. *Literature and the Reader: Research in Response to Literature, Reading Interests, and the Teaching of Literature*. Urbana, IL: National Council of Teachers of English.

Quinn, Tom. 1984. "The Prime of Ms. Nancie Atwell." *Esquire*, December, 252–260.

Rief, Linda. 1992. *Seeking Diversity: Language Arts with Adolescents*. Portsmouth, NH: Heinemann.

Romano, Tom. 1987. *Clearing the Way: Working with Teenage Writers*. Portsmouth, NH: Heinemann.

Rosenbaum, J. 1976. *Making Inequality: The Hidden Curriculum of High School Tracking*. New York: Wiley.

Rowe, Mary B. 1974. "Wait-Time and Rewards as Instructional Variables, Their Influence on Language, Logic, and Fate Control." *Journal of Research in Science Teaching* 11: 81–94.

Smith, Frank. 1982. *Writing and the Writer*. Portsmouth, NH: Heinemann.

———. 1984. *Reading Without Nonsense*. New York: Teachers College Press.

———. 1985. *Reading Without Nonsense*. 2d ed. New York: Teachers College Press.

———. 1986. *Understanding Reading*. Hillsdale, NJ: Lawrence Erlbaum.

———. 1988. *Joining the Literacy Club*. Portsmouth, NH: Heinemann.

Sitton, Rebecca. 1996. *Spelling Sourcebook Reviews for High-Use Writing Words: 1–400*. Spokane, WA: Egger Publishing.

Staton, Jana. 1980. "Writing and Counseling: Using a Dialogue Journal." *Language Arts* 57: 514–518.

Staton, Jana, Roger Shuy, Jane Kreeft, and Leslee Reed. 1982. "Analysis of Dialogue Journal Writing as a Communicative Event." NIE-G-80-0122. Washington, D. C.: Center for Applied Linguistics.

Stafford, William. 1991. "What's in My Journal?" From *Passwords*. New York: HarperCollins.

Stevens, Wallace. 1951. "The Noble Rider and the Sound of Words." In *The Necessary Angel: Essays on Reality and Imagination*. New York: Alfred A. Knopf.

Stevenson, Robert Louis. 1992. "Bed in Summer." In *A Child's Garden of Verses*. New York: Knopf.

Thomas, Dylan. 1957. "A Refusal to Mourn the Death, by Fire, of a Child in London." From *The Collected Poems of Dylan Thomas*. New York: New Directions.

Vonnegut, Kurt. 1984. *Palm Sunday*. New York: Dell.

Vygotsky, Lev. 1962. *Thought and Language*. Cambridge: MIT Press.

Wallace, Ronald. 1983. "You Can't Write a Poem About McDonald's." From *Tunes for Bears to Dance to*. Pittsburgh: University of Pittsburgh Press.

Weaver, Constance. 1994. *Reading Process and Practice: From Socio-Psycholinguistics to Whole Language*. 2d ed. Portsmouth, NH: Heinemann.

———. 1996. *Teaching Grammar in Context*. Portsmouth, NH: Boynton/Cook.

White, E. B. 1974. *Charlotte's Web*. New York: HarperCollins Children's Books.

Whitehead, Frank. 1977. *Children and Their Books*. London: Macmillan.

Wilde, Jack. 1989. "Interview with Thomas Newkirk." In *Workshop 1: Writing and Literature*, edited by Nancie Atwell. Portsmouth, NH: Heinemann.

Williams, William Carlos. 1963. *Paterson*, Book 1. New York: New Directions.

Zinsser, William. 1990. *On Writing Well: An Informal Guide to Writing Non-Fiction*. 4th ed. New York: Harper and Row.

INDEX